C000162810

Luiz Moutinho & Geoff Southern

Strategic Marketing Management

A Business Process Approach

CENGAGE
Learning™

Australia • Brazil • Japan • Korea • Mexico • Singapore • Spain • United Kingdom • United States

SOUTH-WESTERN
CENGAGE Learning™

Strategic Marketing Management
Luiz Moutinho & Geoff Southern

Publishing Director: Linden Harris

Publisher: Stephen Wellings

Development Editor: Jennifer Seth

Content Project Editor: Alison Cooke

Head of Manufacturing: Jane Glendening

Production Controller: Paul Herbert

Marketing Manager: Vicky Fielding

Typesetter: Pre-Press PMG

Cover Design: Adam Renvoize

© 2010, Cengage Learning EMEA

ALL RIGHTS RESERVED. No part of this work covered by the copyright herein may be reproduced, transmitted, stored or used in any form or by any means graphic, electronic, or mechanical, including but not limited to photocopying, recording, scanning, digitizing, taping, Web distribution, information networks, or information storage and retrieval systems, except as permitted under Section 107 or 108 of the 1976 United States Copyright Act, or applicable copyright law of another jurisdiction, without the prior written permission of the publisher. While the publisher has taken all reasonable care in the preparation of this book, the publisher makes no representation, express or implied, with regard to the accuracy of the information contained in this book and cannot accept any legal responsibility or liability for any errors or omissions from the book or the consequences thereof.

For product information and technology assistance, contact **emea.info@cengage.com**.

For permission to use material from this text or product, and for permission queries, email **clsuk.permissions@cengage.com**.

Products and services that are referred to in this book may be either trademarks and/or registered trademarks of their respective owners. The publishers and author/s make no claim to these trademarks.

The Author has asserted the right under the Copyright, Designs and Patents Act 1988 to be identified as Author of this Work.

British Library Cataloguing-in-Publication Data
A catalogue record for this book is available from the British Library.

ISBN: 978-1-84480-000-1

Cengage Learning EMEA
Cheriton House, North Way, Andover, Hampshire. SP10 5BE.
United Kingdom

Cengage Learning products are represented in Canada by Nelson Education Ltd.

For your lifelong learning solutions, visit
www.cengage.co.uk

Purchase your next print book, e-book or e-chapter at
www.ichapters.co.uk

Printed by Seng Lee Press, Singapore
1 2 3 4 5 6 7 8 9 10 – 11 10 09

Contents

Part 4
Keeping existing customer processes (order fulfilment) 157

Part 5
Getting new customer processes (order acquisition) 239

Part 6
Organizational development and co-ordination (infrastructure processes)   311

List of contributors

Alexis Barlow, *Glasgow Caledonian University*

Alexis has been with Glasgow Caledonian University for 6 years and is currently in the Strategy, Operations and Leadership group of the Business School. She has a BA in Business Information Management and a teaching qualification in PGC Advanced Academic Studies. More recently, she was awarded a PhD for her work on the 'Strategic Role of Internet-Related Technologies in Supply Chain Networks' from the University of Newcastle Upon Tyne.

Alexis's main fields of interest are related to recent developments in information systems, aligning information systems with business strategy and using IS to exploit opportunities, value and competitive advantage across supply chains. She is a member of the British Academy of Management (BAM) and e-BRN.

Her current research focuses on the impact of e-business technologies on supply chain management, in particular, concentrating on opportunities such as developing and co-ordinating supply chain processes, integration and information sharing, and advancing supply chain relationships. She is also looking at limitations such as cultural, social and security factors and the implications of e-business for supply chains in terms of power relations, structure, etc.

Charles S. Chien, *Feng Chia University*

Charles S. Chien is Associate Professor of Marketing and Director of the Department of International Trade and Business at Feng Chia University, Taiwan. He was a Visiting Scholar at the Department of Business and Management, University of Glasgow, Scotland, UK. He holds a PhD in Marketing from the University of Wales, UK. His main academic interests are in relationship marketing, customer relationship management and cross-cultural management. He has carried out extensive consultancy regarding Taiwanese firms' marketing strategies in mainland China.

Tony Conway, *Salford Business School*

Tony Conway is a Senior Lecturer in Marketing at Salford Business School and specializes in services marketing, particularly within the Not-For-Profit Sector. He has published many journal articles, text contributions and conference papers on Public Sector, Relationship and General Services Marketing Management. He is Director of the Centre for Research in Marketing at the University.

Fiona Davies, *Cardiff University*

Fiona Davies is a Lecturer in Marketing at Cardiff University, where she teaches at both undergraduate and postgraduate levels. She has co-authored two books and has published extensively in a range of academic journals, e.g. the *Journal of Business Research, the European Journal of Marketing* and the *Journal of Retailing and Consumer Services*. Her current research interests are in consumer behaviour, social marketing and the effects of sponsorship.

Peter Duncan, *Glasgow Caledonian University*

Peter Duncan is a Lecturer in the Division of Strategy, Innovation and Enterprise, Caledonian Business School, Glasgow Caledonian University. His teaching currently focuses on the strategic use of information systems and on the management of intellectual capital. He has published in a number of academic journals, particularly regarding the impact of information systems on firms in the legal services sector. He also acts as reviewer for the *European Journal of Information Systems,* the *International Journal of Business Science and Applied Management* and the *International Journal of Information Technology and Management*, as well as the e-Business and e-Government Special Interest Group of the British

Academy of Management. Peter's current research interests include the impact of information systems on professional services firms and SMEs.

David Edgar, *Glasgow Caledonian University*

Dr David Edgar is Professor of Strategy and Business Transformation and Head of the Division of Strategy, Innovation and Enterprise at Caledonian Business School. His main areas of research and teaching are in the field of strategic management, specifically business uncertainty and complexity, organizational analysis and process improvement, and e-business strategy and knowledge management.

He has a wide range of academic experience, from programme development to international collaboration and has an excellent network of colleagues in both academia and industry.

Dr Edgar is currently on the editorial board of four journals and regularly reviews for a further seven. In addition, he regularly contributes to conference organizing committees and acts as a reviewer for a range of conferences.

David's consultancy experience is in the area of soft systems methodology, organizational analysis, business processes analysis and design, scenario planning and strategic planning/reviews. He has worked with a wide range of private and public sector organizations, including NTL, Telewest, NHS, Local Councils, Aristo Hotels and IBM. The consultancy expertise is supported by and complemented by Dr Edgar's research interests. In recent years these have become contextualized around the strategic development of organizations in complex and transitional environments and have involved working with colleagues in a range of countries and industry sectors.

Kevin Grant, *Glasgow Caledonian University*

Kevin Grant is currently a Senior Lecturer at Glasgow Caledonian University (from 2001) and since 1992, when he joined academia, he has been a university-based consultant: a lecturer and programme, leader at Napier University, a Head of Department and then Head of the Business School at Bell College of Technology, now merged with the University of Paisley. He acts as a reviewer to several high-quality academic journals, including the *European Journal of Information Systems, Omega* and the *International Journal of Electronic Business*, as well as serving as a committee member and reviewer for a range of prestigious national and international conferences. Kevin has over 30 academic publications, in the areas of IS/IM, education and policy, many of which have featured in the *International Journal of Information Management*, the *International Journal of Electronic Commerce Research* and the *International Journal of Educational Management*. Key IS/IM consultancy projects have been: business systems analysis with a private health company; business process re-engineering and information systems development strategy for the Foreign and Commonwealth Office; investment management IT strategy for a large Scottish financial institution; and business analysis of the automation of the business lending unit for a large Scottish bank and the management of a knowledge networks system for the Scottish Health Service.

Kunhuang Huarng, *Feng Chia University*

Kunhuang Huarng is Professor of International Trade and Chief Librarian of University at Feng Chia University, Taiwan. He received his PhD degree in computer science from Texas A&M University, College Station, USA. He then combined the post of Library Director with a post in the Department of Finance in Chaoyang University of Technology, Taiwan. Since 2001, he has been with the Department of International Trade, Feng Chia University, Taiwan, where he has been a professor since 2002; he worked as Associate Dean, the College of Business and also as the Director of Electronic Commerce Research Institute. Professor Huarng is a member of Upsilon Pi Epsilon; the Editor of the *Journal of Economics and Management*; the Associate Editor of the *Journal of Modelling in Management, Advances in Doctoral Research in Management* and the *International Journal of Culture, Tourism and Hospitality Research*; and the Guest Editor of the *Portuguese Journal of Management Studies*. Professor Huarng has published more than 100 journal and conference papers. He was listed in Marquis Who's Who in the World in 1996. His current research interests include computer modelling and e-commerce.

Andrzej Huczynski, *University of Glasgow*

5   Corporate structure, network and knowledge
     management   74

Andrzej Huczynski graduated from the London
School of Economics and Political Science (University
of London) and holds a PhD from Glasgow University. He has held posts at Westminster and Edinburgh
universities and has published in the field of organizational behaviour, management knowledge and teaching methods. His current research and teaching is
focused on influencing skills.

Graeme D. Hutcheson, *University of Manchester*

3   Environmental scanning and strategy   34
7   Marketing measurements and analysis   132

Graeme Hutcheson is currently working at the School
of Education, Manchester University, UK teaching
postgraduate classes in research design and statistical
analysis. He completed his PhD at the University of
Manchester and has held posts at Strathclyde and
Glasgow universities. His major interest is in the
use of quantitative methods and the application of
statistical models, particularly generalized linear
models.

László Józsa, *Széchenyi István University*

14   Innovation management: market timing and
      solution planning   289

László Józsa is Associate Professor of Marketing,
Széchenyi István University, Győr, Hungary. He
completed his PhD at the Hungarian Academy of
Sciences in 1994 and held posts at University of
Veszprém, University of West Hungary, and Budapest College of Economics. In this period he has
also held visiting posts at Case Western University,
the University of Wales, the University of Leon, and
the University of Glasgow. He is the Director of the
Marketing Master Program in Győr. Józsa has published six books in Hungarian and two in English,
and has published extensively in academic journals
in Hungary, and in the *Journal of Euromarketing*.
   Józsa's current research interests include strategic
planning in marketing and marketing communication.
He is a member of the editorial boards of the *Hungarian Journal of Marketing and Management* and *ADRM
- Advances in Doctoral Research in Management*.

Philip J. Kitchen, *University of Hull*

13   Reputation management: corporate image
      and communication   270

Professor Kitchen has been working in academia
since 1984. Prior to joining the academic community, he was a senior manager in the retail industry in the UK. He is managing director of his own
consultancy company and was senior director in a
management training group. Since then, he has carried out research and consultancy with multinational
firms in the European Community, the USA , and
the Pacific Rim. He has worked extensively with organizations in the communications industry such as
the IPA, CIPR and PRCA in the UK and with their
counterparts overseas.
   Professor Kitchens's first degree is in the humanities. Subsequently, he has completed an MSc
in marketing at UMIST, and graduated with a Master of Business Sciences at Manchester Business
School. After commencing his academic career, he
completed a PhD in marketing at Keele University.
   Following a number of academic appointments,
Professor Kitchen was appointed as the founding Professor of Strategic Marketing at the Business School, University of Hull, where he was also
founder and Director of the Research Centre for
Marketing and Communications (CMC) (2001-
2006) and later founder and Director of the Current
Research Centre for Marketing, Communications
and International Strategy (CMCIS) (2007). He
is also Affiliated Professor at ESC Rennes, France,
and Visiting Professor in Italy, Spain and Malaysia.
   At Hull, Professor Kitchen teaches an executive
short course, MBA, MSc and undergraduate degree
levels in the fields of marketing management and
marketing communications.
   His current research interests include marketing
management, marketing theory, marketing communications, branding, the future of marketing, consumer and organizational behaviour and corporate
social responsibility. While primarily interested in
qualitative research approaches, he has also supervised PhD students in the quantitative domain.

Simon Knox, *University of Cranfield*

18   Strategic brand management   395

Simon Knox is Professor of Brand Marketing at the
Cranfield School of Management in the UK and is

a consultant to a number of multinational companies, including McDonald's, Levi Strauss, Johnson-Diversey, BT and Exel. Before joining Cranfield, he pursued a career in marketing of international brands, which comprised a number of senior roles in Unilever plc, covering both detergent and food products.

Since joining Cranfield, Simon has published over 100 papers and books on strategic marketing and branding and is a regular speaker at international conferences. He is currently leading a research team looking at the impact of corporate social responsibility on brand management. His recent books include: *Competing on Value*, FT Pitman (UK, Germany, the USA and China), *Creating a Company for Customers,* FT Prentice-Hall (UK, Brazil and India) and *Customer Relationship Management*, Butterworth-Heinemann.

Carlos Lucas de Freitas, *Universidade Catolica Portugesa*

Carlos Lucas de Freitas is Assistant Professor of Marketing and Management in the Faculty of Philosophy of Braga in the Universidade Catolica Portugesa, and holds professorial posts at the Technical University of Lisbon and with the MIT management programmes in Portugal (in association with the Portuguese Ministry of Science, Technology, and Higher Education).

His teaching and research areas include international management, marketing management, services marketing, and marketing and consumer behaviour.

Stan Maklan, *Cranfield School of Management*

Stan Maklan is an experienced academic, marketer and management consultant with senior, international line management experience in blue chip consumer and business marketing companies.

Stan spent the first 10 years of his career in marketing with Unilever Canada, UK and Sweden, where he was Marketing Director of its toiletries business. He spent the following 10 years as a management consultant concentrating on customer relationship management and online marketing with global leaders in information technology such as Computer Sciences Corporation (CSC) and Sapient.

Stan was appointed a Senior Lecturer in Strategic Marketing in 2006, focusing upon customer relationship management, corporate branding and evaluating marketing effectiveness. He is the Academic Director of Cranfield's Return on Marketing Investment Club and works closely with Cranfield's Customized Executive Development's clients in a wide range of industries: telecommunications, computing, consumer products, defence, automotive, electricity, water and professional services. Stan has co-authored a best-selling management book (*Competing on Value*) about corporate brand development, and a case-history-based book about customer relationship management.

Stan was awarded honours for academic excellence when he obtained a Master of Business Administration from the University of Western Ontario and from the Ivey School of Management (Canada) and has a Bachelor of Science (Economics) from the Université de Montréal. His PhD is from Cranfield University.

Luiz Moutinho, *University of Glasgow*

Luiz Moutinho is Professor of Marketing at the University of Glasgow. He completed his PhD at the University of Sheffield in 1982 and has held posts at Cardiff Business School, University of Wales College of Cardiff, Cleveland State University, Ohio, USA, Northern Arizona University, USA, and California State University, USA, as well as visiting professorship positions in Taiwan, Lithuania, Slovenia, Portugal, New Zealand and Brazil. For over a total of 17 years he was Director of Doctoral Programmes at Confederation of Scottish Business Schools, Cardiff Business School and School of Business and Management, University of Glasgow. Luiz Moutinho has been a full professor of marketing since 1989 and was appointed in 1996 to the Foundation Chair of Marketing at the University of Glasgow. He has published 19 books and has published extensively in academic journals both in the UK and the USA, e.g., *Journal of Business Research* and *European Journal of Marketing*.

Moutinho's current research interests include mathematical and computer modelling in marketing, consumer behaviour and marketing of services. He is the Editor of the *Journal of Modelling in Marketing and Management* (JM2).

Andrew J. Newman, *Manchester Business School*

Andrew Newman joined Manchester Business School from UMIST in August 2003 as a lecturer in retail operations and customer behaviour. Before re-entering academic life, and undertaking a PhD at Manchester Metropolitan University in 1997, Andrew gained more than 20 years' commercial experience with British Airways in the areas of marketing and customer services. He has published articles in a range of journals, including the *European Journal of Marketing* and the *Journal of Retailing and Consumer Services*. His latest book is entitled *Retailing: Environment and Operations* and is published by Thomson Learning.

Andrew's teaching interests are retail operations, retail strategy, retail environments and customer behaviour. His principle research interests include retail store environments and consumer behaviour, business process change, retail strategy formulation and the internationalization of retail institutions. Andrew has raised considerable amounts of research income for MBS and is also the Chair of a special interest group (SIG) in retailing at the British Academy of Management.

Judit Pakai, *University of West Hungary*

Associate Professor at Faculty of Wood Industry, University of West Hungary, Sopron, Judit Pakai completed her PhD at the Hungarian Academy of Sciences in 1998 and held posts at the University of West Hungary. She has published in academic journals in Hungary.

Judit's current research interests include strategic product planning in the wood industry.

Erik M. van Raaij, *RSM Erasmus University, Rotterdam*

Erik van Raaij is Assistant Professor of Purchasing and Supply Management at RSM Erasmus University, Rotterdam. He holds an engineering degree in business and a PhD in marketing from the University of Twente, The Netherlands. Before joining RSM, he held posts at Eindhoven University of Technology, Cass Business School (London) and the University of Twente. He has also been a freelance consultant/trainer for companies including Rank Xerox, the Dutch Post, Philips, Ballast Nedam, Ericsson and 3M. His work has been published in many international academic journals, such as the *Journal of Business Research, Industrial Marketing Management,* the *Journal of Purchasing and Supply Management, Computers & Education,* the *European Journal of Marketing* and *Marketing Intelligence & Planning.*

Current course offerings include Strategic Sourcing (MSc) at RSM and Marketing (EMBA) at Cass Business School. Erik van Raaij has received several awards and commendations for teaching excellence. His current research interests include new technologies in purchasing and marketing; value, cost and profitability in business-to-business relationships; and market orientation.

W. Fred van Raaij, *Tilburg University*

Fred van Raaij is Professor of Economic Psychology at the University of Tilburg, The Netherlands. He completed his PhD at the University of Tilburg in January 1977 and has held positions at the University of Twente, The Netherlands; University of Illinois at Urbana-Champaign, USA; and Erasmus University of Rotterdam, The Netherlands. These positions were professorships in economic psychology and marketing management. He has a honorary degree from the Helsinki School of Economics, Finland. His interests are in the interface between economics and psychology: consumer behaviour, investor behaviour, entrepreneurship, marketing communication and consumer confidence. He was the founder and first Editor of the *Journal of Economic Psychology*, and member of the editorial board of the *Journal of Consumer Research,* the *Journal of Consumer Psychology* and the *International Journal of Research in Marketing*. He was Chairman of the Dutch Consumentenbond (consumer association) and the Genootschap voor Reclame (advertising association). He has published over 20 books and numerous articles in scientific journals. van Raaij's current research interests include consumer financial behaviour and the effects of implicit learning.

Paulo Rita, *ISCTE Business School*

Dr Paulo Rita is currently Director of the Management Research Centre (MRC) and Associate Professor of Marketing at ISCTE Business School, Lisbon, Portugal. He obtained his PhD in marketing at Cardiff Business School, University of Wales, UK, and subsequently a postdoctorate on web marketing at the University of Nevada, Las Vegas, USA. He was Director of the Doctoral Program in Marketing at ISCTE Business School in 2000–2001.

His current research and teaching interests are focused on web marketing and e-commerce, intelligent and decision support systems in marketing, consumer behaviour, and marketing for hospitality and tourism.

Dr Rita has published several books, including *Expert Systems in Tourism Marketing* (1996), co-authored with Luiz Moutinho and Bruce Curry (published by the International Thomson Business Press), and *Computer Modelling and Expert Systems in Marketing* (1994), co-authored with Luiz Moutinho, Bruce Curry and Fiona Davies (published by Routledge).

In addition to presenting refereed papers at international conferences, he has also had book chapters and articles published in refereed journals, such as the *Service Industries Journal,* the *European Journal of Marketing,* the *Journal of International Consumer Marketing, Annals of Tourism Research,* the *International Journal of Contemporary Hospitality Management* and *Marketing Management*, among others.

He is also a member of the editorial board of several academic journals, and has supervised and examined a number of PhD theses and master dissertations.

Geoff Southern, *University of Glasgow*

Geoff Southern is Director of MSc Programmes in Management at the University of Glasgow. An engineer by training, he combined study with work in the electrical construction and machine tool industries before going on to complete a PhD in shipbuilding. Following a period in the UK at the National Ship Research Institution, he entered academia and has researched and taught at Newcastle and Hull universities before joining the University of Glasgow to teach operations management in the Business School.

At Glasgow, he was Director of the MBA programme before being appointed to his present post as Director of the MSc in Management. Under his direction, the programme has grown from 28 to about 200 students in about 4 years, and the number of specialist streams has increased from two to eight. In 2008 the programme received a Queen's Award for Excellence. He now concentrates on innovative teaching and programme design to satisfy the ever-increasing demands of international management students.

Merlin Stone, *Bristol Business School*

Merlin Stone is one of the UK's top consultants, lecturers and trainers in marketing, sales and service. He is a Director of Nowell Stone Ltd, an organizational development and consulting company specializing in improving capabilities in customer management and of The Database Group Ltd, specialists in managing customer databases. He is Research Director of WCL, specialists in public sector change management. He has written more than 30 books. He is Professor of Marketing at Bristol Business School and a Visiting Professor at Brunel, Leicester, Luton, Portsmouth and Southampton Business Schools. He is author or co-author of many articles and 30 books on transforming marketing, sales and customer service capabilities, including *Up Close and Personal – CRM @ Work, Customer Relationship Marketing, Successful Customer Relationship Marketing, CRM in Financial Services, Key Account Management in Financial Services, The Customer Management Scorecard, Consumer Insight, Marketing Revolution* and *Business Solutions on Demand*. He is a Fellow of the Chartered Institute of Marketing and a Founder Fellow of the Institute of Direct Marketing. He is also on the editorial advisory boards of the *Journal of Financial Services Marketing*, the *Journal of Database Marketing and Customer Management Strategy*, the *Journal of Targeting, Measurement and Analysis for Marketing* and the *Journal of Direct, Data and Digital Marketing Practice* (the journal of the Institute of Direct Marketing). He writes regularly for three trade publications: *B2B Marketing, Database Marketing* and *Direct Marketing International*, and contributes to several others. He has a first-class degree and a doctorate in economics from Sussex University.

Harry J. P. Timmermans, *Eindhoven University of Technology*

Professor Timmermans was appointed Professor of Urban Planning at the Eindhoven University of Technology, The Netherlands, in 1985. He currently is Head of the Urban Planning Group and Director of the European Institute of Retailing and Services Studies (EIRASS). His research interests concern the development of models of spatial choice behaviour and the development of decision support systems in a variety of application domains, including transportation, retailing, tourism and recreation, and housing. One of his most recent research endeavours concerns the development of Albatross, currently the only fully operational rule-based, computational process model of travel demand, developed for the Dutch Ministry of Transport. He has authored or co-authored close to 200 refereed articles in geography, transportation, urban planning, marketing, artificial intelligence, tourism and applied computer science.

Professor Timmermans is Founder Editor of the *Journal of Retailing and Consumer Services,* and has acted as (European/Associate) Editor of *TESG, Geographical and Environment Modelling* and *Leisure Sciences*. He is serving on the editorial board of many journals, including *Geographical Analysis, Transportation Research, Tourism Analysis* and *Sistemi Urbani*.

Tom Watson, *Bournemouth University*

Dr Tom Watson is Deputy Dean of Education and Reader in Communications at The Media School at Bournemouth University, UK. Previously, he was Associate Professor in Communication and Head of the School of Communication at Charles Sturt University in Australia from 2003 to 2006.

Before entering academic life, Tom's career covered journalism and public relations in many countries, including Australia and the UK. He ran a successful public relations consultancy in England for 18 years and was Chairman of the UK's Public Relations Consultants Association from 2000 to 2002. Tom is a member of the Commission on Public Relations Measurement and Evaluation and a Fellow of the Chartered Institute of Public Relations in the UK.

He was awarded his PhD in 1995 by Nottingham Trent University for research in models of evaluation in public relations. With Paul Noble, he wrote *Evaluating Public Relations*, which was published in 2005 by Kogan Page and has been translated into Russian, Korean and Japanese. A revised second edition was published in 2007.

James Wilson, *University of Glasgow*

Dr James Wilson is a Senior Lecturer in Operations Management in the Department of Management at the University of Glasgow. His teaching interests are primarily in project management and the applications of IT in management and business. He also teaches finance to non-finance students using a pragmatic approach.

His research interests include the development and evolution of production management systems; Ford's use of the assembly line in producing the Model T with significant archival research and analysis of original source data; developments in production control practices following from Frederick Taylor's ideas; and the interaction between computing technology and its evolving applications to manufacturing control systems.

Len Tiu Wright, *De Montfort University*

Len Tiu Wright is Professor of Marketing and Research Professor at De Montfort University, Leicester and Visiting Professor at the University of Keele. She has held full-time appointments at the universities of Keele, Birmingham and Loughborough and visiting lecturing positions with institutions in the UK, e.g. Cambridge University and overseas.

Len Tiu has consultancy and industrial experience and has researched in the Far East, Europe and North America. Her writings have appeared in books, in American and European academic journals and at conferences where some have gained best paper awards. She is on the editorial boards of a number of leading marketing journals. She is the Founding Editor of *Qualitative Market Research – An International Journal*, (published by Emerald).

Preface

Work by a number of researchers on the concept of process-based management came to fruition in the early 1990s, and by the middle of the decade a plethora of texts aimed at practicing managers reflected both the interest in the approach and the number of organizations attempting to follow it. Hammer and Champy's article in the *Harvard Business Review* (1990) and Davenport and Short's paper in the *Sloan Management Review* (1990) were seminal. Both defined the scope and nature of business process re-engineering (BPR) and opened a debate about the best method of applying it. That debate continues today.

Although we have titled this book *Strategic Marketing Management*, its content draws heavily on BPR, a term which, in the past 10 years, has caught the imagination of the business and commercial world. The title was conferred, or at least popularized, by Hammer and Champy in 1990. Why, then, did we not specifically use the term BPR in the title of the book or a chapter?

Until the advent of the process-based approach, the practice BPR of management was structured around functional departments that called upon the specialist skills of marketing, operations, finance and human resource management. Such organizational structures derived from historical work on division of labour and economies of scale by Adam Smith, developed later, some would say to excess, by the fathers of the school of scientific management, Taylor and Ford.

Proponents of BPR argue that this resulted in the erection of 'Chinese walls' around functional silos, impeding the natural flow of ideas, information and physical material to complete a business transaction and deliver value to the customer. In their view, business processes cross the boundaries of function-based departments. Some even argue that in the future, traditional management functions will become redundant, processes will be managed by multi-functional teams, and functional specialists will be a thing of the past.

We would council caution, and counter-argue that BPR, while it has its merits, also has disadvantages. In the evangelical rhetoric that has accompanied BPR, we are in danger of diminishing the value of specialization associated with the word *management* rather than with the word *business*. Comparing the two in terms of other words used to define their meanings in a dictionary, and in terms of words having connotations with them, we see that they are perceived differently (see table). The word *business* carries a much greater connotation of excitement than *management*. Its value as a marketing tool is indicated by using a simple count of UK universities using it in their relevant departmental titles. Thirty-eight use it, while only ten use *management*, and two universities use both.

But business is what we do, and management is how we do it. It follows that in management we need to be more methodical, and perhaps bureaucratic, to draw together and analyze information in a more scientific manner to better inform business decisions. Functional management specialists will therefore still be needed to support the business, and perhaps to analyze the business processes identified by the business minds.

Comparison of
business *and*
management

	Dictionary definitions	**Words having connotations**
Business	Trade, commercial transactions	An art, creative, strategic, exciting, entrepreneurial, fast moving
Management	Guiding the running of a business, contrive, succeed despite difficulties, administration (from the word *manage*)	A science, methodical, operational, boring, bureaucratic, slow moving

The questions need to be asked:

What place is there in the new process-based approach for specialists in the functional management disciplines that have underpinned business for so long?

and

What skills and techniques can functional specialists bring to the business process party to add value to the new approach?

This text will attempt to answer these questions, for the marketing specialism, by considering the place of strategic marketing within a process-based framework, and the role of process-based management in strategic marketing.

Dedication

To Z

—Luiz

To wife and Registrar Marie BA (weddings by appointment), and children Dr Iain and Dr Ruth. Thank you for everything.

—Geoff

To all our contributors, thank you for your infinite patience.

—Both of us

About the book

Organization of the text: a business process map

This textbook is divided into seven parts. With each part it moves progressively through the business processes generic to all organizations, both direct value adding and service support processes according to Porter's terminology. A process map illustrating these processes and the structure of the textbook is shown in the figure on the following page. Each chapter indicated in the map has been written by a specialist in marketing, supported by a co-author in another cognitive area of management. In this way we have attempted to introduce a cross-fertilization of ideas in much the same way as BPR tries to.

In Part 1, the aim is to introduce the reader to process-based management and to consider the implication of this to the marketing function. In the conclusion of Part 1, the introduction to business processes concludes with further consideration of the aspect of business processes most closely related to marketing, that of customer-focused management.

In any organization, one fundamental process involves predicting and managing the future. Part 2 concentrates on processes aimed at this. It includes chapters on strategic aspects of environmental scanning and demand management.

Part 3 covers the service support process of data management. It includes chapters on strategic corporate knowledge, information systems and marketing measurement and analysis.

Part 4 turns to the direct value adding process of order fulfilment and looks at the value chain, managing customer relationships, operations programming and distribution systems.

Part 5 looks at the core marketing process, that of acquiring customers. This is divided into three areas: the market-to-collection process, the management of reputation and the management of innovation.

Part 6 returns to supporting processes, but fundamentally important ones grouped under the umbrella of infrastructure. These are all concerned with organizational development and co-operation, and include organizational learning, planning and finance, but in the final chapter of this part, cross-boundary and global management factors are also considered.

Finally, in Part 7, a single chapter, the future is considered and the editors of the text attempt to predict future trends in process-based marketing management.

Each chapter is supported with 'process in action' notes to illustrate how organizations could, or do, use the theory and concepts described in the chapter. Learning is best gained by enquiry, so each case is accompanied by questions to get the reader to develop arguments further, or, in the case of 'live' organizations, to find out more.

Strategic Marketing Management: A Business Process Approach. Outline chapter plan.

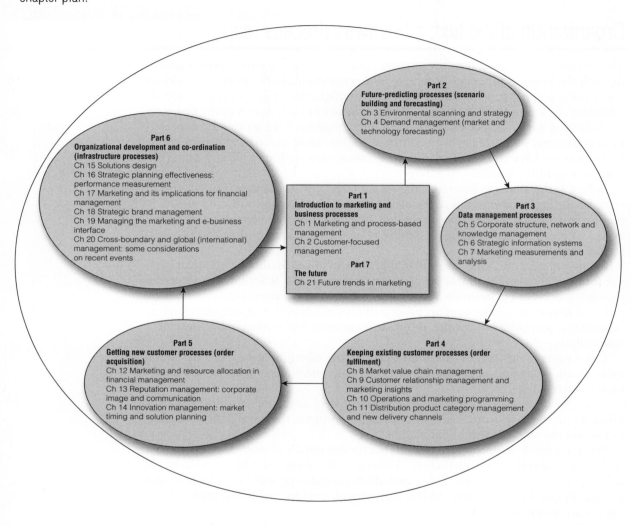

Part 2
Future-predicting processes (scenario building and forecasting)
Ch 3 Environmental scanning and strategy
Ch 4 Demand management (market and technology forecasting)

Part 6
Organizational development and co-ordination (infrastructure processes)
Ch 15 Solutions design
Ch 16 Strategic planning effectiveness: performance measurement
Ch 17 Marketing and its implications for financial management
Ch 18 Strategic brand management
Ch 19 Managing the marketing and e-business interface
Ch 20 Cross-boundary and global (international) management: some considerations on recent events

Part 1
Introduction to marketing and business processes
Ch 1 Marketing and process-based management
Ch 2 Customer-focused management

Part 7
The future
Ch 21 Future trends in marketing

Part 3
Data management processes
Ch 5 Corporate structure, network and knowledge management
Ch 6 Strategic information systems
Ch 7 Marketing measurements and analysis

Part 5
Getting new customer processes (order acquisition)
Ch 12 Marketing and resource allocation in financial management
Ch 13 Reputation management: corporate image and communication
Ch 14 Innovation management: market timing and solution planning

Part 4
Keeping existing customer processes (order fulfilment)
Ch 8 Market value chain management
Ch 9 Customer relationship management and marketing insights
Ch 10 Operations and marketing programming
Ch 11 Distribution product category management and new delivery channels

Walk-through tour

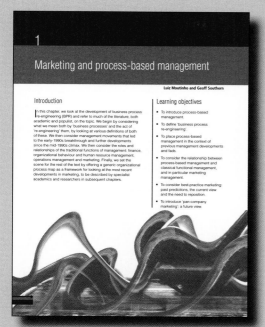

Introduction Each chapter starts with an introduction to the kinds of principles and issues you will meet in the chapter.

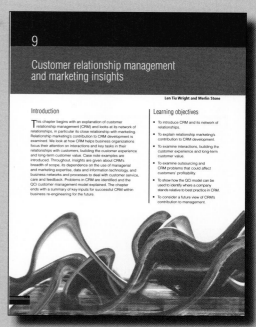

Learning objectives Appear at the start of every chapter to help you monitor your understanding and progress through the chapter.

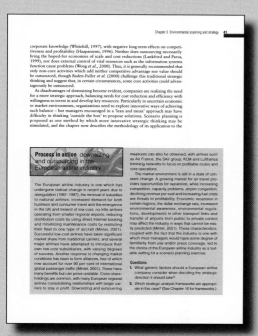

Process in action Each chapter contains in-depth case studies to reinforce principles outlined in each chapter.

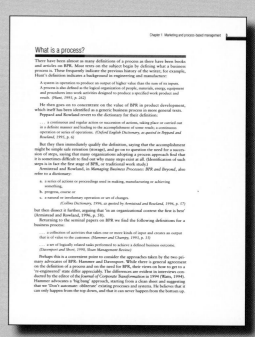

Quotes Each chapter contains quotes from different experts about the principles detailed in the book.

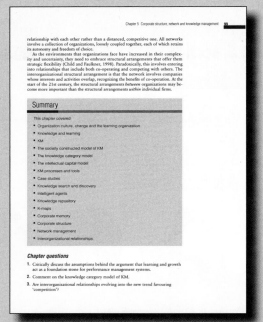

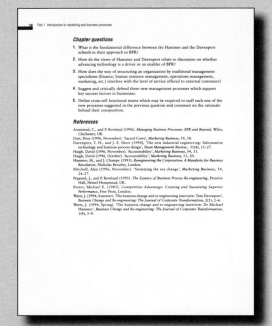

Summary Each chapter ends with a comprehensive summary that provides a thorough recap of the key issues in each chapter, helping you to assess your understanding and revise key content.

Questions Are provided at the end of each chapter and Process in action to help reinforce and test your knowledge and understanding, and provide a basis for group discussions and activities.

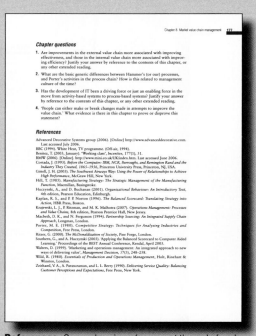

References Comprehensive references at the end of each chapter allow you to explore the subject further, and act as a starting point for projects and assignments.

Part one

Introduction to marketing and business processes

1 Marketing and process-based management

2 Customer-focused management

Process-based management, the core concept and the essence of the positioning of this text, is capable of ensuring truly customer-focused management.

Chapter 1 analyzes key antecedents of process-based management (PBM), i.e., management trends in the role and relationship of the traditional management functions, and offers an organizational process map as a framework for looking at the most recent developments in marketing. This chapter also places PBM in the context of previous management developments and fads to consider the relationship between PBM, process-based marketing management and analyses, and best-practice marketing. The 'process in action' notes in this chapter look at the way IBM changed their strategy from being a 'supplier of electronic boxes' to a 'provider of business solutions', and how their approach to re-engineering (and that of Unipart and Xerox) resulted in a change of structure to focus more on markets and customers.

Chapter 2 complements Chapter 1 by looking at how customer-focused management goes hand in hand with PBM, i.e., optimizing processes by keeping the customer in mind. It stresses the concepts of the creation of customer value, customer-facing processes, market sensing, and customer linking and value assessment. The 'process in action' note looks at customer-perceived problems in the US health industry, specifically a sense of bureaucracy in consumers at a time of high personal stress, and out-of-control costs and inability to detect fraud against insurance companies and state authorities funding the service. The note explains how Microsoft offers off-the-shelf solutions to these problems by using web technology and what they term 'service-oriented architecture'.

1

Marketing and process-based management

Luiz Moutinho and Geoff Southern

Introduction

In this chapter, we look at the development of business process re-engineering (BPR) and refer to much of the literature, both academic and populist, on the topic. We begin by considering what we mean both by 'business processes' and the act of 're-engineering' them, by looking at various definitions of both of these. We then consider management movements that led to the early-1990s breakthrough and further developments since the mid-1990s climax. We then consider the roles and relationships of the traditional functions of management: finance, organizational behaviour and human resource management, operations management and marketing. Finally, we set the scene for the rest of the text by offering a generic organizational process map as a framework for looking at the most recent developments in marketing, to be described by specialist academics and researchers in subsequent chapters.

Learning objectives

- To introduce process-based management.

- To define 'business process re-engineering'.

- To place process-based management in the context of previous management developments and fads.

- To consider the relationship between process-based management and classical functional management, and in particular marketing management.

- To consider best-practice marketing: past predictions, the current view and the need to reposition.

- To introduce 'pan-company marketing': a future view.

What is a process?

There have been almost as many definitions of a process as there have been books and articles on BPR. Most texts on the subject begin by defining what a business process is. These frequently indicate the previous history of the writer; for example, Hunt's definition indicates a background in engineering and manufacture:

> A system in operation to produce an output of higher value than the sum of its inputs. A process is also defined as the logical organization of people, materials, energy, equipment and procedures into work activities designed to produce a specified work product and result. *(Hunt, 1993, p. 262)*

He then goes on to concentrate on the value of BPR in product development, which itself has been identified as a generic business process in more general texts. Peppard and Rowland revert to the dictionary for their definition:

> . . . a continuous and regular action or succession of actions, taking place or carried out in a definite manner and leading to the accomplishment of some result; a continuous operation or series of operations. *(Oxford English Dictionary, as quoted in Peppard and Rowland, 1995, p. 6)*

But they then immediately qualify the definition, saying that the accomplishment might be simple safe retention (storage), and go on to question the need for a succession of steps, saying that many organizations adopting a process approach find that it is sometimes difficult to find out why many steps exist at all. (Identification of such steps is in fact the first stage of BPR, or traditional work study.)

Armistead and Rowland, in *Managing Business Processes: BPR and Beyond*, also refer to a dictionary:

a. a series of actions or proceedings used in making, manufacturing or achieving something,

b. progress, course or

c. a natural or involuntary operation or set of changes.

> *(Collins Dictionary, 1996, as quoted by Armistead and Rowland, 1996, p. 57)*

but then dissect it further, arguing that 'in an organizational context the first is best' (Armistead and Rowland, 1996, p. 58).

Returning to the seminal papers on BPR we find the following definitions for a business process:

> . . . a collection of activities that takes one or more kinds of input and creates an output that is of value to the customer. *(Hammer and Champy, 1993, p. 35)*

> . . . a set of logically related tasks performed to achieve a defined business outcome. *(Davenport and Short, 1990, Sloan Management Review)*

Perhaps this is a convenient point to consider the approaches taken by the two primary advocates of BPR: Hammer and Davenport. While there is general agreement on the definition of a process and on the need for BPR, their views on how to get to a 're-engineered' state differ appreciably. The differences are evident in interviews conducted by the editor of the *Journal of Corporate Transformation* in 1994 (Watts, 1994). Hammer advocates a 'big bang' approach, starting from a clean sheet and suggesting that we 'Don't automate: obliterate' existing processes and systems. He believes that it can only happen from the top down, and that it can never happen from the bottom up.

Davenport, however, stresses the compatibility of BPR with more incremental approaches to change, such as continuous improvement within total quality management (TQM). (These differences reflect the two established classic approaches to managing change, respectively, systems intervention and organizational development.) Davenport also seems to emphasize that technology is a driver of change, while Hammer considers it to be an enabler, although both come from a background in technology.

Hammer and Champy, in their first text (1993), cite four recurring processes, defining them by the state change implied. We would like to modify these slightly and propose them as primary processes for any organization, and perhaps add a further one.

- *Product development*, which they defined by the state change 'concept to prototype'. The only change we would make to this is to make it **'service-product development'**. However, it could also be incorporated into the order acquisition process discussed below.
- *Sales*, which they defined by the state change 'prospect to order'. We would widen this to **'order acquisition'** to include all publicity and brand management activities.
- *Order fulfilment*, which they defined by the state change 'order to payment'. We would not wish to change this definition.
- *Service*, which they defined by the state change 'inquiry to resolution'. We would argue that this is, in effect, a supporting process to order acquisition and order fulfilment, and hence class it as a second-level process.

These processes relate to Porter's generic value chain, where the primary activities of inbound logistics, operations, outbound logistics, marketing and sales, and service are supported by the activities of firm infrastructure, human resource management, technology development and procurement (Porter, 1985). However, Porter defines service as a primary process.

We would include three further generic processes in our list which, although not direct adders of value in the Porter mode, are essential as either directing or supporting processes. These are:

- **Organizational development and co-ordination**, perhaps classed by Porter as firm infrastructure activities. It includes the management activities of strategic development, planning and control, as actioned by a strategic plan and the budgetary control system.
- **Predicting futures**, needed to support both strategic and operational processes.
- **Data management**, also essential for strategic and operational process support.

These generic processes will be used as the framework for this book and will offer a vehicle through which experts may elaborate on what the concepts, theory and techniques of their specialization offer to the re-engineered organization.

What is business process re-engineering?

Having defined what a business process is, we now need to consider the 're-engineering' part of BPR. Hammer and Champy's definition has become the most cited:

> Re-engineering is the fundamental rethinking and radical design of business processes to achieve dramatic improvements in critical, contemporary measures of performance, such as cost, quality, service and speed. *(Hammer and Champy, 1993)*

Asked in 1994 to respond to people who say there is actually nothing new in BPR, Hammer replied, 'I'd say they're probably right!'

Indeed, in many texts on BPR, the established techniques of system analysis and development are described and called upon. These include techniques of work study (method study and work measurement) begun by Tailor and Ford in the 1920s, TQM concepts and techniques from the 1970s and systems thinking and change management material from the 1980s.

Hammer used TQM to illustrate his view of the novelty of BPR, saying:

> Re-engineering borrows two concepts from the quality revolution, namely the focus on customers and the notion of process. They are not original to re-engineering. Those I think, go back a long way, but certainly they are the fundamentals of the quality revolution. What's new about re-engineering is its radical nature. The notion of a clean sheet. . . . So that's what I think is really distinctive and new about it. *(Business Change and Re-engineering, Vol 1 No 4, Spring 1994)*

However, as we have already seen, other advocates of BPR, including Davenport, have a less radical view and see a greater role for employing existing management concepts and techniques in the analysis of processes, and in the implementation of new or amended ones. Davenport, in response to Hammer, says:

> . . . he [Hammer] takes a very strong view of the differences and almost the opposition between re-engineering and the more incremental approaches to change – things like quality and so on. My experience has been very much that these are very compatible approaches to change and in fact most organizations end up mixing and matching and combining them, even on a single project. *(Business Change and Re-engineering, Vol 2 No 1, Summer 1994)*

Since 1990, developments in supply chain management and performance management have built on the BPR foundation. In supply chain management an holistic approach to Porter's value chain has been adopted, and in performance measurement the 'balanced scorecard' approach, concentrating on developing measures to support improvement, has been introduced. Moreover, in these developments, the underlying principles of BPR, i.e.,

> **concentrating on processes** and the change in mindset from specialist (knowledge-based) silos to cross-functional completion

and

> **focusing on customers** throughout the organization's supply chain

are still being applied.

The role of traditional management functions in BPR

Let us now consider the relationship between the traditional functions of management and our generic business processes, in other words, where the work was done and who was primarily responsible.

- **Service-product development** was usually undertaken by a specialist department calling upon expertise from all departments on a need basis, or by a cross-functional team drawn from existing departments. Concepts of simultaneous engineering, particularly in the manufacturing sector, could even be regarded as a forerunner of BPR.

- **Order acquisition** was primarily a concern of the sales and marketing functions, supported by the order-fulfilment process to ensure that existing customers return.
- **Order fulfilment** was primarily a concern of the operations function. This consists of subsystems to define resource needs, to acquire resources and to schedule use of resources. Inputs to the function consist of forecasts of activity levels and work standards. Outputs consist of resource usage plans, which are then incorporated into financial budgets and HRM plans.
- **Organizational development and co-ordination** was usually undertaken by strategy and finance departments. The operating mechanism for this, at least in the short-to-medium term, is the budgeting process, where inputs come from marketing (activity levels, external) and operations (resource costs).
- **Predicting futures** was usually undertaken by the marketing function to predict demand for activities and by the operations function to predict the supply of them, both supported by the data management process.
- **Data management** was usually undertaken by a specialist department; it supports every other process.

The relationship between marketing and BPR

Ever since the concept of process management hit business, activities traditionally undertaken by the marketing function have been prime candidates for re-engineering. This is driven by the idea, inherent in process management, that decisions and actions

Process in action IBM

IBM has created a number of customer-focused business units. These include industry solution units, which focus on the needs of larger customers within specific sectors, such as banking or retailing, and which operate on a regional or even global basis; product sales units, which specialize in particular technologies; and a global services unit, which is, effectively, a consultancy.

Two key points
First, each of them 'does' their own marketing. They have their own budgets and most activities of the traditional marketing department are dispersed across them, popping up as elements of customer relationship management (CRM). However there are some specialist marketing units, such as IBM Direct, which works with segment managers to execute customer communication initiatives, and some specialist training programmes such as IBM's 'Marketing profession'.

Second, the centrifugal tendencies created by myriad different business units have to be countered. For IBM, CRM is a part of the answer, designed to offer customers the full power of IBM's global resources. At the same time, the job of brand management and advertising strategy has been reclaimed by the head office.

One by-product is that advertising is now all but completely separate from the marketing department. The marketing director is now focused primarily on sales channels plus a relatively small number of specialist marketing support functions, such as a rapidly growing telemarketing operation.

There is a separate advertising manager, whose main focus, however, is on media effectiveness, not content, and sits not in the marketing department but in communications and corporate affairs.

Question
IBM believed that their business had changed, from being sellers of 'computer boxes' to being 'providers of business solutions'. How does the reorganization described above support this belief?

should flow horizontally across an organization from supplier inputs to customer outlets, rather than flowing up and down functional departments.

Marketers are nowhere to be seen in the directors' chairs of FTSE 100 companies, or, indeed, of the top Fortune 500 in the US and Europe, as a CIM study revealed in 2001. Accountants, not marketers, dominate in the boardrooms of leading UK and US companies, indicating that marketing is still undervalued by those directing business. It is vital that senior management views marketing as a value driver.

> You have to be expert not only in your silo of marketing, but to be able to demonstrate a skill, knowledge and understanding of how the organization works as a whole. It's a case of thinking organizationally and seeing the bigger picture. *(Chris Pearce Institute of Directors)*

Organizational boundaries are becoming less important. One of the hallmarks of the new process-driven business of particular relevance to marketing is the intense struggle to work out what it really means to be customer facing.

Best-practice marketing: past predictions

A few years ago, the marketing function was in the midst of a revolution. Influential advisers such as McKinsey and Coopers & Lybrand were arguing that marketing was in 'a mid-life crisis' or 'at the crossroads'. A veritable army of trends, business buzzwords and new concepts looked set to transform the face of marketing. Recession and cost cutting were leading to the downsizing and delayering of the marketing department. BPR and TQM would mean that the marketing department would be absorbed into horizontal processes such as order generation and order fulfilment. Cross-functional team working would leave marketing increasingly as a secondary, support function. The rising importance of the delivery channel would prompt the increasing integration of sales and marketing. Internationalization and global branding were forcing national marketing departments to cede their territorial powers to global centres of strategic brand management, leaving local marketers as mere tactical implementers. And, of course, the rise of 'total-company' marketing would end up with the diffusion of marketing across the whole company.

Looking back, it's easy to see that not all of these trends could come to pass; many contradict each other. Yes, there have been some high-profile reorganizations. For example, Unilever subsidiary Elida Gibbs caused quite a stir when they abolished the role of marketing director and redivided the marketing department into brand development, innovation and category management. But far from dying, brand managers (or to be more exact, product managers, who outnumber brand managers 10 to 1) are not only alive and kicking but increasing their influence within the organization. Despite widespread talk about the downgrading of the product manager's role, the opposite appears to be happening. 'The revealed trend is one of increasing responsibility, particularly business or profit responsibility.' This is particularly the case in industrial and business-to-business firms, where the trend is pushing them towards the leading edge in terms of future developments of the role.

Much of the debate about 'the future of the marketing department' and 'the death of the brand manager' has been fast moving consumer goods (FMCG)-centric. Later adopters of product management are seeing things turn out differently. Many of the best performers are the ones who haven't taken their eye off the ball with reorganizations and restructurings, but have simply continued doing a classical job classically well. On the other hand, many companies have introduced well-meaning vision and mission changes, only to find their implementation stifled by traditional organizational structures which simply cannot come to grips with the changes that are needed.

There's an alternative explanation, however, and that is that successful change is so damned difficult.

> There's invariably a curve. Where major change is involved, it takes some time for people to understand and accept it. . . . This is especially the case if it could be construed as a paradigm shift. There is no single way forward, and no obvious place for people to look for a model. *(Mitchell, 1996)*

Best-practice marketing: the current view

Marketing itself is now in need of rejuvenation. Many marketing departments have turned into bureaucratic 'sweatshops', and innovation is seen as a 'holy grail' solution. But the fundamental problem is that marketing is in danger of losing its necessary and vital potency. This increasingly makes tough demands on all marketing in all companies all of the time, and means that everyone in the company, and certainly in the marketing department, has to be totally committed to 'innovation'. And that is what competitive marketing should have been in the first place; marketing subsumes – or should subsume – innovation.

Marketing, as a management function, in subsuming innovation, is becoming more ethically responsible, value oriented, broadened, conservation oriented, flexible and anticipatory. The marketing concept will be broadened to include the social responsibility of organizations – a belief that an organization has an obligation to society to preserve and protect the environment and to contribute to a better quality of life for all citizens. This can create a moral dilemma. Increasingly, the burden is falling on marketing managers to make the right ethical calls and to forge strategies which avoid causing offence. But to which moral or ethical value system should marketers be held accountable? This is not simply a semantic point. It can be a nightmare to get the balance right. For example, is it morally acceptable to promote alcohol, fast cars, furs and field sports? Is it acceptable to advertise sanitary products, formula milk for babies, fatty foods or slimming products? How should a responsible, 'accountable' marketing organization behave? A wide variety of products and services are constantly under the spotlight (Haigh, 1996).

Marketing also provides direct interaction with customers in aspects of perceived quality which many companies attempt to embed into a 'brand'. Because consumers are more quality conscious, value-creating marketing and value-added marketing will become the predominant approaches. These approaches represent an entire system that includes speed, convenience, follow-up and an obsessive pursuit of consumer satisfaction. The new neo-marketing philosophy is essentially customer-centric. Companies once hailed as masters of brand management let their systems harden into a form of corporate sclerosis. The easy times of the 1980s made them complacent and helped them to forget that not only were their brands their *raison d'être* but that brand care and attention should come from the very top.

'Living the brand' entails building an understanding of the brand among one's own employees before communicating the brand promise to consumers. (This concept has similarities to the implementation phase of BPR, and shares the same fundamental principles of communication, ownership and empowerment.) The traditional organizational model, which has one department as brand custodian and another as people custodian, simply does not fit with world-class brand building. The most progressive companies increasingly work in a networked or cross-functional way. This enables the company to look at the way in which the brand promise is delivered in a holistic way. It also ensures that the way in which people are hired, trained, measured and rewarded fits with the brand.

Best-practice marketing: the need to reposition

The argument now goes that marketing has become too remote from the pulse of the organization. Marketing has failed to market itself. It has failed to pick up on major trends in its sphere of operations. These include:

- *Global competition*. Marketing has been too nationally focused and worried more about turf protection rather than contributing to real business success.
- *New technologies*. Information technology has created new, real-time information flows about markets, which in many cases bypass marketing departments.
- *Service revolution*. Lack of product differentiation has put a premium on service delivery. But, again, areas such as warranties and customer support often come under departments other than marketing.
- *Confident, powerful buyers*. Retailers are flexing their increasingly powerful muscles, while end users are becoming far more conscious of value for money. This puts the concept of branding in the spotlight.
- *Lack of innovation*. Too often, brand extension has been a substitute for true innovation.

As a result, many marketing departments are now being examined, analyzed and turned inside out. They can no longer avoid getting swept up by the latest management thinking about how companies operate, which is that rigid functional silos which focus solely on their own operations should be replaced by a more fluid, cross-functional way of working.

That means that words such as *measurement* and *accountability* are beginning to be applied to marketing, which has for too long been regarded as something of a budgeting black hole.

But it by no means signals marketing's demise. If anything, companies have begun to realize that marketing is almost too important to be left to the marketing department alone; it has to be something that is a core competence of that company. At software giant Microsoft, everyone in the organization is having to become customer facing, working to make sure that the company presents a consistent face at every point of contact.

Recognizing marketing as integral rather than a discrete function requires judgement, methodology, information and a focus on the development of the business. It has to be driven by a passion for what the customer wants and be led by the market to take the company forward.

Marketing accountability embraces two quite different concepts. One is transparency, the most obvious manifestation of which is financial transparency. This has been separated out for particular scrutiny in the past few years as clients have sought to extract the best possible value from their marketing budgets.

However, the concept of transparency extends beyond cost, into content, which leads to the second aspect of accountability: responsibility. Who should be held accountable for maintaining ethical and moral standards? Should it be the company, the agency, the regulator or the end consumer? We hear a lot about ethical companies, the role of the regulatory system and the rights of the individual. We also see moral judgements appearing with increasing regularity as an increasing number of issue campaigns are launched: 'right to life', 'meat is murder', 'cars cause asthma', 'breast is best' and so on.

The most important point to bear in mind is that we must make the word *marketing* really mean that vital, imaginative, forward-thinking insightful world that comes to mind when we say *innovation*; otherwise, the marketing function really will be overcome by 'bureaucratic' statistics. So, there is a need once again to create true marketing departments that are naturally and instinctively 'innovative' without pinning the word on the door. Such environments would have:

- Inspirational leadership, in touch with consumers and their 'real' world.
- Space, time and freedom for passionate individuals to pursue genuinely new thinking – with a tolerance for failure.
- Multi-dimensional stimulation that would appeal to and motivate the senses as well as the mind.
- State-of-the-art technology that would provide every statistic and necessary information on customers, habits, attitudes, trends – in fact, everything that is relevant to the efficient perusal of a marketer's vision. (Dart, 1996)

Marketing as a process: pan-company marketing (PCM)

As was the case with TQM, when quality was recognized as a total company responsibility, marketing needs to adopt the policy of becoming 'pan-company'. Pan-company marketing (PCM) unifies the activities of the whole company to win customer preference and in doing so becomes more effective and efficient. The customer becomes the driver of the business. This relates to BPR and the principle of focusing on the customer.

Designing and focusing all aspects and/or functions of the business towards delivering value to the customer is what differentiates a PCM company from a company that exhibits good marketing practice. In a PCM company, every employee has a role to play in the marketing effort.

Overall success in PCM depends upon a company having core products or services that meet and anticipate customer needs, and systems and processes that add value to the customer, plus a culture that empowers employees, encourages creativity and is essentially entrepreneurial in nature. Once again, this relates to a BPR principle: that of taking an holistic approach.

The ability and willingness to change company-wide systems and business processes if they do not add value to customers are also essential.

Marketing has moved from being merely transaction-based to developing long-term profitable relationships with customers and key influencers.

Successful PCM requires a senior executive team that is intent on developing a customer-centric company that lives and breathes a commitment to the customer. Through their actions, senior executives can ensure that the whole company is designed for customers, that is, all people, processes and systems focus on the customer.

The key is that the vision – the customer-centric approach – must permeate everything that the company does. In customer-centric companies, management must:

- Share the PCM vision.
- Communicate the importance of the customer to staff.
- Promote the practice of customer value management.
- Ensure the organizational structure and systems are customer-centric.
- Integrate branding.
- Champion marketing as a process in which the whole company participates.
- See every interaction with a customer as a learning opportunity.
- Develop and encourage flexible cross-functional teams to deliver value to the customer.
- Align performance and appraisal systems to improve and increase customer value.
- Reward employees for improving and increasing customer value.
- Motivate and support employees in their work.
- Empower front-line employees to deal with and manage customers.
- Reward information sharing and knowledge transfer – across functions and also across teams.
- Develop education and training programmes that are focused on the customer and integrated customer management.

(There are indications here of a fundamental principle of supply chain management: that of internal customers, serving each other in a value-adding supply chain, leading to the eventual consumer of the product or service offered by an organization.)

Companies such as Xerox and Unipart have struggled with many of these issues – and come up with similar answers. Both of them, for instance, are devoted to the creation of PCM cultures focused on a single corporate brand which is managed centrally, and separately, from most other marketing activities.

Process in action Unipart

To face the customer in the best way, Unipart has created separate divisions, each with their own marketing departments. One focuses on relationships with major car company clients; a 'demand chain management' division offers integrated logistics services; and Unipart International is responsible for designing, developing and marketing its branded automotive parts.

The core operational marketing activity for its spare parts business is now conducted not by a marketing department but by eight different 'cells', which bring engineers, purchasing staff and product managers together into cross-functional teams. These cells make key decisions relating to range, price, packaging, promotion and specification.

Advertising *per se* is handled by yet another body. In other words, like IBM, what's called the marketing department is now much more keenly focused on channel management.

Question

1. What business processes have been re-engineered in Unipart, and how has this affected their communications with customers?

Likewise, Unipart group Chief Executive John Neill is famous for his backing of the thesis that marketing is too important to be left to the marketing department.

Like IBM, both companies have also struggled with what it means to be customer facing. As a result, their marketing activities are now dispersed across a range of business units with the help of centralized strategic brand communication and tactical marketing support units.

Xerox's struggle to be customer focused has also led to the development of a number of product units, responsible for everything from new product development (NPD) to the final delivery of products such as printers or networked copies. There are also special 'small is beautiful' customer business units whose task is to keep close to customers in relatively small geographical areas, or at a corporate level, such as Siemens in Germany or Thomson in France. Getting the 'conversion layer' between production-oriented management decisions and customer-facing units is critical.

The 20th century may well have marked the end of the marketing department. It has thrown up some common, recognizable problems:

- Aversion to risk taking, with the result that the creative onus is passed to outside suppliers, such as ad agencies.
- Brands proliferate in a bid to increase the power base, both of the brand managers and their creative network.
- Brands compete in the same company for resources.
- Delegating brand decisions to junior managers fails to foster continued brand know-how as well as smother real innovation.

There is no single answer. Whatever the route, brands have to be the signposts for everyone in the company. Marketers become 'added-value coaches' across organizational business teams, while they also keep abreast of consumer/market changes that could rewrite the brand script.

Recently, doubts about the roles of the marketing department, accountability and marketing's influence at board level have been growing. For example, one unavoidable message is that brand building is as much a process of 'from the inside out' as

Process in action Xerox

Xerox has three key processes: 'time to market', which is responsible for upstream product development, including working out what the market wants; 'supply chain', which includes most other traditional operational marketing and selling activities, plus installation and after-sales administration; and finally 'customer service'.

There are also supporting structures, such as a management layer, and an infrastructure layer, which includes market communications. And again, like IBM, Xerox found the need to stop product and

customer business units from becoming, as it were, 'too' customer focused. So, having experimented with dispersing the role of a strategic marketing planning group, IBM reverted to integration, recognizing the need for an 'umbrella' to make sure that market gaps are identified on the one hand, and that efforts aren't duplicated on the other.

Question
1. How well do the Xerox key processes fit the generic processes defined by the authors previously: service-product development, order acquisition, order fulfilment (all direct value adders), and organizational development and co-ordination, predicting futures, and data management (all supporting processes)?

it is 'from the outside (i.e., the market) in'. Somehow, successful brands seem to embody and express the vitality and vision of the corporate culture that created them. If so, the art of building truly great brands is bigger, broader, more subtle and more complex than most marketers have yet achieved.

An uncomfortable thought? Perhaps. But it's exhilaratingly full of new possibilities too. 'Upstream' processes like NPD begin to look very different to 'downstream' customer-facing activities, such as customer service; strategic issues such as market segmentation and targeting find themselves separated from operational tasks such as pricing and promotions. Traditional distinctions between product, service and delivery/distribution dissolve into new all-embracing concepts like 'customer solutions'. In some manufacturing companies, the traditional functions of product design and production have already been merged under the umbrella of simultaneous engineering. Familiar job titles disappear to be replaced by a bizarre assortment of new tags such as 'development manager, market to collection' or 'manager, customer satisfaction, quality and re-engineering'. In short, the marketing department of old finds itself sliced, chopped and dispersed across the whole business.

Summary

- Business process re-engineering (BPR) is the. . . fundamental rethinking and radical design of business processes to achieve dramatic improvements in critical, contemporary measures of performance, such as cost, quality, service and speed. *(Hammer and Champy, 1993)*

- BPR draws upon concepts and techniques from other management strands of thought. It encompasses ideas from, e.g., systems thinking, total quality management (TQM) and supply (and value) chain management.

- BPR takes an holistic approach to management, which concentrates on processes while also focusing on customers.

- The authors of this chapter have identified six generic business processes: service-product development, order acquisition, order fulfilment, organizational development and co-ordination, predicting futures and data management.

- These encompass traditional functions of management, but put into practice a culture of cross-functional completion rather than one of a specialist-silo mentality with responsibility handovers.

- Marketers need to reposition themselves from a mentality of specialist-silo thinking to one which either drives or supports generic business processes.

- Whether driving or supporting, this will involve them in taking the lead in developing and improving a customer-centric approach in all processes identified in a company.

- Marketers must develop the concept of pan-company marketing (PCM) to ensure that both individual employees and business processes continue to be focused on both current customer demands and on future customer needs.

Chapter questions

1. What is the fundamental difference between the Hammer and the Davenport schools in their approach to BPR?

2. How do the views of Hammer and Davenport relate to discussion on whether advancing technology is a driver or an enabler of BPR?

3. How does the way of structuring an organization by traditional management specialisms (finance, human resource management, operations management, marketing, etc.) interfere with the level of service offered to external customers?

4. Suggest and critically defend three new management processes which support key success factors in businesses.

5. Define cross-cell functional teams which may be required to staff each one of the new processes suggested in the previous question and comment on the rationale behind their composition.

References

Armistead, C., and Rowland, P. (1996) *Managing Business Processes: BPR and Beyond*, Chichester, UK: Wiley.

Dart, P. (1996, November) 'Sacred Cows', *Marketing Business*, 54:58.

Davenport, T. H., and Short, J. E. (1990) 'The new industrial engineering: Information technology and business process design', *Sloan Management Review*, 31(4):11–27.

Haigh, D. (1996, November) 'Accountability', *Marketing Business*, 54:31.

Haigh, D. (1996, October) 'Accountability', *Marketing Business*, 53:20.

Hammer, M., and Champy, J. (1993) *Reengineering the Corporation: A Manifesto for Business Revolution*, London: Nicholas Brearley.

Mitchell, A. (1996, November) 'Stemming the sea change', *Marketing Business*, 54:24–27.

Peppard, J., and Rowland, P. (1995) *The Essence of Business Process Re-engineering*, Hemel Hempstead, UK: Prentice Hall.

Porter, M. E. (1985) *Competitive Advantage: Creating and Sustaining Superior Performance*, London: Free Press.

Watts, J. (1994, Summer) 'The business change and re-engineering interview: Tom Davenport', *Business Change and Re-engineering: The Journal of Corporate Transformation*, 2(1):2–6.

Watts, J. (1994, Spring) 'The business change and re-engineering interview: Dr Michael Hammer', *Business Change and Re-engineering: The Journal of Corporate Transformation*, 1(4):5–9.

2

Customer-focused management

Erik M. van Raaij, W. Fred van Raaij and Harry J.P. Timmermans

Introduction

Process-based management and customer-focused management go hand in hand. Harrington (1991) defines a 'process' as 'an activity or group of activities that takes an input, adds value to it and provides an output to an internal or external customer' (p. 9). Harrington thus considers a process to be necessarily customer oriented. In this chapter, we therefore assume that a process-based organization needs to be customer focused, because it needs to define its processes with the internal or external customer in mind. Customer-focused management thus is providing an added value or output that is wanted or requested by a customer. See Figure 2.1.

In this chapter, we will discuss what it means to be customer focused in a process-based organization. One of the key elements is the creation of customer value. As we have seen

Learning objectives

- To understand the link between process-based and customer-focused management.

- To understand which customers to focus on [target group(s)].

- To understand which business processes are crucial to make an organization customer focused.

- To understand which resources an organization needs in order to be customer focused.

from the definition of a process, the activities performed in the process should be adding value to the process inputs. The only entity to judge whether sufficient value has been added is the customer. The customer will perform this judgement on the basis of their product or service needs and service expectations. The success of an organization is determined by the extent to which customers value the organization's process output over and above the outputs of competing organizations. Issues of customer perceived value are discussed in section 2 of this chapter.

Section 3 defines what customer-focused management entails. In addition to an organization structure built around customer-facing processes, there are implications for managerial decision-making, performance management and organizational culture.

In section 4, the key processes in customer-focused organizations are sketched. These six processes are: market sensing and prediction, customer selection, value conception, value generation, customer linking and value assessment. Through these processes, organizations learn about customers and improve their offerings to keep loyal customers and to increase customer satisfaction.

Section 5 describes the key resources in customer-focused organizations. These resources are clustered as customer-focused assets, customer-focused capabilities and customer-focused culture.

Key issues for this chapter:

- Customer-focused management
- Customer value
- Market orientation.

Figure 2.1
A simple process diagram

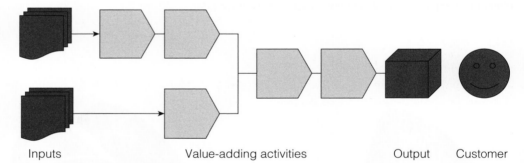

Inputs   Value-adding activities   Output Customer

Customer focus, customer value and customer satisfaction

Process design should always start with the customer in mind. Decisions about what inputs to use, what activities to include in the process, in what sequence and the quality level and depth with which these activities are carried out all impact on the nature, the quality and the cost of the added value and process outputs. Differentiation in the output is determined by differentiation in inputs and processes.

Let's take the restaurant service process as an example. Inputs include raw materials (such as food ingredients), people (such as waiting staff and cooks) and physical assets (such as the building, the kitchen equipment and the furniture). A top restaurant will differentiate itself from a side-street diner by using a top chef, a large number of well-trained staff, top ingredients and a spacious dining room with stylish furniture. Apart from differentiation on these inputs, the top restaurant will differentiate itself on the service process. It will, for instance, offer table reservations, valet parking, cloakroom services, wine advice and à la carte dining, and the chef may go around the tables to talk to the guests. As a customer, we only see the differences in the front-end processes, but the back-end processes – such as buying food items, food preparation and menu planning – will also differ significantly between the top restaurant and the side-street diner.

Variations in inputs and processes lead to variations in outputs. These outputs are usually not individual goods or services, but a bundle of goods and services, such as a marketing textbook that comes with a supporting website or a packaging machine sold together with a service contract. In marketing, these product bundles are called 'offerings'. When customers make purchase decisions, they choose between offerings, and in order to choose, they form expectations about the value of each of the competing offerings. These value expectations are a function of the expected benefits of the offering and the expected total cost of the offering. It is important to note that customer-*perceived* value, *perceived* benefits and *perceived* costs are key here. Perceived costs include the price to pay and the customer time and effort to obtain the benefits. This creates a challenge for suppliers, as different individual customers will have different perceptions of benefits, costs and value. How can an organization accurately design its processes if each individual customer has their own perceptions of the value of process outputs? Should processes be standardized to serve the average customer or should processes be flexible to be able to serve each individual customer differently?

This is the first and foremost key issue for customer-focused management: the decision regarding which customers to focus on. No organization can be customer focused without choosing what customers or groups of customers to focus on. The answer lies in segmentation and targeting. The customer-focused organization needs to study the different needs, attitudes and behaviours within a market and then analyze whether there are distinct segments of customers with similar needs, attitudes and behaviours. If there exist such distinct market segments, the organization needs to determine the attractiveness of each segment by looking at segment size, growth, homogeneity, profitability and risk, as well as the organization's objectives and resources. The organization can then choose to (1) target individual customers, (2) target a single market segment, (3) target a selection of segments or (4) target the market as a whole with an undifferentiated, often low-price offering. In these four different situations, being customer focused means different things, as can be seen in Table 2.1. If a segment is homogeneous, the customers in a segment are similar to the 'average' customer of that segment.[1]

The four types of targeting strategy and customer focus (Table 2.1) are 'ideal types'; in reality, firms employ variations and combinations of these four types. The private banking sector of a retail bank branch, for example, may focus primarily on one customer segment: high-net-worth individuals in a particular geographical region. But for those high-net-worth individuals, it may strive to offer customized solutions. Some of the bank's business processes will be standardized for the 'average' high-net-worth individual (such as marketing communications processes), while other processes will be flexible, customizable processes (such as account management for the personal savings and investments advisory process).

Customer satisfaction

The prime measure of success for a customer-focused organization is customer satisfaction, as the customer is the ultimate judge of process performance. This applies to both internal and external customers. For external customers, the organization should be primarily interested in the level of satisfaction of its target customers.[2]

The way satisfaction is measured should match the idea of a core service product complemented with augmented products/services. With respect to the core product, satisfaction can be measured as the degree to which the product satisfies the need(s) of the customer. A flight that takes the customer and their luggage from Amsterdam to Glasgow is a satisfactory core service if the flight arrives on time and if Glasgow was indeed the intended destination of the customer. With respect to the augmented product elements, satisfaction can be measured as the degree to which the various elements have satisfied the quality expectations of the customer. Was the food up to

Table 2.1
Four types of customer focus

Targeting strategy	Type of customer focus	Implications for process design
Customization	Focusing on each customer as an individual	Flexible, customizable processes
Single segment concentration	Focusing on one specific type of customer	Processes standardized for the 'average' customer of the chosen segment (one target group)
Differentiated marketing	A differentiated focus on a selection of different customer types	Differentiation in processes to cater for a variety of 'average' customers (several target groups)
Undifferentiated (mass) marketing	An undifferentiated focus on all customers	Processes standardized to appeal to the broadest number of customers

---

[1] In some instances, for instance for luxury products, it is better to use in advertising a somewhat 'above average' customer who is perceived as a reference person for the members of that segment. Thus, the models shown in automobile advertising are usually younger than the average member of the particular target group.

[2] This does not mean that customers who do not belong to the target segment can be neglected or ignored. Dissatisfaction among non-target customers can severely disrupt service provision to target customers.

expectations? Were the airhostesses friendly? Were there sufficient newspapers on the flight? Behind the core product, as well as the augmented product, elements are the different business processes. Customer-satisfaction measurement should provide insights into whether these processes deliver the required/expected outputs.

Customer value

Customer-perceived value is one of the drivers for customer satisfaction. Perceived value refers to the trade-off between perceived benefits and perceived costs. Benefits include the benefit of satisfying the core need or solving the core problem. Benefits also include supplementary benefits, such as brand-image benefits, security benefits, social benefits and convenience benefits. A pair of jeans satisfies the core benefit of protecting against the cold, but a 'cool' pair of jeans supplies additional brand-image benefits and the benefit of belonging to a social reference group. Accounting software supplies the core benefit of being able to prepare company accounts, but an accounting module integrated in the company management information system supplies additional benefits of convenience and speed. The other side of the value equation concerns costs. Costs include not only the price on the price tag but also monetary and non-monetary costs to find information about the product, purchase the product, use the product, service the product and dispose of the product. The non-monetary costs include time costs (to find the product and to learn how to operate the product), social costs (whether others will accept and positively evaluate the product or brand) and psychological or behavioural costs (doubts about whether the product will function as promised, uncertainties about potential harmfulness of the product and annoyances about waiting times).

In many cases, it is about not just the customer-perceived benefits and costs related to the offering itself, but also benefits and costs related to the supplier or store. In consumer markets, the benefits of the pair of jeans may be augmented by perceived benefits of the store, such as store image, convenient location or friendliness of staff. Perceived costs related to the store could include parking difficulties or inflexible return policies. In business markets, perceived benefits related to the supplier could be electronic ordering and invoicing, while supplier-related costs could include strict payment terms or low-delivery reliability.

The level of customer satisfaction with an offering is determined by the – positive or negative – difference between expected value before consumption[3] and perceived value after consumption. *A priori* expectations are formed on the basis of customer needs, prior experience, marketing communications and word of mouth. *A posteriori* performance evaluations are formed on the basis of product performance, service product consumption experience, post-purchase marketing communications and post-purchase word of mouth. The customer-focused organization is aware of the various factors that influence the formation of value expectations and value perceptions and tries to manage these processes through an interactive dialogue with the customer. Too-high customer expectations, for instance those based on puffery advertising, may lower satisfaction. 'Managing expectations' in personal contacts with customers and with realistic advertising also contributes to customer satisfaction.

Customer value can be increased through product bundling and cross-selling. The core product can often be complemented with additional products and services. Buying a jacket in a fashion store is often the starting point for buying nicely fitting shirts

---

[3] The customer does not always consciously process customer expectations before consumption. It may often be the case that the customer concludes only afterwards that performance was below expectations.

and ties as well. Products and services may become an integrated 'package' with warranties, maintenance and updates. Customers want to have uninterrupted printing without breakdowns rather than just possessing a printing machine. This means that the product, be it a printer, a heater or a car, becomes part of a more widely-defined service such as uninterrupted printing, climate control or mobility. Customers judge the quality of this broadly-defined service rather than the quality of the hardware component. With increasing product sophistication, customers will judge the quality at the systems level, which is a higher level of abstraction than the product level (van Raaij and Poiesz, 2003; Poiesz and van Raaij, 2007). At this higher level, the concern is not about satisfaction with separate items but about satisfaction with the system as a whole. For business-to-consumer clients, it even concerns the well-being of clients. For business-to-business clients, the provided services may be completely integrated in the value generation system of the client.

An integrated package or bundle may consist of additional products within the same domain or in other domains. The travel agent of the future may not only sell a holiday trip, but also sell holiday items such as maps and travel guides, offer travel insurance, lease sports equipment and care for the home when the customer is on holiday. Customers obtain a clear benefit if these additional items are integrated with the core product. And the value of the customer will increase considerably for the travel agent. In some cases, especially in the case of bundling of products and services, the total offering is achieved through business partnerships and alliances. An airline will, for instance, use a third-party logistics provider to deliver lost luggage to the customer's home or hotel. The service quality of such a business partner will impact the customer's perception of the service quality of the airline. As firms are increasingly outsourcing non-core activities and using business partners to offer total solutions to customers, the brand holder should be aware of the carry-over effects of service failure of one of the partners on the quality perception of their brand.

Loyalty and lifetime value

The pay-off from higher levels of customer satisfaction lies in higher levels of customer loyalty. Customer loyalty is a two-dimensional construct (Dick and Basu, 1994). On the one hand, there is an attitudinal dimension to loyalty: the degree to which someone feels loyal towards a product, a brand or a service provider. On the other hand, there is a behavioural dimension: the degree to which someone repeatedly selects a product, brand or service provider. Attitudinal loyalty and behavioural loyalty do not necessarily go together. When there is a lack of alternatives, there may be behavioural loyalty without attitudinal loyalty. When there is restricted supply of the preferred alternative, there may be attitudinal loyalty without behavioural loyalty. Loyalty programmes are only one source of customer loyalty (and not necessarily the most effective one). Some other sources of customer loyalty are excellent service, personal relationships between buyer and seller, integrated packages of products and services, convenience and technological lock-in (e.g., through the integration of information systems). In the model of Poiesz and van Raaij (2007), product bundling and integration and long-term customer relationships are the major drivers of customer value.

In the first stage, customers may be experimenting with the company through trial of products and services. If satisfied, they may increase their loyalty up to 100 per cent, which means that they buy all products within a category or domain with a particular company. Customers also differ in the number and value of products they buy. 'Heavy' customers buy a large share of the company's output. Heavy buyers may constitute 20 per cent of all customers and buy 80 to 90 per cent of the output of a company (van Raaij *et al.*, 2003). It is clear that these heavy buyers are very valuable for the company and should be retained with special privileges if needed. A company should invest in these customers to keep them satisfied and loyal.

Customer loyalty has an impact on a financial performance indicator: customer-lifetime value (CLV). CLV (Figure 2.2) is the monetary value of expected revenues minus expected costs for the expected duration of the relationship with an individual customer. According to Heskett *et al.* (1994), the lifetime revenue stream from a loyal pizza eater can be as much as $8 000 and from a loyal Cadillac owner, $332 000. The potential lifetime value of a customer can justify investments in customer loyalty. Again, we stress the point of targeting the 'right' customer. The right customers are those with a good fit between the company's offerings and the customer's needs and with an interest in building a long-term relationship (Reinartz and Kumar, 2002).

CLV analysis is a form of prospective customer-profitability analysis. More on customer-profitability analysis can be found in Chapters 9 and 12.

Customer-focused management defined

With the main performance indicators for the customer-focused organization now defined, we turn our attention to customer-focused management. The key question is how to manage the organization in such a way that target customers are satisfied with the organization's offerings. All customer interactions with the organization or with any of the organization's products are moments of truth for the generation of customer satisfaction or dissatisfaction. The first task for management, therefore, is to identify and optimize the customer-contact moments and touchpoints with the organization.

Organization structured around customer-facing processes

All activities within an organization's processes can be categorized as either front-office activities (with customer interaction) or back-office activities (without customer interaction) (see Figure 2.3). Typical front-office activities are customer service and sales activities, while typical back-office activities are planning, purchasing and manufacturing activities.

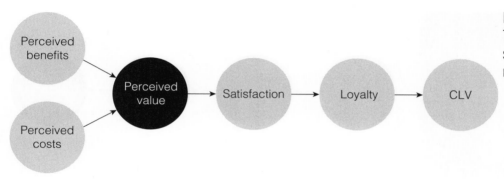

Figure 2.2
The value –
satisfaction – loyalty
relationship

When designing business processes with front-office activities, it is important to take customers and their needs as the starting point. One of the basic tenets of business process thinking is to organize for a single point of contact for the customer. After all, one major source of delays, errors and customer dissatisfaction is the hand-over from one representative to another (Davenport, 1993). There are two different ways to organize for such a single point of contact: One solution is to introduce account managers, or account teams, who represent the customer and take the customer's service requests through the different parts of the (functional) organization. The other solution is to radically redesign the organization around customer-facing processes instead of around functions. New 'departments' in such a redesigned organization could, for instance, be 'customer-solution development', which would include customer prospecting, translation and order generation; 'customer-order fulfilment', which would include order taking, assembling, shipping, installation and billing; and 'customer-enquiry resolution', which would include complaint handling, repairs and returns (cf. Shapiro *et al.*, 1992).

This has implications for an organization's information system as well. The customer-focused organization should organize its information system with the customers as the central units. The information system of a hospital should be based not on departments and specialist doctors but on (segments of) patients and the processes that are needed for their medical treatment. Exactly what activities are called for in such customer-facing processes is determined by a thorough analysis of target customers' needs. The identification of new target segments and the development of customer needs within existing segments necessitate continuous adaptations of such customer-facing processes.

Decision-making based on customer insights

Organizing around customer-facing processes is one aspect of customer-focused management; customer-focused decision-making is another. Customer-focused decision-making means, first of all, that the customer viewpoint is included in the decision-making process of the supplying organization. Consequently, information about the impact of a decision on customer satisfaction should be available and used.

A customer-relational database is necessary to store the relevant customer information, to analyze this information and to use this information for and in customer contacts. A customer database contains the names of contact persons, customer address, customer history on the contents and value of earlier transactions and customer satisfaction with delivered products, services and problem solutions. It could

Figure 2.3
Business processes drive the value – satisfaction – loyalty chain

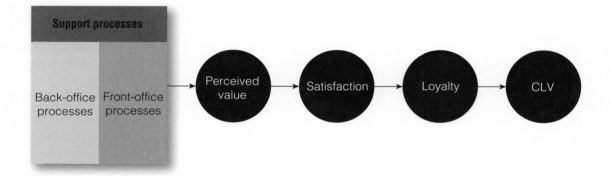

also contain information on how customers react to product offerings, salesperson contacts and direct mail.

A customer database can be used to select customers with a certain profile (characteristics) for direct mail and other contacts in order to increase the likelihood of a positive response to these proposals. It can also be used to find similar customer profiles to predict the behaviour of a particular customer based on the behaviour of similar customers. For some products there is a clear hierarchy of purchase (product ladder): these products are bought in a regular sequence. If this is the case, the next purchase of customers may be predicted. For instance, most bank clients start with a regular account and buy savings and credit products next. At the third stage, they may buy mutual funds and stocks.

Performance management based on customer satisfaction

This means that within the array of possible performance indicators, customer satisfaction and customer retention should play prominent roles. This applies not only to organization-wide performance management, but also to performance evaluation and assessment of departments, teams and individuals. Everyone in a process-based organization has customers. For employees operating in back-office processes, these will be internal customers, while for front-office personnel, these will be external customers. For many processes, there will be both internal and external customers.

When customer satisfaction and customer retention are used for evaluation and rewards, it is imperative to design a reliable customer-satisfaction measurement instrument. Data on customer retention can be acquired from the customer database.

Culture centred around the creation of customer value

Another crucial element of customer-focused management is developing and nurturing an organizational culture based on the creation of customer value. The concept of organizational culture refers to the shared norms, values and beliefs within the organization. These norms, values and beliefs should be based upon what the target customers need and expect from the organization. Norms, values and beliefs can be developed on the basis of selection of personnel, by behavioural examples set by senior managers, by storytelling and by a clear and consistent performance evaluation system based on customer value, customer satisfaction and customer retention.

Key processes in customer-focused organizations

One of the classic ways of looking at an organization as a collection of value creating processes is by the use of Porter's value chain model. While the value chain model is still useful and relevant, we prefer to use a slightly different lens to look at the customer-focused organization. Central to the customer-focused organization is its capacity to *learn* about customers and translate this learning into offerings that provide value and satisfaction to target customers (Day, 1994; Slater and Narver, 2000; van Raaij, 2001). The first thing such an organization needs to do is to develop foresight and create an image of the future. The organization needs to develop a continuous process of 'market sensing and prediction'. Based on management's vision of the future, it needs to decide which customer segment(s) to focus on. This marketing strategy formulation process is called 'customer selection'. The customer selection process defines *where* the organization wants to compete. For each customer segment, the organization needs to define *how* to compete, i.e., what type of value proposition to place in the market. This 'value conception' process is based on an analysis of customer needs, the value propositions of competitors and the identification of value gaps in the market.

Once decisions about where and how to compete are made, the organization needs to define and execute its 'value generation' processes. These are the primary processes of the organization. The exact shape of these value generation processes will depend on the type of firm. For a typical manufacturing firm, for instance, these processes will include product development, sourcing, production, order fulfilment and after-sales service.

Partly in parallel to the value generation processes, the organization needs to engage in a 'customer-linking' process. The customer-linking process includes all activities aimed at keeping and developing target customers. The 'value assessment' process, finally, is comprised measurement, evaluation and feedback activities, such as customer-satisfaction measurement, value analysis and customer-profitability analysis. The sequence of these six key processes of customer-focused organizations is depicted in Figure 2.4.

Market sensing and prediction

Market sensing and prediction cannot be performed with an occasional focus group or survey. Market sensing means that the market is continuously monitored by both customers and competitors. Autonomous developments in culture and society should be monitored as well. This may be called 'environmental scanning'. There are several sources for this monitoring information. Some companies have regular surveys on customer satisfaction, in general and for particular products. Some other companies subscribe to the services of 'trend watchers'. And other companies have a systematic way of collecting information from salespersons, repair mechanics and other persons who are in close contact with customers. Still another source of information are conferences with the presentations of the results of scientific research. We may call this monitoring of markets and society: market intelligence rather than market research.

Scenario planning involves the development of 'possible futures', often 3 to 5 years ahead. This means that present trends are analyzed, combined and integrated to likely future situations. These trends constitute demographic, economic, environmental, legal, social, cultural, political and technological developments and their impact for particular industries. Scenarios are sometimes labelled as 'optimistic' or 'pessimistic', depending on the projected developments. Scenarios may also be rated as more or less likely to happen. 'Doom scenarios' may be developed to prepare for 'crisis situations'. Likely scenarios are developed to take policy measures to be better prepared for the future.

Figure 2.4
Key processes in customer-focused organizations

| Market sensing and prediction | Customer selection | Value conception | Value generation | Customer linking | Value assessment |

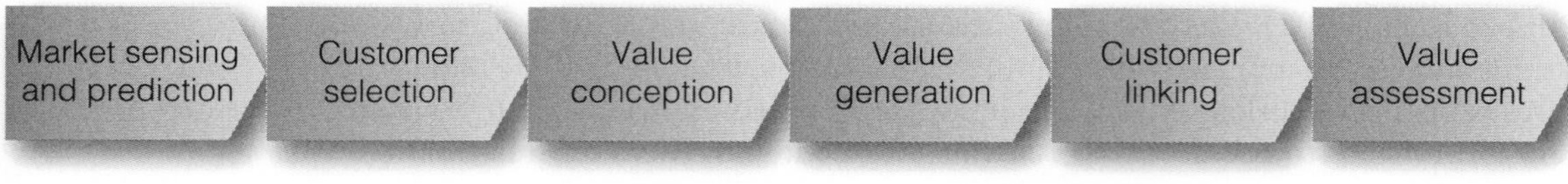

Customer selection

Customers are mainly selected on the basis of their (potential) profitability. The profitability depends on the customer value they represent and whether they can be served because their needs and desires 'match' with the company's products and services. Targeting young people is mainly done because they are potentially profitable.

What to do with non-target customers who buy the company's products? Apparently they are attracted for some reasons that have not yet been distinguished by the company. Non-target customers may also be a signal that a new market segment is emerging. If markets, technology and consumers change rapidly, targeting strategies may become obsolete in a short time. If consumers are able and willing to book their own trips through the Internet, the travel agent has to change their marketing strategy. Either the travel agent starts with Internet selling as well or tries to add value in the traditional channel. It is important for companies to track the emergence of new segments.

Some customers remain unprofitable, even after satisfactory services are provided to them. What about asking them a higher price or even 'firing' these customers? Retail banks often have a group of unprofitable customers who keep a bank account but do not use this account regularly and do not receive their monthly salary in this account. In this case, the retail bank may charge these customers a higher rate (price discrimination) or discontinue the relationship (van Raaij, 2005). The higher rate is often a signal for these customers to stop the relationship.

Value conception

Companies should look for value gaps in the competitive value space. Which consumer segments are not yet sufficiently served? Which segments are ignored in the market? Which value conception can be offered that is different from value conceptions offered by competitors? In the hotel market, Formule 1 hotel in France found a segment of travellers who need a comfortable but cheap bed for one night on their trips. These travellers do not require fancy lounges or restaurants. The Formule 1 concept is to offer a room with a high-quality bed to sleep for a low price in a hotel not far from the motorway, but curtail as much as possible on food services and meeting rooms. This distinguishes Formule 1 hotels from the standard 3- to 5-star hotels with lounges and restaurants. Often this requires a new market definition. An automobile company is not only in the market for selling cars, but in the market of mobility, including leasing cars and other modes of transport. By redefining the market, new market possibilities can be distinguished. Or it requires a closer look to customers and their problems and dissatisfactions. It is crucial to combine these market insights with a deep insight in the organization's strengths and weaknesses.

Value generation

The value generation processes are the organization's primary processes. An organization implements its value conception by means of its primary processes. The primary processes have to be organized in such a way that the value conception can be effectively and efficiently produced. In the case of Formule 1 hotels, rooms are sold face-to-face at a counter or, at the late hours, through a machine. The same is true for basic meals such as a breakfast. Room cleaning is another function that is done efficiently during the day.

An organization's value generation processes should generate value for both the customer and the provider. For the customer, the ratio between perceived benefits and perceived total cost of the offering should outperform those of competing offerings. For the provider, the total value of current revenues and expected future revenues from the customer should outweigh the costs of providing the services to that customer. This implies that the process-based, customer-focused organization needs to design its primary processes with the following parameters in mind:

- The cost/benefit value space targeted with the offering.
- The impact of alternative process designs on total perceived costs to the customer.
- The impact of alternative process designs on customer-perceived benefits.
- The impact of alternative process designs on attainable prices.
- The impact of alternative process designs on direct product costs.
- The impact of alternative process designs on indirect (overhead) costs.

From a range of alternative process designs, the provider can compare how much value each alternative is expected to provide for the customer and for the organization. Much of this thinking has already been incorporated in product design, where value engineering techniques are used to optimize perceived value of the product vis-à-vis cost of production. This value engineering philosophy also needs to be applied to process design, not only in service organizations, but also in manufacturing companies. Physical goods generate only part of the value as perceived by the customer. To a large extent, perceived customer value is generated in customer-interaction processes. However well the physical product may be engineered for optimal value, all processes around the core product also need to be value engineered.

Consider a supplier of building materials to construction firms. We may expect that many such suppliers have optimized their production processes for maximum margin on their products. But how many will have analyzed their ordering and billing processes for maximum value? In a traditional situation, when a construction firm has a need for building materials on a construction site, the overseer will call around for quotations, select the cheapest supplier, write out a purchase order, check incoming materials against the order and send a materials receipt form to the administration office, then the office checks the purchase order, materials receipt form and invoice and sends payment to the supplier. The supplier checks the payment against the invoice. If the supplier were to do a value engineering analysis of this process, it may well conclude that both the customer and the supplier incur high costs in processing purchase orders and that margins are low because competition is on price only. By offering a year contract to customers and electronic ordering, the supplier may be able to occupy a gap in the competitive value space, compete on service instead of price, reduce total cost for the customer (and thus increase customer-perceived value) and reduce total cost of service provision.

Process-based, customer-focused organizations will regularly analyze all their business processes in order to look for new ways of creating value for customers and for themselves.

Customer linking

While the primary processes of the organization are concerned with the generation of day-to-day value for both customer and supplier, customer-linking processes are concerned with generating future value. The customer-focused organization understands that future performance depends to a large extent on the ability to retain profitable customers. We have seen before that there are many sources of customer loyalty. Customer-loyalty programmes ('airmiles') are but one source and contribute to customer retention only when used as a complement to good quality products and services. Customer linking therefore entails much more than a customer-loyalty programme.

Customer-focused organizations that engage in customer linking recognize that high-quality products and services are a necessary, but not sufficient, condition for success. Customer linking adds an extra layer to the exchanges between buyer and seller. Technology can play a key role in customer linking. Many companies use permission-based email marketing as a customer-linking tool. In business-to-business relationships, web-based sales and procurement systems, as well as traditional Electronic Data Interchange, are used as customer-linking tools (Poiesz and van Raaij, 2007).

Value assessment

The value assessment process measures to what extent value is created for the customer as well as for the organization, in the short term and the long term. Measurements include customer satisfaction, customer-perceived value and customer profitability. These assessments of both value *for* the customer and value *of* the customer can be used as inputs for future customer selection, value conception, value generation and customer-linking processes.

Key resources in customer-focused organizations

For an organization to be able to excel in the six key processes of customer-focused organizations (Figure 2.4), it needs to have a set of specific resources at its disposal. Resources come in different types: assets, capabilities, competencies and culture. These resources are particularly valuable if they are convertible, rare among competitors, hard to copy and if there are no perfect substitutes (Srivastava *et al.*, 1998). Following the resource classification of Stoelhorst (1997), we define assets as resources to which the firm can claim property rights, capabilities as the firm's ability to co-ordinate activities, competencies as specialist knowledge, and culture as the norms and values that give direction to the actions of the firm.

With respect to competencies, the customer-focused organization will need to have specialist knowledge in the area(s) of its products or services in order to create distinctive value for customers. These product-related competencies will be specific to the industry and to the organization. There is thus little we can say in general terms about these competencies. Examples of such competencies would be a competency in financial derivatives trading for a financial institution, a competency in supply chain optimization for a retailer or a competency in chip design architecture for a semiconductor manufacturer.

Assets, capabilities and culture will also be to a large extent product/market specific, but there are some assets, capabilities and culture that are related to customer-focused organizations in general. These generic customer-focused resources are discussed below.

Customer-focused assets

Organizational assets can be financial, physical, legal, human, relational or informational assets (Hunt and Morgan, 1995). For the customer-focused organization, the following assets are particularly relevant:

- Physical assets: ICT systems (e.g., relational databases, knowledge management systems)

- Relational assets: relationships with stakeholders (customers, suppliers, competitors, channel partners)
- Informational assets: market/customer knowledge

The customer-focused organization needs a physical infrastructure for collecting, storing, analyzing and disseminating information about markets and customers. In today's digital age, this infrastructure is made of personal computers, servers and relational databases. Three important qualities of such an infrastructure are accuracy, accessibility and capacity. The infrastructure needs to be designed in such a way that data is captured only once and at the source and that data redundancy and duplication are avoided. Once stored, the data should be accessible to those who want to retrieve and/or process it. And third, the infrastructure should have sufficient capacity for data storage and information processing.

The customer-focused organization needs relationships with outside parties in order to learn about its markets. Strong relationships with external parties can leverage an organization's market orientation (Martin and Grbac, 2003).

Besides physical assets and relational assets, the customer-focused organization will also need to invest in informational assets. In particular, it will need to invest in market knowledge and customer knowledge. This knowledge is needed in order to make sound decisions about what customers focus on and what value dimensions to exploit to achieve a competitive advantage.

Customer-focused capabilities

For the customer-focused organization, the following capabilities are particularly relevant:

- Information processing capability
- Learning capability.

An information processing capability is based on knowledge, experience and routines in the following areas: data collection, interpretation, selection, dissemination, use, retention (storage) and retrieval. Such routines may be formalized and captured in procedures and forms, e.g., procedures for customer-satisfaction surveys or standardized supplier evaluation forms. A learning capability is based on routines in areas such as innovation, continuous improvement and plan-do-check-act cycles.

These capabilities need to be managed and nurtured in order to remain sources for competitive advantage in the customer-focused organization. Important elements in this nurturing process are training of employees, identification of best practices and regular evaluation of processes and procedures. The physical and relational assets identified above should serve to support these capabilities, while the capabilities in turn serve to strengthen the organization's informational assets.

Customer-focused culture

At the deepest level of the organization, the set of shared beliefs should be those of a:

- Market-oriented culture
- Service-oriented culture

Homburg and Pflesser (2000) distinguish four interrelated components of organizational culture: shared values, behavioural norms, artefacts and behaviours.

The fourth component, behaviours, is already captured in the processes of the organization (discussed in section 4 of this chapter). Values represent general guidelines of what is desirable in an organization, norms are expectations about behaviour in an organization and artefacts are perceptible manifestations of culture that carry symbolic meaning, such as stories, arrangements, rituals and language (Homburg and Pflesser, 2000). The customer-focused organization is supported by values such as innovativeness and flexibility, openness of internal communication, interfunctional co-operation, respect and excellence (Homburg and Pflesser, 2000; Skålén and Strandvik, 2005). Organizational norms about which behaviours are right and which are wrong can be explicit or implicit, and develop over the years, based on the shared values. The organizational culture 'shines through' in the language that organization members use, the rituals they go through (e.g., customer events), arrangements such as discussion areas to support internal communication and stories about failures and successes in innovation and customer service.

The notion that organizational cultures can be created and managed is not generally supported (Harris and Ogbonna 1999; Skålén and Strandvik, 2005). Organizational cultures are the outcome of many years of evolution and are shaped by the behaviours of the organizational leaders, by recruitment and selection of employees and by the reward system of the organization.

Process in action health and human services in the USA

(See Microsoft web page, 9 Sept 2006, http://www.microsoft.com/industry/government/consumercenteredhumanservices.mspx)

Improvements in information technology (IT), primarily in data storage and retrieval and distributed networks, have opened opportunities for Health and Human Services (HHS) providers to adopt a more customer-focused approach to consumer relationships. In HHS systems, other than where the consumer pays at the point of consumption, there are two categories of customers: the consumer and the paying customer. In the case of insurance-funded system, the payer is the insurance company, and thence their consumers *en masse*. In the case of taxation-based systems, it is the national or local government, and thence the taxpayer. Hence, the quality of service is measured in terms of value, say number of consumers treated or cured, by the paying customer, and in terms of confidence, convenience, availability and comfort, in addition to technical competence, by the consumer.

Investment in IT systems in the US HHS system has primarily been driven by recent increasing costs to the paying customers. At 16 per cent of gross domestic product (see web page), health-care costs are considered to be out of control. In addition, Social Services, a related part of the health-related human ecosystem, comprises 40 per cent of state funding. HHS agencies are coming under severe pressure from both national and local government to demonstrate that they deliver good value. They are also becoming increasingly accountable for tracking consumers throughout the global system to prevent fraud and deliver information on outcomes. IT application appears to be central to delivering these requirements, but piecemeal, function-based applications in the 1980s met with little success due to problems with technology. Attempts to transfer IT systems across functional boundaries failed and such systems were often redundant before deployments were completed. However, technology, and IT system design in general, is now better.

Investment in IT systems also offers an opportunity to reduce many shortcomings in the service quality dimension of the HHS system by increasing customer focus and breaking between functional silos. In both health and human divisions, citizens rely on multiple disciplinary agencies, each with its own IT system, and hence care is currently inconsistent with poor co-ordination between providers. This also results in confusion, redundancy and frustration for families and individuals who must navigate the resulting bureaucratic system when seeking the urgent help they may need. State and national funding complexities make the situation even worse. Customer-focused management, or case management, seems to offer solutions.

Microsoft claims to offer such solutions with commercial off-the-shelf solutions which incorporate web technology and what they term 'service-oriented architecture'. States are beginning to use evolving standardized packaged software to interconnect different agencies, thus adding functionality to each of them. Microsoft claims that it is getting easier to undo the morass of disconnected silos and at last to realize the vision of connected human services. They offer to work with service providers to increase value to all customers. The web-based systems concentrate on case management to deliver the following critical changes:

- From a functional perspective to a process orientation
- From a build-to-last model to a build-to-change model
- From application (functional) silos to loosely coupled, orchestrated solutions.

Microsoft's architectural vision consists of four major components:

- **Portal architecture,** the entrance to the system which must be user-friendly for system users and be secure in holding personal and sensitive information.
- **Core business solutions,** the business applications which share the common data. These support the management of consumer status, both medical and social welfare systems.
- **Integration and business intelligence store,** the 'hub' of the systems: data management and integration of interlocking HHS systems.
- **Business and technology management,** the applications tools required to manage the HHS administrative functions.

Microsoft refers to four US examples of where this work is being applied:

1. The city of Richmond, Virginia, has developed an integrated child welfare system which is now being enlarged to include additional family services, such as adoption and foster care, and adult protective services.
2. The District of Columbia has implemented a web-based access system for social workers.
3. The state of Alabama has used a similar system to improve case management for substance abuse and mental health patients.
4. The Commonwealth of Kentucky is building a master client index to provide a common view of citizen services across multiple public health programmes.

Common to all their initiatives is the building of a central-shared database for a range of HHS providers and the use of the web to increase the availability of this data to caseworkers in the field.

Questions

1. What does each of the two categories of customers identified in this case, consumers and paying customers, want from the systems approach discussed here?
2. How does the theory from this chapter relate to and inform the systems advocated by Microsoft, and how can it contribute to satisfying the customers of the HHS systems?

Summary

- The customer-focused organization is in essence a learning organization.

- Through its processes of market sensing and prediction, customer selection, value conception, value generation, customer linking and value assessment, it continuously learns about markets and customers (cf. Day, 1994).

- The customer-focused organization builds its sustainable competitive advantage on a set of rare and inimitable resources.

- These resources help the organization to create efficiencies in its business processes, which translate into positional advantages in its markets.

- These positional advantages translate into superior performance outcomes.

- Continuous reflection upon the performance achieved on the basis of the resources and the business processes drives a process of continuous learning (see Figure 2.5).

Chapter questions

1. Explain why and how business processes drive the value-satisfaction-loyalty chain.

2. Critically analyze some of the key processes emerging in customer-focused organizations.

3. What can organizations learn from their customer database to serve these and other customers better?

4. Discuss the complications for an organization of having a customer-focused culture.

Figure 2.5
Resources –
processes –
performance (based
on Stoelhorst and
van Raaij, 2004)

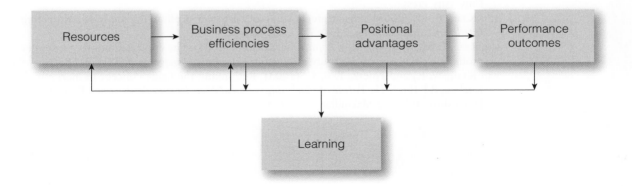

References

Davenport, T. H. (1993) *Process Innovation: Reengineering Work through Information Technology*, Boston, MA: Harvard Business School Press.

Day, G. S. (1994) 'Continuous learning about markets', *California Management Review*, 36:9–31.

Dick, A. S., and Basu, K. (1994) 'Customer loyalty: Toward an integrated conceptual framework', *Journal of the Academy of Marketing Science*, 22(2):99–113.

Harrington, H. J. (1991) *Business Process Improvement: The Breakthrough Strategy for Total Quality, Productivity, and Competitiveness*, New York: McGraw-Hill.

Harris, L. C., and Ogbonna, E. (1999) 'Developing a market oriented culture: A critical evaluation', *Journal of Management Studies*, 36(2):177–196.

Heskett, J. L., Jones, T. O., Loveman, G. W., Sasser, W. E. Jr., and Schlesinger, L. A. (1994) 'Putting the service-profit chain to work', *Harvard Business Review*, 72:164–174.

Homburg, C., and Pflesser, C. (2000) 'A multiple-layer model of market-oriented organizational culture: Measurement issues and performance outcomes', *Journal of Marketing Research*, 37:449–462.

Hunt, S. D., and Morgan, R. M. (1995) 'The comparative advantage theory of competition', *Journal of Marketing*, 59:1–15.

Martin, J. H., and Grbac, B. (2003) 'Using supply chain management to leverage a firm's market orientation', *Industrial Marketing Management*, 32:25–38.

Poiesz, T. B. C., and van Raaij, W. F. (2007) *New Synergies in Marketing: The Virtual Guardian Angel*, Cheltenham, UK: Edward Elgar.

Reinartz, W., and Kumar, V. (2002) 'The mismanagement of customer loyalty', *Harvard Business Review*, 72:4–12.

Shapiro, B. P., Rangan, V. K., and Sviokla, J. J. (1992) 'Staple yourself to an order', *Harvard Business Review*, 70:113–122.

Skålén, P., and Strandvik, T. (2005) 'From prescription to description: A critique and reorientation of service culture', *Managing Service Quality*, 15(3):230–244.

Slater, S. F., and Narver, J. C. (2000) 'Intelligence generation and superior customer value', *Journal of the Academy of Marketing Science*, 28(1):120–127.

Srivastava, R. K., Shervani, T. A., and Fahey, L. (1998) 'Market-based assets and shareholder value: A framework for analysis', *Journal of Marketing*, 62:2–18.

Stoelhorst, J. W. (1997) 'In Search of a Dynamic Theory of the Firm: An Evolutionary Perspective on Competition under Conditions of Technological Change, with an Application to the Semiconductor Industry'. Unpublished dissertation, Enschede, The Netherlands: Twente University Press.

Stoelhorst, J. W., and van Raaij, E. M. (2004) 'On explaining performance differentials: Marketing and the managerial theory of the firm', *Journal of Business Research*, 57(5): 462–477.

van Raaij, E. M. (2001) 'The Implementation of a Market Orientation: Designing Frameworks for Managerial Action'. Unpublished dissertation, Enschede, The Netherlands: Twente University Press.

van Raaij, E. M. (2005) 'The strategic value of customer profitability analysis', *Marketing Intelligence and Planning*, 23(4):372–381.

van Raaij, E. M., Vernooij, M. J. A., and van Triest, S. (2003) 'The implementation of customer profitability analysis: A case study', *Industrial Marketing Management*, 32:573–583.

van Raaij, W. F., and Poiesz, T. B. C. (2003) 'Rethinking the value concept in marketing', Kitchen, P. J. (Ed.), *The Future of Marketing: Critical 21st Century Perspectives,* Basingstoke, Hampshire: Palgrave Macmillan, pp. 41–58.

Part two
Future-predicting processes (scenario building and forecasting)

3 Environmental scanning and strategy

4 Demand management (market and technology forecasting)

Predicting the future is a fundamental process in planning; without a prediction there can be no plan.

Chapter 3 introduces environmental scanning and strategy and discusses methodologies designed to tackle situations of uncertainty – scenario planning and knowledge-based systems. It encourages managers to break from the confines of traditional thinking and challenges their assumptions in the process of strategy formation. The 'process in action' note demonstrates how the approach is applied to downsizing and outsourcing in the European airline industry at a time when a number of factors may affect the industry in ways that cannot be easily predicted by traditional forecasting techniques.

Chapter 4 discusses demand management (market and technology forecasting). It also questions if organizations are able to forecast their capabilities and raises issues related to the aggregation and interpretation of functional forecasts. Two 'process in action' notes demonstrate the importance of forecasting. The first is historical (1838) and is concerned with how Brunel correctly forecast the best type of ships to cross the Atlantic at a time of technological revolution. The second is concerned with air transport today, where two major competitors, Airbus and Boeing, have adopted entirely different strategies in developing new products. Only history will determine which company got their forecasts correct.

3

Environmental scanning and strategy

Fiona Davies, Luiz Moutinho and Graeme D. Hutcheson

Introduction

Today's rapidly changing market and technological environment present many challenges for managers and may necessitate radical changes in the way that management strategy is formulated. Yet, in situations of uncertainty, the tendency is to return to the familiar, to draw on past experience and tried and tested methodologies. As this may not provide an optimal solution, managers may benefit if they are trained in techniques to give them the confidence and ability to go beyond what they know, in order to develop more effective and innovative strategies. One such technique that is already employed to good effect by major companies (e.g., 3M and Hewlett Packard; see Legare, 1998) is scenario planning, an approach to developing strategy which encourages managers to break from the confines of traditional perspectives. In this chapter, both the process of strategy formulation and the output are considered, in order to assess not only whether far-sighted, innovative and effective strategies are produced but also what benefits are gained from the process of strategy formation itself. Furthermore, the strategies emerging from the exercise are recorded in the form of rules in a knowledge-based system (KBS), and it is also considered whether there is added value in capturing information in this way.

Learning objectives

- To build awareness of the importance of scanning due to changing markets and environmental uncertainty.

- To discuss key issues related to scenario planning.

- To demonstrate the use of knowledge-based systems in the area of scenario planning.

- To highlight important managerial implications for companies considering the use of scenario planning.

The literature review which follows gives a rationale for the use of scenario planning, discussing the process and its benefits and use, before moving on to consider KBS and how they can aid scenario planning. The chapter then continues with a brief background to a scenario planning exercise, followed by detailed discussion of the exercise itself.

Changing markets and environmental uncertainty

As Baden-Fuller *et al.* (2000) point out, rapidly changing markets and technologies may necessitate changes in strategic management thinking, and an effective response may mean being unafraid to challenge traditional methodologies and paradigms. However, Wilson (1999) points out that managers facing volatile situations naturally tend to draw on their own experience and intuition, to draw parallels with situations they have faced before and to use decision rules based upon these. He identifies a need for strategic planning techniques which challenge traditional company perspectives and priorities, rather than reinforcing them, and calls for organizations to be constantly challenged to focus on strategy and competitiveness – otherwise, the tendency is that new strategic planning initiatives will only be considered when the company is facing threats to its profitability or even survival. Whitehill (1997) points out the ease with which new companies can now analyze products and services available in the marketplace and acquire the appropriate tangible assets and resources to enter the market and match or better existing offerings. Yet a focus on established products, practices and perspectives may well blind companies currently in the market to such emerging opportunities – until competitors have exploited them. Wilson (1999) cites examples such as IBM, whose 1986 strategic review did not question the company's reliance on computer mainframe products despite the emerging personal computer (PC) market, and Marks and Spencer, whose 1985 review of information technology (IT) requirements made minimal recommendations for change in order not to disturb the established culture of the firm.

So the first requirement for managers to be able to respond effectively to environmental and market developments is that they should recognize such developments as important. They then need to develop adequate techniques, frameworks and methodologies to deal with these developments, their possible impact and suitable responses (Wilson, 1999). Ashill and Jobber (2001) found that managers recognized three components to this problem:

- They might lack information on environmental factors and so cannot predict what was going to happen.
- Even when they could predict likely changes, they might not be able to predict the impact of such changes on their company or decision-making.
- Even when they could predict the impact, they might still not know how best to respond effectively.

These components correspond closely to the three types of uncertainty identified by Milliken (1987, 1990): state uncertainty (the environment is unpredictable), effect uncertainty (the impact is unpredictable) and response uncertainty (range, utility and/ or consequences of responses are unpredictable). Different types of environmental uncertainty (e.g., political, macroeconomic, competitive, technological) may have vastly different strategic implications for a company.

Scenario planning

Furrer and Thomas (2000) have devised a framework, the 'rivalry matrix', which categorizes strategic modelling approaches according to their suitability in particular types of environment and the number of decision variables involved. In uncertain environments, they recommend that with a large number of decision variables, rigorous modelling is impossible due to the level of complexity and decision frameworks such as Porter's (1980) five forces are required. However, if a small number of critical decision variables can be isolated, one recommendation is the use of scenario planning (others being simulation modelling and system dynamic modelling). This is an approach that recognizes today's rapidly changing market and environmental conditions and the difficulties these pose for strategic planning. Instead of trying to make accurate predictions and formulate one optimal strategy, scenario planning encourages the construction of several possible 'alternate futures' (Simpson, 1992) and the planning of strategy in response to each. The technique is employed by many major companies, such as 3M, British Airways, Hewlett Packard, ICI and Levi Strauss (Anonymous, 1988; Legare, 1998). Key decision-makers within the company offer opinions on the most important environmental trends, greatest uncertainties and decisions which will impact most greatly upon the company, in order to aid the construction of credible, consistent and challenging scenarios. Once scenarios have been formulated, the company organizes a workshop or brainstorming session, ideally with a diverse group of participants. Such participation will utilize more fully the knowledge within the company, and should be encouraged, as broader participation in decision-making has been shown to correlate with higher company performance (Papadakis, 1998). Alternatively, a diverse group may be involved from the beginning in identifying the environmental and industry drivers, which will impact the future, and constructing alternative scenarios (Mercer, 1995). In responding to scenarios, there are two possible starting points (Thomas, 1984):

- From the company's current strategy, to examine how it would hold up in the situation envisaged in each scenario.
- From the future envisaged in the scenario, to examine the necessary strategies for survival and profitability in that situation.

The scenario planning approach differs from others in using 'storylines' to describe different futures (Schoemaker, 1993); Wright (2000) sees this as being easier to 'connect with' than the diagrams and figures that form the basis of more traditional planning methodologies. It also enables the incorporation of more subjective elements and macro-environmental variables that could not easily be included in computer simulations due to the difficulty of expressing them quantitatively or defining them within the boundaries of the simulation (Schoemaker, 1997). It is wider in scope than contingency planning, which looks at only one uncertainty at a time, and sensitivity analysis, which considers change in one variable only and cannot cope with major environmental changes which affect several variables (Schoemaker, 1997).

Phelps *et al.* (2001) found some evidence that the use of scenario planning improved decision-making and could also impact company performance. However, advocates of the technique stress that its greatest value lies in the long-term changes to participants' viewpoints which are engendered by the creative thinking required (Mercer, 1995; Schoemaker, 1995). As managers broaden their outlook to different ideas of what the future may hold, they become less certain about the rightness of their decision-making. The process of considering alternative futures and brainstorming with others who have different perspectives broadens participants' thinking, combats marketing myopia and opens their minds to new possibilities – as long as they are willing and motivated to engage fully in the process. Verity (2003), in examining why scenario planning has not been more widely adopted, states that managers have difficulty in accepting the idea of an unpredictable future about which they cannot make confident and clear judgments.

Bood and Postma (1997) divide the functions of scenarios into two clusters: more traditional ones which provided the impetus for the development of the methodology (evaluating and choosing strategies, synthesizing different types of data about the future, exploring the future and identifying opportunities) and those which have only come to be realized as the methodology has been used (generating or increasing awareness of environmental uncertainties, challenging managerial thought patterns and stimulating organizational learning). They point out the usefulness of challenging scenarios in dissolving four 'bottlenecks' to organizational learning: cognitive inertia (the tendency to think in accordance with existing rules, norms and assumptions), the time-lapse between practical strategy implementation and effect of the strategy being seen, 'groupthink' and the inability to reach an agreement due to conflicting thinking between managers. Which of the last two is more likely in any situation will depend on how convergent is the thinking of the various decision-makers involved, and the authors stress the necessity of achieving a balance in this respect when choosing participants. In particular, the use of outsiders as well as internal managers should help to guard against 'groupthink' and tendencies to conform to organizational norms, which may override an individual's natural inclinations (Verity, 2003).

An environment of increasing turbulence enhances the need for companies to have a vision for their future (Oosthuizen, 2000). O'Brien and Meadows (2000, 2003) found that such a vision was typically imposed by communication from the top, rather than being developed participatively. A robust vision cannot be independent of the future environment, and thus scenario planning would seem to have a place in visioning, although few companies use it as yet (O'Brien and Meadows, 2000). O'Brien and Meadows (2001) tested a scenario-based methodology (CHOICES) for visioning in the public domain and found that the development of future scenarios helped participants to have a broader view of the future and to develop stronger and clearer vision statements.

Various authors have suggested how scenario planning can be integrated into an organization's planning procedures. Schoemaker (1997) proposes its combination with competitor analysis to identify the requirements for success in particular market segments in each future scenario. Verity (2003) describes models developed by different management consultancies, using expert judgment, cross-impact analysis and trend-impact analysis, to provide simulations of the future; she suggests that the very flexibility of the scenario planning process limits its acceptability to managers, resulting in this type of incorporation into a more formal approach. Courtney (2003) distinguishes between vision-driven and decision-driven scenario planning, the latter being an adaptation of the process to more short-term strategic decision-making, when there is some level of uncertainty that makes it worth developing alternative scenarios (e.g., a new product launch when consumer demand and competitor reaction are uncertain). Strauss and Radnor (2004) seek to satisfy both strategic and operational demands by blending scenario planning with 'roadmapping' – having identified a future scenario, the organization moves to the micro level to describe in detail what customers would require in that situation and what technological development that would entail. The authors recognize the difficulties, not to mention time and resources, inherent in combining such different levels and perspectives, but believe that benefits will accrue in turbulent conditions when the wrong decision could have drastic consequences.

Millett (2003) emphasizes the necessity of adapting the scenario approach to the culture of the company and its particular problems and recommends the use of automation to reduce time and costs. Gnyawali and Grant (1996) also stress the value of a high-quality information system which interacts with the scenario planning process in optimizing its contribution to organizational learning. Automation allows outline scenarios, the information and assumptions on which they are based, and the strategic decision-making process to be recorded for the future. Scenarios can then be revisited when new environmental developments occur. Artificial intelligence, in the form of a KBS, could be an appropriate medium for such automation. Thus, the next section examines the use of KBS in marketing strategy formulation, assessing their potential for use in scenario planning.

Knowledge-based systems in marketing and scenario planning

A KBS, or expert system (ES), consists of software that can store and interpret knowledge, thus providing 'expert' advice to users and acting as an aid to decision-making. The basic ES model is a rule-based system, which tests a new problem situation against a database of rules formulated by experts. Curry (1992) listed the benefits of such models as the transparency of the rules, which are written in a form similar to natural language; the facility for qualitative reasoning; user-friendliness; and the provision of explanations for the advice given. Cavusgil and Evirgen (1995) stressed the importance of management being able to 'play out' different 'what if?' scenarios. The role of an ES was perceived as an aid for decision-makers, rather than as a replacement for them. Curry (1996) suggested that ES help management to evaluate their thinking and to reflect upon their decision-making criteria and processes, while Stone and Good (1995) found that the use of ES fostered an environment that enriched the management structure and improved the speed of decision-making. Many marketers were keen to investigate the benefits of ES technology; Sing-Chang *et al.* (1995) noted its increasing use by marketing managers in formulating strategic marketing decisions, including the recommendation of strategic options, while in Stone and Good's (1995) survey of 117 US marketing executives, all reported the successful use of ES in their organizations.

ES development and use, however, can bring its own problems. Cavusgil and Evirgen (1995) suggested international marketing as a suitable domain for ES, due to the scarcity of expert knowledge and the complexity and uncertainty of the international marketing environment. These factors not only support the potential usefulness of an ES, but also point to what many authors have identified as the main difficulty in ES development, that of knowledge acquisition, which involves both identifying appropriate expertize and enabling it to be expressed in a rule-based format. Dubelaar *et al.* (1991) pointed out that both factual and procedural knowledge needs to be encoded and that, as knowledge is always evolving and being added to, there needs to be a facility for updating the system. Li *et al.* (2000) found dissatisfaction among managers with current computer-based systems designed to aid marketing strategy decision-making, the most common complaints being limitations to their support capabilities, function and scope and an inability to couple strategic analysis with managerial judgment, deal with uncertainty or meet managers' real needs.

Dramatic increase in ES use within manufacturing organizations led to more rigorous assessment of their value, and recommendations (Guimaraes *et al.*, 1995; Yoon *et al.*, 1995) to increase the likelihood of project success and user satisfaction, including:

- Adding problem difficulty as a criterion for ES applications selection.
- Shaping end-user attitudes and expectations regarding ES.
- Increasing ES developer training to improve people skills.

Others seeking to overcome the limitations identified by Li *et al.* (2000) in the use of ES in the domain of marketing strategy have sought to integrate ES with other support technologies such as decision support systems. Some (Li, 2000; Li and Davies, 2001; Li *et al.*, 2002) went further in developing hybrid systems which used group Delphi to ensure that multiple opinions were represented at the knowledge elicitation stage, a forecasting module based on an artificial neural network, fuzzy logic to deal with ambiguity and uncertainty, integrated with an ES to hold domain knowledge and provide reasoning capabilities. Evaluation of these suggested that the integration of these different techniques improved managerial confidence in the system output and encouraged strategic thinking.

This chapter, therefore, revolves around the reinforcement of the relevance of scenario planning when combined with the end-use of a KBS as antecedent managerial tools for strategic decision-making. Apart from the objective associated with this methodology of increasing the effectiveness of management decisions, this approach is also designed to stimulate strategic thinking processes and the design of innovative strategies. The emphasis put on the value of capturing information should be paramount; this issue is critical when modelling uncertainty and, more specifically, uncertainty reasoning. The methodology related to the elicitation of the information and the capitalization on the background knowledge of the participants, as well as the socio-metric mechanisms associated with consensus decision-making, are all designed to challenge current mindsets. The combination of scenario planning and the utilization of an ES is also linked with the awareness and implementation of contingency planning. The synthesizing of the pertinent information into scenario factors, combinations and options and the stimulation of strategic reasoning capabilities are all good instruments to minimize corporate 'bottlenecks' and corporate inertia. Figure 3.1 depicts the influence that a methodology-linking scenario planning with the design of a KBS has on strategic decision-making.

In the study now described, an in-depth discussion of future scenarios, with a facilitator present, met the need for multiple inputs to the knowledge base. As the input was text based, the subjective and descriptive elements of scenarios were maintained, while also having the facility to deal with quantitative input. Furthermore, the system was able to deal with uncertainty as to the future environment because its rule base, based on scenario development, contained details of several 'alternative futures'. It also has the potential to be added to as required through the development of new rules. The domain of the system is one in which the changing environment has created a great deal of uncertainty and is now discussed.

The practice of downsizing, initially a reaction to economic recession in the late 1980s and early 1990s, has left a lasting impact on business culture. Concerns about profitability continue to lead companies to shed staff, citing reasons such as business process re-engineering, increased automation and improved staff utilization, and the increasing availability and affordability of technology aids greatly in this pursuit of leanness. Companies 'staffing for profitability' may have only a small core of permanent staff, using 'contingent' employees to vary the size of the workforce as demand necessitates (Van Horn-Christopher, 1996), or they may outsource one or more business functions to outside firms. Outsourcing may be driven by vision and function as well as economics: though cost control is the most commonly cited reason for outsourcing, others include a focus on core competencies, improving access to and utilization of new technologies (Kakabadse and Kakabadse, 2002), lack of expertise, difficulty of keeping technology up-to-date and the wish to improve flexibility or supply chain capabilities (Wong *et al.*, 2000). The most commonly outsourced functions are legal work, shipping, production and manufacturing, logistics and information systems (Lankford and Parsa, 1999; Wong *et al.*, 2000).

Turning to the industry considered in this chapter, it is widely recognized that airline companies must be part of the global network if they are to remain competitive. Rationalization might be viewed as a logical response to the increasingly uncertain environment confronting airline firms, and there may be technologies or business functions available from outsourcers that may complement the company's strategic strengths and core competencies. The decision to outsource can therefore lead to competitive advantages, so effective management of the outsourcing relationships is an organizational imperative.

Both downsizing and outsourcing, however, have long-term dangers; they may lead to increased worker insecurity, lower morale and a decline in motivation and loyalty (Cooper, 1998), a culture of risk avoidance (Love, 1998) and loss of

Figure 3.1

Influence of the link between scenario planning and the development of a knowledge-based system on strategic decision-making

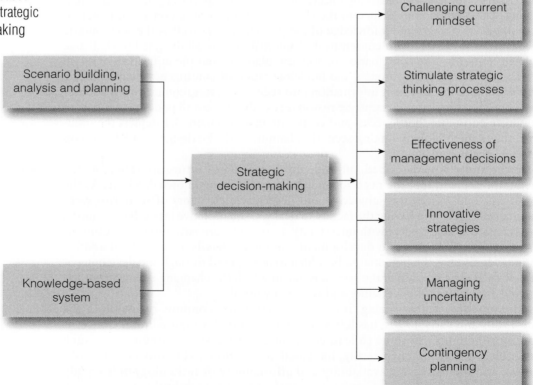

corporate knowledge (Whitehill, 1997), with negative long-term effects on competitiveness and profitability (Haapaniemi, 1996). Neither does outsourcing necessarily bring the hoped-for economies of scale and cost reductions (Lankford and Parsa, 1999), nor does external control of vital resources such as the information systems function cause problems (Wong *et al.*, 2000). Thus, it is generally recommended that only non-core activities which add neither competitive advantage nor value should be outsourced, though Baden-Fuller *et al.* (2000) challenge this traditional strategic thinking and suggest that, in certain circumstances, some core activities could advantageously be outsourced.

As disadvantages of downsizing become evident, companies are realizing the need for a more strategic approach, balancing needs for cost reduction and efficiency with willingness to invest in and develop key resources. Particularly in uncertain economic or market environments, organizations need to explore innovative ways of achieving such balance – but managers encouraged in a 'lean and mean' approach may have difficulty in thinking 'outside the box' to propose solutions. Scenario planning is proposed as one method by which more innovative strategic thinking may be stimulated, and the chapter now describes the methodology of its application to the

Process in action downsizing and outsourcing in the European airline industry

The European airline industry is one which has undergone radical change in recent years due to deregulation (1987–1997), the removal of subsidies to national airlines, increased demand for both business and consumer travel and the emergence in the UK and Ireland of low-cost, no-frills airlines operating from smaller regional airports, reducing distribution costs by using direct Internet booking and minimizing maintenance costs by restricting their fleet to one type of aircraft (Mintel, 2001). Successful low-cost airlines have taken significant market share from traditional carriers, and several major airlines have attempted to introduce their own low-cost subsidiaries, with varying degrees of success. Another response to changing market conditions has been to form alliances, four of which now account for over 90 per cent of international global passenger traffic (Mintel, 2001). These have many benefits but can prove unstable. Cross-shareholdings are common, with many European regional airlines consolidating relationships with larger carriers to stay in profit. Downsizing and outsourcing measures can also be observed, with airlines such as Air France, the SAir group, KLM and Lufthansa trimming networks to focus on profitable routes and core operations.

The market environment is still in a state of constant change. A growing market for air travel provides opportunities for expansion, while increasing competition, capacity problems, airport congestion, declining revenue per seat and increasing fuel costs are threats to profitability. Economic recession in certain regions, the dollar exchange rate, increased environmental awareness, environmental regulations, developments in other transport links and transfer of airports from public to private control may affect the industry in ways that cannot be easily predicted (Mintel, 2001). These characteristics, coupled with the fact that the industry is one with which most managers would have some degree of familiarity from use and/or press coverage, led to the choice of the European airline industry as a suitable setting for a scenario planning exercise.

Questions

1. What generic factors should a European airline company consider when deciding the strategic direction it should take?

2. Which strategic analysis frameworks are appropriate in this case? (See Chapter 16 for frameworks.)

airline industry. The analysis concentrates particularly on scenarios where downsizing or outsourcing is, or could be, recommended, in order to judge whether scenario planning has enabled participants to think more creatively and innovatively.

Methodology

The ES was constructed from decision rules that were elicited using a set of scenarios based on the European airline industry. Participants were practising managers in major companies.

The scenarios constructed dealt with a number of critical environmental and competitive dimensions that had been identified by the course leaders and modified through discussion of these factors in teaching sessions on environmental scanning. A list of 37 factors was identified in 1998 and increased to 40 in future years following suggestions from participants. Each factor was defined and given a description. Four example factors are shown below:

- **Fixed costs:** Total costs that do not change with volume but might change on a per-unit basis.
- **Variable costs:** Total costs that change with volume but are fixed on a per-unit basis.
- **Quality of suppliers:** Attributes of suppliers including aspects such as speed, reliability and consistency.
- **Partnership agreements with suppliers:** The set of relationships that improve the value chain and go beyond a contractual arrangement.

The groups were introduced to all the factors and these were explained so that everyone was familiar with the definitions and agreed with them.

In the scenarios, these factors were allowed to assume three different values. They could increase, remain the same or decrease. This rather restrictive set of conditions was necessary in order to simplify the programming of the ES and allow it to be constructed and validated within the time limits imposed by the course. The four factors above were allowed to vary as follows:

- **Fixed costs:** In future, are fixed costs likely to increase, remain the same or decrease?
- **Variable costs:** In future, are variable costs likely to increase, remain the same or decrease?
- **Quality of suppliers:** In future, is the importance of the quality of suppliers likely to increase, remain the same or decrease?
- **Partnership agreements with suppliers:** In future, is the importance of partnership agreements with suppliers likely to increase, remain the same or decrease?

The scenarios identified a set of conditions and it was the task of the participants to decide on a course of action given these conditions and provide reasons for the action taken. Each scenario was designed using a subset of only five factors. This requirement was imposed to provide some control over the specificity of the ES. If a scenario contained only one rule – e.g., a rule about what action to take if fixed costs increase – then this action would be identified in all cases where fixed costs increase. On the other hand, if a scenario was based on many rules – e.g., a specific response for each of the 40 factors – then the resulting action would only be identified for this very specific case. Too few rules in the scenario tend to make the recommendations numerous and too general, whereas too many rules tend to make the recommendations too specific and rare.

It was not the intention to construct an exhaustive ES that dealt with all possible combinations of factors. Clearly, this would have led to an extremely large knowledge base, much of which would have to be based around unlikely or even impossible scenarios. Scenarios were based around optimistic, pessimistic and neutral predictions about the future, and unusual and specific incident scenarios (e.g., what would happen if the euro plunged in value compared to the dollar?). Some scenarios were provided by the course leaders, while others were modified or constructed entirely by the participants.

This chapter now goes on to analyze the ES rule base, examining the thinking of these international managers on scenarios where downsizing/outsourcing is appropriate and on alternatives to downsizing/outsourcing, while also critically appraising the outputs provided by the group in order to assess the benefits of the exercise.

Process in action the European airline industry–expert system building

An example of a scenario is provided below:

The following scenario predicts how five factors will change in future.

- *The **importance of IT** is likely to **increase**.*
- *The importance of **risk spreading** is likely to **increase**.*
- ***Resources available** are likely to **decrease**.*
- *The importance of **communication mechanisms** are likely to **decrease**.*
- *The importance of **maximizing the value chain** is likely to **increase**.*

Participants were asked to provide recommendations based on these conditions and also provide a reason for them. For example, the recommendation made for the above scenario might be to:

- Use an IT-based outsourcing strategy.
- Invest in technology and automation.

with the reason for this action being:

- Emphasis in future is likely to be on technology and the need to spread risk while at the same time maximizing the value chain.

The participants were divided into groups and provided with the following instructions about how to complete the scenarios.

Guidance for completing rules
The scenarios provided give the conditions that apply for a particular company. You are required to decide on a course of action and provide a reason for this action. In order to provide some context for your recommendations, the company we are to consider is

a European airline with more than 500 employees, catering for the mass-market (for example, easyJet or RyanAir). We will be concerned with recommendations made in response to predictions about how the factors are likely to change in the future (about 2–4 years).

Recommendations and rules need to be agreed upon by the entire group; as all recommendations and reasons will be added to the ES by the elective organizers (in a limited amount of time), please provide brief notations.

Avoid the obvious and circular reasoning, such as:

Scenario
- *The **Asian market** share is likely to **increase**.*
- *The importance of **mergers and acquisitions** is likely to **increase**.*

- *The importance of **strategic alliances** is likely to **increase**.*
- *The importance of **defranchizing** is likely to **increase**.*
- *The importance of **share of voice** is likely to **increase**.*

Questions

1. What other factors might influence the future of the European airline industry?

2. What additional scenarios do you think should be considered?

3. How can the optimization of complexity and value of the analysis be considered?

Recommendation

- *Make more strategic alliances increase advertising budget.*

Reason

- *The importance of strategic alliances and share of voice is likely to increase.*

Once rules and reasons had been agreed upon in the group, the rule was added to the rule base. Table 3.1 shows the progressive development of the rule base over 3 years. The workshop thus fulfilled to some extent the recommendation of managerial involvement in scenario design. It was hoped that the diversity of backgrounds and nationalities would guard against any danger of 'groupthink', but in case it did not, or conflicting ideas threatened the group's progress, one of the authors acted as a group facilitator, challenging or peacemaking as deemed necessary.

Table 3.1
Progressive development of rule base

	1998	1999	2000
Preformulated scenarios	10	10	10
Participant-designed scenarios	30	23	16
Total scenarios (number of rules)	40	73	99

Analysis of the rule base

The analysis of the final 99-rule ES is now considered, examining the rules recommending downsizing or outsourcing in order to reveal the market conditions in which these measures are thought to be appropriate. A comparison of these with conditions which have traditionally led to downsizing, coupled with an appraisal of other solutions suggested under such conditions, will indicate how successful the scenario planning methodology has been in encouraging more innovative managerial thinking.

Table 3.2 details the factors most commonly used in scenario building, with an indication of how they were set to vary. These cover the major areas discussed in the foregoing analysis of the European airline industry, and in most cases, all three possible variations have been used, thus indicating that a wide range of alternatives have been considered. Of the 99 rules, 45 recommended downsizing or outsourcing, either generally or more specifically, and Table 3.3 shows the major factors causing such recommendations.

Table 3.2

Factors most often used in scenario building

Factor	How often used	Decreasing	Staying the same	Increasing
Importance of salaries	26	2	11	13
Market turbulence	25	7	7	11
Staff quality	22	11	1	10
Importance of product quality	21	4	—	17
Fixed costs	20	5	4	11
Rate of innovation	20	4	1	15
Importance of core activities	18	4	8	6
Importance of skill needs analysis	18	3	4	11
Profits	17	7	4	6
Importance of quality of suppliers	17	5	2	10
Importance of customer satisfaction	17	5	2	10
Performance	16	4	4	8
Competitor strength	15	1	—	14
Importance of global integration	15	4	1	10
Resources available	15	8	4	3
Variable costs	14	4	6	4
Union pressure against downsizing	14	5	—	9
Importance of product complexity	14	4	3	7
Importance of an IT strategy	14	—	2	12
Productivity	13	5	7	1
Importance of spreading risk	13	3	1	9
Importance of having access to world-class capabilities	9	—	—	9

Table 3.3
Factors most frequently leading to a recommendation of downsizing/ outsourcing

Type of recommendation/factor	Number of times this factor led to recommendation	
	Number	%
General downsizing or outsourcing (16 rules)		
Increased importance of business process re-engineering	3	20
Increase in competitor strength	3	20
Increased importance of global integration	3	20
Increased market turbulence	3	20
Decreased profits	3	20
Increase in importance of quality of suppliers	3	20
Increased importance placed on spreading of risk	3	20
Decrease in staff quality	3	20
Increased union pressure	3	20
IT outsourcing (8 rules)		
Increased importance of IT strategy	6	75
Increase in rate of innovation	4	50
Increased importance of skill needs analysis	4	50
Selective outsourcing (21 rules)		
Increase in importance of product quality	4	19
Decrease in staff quality	4	19
Increased importance of core activities	3	14
Increased importance placed on customer satisfaction	3	14
Increase in fixed costs	3	14
Decrease in productivity	3	14
Increase in importance of quality of suppliers	3	14
Decrease in resources available	3	14

Table 3.3
(Continued)

Type of recommendation/factor	Number of times this factor led to recommendation	
All downsizing/outsourcing recommendations (45 rules)		
Increased importance of IT strategy	8	18
Increase in fixed costs	7	16
Decrease in staff quality	7	16
Increase in competitor strength	6	13
Decreased profits	6	13
Increase in importance of quality of suppliers	6	13
Decrease in resources available	6	13
Increased importance placed on spreading of risk	6	13
Increased importance of skill needs analysis	6	13
Increase in rate of innovation	5	11
Increased market turbulence	5	11

Downsizing/outsourcing can be seen here as a response to a more uncertain and competitive environment, as a measure to improve the cost structure and hence profitability of the firm, or as a way of coping with a shortage of skilled staff or required resources. These are in line with much general corporate practice. General downsizing may be a result of business process re-engineering and/or integration. Outsourcing of IT functions was the most frequent single recommendation when IT and innovation was seen as increasing in importance but the firm did not have in-house resources to develop its IT function competitively. Other selective outsourcing referred frequently not only to 'non-core activities' but also to staff outsourcing, when staff of the required calibre could not be recruited profitably. This fits with Van Horn-Christopher's (1996) predictions of increasing 'Staffing for Profitability'.

Examining the reasons given for downsizing/outsourcing shows some tendency to accept traditional thinking that they will improve the airline's cost structure, e.g., 'need to downsize to improve productivity and profits', 'gain a competitive advantage by reducing costs', 'to reduce fixed costs/variable costs/cost base' (used many times). In one 'status quo' scenario, where costs (including salaries), profits and market turbulence were all set to stay the same, outsourcing of non-value-added activities (along with investing in more routes and aircraft) was recommended as a 'growth/cost reduction strategy'. However, other recommendations show more strategic thinking, with some appreciation of the risks of losing company knowledge, for example:

- Outsource risky technologies to allow the airline to concentrate on strategic competencies and master leading-edge technologies.
- Outsource parts of the value chain to providers who will give extra value, while preserving corporate knowledge.
- Outsource less productive routes in order to improve routing efficiency.
- Outsource activities which are no longer adding incremental value.
- Downsize in order to be able to invest in training for the retained workforce (when skill needs and costs were increasing).

The most common alternative strategy recommended when the factors in Table 3.2 occurred in a particular scenario was some type of partnership (joint venture, alliance, merger or collaboration), which is in line with current industry trends. These covered both partnerships with other airlines, to enhance market/route coverage or to access expertise that was lacking, and partnerships with suppliers. Where resources allowed, investment, in-house research and development, and training/retraining of staff were recommended – but in any situation where the scenario indicated limited resources, financial pressures, or a more uncertain or competitive marketplace, downsizing or outsourcing was the strategy of choice. In only one case was the opposite strategy of bringing outsourced functions back in-house recommended, in a highly competitive situation where the importance of product quality was increasing but customer satisfaction decreasing, and it was thought that closer control of quality was required to boost customer satisfaction.

The full list of recommendations was also scrutinized for more innovative strategies, some of which foreshadow more recent airline moves:

- Collaborative new product development, flexible manufacturing, a preferred supplier network – to deal with increasing importance of innovation and increasing product complexity.

Process in action the European airline industry– implications for the airline industry

Discussion of the various scenarios resulted in the development of a database of suggested strategic options, some very industry-specific while others are more general and need to be interpreted in terms relevant to the industry. Although participants did not come from the airline industry, their discussions produced several strategic ideas which have since emerged in reality, e.g., the founder of easyJet has set up easyRentacar, Air France has offered share options to employees and RyanAir announced in 2001 its plans for a continental hub at the minor Belgian airport of Charleroi. For the database to be of use to an airline, it would first require validation by company or industry experts. Also, the list of relevant factors should be checked for omissions, in the light of recent airline industry research; airlines may wish to add factors such as market growth rate and extent of environmental regulation. The ES recommendations could then serve as a useful starting point for strategic discussion.

Questions

1. What is the value of this strategy in devising the strategy of an organization?

2. What are the advantages, disadvantages and dangers of using it in this specific context?

- Business process re-engineering, retraining the freed staff in customer service skills (language, globalization) – when a stronger market orientation was required.

- Sharing common services with other industry players.

- Starting alliances with economy airlines outside Europe – where the importance of a new competitive structure is increasing.

- Reviewing human resources (HR) policies, introducing a stock-option plan or profit-sharing – to deal with decreasing staff quality.

- Team building training, developing brainstorming capabilities – where importance of customer satisfaction and the value chain is increasing.

- Developing alliances with travel agencies, car hire companies, local tour operators, etc. – where importance of value chain is increasing.

- Using low-cost hubs – where profits are decreasing but competition is increasing.

- Vertical integration through supplier acquisition, rewards/penalties for suppliers – to deal with decreasing supplier quality.

Implications for companies considering the use of scenario planning

The use of scenario planning in this context has highlighted both benefits and potential problems. The participants testified to the emergent benefits outlined by Bood and Postma (1997), in that they became more aware of environmental uncertainties and their possible implications, while discussion with peers from different backgrounds gave alternative perspectives and stretched their thinking. The ES proved extremely useful as a quick method of recording complex information and allowing its retrieval, while the requirement to draft chosen strategies in terms of ES rules with appropriate reasons was useful in clarifying thinking and achieving group consensus. However, examination of the database shows many instances of 'circular reasoning', where one or more of the scenario conditions are repeated as a reason for the chosen action – this indicates some reliance on traditional 'rules of thumb'. The fact that this happened even when a facilitator was present some of the time to encourage deeper thinking shows how easy it is to fall back unquestioningly on 'received wisdom' and highlights the importance of constantly challenging this practice.

Reliability and validity

The reliability of the system and consequent methodology lies in the longitudinal approach taken (collected over 3 years on exactly the same factors and scenarios) as well as on the cross-sectional myriad of practitioner profiles who took part in the exercise (a considerable number of international managers from a multiplicity of cultures, industries, managerial functions and educational and demographic backgrounds).

The validity associated with method and the final ES prototype was measured through a validation procedure involving the presence each time (each year with different groups of participants) of two experts – one an academic specializing in outsourcing/downsizing and the other an industry expert – who have dissected the different features of scenario construction, strategic inputs/recommendations and subsequent strategic reasoning. Furthermore, the elicitation of knowledge provided by the participants and the requests and allowance for the provision of self-designed scenario options have all provided the necessary stimulation and involvement on the part of the system users, which can also be seen as an important element underwriting the validity of the methodology and the resulting knowledge-based system.

Managerial implications

Multiple-scenario analysis is praised for the radically different stance it takes towards environmental uncertainties. Whereas trend-projecting forecasting techniques try to abandon any uncertainty by providing managers with only one forecast, multiple-scenario analysis deliberately confronts managers with environmental uncertainties by presenting them with several fundamentally different outlooks on the future. Scenarios focus attention on causal processes and crucial decision points, can serve as a background for the evaluation and selection of strategies, and can also provide a framework within which all the various factors and information can be more effectively and easily judged by the decision-maker. Furthermore, and better than any other future-oriented tool, scenarios offer the possibility to integrate various kinds of data in a consistent manner. Good scenarios enlarge managers' understanding as to what is significant versus ephemeral. This allows for anticipation of the unexpected and provides for an early warning system. Organizations may even develop several contingency plans on the basis of the scenarios or an environment-monitoring system. By exploring and anticipating the future, scenarios can help to identify major changes and strategic problems an organization will be facing in future as well as to generate strategic options to effectively deal with them.

These findings reinforce the main objective of any ES, which is to act as a decision aid for a human problem-solver and decision-maker. This particular rule-based prototype could be intertwined with the more recent form of an ES in case-based reasoning, which uses previous cases similar to the current problem situation to find solutions. This form of ES allows the user to access the experience of experts and the database of previous cases to analyze the current cases and determine the outcome. Organizations are using expert and KBS in order to reduce the learning curves of processes. These systems can be used to build scenarios, test understanding of the industry and 'test' the internal knowledge of the managers. They are only as good as the designs and the quality of inputs and should be used to guide the business in taking strategic actions. Reasoning from knowledge is an area in which computer programmes can exceed human performance, as the computer does not contain a bias for information. The structure of knowledge is important when developing the ES, as knowledge that is not used over time in the hands of individuals can become distorted, 'corrupt' and forgotten. The advantage of KBS is that the system can identify links between pieces of information well before an individual can make the connection due to the unbiased nature of the system as well as its ability to contain so much more information than a person's brain. Furthermore, the construction of small-scale applications such as this one, focusing on specific problem areas and using an ES shell, does not require extensive programming knowledge and can be carried out concurrently with the discussion of scenarios. This allows speedy and effective development and validation.

Conclusions

The main contribution of this research study can be encapsulated by stating that strategic decisions taken by senior managers can be enhanced and become more effective in terms of accuracy, goal-reaching capabilities and risk minimization, through the utilization of an environmental scanning methodology (in this case, scenario planning) coupled with the application of artificial intelligence (e.g., an ES). Furthermore, the heuristics involved in strategic (long-term) decision-making can benefit from the challenge confronting current mindsets, the stimulation of new assumptions, the triggering of innovative thought processes and the predisposition to plan for contingencies, as well as a more concerted way to manage the intricacies of uncertainty.

Dedicated ESs similar to that detailed here have been applied to the oil, automotive and tourist industries and were also the subject of a workshop of top academics in Scotland that considered the use of environmental scanning and KBS (Davies, *et al.,* 2001).

Summary

- This chapter delves into the analysis of changing markets and environmental uncertainty.

- It focuses on the discussion and application of scenario planning, and it connects a branch of artificial intelligence (AI) with utilization of scenario planning.

- The chapter uses a case study approach – in this case, the example of downsizing and outsourcing in the European airline industry.

- It shows the particular methodology used to construct the ES from decision rules that were elicited using a set of scenarios based on the European airline industry.

- Strategic implications for this particular industry as well as key implications for companies considering the utilization of scenario planning are also discussed. Reliability and validity issues are also presented.

Chapter questions

1. Comment on the three types of uncertainty identified by Milliken (1987, 1990).

2. Discuss the benefits for an organization of adopting a scenario planning approach.

3. Critically analyze the role of KBS/ES as an aid for management decision-making, as they can be applied to any sector ranging from retailing, banking and automobiles to health and utilities.

References

Anonymous (1998) 'Scenario planning', *Business Europe,* 38(5):9–10.
Ashill, N. J., and Jobber, D. (2001) 'Defining the domain of perceived environmental uncertainty: An exploratory study of senior marketing executives', *Journal of Marketing Management,* 17(5/6):543–558.

Baden-Fuller, C., Targett, D., and Hunt, B. (2000) 'Outsourcing to outmanoeuvre: Outsourcing re-defines competitive strategy and structure', *European Management Journal,* 18(3): 285–295.

Bood, R., and Postma, T. (1997) 'Strategic learning with Scenarios, European', *Management Journal,* 15(60):633–647.

Cavusgil, S. T., and Evirgen, C. (1995) 'Use of expert systems in international marketing: An application for co-operative venture partner selection', *European Journal of Marketing,* 31(1):73–86.

Cooper, C. (1998, February) 'Working in a short-term culture', *Management Today,* p. 5.

Courtney, H. (2003) 'Decision-driven scenarios for assessing four levels of uncertainty', *Strategy and Leadership,* 31(1):14–22.

Curry, B. (1992) 'Constructing a knowledge base for a marketing expert system', *Market Intelligence and Planning,* 10(11):12–20.

Curry, B. (1996) 'Knowledge-based modelling for strategic decisions', *Market Intelligence and Planning,* 14(4):24–28.

Dubelaar, C., Finlay, P. N., and Taylor, D. (1991) 'Expert systems: The cold fusion of marketing?', *Journal of Marketing Management,* 7(4):371–382.

Furrer, O., and Thomas, H. (2000) 'The rivalry matrix: Understanding rivalry and competitive dynamics', *European Management Journal,* 18(6):619–637.

Gnyawali, D. R., and Grant, J. H. (1996) *Strategy and Leadership,* 24(3):28–34.

Guimaraes, T., Yoon, Y., and O'Neal, Q. (1995) 'Success factors for manufacturing expert system development', *Computers and Industrial Engineering,* 28(3):545–559.

Haapaniemi, P. (1996, July/August) 'The people/performance paradox', *Chief Executive Magazine,* pp. 4–15.

Kakabadse, A., and Kakabadse, N. (2002) 'Trends in outsourcing: Contrasting USA and Europe', *European Management Journal,* 20(2):189–198.

Klein, M. R. (2002) 'An expert system for evaluating the make or buy decision', *Computers and Industrial Engineering,* 26(2):151–177.

Knill, B. (1996) 'The many faces of downsizing', *Material Handling Engineering,* 51(3):73–74.

Lankford, W. M., and Parsa, F. (1999) 'Outsourcing: A primer', *Management Decision,* 37(4): 310–316.

Legare, T. L. (1998) 'Strategic dialogue', *Marketing Research,* 10(1):14–19.

Li, S. (2000) 'Developing marketing strategy with MarStra: The support system and the real-world tests', *Marketing Intelligence and Planning,* 18(3):135–143.

Li, S., Davies, B., Edwards, J., Kinman, R., and Duan, Y. (2002) 'Integrating group Delphi, fuzzy logic and expert systems for marketing strategy development: The hybridisation and its effectiveness', *Marketing Intelligence and Planning,* 20(4/5):273–284.

Li, S., and Davies, B. J. (2001) 'GloStra – a hybrid system for developing global strategy and associated Internet strategy', *Industrial Management and Data Systems,* 101(3/4):132–140.

Li, S., Kinman, R., Duan, Y., and Edwards, J. S. (2000) 'Computer-based support for marketing strategy development', *European Journal of Marketing,* 34(5/6):551–575.

Love, B. (1998) 'How our jobs have changed', *Folio: The Magazine for Magazine Management,* 27(5):46–55.

Mercer, D. (1995) 'Simpler scenarios', *Management Decision,* 33(4):32–40.

Millett, S. M. (2003) 'The future of scenarios: Challenges and opportunities', *Strategy and Leadership,* 31(2):16–24.

Milliken, F. J. (1987) 'Three types of uncertainty about the environment: State, effect and response uncertainty', *Academy of Management Review,* 12:133–143.

Milliken, F. J. (1990) 'Perceiving and integrating change: An examination of college administrators' interpretation of changing demographics', *Academy of Management Journal,* 33:42–63.

Mintel (2001) *Airlines,* London: Mintel International Group Limited.

O'Brien, F. A., and Meadows, M. (2000) 'Corporate visioning: A survey of UK practice', *Journal of the Operational Research Society,* 51(1):36–44.

O'Brien, F. A., and Meadows, M. (2001) 'How to develop visions: A literature review and a revised CHOICES approach for an uncertain world', *Journal of Systemic Practice and Action Research,* 14(4):495–515.

O'Brien, F. A., and Meadows, M. (2003) 'Exploring the current practice of visioning: Case studies from the UK financial services sector', *Management Decision,* 41(5):488–497.

O'Brien, F. A., and Meadows, M. (2004) 'Scenario planning – lessons for practice from teaching and learning', *European Journal of Operational Research,* 152(3):709–722.

Oosthuizen, H. (2000) 'Developing strategy – do we really need a new paradigm?', *South African Journal of Business Management,* 31(1):9–16.

Papadakis, V. M. (1998) 'Strategic investment decision processes and organizational performance: an empirical examination', *British Journal of Management,* 9(2):115–132.

Pettigrew, A., Massini, S., and Numagami, T. (2000) 'Innovative forms of organising in Europe and Japan', *European Management Journal,* 18(3):259–273.

Phelps, R., Chan, C., and Kapsalis, S. C. (2001) 'Does scenario planning effect performance? Two exploratory studies', *Journal of Business Research,* 51(3):223–232.

Porter, M. E. (1980) *Competitive Strategy: Techniques for Analyzing Industries and Competitors,* New York: The Free Press.

Runnion, T. (1993) 'Outsourcing can be a productivity solution for the '90s', *HR Focus,* 70(11):23.

Schoemaker, P. J. H. (1993) 'Multiple scenario development: Its conceptual and behavioural foundation', *Strategic Management Journal,* 14(3):193–203.

Schoemaker, P. J. H. (1995) 'Scenario planning: A tool for strategic thinking', *Sloan Management Review,* 36(2):25–40.

Schoemaker, P. J. H. (1997) 'Disciplined imagination: From scenarios to strategic options', *International Studies of Management and Organization,* 27(2):43–70.

Simpson, D. G. (1992) 'Key lessons for adopting scenario planning in diversified companies', *Planning Review,* 20(3):10–22.

Sing-Chang, S., Kalafatis, S., and Yeghiazarian, A. (1995) 'Artificial intelligence in marketing: A review', *Journal of Targeting, Measurement and Analysis for Marketing,* 3(3):200–211.

Stone, R. W., and Good, D. J. (1995) 'Expert systems in the marketing organisation', *Industrial Management and Data Systems,* 95(4):3–7.

Strauss, J. D., and Radnor, M. (2004) 'Roadmapping for dynamic and uncertain environments', *Research Technology Management,* 47(2):51–57.

Thomas, C. W. (1994) 'Learning from imagining the years ahead', *Planning Review,* 22(3):6–11.

Thomas, H. (1984) 'Strategic decision analysis: Applied decision analysis and its role in the strategic management process', *Strategic Management Journal,* 5(2):139–156.

Van Horn-Christopher, D. A. (1996) 'Will employee meltdown mean a "contingent" workforce?', *Business Forum,* 21(3/4):11–13.

Verity, J. (2003) 'Scenario planning as a strategy technique', *European Business Journal,* 15(4): 185–195.

Whitehill, M. (1997) 'Knowledge-based strategy to deliver sustained competitive advantage', *Long Range Planning,* 30(4):621–627.

Wilson, D. F. (1999) 'Competitive marketing strategy in a volatile environment: Theory, practice and research priorities', *Journal of Strategic Marketing,* 7:19–40.

Wong, Y., Maher, T. E., Nicholson, J. D., and Gurney, N. P. (2000) 'Strategic alliances in logistics outsourcing', *Asia Pacific Journal of Marketing and Logistics,* 12(4):1–21.

Wright, A. D. (2000) 'Scenario planning: A continuous improvement approach to strategy', *Total Quality Management,* 11(4/5/6):S433–S438.

Yoon, Y., Guimaraes, T., and O'Neal, Q. (1995) 'Exploring the factors associated with expert systems success', *MIS Quarterly,* 19(1):83–106.

4

Demand management (market and technology forecasting)

Geoff Southern and Luiz Moutinho

Introduction

Forecasting is fundamentally important in any organization, but forecasting methods are mainly applied to predict market demand. Although this chapter will concentrate on demand forecasting, in other words techniques to forecast what the organization will be asked to do by customers, it should also be noted that an organization must also be able to forecast its capabilities. Resources must be planned and managed to deliver the demand forecasted. Then both demand and organizational capability must be reconciled and used to forecast the financial performance of the organization. As the 'bottom line', this is perhaps the most important thing to be forecast in the organization, although it really represents an aggregation and interpretation of other functional forecasts.

Forecasting requirements are related to the strategy level of decisions they inform. These are in turn related to planning time horizons, and hence forecasts are needed for different time spans. This relationship drives the specification of business decisions which must be made and the factors that need to be forecast (Figure 4.1) to inform them. Table 4.1 indicates the

Learning objectives

To understand the concepts and techniques of:

- Qualitative (or judgemental) forecasting

- Quantitative forecasting

and to select and apply them appropriately in specific contexts.

nature of this relationship and some of the factors to which the forecasts and strategic decisions are applied.

Most market demand forecasts fit into the long- and medium-term categories and are, in effect, used to produce yearly (and perhaps once every 5 years) budgets, but these are in turn used to specify monthly budgets that are in effect operating plans. Forecasting is therefore essential to both long-term strategic planning and short-term scheduling and operational control – in fact, to all business processes of the organization.

This chapter will:

- Describe the fundamental principles underlying different ways of forecasting and in what situation they will be of most value.
- Attempt to place these different ways of forecasting into different categories.
- Consider how a forecasting system should be designed to suit a specific context.

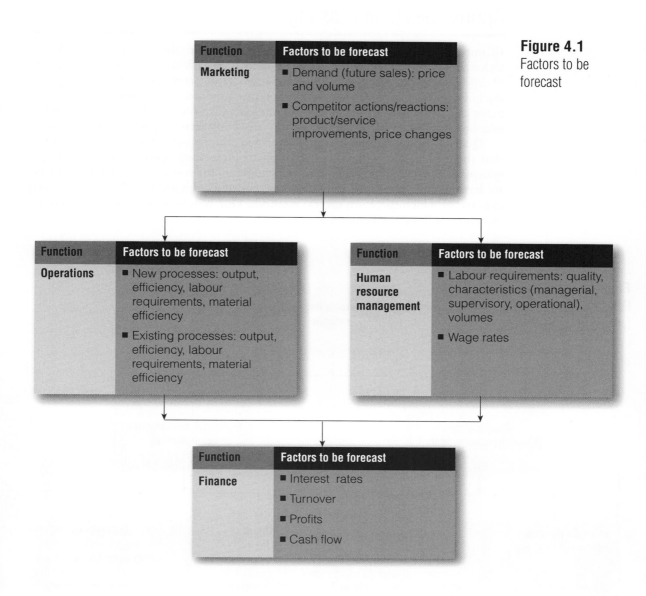

Figure 4.1
Factors to be forecast

Table 4.1
Typical factors to be
forecast related to
time

Forecast type (time base)	Decision and forecast factor
Long term (strategic)	Product portfolio: focus and range Operating system design: facility location, process design, capacity requirements
Medium term	Product volumes: operating mix, volumes created/ purchased
Short term	Scheduling: products made, services delivered, inventory requirements, workforce tasks allocated

Approaches to forecasting

Chambers *et al.* (1979) classified forecasting methods into three categories: qualitative techniques, time-series analysis and causal models. In each category, there are a number of different forecasting models. In demand forecasting, some are suitable for forecasting initial sales and others for forecasting repeat purchases. Consequently, one should make clear the differentiation between models which favour adoption (early market take-up) and those which favour diffusion (steady market growth or continuation).

'Qualitative techniques' are also termed *judgemental forecasting*. We think that these methods, which basically consist of seeking opinion and analyzing it systematically, should be subdivided depending on the source of information. Hence we have divided this category into asking customers (market research), and asking experts, of which there are several methods. Our system of forecasting typology is therefore as shown in Figure 4.2.

Figure 4.2
Forecasting
typology:
classification
of methods

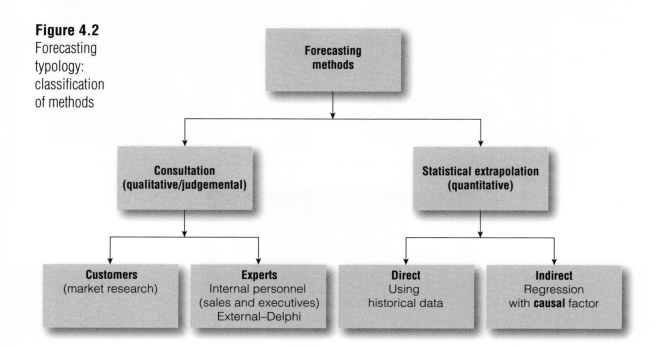

Consultation: asking the customers (market research)

Market research is a systematic approach to determine consumer interest in a product or service by creating and testing hypotheses through data gathering surveys. It is good for identifying product or service features that are or may be attractive to the customer, but not necessarily good for directly forecasting total demand. People are ready to give an opinion on product or service features, but less willing to say whether they will buy something if it is offered. It should also be noted that demand results from a need or desire for the product or service plus the ability to pay, so measures of both desire and income are needed to forecast demand by these methods, and all of the people are not willing to divulge their income honestly.

Market research is usually conducted by survey. Survey design is important, the objective being to get as much information that is relevant to decisions we have to make, at as low a cost as possible. Surveys can be small in sample size, e.g., using focus groups and asking open-ended questions (i.e., asking for descriptive answers) to gather richer information. At the other extreme, the sample can be very large, e.g., using public surveys and asking closed questions (i.e., asking 'yes' or 'no', or 'would you prefer A or B' questions). These are extremes, and most market research exercises adopt a combination of techniques. So, there are several generic decisions that must be addressed in designing the research. These are briefly mentioned:

Should the survey questionnaire:

- Have open or closed questions?
- Be long or short? You are asking people for their time, so it must not be too long. Incentives to complete it may be useful here, but care must be taken that they do not influence respondents into giving answers that they think the questioner wants to hear.
- Have bias? Are the questions loaded in that they indicate the preference of the questioner or their organization? Of course they should not be.

How should we conduct our survey?

- What method of delivery should we employ – post, phone, street survey, or focus group? All these have cost implications, and responses to some methods may depend on interviewee interest and hence be positively or negatively self-selecting.
- What degree of 'friendliness' should we adopt?

What should our sample be?

- How big? We can use statistical methods to decide our sample size, and how it can be stratified (divided up by generic features) to relate to the total population of potential customers? There is also a trade-off here between the cost of the exercise and the value of the information gathered.
- How relevant? Again rhetorical, it should be relevant to the information we need. For example, it may be better to conduct a survey on luxury goods in a prestige shopping precinct, where shoppers are more likely to have the means of purchase than in an everyday supermarket.

Whatever the design of the survey, it is always worth conducting a pilot study to test it. Market research exercises are expensive, and faults can be minimized in a pilot before costs escalate.

Consultation: asking experts

Known as *Judgement Methods*, these rely on the experience and knowledge of experts assimilated from a combination of specialist study and life experience. We are really asking experts to tell us about possible occurrences or developments – which may lead to discontinuities or sudden changes in trend of demand – that will change the way we do business. Expert sources include:

- The organization's sales force – forecasts compiled from estimates of future demands made periodically by members of the company's sales force.

- Executives – opinions, experience and technical knowledge of one or more managers are summarized to arrive at a single forecast.

- External experts – experts in, for e.g., technology, finance (economics) or fashion, who are external to the organization.

There is a need here to stimulate discussion among the experts so that they can consider each other's viewpoints before arriving at some form of consensus. However, problems sometimes arise when the presence of 'high status' experts results in 'groupthink'. Such status can come from academic standing or organizational power. Persuasiveness of such experts, resulting from their perceived status, can result in focus being placed too soon on a limited number of possible outcomes. It is therefore advisable to keep experts apart during the consultation process. Also, the time of experts is very expensive, and this makes it very costly to conduct what, in effect, would be a super focus group. A technique called the Delphi method overcomes this problem. This is a process for gaining consensus from a group of experts while maintaining their anonymity. It consists of using an initial questionnaire to gather views, followed by iterative cycles of preparing a report and seeking more views on that report. It is particularly useful when employing external experts to predict environmental changes, e.g., economic and legal changes, and technological and fashion developments. The process is shown diagrammatically in Figure 4.3.

Figure 4.3
The Delphi method

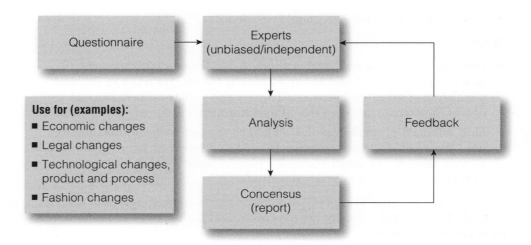

Statistical extrapolation: use of causal relationships – linear regression

Linear regression is a technique where one variable (the dependent variable) is related to one or more independent variables by a linear equation. We want to forecast the dependent variable, but factual information may already be available for the independent variable, or someone else may be forecasting the future behaviour of it. It follows that all we need to know is how the dependent variable behaves when the independent variable changes, or in other words the regression relationship (or line of best prediction). Table 4.2 gives illustrations of this relationship.

The method of arriving at the 'line of best prediction' to be used for linear regression is shown in Figure 4.4. The aim in defining this line is to minimize the forecast errors which would have resulted from existing (known) data, and to use this to convert known future data for the independent variable into a forecast, which we need, for the dependent variable.

Linear regression assumes a very simple view of relationships. 'Life' very seldom 'happens' in straight lines, as demonstrated by the classic supply/demand elasticity curve from economics and by the classic product life cycle curve. Linear relationships can only be assumed as approximations over certain sections of these curves, so polynomial curve fitting computer programs can sometimes be used to identify more complex equations to use for forecasting. The following historic case illustrates the principle that relationships cannot always be defined by straight lines.

Causal variable (independent)	Dependent variable	Source of data on causal variable	External factors affecting relationship
Advertising budget	Sales of goods or services being advertised	Internal organization plans	Economy Effectiveness of spend Fashion and technology
Price	Demand (sales)	Internal proposal	(The classic economics elasticity of demand curve)
House brick sales	Planning permissions granted or pending (in short term) Land purchased by house builders (in longer term)	Local government records (planning permissions) Land ownership records (national registration system)	Economy Changes (fashion- or technology-driven) in building materials or styles

Table 4.2
Causal relationships and data sources for independent variables

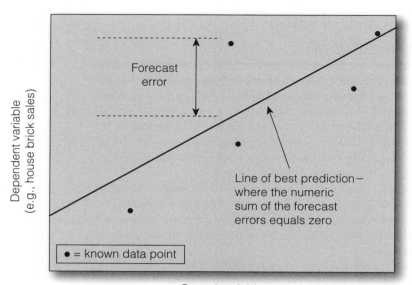

Figure 4.4
Regression –
method of finding
line of best
prediction

Process in action Brunel and the Atlantic

In the early days of steam ships it was thought that steam-driven vessels could never cross the Atlantic because they were incapable of carrying enough fuel (coal) for the long journey. However, ship designers were assuming a linear relationship between the dimensions of the ship and the amount of coal it could carry, i.e., increasing the length by 10 per cent increased the coal capacity by 10 per cent. Brunel realized that this was not true and that the relationship between dimension and volume was cubic, i.e., increasing the length by 10 per cent increased the

volume (and coal-carrying capacity) by 1.1 to the power of 3 or 33 per cent. Using similar logic, if he increases the length by 10 per cent, the area in contact with the water, creating 'drag' and increasing fuel usage, increases by 1.1 to the power of 2 or 21 per cent. With a positive difference of 12 per cent in the relationship between coal-carrying capacity and extra fuel needed for every 10 per cent increase in linear dimension, all Brunel had to do was build larger ships.

Working on this principle, and on his faith that he could build ships large enough, Brunel changed the face of shipbuilding when he built the Great Western. (But it still had sails, just in case.)

Question
1. If it was that simple, why did others not do it?

Statistical extrapolation: use of historic behaviour of data (time-series analysis)

When using time-series analysis, the methods rely on past demand or performance to predict what will happen in the future, assuming there will be no discontinuities in the business environment.

The methods are based on a fundamental assumption that variability in demand comes from four sources:

- *Underlying* trend
- *Economic or trade* cycle
- Seasonality (this may coincide with the trade cycle)
- Randomness.

We will illustrate the principles of time-series methods by starting at the simplest techniques and then progressively building on these to illustrate more complex methods. However, the following principles should be noted throughout the build-up:

- Techniques strive to smooth out the effect of randomness of the demand data.
- At the same time, natural trends and patterns must be factored into the forecast as much as possible.
- As a result, there is a trade-off between smoothing out the randomness and incorporating trend and natural cycles.
- In time-series methods, the future is divided into useful time periods – days, weeks, year quarters or years – depending on the planning horizon and stability of the business, the degree of seasonality in the data to be forecast and the accuracy of forecast needed. Again, there is a trade-off here.
- Time-series analysis generates an ongoing forecasting system for short-term forecasting. Few organizations operate in an environment stable enough for it to be used to generate long-term predictions. Its main use is therefore to inform short-term operating decisions.
- A time-series method is selected by testing it on historical data which is already available, first finding a method which would have given reasonably good forecast figures and then improving it iteratively. This will be discussed at the end of the description of the various methods.

Smoothing out randomness

The simplest time-series method is the naïve forecast – a forecast for the next time period that equals the demand for the current period. While this follows an underlying trend in the data, it reacts immediately to randomness. However, it is simple and useful where randomness is very small. This is rarely the case.

Let us therefore try to smooth out the effects of randomness. One way to do this is by using a moving average. The simple moving average (SMA) demonstrates the principle involved. Figure 4.5 demonstrates how a four-period SMA is calculated. It can be seen that randomness in demand is smoothed, but that reaction to trend is also suppressed. Any number of periods can be used as the base for the SMA, but using more periods both smoothes reaction to randomness, which we want, and suppresses further the reaction to trend, which we do not want. Yet again the fundamental trade-off of the technique needs to be considered.

One way to increase the effect of trend on our forecast is to give greater weighting to more recent periods. The weighted moving average (WMA) technique gives us a simple way of doing this. It is illustrated in Figure 4.6.

The WMA method deals with the SMA method and incorporates it into our forecast, and we can change the weighting factors and the number of periods to improve the performance of the forecasting system. In fact, there is a clever way of doing this called the exponentially WMA (EWMA) technique. The simple formula used here is:

$$\text{Prediction} = \alpha \times \text{last outcome} + (1 - \alpha) \times \text{last prediction (i.e., for last outcome)}$$

It is obvious that we must make some simple estimates to start the technique off, but once started predictions become self-generating. Calculations are simplified and each prediction 'rolls over' into the next one.

α is known as a smoothing constant and is a number between 0 and 1. As α nears 1, we have a naïve forecast; we overreact to randomness and suppress consideration of trend. As α nears 0, we have an SMA forecast, covering all periods back to infinity (or as near as we can get to it). By changing α, we can thus simulate using different weighting factors very quickly to find one which would have given us good forecast results in the past.

Figure 4.5
Simple moving average calculation (Four periods)

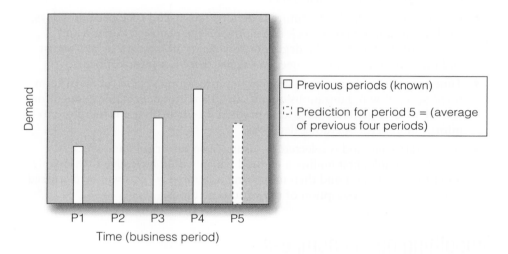

Figure 4.6
Weighted moving average calculation (Four periods)

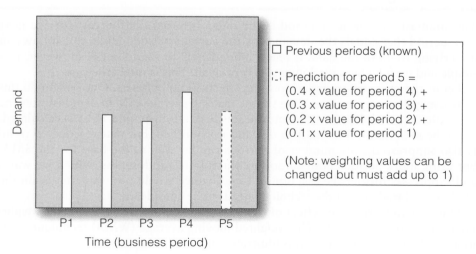

Incorporating trend

In dealing with trend, we use some type of SMA to give us a baseline forecast, and in addition, we calculate an element to adjust for the trend. A simple method of doing this is illustrated in Figure 4.7. In this case, a four-period SMA is used to calculate the baseline forecast, and the estimate of the trend is simply the difference between the last and the first period divided by the time span of the SMA.

In fact, much more complicated methods of dealing with the underlying trend are generally used. One such method is the double exponentially WMA (DEWMA). (This is also called the *trend-adjusted exponentially smoothing method*.) Here the baseline element of the forecast is calculated using the EWMA method, and a second element for the trend is found using another smoothing factor, β. This allows fine-tuning of the forecast system design by trying different values of both α and β until a good system results.

Incorporating business cycles and/or seasonality

In order to compensate for the effects of business cycles or seasonality on demand, we need to identify where the effect takes place and then separate the seasonal factor for separate analysis. The generic procedure is as follows:

- Identify the seasons.
- Deseasonalize the data and deal with it as previously discussed (the trend adjustment method).
- Calculate, separately, a seasonal adjustment for each season (it can be +ve or −ve) and add it to the outcome of the previous stage.

Note that weighting can also be applied here.

Figure 4.7
Moving average plus trend adjustment

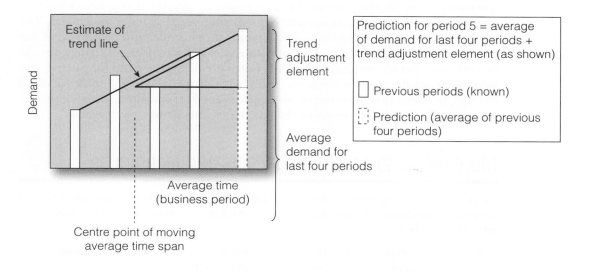

Fitting time-series methods and measuring how well they continue to perform

So far we have demonstrated the basic principles of time-series methods. Applied systems are much more complicated. When applied, they must be tested against previous data and 'tuned' by changing weighting factors to optimize reaction to changes (in the environment) against smoothing out reaction to these changes. As we have already indicated, we use errors in forecasts to indicate how good our forecasting system is. A forecast error is the difference between the forecast we made and what really happened. (When using simulation to design a new forecasting system, it is the difference between the forecast we would have made and what really happened.) Thus, we have a forecast error for every forecast we make, giving us a statistical distribution of forecast errors. We are then interested in two aspects, and associated measures, of this distribution:

- **Measure 1:** where the mean of this distribution lies relative to zero error; this is called the *bias* and indicates how well we are predicting any trend or pattern across time. There may be a lead or lag in the trend prediction. The most popular measures of bias are the cumulative sum of forecast errors (CFE) and the average forecast error (= CFE/n, where n = number of data points).

- **Measure 2:** of the spread of the distribution, indicating how well we are smoothing out the random elements. There are three methods of measuring the spread of the error distribution: the mean square error, the standard deviation and the mean absolute deviation. Although the formulas are different, the underlying principle of all three is the same; that the sign (+ or −) of the error is ignored in some way when finding their average.

We want to minimize both of these measures, but as one rises, the other falls, so a compromise is needed. If we are using exponential weighting, the easiest way, then we will test which weighting factors give the best compromise between our measure for bias and our measure for spread. (Computer forecasting systems allow us to do this very quickly.) These will be the factors we use, and we start applying the system in practice.

Having specified the design of our forecasting system, we now need a mechanism to test that it is still working well. External influences in the environment may introduce sudden or even step changes in demand trends or patterns with which our system cannot deal. We therefore use a *tracking signal*, a measure that indicates whether our method of forecasting is accurately predicting actual changes in demand. The most effective way of doing this is to constantly monitor the ratio of the bias of our predictions to their spread, i.e., Measure 1/Measure 2. If this does not change, we can be fairly sure that our original trade-off between predicting the trend (or pattern) and smoothing out the random elements is still being maintained. If the tracking signal changes, we know that the system is no longer as good at forecasting demand, and we need to go back and start designing the time-series forecasting system again.

More recent forecasting concepts and techniques

More recent developments in forecasting generally attempt to combine judgemental approaches with data-processing techniques such as regression and time-series methods. This can be by:

- Factoring expert knowledge into 'automatic' decision-making techniques (e.g., simulation methods, expert systems, neural networks).

- Collating and analyzing the plethora of data that can now be collected automatically by computer database systems (e.g., data mining).
- Go beyond the simplistic two-factor regression approach to look at multi-factor relationships (e.g., conjoint analysis).
- Combining expert systems methodology and statistical extrapolation (e.g., rule-based forecasting, judgemental bootstrapping).

This section will describe and briefly evaluate these concepts and techniques.

Simulation methods

Checking whether a proposed forecasting system will work will often involve field research. The cost, the time involved and other problems associated with field experimentation often preclude a method as a source of information for particular situations. In such instances, it is often desirable to construct a model of an operational situation and obtain relevant information through the manipulation of this model. This manipulation, called *simulation*, describes the act of creating a complex model to resemble a real process or system and experimenting with this model in the hope of learning something about the real system.

Simulation represents a general technique that is useful for studying marketing systems, and is one of the most flexible methods in terms of application. Simulation models have been formulated to serve two management functions: planning, and monitoring and controlling operations.

Marketing simulations can be conveniently divided into three classes (Doyle and Fenwick, 1976). The first deals with computer models of the behaviour of marketing system components, the second with computer models on the effect of different marketing instruments on demand, and the third with marketing games.

Expert systems

An expert system, simply defined, is a computer program which contains human knowledge or expertise that it can use to generate reasoned advice or instructions. The development of expert systems stems from earlier work on artificial intelligence (AI). AI models have emerged in the last few years as a follow-up to simulation, attempting to portray, comprehend and analyze the reasoning in a range of situations. Although the two methods of AI (expert systems and neural networks) are, in a certain sense, 'simulations', because of the importance and the potential of these methods, we have introduced them under a separate stand-alone heading. The knowledge base of an expert system is usually represented internally in the machine as a set of IF . . . THEN rules, and the 'inference engine' of the expert system matches together appropriate combinations of rules in order to generate conclusions.

In determining whether a particular marketing domain is suited for this methodology, the following checklist is useful:

- Are the key relationships in the domain logical rather than computational? In practical terms, the answer requires an assessment of whether the decision area is knowledge-intensive (e.g., generating new product areas) or data-intensive (e.g., allocating an advertising budget across media).

- Is the problem domain semi-structured rather than structured or unstructured? If the problem is well-structured, a traditional approach using sequential procedures will be more efficient than an expert system approach. This would be true, e.g., when the entire problem-solving sequence can be enumerated in advance.

- Is knowledge in the domain incomplete? If the problem is well-structured, a traditional approach using sequential procedures will be more efficient than an expert system approach. This would be true, e.g., when the entire problem-solving sequence can be enumerated in advance. Moreover, for highly unstructured domains, expert system performance may be disappointing because the available problem-solving strategies may be inadequate.

- Is it difficult to identify all the important variables or to specify fully their interrelationships? Expert systems are particularly applicable in domains with incomplete knowledge.

- Will problem-solving in the domain require a direct interface between the manager and the computer system? A direct interface may be necessary in situations calling for online decision support. Such situations are generally characterized by a high level of decision urgency (e.g., buying and selling stocks) or complexity (e.g., retail site selection).

Expert systems are particularly useful in these contexts because of their flexible and 'friendly' user interaction facilities, coupled with their ability to explain their reasoning (Rangaswamy *et al.*, 1989). A number of expert systems in marketing have been developed over the years, in particular focusing on the following domains: marketing research, test marketing, pricing, generation of advertising appeals, choice of promotional technique, selection of effective sales techniques, negotiation strategies, site selection, allocation of marketing budget, promotion evaluation, strategic positioning, strategic marketing, assessment of sales territories, brand management, marketing planning, international marketing, bank marketing, tourism marketing and industrial marketing (see Curry and Moutinho, 1991).

The greatest single problem with regard to the effectiveness and applicability of expert system models in the marketing context concerns the construction and validation of the knowledge base.

Neural networks

Neural networks are designed to offer the end-user the capability to bypass the rigidity of expert systems and to develop 'fuzzy logic' decision-making tools. Several authors claim that neural networks provide the user with the ability to design a decision-support tool in less time and with less effort than can be accomplished with other decision-support system tools. Neural networks have been successfully applied in the following marketing areas: consumer behaviour analysis (Curry and Moutinho, 1993), market segmentation, price modelling (Ellis *et al.*, 1991), copy strategy and media planning (Kennedy, 1991).

Neural networks use structured input and output data to develop patterns that mimic human decision-making. Input data are compared to relative output data for many data points. The relationships between the input data and output data are used to develop a pattern that represents the decision-making style of the user. The development of patterns from data points eliminates the need to build rules that support decision-making. Unlike expert systems, which require user intervention to accommodate variable changes within the model, the neural network is capable of retraining, which is accomplished through the addition of new input and output data.

An important strength of this method is its ability to bring together psychometric and econometric analyses so that the best features of both can be exploited. Whereas expert systems are good at organizing masses of information, neural networks may prove capable of duplicating the kind of intuitive, trial-and-error thinking marketing managers typically require. The accuracy of the neural network is not as high as of other methods, yet it has the ability to learn from increased input/output facts and the ability to address data that other decision-support systems cannot handle logically.

Data mining

Analyzing large databases has become known as *data mining,* and businesses hope it will allow them to boost sales and profits by better understanding their customers. The analysis of databases is not new – what is new and challenging is the extraordinary size of these databases.

The availability of huge databases began with scanner purchase data. Estimates suggest that marketing managers in packaged goods companies are inundated with 100 to 1000 times more bits of data than even a few years ago because of the adoption of scanner technology in their channels of distribution. Some data mining techniques also arose in response to 'database marketing' or 'direct marketing' (e.g., by catalogue vendors or coupon distribution providers) in which a company is trying to form relationships with its individual customers as marketing attempts to proceed from 'mass' (one media message for all potential buyers) to 'segments' (some targeting and positioning differences) to 'one-to-one' marketing. In order to achieve such tailored market offerings, a company has to know a great deal about its customers – hence, the database contain many pieces of information on each of the company's many customers.

Traditionally, a company's database would have contained only current business information, but many now contain historical information as well. These 'data warehouses' literally dwarf those available even a few years ago. For example, Wal-Mart has contracted with NCR Corporation to build a data warehouse with 24 terabytes (1 terabyte = 1000 gigabytes) of data storage, which will make it the world's largest data warehouse. The system will provide information about each of Wal-Mart's 3000-plus stores in multiple countries. Wal-Mart plans to use the information to select products that need replenishment, analyze seasonal buying patterns, examine customer buying trends, select markdowns and react to merchandise volume and movement.

In response to the increasingly massive data sets, firms have been working to create increasingly sophisticated data mining technologies (hardware and software) to analyze the data. Data mining uses *massively parallel processing* and *symmetric multiprocessing* supercomputer technologies (during which multiple data points and subroutines may be processing simultaneously, compared with old-fashioned 'serial' processing, in which one datum is processed after another). These huge machines support 'relational' database programs that can slice massive amounts of data into dozens of smaller, more manageable pools of information.

Sometimes these intensive approaches are applied to databases that are being analyzed with fairly traditional statistical techniques. For example, regression is still a premier analytical tool, because many predictors can be used to capture complex consumer decision-making and market behaviour – forecasting sales as a function of season, price, promotions, sales force, competitor factors and delivery delays. Other popular techniques of data mining include cluster analysis for segmentation and neural networks. Businesses regularly use data mining analytical tools to mathematically model customers who respond to their promotional campaigns versus those who do not. The effects of direct mailing efforts, e.g., are easily measured and compared as a function of customer information (demographics such as age, household size, income) and purchase behaviour (past buying history, cross-sales). Data mining can also be used to measure incremental business (additional traffic, sales, profits) that may be directly attributed to a recent promotion by deliberately withholding the promotional mailing from a 'control' group (an 'experimental' technique).

In addition to standard techniques being applied to these huge data sets, marketing research methodologists are creating techniques and software, especially for data mining analyses on large data sets. Sales of such customer management software are currently growing at five times the rate of the overall software market, as managers struggle to track every encounter with each customer, to facilitate call-centre interactions between customers and customer service representatives, and to manage internal customers, such as one's sales force. Some of these relational database systems include NCR's Teradata system, Unix or Windows NT machines, IBM's Intelligent Miner, and SAS's Enterprise Miner. Other software companies offer 'content aggregator' services that synthesize multiple databases – company financial information, histories, executive profiles and the like.

Conjoint analysis

This technique is concerned with the joint effects of two or more independent variables on the ordering of a dependent variable. Conjoint analysis, like multidimensional scaling, is concerned with the measurement of psychological judgements, such as consumer preferences. Products are essentially bundles of attributes, such as price and colour. For example, conjoint analysis software generates a deck of cards, each of which combines levels of these product attributes. Respondents are asked to sort the cards generated into an order of preference. Conjoint analysis then assigns a value to each level and produces a 'ready-reckoner' to calculate the preference for each chosen combination. The preference logic of conjoint analysis is as follows. The respondent had to base their overall ranking of the versions on an evaluation of the attributes presented. The values that the individual implicitly assigns each attribute associated with the most-preferred brand must, in total, sum to a greater value than those associated with the second most-preferred brand. The same relationship must hold for the second and third most-preferred brands, the third and fourth most-preferred brands and so forth. The computation task then is to find a set of values that will meet these requirements.

Potential areas of application for conjoint analysis include product design, new product concept descriptions and testing, price/value relationships, attitude measurement, promotional congruence testing, the study of functional versus symbolic product characteristics, ranking a hypothetical product against existing competitors already in the market and suggesting modifications to existing products which would help to strengthen a product's performance.

The limitations of conjoint analysis are quite clear when, e.g., we are using this technique to predict trial rate. These include:

- Utility measurement rather than actual purchase behaviour is used as the predictor. The configuration of elements used in the concepts may not be complete.

- In the case of a new product that differs substantially from its principal competitors, the same elements cannot be used for aggregating utilities.

- The effects of promotion and distribution effort on competitive reaction are not considered.

- Perceptions from a concept statement and those from the actual product may differ.

- New products may take several years to reach the market, during which time customer preferences and competitive products may have undergone substantial changes. Conjoint analysis has been applied widely on consumer research (Vriens, 1994), in advertising evaluation (Stanton and Reese, 1983) and other commercial uses (Cattin and Wittink, 1982).

Rule-based forecasting

Going further than expert systems, rule-based forecasting (RBF) draws upon features of both expert systems and statistical extrapolation by using rules to combine forecasts from simple extrapolation outcomes. Weights for combining the rules use statistical and domain-based features of time series. RBF was originally developed, tested and validated only on annual data. One of RBF's primary advantages is the existence of domain knowledge. Automatic identification provided for time-series features that had previously been identified using judgement, therefore improving reliability. RBF can still benefit from the use of prior findings on extrapolation, so one would expect that it would be substantially more accurate than random walk (a mathematical formalization of a trajectory that consists of taking successive random steps) and more accurate than combining equal weights.

Judgemental bootstrapping

Judgemental bootstrapping is an extension of expert system methodology that creates structured procedures from the subjective judgements of experts. It is most useful for repetitive and complex forecasting problems where regression can play a part. In the technique, methodology and information that experts use are studied by asking them to make predictions and decisions in a number of diverse real or hypothetical situations, in effect in simulations. The outcomes of this study are then converted into a regression-based system relating the expert subjective judgements to the information used.

The underlying argument for using this process is one of consistency and cost. Once a 'bootstrapping' system has been devised, it can be applied more consistently and more cheaply than using the experts again.

Based on a review of 11 situations, Armstrong (2001) asserted that 'bootstrapping was more accurate than unaided judgement (the normal method for these situations) in eight of the 11 comparisons, with two tests showing no difference, and one showing a small loss. The typical error was about 6 per cent. The failure occurred when experts used incorrect rules'.

Judgemental bootstrapping has the additional advantage of creating transparency. For instance, it makes the weighting systems used by experts in their judgements more transparent and open to scrutiny and hence an improvement. It can reveal factors within the prediction decision process that were not obvious, such as the physical appearance of people in creating demand in certain situations. While not as complex as full expert systems, the judgemental bootstrapping process can offer many of the advantages with less of the complexity or cost.

Choosing the forecasting system

When selecting a forecasting technique, usually for new products, there are three principles to consider.

- The first principle is to match the methodology with the situation. The degree of newness of the product, e.g., is crucial, as are product and market characteristics, the forecaster's ability, the cost, the urgency and the purpose for which the forecast is needed.

Process in action Airbus and Boeing – who is right?

The two major western aircraft manufacturers, Airbus and Boeing, have adopted entirely different strategies in developing new products. Airbus was nearing completion (in 2006) of the design of the 380, a 555-seat double-deck, wide-body aircraft which is ideal for carrying many people over long distances. The 380 entered production in August 2006 and Airbus is hoping that it will be preferred to the Boeing 747, the ubiquitous 'Jumbo Jet'. Boeing, perhaps spurred on by the fact that in 2003 Airbus secured more orders than them, have decided to develop the 7E7 Dreamliner, a much smaller aircraft with 200 to 250 seats, to replace their ageing 757 and 767 ranges. Both companies argue that they are developing and incorporating new technology into their new products to make them more ecologically friendly, i.e., cleaner and more fuel-efficient.

Airbus has a long tradition of international collaboration stemming from their beginnings as a consortium of British, French, German and Italian companies producing different sections of the airframe. They plan to exploit their managerial competence in this area to outsource aircraft parts from other countries, e.g., China, perhaps in the hope that this will gain orders from national flag-carrying airlines, although the World Trade Agreement may prevent countries subsidizing airlines in the future. Boeing is a little more introspective, manufacturing the airframe in the USA and only outsourcing some engines from outside.

Airbus estimate the demand for the 380 product type at 1100 over its lifetime. Boeing estimate the demand at 320. Who will be right?

Questions

1. Which generic forecasting techniques will Airbus and Boeing have used to make their decisions?

2. How will the development lead-time for new-concept aircraft have influenced their decision?

3. What aircraft service factors will the companies need to take into consideration, and how will this affect their decision? How can the actions of each company in this area affect sales?

4. Which company has made the best decision?

- The second principle is 'don't rely on the business environment not to change'. At least two forecasting methods should be used, usually one assuming that the environment will not change (regression or time series) and the other assuming that it will. One technique will check on the other.

- The forecaster must be able to override a decision stemming from the application of a formal technique when information coming from outside the model clearly shows that the technique's forecast may be at fault.

There are powerful arguments for combining forecasts by different techniques. Methods are selective in the information they use, so that a combination of methods would incorporate more information and improve accuracy. Doyle and Fenwick (1976) advocate this and produce evidence of improved accuracy.

Summary

- Forecasting is essential to any planning process. Market forecasts are used for resource requirement planning and acquisition for all company activities.

- Forecasts can be based on statistical data or on judgement.

- Statistical forecasting involves extrapolation of the time-based behaviour of a factor under consideration, or consideration of the relationship with a causal factor, to predict future demand.

- Judgemental forecasting calls upon the domain knowledge of managers or specialized technical and market experts to predict future events or trends.

- Statistical forecasting is of most value to an organization when the operating environment remains stable. Judgemental forecasting is of most value in predicting changes in the environment which will change existing demand trends.

- Forecasters should use both approaches together.

- Consideration should be given to the trade-off between complexity and user understanding and ease of application. Added complexity can cause users to overlook errors and to apply the methods improperly.

Chapter questions

1. Summarize the findings of these researchers for the chief executive officer of an aircraft manufacturer, indicating the value of both statistical and judgemental approaches to forecasting.

2. Comment on the forecasting method called 'judgemental bootstrapping'.

3. Explain the reasoning behind RBF.

4. Critically comment on the following statement: 'Organizations should integrate judgemental and statistical forecasting methods.'

References

Armstrong, J. S. (2001) 'Judgmental bootstrapping: Inferring experts' rules for forecasting', in Armstrong, J. S. (Ed.), *Principles of Forecasting*, Norwell, MA: Kluwer Academic Publishers. pp. 171–192.

Cattin, P., and Wittink, D. R. (1982) 'Decision making with imprecise probabilities: Dempster–Shafer theory and applications', *Water Resources Research*, 28(12):3071–3083.

Chambers, J. D., Mullick, S. K., and Smith, D. D. (1979, Summer) 'Commercial use of conjoint analysis: A survey', *Journal of Marketing*, pp. 44–53.

Curry, B., and Moutinho, L. (1991) 'Forecasting of curves using a Kohonen classification', *Journal of Forecasting*, 17:429–439.

Curry, B., and Moutinho, L. (1993) 'Expert systems and marketing strategy: An application to site location decisions', *Journal of Marketing Channels*, 1(1):23–27.

Doyle, P., and Fenwick, I. (1976, April) 'Business failure prediction using rough sets', *European Journal of Operational Research*, 11(4):263–280.

Ellis, R., LeMay, S., and Arnold, D. (1991, June) 'Sales forecasting using a combination of approaches', *Long Range Planning*, pp. 61–64.

Kennedy, M. S. (1991) *In the Wake of Chaos: Unpredictable Order in Dynamical Systems*, Chicago: University of Chicago Press.

Rangaswamy, A., Eliahberg, J. B., Raymond, R., and Wind, J. (1989, November) 'Rough sets', *Communications of the ACM*, 38(11):88–95.

Stanton, W. W., and Reese, R. M. (1983) *Strategic Management and Organisational Dynamics*, London: Pitman.

Vriens, M. (1994) 'Some developments in the theory and applications of media scheduling method', *Operational Research Quarterly*, pp. 291–305.

Part three

Data management processes

5 **Corporate structure, network and knowledge management**

6 **Strategic information systems**

7 **Marketing measurements and analysis**

Data management is a major process in the planning and control of organizational activities. It fuels predictions, enables plans to be formulated and monitors and controls activities to those plans.

Chapter 5 tackles the topic of strategic corporate knowledge by examining organizational learning, knowledge management and sharing networks. This trilogy is associated with visionary management strategies where the creation of interdisciplinary knowledge is crucial. Topics covered include the value chain, environmental volatility, isolation and interorganizational relationships. Short 'process in action' notes on many companies are used to demonstrate these linkages and how organizations have attempted to exploit them. A longer note describes how the new chief executive officer (CEO) of Oticon, a Danish manufacturer of hearing aids, totally restructured the company to create what he termed the 'spaghetti organization' to enhance corporate knowledge.

Strategic information systems (SIS) are covered in Chapter 6. SIS are a major resource within organizations, affecting the effectiveness of decision-making. The discussion covers issues such as intelligent data and competitive advantage. In the 'process in action' note, key business advantages derived from SIS are illustrated in a simple example: the authoring and selling of children's fiction. The example uses a fictitious author to illustrate how a business idea enabled him to get closer to his customers and add value to the business process of selling books.

Finally, Chapter 7 discusses marketing measurement and analysis. It focuses on the use of generalized linear models (GLMs), measurement scaling and model-fit statistics. The 'process in action' note on forecasting ice cream consumption demonstrates the application of GLM theory by modelling continuous data on ice cream consumption (in pints per capita), the price of ice cream (in dollars per pint), the weekly family income (in dollars) and the mean outdoor temperature (in degrees Fahrenheit).

5

Corporate structure, network and knowledge management

Luiz Moutinho, Andrzej Huczynski and Geoff Southern

Introduction

The overall purpose of this chapter is to examine the areas of organizational learning, knowledge management (KM) and organizational knowledge sharing networks as a critical strategic 'tripod'. The tripod is designed to provide sustainable antecedent stages to the formulation of visionary management strategies, therefore triggering high levels of organizational performance. The chapter is consequently divided into three major building blocks – organizational learning, KM and organizational knowledge sharing – which reflect the way we perceive linkages between them in terms of conceptual developments encapsulated by the synergetic combination of three perspectives.

Learning objectives

To provide the students with:

- An understanding of the concepts of organizational learning.

- An ability to reflect upon different facets of knowledge management.

- Understanding of, and an ability to analyze, strategic aspects of inter-firm collaboration.

Organizational learning

Learning is a continuous personal transformation. It is a cyclic and cumulative process of the continuous actualization of your knowledge (adding new things to your knowledge repertoire), in order to change your behaviour so you can function and act better. An organization that does not learn continuously and is not able to continuously list, develop, share, mobilize, cultivate, put into practice, review and spread knowledge will not be able to compete effectively.

Learning organizations have the ability to learn and facilitate all facets of the learning process and thus continuously transform themselves.

Knowledge management

A firm's long-term success and survival increasingly depends less on particular products and more on an organization's distinctive capabilities to develop, share and utilize scientific and technological knowledge. KM strategies should, therefore, be focused on strengthening interorganizational processes and building core organizational capabilities so that knowledge is consistently and strategically developed.

KM – through learning organizations – can represent a golden opportunity for the creation of interdisciplinary knowledge.

- The creation of an organization in which KM activities, such as knowledge creation, transfer and use, are of high priority seems to be the golden solution.

- Knowledge is a sustainable source of economic growth, as it does not deplete over time like the other factors of production. Knowledge generates more knowledge because ideas spark new threads of possibilities to explore.

- Knowledge influences a firm's decision with regard to strategy, competitors, customers, distribution channels and product/service life cycles.

- Knowledge sharing is common among firms that are part of a value chain. Firms that are working closely with their suppliers can gain knowledge in production processes and procedures that will help to improve efficiencies.

- The overall purpose of KM is to maximize the enterprise's knowledge-related effectiveness and returns from its knowledge assets to renew them continuously.

Organizational knowledge sharing

The environmental volatility experienced by many organizations in the early years of the 21st century has encouraged many of them to abandon isolationism and a focus on looking inside at themselves in favour of collaboration, looking outside and establishing interorganizational relationships.

The advantage possessed by a hierarchical firm over a marketplace full of independent contractors has been eroded. Many companies have removed some of their activities to pursue a common strategy. These non-market, non-bureaucratic organizational relationships are becoming highly significant features.

Organization culture, change and the learning organization

Culture and change

Consideration of organization culture came to prominence in the early 1980s. Earlier work summarized by Handy in his bestseller *Understanding Organizations* (1976) classified organizations in terms of power, role, task and person. These concepts are still described in some detail in current standard texts (e.g., Mullins, 2007). Handy hypothesized that organizations naturally develop from a power-based culture in entrepreneurial (start-up) firms, driven by growth to define standard procedures and job descriptions which are indicative of a role-based culture, then concentrate on jobs and projects in a task-based culture and finally move towards a person-based culture where the organization exists to serve and support the individuals within it. Of course, organizations do not jettison existing culture on moving to the next stage, but rather accumulate a hybrid of all four categories.

Research in the 1980s suggested that a strong organizational culture is a powerful lever for guiding workforce behaviour and is indicated by the values, myths, heroes and symbols of an organization. Peters and Waterman, in their seminal work *In Search of Excellence* (1982), attributed organizational success at least partly to applying the McKinsey '7-S' framework, where shared values, the first S, are central and hold together the other elements of success: strategy, structure, systems, style, staff and skills. Schein (2004) observed that there are three levels of organizational culture: surface manifestation, organization values and basic (individual) assumptions. Surface manifestations are indicative of underlying organizational values, which can differentiate one organization from another and which are themselves comprised basic assumptions of individuals. Subsequent consideration of surface manifestations of culture has resulted in extensive lists of cultural elements (e.g., see Buchanan and Huczynski, 2004, Chapter 19), but the basic assumptions of individuals are invisible, taken for granted and difficult to appraise. In practice, an individual undergoes the process of socialization on joining an organization, 'the process whereby an organization seeks to influence the individual to adopt its values and outcomes' (Handy, 1976, p. 142). The effect of organizational culture and values is evident in the mission statements and web pages of many companies, e.g., Scottish Power (http://www.scottishpower.plc.uk/pages/aboutus_ourvalues.htm).

In the late 1980s and 1990s, attention moved to consideration of how to manage change in organizations. There are two schools of managing change: the systems intervention (SI) school, which tends to consider organizations as hard bureaucratic or technical systems, and the organizational development (OD) school, which thinks of them as softer socio-political and economic systems (Paton and McCalman, 2008). Change in the SI school is analyzed and planned at higher management levels, and implementation is supported by communication and persuasion. Change in the OD school is driven from the bottom and requires a culture that looks for improvement and individuals who are empowered to seek it. Referring to previous comments on classification of organizations in terms of power, role, task and person, one can relate the SI approach to power and role and the OD approach to task and person. The OD school, therefore, encourages the study of the culture of an organization as part of the change process, attempting to identify where an organization wants to be in terms of culture, where it is now and how to manage the transition. This process is embodied in a classic framework for analysis, Pugh's (1983) OD matrix, which considers current states of behaviour, structure and context at the individual level, group level, intergroup level and organizational level, looking for improvements and suggesting mechanisms to effect them.

Out of the OD approach to managing change has evolved the concept of the 'learning organization'. Senge has defined the learning organization as a place 'where people continually expand their capacity to create the results they truly deserve, where new and expansive patterns of thinking are nurtured, where collective aspiration is set free, and where people are continually learning how to learn together' (1990, p. 1). The value of this approach to internal OD in organizations where learning itself is the key product delivered to customers is obvious but can be overlooked.

It is now recognized that learning and growth are central to the improvement and continuing success of all organizations, and they act as a foundation stone for performance management systems such as the balanced scorecard (Kaplan and Norton 1996) and its derivatives, employed in both business and customer service, which in turn will lead to better financial results.

An organization is more successful if its employees learn more quickly and implement and commercialize knowledge more rapidly than the workers of the competitive organization. An organization that does not learn continuously and is not able to continuously list, develop, share, mobilize, cultivate, put into practice, review and spread knowledge will not be able to compete effectively. That is why the ability of an organization to improve existing skills and acquire new ones forms its most tenable ability.

Knowledge and learning

Knowledge is a function of information, culture and skills (Rampersad, 2001):

$$<\text{Knowledge}> = f (< \text{Information} >, < \text{Culture} >, < \text{Skills} >)$$

The function f specifies the relationship between knowledge on the one side and information, culture and skills on the other. In this context, *information* comprises the meaning given to data or information obtained according to certain conventions; this is also known as *explicit knowledge* (Nonaka and Takeuchi, 1995). On the one hand, *culture* is the total amount of standards, values, views, principles and attitudes of people that underscore their behaviour and functioning. On the other hand, *skills* are related to the capability, ability and personal experience of people; it relates to what people can do, know and understand. The knowledge components of culture and skills represent *implicit knowledge*, which depends on the individual and is stored in the minds of people. This concept is difficult to describe, is based on experience and is practical in nature. It finds its source, among other things, in associations, intuitions and fantasies. Explicit knowledge, on the contrary, is not dependent upon the individual, is theoretical in nature and is specified as procedures, theories, equations, manuals, drawings, etc. This knowledge is mainly stored in management information and technical systems, and organizational systems. The central question here is: How can knowledge be transformed into new behaviour? Thus, how can people learn effectively so that they can function better? If knowledge is to lead to competent action, then learning should receive special attention, and the organizational culture and structure should stimulate and support this.

Knowledge ages rapidly and is liable to wear. That is why one should consistently learn. *Learning is a continuous personal transformation.* It is a cyclic and cumulative process of the continuous actualization of your knowledge (adding new things to your knowledge repertoire) in order to change your behaviour so you can function and act better. It is a permanent change in your knowledge and behaviour partly due to repeated experiences. Here the intention is improving the quality of your thinking and acting. In view of the increasing shift from *lifetime employment* to *lifetime employability*, people must make sure that their knowledge is up-to-date.

It is, therefore, imperative to constantly know which knowledge is essential, where it is available in the organization, which associate possesses this skill, how this knowledge can be adequately utilized, how it can be shared, how this provides added value and how it can be maintained. The knowledge infrastructure within the organization must be organized in such a way that effective teamwork, creativity, positive thinking, self-confidence and a good learning environment are stimulated by, e.g., the use of computers, Internet and intranet, design of a knowledge bank, presence of a library, continuous training, an auditorium, organization of brainstorm sessions and review meetings. With regard to this, it can also be mentioned that the ability of an organization to learn by experience depends upon the willingness of its employees to think about problems, the opportunities presented to associates to identify and solve common problems together, the willingness to intervene preventively and the existence of a working atmosphere where every employee feels responsible for the company's performance. In practice, organizations especially seem to learn if employees have a sense of direction through a collective ambition (mission and vision) and work with all their might to realize this ambition. Because of this, employees feel a strong common bond, which motivates them to learn together. With these aspirations, employees are also willing to share their knowledge with their colleagues and match their personal objectives with those of the organization. Through this, *learning organizations* emerge in which learning is collective and based on personal and collective ambition.

Learning organizations have the ability to learn and facilitate all facets of the learning process and thus continuously transform themselves. Such organizations consist of teams with balanced learning styles and people whose personal ambition corresponds to that of the organization. Because of this, employees have a positive attitude towards improving, changing and learning. Learning organizations also consist of people who constantly learn from their own mistakes, share knowledge and communicate openly with each other. These organizations have leaders who coach, help, inspire, motivate, stimulate and intuitively make decisions, and have processes that are constantly reviewed based on performance measures and feedback. The management of the knowledge stream within the organization is essential for this, as is changing the way we think and deal with each other. According to Peter Senge (1990), people must give up their traditional way of thinking, develop their own skills and be open to change, understand how the whole organization functions and formulate the shared vision of the organizations that are also based on people's experiences. In practice, it shows that the tempo with which the abilities of an organization increase are to a greater degree determined by the efficiency with which one learns from experiences. In order to obtain an optimum learning effect, people should have a certain educational level and specifically get the chance to acquire experience; this is because people with experience learn more rapidly. Therefore, it is important to accept that every employee is able to learn and is motivated to do so, that learning is not a passive but an active and continuous process and that associates need guidance in this process.

Knowledge management

A firm's long-term success and survival increasingly depends less on particular products and more on an organization's distinctive capabilities to develop, share and utilize scientific and technological knowledge (Coombs, 1996). Given the intangible nature of knowledge in organizations, knowledge development will tend to occur at random and be unsystematic.

KM strategies should, therefore, be focused on strengthening interorganizational processes and building core organizational capabilities so that knowledge is consistently and strategically developed.

A very comprehensive definition of knowledge was given by Davenport and Prusak (1998, p. 5):

> Knowledge is a fluid mix of framed experience, values, contextual information and expert insight that provides a framework for evaluating and incorporating new experiences and information. It originates and is applied in the minds of knowers.

What is knowledge?

Knowledge belongs to the family of steadily increasing invisible corporate assets that include management systems, patents, brand identity and corporate reputation. In the era of knowledge-based economies, it remains easier to understand knowledge in terms of what it is not by distinguishing data, information and knowledge. In general, data are raw facts, while information is an organized set of data. Knowledge is meaningful information or the understanding, awareness and familiarity acquired through study, investigation, observation or experience over the course of time (Zeleny, 2000).

There are two main types of knowledge – explicit and tacit. Everyone has explicit and tacit knowledge. Explicit knowledge is described in formal language, like mathematical expressions and statements in textbooks. It consists of technical knowledge or 'know-how'. Tacit knowledge is automatic, resembles intuition and is oral. It is often taken for granted and may be considered less valuable than explicit knowledge. The effective utilization of tacit knowledge is essential for competitiveness, but the problem is that tacit knowledge is difficult to capture. It is highly personalized, context-sensitive and very hard to measure and manage.

Basically, a company has to manage the change and allow the culture to move towards a structure that enables the organization to transform tacit knowledge into explicit knowledge in order to develop the knowledge cycle and make knowledge available and accessible company-wide (Burk, 1999).

Other authors have sought to take a process-based rather than a project-based perspective to the definition of KM. Liebowitz (2000) presented a nine-step approach to KM:

- Transform information into knowledge
- Identify and verify knowledge
- Capture and secure knowledge
- Organize knowledge
- Retrieve and apply knowledge
- Combine knowledge
- Create knowledge

- Learn knowledge
- Distribute/sell knowledge.

KM is driven by the need to enhance:

- Intellectual asset management
- Operational efficiency
- Customer and competitor intelligence
- Continuous improvement
- Organizational learning
- Innovation in products and services
- Time to market.

In general, one of the most important issues in KM is the organization, distribution and refinement of knowledge. Knowledge can be generated by data mining tools, be acquired from third parties and be refined and refreshed. The collected knowledge can then be organized by indexing the knowledge elements. This knowledge is then integrated into a knowledge base and distributed to the decision support applications. The insights resulting from the decision support applications are used to refine the existing knowledge and feedback into the knowledge organization.

Another important issue is knowledge presentation. This refers to the ways in which knowledge is displayed to the organization's members. In general, an organization may devise different procedures to format its knowledge base. Because of the different presentation styles, organization members often find it difficult to reconfigure, recombine and integrate knowledge from distinct and disparate sources. Information technology (IT) and the Internet have enabled and increased this sharing of knowledge, and new emerging technologies can further advance it.

The need for organizations to survive in a changing environment has led to the development of the concept of the 'learning organization'. Pedler *et al.* (1998) proposed the following definition of a learning organization:

> An organization which facilitates the learning of all its members and continuously transforms itself.

A learning organization is one which:

- Has a climate in which individual members are encouraged to learn and to develop their full potential.
- Extends this learning culture to include customers, suppliers and other significant stakeholders.
- Makes human resource (HR) development strategy central to business policy.
- Is in a continuous process of organizational transformation.

In summary, a learning organization is one in which the learning strategy is more than a HR or staff development strategy; it is a core component of all operations.

KM – through learning organizations – can represent a golden opportunity for the creation of interdisciplinary knowledge. A learning organization works to create values, practices and procedures in which learning and working are synonymous throughout the organization.

> The creation of an organization in which knowledge management activities, such as knowledge creation, transfer and use, are of high priority seems to be the golden solution.

Although knowledge cannot be totally extracted from the minds of individuals, Davenport and Prusak (1998), as well as Kluge *et al.* (2001), argue that organizations can collect some embedded knowledge through documents, reports, repositories, routines, processes, procedures, practices, norms, apprenticeships, job rotation and mentoring.

There are several reasons why knowledge plays an important part. First, knowledge is considered to be one of the drivers for innovation (Davenport and Prusak, 1998; Information technology Advisory Group, 1999; Kluge *et al.*, 2001). Through technical know-how and know-who, product design, marketing presentation, understanding the customer and creativity, firms are able to introduce to the market innovative services and products ahead of their competitors.

Second, knowledge is a sustainable source of economic growth, as it does not deplete over time like the other factors of production (Davenport and Prusak, 1998). Knowledge generates more knowledge because ideas spark new threads of possibilities to explore. Firms that are knowledge-rich, knowledge-oriented and avid learners will have moved on by the time competitors have managed to emulate their initial level of quality, creativity or efficiency.

Third, as Davenport and Prusak (1998) pointed out, knowledge is close to the action. In other words, knowledge influences a firm's decision with regard to strategy, competitors, customers, distribution channels and product/service life cycles.

Lee and Al-Hawamdeh (2002) described the results of a survey undertaken by Ernst and Young (see Kirby and Harvey, 1997), which identified six types of knowledge relevant for any company: (1) knowledge about customers, (2) knowledge about best practices and effective processes, (3) knowledge about the company's own competencies and capabilities, (4) knowledge about the company's own products and services, (5) knowledge about the market trends and (6) knowledge about competitors. Firms that have come up with some innovative solution to tackle one or more of these six areas – while the rest of the industry have not – are able to charge premium prices for their products and services or enjoy lower costs. This is why firms are very protective of their knowledge and reluctant to share it.

Knowledge sharing is common among firms that are part of a value chain. Firms that are working closely with their suppliers can gain knowledge in production processes and procedures that will help to improve efficiencies. By exchanging ideas with distributors, retailers and end-users, a firm can learn about marketing, product development and design.

Some organizations have opted to collaborate with competing firms to tackle new business opportunities. The literature has termed this phenomenon 'co-operation' (Nalebuff and Brandenburger, 1996). In one research study, Loebecke *et al.* (1999) focused on the value of interfirm knowledge transfer. For them the ability of the firm to manage the process of knowledge sharing, consisting of synergy and leveragability, is crucial to the firm's decision as to whether to share knowledge or not.

Synergy is defined by the authors as the 'extent to which co-operation yields an additional value from interdependent knowledge sharing beyond the sum of the parties' individual knowledge' (Loebecke *et al.*, 1999, p. 18). *Leveragability* is the increase of knowledge value by one of the parties after exploiting the shared knowledge 'on its own' beyond the co-operation agreement. *Negative reverse-impact* is defined as the value of the company's individual knowledge lost after sharing it with the other party.

The literature on organizational learning and KM over the last decade has been extensive and far-reaching. The overall purpose of KM is to 'maximize the enterprise's knowledge-related effectiveness and returns from its knowledge assets to renew them continuously' (Wiig, 1997). How this purpose may be accomplished in different enterprises will depend on their culture, priorities and capabilities (Teece, 2000). It follows, therefore, that KM may be carried out differently depending on differing needs and requirements in different environmental situations.

If it is done primarily by focusing on intellectual assets available and through the creation and maintenance of 'knowledge repositories', the model of KM adopted is the *intellectual capital* mode. If, however, it is done through the development of new knowledge and the delivery of improved knowledge access that is shared through user-friendly tools, then the *knowledge category* model is adopted. If it is carried out primarily through enhancement of the organizational knowledge environment in which social learning and development is conducted continuously, then the *socially constructed* model applies.

Therefore, depending on the purpose for which it is intended, it is possible to categorize KM models as the knowledge category models (Nonaka and Takeuchi, 1995), intellectual capacity models (Baker, 2000) and socially constructed models (Demarest, 1997).

The socially constructed model of knowledge management

The socially constructed model emphasizes four key dimensions of KM. They include the construction of knowledge within the organization and the embodiments of knowledge through a process of social interchange. These are followed by a process of dissemination of the espoused knowledge throughout the organization and, finally, the economic use of the knowledge with regard to organizational outputs (Demarest, 1997).

It attempts to enhance the knowledge environment and encourage the development of a knowledge-driven organization that actively promotes learning in a social context.

Within the context of a socially constructed model, knowledge is considered a 'process of knowing' (Allee, 1997) or an activity that plays the role of the product or of fodder for sense-making (Dervin, 1998). This is because of the emphasis laid on the aspect of learning as an ongoing activity in this model.

In this social perspective, organizational learning is based on a cultural as opposed to a cognitive approach. This is because organizations learn not as an individual or individuals but as a collective. In addition, the location of knowledge in this social perspective is in the knowing and not inside or outside the minds of individuals (Ortenblad, 2001).

A learning organization shall be defined as:

> An organization that creates, acquires and communicates information and knowledge, behaves differently as a consequence and produces organizational results from doing so.
> (*Huber, 1991 and King, 1999,* as cited in King, 2001)

The knowledge category model of knowledge management

In this model, knowledge is categorized into discrete elements capable of being converted from one form to another and in the process of facilitating the change process required in an organization. The model of KM that is applicable in this context is the knowledge category model, which categorizes knowledge as either tacit or explicit (Nonaka and Takeuchi, 1995), codified or uncodified (Boissot *et al.*, 2007) and programmed or questioned (McLaughlin and Harris, 1993).

This model essentially involves the identification of and continuous conversion between various categories of knowledge along increasing ontological levels in order for knowledge creation to occur in organizations.

Within this model, knowledge appears to take on the properties of a fluid, capable of changing readily from one form to another and vice versa.

This model of KM addresses a higher level of learning mode, which may be referred to as the managing mode that makes it possible to understand the context, relationships and trends between the members of an enterprise. In this mode of learning, there exists a 'communal form or learning dynamic' (Allee, 1997).

The knowledge category model addresses learning as a functional activity, because in this model, learning is carried out for the purpose of creating new knowledge.

A prime consideration of the knowledge category model relates to the process of knowledge creation. Based on the theory developed, knowledge is created through the interaction between tacit and explicit knowledge (Nonaka and Takeuchi, 1995). *Tacit knowledge* is defined as personal, context specific and hard to materialize and communicate, whereas *explicit knowledge* is transmittable in formal systematic language (Polanyi, 1997).

Within this context, four models of knowledge conversion occur. The first is the conversion from tacit knowledge to tacit knowledge, or *socialization*. The second is the conversion from tacit knowledge to explicit knowledge, or *externalization*. The third is the conversion from explicit knowledge to explicit knowledge, or *combination*. The fourth is the conversion from explicit knowledge to tacit knowledge, or through *internalization* (Nonaka and Takeuchi, 1995).

Each of these modes of knowledge creation – socialization, externalization, combination and internalization – play equally significant roles in learning.

The intellectual capital model of knowledge management

Intellectual capital theory represents the fusion between two streams of thought: the management of knowledge and information and the measurement of the total value of an organization in terms of financial capital and intellectual capital (Roos *et al.*, 1997). The financial capital that is measurable and captured in the balance sheets is essentially physical and monetary capital. The intellectual capital, which is 'hidden', may be categorized as either *human capital* – competence, attitude and intellectual agility – or *structured capital* – relationships, organization, renewal and development (Roos *et al.*, 1997).

The intellectual capital model primarily involves what Allee (1997) describes as the data and procedural model of learning because it is geared towards identifying what knowledge resides in an organization. Thus, the measurement of intellectual capital that is indicative of the amount of collective learning in an organization is the main contribution of the intellectual capital model of KM to organizational learning.

The inherent limitation of the intellectual capital model is its tendency to downplay the importance of tacit knowledge and view both tacit and explicit knowledge as being equally important. This apparently is because if tacit knowledge is critical then intellectual capital is 'intangible and unexplainable' (Roos *et al.*, 1997).

A summarized version of these differences is listed in Table 5.1.

Integration of different models of knowledge management

The different models of KM differ considerably in their focus and on issues that relate to the conception of knowledge and the mode of learning incorporated. The socially constructed model involves a continuous process of learning in a learning-based environment. The knowledge category model, on the other hand, focuses on the transformation process of knowledge in a firm that has within it 'a system of knowledge'. It tends to focus more on issues that relate to creation of knowledge as opposed to enhancing social interaction involved in developing knowledge. The intellectual capital model focuses on identifying and exploiting knowledge-based assets.

The intellectual capital model assumes knowledge to be something tangible that can be readily stored, retrieved and measured. Within the context of the knowledge category model, knowledge can readily change from one form to another and therefore exhibits fluid-like properties. In the socially constructed model, knowledge may be conceptualized as the 'process of knowing'.

The mode of learning adopted in each of these models differs significantly. In the intellectual capital model, a data and procedural mode is used, whereas in the knowledge category model, both the functional and the managing mode apply. The socially constructed model, on the other hand, adopts a double-loop transformational learning mode.

The three models discussed are aimed at enhancing organizational capability and increasing competitive advantage. The knowledge category model provides an excellent technique to understand the learning processes involved in each of the modes of knowledge conversion. A clear understanding of this will enable managers to sustain growth and development in a dynamic environment. The intellectual capital model plays an important role in identifying the sources of knowledge competency through both human and structural capital considerations that make up the intellectual capital of an organization.

Society is entering into an era where the future will be determined by people's ability to wisely use knowledge, a precious global resource that is the embodiment of human intellectual capital and technology. The knowledge-based economy places great importance on the diffusion and use of information and knowledge, as well as

Table 5.1
Differences between different 'knowledge' models

	Intellectual capital model	Knowledge category model	Socially constructed model
Capital of knowledge	Tangible construct or object	Semi-permanent and capable of changing from one form to another	Process of knowing or activity
Mode of learning	Data and procedural	Managing and functional	Deutero or double loop
Main contribution to organizational learning	Provides a basis of *measurement* of organizational learning	Provides a basis of *managing* organizational learning	Provides a basis of understanding the *meaning* of organizational learning

its creation. In this new economy, individuals and companies are obliged to focus on maintaining and enhancing their knowledge capital in order to innovate, and their ability to learn, adopt and change becomes a core competency for survival.

KM is today the subject of much literature, discussion, planning and some action.

Knowledge management processes and tools

KM is perceived as part of corporate culture and a company-oriented method. Core identified KM processes included identification of relevant knowledge (e.g., via benchmarking, knowledge brokers), generation of new knowledge (e.g., project teams, external links), storage of knowledge (e.g., success stories, case studies, databases), distribution of knowledge (e.g., intranet, newsletters, mentoring) and application of knowledge (e.g., coaching, expert opinions).

The five key KM success factors, according to the survey, were corporate culture (openness, autonomy, learning behaviours), motivation (visualization of success, rewards), management support (coaching), structures/processes (roles) and IT (intelligent agents, intranet).

The HR department plays an important role in the sustainable development of employee research abilities, structured thinking, self-reflection, meta-cognition and knowledge communication. Employees should feel motivated, committed, personally involved and incentivized. Change management typically goes through cycles of 'unfreeze, move and refreeze' with successive waves of change propagation and stabilization.

The Fraunhofer Institute conducted a Delphi study (Scholl *et al.*, 2004) in 2001 on the future of KM, focusing on theoretical (e.g., multidisciplinary studies, social network analysis, organizational learning) and practical (e.g., knowledge roles, storytelling, IT systems) advances in KM.

Process in action knowledge management in various organizations

Volkswagen branded its KM programme as ww.deck and even produced a video recording of a song called 'King of Knowledge'.

Celemi's Roche Diagnostics actively cultivates knowledge 'promoters' and 'multipliers'. Many companies have academic partners in KM, such as the University of St. Gallen in Switzerland, which has a benchmarking centre.

Arthur D. Little has formal roles for knowledge stewards (content creation, team building, bio updates), knowledge advocates (representing a practice or group) and knowledge board (overall KM definition and co-ordination). Its intranet, ADL-Link, serves as a portal for accessing case abstracts.

HP Austria tackles a period of decreasing market share in the late 1990s with a change programme to create a 'culture of curiousness', a customer focus programme called 'Customer Voice', and internal knowledge assessments.

IBM Global Services structured its intellectual approach into three segments: environment (vision, strategy, values), management (processes, technology, organization) and incentives/measurements for intellectual capital. 'ShareNet' meetings helped gather 'best of breed' material and methodologies. 'Scouts for knowledge', 'ambassadors for intellectual capital management', reviewers and contributors jointly helped create a quarterly newsletter to sustain the KM message.

Questions

1. To what extent are these initiatives structured and systematic, or unstructured and evangelical?
2. What mix would you suggest to an organization?

'Organizational, technical and emotional barriers are ranked as the most challenging practical problem of KM', according to the researchers. Integration of KM into business processes, cultural change away from command and control, and a better match between IT systems and human factors were other recommendations of the survey.

Producing knowledge internally involves the identification, capture and exploitation of the information, mobilized for use in a particular setting or context. Mobilization is a managing function involving interpretation, dissemination and internalization. The types of knowledge generated and the way in which this is managed is the source for potential competitive advantage.

Generally and in the project context, internal KM provision has also been shown to be asymmetrical and resource intensive.

HR management (HRM) must align the organization's mission with KM objectives. It should create knowledge-sharing expectations, cultivate a culture of caring, promote productive cross-pollinating conversations, integrate knowledge behaviours into everyday life and overhaul appraisal and compensation practices.

This logic requires a combination of persuasive business arguments and effective inducements. At the same time, organizational capital must be protected through legal means such as non-disclosure agreements and access control mechanisms.

Steps must be taken to facilitate knowledge creation/acquisition, codification (e.g., videotapes/databases), distribution (e.g., groupware) and use (e.g., incentives, appetite). HRM must relax controls and allow (even encourage) behaviours that, in the clockwork world of industrial efficiency, never would have been tolerated.

Relationship builder

In addition to human capital, HRM should focus on social capital or the web of relationships. Collective KM requires a relationship orientation. This stretches across four dimensions: rapport (level of comfort, e.g., trust, empathy, respect), bonding (robustness of relationship, e.g., collaborators), breadth (scope of relationship, e.g., transactional) and affinity (level of interest and attraction). These dimensions apply to the entire matrix of relationships between individuals, groups and the parent organization and should be prioritized appropriately. Care should be taken to avoid in-breeding, stagnation and 'groupthink' in these community relationships.

HRM, therefore, needs to be adept at cross-functional team development, cellular structuring, organizational communication, inter-unit resource exchange and inter-firm learning. Relationships extend to not just current but future and past employees – as well as business partners and customers, who can be organized as 'quasi-workforce members'. HR professions should go beyond 'picnic organizers' to 'relationship brokers'.

HRM should cultivate strategies around manoeuvrability to reflect turbulent and unpredictable marketplaces. This requires dealing with fluid work assignments and widespread sharing of organizational information. HRM should be able to rapidly assemble and deploy scientific configurations of human capital – and then disassemble and redeploy them elsewhere. In such circumstances, it is not just the skills and knowledge but the employee attitude, team behaviours and values that matter. Such adoptive performance should encompass the ability to perform in situations of crisis, stress, unpredictability, cultural variance, creativity on demand and dynamic learning. Such assets may also need to be leveraged from external value chains of 'co-production', calling for external team building. Corporate leaders must rely on individuals within the firm to self-organize and design emergent strategies that move the firm forward without waiting for a long-term planning document to guide their decisions. It is argued that one of the most challenging roles for technology with respect to building effective organizational knowledge repositories is to make stored knowledge more visible and accessible.

Facilitating knowledge search and discovery

Many enterprise systems acquire large volumes of knowledge artefacts from multiple and often remote sources. The complexity of interrelated knowledge artefacts stored in these repositories make it often difficult for people to locate relevant artefacts or comprehend and interpret their meaning. Locating relevant knowledge in corporate memories is one of the important objectives of developing and deploying KM systems in organizations. Researchers in the areas of artificial intelligence and information retrieval have been particularly influential in directing the development and evolution of such systems. Search engines and intelligent agents are increasingly becoming evident in the market where they comprise a considerable proportion of the available commercial KM software.

Intelligent agents

Intelligent agents are software programs that act as personal or communication assistants to their users and carry out some sets of operations on their behalf with some degree of independence or autonomy. Intelligent agents that grew from expert systems and artificial intelligence research learn from data input during the course of their performance and modify their behaviour accordingly.

Although knowledge can be embedded in a computerized system using rules or heuristics, it is argued that many knowledge-based systems, expert systems, case-based reasoning systems and software agents may not qualify as KM systems. The position in this case is that KM systems should not be viewed as automating expert tasks, but rather informing about such tasks. As cognitive overload increasingly chokes the effective utilization of codified knowledge in organizations, scholars are pointing to some promising alternative knowledge technologies. Knowledge maps (k-maps) are seen as a particularly feasible method of co-ordinating, simplifying, highlighting and navigating through complex silos of knowledge artefacts. K-maps point to knowledge but they do not contain it. They are guides, not repositories. Typically, they point to people, documents and repositories. The main purpose of k-maps is to direct people where to go when they need certain expertise. In addition to the guiding function, k-maps may also identify strengths to exploit and knowledge to fill. Knowledge discovery involves uncovering previously unknown valid and useful patterns in data for description and prediction purposes. The uncovered patterns in the form of relationships, categories, clusters or trends are described and presented in a mode understandable by humans to help them better predict future behaviour of interest. Making organizational knowledge visible can support improvements and changes to the way knowledge is used, shared and transferred.

Promoting virtual socialization and collaboration

The spiral model of knowledge creation recognizes the crucial importance of socialization in developing and transferring tacit knowledge in an organization. The main aim of technology is enabling and facilitating interaction among people for the purpose of knowledge sharing and collective learning. Communication and collaboration technologies may be classified by the features offered to support group activities from facilitating communication, through to process and task structuring, to regulating interaction.

Stimulating creativity and complex problem-solving

There is a widespread recognition in the KM literature of the importance of creativity and innovation for organizational success in a changing environment.

An organization's adaptive response may be a choice between development and decay. It is argued that great innovations need creative thinking and ideas.

The literature mentions a variety of technologies that can be used to stimulate creativity, such as 'mind games'. This group of technologies is focused on fostering creativity and innovative problem-solving. Most systems are designed to stimulate creative thinking based on the principles of associations and memory retrieval and the use of analogy and metaphor. In multi-participant settings, it is also assumed that generation of creative ideas will be stimulated through participants' interaction, where one idea leads to another and the process tends to build upon itself.

Knowledge has been widely recognized as a critical organizational resource for success in the new economy. Many organizations are trying to capitalize on their organizational knowledge in order to maintain their competitive advantage. This requires mobilizing the collective assemblage of all intelligences that contribute towards building a shared vision, renewal process and direction for the organization.

One of the important objectives of KM is to capture, codify, organize and store relevant organizational knowledge. Capturing and storing knowledge into knowledge repositories is an important part of building organizational memory. The assumption is that tacit knowledge needs to be made explicit and formalized to be shared and used more easily by organizational members. By capturing experiences, case studies, lessons learnt, best practices, failures and successes, heuristics and valuable relationships, organizations also begin to evolve into true knowledge organizations.

Technology can be used as an enabler to support these KM efforts via building computer-based knowledge repositories. The availability of a KM system as a codified knowledge repository should lead to an increase in organizational knowledge and result in improved performance. One of the most challenging research questions with respect to building effective knowledge repositories for organizations is to find technologies (tools and methods) that make stored knowledge more effective.

The concept of knowledge repository

A knowledge repository can be viewed as a form of organizational memory, i.e., a set of stored artefacts that organizations acquire, retain and bring to bear on their present activities in order to avoid future mistakes. A knowledge repository can be studied from two perspectives. The 'content' perspective focuses on the knowledge that is captured and the context in which it is used. The 'repository' perspective focuses on how knowledge is stored and retrieved.

In general, repositories store two types of knowledge:

- Structured concrete information and knowledge in databases, documents and artefacts (e.g., standards, rules).
- The representation of unstructured abstract information and knowledge of human actors (e.g., conceptual lenses, frameworks).

They serve two basic functions: *representation*, presenting the knowledge for a given context, and *interpretation*, providing the frames of reference and guidelines for knowledge application. Computer-based repositories incorporate a variety of knowledge forms ranging from data and text-based documents and models to digital images, video and audio recordings. Applying corporate knowledge repositories will result in improved organizational effectiveness.

The capacity of digital storage in the last decade has increased worldwide at twice the rate predicted for the growth of computing power. Our ability to capture and store data has by far outpaced our ability to process and use it. As more artefacts are added to an organizational store, it becomes clear that there needs to be some sort of mechanism to help organize and search for useful knowledge from these stores. This poses a major challenge for KM, and knowledge mapping is often used to address this (see 'Intelligent agents', p. 87). One of the main purposes of k-maps is to locate important knowledge in an organization and show users where to find it. Effective k-maps should point not only to people but to documents and databases as well. K-maps should also locate actionable information, identify domain experts and facilitate organization-wide learning. They should also trace the acquisition and loss of knowledge, as well as map knowledge flows throughout the organization. Knowledge mapping can offer many benefits, including economic, cultural, structural and knowledge returns. Knowledge mapping can be used to facilitate the visibility of and access to organizational knowledge resources required by its employees.

Understanding knowledge maps

Most definitions of *k-maps* include the idea of tools or processes that help users navigate the silos of artefacts that reside in an organization, while determining meaningful relationships between knowledge domains.

A k-map is understood to be the visual display of knowledge and relationships using text, stories, graphics, models or numbers. K-map examples include knowledge application, knowledge structure, knowledge source, knowledge asset and knowledge development maps. Others identify concept, competency, strategy, causal and cognitive maps. K-maps can also be procedural, concept, competency and social network maps. The analysis of similarities and differences among various types of maps mentioned in the KM literature led us to the following three-class categorization: concept-, competency- and process-based k-maps.

Concept-based knowledge maps

The group of concept-based k-maps or taxonomies includes conceptual k-maps and knowledge structure maps. Both of these provide a framework for capturing and organizing domain knowledge of an organization around topic areas. They represent a method of structuring and classifying content in a hierarchical manner. Concept-based k-maps also allow for internal experts' knowledge to be made explicit in a visual, graphical representation that can be easily understood and shared. Mind maps, as special forms of concept or cognitive maps, provide further ability to express and organize a person's thoughts about a given topic.

Concept maps improve both the visibility and the usability of organizational knowledge. The visibility is typically enhanced by the structure of the concept maps and the use of visual symbols. The visual symbols can be quickly and easily recognized, while the minimal use of text makes it easy to scan for a particular word or phrase. In short, visual representation allows for development of a more holistic understanding of the domain that words alone cannot convey. Concept maps also improve the usability of knowledge as they organize knowledge artefacts around topics rather than functions. Thus, they provide an opportunity to bridge functional boundaries.

Competency-based knowledge maps

Competency-based k-maps cover a group of similar maps including competency k-maps, knowledge source and knowledge asset maps. These maps provide an overview of expertise that resides in the organization along with the identification of entries that possess such expertise. They act as 'yellow pages' or directories which enable people to find needed expertise; visually qualify the existing stock of knowledge of an individual, team or whole organization; and document skills, positions and career paths. Essentially, they are simple graphic balance sheets of a company's intellectual capital.

One of the major benefits of competency-based k-maps is that they make the human capital of the organization highly visible. They can be used to profile a company's workforce across a number of criteria such as domains of expertise, proximity, seniority or regional distribution. They can also be used to depict the stages of development of a certain competence. Competency-based k-maps can also greatly improve the usability of intellectual capital within the organization. When converted into 'yellow pages' and directories, these maps can enable employees to easily find needed expertise within an organization.

Process-based knowledge maps

Process-based k-maps are one of the most commonly used types of k-maps in organizations. They include procedural maps and knowledge application maps. They are similar in that they both focus on work/business processes. Essentially, process-based k-maps present business processes with related knowledge sources in auditing, consulting, research and product development. Any type of knowledge that drives these processes or results from execution of these processes can be mapped. Types of knowledge include tacit knowledge in people, explicit knowledge in databases and process knowledge in organizations.

Process-based k-maps have several benefits. They help to improve the visibility of knowledge in organizations by showing which type of knowledge has to be applied at a certain process stage or in a business situation. These maps also provide pointers to locate this specific knowledge. Process-based k-maps help to improve the usability of knowledge in organizations by forcing participants to identify key knowledge areas that are critical to their business. The analysis of the k-map generates ideas for sharing and leveraging knowledge most suited to the organization and the business context.

Corporate memory

Having spent the 1990s in the throes of reconstructing, re-engineering and downsizing, companies are worrying about corporate amnesia. There was a time when air travellers, in search of timely take-offs and sterling service, would fly with Delta Airways. Then Delta embarked on a cost-cutting and re-engineering programme, reduced its workforce by about a sixth, thus reducing perceptions of service quality. Somewhere along the way, Delta seemed to 'forget' that service was what gave it an edge and lost the loyalty of many customers. That firms should have 'memories' – and that these are strategically important – is not as whimsical as it sounds.

Shrinking companies are at risk of 'corporate Alzheimer's'. The success of a firm depends not only on its skill and knowledge but also on its collective business experiences, successes and failures, culture, vision and numerous other intangible qualities.

Not all the memory loss is a bad thing. One reason why IBM and General Motors were outwitted by younger firms is that they were unable to forget about making mainframe computers or gas-guzzling cars. For every management thinker beginning to worry about corporate amnesia, there are many more urging companies to dump their mental baggage so that they can compete in the 'nanosecond century'. The whole point of re-engineering is to rethink a company's existing processes and systems from the ground up.

All the same, a lot of companies seem to be ending up like Delta. Their processes are more perfect, their systems are sleeker and their workforces are leaner, but they are not noticeably more competitive. A recent survey by the American Management Association found that fewer than half of those companies that had downsized since 1990 went on to report higher operating profits in the years following the move; even fewer saw improved productivity. An unpublished research by Monitor, a consultancy based in Cambridge, Massachusetts, found that nine out of 10 firms that had outperformed their industries over a 10-year period had 'stable' structures, with no more than one reorganization and no change (or orderly change) in their chief executive.

Some experts believe that re-engineering totally disrupts all of a firm's informal networks – the contacts and relationships between employees and the unofficial routines and processes that make a company tick. This matters most in fuzzy, creative processes such as product development. IBM's personal computer (PC) unit has suffered because the company failed to retain staff who worked on previous generations of PCs. A similar loss of 'design memory' has also hampered Ford's Taurus. The original car was a hit because it met the needs of big-car buyers better than most rivals. But the latest Taurus, a product of a constantly re-engineered 'global' design effort, has failed to capture buyers' imaginations. In losing its design memory, it seems, Ford forgot what customers wanted.

Service companies are especially vulnerable to amnesia. Numerous downsized banks, insurers and retail chains have seen their customers' satisfaction plummet. Indeed, America now has a small but rapidly growing group of 'corporate-memory' consultancies, such as the Winthrop Group, also based in Cambridge. Margaret Graham, one of its partners, argues that companies need to grasp the entire history of a product or a project to determine the best strategy. Philip Morris's Kraft Food unit, for instance, based parts of one marketing campaign for its Cracker Barrel cheese on how the product was sold in the 1960s, when its sales were soaring. Coca-Cola, by contrast, forgot the importance of years of image building when it launched

'New Coke' in 1985. Such actions indicate that some firms display a willfulness not to remember. How, then, can firms achieve total recall? A lot of people seem to think the answer lies in technology.

Some of the knowledge and skills of managers can be transferred from individuals to computer networks and databases. This is, in effect, 'management automation'. Similarly, a new generation of 'product data management' software, which ties together the knowledge of product designers and manufacturing engineers, can proof product development against the ill-effects of change. Such tools are already being used by firms such as GM, General Electric and – as part of an effort to sort out its design woes – Ford. The snag is that at present, computers are good only at mimicking formal organizational processes, rather than the information social networks that tend to make up corporate memory.

Memories can be too vivid – and not only for elderly giants such as IBM and GM. One reason why Apple Computers got into such trouble was that it never stopped thinking about itself as a young, cult firm. The hard part is sorting the good memories from the bad.

Organizational knowledge sharing

The developing field

During the last quarter of the 20th century, a considerable amount of management, academic and consultancy time, and thought and effort, was put into altering some of the classical structures of many large organizations that had been in place since the end of 1945. The key features of these structures would have been familiar to Max Weber (1947) who had written about the benefits of bureaucratic organization at the start of that same century. Features of classical structures included head office determining strategy and its implementation; controlling several business units which operated in similar ways, but separately; everybody knowing their place on the organization chart; and a leadership philosophy which emphasized command-and-control. Those characteristics produced many benefits for the organizations concerned. Those with the greatest knowledge directed those with less; there was less dependence upon individuals who could leave at any time; discipline could be exercised down the chain of command; specification improved performance; there was clear responsibility for duties; stability and consistency of service was possible; past mistakes could be avoided in the future; the work was easily allocated; and managers exercised power. There are many positive aspects to bureaucracy, and that is why so many large organizations continue to be structured in this way today.

However, even from the earliest times, the negative aspects of bureaucracy were recognized. Jean Claude Marie Vincent de Gournay, who became France's administrator of commerce in 1751, complained about the excessive government regulations of the time, which he believed depressed business activity. He described the government as being run by insensitive creators and enforcers of rules, who neither knew nor cared about the effects of their actions on others. Gournay used the term *bureaucratie*, which means 'government by desks or offices' (Starbuck, 2005).

Starbuck notes the long-standing tension between innovation and bureaucracy. He says that when promising ideas fail to make it to market, or when nimble start-ups thwart a major competitor, it is excessive layers of management and slow-moving bureaucratic processes that are frequently identified as the culprits. With an increase in political, economic, social and technological volatility, many bureaucracies found that they were unable to respond swiftly enough. This threatened their profitability and even their continued existence. Increases in e-business, the requirement for perpetuation innovation and challenge of global competition, all posed new challenges. Within these organizations, there was also a stress on job satisfaction amongst employees. For these and some other reasons, there came the pressure to reform existing structures. In a situation where innovation is required, bureaucracies produce predictability. When companies need commitment to change from employees, bureaucracies provide only compliance. The problem is: How does one foster innovation, yet retain some sort of predictable operation? How does one bring different employees together, while allowing them to pursue their individual specialisms? How does one give employees freedom to share knowledge while simultaneously retaining management control? These were the questions to which organizations sought answers in the last quarter of the 20th century.

Internal experiments

In that period, the solutions to these problems of knowledge sharing were focused inside organizations. To ameliorate the worst dysfunctions of bureaucracy, many companies opted to introduce teamworking into their bureaucratic structures. Hayes (1997, p. 1) noted that 'To an ever-increasing extent, modern management has become focused on the idea of the team. Management consultants propose organizational restructuring to facilitate teamwork; directors make policy statements about the importance of the team to the organization; and senior managers exhort their junior staff to encourage teamworking in their departments.' Both tacit and explicit learning can be shared among team members. Proctor and Mueller (2000, p. 7) summarized statistics which reveal the remorseless organizational trend towards group and teamworking all around the world, and in virtually all industries. In the USA, 54 per cent of 600 leading enterprises used self-directed teams (Osterman, 1994). The EPOC survey of European workplaces showed that some sort of teamwork existed in 36 per cent of them (Benders and Van Hootegem, 1999; Benders et al., 2001). The British 1998 Workplace Employee Relations Survey found that 54 per cent of employees in the core workforce who manufactured a product or provided a service worked in some form of a team (Culley et al., 1998). In Australia, the percentage of employees working in formal teams rose from 8 to 47 per cent in the 1988–1991 period (Ozaki, 1996). By 1995, 47 per cent of manufacturing workplaces with over 100 employees reported that they had some form of semi-autonomous teamworking (Morehead et al., 1997). It has been reported that headhunters are increasingly being asked to assemble teams of top executives and that managers themselves are expected to be good at putting together teams (Nadler, 2006). It is argued that the modern organization is no longer a network of individuals, but rather a network of interconnected teams (Kazlowski and Bell, 2003). Interest in 'super teams' continues as companies attempt to exploit this work arrangement to its limit and manage the knowledge that is embedded within these teams (Evans and Wolf, 2005; Fischer and Boynton, 2005; Guimera et al., 2005). Instead of grafting teamworking onto existing bureaucratic structures, a very small number of companies have chosen to embark on radical, structural change.

A popular way of interconnecting individuals and sharing their functional knowledge and expertise, while retaining intact the bureaucratic structure of departmental silos or 'chimneys', has been the cross-functional team. Such teams can operate within a matrix structure, which is a type of organization design that combines two different, traditional types of structure, usually a functional structure and a project structure, which results in an employee being part of both a functional department and a project team and, in consequence, having two reporting relationships. In Europe after 1945, it was Philips, a Dutch electrical giant, which championed this organizational form, structuring itself on the basis of both product and country simultaneously. By 1991, the company was in deep financial trouble and reviewed its structural arrangements. It had experienced problems of accountability (was the country boss or product head responsible for the profit-and-loss account?) and struggles for power between country heads and business bosses (consumer electronics, medical products). Bartlett and Ghoshal (1990) concluded that matrix structures led to conflict and confusion, that the proliferation of channels created informational log jams, that multiple committees and reports bogged down the organization, and that overlapping responsibilities produced turf battles and a loss of accountability. Academic commentators have described the matrix structure as one of the least successful organizational forms.

Process in action Oticon – the strategy view

Around 1990, Oticon, a hearing aid manufacturer based in Copenhagen, was facing tough competition from larger companies who were capable of investing millions of US dollars in facilities. They had to find a new way to compete, and they decided to adopt a strategy of 'reworking' their entire organization. They decided to tackle the dangers of creeping bureaucracy by developing a paperless organization, revolutionary at the time. But perhaps underlying this initiative was a more fundamental change in strategy from subscribing to the prescriptive strategy school to subscribing to the descriptive one.

Oticon's objectives were to active improvements on three fronts: creativity, speed and productivity. They identified four organizational changes that were needed to achieve the improvements:

- In employee outlook, a 'mono-job' to a 'multi-job' mentality.

- Organizationally, from a hierarchical structure to what the CEO called a 'spaghetti' organization.

- Spatially, from a traditional individual-office layout to an open-plan office, including the introduction of mobile workplaces, again predicting the concept of flexible workspaces by 'hot-desking'.

- A change in communication methods, and mentality, from writing (e-mails and memos) to talking.

The primary change was, therefore, from a task-based organization to a project-oriented one. Each employee might be involved in several projects, not limited by departmental boundaries, and doing different things in each. (The only paper record of the project would be a one-page description.)

The organization changed from one driven by procedure to one driven by performance in completing the projects. The overall aim of the changes was to be 30 per cent more efficient in 3 years; hence it was called the '330 project'.

In summarizing the changes, Lars Kolind, CEO, said that the new organization was integrated, not structured, and that the open plan meant that there was no hiding place in bureaucracy for employees and that managers were on stage all the time. Some managers initially disliked this, but he preferred being able to go right to a problem and getting it solved. The greatest risk in any such project was not taking it all the way.

Questions

1. How do you think the changes in Oticon affect how people relate to each other?

2. How will the changes affect how employees consider the ownership of knowledge within the company?

Ruizendaal, head of corporate strategy at Philips, stated that creating a new organization structure simultaneously created new problems. Under its 'One Philips' slogan, the company encouraged its employees to work across different business units and rewarded business initiatives that created value for the company by staff collaborating with each other beyond their immediate units. Again, sharing knowledge across boundaries was the objective. Philips expected their staff to move between different geographical regions and product areas. Transferring people was a way of transferring knowledge. In 2005, Philips ran workshops for its top 1000 managers, who had been brought together to discuss issues that cut across organizational boundaries (*The Economist*, 2006b).

Interorganizational relationships

The environmental volatility experienced by many organizations in the early years of the 21st century has encouraged many of them to abandon isolationism in favour of collaboration, looking outside, to establish interorganizational relationships from which they can mutually learn and prosper. 'Partnering' in all its various forms has become the buzzword. Consideration of structural alternatives to bureaucracy has increasingly focused on co-operative relationships between organizations intended to develop new, joint strategies in which the participants can maximize the specialist knowledge that they possess.

In the past, it made economic sense to have all those involved in the manufacture of a product or the provision of a service together in a single, hierarchically ordered organization – the people in production, marketing, accounts, research and development (R&D), HR, sales, etc. Having them all together reduced the time for co-ordinating their activities. However, the gains from this arrangement have to be balanced against the costs of managers ignoring dispersed information and knowledge. A hierarchical company has to be able to do things more efficiently than buying these services individually on the open market. Technology, however, has shifted the balance of advantage away from company hierarchies and towards markets and individuals. Faster, cheaper telecommunications and the Internet have dramatically reduced the costs. The advantage possessed by a hierarchical firm over a marketplace full of independent, expert contractors has been eroded. Many companies have removed some of their operations from within their hierarchy and have subcontracted them into the marketplace to be performed in countries such as India and China. This has allowed them to focus on those functions in which they possess a competitive edge.

Interorganizational relationships involve two or more organizations sharing resources and activities to pursue a common strategy. Towards the end of the 20th century, considerable attention came to be focused on these relationships (Oliver and Ebers, 1998). Powell (1987, p. 67) observed that, 'By looking at the economic organization as a choice between markets and contractual relations on one side, and at conscious planning within a firm on the other, we fail to see the enormous variety that forms of co-operative arrangements can take.' His view was that these organizational relationships, which were neither market driven nor bureaucratic, were becoming increasingly important as economic arrangements. Rubery *et al.* (2002) offered three explanations for the increase in the number of organizational forms that were simultaneously permeable and complex. First, there have been reductions in costs for managing subcontracted or shared activities due to cheaper new technologies. This has reduced the cost of running a less-integrated firm (Williamson, 1985; Semlinger, 1991; Schendel, 1995; *The Economist*, 2006a, 2006b). Second, there has been a new emphasis on competences, leading to organizations focusing increasingly on the things in which they do well and subcontracting all other non-core activities to specialists who are equally focused. Some companies also choose to link up with others so as to be able to expand into new sectors (Penrose, 1959; Montgomery, 1995). Third, the new arrangements provide a way for firms to acquire knowledge and gain learning in situations where these are crucial to maintaining competitiveness (Cooms and Ketchen, 1999). The motivation of organizations to learn, and to acquire and use knowledge, is a recurring theme in the literature.

Many organizations had adapted their relationships with their trading partners, enthusiastically embracing new and different forms of combinations. Here, we use the term 'interorganizational relationships' to refer broadly to a variety of different co-operative relationships which involve two or more organizations. de Wit and Meyer (2005) listed the most common examples. These included contractual arrangements between two or more organizations (e.g., research consortium, export partnerships, licensing agreements, co-branding alliances), while others represented equity-based arrangements (e.g., shared payment systems, construction consortiums, joint reservation systems, new product joint ventures, cross-border joint ventures and local joint ventures). Let us consider the most popular in a little more detail.

Unilateral agreement

What distinguishes a unilateral agreement is that it involves one firm providing another on a close basis with a specific service, primarily for a financial return. For example, one firm may provide management consultancy services, marketing advice and technical inputs. The connection between the two firms is strictly financial. Because the service is being paid for by one of the partners, the level of interdependence between the two entities is very limited.

If one of the parties is unhappy with the relationship, it can terminate it and find another, more suitable partner. Because one of the firms already possesses the necessary expertise and knowledge, the other one does not have to duplicate it.

Subcontracting

Subcontracting involves an organization handing over to others some of its internal functions, which it then buys back from them as services. These functions are put out to tender, and the chosen company supplies these services. The types of functions subcontracted by tendering often include cleaning, transport logistics, IT, payroll, facilities management and customer support. These contracting-out organizations do not normally own their subcontractors. Subcontracting blurs a firm's existing boundaries, representing neither the familiar market contract nor the hierarchical, vertically integrated structure. In the UK, Boots, the chemist, a health and beauty products retailer, signed a 7-year, £400 million contract with Xchanging, the business services company. Xchanging will be responsible for various aspects of the company's travel, marketing, resourcing, facilities management and workplace services. It will also manage the transactional procurement activities, such as order raising and invoice processing, within the Boots Operational Processing Centre in Nottingham, England, which manages £800 million of expenditure (*Personnel Today*, 2005; *The Economist*, 2006c). This relieves the company from engaging in these activities and leaves it free to concentrate on those tasks that it is most skilled in.

Strategic alliance

Another popular interorganizational form is the strategic alliance. This involves two firms co-operating in order to realize commercial goals for their mutual advantage. In this case, the contractual relationship is highly formalized and has a legal element. Two companies are likely to begin by creating an alliance to progress a specific project. Later, depending on success, they may expand their co-operation to cover other activities in a number of different areas. The airline industry contains several such alliances. Alliances have been popular in uncertain industries such as biotechnology, as well as in distant geographical markets (Reuer, 1999). The aim here is to minimize risk and to draw upon the expertise of the alliance partners.

Strategic alliances may be formed in order to facilitate organizational learning within its constituent members. Each one may want to learn from the other so as to develop its knowledge, skill and expertise in an area in which it is not strong. Alliances can also be created to help each company obtain the specific competencies and resources that it needs to survive and prosper. Rapidly changing technologies and accelerating globalization mean that a specific company may no longer have the time to develop its own expertise in these areas alone.

Despite their popularity, alliances are rarely successful (Koza and Lewin, 1999). This interorganizational arrangement has problems, and managing and developing alliances over time presents challenges. A study of banking alliances by ul-Haq (2005) looked at 23 years of the growth and decline of three life cycles of alliances. Lank (2005) considered the positive side of alliances and focused on the structures, processes, roles, skills, tools and techniques that enabled people to collaborate in partnerships to achieve successful joint outcomes. Suen (2005), in contrast, considered the negative aspects of strategic alliances, looking at the influences on the partners' attitudes and at what triggered non-co-operative impulses among them.

Joint venture or consortia

In this relationship, each organization retains its independence, but they form a new company which is jointly owned and managed. The relationship between the two firms is formal. Shareholding arrangements or asset-holding agreements determine responsibilities. Joint ventures are regularly reported in the financial press. One well-known joint venture was established between Switzerland's Nestle and America's General Mills with respect to breakfast cereals. Other parts of both businesses remained separate from this venture (Anand, 1999; Mitchell, 1999). From the late 20th century, European companies have been eager to set up joint ventures with Russia, India and particularly China. The Europeans provide expertise and investment, while their partners supply access to markets, labour and political awareness. By partnering with local firms, they can draw upon their knowledge of the unique characteristics of the market being targeted and its customers.

Network organization

Network organizations are much discussed in the academic and business literature and frequently arise because a company lacks the knowledge and resources that it needs. It must go beyond its own boundaries to meet its requirements. The expertise and competences that are required are spread across a range of different organizations. Other companies have the same problem. So they form themselves into a grouping of equal agents that enjoy informal relationships with each other

(Thompson *et al.*, 1991). They enter into this relationship expecting it to be long term rather than short term and that there will be a sharing of information, a mutual dependency between the members, and long-term, rather than short-term, gains. The different parties constituting the network expect to learn from each other over the long term. All are underpinned by mutual trust. Networks need to be considered not only from the perspective of their individual components but also from that of the whole (Ebers, 1999).

Although a fashionable concept today, networks go back centuries to a time when entrepreneurs and traders engaged in repeated transactions with their suppliers, distributors, employees and customers (Child and Faulkner, 1998). In those days, the parties communicated using speech and writing and developed trust by gaining experience of each other over a long period of time. What recent developments in electronic communications have done is to transform the linkages between a company and customers and suppliers and thus modify the previous relationships. Electronic linkages have allowed vendors to work as close partners with the companies that they supply. Additionally, the availability of online information in the form of price-comparing websites has allowed customers to decide between different retailers and suppliers. An added dimension is that customers and suppliers are increasingly treated as sources of vital information who can help a company achieve its goals.

A study of over 400 companies in Europe revealed an increase in interorganizational co-operation between firms with respect to joint purchasing, shared R&D and marketing information. Subcontracting and strategic alliances increased by about 60 per cent (Pettigrew and Fenton, 2000). Storey's (2001) study of 2700 British firms showed a 61 per cent increase in those sharing knowledge with their suppliers and 41 per cent sharing it with 'other organizations in the network'. In the USA, General Electric collaborated with its major suppliers, sharing monthly sales data with 25 of them. They planned jointly, co-ordinating data on sales, scheduling, production and design, and could thus respond rapidly to changes in demand and production schedules. This form of KM and knowledge sharing is increasing in importance.

Back to the future or something entirely new? Some commentators argue that networks of different organizations represent a separate and different structural arrangement that has only been with us for the last two decades (Miles and Snow, 1986; Powell, 1987; Snow *et al.*, 1992; Hinterhuber and Levin, 1994; Ebers, 1999). These networks differ greatly in form. Some are dominated by a single, large organization at its hub, which subcontracts its production functions except those deemed to be strategically vital and close to its core competence. Other networks consist of similarly sized companies operating as equal partners with no one firm controlling what goes on within the network. The network partners change constantly and have different amounts of power with which to impose their will (Child and Faulkner, 1998). In Child's (2005) view, an electronically linked network, i.e., a virtual organization, was most likely to be a dominated network. At its centre, it had a brand name that denoted quality and possessed market appeal. The company at the centre controlled the information systems. Organizations such as Nike and the Dell Computer Corporation would represent examples of this structural form.

The co-operative, organizational entity that consists of different component parts, and which represents the network itself, is based upon the relationships between the firms that together form its sub-structure. Nohria's (1992) study of small firms developing computing and biotechnology in Silicon Valley in California showed that companies created lateral and horizontal linkages between each other, which finally formed into a network. These companies preferred to have a collaborative relationship with each other rather than a distanced, competitive one. All networks involve a collection of organizations, loosely coupled together, each of which retains its autonomy and freedom of choice.

As the environments that organizations face have increased in their complexity and uncertainty, they need to embrace structural arrangements that offer them strategic flexibility (Child and Faulkner, 1998). Paradoxically, this involves entering into relationships that include both co-operating and competing with others. The interorganizational structural arrangement is that the network involves companies whose interests and activities overlap, recognizing the benefits of co-operation. At the start of the 21st century, the structural arrangements *between* organizations may become more important than the structural arrangements *within* individual firms.

Summary

This chapter covered:

- Organization culture, change and the learning organization
- Knowledge and learning
- KM
- The socially constructed model of KM
- The knowledge category model
- The intellectual capital model
- KM processes and tools
- Case studies
- Knowledge search and discovery
- Intelligent agents
- Knowledge repository
- K-maps
- Corporate memory
- Corporate structure
- Network management
- Interorganizational relationships.

Chapter questions

1. Critically discuss the assumptions behind the argument that learning and growth act as a foundation stone for performance management systems.

2. Comment on the knowledge category model of KM.

3. Are interorganizational relationships evolving into the new trend favouring 'competition'?

References

Alderman, J., and Navach, J. (2005) *Demand Value Chain*, Charter Consulting Inc., pp. 1–7.

Allee, V. (1997) *The Knowledge Evolution*, Newton, MA: Butterworth-Heinemann.

Anand, J. (1999, October 25) 'How many matches are made in heaven?', Mastering Strategy Part 5, *Financial Times*, pp. 6–7.

Baker, R. J. (2000) *Why Intellectual Capital Is the Chief Source of Wealth*, Chichester, UK: Wiley.

Bartlett, C., and Ghoshal, S. (1990) 'Matrix management: Not a structure, a frame of mind', *Harvard Business Review*, 68(4):138–145.

Benders, J., and Van Hootegem, G. (1999) 'Teams and their context: Moving the team discussion beyond existing dichotomies', *Journal of Management Studies*, 36(5):609–628.

Benders, J., Huijgen, F., and Pekruhl, U. (2001) 'Measuring groupwork: Findings and lessons from a European survey', *New Technology, Work and Employment*, 17(3):204–217.

Berry, M. (2006, January) 'HR boss quits in-flight caterer after seven months of conflict', *Personnel Today*, 31:4.

Bjorn-Andersen, N., and Turner, J. (1994) 'Creating the twenty-first century organization: The metamorphosis of Opticon' in Baskerville, R., *et al.*, (eds.), *Transforming Organizations with Information Technology*, Amsterdam: Elsevier.

Boissot, M., MacMillan, I., and Han, K. S. (2007) *Explorations in Information Space: Knowledge, Agents, and Organizations*, Oxford, UK: Oxford University Press.

Buchanan, D., and Huczynski, A. (2004) *Organizational Behaviour: An Introductory Text* (5th edn.), Harlow, UK: FT Prentice Hall.

Burk, M. (1999) 'Knowledge management: Everyone benefits by sharing information', [Online]. http://www.fhwa.dot.gov/km/prart.htm. Last accessed 27 July 2009.

Callahan, C. V., and Pasternack, B. A. (1999, October) 'Corporate strategy in the digital age', *Strategy and Business*, 15:10–14.

Child, J. (2005) *Organization: Contemporary Principles and Practice*, Oxford: Blackwell.

Child, C., and Faulkner, D. (1998) 'Networks and virtuality', in *Strategies of Co-operation: Managing Alliances, Networks and Joint Ventures*, Oxford, UK: Oxford University Press, pp. 113–142.

Coase, R. H. (1937) 'The nature of the firm', *Economica*, 4(16):386–405.

Cooms, J. G., and Ketchen, D. J. (1999) 'Explaining interfirm co-operation and performance: Toward a reconciliation of predictions from the resource-based view and organizational economics', *Strategic Management Journal*, 20:867–888.

Coombs, Rod (1996) 'Core competences and the strategic management of R&D', *R&D Management,* 26(4):345–355.

Culley, M., O'Reilly, A., Millward, N., Forth, J., Woodland, S., Dix, G., and Bryson, A. (1998) *The 1998 Workplace Employee Relations Survey: First Findings*, London: Department of Trade and Industry.

Davenport, T., and Prusak, L. (1998) *Working Knowledge: How Organisations Manage What They Know*, Boston, MA: Harvard Business School Press.

Demarest, M. (1997) 'Understanding knowledge management', *Long Range Planning*, 30(3): 374–384.

Dervin, B. (1998) *Rethinking Communication: Paradigm Exemplars*, UK: Sage.

Ebers, M. (ed.) (1999) *The Formation of Inter Organizational Networks*, Oxford, UK: Oxford University Press.

The Economist (2006a, January 21) 'The new organization', A Survey of the Company, pp. 3–5.

The Economist (2006b, January 21) 'The matrix master', A Survey of the Company, p. 6.

The Economist (2006c, January 21) 'Partners in wealth', A Survey of the Company.

Evans, P., and Wolf, B. B. (2005) 'Collaboration rules', *Harvard Business Review*, 83(7–8): 96–104.

Fischer, B., and Boynton, A. (2005) 'Virtuoso teams', *Harvard Business Review*, 83(7–8): 116–123.

Foss, N. J. (2003) 'Selective intervention and internal hybrids: Interpreting and learning from the rise and decline of the Oticon spaghetti organization', *Organization Science*, 14(3):331–349.

Griffiths, J. (2005, March 16) 'A marriage of two mindsets', *Financial Times*, p. 15.

Guimera, R., Uzzi, B., Spiro, J., and Amaral, L. A. N. (2005) 'Team assembly mechanisms determine network structure and performance', *Science*, 308(5722):697–702.

Handy, C. B. (1976) *Understanding Organizations*, Harmondsworth, UK: Penguin Books.

Handzic, M. (2004) 'Knowledge management – through the technology glass', in *Series on Innovation and Knowledge Management* (Vol.2), Singapore: World Scientific.

Hayes, N. (1997) *Successful Team Management*, London, UK: Thompson Business Press.

ul-Haq, R. (2005) *Alliances and Co-Evolution*, Hampshire, UK: Palgrave Macmillan.

Hinterhuber, H., and Levin, B. (1994) 'Strategic networks – the organization of the future', *Long Range Planning*, 27(3):26–53.

Information Technology Advisory Group (1999) 'The Knowledge Economy'. [Online]. www .moc.gvot.nz/pbt/infotech/itag/publications.html.

Kaplan R. S., and Norton, D. P. (1996) *The Balanced Scorecard: Translating Strategy into Action*, Cambridge, MA: HBS Press.

Kazlowski, S. W. J., and Bell, B. S. (2003) 'Work groups and teams in organizations', in Borman, W. C., Ilgen, D. R., and Klomoski, R. J. (eds.), *Handbook of Psychology: Industrial and Organizational Psychology* (Vol. 12), London: Wiley, pp. 333–375.

King, W. R. (2001) 'Strategies for creating a learning organisation', *Information Systems Management*, Winter, 12–20.

Kirby, J., and Harvey, D. (1997) *Executive Perspectives on Knowledge in the Organisation*, Cambridge, MA: Ernst & Young.

Kluge, J., Stein, W., Licht, T., and Bendler, A. (Mckinsey and Company) (2001) *Knowledge Unplugged*, London: Palgrave Macmillan.

Koza, M. P., and Lewin, A. Y. (1999, November 1) 'Putting the S-word back in alliances', Mastering Strategy Part 6, *Financial Times*, pp. 12–13.

Lank, E. (2005) *Collaborative Advantage*, Hampshire, UK: Palgrave Macmillan.

Lee, L., and Al-Hawamdeh, S. (2002) 'Factors impacting knowledge sharing', *Journal of Information & Knowledge Management*, 1(1):49–56.

Lengnick–Hall, M., and Lengnick-Hall, C. (2003) *Human Resource Management in the Knowledge Economy: New Challenges, New Roles, New Capabilities*, San Francisco: Berrett-Koehler Publishers.

Liebowitz, J. (2000) *Building Organisational Intelligence: A Knowledge Management Primer*, Boca Raton, FL: CRC Press.

Loebecke, C., Van Fenema, P., and Powell, P. (1999) 'Co-opetition and knowledge transfer', *The DATABASE for Advances in Information Systems*, 30(2):14–15.

Marchington, M., Grimshaw, D., Rubery, J., and Wilmott, H. (eds.) (2005) *Fragmenting Work: Blurring Organizational Boundaries*, Oxford, UK: Oxford University Press.

McLaughlin, I., and Harris, M. (eds.) (1993) *Technological Change at Work* (2nd edn.), Oxford, UK: Oxford University Press.

Mertins, K., Heisig, P., and Vorbeck, J. (2003) *Knowledge Management: Concepts and Best Practices,* (2nd edn.), Berlin: Springer Verlag.

Metaxiotis, K., and Psarras, J. (2003, December) 'Applying knowledge management in higher education: The creation of a learning organisation', *Journal of Information and Knowledge Management*, 2(4):353–359.

Miles, R. E., and Snow, C. C. (1986) 'Organizations: New concepts for new forms', *California Management Review*, 28(3):62–73.

Mitchell, W. (1999, October 18) 'Alliances: Achieving long term value and short term goals', Mastering Strategy Part 4, *Financial Times*, pp. 6–7.

Molina, M., and Yoong, P. (2003, December) 'Knowledge shaping in a co-operative environment: The case of business clusters', *Journal of Information and Knowledge Management*, 2(4):321–341.

Montgomery, C. A. (1995) *Resource-based and Evolutionary Theories of the Firm: Towards a Synthesis*, Toronto, Canada: Kluwer Academic Publishers.

Morehead, A., Steele, M., Alexander, M., Stephen, K., and Dufflin, L. (1997) *Changes at Work: The 1995 Australian Workplace Industrial Relations Survey*, Melbourne: Longman.

Mullins, L. J. (2007) *Management and Organizational Behaviour*, Harlow, UK: FT Prentice Hall.

Nadler, D. A. (2006) *Building Better Boards: A Blueprint for Better Governance*, Chichester, UK: Wiley.

Nalebuff, B., and Brandenburger, M. (1996) *Co-operation*, London: HarperCollins Publishers.

Nohria, N. (1992) 'Is a network perspective a useful way of studying organizations?', in Nohria, N., and Eccles, R. G. (eds.), *Networks and Organizations*, Boston, MA: Harvard Business School Press.

Nonaka, I., and Takeuchi, H. (1995) *The Knowledge-Creating Company*, New York: Oxford University Press.

Oliver, A., and Ebers, M. (1998) 'Networking network studies: Analysis of conceptual configurations in the study of inter-organizational relationships', *Organization Studies*, 19(4): 549–583.

Ortenblad, A. (2001) 'On differences between organisational learning and learning organisation', *The Learning Organisation*, 8(3):125–133.

Osterman, P. (1994) 'How common is workplace transformation and who adopts it?, *Industrial and Labour Relations Review*, 47:173–188.

Overall, S. (2005, March 29) 'Employers hide in the shadows', *Personnel Today*, p. 10.

Ozaki, M. (1996) 'Direct participation in work organization: A survey of recent international developments', *The Economic and Labour Relations Review*, 7(1):5–28.

Paton, R. A., and McCalman, J. (2008) *Change Management: A Guide to Effective Implementation* (3rd edn.), London, UK: Sage.

Pedler, M., Boydell, T., and Burgoyne, J. (1998) *Learning Company Project Report*, Sheffield: Training Agency.

Penrose, E. (1959) *The Theory of the Growth of the Firm*, Oxford: Blackwell.

Personnel Today (2005, June 7) 'Boots signs £400 m outsourcing deal', p. 4.

Peters T. J., and Waterman L, R. H. (1982) *In Search of Excellence: Lessons from America's Best Run Companies*, New York: Harper Row.

Pettigrew, A. M., and Fenton, E. M. (eds.) (2000) *The Innovating Organization*, London: Sage.

Polanyi, M. (1997) *The Tacit Dimension: Knowledge in Organisations*, London: Butterworths.

Powell, W. W. (1987) 'Hybrid organizational arrangements: New form or transitional development?', *California Management Review*, 30:67–87.

Proctor, S., and Mueller, F. (2000) 'Teamworking, strategy, structure, systems and culture', in Proctor, S., and Mueller, F. (eds.), *Teamworking*, Macmillan, pp. 3–24.

Pugh, D. (1983) *People in Organizations*, Harmondsworth, UK: Penguin Books.

Rampersad, H. K. (2001) *Total Quality Management: An Executive Guide to Continuous Improvement*, New York: Springer-Verlag.

Rampersad, H. K. (2002) *Total Performance Scorecard; een speurtocht naar zelfkennis en competentieontwikkeling van lerende organisaties*, Schiedam: Scriptum Management.

Reuer, J. (1999, October 4) 'Collaborative strategy: The logic of alliances', Mastering Strategy Part 2, *Financial Times*, pp. 12–13.

Rivard, S., Bennoit, A. A., Patry, M., Pare, G., and Smith, H. A. (2004) *Information Technology and Organizational Transformation*, Oxford: Elsevier / Butterworth-Heinemann.

Roberts, J. (2005) *The Modern Firm*, Oxford University Press.

Roos, J., Roos, G., Edvinsson, L., and Dragonelli, N. C. (1997) *Intellectual Capital-Navigating in the New Business Landscape*, Hampshire and London: Macmillan Press Ltd.

Rubery, J., Earnshaw, J., Marchington, M., Cooke, F. L., and Vincent, S. (2002) 'Changing organizational forms and the employment relationship', *Journal of Management Studies*, 39(5):645–672.

Schein E. H. (2004) *Organizational Culture and Leadership*, San Francisco: Josey Boss.

Schendel, D. (1995) 'Introduction to "technological transformation and the new competitive landscape"', *Strategic Management Journal*, 16:1–6.

Scholl, W. C., Meyer, K. B., and Heisig, P. (2004) 'The future of knowledge management: An international Delphi study', *Journal of Knowledge Management*.

Semlinger, K. (1991) 'New developments in subcontracting: Mixed market and hierarchy', in Amin, A., and Dietrich, M. (eds.), *Towards a New Europe: Structural Changes in the European Economy*, Cheltenham: Edward Elgar.

Senge, P. M. (1990) *The Fifth Discipline: The Art & Practice of the Learning Organization*, New York: Doubleday.

Sharma, R. K. (2003, December) 'Understanding organisational learning through knowledge of management', *Journal of Information and Knowledge Management*, 2(4):343–352.

Smyth, H., and Long-Bottom, R. (2005, April) 'External provision of management information systems: The case of the concrete and cement industries', *European Management Journal*, 23(2):247–259.

Snow, C. C., Miles, R. E., and Coleman, H. J. (1992) 'Managing 21st century network organizations', *Organizational Dynamics*, 20:5–20.

Starbuck, W. H. (2005) 'Bureaucracy becomes a four letter word', *Harvard Business Review*, 83(10):17.

Storey, J. (2001, November 12) 'When internal boundaries become network relationships', in Mastering People, Part 6, *Financial Times*, pp. 6–8.

Suen, W. W. (2005) *Non-Co-operation: The Dark Side of Strategic Alliances*, Palgrave Macmillan.

Teece, D. J. (2000) 'Strategies for managing knowledge assets: The role of the firm structure and industrial context', *Long Range Planning*, 33:35–54.

Thompson, G., Francis, J., Levacic, R., and Mitchell, J. (eds.) (1991) *Markets, Hierarchies and Networks: The Co-ordination of Social Life*, Milton Keynes, UK: Sage / Open University Press.

Weber, M. (1947) *The Theory of Social and Economic Organizations*, translated and edited by Henderson, A. M. and Parson, T., New York: Free Press.

Wiig, K. M. (1997) 'Integrating intellectual capital and knowledge management', *Long Range Planning*, 30(3):399–405.

Williamson, O. E. (1985) *The Economic Institutions of Capitalism*, New York: Free Press.

de Wit, B., and Meyer, R. (2005) *Strategy Synthesis*, London: Thomson Learning, p. 161.

Zeleny, M. (2000) 'Knowledge vs information', in *The IEBM Handbook of Information Technology In Business*, London: Thomson Learning, pp. 162–168.

6

Strategic information systems

Alexis Barlow, Peter Duncan, Kevin Grant and David Edgar

Introduction

In any discussion of strategic information systems (SIS), it is logical, sensible and necessary to establish the foundations of what we mean by information, information systems and strategy. Information is a major resource within organizations that is used for a range of activities and, as such, needs to be appropriately managed. Information must be made available in the correct format to the right people at the right time. Information technology (IT) and information systems (IS) are not new; they have always existed in organizations (Galliers and Baker, 1994; Ward, 1995), providing for the capture, storage, processing and transmission of information. A key activity within organizations that requires appropriate and timely information is decision-making. Decision-making can be regarded as a process involving three main stages: intelligence, design and choice (Newell and Simon, 1972). The *intelligence* stage entails discovering some problem or opportunity that needs to be addressed; the *design* stage requires the decision-maker to use available resources to develop alternative solutions to the problem or opportunity; and the final stage involves the decision-maker's making a *choice* and deciding which solution to implement.

Learning objectives

- Introduce the concept of strategic information systems.

- Introduce the concepts of competitive advantage.

- Introduce and evaluate the business impact and value adding strategic information systems may have on businesses today.

- Describe the key stages and processes businesses can adopt to think about and introduce strategic information systems.

The advanced information and communications technologies currently available provide a host of opportunities with a myriad of configurations of IT and IS, dramatically expanding what Groth (1999, p. 34) calls the 'constructible space' of organizations, that is, the organization's ability to redefine its structure and the nature of its competitive advantage. An example of this is provided by Werbach (2005), who argues that whereas in the 19th century the telegraph quickly became ubiquitous and lost its value as a potential source of competitive advantage (among New York stock traders), the current telephone technology development of voice over Internet protocol (or VoIP) 'will become strategically more significant over time' and allow firms to 'rethink their entire businesses' (pp. 146–147). Both Groth's and Werbech's views highlight that, as Porter and Millar (1985) noted in their seminal article, information changes the way you compete – and the strategic use of IS has become a key challenge for today's organizations.

Over the years, IT/IS have changed both the fundamentals of business strategy and also the nature of 'doing' business (the day-to-day operations). Throughout the last 30 years or so, the application of relevant and appropriate technology has changed how businesses perceive what technology can do for them. This chapter explores what ISs are, how they have evolved and how they help organizations gain a competitive edge.

Acronyms used in the text

BIS	Business intelligence system(s)
DSS	Decision support system(s)
EDI	Electronic data interchange
ERP	Enterprise resource planning
GDSS	Group decision support system(s)
GIS	Geographic information system(s)
IMS	Information management strategy
IRT	Internet-related technologies
IT	Information technology
ITS	Information technology strategy
IS	Information system(s)
ISS	Information systems strategy
MDSS	Marketing decision support systems
MIS	Management information system(s)
MkIS	Marketing information system(s)
SAM	Strategic alignment model
SCN	Supply chain network(s)
SIS	Strategic information system(s)
SISP	Strategic information systems planning
TPS	Transaction processing system(s)

Key concepts

This section will provide definitions of a number of key concepts that are closely related to SIS and are used widely within a wide range of business sectors and are referred to throughout the chapter.

Strategy

Strategies are the business policies intended to match the activities of the organization to those of the environment within which it operates, and they are the means the organization uses to attain its long-term objectives. A good strategy co-ordinates the activities of all parts of the organization, and ensures that the various activities are well integrated.

Strategic formulation

Strategy is the direction and scope of an organization over the long term. It describes how the resources of the organization should be configured within a changing environment to meet the needs of the markets and fulfil stakeholder expectations. At the same time, it should encourage creative thinking and innovation so that the organization does not come to a standstill. This is relevant for business strategy and IS/IT strategy, as well as any other strategy of the organization.

IS/IT

A distinction between IS and IT is necessary for a meaningful discussion and helps in clarifying many of the important issues regarding alignment of business and information strategies. The differentiation between IS and IT is essential when developing IS/IT strategies because the technology structure is never enough to ensure the successful alignment of IS/IT and business strategies. The definitions used for IS and IT stem from Ward and Peppard (2003):

- *Information systems*, or *IS*, refers to how information is gathered, processed, stored, used and disseminated by the organization. The IS strategy defines the organization's requirement for information and systems to support the overall strategy of the business.

- *Information technology*, or *IT*, refers to hardware, software and telecommunications networks technology. The IT strategy is concerned with how the organization's demand for information and systems will be supported by technology.

Strategic information systems planning

The purpose of developing an IS/IT strategy should be to ensure that the value delivered from IS/IT investments is as high as possible. According to Ward and Peppard (2003) this can be achieved by aligning the IS demand to the business strategy and at the same time searching for opportunities for IS/IT to improve the overall competitiveness.

Competitive advantage

According to the capabilities approach to organizational performance, the essence of business success is choosing the right capabilities to build, managing them carefully and exploiting them fully. The distinctive competences of a company must be based on some capabilities that others find difficult to emulate and set it apart from competitors in the industry. According to Porter (1985), these competences must either be geared towards developing superior cost characteristics, or differentiation through creating some distinctive added value (as perceived by the customer). Competitive advantage is based on fully utilizing these competences and sustaining them by being able to respond to evolving opportunities. If a capability is to be of long-term value to the organization, it has to be something quite complex, hard to define and not associated with any particular individual. Capabilities such as organizational architecture, reputation, corporate culture, collective learning or business processes can possibly be sustainable, since they are difficult for rivals and potential competitors to either identify or replicate.

Information systems defined

Before exploring the strategic use of IT/IS, it is useful to understand the foundations of what a system is, what its purpose is and, therefore, how businesses can use such systems to add value to their operations.

One view of a 'system' is 'a set of elements or components that interact to accomplish goals' (Stair and Reynolds, 2006, p. 740). IS are socio-technical systems (in other words, they straddle both human and technological dimensions) consisting of hardware, software and communications technologies (the IT components) as well as data, procedures and people. In general terms, the goals of IS are to 'gather, process, store, use and disseminate information' (United Kingdom Academy of Information Sytems, 1999). Although IT could refer to non-computer technologies, such as pen and paper (hardware) and writing systems (software), for the purposes of this chapter *IT* refers to the use of computer-based IS and related technologies.

So, what does an IS do? In simple terms, it converts data into information and allows such information to be interpreted in such a way that allows for enhanced knowledge of an issue or situation. In this respect, 'data' (or 'facts') are the raw material (input) for an IS, which is processed (or transformed) into 'information' – the output of the system. The processing from data into information can be via a number of techniques (based on Davenport and Prusak, 2000, p. 4) such as:

- **Contextualization** – by examining why the data were collected
- **Categorization** – by units of analysis (e.g., by product or shop)
- **Calculation** – by analysis using mathematical or statistical techniques
- **Correction** – by removing errors from the data ('garbage in – garbage out')
- **Condensing** – by summarizing or condensing the data.

These techniques may be combined. For example, the total sales per day per shop (a figure for a particular *category/unit of analysis*) will be *calculated* to provide a *condensed* summary of all the individual transactions made in the shop on a particular day to inform decision-makers regarding the shop's profitability (*context*).

A system may also provide feedback, e.g., error reports if data are incorrectly entered, leading to refinement of the input or processing tasks (Stair and Reynolds, 2006). It is the final product of the data processing, the resulting information, that is used to help make decisions and which forms the basis of knowledge which underpins the rationale and justification for such decisions.

Information is therefore a major resource within organizations that is used for a range of activities. It needs to be appropriately managed and interpreted within the context of the organization, and the purpose for which the data and information are being used. Such information must be made available in the correct format, to the right people, at the right time. It should have 'added value beyond the value of the facts [data] themselves' (Stair and Reynolds, 2006, p. 732), and its role is to 'inform' the recipient or user, giving the potential to change the actions of the recipient (Davenport and Prusak, 2000) and thus add value to the organization's activities.

To understand the conversion process it is necessary to understand what an IS is. While IT is relatively straightforward and clearly defined, IS, in this case computer-based IS, is more complex in that information may potentially be 'anything that can be digitized' (Shapiro and Varian, 1999, p. 3) and might include numbers, text, sounds (e.g., the spoken word or music) and static (photographs) or dynamic (movies) images, or a combination of these, such as a movie with the soundtrack and subtitles (Vonage, 2005).

IS have a vital role to play in making information available that will support and inform decision-makers and decision-making and thus the achievement of competitive advantage. Robson (1997) explored the role of IS at each stage of the decision-making process (Newell and Simon, 1972; outlined in the introduction to this chapter), and highlighted that at the intelligence stage, IS can provide information on the current situation and provide warnings (e.g. through reporting on exceptional events). At the design stage it can help present forecasts and predictive models to explore the consequence of decisions made. Ultimately, at the choice stage, IS can perform risk analysis on alternative options for alternative futures, and offer feedback or allow for reflection.

The following discussion draws on Anthony's (1965) three levels of decision-making in the organization (strategic, tactical and operational). Decision-making support can be offered to the *strategic* or top management, making decisions concerning longer-term goals and plans, and about issues that impact the future growth and profitability of the organization. These decisions tend to have a wider scope, be more complex, be unstructured (in that there may be no 'ready-to-go' plan about how to tackle the issue) and have a high degree of uncertainty. The information required for these types of decisions tends to be external information regarding the environment, the marketplace, competitors, supplier, customers and the like. Examples of strategic decisions are joint ventures into new areas, new product initiatives and expansion into new international markets.

On the other hand, *tactical* or middle managers are involved in supporting the strategic goals of the organization. The decisions made by tactical or middle management tend to be semi-structured and have a more medium-term impact on the organization. Examples of tactical decisions are selecting suppliers of materials or pricing products.

At the third and final level, *operational* or line managers are involved in decisions that affect the day-to-day running of the organization. Operational decisions tend to be much more structured and there is a routine or process in place to help decision-makers deal with the situation, such as taking a customer order. They have a narrower scope and shorter-term impact. The information required for operational decisions is largely internal. Examples of operational decisions are inventory control, order processing and customer billing.

As well as supporting decisions, IS are increasingly being used to make decisions. They are being used more and more for automating operational decisions which are routine and follow clearly defined rules. For example, the reordering of stock can be conducted automatically as stock levels fall below a particular level. Such systems increase the efficiency and effectiveness of organizations – a concept discussed later (under the heading of 'Role of Information Systems in Strategy'). However, before this, it is useful to understand how IS are categorized and what the role of IS has been as they have evolved over time.

Classifying information systems

IS can be classified in a number of different ways. By looking at a particular system or application from several different perspectives (classifications) it is possible to build up a clearer picture of what the system does, or could do.

Two possible methods of classification have been mentioned already. First, not all IS require the involvement of IT, and one distinction can be made between manual and computer-based IS (Stair and Reynolds, 2006). Second, IS can be aimed at supporting decision-makers at different levels of organization – strategic, tactical or operational. As noted above, there are distinctions between the three levels based on, e.g., the nature of the decision (structured/unstructured) and the nature of the information required from internal or external sources.

IS may be public or private and consist of formal or informal information-handling techniques (after Davis and Olson, 1984). In this case, 'public' and 'private' refer to who can access the system – public provides access across a number of users, whereas private refers to use by a single person (see Table 6.1).

The IT application is 'neutral' and merely a tool for the user to use. So, e.g., a database application such as Microsoft Access could be used by you at work to create your own key contacts database which only you will see (private). There will have to be at least some level of formality in how you create the database itself (requirements to create 'fields' such as name, address and so on). On the other hand, you may also be working with a company-wide (public) database of names, telephone and e-mail details of employees which is accessed by all employees (internal), and perhaps customers or potential customers via the corporate website (external).

This last point suggests another way of classifying IS – is the focus internal to the organization, or external? However, this distinction is increasingly becoming blurred as many organizations attempt to integrate their internal processes with the processes of their customers or clients using Internet technologies. The potential benefits from such integration are considerable. For example, dealerships who stock Harley-Davidson motorcycles found that the processing time for routine warranty claims was reduced from around a month with a paper-based system to 48 hours using a web-based extranet system (Kalin, 1998). (Internet-based systems are discussed in greater detail later in this chapter.)

Another way of classifying IS is by traditional business function, e.g., financial IS, accounting IS and so on for other functions such as human resources and marketing (cf. Oz, 2004; Stair and Reynolds, 2006).

	Formal	*Informal*
Public	Historical financial data or online corporate address book	The 'grapevine'
Private	Your own 'key contacts' database	Handwritten scribbles on the back of an envelope

Table 6.1 Generic classification of information systems

One final way of classifying IS relates to the system's complexity and the purpose it serves (Stair and Reynolds, 2006, p. 21). Typical classes of IS include (based on Marakas, 2003; Oz, 2004; Stair and Reynolds, 2006):

Transaction processing systems (TPS) deal with the data generated by the organization's transactions with other parties. These are typically customer-facing and record order details, credit card transactions and so on.

Management information systems (MIS) is a generic label for those IS which support management across all levels of the organization. Key outputs of such systems are management reports. Some of the other systems described below also support management, and sometimes they may be seen as 'sub-species' of MIS.

DSSs support middle and senior managers, and focus in particular on facilitating decision-making (in contrast to the more report-oriented focus of MIS). As discussed earlier, making a decision involves choosing a particular option from a range of alternatives, and a key aspect of DSS is the ability to play 'what if' and see what impact your changes make on the system's predicted outcome. What if sales increased by 10 per cent next year instead of 8 per cent? What if the marketing budget is cut by 3 per cent in the next quarter? These systems can be expensive and highly sophisticated using complex mathematical and statistical formulae – but the most commonly used DSS tool is the humble spreadsheet.

DSSs support individual decision-makers. In contrast, **Group decision support systems (GDSS)** support, as the name suggests, the decision-making activities of groups. There are, potentially, considerable cost savings to be made by using GDSS-related technologies such as video-conferencing to alleviate the need for staff to travel long distances to attend meetings (e.g., from Vancouver to Hong Kong). You are likely to be familiar with sending your friends and family SMS text messages via your mobile phone. There is increasing *business* use of text messaging to keep groups in touch with each other to facilitate faster decision-making. For example, reminders or details of changes to decision deadlines can be quickly sent to a group – people 'on the move' may be easier to reach via their mobile phone than by e-mail. For some examples of how text messaging can be used in business see TextAnywhere (2005).

Executive information systems (EIS) [or executive support systems (ESS)] can be seen to combine aspects of MIS and DSS. The key difference is that EIS/ESS supports the top level managers in the organization who are making strategic 'bet the business' decisions about the organization.

Where there is a clear pattern or structure to decision-making, IS such as TPS may be able to automate part, or all, of the process. However, where there is no pattern to follow (unstructured), such systems may be of little benefit, and a person's skill and expertise are crucial. **Expert systems** attempt to capture this human expertise through a range of techniques such as case-based reasoning (finding past cases most similar to the current situation and using them to decide what should be done in the current situation). Potentially, expert systems could save an organization from paying for expensive experts – and the system (and its expertise) could be shared throughout the company (a human expert would find it hard to be in five places at once).

Geographic information systems (GIS) are IS which have a map as a key component. The next time you are in a taxicab, look and see if there is a GIS on board that is helping the driver plan their route. The map may be augmented with the up-to-date location of speed cameras, which may also inform decision-making regarding not only which route to take, but also speed.

The discussion above outlined a number of the principle IS which an organization may use, but there are others such as business intelligence systems (BIS) and enterprise resource planning (ERP) systems. As noted, it can be useful to consider IS from several different perspectives to investigate what benefits may be gained. However, the distinctions between the various classifications may be blurred. For example, we have marketing information systems (MkIS) (Talvinen, 1995; Kotler and Keller, 2006) based around the **marketing function**, and **marketing decision support systems** (MDSS) (Talvinen, 1995; Wöber and Gretzel, 2000) providing decision support specifically for the marketing function. Kotler and Keller (2006, p. 73) suggest that MkIS should be developed from internal company records (incorporating data from the order-to-payment cycle and sales which would typically be generated through TPS), marketing intelligence (an analysis of *existing* data regarding trends and signals from the external environment – relating to BIS) and market research (conducting *new* research into market trends).

In summary, IS can be classified from a number of different perspectives such as:

- Manual or computer-based
- Level of decision-making (strategic, tactical or operational)
- Formal or informal
- Public or private
- Internal or external
- By business function
- Complexity/purpose (TPS, MIS, DSS and so on).

The evolving role of information systems

Having classified how IS can be described, to help us to further understand the nature of IS in organizations and their role in strategic decision-making, it is useful to understand how the role of IS has evolved and the benefits they can yield for organizations.

Many authors, such as Somogyi and Galliers (1987) and Ward and Peppard (2003), identify three different eras in the evolution of the role of IS and technology in organizations. Ward and Peppard (2003) define the three eras as:

- Data processing (DP) – from the 1960s onwards
- Management information systems – from the 1970s onwards
- Strategic information systems (SIS) – from the 1980s onwards.

The three eras overlap; DP continued to mature as MIS emerged, and MIS continued to mature as SIS emerged. Some organizations are still at the MIS stage, while others have entered and maximized their 'value adding' in the SIS era. As such, IS can add value if the organization is mature enough to handle the effective strategic alignment of technologies to their business strategy.

Historically, the use and perception of IT/IS was connected with information and knowledge, in an attempt to determine and discover what was going on in the business, to help managers to manage more effectively and to enhance communication and improve decision-making within the business. As the technology matured and businesses started to develop the skills of managing technology and information, the focus moved from what the business was doing on a day-to-day basis, to a more long-term focus on how the business worked, i.e. its business processes. This trend was connected with looking at business processes and used technologies and information to redesign existing ways of working to ensure consistency, uniformity and that systems and processes were followed, monitored by specific ISs. As a greater understanding of the business developed by knowing and understanding the business processes, individuals within the company started to think that new ways of working were possible with technology and the effective use of information. This business process optimization era was concerned with improving existing processes in the business. The term *BPR* (business process re-engineering, later redesign) was coined to show this application of technology and information to fundamentally challenge what businesses did and how they did it.

It is worth noting that technology is essentially a business tool. As such, the IT and IS dimensions of business tend to reflect the underlying strategic developments and priorities of the business. This is seen in two core areas: the drive for efficiency and the need to differentiate or drive for effectiveness. So while the early use of technology and IS was geared towards streamlining organizations, managing scale economies, coping with globalization, global communications and making processes more efficient, more recent use has revolved around knowledge management, customer relationship management, innovation and managing complex adaptive systems. These latter uses are geared towards gaining a competitive advantage through personalizing products, being more outward-looking, and being more effective in the operations of the business. In this respect, developments in IS and IT use can be seen to be aligning with (and in some cases driving) the general business strategy of the organization.

As such, the fundamental challenge of rethinking business design encouraged organizations to rethink their use of IS and seek to support the business in a strategic way, supporting business innovation and action in an attempt to secure business objectives. The notion of SIS was born.

The development of SIS was fuelled by Porter's competitive strategy framework (Porter, 1980, 1985). On the basis of Porter's (1980) model of five competitive forces, researchers explained how IT supports and enables Porter's four generic differentiation strategies (cf. Somogyi and Galliers, 1987). Similarly, IS were seen as a key element in optimizing the company's value chain (Porter, 1980), mainly through better co-ordination of involved activities. Porter and Millar (1985) argued, based on their proposed information intensity matrix, that IS will play a strategic role in industries characterized by high information intensity in both the value chain and the product.

Unfortunately, the term *strategic information system* was coined. Many believe SIS to be a particular type of information system, like a MIS or a TPS. They are not. In its simplest form, SIS refer to any IS that exists in the organization that, if used in a different way, can change, support and inform the strategic goals and objectives of a business, or influence its ability to manipulate the environmental relationships it has (e.g., with customers or suppliers). Ultimately, the goal is to gain and sustain a competitive advantage or reduce a competitor's advantage, either by reducing costs (efficiency) or by offering more or different features (effectiveness).

It is useful to note that Ward and Peppard (2003) define four main types of SIS:

- Systems that share information with customers and/or suppliers.
- Systems that facilitate improved integration of internal processes.
- Systems that enhance the development of products and services.
- Systems that provide relevant strategic information to executive management.

These systems can be used to add value for the different stakeholders and allow for opportunities to gain strategic rent. In summary, SIS are connected with the most appropriate and relevant use of information, systems and information systems which contribute significantly to the achievement of an organization's overall objectives. This is achieved by changing the way it does something, usually by maximizing the internal competencies of the firm – a competitive stance founded in the resource-based view of strategy (Hamel and Prahalad, 1994). This gains (or sustains) a competitive advantage for a business, and enables it to be an effective competitor.

Now that we understand the evolving role of IS, we can look at a number of ways in which such systems can be used to support the strategic developments of organizations and then explore how one aligns the systems with the strategic aspirations of the organization.

Role of information systems in strategy

SIS are playing an increasingly significant role in the future direction of organizations and their organizational strategies. A major development in recent years that has led to a change in the nature of business and a range of innovative applications have been the Internet and the WorldWideWeb (the Web). Porter (2001) regards the Internet as a powerful tool that can provide opportunities for enhancing the competitive position of organizations. This can be achieved by building barriers against new entrants, changing the basis for competition, changing the balance of power in supplier relationships, tying in new customers, switching costs and creating new products and service (Somogyi and Galliers, 2003).

The area of SIS can help organizations today in a variety of ways. The main ways are given in Table 6.2.

We can see how information systems, in this case the Internet, can be used as a strategic tool. The example also shows that you need to have a decent selling proposition which is valued by the consumer and that there needs to be a solid business plan with clear revenue streams (one of the factors that many casualties of the dot.com crash did not ensure). In this respect, the strategy is clear and the business model appropriate – the technology and IS simply facilitate and enhance the operation.

Once a company or an individual achieves a competitive advantage from an innovative application of relevant and appropriate technologies, usually as the first mover, keeping it is hard. This is because the technology is available to all and it could be used by a new business in the same way; thus, the second mover, if they do it correctly and better, will also gain a competitive advantage. Therefore, the

Table 6.2
Potential
applications of
strategic information
systems

- **Innovative applications (A):** Create innovative applications that provide direct strategic advantage to organizations.

- **Competitive weapons (B):** Information systems themselves are recognized as a competitive weapon.

- **Changes in processes (C):** IT supports changes in business processes that translate to strategic advantage.

- **Links with business partners (D):** IT links a company with its business partners effectively and efficiently.

- **Cost reductions (E):** IT enables companies to reduce costs.

- **Relationships with suppliers and customers (F):** IT can be used to lock in suppliers and customers, or to build in switching costs.

- **New products (G):** A firm can leverage its investment in IT to create new products that are in demand in the marketplace.

- **Competitive intelligence (H):** IT provides competitive (business) intelligence by collecting and analyzing information about products, markets, competitors, customers and environmental changes.

SOURCE: ADAPTED FROM TURBAN ET AL. (2004).

technology is not the barrier to entry, unless the first mover patents it, but this takes time and it is hard to patent an idea or concept like Peter Barlow Edgar's innovative idea.

So, at least in the short term, a business can ensure that their SIS continue to add value to the business by:

- Making them unique
- Making it hard to imitate the physical technology, the process and how the technology has been introduced to the organization
- Use of patentable technology
- Linking innovative, creative ideas with organizational culture and core competencies supported and being supported by technology.

From the example used we see that organizations can seek to build relationships with clients and develop strategic networks that allow for external as well as internal efficiencies and effectiveness, in essence representing the demand side (Internet) and supply side (supply chain). Two key areas that lend themselves to the pursuit of competitive advantage through efficiency and effectiveness are how IS is used as part of the Internet revolution and how the organization develops IS throughout its supply (or value) chain in its business processes. These two areas are discussed next.

Process in action IS and strategy in action – the author example

Many of the former key business advantages from SIS can be illustrated with a simple example, in this case the authoring and selling of children's fiction. The example uses a fictitious author, called Peter Barlow Edgar.

Let's assume that Peter Barlow Edgar, the author of the *Tractor and the Farm* series of books, is writing his books today, and that he wants to use the Internet to help make additional money, as he does not like giving a percentage of the money from each book sold to the publisher, the printer, the book distribution company and the book shop, who would actually sell the book, which is the way authors currently develop books and get them to the marketplace. Let's also assume that his latest book, *The Big Red Tractor in Farmer Smith's Farm* ('*The Big Red Tractor*') retails from a book shop for £11.50. That cost, which the buyer pays, is made up of the following elements:

1. Book shop (to cover costs and to make a profit), £3.50 per book
2. Book distribution company (to cover costs and to make a profit), £2.50 per book
3. Printer (to cover costs and to make a profit), £2.50 per book
4. Publisher (to cover costs and to make a profit), £2.00 per book
5. Author, £1 per book

As you can see, the author is only making £1 per book, with the rest of the supply chain making their living from his work.

Let us assume that things are different and the author has studied SIS. His goal is still the same: to sell as many copies of *The Big Red Tractor* as he can, to make money, using the Internet and websites to sell his books to individuals who love to read books about tractors.

After studying SIS, the author thinks that he can use the Internet and websites to sell his books in a different manner than the mercantile model of selling books, as described above. This we call an innovative application of technology – to do something different that the technology is able to and capable of doing. The reader and the author of the book enter into a common relationship supported by technology, which in this case is the Web (A in Table 6.2). The author quickly realizes that his innovative idea changes the way people buy books and how authors can get their books to the marketplace (C in Table 6.2).

Peter Barlow Edgar sets up a website for people interested in tractors and farms and story telling. He quickly develops an interactive and dynamic website, that records people who visit the website and are really interested (by asking them to complete a contact form and asking what they are interested in). This is called customer intelligence (H in Table 6.2). As more and more people visit the website, Peter Barlow Edgar thinks to himself, how do I build a better relationship with these people, in order to sell my books? He realises that it is not the technology that is the key but the interaction and the relationship between him and the people who want to read his books that is the key (F in Table 6.2). He quickly gets to work, writing two chapters of the next adventures of the Big Red Tractor. But instead of writing all the other chapters of the story and trying to convince a publisher to publish them in a book, he contacts via e-mail, all the people who have completed the contact form and says to them that he has written two chapters about the latest adventures of the Big Red Tractor. Interestingly, many of the people that he had e-mailed and who were interested in the adventure printed out the two chapters he wrote.

Remember that these readers are avid followers of tractors who can afford home computers and printers, so they have high disposable incomes to spend on hobbies, such as reading.

They were asked to comment on and provide ideas about the two chapters; not all of them will respond, but many do. They provide a great deal of feedback directly to Peter Barlow Edgar (C in Table 6.2). The author now has a new e-mail list of people who are very interested in books about a Big Red Tractor (H in Table 6.2) and many ideas to develop subsequent chapters.

This time he does write all the remaining chapters of the story, using many of the ideas provided to him by the community. But this time he develops a secure site that can only be accessed by a password, which is needed to access and download the remaining chapters (A and B in Table 6.2).

This time he e-mails a second list, one that has all the people who responded back to him regarding the first two chapters. He e-mails them saying that he has taken on board many of the ideas and that the 12 remaining chapters can be accessed via the Web for a small subscription fee. Once the fee is paid, by credit or debit card, an e-mail is sent to them that allows access to the new chapters. However, the author knows that he cannot charge too much for the remaining chapters, as book publishing is a highly competitive market. He knows from his own experience and market intelligence that, in the shops, books sell for about £11.50. So he decides to sell the book for £4.50 to secure demand and sales. In addition, he is anticipating a strong response from people who responded with feedback, as he knows they will be interested to see if any of their original ideas and suggestions have been incorporated in the story and the remaining chapters (F and G in Table 6.2).

In the 10 days following this e-mail campaign, he is inundated with requests for passwords; people feel that paying £4.50 is great value as they feel they are saving £7. Remember, they receive the PDF files and print the chapters out themselves, so the author does not incur any printing and reproduction costs. As you would expect in this new relationship (A and B in Table 6.2), Peter Barlow Edgar is also very happy. Before, he received £1 per book; now he gets £4.50, which is a profit increase of over 400 per cent. That is what we call 'good business', as both the customer and author seem happy. The people who lose out are intermediaries, who, given the technology and the customer interaction and relationship, are no longer needed as much as they once were.

Interestingly, as we leave Peter Barlow Edgar thinking about his next book, he starts to reflect on what has happened and the changes to the way he earns a living that have occurred. Then he has another great idea: maybe these people would be interested in buying a model of the Big Red Tractor. He sends an e-mail to a company that manufactures models and suggests that they pay him a fee to put a link on his secure website, which is accessible only with a password, to buy a model kit of the Big Red Tractor. This is an example of A and D in Table 6.2. When he finishes his e-mail to the model manufacturers, his e-mail inbox makes a sound, indicating a new message has just been received. It is from his friend in the USA, Nancy, who asks if she can have a copy of the chapters so she can read them. Peter Barlow Edgar realizes that he can sell the book to the Americans in the same way he has sold it in the UK, without physically having to go to America; the cycle starts all over again.

Questions

1. How has Peter's business idea enabled him to get closer to his customers? What generic aspects or type of marketing approach has he used?

2. Has this been driven by the technology, or has technology just enabled him to do what could have been done anyway? How has IT added value to the business process of selling books?

Internet revolution

Enabling many of the current advancements in IS has been the development of the Internet and related applications. The Internet is a network of networks 'made up of many separate but interconnected networks belonging to commercial, educational and government organizations, and Internet service providers' (Begg and Connolly, 2002). The origins of the Internet can be traced back to a US military project commissioned by the US Department of Defense in 1969 to develop a national communication system for the US military that would maintain communications integrity in the event of a national emergency. The Internet was commercialized in 1992, and by mid-1994, the Internet had connected an estimated two million computers in more than 100 countries (Internet.com). One of the main drivers that has led to such an increase in commercial and business usage of the Internet is the Web, a global information sharing architecture that provides a 'point and click' means of exploring the immense volume of pages of information residing on other computers on different networks connected to the Internet (Berners-Lee, 2000).

Since its commercialization, the Internet has evolved through a number of phases. Jelassi and Enders (2005) used Perez's (2002) 'Life Cycle of Technological Revolutions' to develop a model of the different stages through which technological revolutions move as their diffusion increases. These are summarized and illustrated in Table 6.3.

Developments in the Internet can be related to each of the stages. The Internet was commercialized in the 1990s, and the 'Irruption' stage began as innovations gradually started appearing. The Internet boom or 'frenzy' stage probably began in 1995 with the launch of Amazon.com, one of today's most well-known online retailers, and rapidly advanced with the multiplication of dot.coms in the late 1990s due to low barriers of entry and the ability to raise capital without demonstrating viability. However, market sizes and revenues had been artificially inflated, there had been few sustainable business models created and there was less value or profits created than anticipated. The Internet boom finally crashed in February 2000. The Internet is currently in the 'Synergy' stage as organizations are realizing that they need to

Stages	Description
Irruption	▪ New technology slowly penetrates economy ▪ Innovative products and services based on technology appear
Frenzy	▪ Greater opportunities of technology are explored ▪ Investors become increasingly confident and excited ▪ Organizations generate quick and easy profits ▪ Process continues and quickens until it reaches a bubble point
Crash	▪ Investors lose confidence and pull out funds ▪ Bubble deflates ▪ Stock market collapses
Synergy	▪ Time of quick and easy profits has passed ▪ Organizations concentrate on generating economies of scale and scope ▪ Return to business fundamentals, e.g., value creation, sustainable competitive advantage
Maturity	▪ Market saturation and mature technologies ▪ Growth opportunities limited

Table 6.3
Stages of technological revolutions

SOURCE: ADAPTED FROM JELASSI AND ENDERS, 2005, p. 11.

return to business fundamentals. Although the Internet is a powerful set of tools, it must be used to build on the proven principles of effective strategy (Porter, 2001).

The four P's of the classic 'marketing mix' (product, price, place and promotion) (Kotler and Keller, 2006) have been altered by the advent of the Internet (the Web and e-mail), providing a new channel for marketing and doing business, and its own Internet marketing literature (cf. Chaffey *et al.*, 2003). Many of us may have bought books from Amazon or cheap airline tickets from easyJet, or bought/sold common (or not-so-common) items on eBay.

In their book *Blown to Bits: How the New Economics of Information Transforms Strategy*, Evans and Wurster (2000) provide interesting insights into the changing nature of marketing and the role of IS. They argue that the transfer of information is a 'trade-off between richness and reach' (p. 23). **Reach** refers to the number of people who share particular information, with *richness* being a more complex concept combining: *bandwidth* (the volume of information transferred per time period), *customization* (fitting information to the recipient's particular requirements), *interactivity* (two-way exchange between parties involved), *reliability* (relating to sharing information with trusted partners, or not, as the case may be), *security* and *currency* (after Evans and Wurster, 2000, p. 25).

Traditionally, organizations have had a choice – to increase the reach of their products or services at the expense of the richness of the product or service, or vice versa. The concepts can be applied to various dimensions of a product or service, such as its marketing, as well as the nature and delivery of the product or service itself. Evans (2000, p. 37) gives the following example from marketing:

> Newspaper advertisements reach a wide range of possible customers but have a limited, static content. Direct mail or telemarketing are a bit richer in customization and interactivity but are much more expensive, and, therefore, have to be targeted . . . . A salesman giving his pitch offers the highest level of customization, dialogue and empathy but with only one customer at a time.

However, Evans and Wurster (2000) argue that with the advent of powerful information and communication technologies (such as the Internet), this historic trade-off between richness and reach may no longer apply. Although there may still be a trade-off as before, technologies such as the Internet allow *both* the reach and richness dimensions to operate at higher levels than before, allowing a sea change in the strategic opportunities available.

Increased reach implies greater choice on the part of the consumer. With the Internet, this choice extends beyond the number of possible service providers to include the possibility of purchasing 24 hours, 7 days a week, 365 days a year. The extended reach may, e.g., benefit the consumer through the ability to find precisely what is required and/or the lowest cost, perhaps via websites which allow an easy comparison of prices/products across a range of vendors (cf. Levitt and Dubner, 2005 regarding life insurance prices; or try it yourself at Kelkoo (http://www.kelkoo. co.uk/)).

Competing on richness has two dimensions – richness with respect to the *consumer*, or the *product/service* (Evans and Wurster, 2000, p. 149). With respect to the consumer, this refers to customer-specific marketing to a 'segment of one' (Evans and Wurster, 2000, p. 149). Increasing the richness of the product or service might include increasing the availability of technical and product/service information as well as 'branding' of the product, service or the firm itself.

However, just because these technological opportunities exist does not replace 'common [business] sense' and considered judgement. For example, extending choice 'beyond a certain point implies bewilderment' (Evans and Wurster, 2000, p. 64) and the search costs may be too 'exhausting to be exhaustive, and people rarely do it' (Evans and Wurster, 2000, p. 103). Personalized advertising which is regarded by consumers or potential consumers as 'junk mail' may undermine rather than enhance a firm's relationship with its customers (Zuboff and Maxmin, 2002, p. 265). Porter (2001) suggests there should be a retrenchment in strategic thinking to the core disciplines of business and strategy, from which new business opportunities relating to the Internet and allied technologies will spring. As Shapiro and Varian (1999, pp. 1–2) note: 'Technology changes. Economic laws do not.'

Role of information systems in supply chain management

Supply chain refers to all those business processes that create and deliver a product or service, from concept through development and manufacturing or conversion, into a market for consumption (Poirier and Bauer, 2001). The Global Supply Chain Forum identified eight key processes that make up the core of supply chains: customer relationship management, customer service management, demand management, order fulfilment, manufacturing flow management, procurement, product development, and commercialization and returns. These processes are based on a manufacturing company and would obviously vary depending on the type of organization and the nature of the industry. Supply chain management requires the integration of key supply chain processes and associated information flows (The Global Supply Chain Forum, 2003).

Supply chains have moved from being an ancillary concern to a major component of organizational strategies (Lancioni *et al.*, 2003). This is due to a range of factors, including increasingly competitive business environments. Organizations are increasingly globalizing and customers have become more demanding, expecting shorter response times, shorter product cycle times and greater customization of products. In order to remain competitive, supply chains have to be more dynamic and responsive. Maximum value needs to be exploited from supply chains to drive competitive growth, competitive advantage and profit.

The focus of supply chains should not only be on one organization. Organizations are increasingly involved in mergers, acquisitions, strategic alliances, collaborations or outsourcing, with the aim of generating new products or developing products more quickly from conception to marketplace, increasing organizational size, accessing other organizations' core competencies or new markets, enhancing the organization's position in an existing market or decreasing organizational risk (Cohen and Mankin, 2002; Manchester, 2003). Consequently, products and services are more and more likely to go through the supply chains of a number of organizations (suppliers, manufacturers, distributors, retailers, customers) before reaching the end customer. The different supply chains will collectively contribute to the value and cost of end products or services and the level of customer satisfaction. Maximum competitive advantage will be achieved by focusing on a network of supply chains rather than individual supply chains.

SIS are playing a greater role in advancing supply chains and supply chain networks (SCN). In particular, the Internet provides a worldwide, standardized, low-cost infrastructure that is easily accessible, and the Web offers a simple mechanism for sharing information between different organizations and people. Many organizations have used the Internet to develop organizational networks such as intranets and extranets. Intranets are used for sharing information between employees within the boundaries of an organization, while extranets extend information access to external partners such as suppliers and customers (see Table 6.4).

Moreover, the Internet can be used to support a range of technologies such as e-mail, collaboration tools, ERP systems, document management workflow systems, and electronic data interchange (EDI) that can be used for conducting supply chain processes and activities.

There are many strategic benefits in using Internet-related technologies (IRTs) for supply chains and SCNs. First, IRTs can enable supply chain processes to be developed and streamlined. Second, the technology supports the integration of supply chain processes internally and externally with business partners. This can lead to more co-ordinated and coherent SCNs. Benefits can be achieved in the form of improved visibility, timely information and material flows, superior inventory management, better decision-making, optimized performance and enhanced levels of customer service and responsiveness. Internet technology can also contribute to organizations' abilities to provide on-demand SCNs. Real-time information is being shared up and down the network, allowing organizations to sense and respond readily to changes in the marketplace.

Using IRTs across SCNs may also raise many concerns or issues. For example, organizations may be concerned that the technology will change the relative level of power that different supply chain players have across the SCN. Moreover, they are likely to be concerned with ensuring that the information that is being shared across the SCN remains secure and only accessible by the relevant parties.

Supply chain: current applications

There are many applications of IRTs appearing across supply chains and SCN. Early adopters of the Internet focused on its use for transacting with customers through e-commerce. e-Commerce is the process of buying and selling online. There has been a huge increase in e-commerce in fields such as retailing, publishing and entertainment.

A more recent drive has been in the area of e-business. e-Business embraces all those front-end and back-end applications that enable organizations to conduct these transactions. Early adopters of e-business applications typically focused on self-service applications, internal processes and improved cost reductions and administrative efficiencies (Ash and Burn, 2003). More advanced users are now widening their efforts to higher-level operational and strategic processes. The focus has shifted to gaining strategic

Table 6.4
Distinctions between intranet, extranet and the Internet

Intranet	Sharing of information within the firm
Extranet	Sharing of information with key partners (e.g., clients or suppliers)
Internet	Sharing information with clients, prospective clients and other interested parties outside the organization; usually conducted via a 'public access' website

advantage through an evolutionary model of organizational change (Farhoomand and Wigand, 2003). Moreover, organizations are now recognizing the benefits that can be sought through deploying the technology in business-to-business communication and have begun concentrating their efforts on integrating interorganizational supply chain processes with external business partners (Ash and Burn, 2003).

A range of prominent e-business applications are appearing. These include areas such as customer relationship management, customer service, marketing, order fulfilment, logistics, materials replenishment and procurement. Cagliano *et al.* (2003) explored the adoption of IRT in supply chain processes by using a large sample of European manufacturing firms in three main categories of supply chain processes: e-commerce (sales, customer service and support), e-procurement (purchasing activities), e-operations (order processing, tracking, production planning and scheduling, inventory management, transportation planning). Their findings illustrated that the adoption of the Internet varies from partial adoption to complete adoption through the supply chain, and applications tend to start with external processes and subsequently integrate internal ones. Only the most advanced organizations have adopted the Internet in all three categories, providing the greatest pay-offs.

A few examples of e-business applications can be provided. Ford Motor Company has a web-based order fulfilment system that can be accessed by their key dealerships. The system streamlines the order fulfilment process by allowing dealers to order vehicles, determine the make-up of vehicles, cancel orders and access other dealers' orders online. There are many benefits to using an online system, including a greater depth of information available regarding the availability of cars. This leads not only to increased choice for the customer and their vehicle requirements being better met, but also to reduction in inventory and obsolescence of stock. Furthermore online reports and greater analysis can support and improve future business planning.

Another example is the legendary extranet transportation application provided by Federal Express (FedEx). FedEx is the largest express transportation company in the world, with about 30 per cent of the market share and annual revenue in excess of $19 billion (Farhoomand *et al.*, 2003). They were one of the first organizations to make an easy-to-use extranet system and tracking service available to customers for arranging the delivery of goods and for tracking the progress of goods to their destination. This has the advantages of providing an all-around better level of service to customers and increasing the likelihood that customers will continue to choose their services.

Another application area that has grown considerably in recent years is e-procurement. One of the biggest costs for organizations is business-to-business procurement, with many organizations spending 50 to 60 per cent of their revenue on goods and services (Kalakota and Robinson, 2001; Presutti, 2003). e-procurement involves automating the procurement process for procuring goods and services used directly in the production process or indirectly to support the production process, and is aimed at improving performance. It can positively impact the competitiveness and profitability of organizations by allowing requisitions to be processed more quickly, reducing search times for employees, controlling corporate-wide spending, improving strategic sourcing of suppliers and reducing material costs and inventory levels (Ariba, 2004; Pressuti, 2003; Subramaniam and Shaw, 2002). Factors such as the level of standardization in the products being procured and the participation of suppliers may, however, limit the value of e-procurement.

From the former it is clear that IT and IS are critical strategic weapons of the 21st century. The next section explores how organizations align such a weapon to the achievement of an organization's strategic goals.

Strategic alignment and strategic information systems planning

IS strategies have been attracting interest from the 1970s (Table 6.5), and since then many terms have been used to address the alignment of IS and business strategy. A frequently used term is SIS planning (SISP). Numerous authors have defined SISP in slightly different ways because of the rapidly changing environment of the IS/IT field. One of the most regularly used definitions, and the one used in this work, stems from Earl (1993), who stated that SISP should target the following areas:

- Aligning investment in IS with business goals.
- Exploiting IT for competitive advantage.
- Directing efficient and effective management of IS resources.
- Developing technology policies and architectures.

The first two areas are concerned with information systems strategy (ISS) (how the organization can organize, manage and exploit its information, systems and IS), the third is concerned with information management strategy (IMS) (why an organization should be doing what it is doing) and the fourth with IT strategy (what sort of

Table 6.5
Historical development of SISP

IS role	Issues	Terms	Typical definitions
Data processing	*Technical issues* Computer efficiency and automation	—	Alignment not an issue
Management information systems	*Business issues* Strategy, resource allocation, management support	Alignment co-ordination linkage	'Co-ordination, which can be achieved when the ISS is derived from the organization strategy' (Lederer and Mendelow, 1989, p. 6)
Strategic information systems	*Competitive Issues* Competitive advantage, innovation, technology	Alignment fit integration balance	'The internal fit and functional integration between business strategy and IS/IT strategy and how this integration is important to gain a competitive advantage' (Henderson and Venkatraman, 1993)
Knowledge management	*Organizational issues* Group interaction, organizational learning, change management	Fusion fit integration harmony	'Continuous process of conscious and coherent interrelation of all components and personnel of the business and IT in order to contribute to the organization's performance over time' (Ekstedt *et al.*, 2005, p. 1)

The authors would like to acknowledge the contribution Markus Tesucher has made to the development of this table.

physical infrastructure, in terms of hardware, software and telecommunications, is needed to support the ISS).

The definition of SISP of Doherty *et al.* (1999), which is based on the work of Michael Earl, concludes that SISP is the process of identifying a portfolio of computer-based applications to be implemented which is both highly aligned with corporate strategy and has the ability to create an advantage over competitors.

Literature on the alignment of IT/IS with business has tended to mirror the developments in the evolution of IS (see Table 6.5).

The last two views, especially the penultimate one, come closer to Henderson and Venkatraman's (1993) alignment model in that it covers elements of information management (third point) and information technology strategy (ITS) (fourth point). The strategic alignment model (SAM) was developed by Henderson and Venkatraman (1993) (see Figure 6.1). It conceptualizes strategic alignment in terms of two dimensions: strategic fit (between the internal and external domain, something with which Earl does not agree) and functional integration (between the business and IT domain).

The core of the model in Figure 6.1 is that, in order to generate value, all four quadrants must be co-ordinated 'accordingly'. Smaczny (2001) criticizes the model for its mechanistic, sequential view of the strategic planning within a company. Rather, Smaczny feels that strategic planning should be organic, emergent and fluid. One could, however, argue that the SAM only describes the alignment conceptually, and does not inherently prescribe a way of operationalizing the alignment as a process; in other words, it is good at suggesting what needs to happen, but weak at suggesting how it is to happen. Almost all later models (cf. Broadbent and Weill, 1993; Luftman, 2000), which sought to develop and enhance SAM, are firmly based on the original model, with the same ideological, noun-holistic (substantive view) of a business.

Figure 6.1
Strategic alignment model

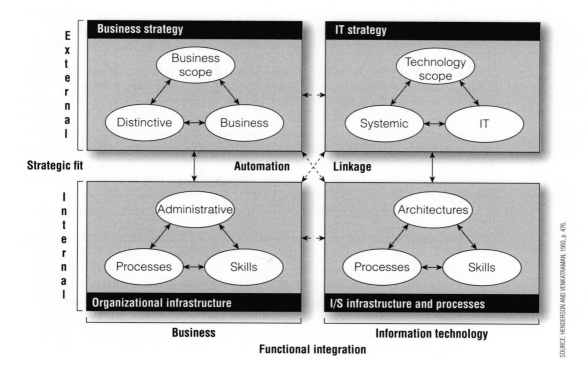

SOURCE: HENDERSON AND VENKATRAMAN, 1993, p. 476.

However, to assist managers in implementing a SAM, several tools and techniques can be used to inform the strategic planning process; the most notable ones are:

- Critical success factor analysis can be used to identify those competencies (or pressure points) where the organization must excel in order to outperform the competition, e.g., customer service, market image. It can be used to interpret the business objectives in terms of actions required and where technology can be used to identify the key information and application needs of the organization, as well as for assessing the strengths and weaknesses of existing systems.

- Porter's five forces analysis can be used to analyze the interactions with customers, suppliers and competitors, and evaluate the threat of new entrants and substitute products. The implications from these forces have to be understood in order to avoid being disadvantaged by them and to recognize opportunities to gain competitive advantage.

- Porter's value chain analysis considers industry information flows and how they affect the business. The objective is to identify strategically important applications that directly support chosen business strategies or enable new business strategies to be developed and implemented and to improve the position of the organization within the industry value chain. This involves looking at the primary (e.g., sales, distribution) and secondary activities (e.g., human resource management, IT) of a business and searching for ways to link them together.

- SWOT analysis, where the critical strengths, weaknesses, opportunities and threats are brought together, is a very useful step in all strategic formulation, because a strategy that is not based on a combination of internal strengths and external opportunities is not likely to be efficient.

- The Boston Consulting Group Matrix can be used to determine whether the business's portfolio of products is balanced within the overall strategy and whether the linkages between the various businesses are sound in the long term. Each quadrant looks at the IT/IS provision (factory, support, turnaround and strategic).

All these techniques have a common theme of looking internally and externally to find innovation and new, better ways of doing things, usually supported by appropriate and relevant technology. They require that people with knowledge of the business and its environment, as well as the technology, use them. All the tools and techniques described can be used for the business strategies of the organization, and equally to create the IS/IT subsets of the business strategies. If the IS/IT managers use the same set of models and tools as the rest of the organization, they can become actively involved in determining the future potential that IS/IT has to offer the organization.

According to Earl's (1989) multiple methodology, SISP consists of three stages:

- **Develop an information systems strategy that is concerned with what to do.** The outcome is the long-term, directional plan of what to do with IT. It should be business led and demand oriented and concerned with exploiting IT for the good of the business. This part of SISP is mainly a business management issue.

- **Develop an information technology strategy that is concerned with how to do it.** The result is a technology framework or architecture that shapes and controls the IT infrastructure and at the same time supports business needs. This part of SISP is mainly the concern of the IT functional department.

- **Develop an information management strategy.** The outcome is an IS/IT governance model where the structure between the corporate centre and business units, as well as the role and structure of users, is defined. Management responsibilities and processes should also be stated and the arrangement has to be such that the needs of the business and the chosen technological infrastructure are aligned.

Earl (1989) suggests that both top-down and bottom-up methods should be used for SISP, as this gives a comprehensive overview of the situation from all angles and stakeholders.

Accordingly *top-down* methods should be used to clarify business strategies and needs as well as the potential contribution of IT applications. This should result in the alignment of IT and IS investment with business needs. *Bottom-up* methods should be used to discover gaps and map where an enterprise is in IS terms. The result should be improved specialist-user relationships and knowledge of where IT is important for the competitive functioning. The third part of the methodology is termed *inside-out*. This implies designing an organizational and technological environment that enables innovations to happen, thus making it possible to gain competitive advantage from IS/IT. This is sometimes thought of as 'thinking out of the box' and 'breaking the china'.

Galliers (1991) further developed the Earl framework and states that IS/IT strategy has four distinct components: the information strategy, the ITS, the information services strategy and the change management/implementation strategy.

The first three categories are comparable to Earl's groups; however, Galliers (1991) emphasizes that the appropriateness of the critical assumptions behind the strategy has to be questioned in light of the changing environment and changing perceptions, thereby stressing the emergent part of strategy making. The fourth category in Galliers's model is the change management or implementation strategy, which should identify what organizational change will be needed for the ISS to be successful, and when it should be implemented and by whom, thereby taking into account surprising outcomes, emergent issues and the changing organizational environment.

A new generic management tool, the balanced scorecard, can be used to consider the role of SIS, and the value they can bring to a business.

The balanced scorecard is a strategic management system developed by Kaplan and Norton during the 1990s, which allows businesses to drive their strategies based on measurement and feedback. According to Kaplan and Norton (1996), the balanced scorecard addresses an organization's inability to link its long-term strategy with its short-term actions.

Balanced scorecards can be used to clarify and update the current strategy and communicate it throughout the company, align goals with the strategy and identify strategic initiatives. This can be quite useful when businesses try to align IS/IT strategy to business strategy. The scorecard provides a framework for managing the implementation of strategy and at the same time allowing the strategy to evolve in response to changes in the technological environments.

According to Van Grembergen and Van Bruggen (1997), the balanced scorecard is a useful framework to evaluate IS/IT. Such an evaluation includes assessing the contribution of a specific IS or project as well as the general IS/IT function. However, IS/IT-based perspectives to the balanced scorecard have to differ slightly from the general ones suggested by Kaplan and Norton. The reason for this differentiation is that IS/IT is an internal service supplier where the users are its clients and the contribution is to be considered from management's point of view.

Van Grembergen and Van Bruggen (1997) suggest that the four dimensions of the scorecard for an evaluation of the IS/IT function should be:

- **Measuring corporate contribution.** This dimension should be divided between short-term financial evaluation and long-term evaluation of IS/IT projects and the IS/IT function itself.
- **Measuring user orientation.** This element should be divided between the internal customers of the IT department and the company's customers in the case of interorganizational systems.
- **Measuring operational excellence.** This element should measure the development of new IS and computer operations.
- **Measuring future orientation.** This dimension should measure the preparation of the IS/IT staff for the future, the preparation of the applications portfolio for the future and the effort put into researching new emerging technologies.

Kaplan and Norton (1993) argue that if the balanced scorecard is to become a strategic management system, measurements alone are not enough; the outcome must be used and acted upon by management. Keeping this in mind, Van Grembergen and Van Bruggen (1997) propose the following steps to effectively implement an IS/IT balanced scorecard as a strategic management system:

- Presentation of the concept of the IS/IT balanced scorecard technique to senior management and IT management as necessary.
- Collecting information regarding corporate and IS/IT strategy and IS/IT metrics already in use for performance measurement.
- Developing company-specific IS/IT balanced scorecard according to the principles of Kaplan and Norton.

Thus, the balanced scorecard can enable a strategy-focused IS/IT organization by creating a shared language between IS/IT and the business. Van Grembergen (2000) states that the balanced scorecard methodology also provides a measurement and management system that supports the IS/IT and business alignment process and proposes that this should be done through a cascade of business and IS/IT balanced scorecards. This cascade of balanced scorecards should fuse business and IS/IT, thereby aligning the IS/IT governance process to the corporate governance model and helping the integration of business and IT decisions, resulting in the alignment of IS/IT and business strategy.

Van Grembergen and Saull (2001) recommend constructing business and IS/IT scorecards simultaneously and that this should be looked upon as an evolutionary project with a formal project organization. The scorecard should be considered as a supportive mechanism for IS/IT and business alignment. However, the balanced scorecard is a technique that will not be successful unless business alignment and IS/IT work together and act upon the measurements of the scorecards.

The identification of the relevant objectives and opportunities in the four dimensions of the scorecard is then matched against the needs of the various stakeholder groups of the organization. Resources and actions are directed towards areas that will affect the achievement of future, known business objectives and measured by the value that it actually delivers to the defined stakeholders, thereby developing the strategy. When deployed in this way, the balanced scorecard transforms strategic planning into an ongoing process, which sees the business as a process (a verb) rather than a substantive 'thing' (a noun), which allows business to conceptualize SISP in a different, more complex, adaptive way.

We are going to conclude this chapter by providing a brief overview of some of the emerging technologies. It is the job of the reader to consider how these can impact upon the strategic opportunities for organizations.

Emerging technologies and applications

Organizations should be continually exploring potential applications of emerging and more sophisticated technologies and ways of incorporating them into their SIS infrastructures, in order to gain competitive advantage, sustain position as a cutting-edge organization, gain business value and so on. In particular, mobile and wireless technologies and radiofrequency identification (RFID) tags are expected to be emerging technologies that will play a key role.

Mobile and wireless technologies are already being applied in a variety of business areas, but they have not been fully exploited. Early applications have focused more on customer support and sales. For example, computing engineers are using mobile and wireless technologies to provide customer service and support. They are connecting to customer sites remotely and viewing the internal layout of components in customer machines while analyzing wiring diagrams or maintenance procedures to solve computer hardware problems. Organizations should continually seek out new applications for mobile technologies, as they offer business benefits such as remote access and improved flexibility.

Another technology that is provoking huge interest is RFID tags. These are tags that are attached to products and signal their presence over radio frequencies. The strategic benefits and applications of RFID tags across the supply chain are plentiful, including the ability to track the whereabouts of goods in real time as they pass from factory floors, to warehouses, through distribution chains, to retailers and then at point of sale (Harvey, 2003). It also allows organizations to guard against stock shortages, cut down on theft and monitor their sales more closely and efficiently than before. A further potential application of RFID technologies is for reverse logistics, e.g., the capability to launch a product recall (Dempsey, 2003). This is something that particularly affects food manufacturers and pharmaceutical companies, who must have the capability to create and withdraw specific batches of product from anywhere in the world at a moment's notice.

Pilot schemes have been undertaken in the retail industry. Tesco set up a pilot scheme that attached tags to high-value goods and took pictures of customers as they picked them up from the shelves (Harvey, 2003). Marks & Spencer undertook a month-long trial that used RFID tags to provide an automatic picture of stock levels and the location of individual items (Stewart, 2003). In 2003 Wal-Mart requested that their 100 biggest suppliers begin fitting RFID tags by 2005, and that all the goods supplied by them would be tagged by 2006 (Harvey, 2003; Niemeyer et al., 2003). There are many potential opportunities for using RFID tags for improving the level of corporate intelligence. As RFID tags decrease in price and improve in efficiency, different organizations and a broader range of industries will be looking to implement and use the technology more broadly.

Summary

This chapter has explored the foundations of what we mean by information, information systems and strategy. It has established that:

- Information is a major resource within organizations.

- This information is used for a range of activities and as such needs to be appropriately managed.

- A key activity within organizations that requires appropriate and timely information is decision-making.

- Such decision-making is intimately linked to strategy and strategic development.

The chapter has demonstrated that:

- The advanced information and communications technologies currently available provide a host of opportunities, through a myriad of configurations of IT and IS.

- This allows organizations to gain a competitive advantage through either improved efficiency or enhanced value through greater effectiveness, and in effect expand the opportunities generated through a greater 'constructible space'.

- Over the years, IT/IS has changed both the fundamentals of business and the ways of 'doing' business in a pursuit for greater competitive advantage.

- Such a dynamic will continue to shape the future business landscape, and makes understanding SIS a critical component of any business education.

Chapter questions

1. Discuss the classification of information systems related to the system's complexity and the purpose it serves.

2. Critically analyze the role of information systems in strategy.

3. Comment on the key facets underlying the concepts of strategic alignment and SIS planning.

References

Ansoff, H. I. (1957) 'Strategies for diversification', *Harvard Business Review*, 35(5):113–124.

Anthony, R. N. (1965) *Planning and Control Systems: A Framework for Analysis*, Boston: Harvard Business School Press.

Ariba (2004) Ariba: Enterprise Spend Management Solutions. [Online]. http://www.ariba.com. Last accessed 12 February, 2004.

Ash, C. G., and Burn, J. M. (2003) 'Assessing the benefits from e-business transformation through effective enterprise management', *European Journal of Information Systems*, 12: 297–308.

Begg, C. E., and Connolly, T. M. (eds.) (2002) 'Web technology and DBMSs', in *Database Systems: A Practical Approach to Design, Implementation and Management*, 3rd edn., Harlow: Addison-Wesley.

Berners-Lee, T. (2000) *Weaving the Web: The Past, Present and Future of the World Wide Web by Its Inventor*, London: Orion Business.

Broadbent, M., and Weill, P. (1993) 'Improving business and information strategy alignment: Learning from the banking industry', *IBM Systems Journal*, 32:162–179.

Bucklin, R. E., Lehmann, D. R., and Little, J. D. C. (1998) 'From decision support to decision automation: A 2020 vision', *Marketing Letters*, 9(3):235–246.

Cagliano, R., Caniato, F., and Spina, G. (2003) 'e-Business strategy: How companies are shaping their supply chain through the Internet', *International Journal of Operations & Production Management*, 23(10):1142–1162.

Chaffey, D., Mayer, R., Johnston, K., and Ellis-Chadwick, F. (2003) *Internet Marketing: Strategy, Implementation and Practice*, 2nd edn., FT Prentice Hall.

Cohen, S. G., and Mankin, D. (2002) 'Complex collaborations in the new global economy', *Organisational Dynamics*, 31(2):117–133.

Davenport, T. H., and Prusak, L. (2000) *Working Knowledge: How Organizations Manage What They Know*, Boston: Harvard Business School Press.

Davis, G. B., and Olson, M. H. (1984) *Management Information Systems: Conceptual Foundations, Structure and Development*, 2nd edn., Singapore: McGraw-Hill.

Dempsey, M. (2003, November 26) 'In search of the missing link', in Understanding supply chain execution, *Financial Times*, 2–3.

Doherty, N. F., Marples, C. G., and Suhaimi, A. (1999) 'The relative success of alternative approaches to strategic information systems planning: an empirical analysis', *Journal of Strategic Information Systems*, 8(3):263–283.

Earl, M. J. (1989) *Management Strategies for Information Technology*, Hemel Hempstead: Prentice-Hall.

Earl, M. J. (1993) 'Experiences in strategic information systems planning', *MIS Quarterly*, 17(1):1–24.

Ekstedt, M., Jonsson, N., Plazaola, L., and Molina, S. E. (2005) An Organization-Wide Approach for Assessing Strategic Business and IT. [Online]. http://www.uni.edu.ni/sarec/fec/Sitio/NormanVargas/An%20approach%20for%20assessment%20of%20Business-IT%20strategy%20alignment.pdf. Last accessed 14 March, 2006.

Evans, P. (2000) 'Strategy and the new economics of information', in Marchand, D. A., Davenport, T. H., and Dickson, T. (eds.), *Mastering Information Management: Complete MBA Companion in Information Management*, Financial Times Mastering Series, pp. 37–42, Harlow, UK: Pearson Education.

Evans, P., and Wurster, T. S. (2000) *Blown to Bits: How the New Economics of Information Transforms Strategy*, Boston: Harvard Business School.

Farhoomand, A., and Wigand, R. (2003) 'Special section on managing e-business transformation', *European Journal of Information Systems*, 12:249–250.

Farhoomand, A. F., Ng, P. S. P., and Conley, W. L. (2003) 'Building a successful e-business: The FedEx story', *Communications of the ACM*, 46(4):84–89.

Galliers, R. D. (1991) 'Strategic information systems planning: myths reality and guidelines for successful implementation', *European Journal of Information Systems*, 1(1):55–64.

Galliers, R. D., and Baker, B. S. H. (1994) 'Introduction', in Galliers, R. D., and B. S. H. Baker (Eds.), *Strategic Information Management: Challenges and Strategies in Managing Information Systems*, Oxford, UK: Butterworth-Heinemann. Management Readers Series.

Galliers, R. D., Leidener, D. E., and Baker, B. S. (2003) *Strategic Information Management: Challenges and Strategies in Managing Information Systems*, Woburn, MA: Butterworth-Heinemann.

Groth, L. (1999) *Future Organizational Design: The Scope for the IT-Based Enterprise*, Chichester, UK: John Wiley and Sons. Wiley Series in Information Systems.

Hamel, G., and Prahalad, C. K. (1994) *Competing for the Future: Breakthrough Strategies for Seizing Control of Your Industry and Creating the Markets of Tomorrow*, Boston, MA: Harvard Business School Press.

Harvey, F. (2003, November 26) 'RFID tags: Retailers give a good reception to radio control', in Understanding supply chain execution, *Financial Times*, p. 5.

Henderson, J. C., and Venkatraman, H. (1991) 'Understanding Strategic Alignment', *Business Quarterly*, Winter, 72–78.

Henderson, J. C., and Venkatraman, H. (1993) 'Strategic alignment: Leveraging information technology for transforming organizations', *IBM Systems Journal*, 32(1):472–484.

Jelassi, A., and Enders, A. (2005) *Strategies for e-Business: Creating Value through Electronic and Mobile Commerce Concepts and Cases.* Harlow, UK: FT Prentice Hall.

Kalakota, R., and Robinson, M. (2001) *e-Business 2.0: Roadmap for Success*, Boston: Addison-Wesley.

Kalin, S. (1998) 'The fast lane', CIO *Webbusiness Magazine*. [Online]. http://compnetworking.about.com/gi/dynamic/offsite.htm?site=http%3A%2F%2Fwww.cio.com%2Farchive%2Fwebbusiness%2F040198_harley.html2. Last accessed 10 March, 2006.

Kaplan, R. S., and Norton, D. P. (1993) 'Putting the Balanced Scorecard to work', *Harvard Business Review,* 71(5):134–142.

Kaplan, R. S., and Norton, D. P. (1996) 'Using the Balanced Scorecard as a strategic management system', *Harvard Business Review,* 74(1):75–85.

Kotler, P., and Keller, K. L. (2006) *Marketing Management*, 12th edn., New Jersey, USA: Pearson Prentice-Hall.

Lancioni, R. A., Schau, H. J., and Smith, M. F. (2003) 'Internet impacts on supply chain management', *Industrial Marketing Management,* 32(3):173–175.

Levitt, S. D., and Dubner, S. J. (2005) *Freakonomics: A Rogue Economist Explores the Hidden Side of Everything,* London, UK: Allen Lane.

Luftman, J. (2000) 'Assessing Business-IT Alignment Maturity', *Communications of the AIS,* 4(14):1–51.

Manchester, P. (2003, November 26) 'Outsourcing: Keeping check on a vital partnership', in Understanding supply chain execution, *Financial Times*, 4–5.

Marakas, G. M. (2003) *Decision Support Systems in the 21st Century*, 2nd edn., New Jersey, USA: Pearson Education.

Newell, A., and Simon, H. A. (1972) *Human Problem Solving,* Englewood Cliffs, NJ, USA: Prentice Hall.

Niemeyer, A., Pak, M. H., and Ramaswamy, S. E. (2003) 'Smart tags for your supply chain', *The McKinsey Quarterly,* no. 4. http://www.mckinseyquarterly.com. Last accessed 25 November 2003.

Oz, E. (2004) *Management Information Systems,* 4th edn., Boston: Course Technology, Thomson Learning.

Perez, C. (2002) *Technological Revolutions and Financial Capital: The Dynamics of Bubbles and Golden Ages*, Edward Elgar.

Poirier, C. C., and Bauer, M. J. (2001) *e-Supply Chain: Using the Internet to Revolutionalise Your Business.* San Francisco: Berrett-Koehler.

Porter, M. E. (1980) *Competitive Strategy: Techniques for Analyzing Industries and Competitors,* New York: Free Press.

Porter, M. E. (1985) *Competitive Advantage: Creating and Sustaining Superior Performance,* New York: Free Press.

Porter, M. E. (2001) 'Strategy and the Internet', *Harvard Business Review*, 9(3):62–78.

Porter, M. E., and Millar, V. E. (1985) 'How information gives you competitive advantage', *Harvard Business Review*, July-August, 149–160.

Presutti, W. D. Jr. (2003) 'Supply management and e-procurement: creating value added in the supply chain', *Industrial Marketing Management*, 32:219–226.

Robson, W. (1997) *Strategic Management and Information Systems*, 2nd edn., London: Pitman.

Shapiro, C., and Varian, H. R. (1999) *Information Rules: A Strategic Guide to the Network Economy*, Boston: Harvard Business School Press.

Smaczny, T. (2001) 'Is an alignment between business and information technology the appropriate paradigm to manage IT in today's organisations?' *Management Decision*, 39(10):797–802.

Somogyi, E. K., and Galliers, R. D. (1987) 'Developments in the application of information technology in business', in Galliers, R. D., and Leidner, D. E. (eds.), *Strategic Information Management: Challenges and Strategies in Managing Information Systems*. Oxford, UK: Butterworth-Heinemann. Management Readers Series.

Stair, R., and Reynolds, G. (2006) *Principles of Information Systems*, 7th edn., Boston: Thomson Course Technology.

Stewart, A. (2003, November 26) 'Taking stock of radio tags', in Understanding supply chain execution, *Financial Times*, p. 14.

Subramaniam, C., and Shaw, M. J. (2002) 'A study of the value and impact of B2B e-commerce: The case of web-based procurement', *International Journal of Electronic Commerce*, Summer, 6(4):19–40.

Talvinen, J. M. (1995) 'Information systems in marketing: identifying opportunities for new applications', *European Journal of Marketing*, 29(1):8–26.

TextAnywhere (2005) 'Why Text?' [Online]. http://ws.textanywhere.net/web/WhyText/. Last accessed 10 March 2006.

The Global Supply Chain Forum (2003) 'Definition of Supply Chain Management'. [Online]. http://fisher.osu.edu/logistics/about/mission.html. Last accessed 4 December 2003.

Turban, E., McLean, E., and Wetherby, J. (2004) *Information Technology for Management*. Chichester: Wiley.

United Kingdom Academy of Information Systems (UKAIS) (1999) 'The Definition of Information Systems'. [Online]. http://www.cs.york.ac.uk/ukais/isdefn.pdf. Last accessed 22 September 2005.

Van Grembergen, W. (2000) 'The balanced scorecard and IT governance,' *Information Systems Control Journal*, 2.

Van Grembergen, W., and Saull, R. (2001) 'Aligning Business and Information Technology through the Balanced Scorecard at a Major Canadian Financial Group: Its Status Measured with an IT BSC Maturity Model', *Proceedings of the 34th Annual Hawaii International Conference on System Sciences*, January 2001.

Van Grembergen, W., and Van Bruggen, R. (1997) 'Measuring and improving corporate information technology through the balanced scorecard', *The Electronic Journal of Information System Evaluation*, 1(1).

Vonage (2005) Will VoIP Replace the Telephone System? [Online]. http://www.vonage.co.uk/uk/corp_english/broadcast.html?PR=2005_05_20_2. Last accessed 30 September 2005.

Ward, J. (1995) *Principles of Information Systems Management*. London: Routledge. Routledge Principles of Management Series.

Ward, J., and Peppard, J. (2003) *Strategic Planning For Information Systems*, 3rd edn., Chichester: Wiley.

Werbach, K. (2005) 'Using VoIP to compete,' *Harvard Business Review*, September, 140–147.

Wöber, K., and Gretzel, U. (2000, November) 'Tourism managers' adoption of marketing information systems', *Journal of Travel Research*, 39:172–181.

Zuboff, S., and Maxmin, J. (2002) *The Support Economy: Why Corporations are Failing Individuals and the Next Episode of Capitalism*, New York: Penguin.

7

Marketing measurements and analysis

Luiz Moutinho and Graeme D. Hutcheson

Introduction

In this chapter, we highlight the different types of measurement scales and describe ways in which these can be recorded. We then go on to show how each of these can be analyzed using generalized linear models (GLMs).

Learning objectives

- To identify different types of measurement scales and learn how these can be coded and manipulated.

- To introduce generalized linear models as a method for modelling these data.

- To appropriately interpret model parameters and model-fit statistics.

- To provide a theoretically consistent approach to data analysis.

Measurement scales

There are many ways to categorize data, and a number of different schemes have been proposed that use a variety of categories and subdivisions (cf. Agresti and Finlay (1997), Lindsey (1995), Rose and Sullivan (1993), Sarle (1995) and Tal (2001)). Here we shall distinguish between just three scales of measurement, unordered categorical, ordered categorical and continuous, as these represent the minimum requirement necessary to make decisions about which modelling technique is appropriate to use. It is worth noting that assigning variables to particular scales of measurement is not always obvious, as some data may be legitimately classified in a variety of ways depending on the properties of the attribute, the coding scheme used to represent this attribute, the number of observations recorded, the type of analyses that are planned and the hypotheses that are to be tested. The classification of data into different scales of measurement is not, therefore, an exact science.

Unordered categorical data

Unordered categorical data consist of a number of separate categories that do not have any inherent order. For example, gender is recorded using unordered categories as a person is either male or female. Any person must fall into one or the other of the categories – there is nothing in between. Unordered categorical data consisting of two categories are commonly referred to as *dichotomous*. Other examples of dichotomous categories are success–failure, died–survived, employed–unemployed, yes–no and two-group experimental units (e.g., group A and group B). Unordered categorical data may also have more than two categories, as with blood group (A, B, AB, O), make of car (Ford, Nissan, BMW), residential status (owner-occupied, privately rented, councilrented), experimental group (group A, group B, group C) and religious belief (atheist, Christian, Muslim). These data are commonly referred to as *polytomous*.

Recording the data

An unordered categorical variable can be represented using a numeric system whereby data are reassigned specific numbers which have no intrinsic meaning other than identifying each of the categories. Table 7.1 shows how a polytomous unordered categorical variable indicating the manufacturer of a family's main transport may be represented numerically using a coding scheme. In this example, the coding scheme consists of the numbers 1 through 6; however, the make of car may be represented using any unique numbers. Also included in this table is a frequency count showing the number of respondents who chose each make of car.

Applying mathematical operations

Although numerically 1 is less than 4, and 1 plus 2 does equal 3, such mathematical operations cannot be applied to the codes used to represent the make of car. It is clear that when dealing with the make of car, a Ford (coded 1) is not less than a Jaguar (coded 4) and a Ford (coded 1) plus a Nissan (coded 2) does not equal a

BMW (coded 3), as there is no direct correspondence between the make of car and the coding scheme. As the codes used to represent the make of car are more or less arbitrary, mathematical operations that require an ordered or a measured scale should not be used. For example, greater than and less than relationships do not hold, nor do addition or subtraction.

- A Ford (1) *is not less than* (≮) a Jaguar (4)
- An Alpha Romeo (5) *is not greater than* (≯) a BMW (3)
- A Ford (1) + a Nissan (2) *does not equal* (≠) a BMW (3)
- A Ferrari (6) − a Jaguar (4) *does not equal* (≠) a Nissan (2)

Any statistics using greater than or less than relationships, or addition and subtraction, should not be used on unordered categorical data. When computing an average value, one should therefore not use the median (which uses information about order) or the mean (which uses the actual values of the codes). The measure of average appropriate for unordered categorical data is the mode, which is simply the most frequent category. For the data in Table 7.1, the 'average' family car for the sample is a Nissan (coded 2).

Ordered categorical data

Variables which have a clearly defined underlying ordered categorical distribution are quite rare; however, measurements are frequently gathered and coded in a way that results in ordered data. Ordered categorical data constitute a large percentage of data used in the management field, making their coding and manipulation of particular interest. Ordered categorical data are composed of a number of distinct categories which have an order. For example, a person's highest academic qualification may be a school certificate, a diploma from a college, or a postgraduate degree obtained through prolonged study at a university. These qualifications represent distinct categories in that a person's highest academic achievement will be one and only one of the categories: there is nothing in between. The categories also have an order, in that a school certificate is generally considered to be less advanced than a diploma

Table 7.1
Manufacturer of main family transport: unordered categorical data

Which make of car is your main family transport?		Code 1	Number sold
Ford	❑	1	46
Nissan	❑	2	54
BMW	❑	3	32
Jaguar	❑	4	21
Alpha Romeo	❑	5	12
Ferrari	❑	6	19

and a diploma less advanced than a postgraduate degree. Other examples of ordered categorical data are seniority at work (junior manager, section head, director), judo gradings (yellow, blue and black belts) and poker hands (pairs, triples, full houses, etc.) with perhaps the classic example being found in the armed forces or police service where seniority is explicitly designated by rank.

Recording the data

Ordered categorical data can be recorded from variables having an underlying ordered or a continuous distribution. We will deal with both types here, but will first look at ordered categorical data, which are obtained from a variable having an underlying ordered categorical distribution. The example we will use here is highest academic achievement. The data in Table 7.2 show the highest academic award achieved by a number of people.

The coding scheme used to represent achievement should be regarded as ordered categories, with higher codes representing higher academic achievement. It should be noted that any coding scheme that maintains an ordered relationship between the categories could also have been used. It should also be realized that the differences between adjacent categories need not be standard. The numbers chosen to represent achievement (the code) merely identify relative achievement. For example, an O-level is less of an achievement than a degree, which is itself less of an achievement than a doctorate. The codes themselves do not indicate the actual degree of achievement; they merely identify the position of each qualification in the ordered categories.

A large percentage of the ordered categorical data one encounters will be from variables which have an underlying continuous distribution but have been coded, for whatever reason, as ordered categorical. For example, Table 7.3 shows two variables that have underlying continuous distributions, but are recorded as ordered categorical. A person's mental status may be thought of as having an underlying continuous distribution, as someone could be anywhere on a scale from 'well' to 'impaired functioning'; there are potentially an infinite number of degrees of mental impairment between these extremes. Here the data are recorded using a four-point ordered scale devised more for descriptive convenience than as an attempt to record

Qualification	Code	Frequency
No qualification	1	14
O-level	2	52
A-level	3	28
Degree	4	12
Masters	5	5
Doctorate	6	9

Table 7.2
Highest educational attainment

the underlying distribution as accurately as possible.[1] Similarly, socioeconomic status may be thought of as having an underlying continuous distribution, but the data are recorded using six discrete ordered categories (1, 2, 3, 4, 5, 6). For both of these variables, there is no direct correspondence between the codes used and what is being measured – the codes themselves merely designate ordered categories. It is also the case that the differences between categories may not be standard (i.e., the difference in socioeconomic status between categories 1 and 2 might bear little relation to the difference in socioeconomic status between categories 4 and 5).

Applying mathematical operations

The permissible mathematical operations for ordered categorical data will be illustrated using the example data from Table 7.2. These data represent the highest academic award achieved with higher codes representing higher academic achievement. For these data, information about order is meaningful, which allows statistics that preserve the greater than and less than relationships to be used. Numerically, 1 is less than 2 and 4 is greater than 3. These relationships also hold for the data in Table 7.2 as 'no qualification' represents a lower level of academic achievement than an O-level. Similarly, a 'degree' is a higher achievement than an A-level.

- An O level (2) *is greater than* (>) no qualification (1)
- A degree (4) *is less than* (<) a masters (5)

However, mathematical procedures that add or subtract numbers assigned to the data are not admissible. Numerically, 2 plus 1 equals 3, but this does not apply to achievement, as an O-level plus no qualification does not equal an A-level. Similarly, although 2 multiplied by 3 equals 6, this does not hold for achievement, as an O-level multiplied by 3 does not equal a doctorate (coded 6).

Table 7.3
Continuous variables coded as ordered categories

SOURCE: AGRESTI (1989).

Mental status		Socioeconomic status of parents					
		1	2	3	4	5	6
	Well	64	57	57	72	36	21
	Mild symptoms	94	94	105	141	97	71
	Moderate symptoms	58	54	65	77	54	54
	Impaired functioning	46	40	60	94	78	71

[1] It may be that physicians actually describe mental impairment according to these categories. If this is the case, the four ordered categories given here might be the most appropriate and accurate method of recording mental status.

- An O-level (2) + no qualification (1) *does not equal* (≠) an A-level (3)
- A degree (4) − an A-level (3) *does not equal* (≠) no qualification (1)

Any statistics that use addition or subtraction should not be used with ordered categorical data. When computing the average for such data, one should not therefore use the mean (which uses the actual values of the codes) but can use the median or the mode. For the data shown in Table 7.2, the average highest educational attainment may be represented by the mode (an O-level, coded 2), or by the median (which in this case is also an O-level, coded 2).

Continuous data

A data point (a single observation) on a continuous scale can, in theory at least, assume any value between the highest and lowest points. The only restriction on the number of values possible is the accuracy of the measuring instrument. For example, weight can be measured fairly crudely in pounds using a set of bathroom scales, or can be measured much more accurately in grams using a professional set of medical scales. A person could, at least in theory, assume any weight. This is different to an ordered categorical scale, where categories are distinct.

Recording the data

Some examples of continuous data are relatively simple to record as the information has an easily measured direct numerical representation. For example, Table 7.4 shows average temperature differences measured in degrees centigrade between

Temperature difference (deg C)	Daily gas consumption (kWh)	Temperature difference (deg C)	Daily gas consumption (kWh)
10.3	69.81	15.2	81.29
11.4	82.75	15.3	99.20
11.5	81.75	15.6	86.35
12.5	80.38	16.4	110.23
13.1	85.89	16.5	106.55
13.4	75.32	17.0	85.50
13.6	69.81	17.2	90.02
15.0	78.54		

Table 7.4
Temperature difference and gas consumption

SOURCE: THE OPEN UNIVERSITY (1984).

the inside and outside, and average daily gas consumption for 15 houses in Milton Keynes, in the UK.

Applying mathematical operations

Using the data above in Table 7.4, it can be shown that the greater than and less than relationships can be used:

- 11.4 degrees C *is greater than* (>) 10.3 degrees C
- 69.81 kWh *is less than* (<) 78.54 kWh

Addition and subtraction can also be used:

- 10.3 degrees C + 4.7 degrees C = 15 degrees C
- 99.20 kWh − 11.03 kWh = 88.17 kWh

For continuous data, one may use the mode, median and the mean to represent the average value. Per the data shown in Table 7.4, the mode[2] of daily gas consumption is 69.81, the median daily gas consumption is 82.75 and the mean daily gas consumption is 85.56. The identification of the measurement scale is particularly important as it enables an appropriate technique of analysis to be determined. Here we will show how data taken from the different scales identified above may be analyzed using techniques that form part of the GLM.

Analyzing data using GLM models

GLMs were proposed by Nelder and Wedderburn (1972) and represent a family of statistical tests that can be used to analyze a wide variety of data. They are sufficiently general to be applicable to much social science data and provide a comprehensive set of analytical tools. Of particular importance is the unified theoretical framework that enables certain 'economies of scale' to be realized (for example, the interpretation of the parameter estimates and model-fit statistics are similar, as are model-building techniques and model diagnostics) and a full set of analyses taught within the confines of a typical postgraduate statistics course. Whilst this chapter can only provide an overview of the techniques that comprise the GLM, full details can be found in Dobson (2001), Fahrmeir and Tutz (2001), Gill (2000), Hoffman (2003), Hutcheson and Sofroniou (1999), Lindsey (1997) and McCullagh and Nelder (1989).

The aim of many analyses is to predict (or model) the behaviour of a particular variable. At a very basic level it is possible to predict one variable, to a greater or lesser degree, given information about other variables. For example,

Variable Y can be predicted by Variable X1 and Variable X2.

Variable Y might be wage, educational attainment, test score, share price, success–failure, university chosen or religious affiliation. Variables X1 and X2 could be age, average school grade, gender, nationality, race, attractiveness, weight or attitude to

---

[2]As in this example, the mode is often of questionable value when used with continuous data.

innovation. In short, variables Y, X1 and X2 can be any type of variable recorded on any of the scales described above. Using the concrete example of a particular company's share price, the relationship above could be written as:

Share Price *may be predicted by* Output *and* Market Confidence.

From the relationship above one can deduce that share price may be determined by the company's output and the confidence shown in the market the company operates in. This is not likely to be a perfect relationship, as a number of other variables not represented in the model are also likely to influence share price (such as government policy and exchange rates). The model can be said to consist of three components: the response variable, Y (share price), the explanatory variables, X1 and X2 (output and market confidence) and a function that links the two. These three components form the basis of the GLM, where they are commonly referred to as the random component, the systematic component and the link function.

The GLM can be summarized as:

$$\text{Random Component} \xrightarrow[\text{Function}]{\text{Link}} \text{Systematic Component}$$

with a concrete example being:

$$\text{Share Price} \xrightarrow[\text{Function}]{\text{Link}} \begin{array}{l} \text{Output} \\ and \\ \text{Market Confidence} \end{array}$$

The appropriate link function and analysis technique is dependent upon the level of measurement of the response variable. For example, if the response variable is continuous, the link between the random and systematic components of the model is direct and an OLS (ordinary least squares) regression can be used. If, on the other hand, the response variable is categorical, the link between the random and systematic components of the model is not direct, requiring an analysis technique to be used that does not assume a direct link. The appropriate analysis techniques for the different types of response variables are shown in Table 7.5. All of these techniques are explained in detail below.

Response variable	Link function	Technique*
Continuous	Identity	Ordinary least squares regression
Ordered categorical	Logit	Proportional odds model
Unordered categorical (binary)	Logit	Logistic regression
Unordered categorical (polytomous)	Logit	Multinomial logistic regression

Table 7.5
Generalized linear modelling techniques

*The analysis techniques shown here only provide a minimal set of possible analyses and do not include the full range of GLM models.

Process in action modelling continuous data: ice cream consumption

Modelling continuous data

The data that are to be used here to illustrate the technique are from Koteswara (1970), reported in Hand *et al.* (1994), who present data collected over 30 four-week periods from March 18, 1951 to July 11, 1953. The data show ice cream consumption (pints per capita), the price of ice cream (in dollars per pint), the weekly family income (in dollars) and the mean outdoor temperature (in degrees Fahrenheit). These data are shown in Table 7.6.

Simple OLS regression

The research problem here is to model consumption. For simplicity, here we will only take into account a single explanatory variable, outdoor temperature. The basic relationship we are trying to model is of the form:

Ice cream consumption *may be predicted by outdoor temperature.*

As consumption and temperature are both continuous variables, this relationship can be depicted directly using a scatter-plot (see Figure 7.1).

Table 7.6
Ice cream consumption

Ice cream consumption	Price	Family income	Temperature
0.386	0.270	78	41
0.374	0.282	79	56
0.393	0.277	81	63
0.425	0.280	80	68
0.406	0.272	76	69
0.344	0.262	78	65
0.327	0.275	82	61
0.288	0.267	79	47
0.269	0.265	76	32
0.286	0.282	82	28
0.298	0.270	85	26
0.329	0.272	86	32
0.318	0.287	83	40
0.381	0.277	84	55
0.381	0.287	82	63
0.470	0.280	80	72

➡

Ice cream consumption	Price	Family income	Temperature
0.443	0.277	78	72
0.386	0.277	84	67
0.342	0.277	86	60
0.319	0.292	85	44
0.307	0.287	87	40
0.284	0.277	94	32
0.326	0.285	92	27
0.309	0.282	95	28
0.359	0.265	96	33
0.376	0.265	94	41
0.416	0.265	96	52
0.437	0.268	91	64
0.548	0.260	90	71

Table 7.6
(Continued)

SOURCE: KOTESWARA (1970).

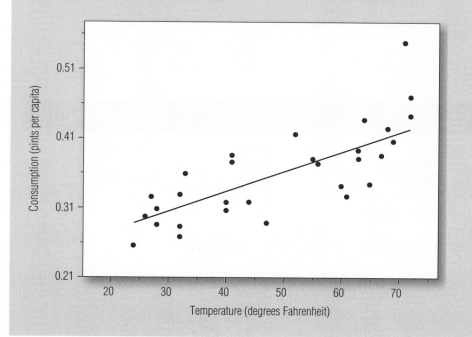

Figure 7.1
An OLS regression model of ice cream consumption and its relationship to outdoor temperature

On the graph, a line is also depicted that has been derived using an algorithm that minimizes the sum of the squares of the distances from each data point to the line (hence it is known as the least-squares technique), producing a line of best fit.

This line describes the relationship between consumption and temperature, and in this case we can see that the relationship is roughly linear and represented quite well by the line.[3] The relationship between consumption and temperature is represented by the slope of the graph. For each unit increase in temperature, consumption is expected to change by a certain amount. This amount is known as the regression coefficient, β. The line of best fit can be described exactly from the regression coefficient and the point where the line crosses the Y axis, α. Readily available statistical software can compute these parameters and these are shown in Table 7.7. From the estimates provided in Table 7.7, one can obtain the intercept (α) and the regression coefficient for temperature (β) to get the equation of the line of best fit. Given a certain temperature (provided that it is within the range of observations recorded during the study), one can predict the amount of ice cream that will be consumed. For example, when the temperature is 50 degrees Fahrenheit, ice cream consumption = 0.2069 + (0.0031 × 50) = 0.3619.

For each unit increase in temperature, per capita consumption of ice cream is expected to increase by 0.0031 pints. This increase in ice cream consumption is the average increase one would expect.

In addition to identifying the parameters α and β, it is also useful to determine how well the model fits the data. Model fit can be determined by comparing the observed scores (the data) with those predicted from the model (the line of best fit). The difference between these two values (also known as the deviation or residual) provides an indication of how well the model predicts each data point. The sum of all the squared residuals is known as the residual sum of squares (RSS) and is essentially a measure of how much the model deviates from the data. A poorly fitting model will deviate markedly from the data and will have a relatively large RSS, whereas a good-fitting model will not deviate markedly from the data and will have a relatively small RSS (a perfectly fitting model will have an RSS equal to zero). The RSS statistic, therefore, provides a way of determining how well the model fits the data. This statistic is also known as **deviance** and is discussed in depth by Agresti (1996, pp. 96–97).

The deviance is a very useful statistic, as it allows the significance of individual and groups of variables within a model to be computed. The significances can be readily obtained by comparing the deviance statistics for nested models. For example, the significance of the relationship between temperature and ice cream consumption can be ascertained by comparing the deviance in the models 'ice cream consumption = α' and 'ice cream consumption = $\alpha + \beta$ temperature'. The only difference between these two models is that one includes temperature and the other does not. Any change

Table 7.7
Regression parameters for a simple regression model of ice cream consumption

	Estimate	Standard error
(Intercept)	0.2069	0.0247
Temperature	0.0031	0.0005
Model: consumption = $\alpha + \beta$ temperature		
Model: consumption = 0.2069 + (0.0031 temperature)		

[3] Although there is a suggestion that the relationship is curvilinear, further analyses (not included in this chapter) reveal that this is not significant. A linear relationship appears to be adequate for these data.

in deviance can therefore be attributed to the effect of temperature. Commonly available statistical software provides these statistics for simple OLS regression models and these are shown in Table 7.8.

For our example of ice cream consumption, the addition of the explanatory variable temperature into the model results in a change in deviance of 0.0755 (RSS_{diff}), which can be assessed for significance using the F-distribution (for a full discussion of this, see Hutcheson and Sofroniou (1999)). It should be noted that this procedure is exactly the same as is used to calculate the t-statistics that are usually provided for each explanatory variable as part of the analysis output. For the model above, the t-statistic for temperature is 6.502, which is directly comparable to the F-statistic. In this case, the square of t equals F ($6.502^2 = 42.28$).

Multiple OLS regression

The model presented above was quite simple in that it only included a single explanatory variable. It is relatively straightforward, however, to extend the OLS regression model to cases where there is more than one explanatory variable. For example, if one was to predict ice cream consumption given outdoor temperature, family income and price, the equation for the regression model would be:

$$\text{Ice cream consumption} = \alpha + \beta1 \text{ temperature} + \beta2 \text{ income} + \beta3 \text{ price}.$$

The parameters for this model shown in Table 7.9 are interpreted in much the same way as for the simple regression model. For example, for a unit increase in price, the amount of ice cream consumed is predicted to go down by 1.0444 pints per

	Estimate	Standard error	t-value	P-value
(Intercept)	0.2069	0.0247	8.375	$4.13e^{-09}$
Temperature	0.0031	0.0005	6.502	$4.79e^{-07}$

From our simple regression model above we can state the relationship between consumption and temperature and the significance of this relationship. Unsurprisingly, it appears that the greater the temperature, the more ice cream is consumed. This relationship is significant.

capita, while taking into account family income and temperature. Similarly, for a unit increase in temperature, consumption is predicted to increase by 0.0035 pints per capita while taking into account price and family income.

Model	RSS	df	RSS_{diff}	F-value	P-value
Consumption = α	0.1255	29			
Consumption = $\alpha + \beta$ temperature	0.0500	28	00755	42.28	$4.79e^{-07}$

RSS represents the deviance in the model

RSS_{diff} is the difference in deviance between the two models

F-statistic = 42.28 on 1 and 28 degrees of freedom

Table 7.8
Measures of deviance for a simple regression model of ice cream consumption

The significance of each parameter and group of parameters for predicting ice cream consumption can be calculated by comparing the deviances of nested models. For example, the significance of price may be obtained by comparing the RSS values for two nested models, one that contains price and one that does not. The change in the RSS value between these two models indicates the effect that price has on the prediction of consumption. A similar procedure is used to ascertain the significance of all parameters in the model. In this case, the deviance statistic of the full model (containing all parameters) is compared to the null model (containing no parameters). The difference between them indicates the effects that all the parameters have on the prediction of consumption.

The calculation of these statistics is shown in Table 7.10. For the models above, the F-value for price is 1.5669 and this is tested on 1 and 26 degrees of freedom, giving a significance value of 0.2218. Price does not appear to be significantly related to consumption (at least within the range of the data collected).

The value of F for this one parameter is analogous to the t-statistic commonly provided by analysis software. The t-statistic computed for price is -1.2518, which corresponds to an F-value of 1.5669 (-1.2518^2). The value of F for all three parameters in the model is 22.1749, which is tested on 3 and 26 degrees of freedom, giving a significance of $P < 0.0001$ (see Hutcheson and Sofroniou (1999) for a discussion of computing F values). Taken

Table 7.9
Regression parameters for a multiple regression model of ice cream consumption

	Estimate	Standard error
(Intercept)	0.1973	0.2702
Price	−1.0444	0.8344
Family income	0.0033	0.0012
Temperature	0.0035	0.0004

Table 7.10
The significance of groups and individual parameters in a multiple regression model of ice cream consumption

Model	RSS	df	RSS$_{diff}$	F-value	P-value
Determining the effect of all three variables					
Consumption = $\alpha + \beta_1$ price + β_2 income + β_3 temperature	0.0353	26			
			0.0902	22.1749	2.45e^{-7}
Consumption = α	0.1255	29			
Determining the effect of price					
Consumption = $\alpha + \beta_1$ price + β_2 income + β_3 temperature	0.0353	26			
			0.0021	1.5669	0.2218
Consumption = $\alpha + \beta_2$ income + β_3 temperature	0.0374	27			

together, all three parameters do enable a better prediction to be made of ice cream consumption.

The OLS regression model for continuous response variables is very versatile and can be adapted in a number of ways to model nonlinear relationships, categorical explanatory variables, interactions and hierarchically structured data. These topics are beyond the scope of this chapter and interested readers should consult the numerous books and articles that deal with these specific topics; cf. Aitken and West (1991), Fox (2002), Hardy (1993), Jaccard *et al.* (1990), Raudenbush and Bryk (2001), Ryan (1997) and Pinheiro and Bates (2000).

Questions

1. Evaluate the models used here and the measures of performance employed.

2. What is the value of the models to an ice cream manufacturer where the weather is very changeable, as in the UK?

Modelling categorical data

The OLS regression model may be applied to continuous response variables, but is not appropriate to use when modelling categorical data. This can be demonstrated using the hypothetical example of whether a sale is made given the years of experience of a sales team. In this case, the response variable is a binary classification of success and the explanatory variable is continuous and represents years of service. A model of 'success' can be represented as:

Success *may be predicted by* the experience of the sales team.

In general, we may expect that the more experience a sales team has, the greater the chance there is that a sale will be made. The scatterplot in Figure 7.2 shows the raw data plotted as empty circles and suggests that this may be the case as the successful sales tend to be clustered more to the right-hand side of the graph. The relationship between success and experience can, however, be more clearly seen using the **probability of success** data, which is shown as filled circles.[4] These data clearly show that the probability of success increases with the experience of the sales team.

From Figure 7.2, it can be seen that the relationship between the probability of success and experience is not linear. As a consequence, the linear OLS regression model shown in the graph does not provide a particularly close fit to the data. Most important, the data are constrained between 0 and 1 (the raw data and the probability measure) but the model is not. At values of experience below 13 years, the model underestimates probability (as the value of probability cannot go below 0, the model actually provides invalid values of probability) whilst it overestimates probability for values of experience above 40 years (again, the model provides invalid values, as probabilities cannot assume values greater than 1). The relationship between the probability of success and years of experience would appear to be S-shaped (sigmoid) rather than linear. Clearly, the linear OLS regression model 'success $= \alpha + \beta$ experience' does not provide an accurate representation of the relationship between the response and explanatory variables and is not, therefore, appropriate for these data.

---

[4]To obtain this graph, experience was categorized and the probability of success calculated for each experience category.

It would be possible, however, to appropriately apply a linear model to these data if the relationship between the probability of success and experience were represented as a straight line. This is what is achieved when the response variable is transformed using a logit (log odds). The logit link transforms the nonlinear relationship

$$\text{probability of success} = \alpha + \beta \text{ experience}$$

into the linear relationship

$$\text{logit (probability of success)} = \alpha + \beta \text{ experience}.$$

Figure 7.3 shows the log odds (the logit) of the probability of success plotted against experience. Of particular interest here is the fact that the data are not now constrained to values between 0 and 1, and a linear model more closely represents the relationship. In essence, the logit has transformed the S-shaped relationship suggested by Figure 7.2 into a linear relationship between the random and systematic component of the model.

It is easy to demonstrate that the logit model provides a better representation of the relationship between success and experience by transforming the predicted values (the model) to show probability rather than the log odds of probability.[5] Figure 7.4 plots the model according to a straightforward measure of probability and clearly shows that the resultant S-shaped model more accurately reflects the relationship between the probability of success and experience than does the OLS regression model shown in Figure 7.2.

Figure 7.2
The probability of success and the experience of the sales team

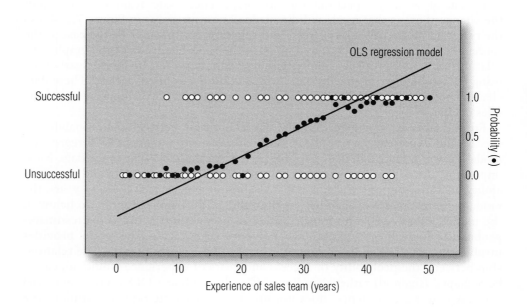

---
[5] For example, a value of -3 on the logit scale can be transformed to a probability by using the inverse of the logit, $e^{-3}/(1 + e^{-3})$, which equals 0.33. Similarly, a value of 2.5 on the logit scale equals a probability of $e^{2.5}/(1 + e^{2.5})$, or 0.924.

Modelling binary data

Logistic regression can be used to model a dichotomous response variable. As the response variable is dichotomous, a logit link is used to link the random and systematic components of the model. The relationship we are to model here is the one between union membership (a member or not) and wage.[6] Using the logit model, this relationship is represented as:

$$\text{logit (probability of being a union member)} = \alpha + \beta \text{ wage}$$

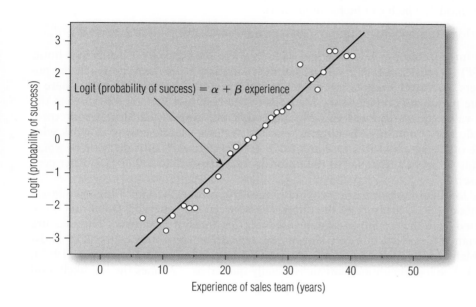

Figure 7.3
The log odds of the probability of success plotted against experience

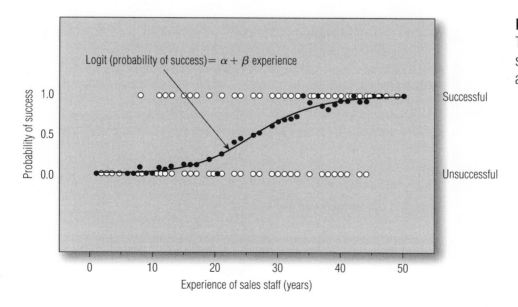

Figure 7.4
The probability of success plotted against experience

[6]These data were obtained from the Current Population Survey (CPS); see Berndt (1991).

This is a very simplified model and merely states that the probability that someone is a union member may be related to the amount they earn. There are clearly many more variables that are likely to play a role in union membership, but these are not included in this example. The scatterplot in Figure 7.5 shows the raw data and the categorized probabilities, and suggests that the probability of someone being a union member increases as wage increases. This is not, however, a particularly strong relationship and it is unclear from the graph whether it is significant.

In order to more accurately quantify the relationship between wage and union membership, we will compute a logistic regression. Table 7.11 shows the parameters for this model, which can be formulated as:

$$\text{logit (probability of union membership)} = -2.207 + (0.072 \times \text{wage})$$

and is interpreted in the following way: As wage increases by 1 dollar per hour, logit (P) increases by 0.072.[7] This is almost identical to the way in which the parameters for an OLS regression model are interpreted. The only difference here is that the parameters relate to the log odds of the response variable rather than the actual value of the response variable. Log odds are, however, difficult to interpret as we do not commonly think in these terms. A more useful statistic to work with are the odds, which in this case are 1.075 ($e^{0.072}$). For each unit increase in wage, the odds of being a member of the union increase from 1 to 1.075 (a 7.5 per cent increase).

The log-likelihood statistic provides a measure of deviance for a logistic regression model (i.e., a measure of the difference between the observed values and those predicted from the model) and can be used as a goodness-of-fit statistic. This measure of deviance for a logistic regression model broadly corresponds to the RSS statistic, which is a measure of deviance for an OLS regression model (see Ryan (1997), p. 267). The log-likelihood statistic is usually quoted as -2 times the log-likelihood

Figure 7.5
Union membership and wage

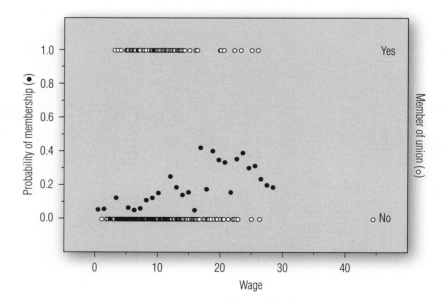

---

[7] Techniques to obtain the confidence intervals associated with these parameters can be found in Sofroniou and Hutcheson (2002).

$(-2LL)$ as this has approximately a χ^2 distribution, thus enabling significance to be evaluated. The interpretation of $-2LL$ is quite straightforward – the smaller its value, the better the model fit (a $-2LL$ score equal to 0 indicates a perfect model where there is no deviance).

Similar to OLS regression, the effect of a particular explanatory variable may be computed by comparing the deviance between nested models (one model including the explanatory variable and the other not) and evaluating significance using the chi-square distribution with the number of degrees of freedom equal to the difference in the number of terms between the two models. For a simple logistic regression model, the effect of the explanatory variable can be assessed by comparing the $-2LL$ statistic for the regression model with that for the null model (see Equation 7.1). These statistics are shown in Table 7.12.

$$-2LL_{diff} = (-2LL_0) - (-2LL_1) \tag{7.1}$$

where $-2LL_0$ is the measure of deviance in the null model $logit(P) = \alpha$, and $-2LL_1$ is the measure of deviance in the model $logit(P) = \alpha + \beta x$.

We have only provided a brief introduction to logistic regression and logit models. More detailed information may be found in Collett (1991), Hosmer and Lemeshow (2000), Kleinbaum *et al.* (2002) and Menard (1995).

The logistic regression model shown above can be generalized to model polytomous ordered and unordered categorical variables. Two techniques that deal with these analytical problems are shown below, the proportional odds model for ordered categorical data and multinomial logistic regression for unordered categorical data.

	Estimate	Standard error	Odds ratio
(Intercept)	−2.207	0.233	
Wage	0.072	0.020	1.075
Model: logit $(P) = \alpha + \beta$ wage			

Table 7.11
Regression parameters for a simple logistic regression model of union membership

Model	Deviance (−2LL)	df	−2LL$_{diff}$	P-value
Logit $(P) = \alpha$	503.084	533		
			12.584	0.0004
Logit $(P) = \alpha + \beta x$	490.500	532		
Model: logit $(P) = \alpha + \beta$ wage				
P is the probability of union membership				
−2LL$_{diff}$ is the difference in deviance between the two models				
Chi-square statistic = 12.584 on 1 degree of freedom				

Table 7.12
Measures of deviance for a simple logistic regression model of union membership

Modelling ordered categorical data

There are a number of methods available to model ordered categorical data: linear-by-linear models, continuation-ratio logits and proportional odds are some of the more widely used. The use of linear-by-linear techniques and continuation-ratio logits is covered by Hutcheson and Sofroniou (1999) and will not be covered in any detail here. The technique we will be dealing with here is the proportional odds model, which can be understood as an extension of logistic regression. A binary logistic regression, models one dichotomy, whereas the proportional odds model uses a number of dichotomies and combines these into a single model.

Recoding the consumption variable from Table 7.6 into three categories ('low', coded as 1 where consumption is below 0.33, 'medium', coded as 2 where consumption is between 0.33 and 0.38, and 'high', coded as 3 where consumption is above 0.38) produces an ordered variable representing the amount of ice cream consumed. As this new coding scheme representing consumption is not continuous, an OLS regression is not an appropriate technique to use. The data can, however, be analyzed as a series of dichotomies, comparing lower with higher groups. In this case, low consumption is compared to medium and high, and then low and medium are compared to high. Using this method of categorizing the data enables the order to be accounted for as comparisons are being made between lower and higher levels of the variable ($Y \leq j$ and $Y > j$) and is unaffected by the actual codes chosen to represent the categories. The model assumes that the effect of the explanatory variables is the same for each cumulative probability and provides a single parameter for the variable. If the errors are independently distributed according to the standard logistic distribution, we get the ordered logit model shown in Equation 7.2.

$$\text{logit } [P(Y > j)] = \alpha + \beta \text{ temperature} \tag{7.2}$$

The parameters for the model 'logit $[P(Y > j)] = \alpha + \beta$ temperature', where P is the probability of being in a higher consumption category, are shown in Table 7.13. As two comparisons have been made in this model, there are two parameters for the intercepts. Of more interest, however, are the parameters associated with the explanatory variable 'temperature'. For each unit increase in temperature, logit $[P(Y > j)]$ increases by 0.128. The log odds of being in a higher consumption category compared to a lower one increases by 0.128. The odds of being in a higher consumption category compared to a lower one increases by 1.137 for each unit increase in temperature. Within the limits of the observations made in this study, each time the

Table 7.13

Parameters for a proportional odds model of ice cream consumption

	Estimate	Standard error	Odds ratio
Comparison (1)	4.993	1.539	
Comparison (2)	7.727	2.068	
Temperature	0.128	0.035	1.137
Model: logit $[P(Y \leq j)] = \alpha + \beta$ temperature			

temperature increases by 1 degree, the odds of consuming more ice cream increase by 13.7 per cent. The hotter it gets, the more ice cream is consumed.

The significance of the overall model and the explanatory variable can be computed in much the same way as for a binary logit model. That is, the deviances are compared between nested models. Table 7.14 shows the deviance statistics for the model and shows that the addition of the variable 'temperature' leads to a significant reduction in the deviance. Temperature is therefore a significant predictor of the category Y.

The proportional odds model shown below included just three categories of the response variable. The model is, however, easy to generalize to greater numbers of categories and also additional categorical and continuous explanatory variables. For more information on the proportional odds model see Agresti (1996), Agresti and Finlay (1997), Clogg and Shihadeh (1994), Fox (2002) and Powers and Xie (2000).

Modelling unordered categorical data

A logit modelling technique that can be used to analyze unordered categorical data is multinomial logistic regression. It is important, however, to distinguish between this model and the log-linear model, a technique that can also be used on categorical data. The basic difference is that a multinomial logistic regression distinguishes between a single response variable and a set of explanatory variables, whereas a log-linear model treats every variable as a response. Multinomial logistic regression is a univariate model that explicitly models a single response variable. The two techniques are, however, similar, as evidenced by the fact that when all explanatory variables are categorical the multinomial logistic regression models correspond to log-linear models. As most applications are concerned with predicting a single response variable,[8] we will concentrate on the multinomial technique; it applies to a single response variable and can be understood as a simple generalization of the logistic regression model. Whilst a full description of log-linear models is beyond the scope of this chapter, detailed information may be found in Agresti (1990), Anderson (1997), Christensen (1997), Simonoff (2003) and Zelterman (1999).

Multinomial logistic regression allows each category of an unordered response variable to be compared to an arbitrary reference category providing a number of logistic regression models. For example, if one were to model which of three supermarkets is likely to be chosen by a customer, two models could be computed,

Model	Deviance (−2LL)	−2LL$_{diff}$	df	P-value
Logit $[P(Y > j)] = \alpha$	60.947			
Logit $[P(Y > j)] = \alpha$ + β temperature	39.052	21.895	1	0.0004
−2LL$_{diff}$ is the difference in deviance between the two models				

Table 7.14 Measures of deviance for a proportional odds model of ice cream consumption

[8]And, it must be said, to maintain consistency with the other techniques presented in this chapter.

one comparing supermarket A with the reference category (supermarket C) and one comparing supermarket B with the reference category. The multinomial logistic regression procedure therefore outputs a number of logistic regression models that make specific comparisons. When there are j categories, the model consists of $j - 1$ logit equations which are fitted simultaneously.

Multinomial logistic regression is basically multiple logistic regressions conducted on a multi-category unordered response variable that has been 'dummy coded'. To demonstrate this technique we will use an example of supermarket choice behaviour (see Hutcheson and Moutinho (1998) and Moutinho and Hutcheson (2000)). The aim of this analysis is to model which supermarket someone is likely to choose given their salary and whether they use a car.[9] The model is of the form shown in Equation 7.3.

$$\log\left[\frac{P(Y = j)}{P(Y = j')}\right] = \alpha + \beta_1 \text{ salary} + \beta_2 \text{ car} \tag{7.3}$$

This equation simply represents a comparison between one supermarket ($Y = j$) and the reference supermarket ($Y = j'$). This is the odds of being in one category compared to the other and is computed as a log, hence this is a logit model (log odds).

The parameters for the model are shown in Table 7.15.

Table 7.15
Parameters for a multinomial logistic regression model of supermarket choice

Supermarket	Parameter	Estimate	Standard error	Odds ratio
	(Intercept)	3.126	0.773	
Kwik Save	Salary	−0.005	0.001	0.995
	Car(l)	−1.662	0.780	0.190
	(Intercept)	3.022	0.741	
Tesco	Salary	0.000	0.001	0.774
	Car(l)	−1.976	0.752	0.139

Model: $\log\left[\dfrac{P(Y = j)}{P(Y = j')}\right] = \alpha + \beta_1 \text{ salary} + \beta_2 \text{ car}$

j' = reference category = Sainsburys

car(l) = use a car, reference category = no car

---

[9]The original data contains many more variables; these have just been chosen for the purpose of illustration.

As the multinomial logistic regression is essentially multiple logistic regressions, the interpretation of the parameters is very similar. The parameters are provided as logits and refer to a comparison between the identified supermarket and the reference category (Sainsburys). For a unit increase in salary, the log odds on someone shopping in Kwik Save compared to Sainsburys goes down by 0.005. For a unit increase in salary, the odds of someone shopping in Kwik Save compared to Sainsburys is 0.995:1. Put another way, Sainsburys attracts wealthier shoppers. For a unit increase in car,[10] the log odds of shopping in Tesco as opposed to Sainsburys is 1.976 lower. For car users compared to non-car users the odds of shopping in Tesco as opposed to Sainsburys is 0.139:1. Sainsburys attracts more car users.

The significance of the overall model and the explanatory variables can be computed in much the same way as for a binary logit model. That is, the deviances are compared between nested models. Table 7.16 shows the deviance statistics for a model including salary and car use and for models where individual and groups of variables have been removed. The significance of the changes in deviance ($-2LL$) are also shown.

You will note that there are 4 degrees of freedom associated with the first comparison, as two parameters have been removed from two models (two separate logistic regressions have been computed, one comparing Kwik Save and Sainsburys and one

Table 7.16

Measures of deviance for a multinomial logistic regression model of supermarket choice

Model	Deviance ($-2LL$)	$-2LL_{diff}$	df	P-value
Determining the effect of all explanatory variables				
$\log\left[\dfrac{P(Y=j)}{P(Y=j')}\right] = \alpha$	124.804			
		45.584	4	<0.0005
$\log\left[\dfrac{P(Y=j)}{P(Y=j')}\right] = \alpha + \beta_1\,\text{salary} + \beta_2\,\text{car}$	79.220			
Determining the effect of salary				
$\log\left[\dfrac{P(Y=j)}{P(Y=j')}\right] = \alpha + \beta_1\,\text{salary} + \beta_2\,\text{car}$	79.220			
		31.986	2	<0.0005
$\log\left[\dfrac{P(Y=j)}{P(Y=j')}\right] = \alpha + \beta\,\text{car}$	111.206			
Determining the effect of price				
$\log\left[\dfrac{P(Y=j)}{P(Y=j')}\right] = \alpha + \beta_1\,\text{salary} + \beta_2\,\text{car}$	79.220			
		11.298	2	0.004
$\log\left[\dfrac{P(Y=j)}{P(Y=j')}\right] = \alpha + \beta\,\text{salary}$	90.518			

---

[10] The variable car has been dummy coded here to indicate no car (0) and car (1), which is the reference category. A unit increase in car therefore provides a comparison between those with a car and those without.

comparing Tesco and Sainsburys), whilst there are 2 degrees of freedom associated with the other models as there is a single parameter removed from the two models. These are combined statistics for the overall model – it should be noted that individual comparisons are also typically provided by analysis packages. That is, while there is an overall significance assigned to the car, there is also an indication of how significant this variable is when distinguishing between individual supermarkets. If, for example, Tesco and Sainsburys are both out-of-town stores which require patrons to use a car, whereas Kwik Save is an in-town store without a car park, the variable car might be significant in the model, but may only show a significant effect when predicting attendance between Tesco and Kwik Save or Sainsburys and Kwik Save, but not Sainsburys and Tesco.

We have only managed to provide a very general and brief introduction to the multinomial logistic regression model here. Further information about this model and other related techniques for analyzing unordered categorical data can be found in Agresti (1990, 1996), Fox (2002) and Venables and Ripley (2002).

Summary

- This chapter has identified key issues in measurement scaling and coding for subsequent statistical modelling.

- It provided an introduction to generalized linear models (GLMs).

Chapter questions

1. Discuss the three components which form the basis of generalized linear models.

2. Which GLM techniques should be applied when:

- The response variable is continuous and the link function is an identity?
- The response variable is ordered categorical and the link function is the logit?
- The response variable is unordered categorical (binary) and the link function is the logit?
- The response variable is unordered categorical (polytonous) and the link function is the logit?

3. What is the measure of deviance that is associated with OLS regression with the GLM approach?

References

Agresti, A. (1989) 'Tutorial on modelling ordinal categorical response data', *Psychological Bulletin*, 105:290–301.

Agresti, A. (1990) *Categorical Data Analysis,* John Wiley.

Agresti, A. (1996) *An Introduction to Categorical Data Analysis,* John Wiley.

Agresti, A., and Finlay, B. (1997) *Statistical Methods for the Social Sciences,* 3rd edn., Prentice-Hall.

Aitken, L. S., and West, S. G. (1991) *Testing and Interpreting Interactions,* 2nd edn., Sage.

Anderson, E. B. (1997) *Introduction to the Statistical Analysis of Categorical Data,* Springer-Verlag.

Christensen, R. (1997) *Log-Linear Models and Logistic Regression,* Springer-Verlag. Springer Texts in Statistics.

Clogg, C. C., and Shihadeh, E. S. (1994) *Statistical Models for Ordered Variables,* Sage.

Collett, D. (1991) *Modelling Binary Data,* Chapman & Hall.

Dobson, A. J. (2001) *An Introduction to Generalized Linear Models,* 2nd edn., Chapman & Hall.

Fahrmeir, L., and Tutz, G. (2001) *Multivariate Statistical Modelling Based on Generalized Linear Models,* Springer-Verlag. Springer Series in Statistics.

Fox, J. (2002) *An R and S-PLUS Companion to Applied Regression,* Sage.

Gill, J. (2000) *Generalized Linear Models: A Unified Approach,* Sage. Quantitative Applications in the Social Sciences.

Hand, D. J., Daly, F., Lunn, A. D., McConway, K. J., and Ostrowski, E. (1994) *A Handbook of Small Data Sets,* Chapman & Hall.

Hardy, M. A. (1993) 'Regression with dummy variables', in Lewis-Beck, M. S. (ed.), *Regression Analysis,* Sage. International Handbooks of Quantitative Applications in the Social Sciences, Volume 2.

Hoffman, J. P. (2003) *Generalized Linear Models,* Allyn & Bacon.

Hosmer, D. W., and Lemeshow, S. (2000) *Applied Logistic Regression.* Wiley-Interscience. Wiley Series in Probability and Statistics.

Hutcheson, G. D., and Moutinho, L. (1998) 'Measuring preferred store satisfaction using consumer choice criteria as a mediating factor', *Journal of Marketing Management,* 14: 705–720.

Hutcheson, G. D., and Sofroniou, N. (1999) *The Multivariate Social Scientist: Introductory Statistics Using Generalized Linear Models,* Sage.

Jaccard, J., Turrisi, R., and Wan, C. K. (1990) *Interaction Effects in Multiple Regression.* Sage. Sage University Paper Series on Quantitative Applications in the Social Sciences.

Kleinbaum, D. G., Klein, M., and Pryor, E. R. (2002) *Logistic Regression,* 2nd edn., Springer-Verlag.

Koteswara, R. K. (1970) 'Testing for the independence of regression disturbances', *Econometrica,* 38:97–117.

Lindsey, J. K. (1995) *Introductory Statistics: A Modelling Approach,* Oxford University Press.

Lindsey, J. K. (1997) *Applying Generalized Linear Models.* Springer-Verlag. Springer Texts in Statistics.

Menard, S. (1995) *Applied Logistic Regression Analysis.* Sage. p. 106. Quantitative Applications in the Social Sciences.

McCullagh, P., and Nelder, J. A. (1989) *Generalized Linear Models,* 2nd edn., Chapman & Hall.

Moutinho, L., and Hutcheson, G. D. (2000) 'Modelling store patronage using comparative structural equation models', *Journal of Targeting, Measurement and Analysis for Marketing,* 8(3):259–275.

Nelder, J., and Wedderburn, R. W. M. (1972) 'Generalized linear models', *Journal of the Royal Statistical Society A,* 135:370–384.

The Open University (1984) MDST242 *Statistics in Society, Unit A5: Review,* 2nd edn., The Open University Milton Keynes. Figure 2.13.

Pinheiro, J. C., and Bates, D. M. (2000) *Mixed-Effects Models in S and S-PLUS.* Springer. Statistics and Computing.

Powers, D. A., and Xie, Y. (2000) *Statistical Methods for Categorical Data Analysis,* Academic Press.

Raudenbush, S. W., and Bryk, A. S. (2001) *Hierarchical Linear Models: Applications and Data Analysis Methods,* 2nd edition, Sage. Advanced Quantitative Techniques in the Social Sciences.

Rose, D., and Sullivan, O. (1993) *Introducing Data Analysis for Social Scientists,* Open University Press.

Ryan, T. P. (1997) *Modern Regression Methods,* John Wiley.

Sarle, W. S. (1995) 'Measurement theory: Frequently asked questions', *Dissemination of the International Statistical Applications Institute,* 4th edn., Wichita: ACG Press, pp. 61–66.

Simonoff, J. S. (2003) *Analyzing Categorical Data,* Springer-Verlag. Springer Texts in Statistics.

Sofroniou, N., and Hutcheson, G. D. (2002) 'Confidence intervals for the predictions of logistic regression in the presence and absence of a variance-covariance matrix', *Understanding Statistics: Statistical Issues in Psychology, Education and the Social Sciences,* 1(1):3–18.

Tal, J. (2001) *Reading Between the Numbers: Statistical Thinking in Everyday Life,* McGraw-Hill.

Venables, W. N., and Ripley, B. D. (2002) *Modern Applied Statistics with S,* 4th edn., Springer.

Zelterman, D. (1999) *Models for Discrete Data,* Oxford University Press.

Part four
Keeping existing customer processes (order fulfilment)

8 **Market value chain management**

9 **Customer relationship management and marketing insights**

10 **Operations and marketing programming**

11 **Distribution product category management and new delivery channels**

Good order fulfilment is at the heart of a successful organization. Without it, customers will not return and the organization will die.

Chapter 8 deals with market value chain management. Topics covered include supply chain management, lean manufacturing, the role of human resources and the increasing importance of technology. In addition, a comparison is made between the operations and marketing viewpoints of supply/value chains. Several 'process in action' notes illustrate how an automotive-part manufacturer was proactive in seeking improvements in the supply chain by working closely with both their customers and suppliers, and how their world-class leadership in their core process, combined with their position in the chain, was exploited to achieve this.

Chapter 9 introduces customer relationship management (CRM) and marketing insights. It explores networks of relationships, in particular within the marketing domain. It also introduces topics ranging from customer experience, long-term customer value and business processes to business re-engineering. In the first of two 'process in action' notes, Gartner's building block model is suggested as a valuable approach to CRM, and four steps to success are identified: set the strategic context, define customers and relationships, create the agenda for change and change the organization. In the second note (using UIA Insurance as an example), the benefits of *not* outsourcing and handling the company's own call centre activities are cited.

Chapter 10 presents operations and marketing programming. It covers issues such as product delivery systems, production systems, functional silos, management integration, conflicts and cultural differences. The first of two 'process in action' notes describe how a multifunctional team in ICI, re-engineered a highly complex industrial process to change not only the process itself but the way the whole industry operated. The second note demonstrates how a combination of product modularization and application of new technology enabled BMW Mini to offer customers greater perceived choice at little extra product cost.

Finally, Chapter 11 presents distribution product category management and new delivery channels. It stresses that the topic is a vital element of marketing strategy as an 'order fulfilment' process. It involves logistics management, channel decisions, channel management, retailing and inventory management. The 'process in action' note describes how a leading retailer, Tesco, categorizes their products and distributes them appropriately using different outlet types and distribution systems.

8

Market value chain management

Geoff Southern and Luiz Moutinho

Introduction

In this chapter, we will begin to consider business processes concerned with achieving customer satisfaction. Many successful businessmen have said that we should aim at more than just satisfying customers. For example, Sir Tom Farmer, founder of the Kwik-fit garage services organization, in setting targets for customer satisfaction coined the phrase 'customer delight'. With such targets, and starting from small beginnings in Edinburgh, Kwik-fit grew to be the leading UK supplier of replacement private vehicle tyres, exhausts and batteries. This was achieved by competing on low price, instant part availability and a fast fitting service conducted by personable and motivated staff. Most of Farmer's success could be attributed to good marketing, combined with astute management of his supply and distribution networks to achieve quick delivery of parts and service at competitive prices.

Learning objectives

- To consider production of goods and services in a historical context.

- To discuss concepts of value-adding market supply chains.

- To consider value-adding market supply chains as business processes.

- To consider the role of the human resource in value-adding market supply chains.

- To discuss the increasing importance of technology in managing value-adding market supply chains.

- To compare the operations and marketing views of supply/value chains.

We will first look at traditional approaches to the goods and service product production process, before taking a generic view of this as a set of business processes. (In fact, there is some repetition here of concepts considered in Chapter 1.) Concepts of value chains are then considered, beginning with Porter's strategic view, before moving onto the more operational supply chain management view and then the 'lean organization' view. The importance of satisfying and motivating the human resource of organizations, employees or internal customers, is considered, and finally the role of technology in managing the supply chain is assessed.

In this chapter, several project case notes from a single company will be used to both illustrate concepts and endorse the learning objectives. The company is John McGavigan Automotive, now part of the Advanced Decorative Systems group (2006), and their products, production processes and place in the automotive supply chain are briefly described below.

Process in action John McGavigan automotive

Introduction to the company

McGavigan manufacture instrument facia components for the automotive industry. Their products are seemingly simple: the part of the dashboard instrument panel that is usually black with graduations painted on it to indicate, e.g., the speed of the car. The primary manufacturing process involves the printing of several identical facia impressions onto large plastic sheets by means of a 'silk screen' method. This is followed by cutting into individual instrument-sized components. The manufacture of the product is more complicated than it appears. Starting with a translucent plastic sheet, several coats of black paint are applied to ensure evenness of appearance from a back lighting system for night driving, followed by additional coats for each of the two or three lighter-tone colours of the indication pattern. As such there are opportunities to produce quality errors of several types, e.g., scratches, paint blemishes from handling before dry or from a paint overload and areas of thin paint and pinholes which can only be seen when driving at night.

McGavigan supply to the instrument suppliers of many world vehicle manufacturers. Main customers are located in the USA, UK, Germany and Japan.

McGavigan's product quality is closely monitored by all vehicle instrument manufacturers to different quality systems; indeed, a quality visit is often indicated by an appropriate national flag flying above the company offices.

McGavigan are a third-tier supply company, after the car manufacturers and the instrument manufacturers. They, in turn, are supplied by plastic sheet manufacturers and by paint manufacturers. Being a third-tier company does not preclude McGavigan from being proactive in managing the supply chain; indeed, they consider themselves to be world-class in the specialized products they manufacture. Furthermore, their position as supplier to most of the world's leading vehicle manufacturers gives them opportunities to transfer any process improvements which they develop and thus enhance their reputation as world leaders. The four examples which follow in this chapter illustrate how McGavigan are proactive in seeking improvements in the supply chain by working closely with both their customers and suppliers, and how their world-class leadership in their core process, combined with their position in the chain, is exploited to achieve this.

Questions

1. Draw a diagram showing McGavigan's position in the supply chain.

2. What power and influence do you think McGavigan have in the supply chain?

Business and production in an historical context

History shows that it is in the nature of economic development that industry starts from a foundation of craftsmanship and individuality of a product or service. In embryo craft-based economies, manufacture began with the receipt of an order. Perhaps *commission* would be a better word than *order*, as the design of the artefact to the wishes of the purchaser was part of the manufacturing process. Purchasers were comparatively rich, and there were relatively few of them. Distinguishing between manufacture and service is difficult here. Although something is made, the situation also displays many facets that we now attribute to a service situation. For example, a wide range of customer requirements were met (heterogeneity), and if customers could not be accommodated immediately they would possibly go elsewhere and the opportunity for a 'sale' was lost. (This is termed **perishability.**)

With economic growth, an increasing number of people could afford to buy artefacts and services that were once thought of as luxury items, although they were usually willing to forgo the individuality still offered to their richer neighbours. As a result, markets grew, introducing economies of scale, first recognized by Adam Smith in his *Wealth of Nations*, and prices became lower, causing markets to grow further. Thus, a cycle of market growth and price reduction came into existence, and factories arose where labour was specialized, making only part of the product or undertaking only part of the service.

Economy of scale enabled owners of factories to implement the policy of division of labour, dividing work into short-duration interconnected tasks and enabling workers completing a task to become specialized, and fast, in continuously employing a very narrow range of skills. In addition, the continuity achieved removed the need to relearn jobs and skills frequently when restarting work, eliminating the learning curve needed to get to peak operational effectiveness. Ultimately, many tasks were mechanically automated to some degree, deskilling the work and improving intrinsic quality by reducing the chance of human error. Some factories gained sufficient markets to become very specialized, make only one product and compete purely on the basis of low price. The underlying secret of successful factory production lay in detailed specification of products and parts, and in the ability to achieve these specifications to ensure changeability of parts. Remington, the US manufacturer, was early in the field, using lessons learned from their existing typewriter factory to improve the manufacture of firearms (Cortada, 1993). Ford also capitalized on the concept of changeability with the Model T car, reducing the price from $825 in 1908 to $395 in 1923, and increasing the production rate from 27 cars per day to 2000 cars per day (BBC, 1994). However, there were always people with more money who would pay higher prices for something completely different, or one of a 'limited edition'. There still are. So, depending on price asked, or volume produced, a range of types of factories emerged.

Where product or service demand was high enough to justify a factory delivering a single product or service, a production system designed around the product was adopted. Here material passed along line-flows of specialized processes in the case of manufacture, or people underwent a standard sequence of treatments in the case of services, until the product or service was completed. Great efforts were made to 'balance flow', designing work stages and tasks in the flow line to have equal duration times, and hence ensure that workers in particular were not left idle, waiting for work. Managerial effort was placed on the design of the flow-line system and on ensuring good workflows. In the case of Ford, the company expanded upstream to ensure supplies of raw materials, and into transport systems in order to ensure that materials and parts arrived at the right time and at the right place.

Where product or service demand was not high enough to justify a continuous flow-line factory to deliver a single product or service, a process-based design was adopted. Here, similar processes requiring similar operator skills were grouped together into departments or work cells. Different parts and products were then routed through the work cells as appropriate until the product or service was completed. This arrangement allowed different parts and products to be made using common plant and people resources. By employing skilled and flexible workers, and by allowing queues to form and subside at each work-cell, resource utilization could be maximized. This factory system was more flexible than the product-based system in that it could cope with a wide range of parts and products, but on the downside it needed a greater skill base and had material spending more time in queues awaiting the next process. This material became known as **work-in-progress stock**. Managerial effort was placed on the design of material queuing systems to optimize the competing costs of resource utilization and work-in-progress inventory. This is analogous to service situations and the design of service delivery systems to optimize resource utilization with the placation of queuing customers.

The principle of specialization, exhibited as division of labour within factories, was also applied to the management of the whole business. With economies of scale, managers of an organization were able to concentrate on specific aspects of management or the business, such as marketing, sales, research and product or service development, production, personnel (human resource management), finance or accounts. At the same time, the scale of the new businesses challenged the ability of managers to plan and control within them. This resulted in the development of pyramid-shaped organizational structures to present managers with a manageable span of control, and to enable policy decisions made at the top of the pyramid to be cascaded down to operational decisions at the bottom. While this development solved the organizational problems of planning and control, it also resulted in a 'silo culture' and hand-over philosophy, with each specialist manager tending to manage up to, and perhaps just beyond the boundary of, their department before handing over the product, project or problem to the next specialist. This tended to induce localized improvements in working practice and productivity improvement that might be detrimental in another part of the business. In short, it inhibited the tendency to think more holistically in the search for bigger business improvements. The tendency to concentrate on localized improvements was also a failing between companies, with those in supply chains concentrating on getting a better deal from their customers or suppliers rather than working together to reduce total costs and improve the service or lower the price to the final consumer, thus increasing the market or the market share to the benefit of both parties.

A seed change in the approach to management

The last quarter of the 20th century saw a seed change in the approach taken to managing organizations. It came with the realization that organizations were more than techno-economic entities, that they were organic in nature and that social and political factors had to be considered when managing them. It was important to consider the political structure of an organization, and to create a culture in which an individual was both motivated to serve customers, internal or external, and to seek out continuous improvement in how this was done.

Early work on motivation theory by luminaries such as Maslow, McGregor and Hertzberg developed into broader considerations by organizational thinkers, such as Handy and Kantor, of how organizations behave (Huczynski and Buchanan, 2001). Relationships between organizational structure, power, managerial style and the culture of organizations were studied. At the same time, organizations still needed to be supported by the application of scientific method in the search for improvement. Hence total quality management (TQM) and business process re-engineering (BPR) approaches gathered favour (see Chapter 10). Here, motivational elements are closely supported by scientific analysis and process control. (Change is sought, in the case of TQM, by incremental improvement, and by a radical step in the case of BPR.) Even more recently, at the end of the century, the concept of integrating marketing and operational activities in support of strategies that deliver value to the customer was developed (Walters, 1999). The concept is supported by the popularity of integrated business performance measurement systems such as the balanced scorecard. These go beyond consideration of pure financial (outcome) performance measures such as return on investment (ROI) and cash flow, to consider non-financial factors which drive these outcomes – factors such as customer relations, internal operational performance, the knowledge and skills of workforce individuals and the organizational competencies of the organization. Indeed, later consideration of the balanced scorecard emphasized its benefit as a 'strategy driver' (Kaplan and Norton, 1996).

The value of these techniques in supporting company strategy, even in stable markets, is self-evident, but now consumer expectation is changing from an emphasis on low-price mass consumer goods and services to one of high-value differentiation. Walters (1999) states that 'value is determined by the utility combination of price and non-price benefits offered'. In other words, a perception of value is created from a bundle of benefits presented, which include not only price, technical specification and conformance to that specification but also others such as availability, on-time delivery and the feelings aroused in the product purchase or service transaction. The identification of non-price performance measures, as espoused by recent performance measurement systems such as the balanced scorecard, supports the strategic concept of value. Walters goes on to analyze the effect of change in expectation, highlighting a recommendation by Hill (1985) in a much earlier work that management should first define the order-winning criteria of the target market, i.e., those where sales are directly proportional to performance, and set manufacturing-based performance goals based on these. Perhaps we should also add that, while doing this, management must also maintain performance on market-qualifying criteria, i.e., those where a threshold level must be maintained for a product or service to even be considered in a purchasing decision. Related to this, and highly relevant to the discussion, is the difference between 'doing the right things', and 'doing the right things right'. If we were not arguing for integrated management and performance management, it could be said that the first of these is the responsibility of strategic marketers, and the second is that of operational managers.

Underlying all the developments discussed here is a deeper consideration of cause–effect relationships in organizations: a study of value and supply chains in the context of lean manufacture and mass customization. These will now be considered in more detail, first for the value chain internal to an organization, then for the external value chain. The role of the human resource and technology in both will then be discussed.

The internal value chain: activities, systems and processes

The value chain that is internal to an organization is primarily concerned with 'doing the right things right', and the efficiency of the internal system of change. All businesses are concerned with a change of state of some kind. Wild (1980) identified four types of transformation, involving a change of state, possession, place or feeling:

- A change of state in its pure form is represented by manufacture.
- A change of possession is represented by shopkeeping and selling.
- A change of place is represented by public transport and trucking, although many trucking companies now take responsibility for the entire distribution process and call it 'supply chain logistics'.
- A change of personal attribute is represented by any transaction adding knowledge, comfort, prestige, etc.

Of course there are no organizations exhibiting a pure change classification; all combine the three generic categories in various ratios. For example:

- Public transport is primarily a change of place, but the traveller must be given a ticket (change of state from paper spool to tickets), and has feelings of comfort and safety on the journey (personal attribute).
- Education is primarily a change of personal attribute, but the student still needs books and handouts (change of state from blank paper sheets to printed document).
- Even in manufacture the customer has pride of ownership and may be involved in the design or personalization of the product (personal attribute), and has to take delivery (possession and perhaps transport).

It therefore follows that the production of goods and services consists of a series of actions that add value in some way to the material items being produced or perhaps to a personal attribute of the end customer. In 1980, Porter presented a generic value chain model that has become generally accepted as how organizations do business.

In his value chain model, Porter (1980) envisaged a sequential series of five primary activities supported by four underpinning activities. These are as follows.

Primary activities

- **Inbound logistics.** More than purchasing, relating to all of the activities in organizing a reliable supply of all the input materials used by an organization.
- **Operations.** The set of activities to achieve the transformation considered above
- **Outbound logistics.** Delivering the product to the customer.
- **Marketing and sales.** Creation of demand and the selling function.
- **Service.** In support of the product after delivery to the customer.

Support activities

- **Procurement.** Of input resources.
- **Technology development.** Both of the product and the process of transformation.

- **Firm infrastructure.** Satisfying the general organizational requirements concerned with legal and internal planning and external liaison activities.
- **Human resource management.** Ensuring that a motivated and appropriately skilled group of people are available in appropriate numbers to fulfil all of the above activities.

Porter's model indicates the emphasis placed at that time on academic study on manufacturing rather than service industries, and in particular on producer-driven rather than market-driven mass manufacture in the 1970s. If we consider job-shop or service situations, or concepts of mass customization discussed later, it seems more sensible to place marketing and sales much earlier in the chain. Here the customer becomes part of the operational activities, helping in the design of the product or service, or selecting from modular options offered, before and during creation of the product or service. The model also tends to infer that activities in the value chain correspond to functional departments, indicating that at that time, functional silos were predominant, with handovers of material, information or client customers. The concept of the 'internal customer' – the next person in line or the internal recipient of the functional service – was central to the TQM philosophy that came to prominence at the same time.

Work in the 1980s on how to plan and manage change introduced systems that considered fundamentally how we do business, and this has ultimately led to the study of business processes and BPR, described in some detail in Chapter 1, where six generic processes were postulated (based on previously published work): product/service development, order acquisition, order fulfilment, organizational development and co-ordination, predicting futures and data management. [Note that other writers on the subject include a further primary process, acquiring payment, but we have already argued in Chapter 1 that this is part of the order fulfilment (order to payment) process.] Table 8.1 shows an attempt to map these generic business processes against Porter's value chain activities, and this shows that the processes that we propose cross the traditional functional boundaries of Porter's model. Furthermore,

Business process	Activity (after Porter)
▪ Product/service development	▪ Technology development
▪ Order acquisition	▪ Marketing and sales
▪ Order fulfilment	▪ Procurement ▪ Inbound logistics ▪ Operations ▪ Outbound logistics ▪ Service
▪ Organization development and co-ordination ▪ Data management ▪ Predicting futures	▪ Firm infrastructure ▪ Human resource management

Table 8.1
Comparison of proposed business processes with Porter's value chain activities

by adopting a process or systems viewpoint in the design of value chains, a more holistic approach is adopted, and global rather than local improvements in productivity are attainable.

Having constructed a business process framework, there is a tendency to deconstruct business into more manageable parts in much the same way as with traditional management functions. A policy of continuous improvement is often adopted, supported by scientific analysis and resource planning techniques such as:

- MRP and queuing theory in the case of batch manufacturing systems.
- Line balancing and just-in-time (JIT) in the case of mass production systems.
- CPM and PERT in the case of project work.
- Queuing theory in the case of retail and 'personal attribute' service industries.

Process in action John McGavigan (contd.)

The internal value chain: the printing process

In the mid-1990s, McGavigan were making full use of quality circles, although they preferred to call them 'improvement circles', to investigate issues of poor quality. One such issue concerned the poor yield rate of parts as a result of problems in the printing process. (This has already been listed in the introduction to the company.) Several product defects were identified, and a statistical analysis of defective parts showed that most problems were associated with print definition (31 per cent) and surface marks (46 per cent). Brainstorming sessions identified several process parameters that could be causing the defective parts. These were as follows:

Poor definition:

- Insufficient or excess paint applied.
- Inaccurate repositioning of parts on subsequent printing operations.

Surface marks:

- Lack of care in handling.

Several solutions to the problems were developed and installed.

- Insufficient or excess paint applied.

The size of mesh was found changing. This was a result of stretching of the mesh, caused in turn by

frame materials expanding differently with changes in the ambient temperature. A standard frame material was specified, and the ambient temperature was controlled.

The optimum viscosity of paint was determined, and a new supply system devised to ensure that it was maintained. (See later case note.)

Careful design and maintenance of the 'wiper', which pushed the paint through the mesh, was ensured, and the optimum pressure was determined and maintained.

- Paint not fully dry before another part is placed on the production stack, and
- Paint drying too quickly causing surface cracking.

The drying tunnel was redesigned so that parts, instead of being fully dried in the horizontal position on a conveyor belt, after surface drying, entered a vertical orientation. This enabled the parts to be dried more slowly and at a lower temperature to ensure that they were fully dried, but not cracked, on leaving the tunnel. (The drying plant was colloquially known as the 'wicket' dryer.)

Questions

1. From where did the knowledge used here to analyze problems come?
2. From where did the knowledge used here to solve problems come?
3. How does the use of quality circles increase corporate knowledge?

- Shift scheduling in the case of service industries.
- Optimization techniques for decisions such as whether to make or buy, traffic routing, facility location and inventory management.
- Work study for internal process improvement.
- TQM and SQC for quality improvement and conformance to specification.

The next case note, considering the printing process at McGavigan's, illustrates how the principles of work study and statistical quality control were employed to improve product quality.

The external value chain: supply chains

The value chain that is internal to an organization is primarily concerned with 'doing the right things', i.e., identifying what the business of an organization is or should be. It involves identifying the core competencies of the business, and market opportunities that can be exploited using those core competencies.

It has already been stated that customers are increasingly expecting greater variety and personal choice in both consumer products and service transactions. Techniques have been developed to help organizations to determine customer expectation, e.g., market research, and analysis frameworks exist to help match what a company delivers to this expectation, e.g., quality function deployment (Krajewski *et al.*, 2007) and the service quality model (SERVQUAL) (Zeithaml *et al.*, 1990). Consumers expect more choice, both in customization of existing products and services and in more frequent development of new products. They also expect faster satisfaction of need and an increasing level of customer service in terms of delivery speed and enjoyment of service encounter (Macbeth and Fergusson, 1994). These expectations are transferred from consumers to original equipment or service providers, and thence to first-, second- and subsequent-tier suppliers. Thus, supply chains are created where constituent organizations must have the ability to deliver in smaller quantities with a shorter lead time, giving customers the freedom and opportunity to change operational day-to-day orders late in the order cycle. However, in order to offer a degree of financial protection to smaller suppliers and confidence in supply for larger customers, such late changes often take place within a framework of a long-term supply contract based on mutual trust.

Macbeth and Fergusson (1994) specify a number of prerequisites for success in supply chains. These include:

- Capable technologies.
- Flexible processes, achieved by simple changeovers in the case of manufacture and by flexible workers in both manufacture and service.
- Effective communication and information processing, involving trusting relationships and good technology (see next sections).

The next two case notes illustrate how companies in the supply chain can work together to add value in terms of product quality and cost reduction. In the first case note, McGavigan work with suppliers, recognizing that if they delegate one task to a supplier, the value added in terms of better intrinsic product quality and increase in yield, more than offsets the increase in material costs. In the second case note, they work with a customer to redefine what they do, but with the same outcomes. In both cases, they add value to the eventual consumer in terms of overall product price.

The human resource in the value chain

'Our greatest asset is our people.'

We have not attributed the above quotation, as it has now become a cliché used by many chief executives in statements to shareholders and the general public alike (Gittell, 2003). However, as with all clichés, it is founded on truth. But, in order to exploit this asset fully, a company must recognize its value by nurturing good relationships.

Process in action John McGavigan (contd.)

The external value chain: working with a supplier

As part of a wider TQM, a quality circle exercise involving the use of Taguchi methods, it was noted that defects due to poor paint adhesion and inadequate paint being applied increased at the end of a 4 hour shift. This was quickly attributed to increased viscosity of the paint, making it more difficult to 'push' through the silk screen in the printing process. At the time, paint was mixed from powder and fluid at the start of each shift in quantities to last the shift. It was agreed that paint should be mixed in smaller quantities, but this would be time-consuming during manufacture and there would be a high possibility of mistakes in the mixing process with the increase in frequency of mixing and working online. On approaching the suppliers of paint, a mutually beneficial agreement was reached to supply the paint ready-mixed in relatively small-quantity cans. Facilities were installed to stir each can before use, and the paint supply process was changed accordingly. The purchase cost of paint was increased, but the total cost of paint application was reduced.

Question

1. Who has benefited from this change of process? How and why?

Process in action John McGavigan (contd.)

Working on specifications with the customer

The final quality inspection process at McGavigan was a simulation of night driving by closely viewing the component in the dark with synthesized back lighting. Many components were scrapped at this stage because of localized unevenness of light distribution or, even more frequently, pinholes in the printing allowing light through. (These faults were usually not identifiable in daytime inspection conditions.) Faults found at this stage contributed greatly to what was already an intrinsically poor product yield rate (proportion of usable product), and the fact that they were discovered at this late stage obviously had serious cost implications as the value added at this stage was complete. On considering the assembled instrument, rather than just the McGavigan component, it was noted that about 30 per cent of the area of the component was covered by the central instrument boss or the outer casing. McGavigan, and in effect their customers, were therefore rejecting 30 per cent of components for faults which the end-users would never see. A proposal was taken to the customer to inspect the component under conditions simulating it fitted in the instrument, and an agreement to reduce prices accordingly on a shared saving basis was agreed. The outcome was the equivalent to an approximate 10 per cent increase in yield, with insignificant cost of process change.

Question

1. Who has benefited from this change of process? How and why?

Gittell (2003), in an analysis of the success of Southwest Airlines, says that one key to its success has been the promotion of '"relational co-ordination" – that is, strong, trusting partnerships between managers and workers that allow all concerned to execute the mind-boggling intricacies of making an airline run smoothly'. However, Southwest Airlines believe that there is a chain of customers from managers, through employees, to customers, and that if work can be fun, all members of that chain will be happier. 'Employees at Southwest Airlines know how to have fun. The airline's 32 000 employees are encouraged to be themselves, "not robots", at work. At their headquarters in Love Field, Texas, every inch of wall space in the five-storey building is filled with mementos of company gatherings and celebrations (Benitez, 2003).'

There are many schools of thought, both academic and practical, that promote the value of the human element within and between organizations in supply chains. For example:

- In TQM – quality circles, quality training, management support.
- In the organizational development school of managing change.
- In BPR – processes, not 'functional silos', centralized and decentralized debate, empowerment, single point of customer contact (familiarity – 'Hello, I'm Geoff, how can I help you? . . .').
- In the balanced scorecard approach to performance management – specific scorecard devoted to learning and growth of an organization, driving all other performance outcomes.

Underlying all these approaches to improvement are generic principles of employee empowerment, employee development and good communication – up, down and horizontal.

The final case note from McGavigan demonstrates how they enriched the working relationships of their employees, and at the same time added to their product and process knowledge, making them better equipped and motivated to search for quality and productivity improvements.

Process in action John McGavigan (contd.)

The human resource in the value chain: getting closer to the customer

In order to get closer together and create a win-win culture at an organizational level, McGavigan and their customers exchanged shop-floor employees for periods of 2 or 3 weeks. By this mechanism, McGavigan employees could see their products being assembled into the next stage of assembly, note any problems intrinsic in this process and bring them back to the quality circle system which they ran internally. The customer employee could also consider difficulties which McGavigan may have had, and bring their knowledge of using the products to the process of solving them. Production workers from both organizations got to know each other better, and a more direct and meaningful supplier–customer relationship was developed.

Question

1. How will this initiative benefit both the supplier and the customer?

The role of technology

No company can ignore technological advances in the way they do things (process developments), the service or manufactured products they deliver, in the logistics of supply and distribution and in the improvement of communications within and between organizations. We can illustrate the need to keep abreast of technological developments by reference to what has happened to McGavigan since the work reported above.

The work reported here so far has concentrated on process improvement, e.g., improvement of existing processes as demonstrated in improvements in the paint application process, and a radical step in the paint-drying process when the 'wicket' dryer was implemented. Such advances were enabling the company to maintain good relationships with their customers by delivering 5 per cent year-on-year cuts in prices, as the customers expected.

However, even at this time, the company's expertise in printing was being used to enter the market for membrane touch-pad control technology, in control panels for microwave cookers and photocopying machines. (These devices consist of two thin membranes with a non-mechanical contact between them.) Furthermore, the introduction of air-bag safety technology into cars allowed the company to develop lightweight car horn switches which could be placed in the centre of the steering wheel. Existing heavy mechanical switches were proving to be very dangerous to the driver when the airbag activated. Thus, innovations in technology were allowing McGavigan to enter existing product markets with highly improved products which superseded previous products.

But even now, new technology in the form of first optical fibre lighting, and then, liquid crystal displays were superseding existing printing technology, which had been the foundation of company success in the past. McGavigan were aware of this and were able to work with their customers in the exploitation of this technology in the design of products which were both aesthetically more pleasing and able to fit into flatter dashboard instruments and allow greater flexibility in the design of the host vehicles. Such collaboration fully exploited improvements in communication in the supply chain, improvements which began a long time ago with the introduction and transmission of digitized images of car dashboard facia to reduce the likelihood of transposition errors when manufacturing the silk screen tools for printing.

The marketing view: demand value chains and customer value creation

Ultimately, the whole point of a supply chain is to create value for the customer; so perhaps the term *demand value chain* is better than *supply chain* from the marketing viewpoint. Achieving a disciplined approach to customer value creation (CVC) requires adopting a number of ideas or philosophies that are new to many companies. Companies must incorporate a specific set of tools and ideas to move along the path towards profitable growth, as indicated in Figure 8.1.

This section focuses on the marketing viewpoint and the concept of the demand value chain (DVC). The DVC represents the foundation of a set of tools that comprise the overall CVC method, and is focused on understanding how value is created and captured with participants along a value chain. The DVC concept relates most directly to business-to-business companies who exist in a relatively complex ecosystem of value-adding transformations among multiple companies who are working together to deliver a product. One of the fundamental ideas in DVC work is to think of participants in the ecosystem as 'markets of one' rather than segments of many, and to develop a deep understanding of how each participant makes money and why.

What is a DVC?

The DVC takes into consideration how and why value is captured as well as the physical product transformations that occur along the way. To describe the concept of DVC, we think of each of the three components of this tool – demand, value, chain – as discrete building blocks that taken together can help companies understand and drive towards the optimal value exchange. We begin by defining the foundation – the chain of goods and services of all the players within the ecosystem.

The chain in Figure 8.2 defines the steps required to deliver goods and service to a source of demand.

The DVC in Figure 8.3 is constructed differently from the typical supply chain. Rather than following the product flow from left to right, the DVC focuses more on

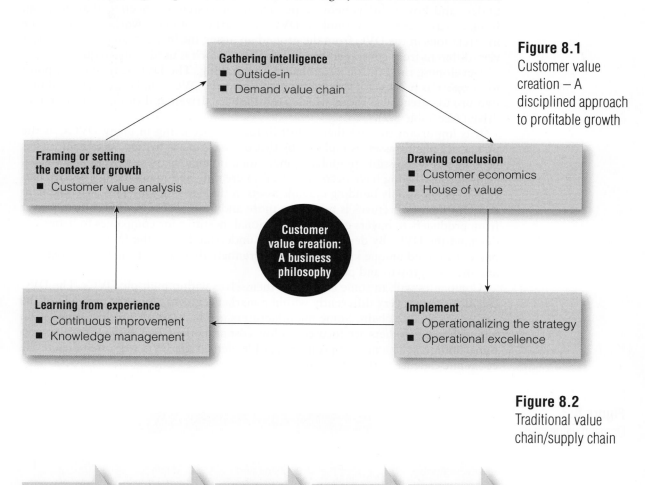

Figure 8.1
Customer value creation – A disciplined approach to profitable growth

Figure 8.2
Traditional value chain/supply chain

the flow of money from right to left. As such, the DVC takes into consideration all those decision-making functions that determine the economics of the chain, including sales and marketing.

Value in the DVC perspective focuses on how economic value is created along the chain and how this value is captured by participants along the chain. By shifting their perspective from traditional supply-side marketing to thinking in terms of DVCs, marketing professionals will be faced with two critical questions they must answer: 'What is driving our product demand?' and 'How are the participants in the value chain deriving value from our products and services?' These questions begin to shift the focus to consider value in quantitative economic terms – 'What is the value received by each of the participants in the value chain?'

Demand defines the need for the value chain to exist in the first place. In many situations, we find that companies do not understand the business they are in because they have not clearly considered the source of demand.

In actuality, the DVC is very complex. The purpose of the DVC, however, is not to predict the forces and factors of consumer demand, but rather to help the company understand how value is being captured in the system of meeting that demand. In many cases, it helps to think of DVCs as 'markets of one'. Working through the interrelations in the DVC from the ground up, using the 'markets of one' concept, is very different from consumer segment analysis (which is used more frequently).

Developing the DVC is a significant undertaking. The DVC is the launch point for a rigorous process for driving profitable growth. DVCs can be characterized into two broad categories: those which are producer driven and those that are buyer driven (see Table 8.2).

It is important to note that a shift in focus is occurring in many DVCs, as the power of tangible assets is replaced by that of intangible activities. As tangible assets become more accessible to global competitors, intangible assets such as knowledge, skills and marketing have become critical to creating and maintaining effective barriers to entry. Simply building tangible assets in the hope that the DVC will maintain constant financial returns is becoming more and more difficult. This shift in power from producers to buyers creates an additional incentive for companies to better understand the DVC. By developing a better understanding of the DVC drivers, companies can build unique knowledge to differentiate themselves from the competition and increase growth and profits.

Companies will, in some cases, find themselves within multiple DVCs. The DVC can also operate very differently within a market segment. Take the example of the automotive value chain. Some manufacturers are focused on product innovation and technology, others are focused on low cost and others may differentiate on customer intimacy. The market positioning of leaders in the DVC will often dictate the economic cadence within the chain.

Figure 8.3
Demand value chain

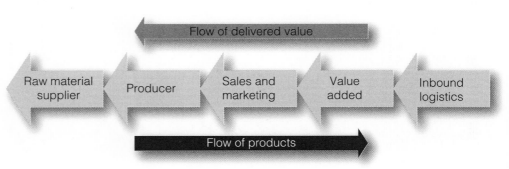

All players are not created equal in the DVC. Power is typically asymmetrical due to concentrated demand, proprietary technology, control of downstream customer access, etc. One of the keys in developing a DVC is to identify these sources of power and understand their impact on your ability to influence desired outcomes.

There is a series of steps to be taken in implementing DVC:

1. **Map the DVC.** The first step in DVC analysis is determining the participants in the specific DVC. As we have mentioned, the DVC should be thought of as an economic ecosystem. Participants work and live together to create value at their respective positions in the chain to deliver value to the end consumer. Understanding who plays in this chain is critical to understanding how value and profits are captured.

   As with most DVC projects, there is considerable learning that occurs by simply mapping the chain, starting with the idea that value flows from right to left. The concepts of thinking from right to left and mapping steps as if the market were made of individual companies, 'markets of one', hold true for the more complex version as well. Once the value chain has been mapped out, the process of identifying where value is created and captured along the chain can begin.

2. **Gather information and generating ideas.** This phase of conducting DVC work is the most iterative in nature. Keep an outside-in mindset: The point here is to get out and talk to customers in person. No other single activity generates more insights than engaging customers in a rigorous process that

Table 8.2
Facets of demand value chains

Parameter	Product based	Buyer based
Triggers of the chain	Industrial capital	Commercial capital
Core strengths	R&D, production	Design, marketing
Entry obstacles	Economies of scale	Economies of scope
Economic sectors	Consumer durables, intermediate goods, capital goods	Consumer non-durables
Examples of industries	Automobiles, computers, aircraft	Apparel, footwear, toys
Type of ownership	Transitional firms	Local firms in developing countries
Network approach	Investment based	Trade based
Network structure	Vertical	Horizontal

is focused on understanding and building value. In addition to 'customers', other stakeholders within the DVC should be included in direct collaboration as well. Add quantitative rigor to quantitative understanding: Developing a thorough quantitative understanding of the DVC may be hard work, but it is always worth the effort. Take an iterative approach.

3. **Quantify economic value.** Conducting the economic analysis becomes iterative and consistent with the level of intelligence collected. The approach is to identify and quantify revenue and cost drivers for each step along the DVC.

4. **Identify and develop solutions.** The payoff for conducting DVC analysis is to uncover and develop solution concepts. When developing solutions, it is typically more effective to find a balanced portfolio of potential ideas. The balancing determinants and their respective weighting criteria should be established prior to engaging in the DVC effort so that identified opportunities are consistent with the company's fundamental strategy, needs and capital plan. The portfolio typically considers both financial attractiveness and probability of success.

   As solution ideas are found and analyzed they should be considered in the context of value delivered above that available from other DVC competitors. In order to create value, the delivered value must be greater than that available from the competitive set. Once the DVC has been mapped, quantified and potential solutions developed it is helpful to summarize findings from a DVC perspective (see Figure 8.4).

Figure 8.4
Example of DVC

	Media planning and budgeting	Creative services	Print production and paper	Logistics	Insertion
% Spend	5.0	6.0	34.0	5.0	50.0
Opportunity prioritization	High	High	Low	Low	High
Value potential	Medium	Medium	Low	Low	High
Suggested solutions (ranking)	Concept (3)	Concept (2)	Concept (6)		Concept (1)
Cycle time	14 weeks		1 week	3 weeks	

5. **Quantify economic value.** One of the benefits to conducting DVC analysis is to develop deeper understandings of demand sources.

6. **Leverage the DVC.** An understanding of the DVC provides a rigorous and quantitative foundation for future profitable growth opportunities. Companies that understand the DVC, their customers' economics and the sources of demand along the chain can create value propositions to quickly distinguish themselves from the competition. Approaching a customer with an understanding of *their business* and a targeted value proposition can quickly facilitate the shift from being viewed as a strategic partner. In order to effectively construct the DVC, companies should use an outside-in approach and use the 'market of one' concepts. Then, by linking DVC to business strategy, management can shift its mindset from 'What do our customers want?' to 'How do we economically satisfy our customers' sources of demand?'

The latest paradigms: lean production, mass customization and mass consumption

Two of the latest management paradigms, or buzzwords, are lean production and mass customization. These may bridge the gap between producer- or operations-driven concepts of supply chains and the marketing concept of customer value chains. Lean production is similar to BPR in that it is difficult to both envisage and define. As with BPR, the language used to define it is evangelical, e.g., the expression *world-class* is often employed with little obvious explanation except in terms of outcomes. In general, it involves delivering better quality, itself subjective, to customers at a lower 'total cost'. It could be argued that McGavigan would remain a lean manufacturing world-class company as long as they deliver the 5 per cent price decrease year by year expected by their customers, improving of course on their quality of product.

Mass customization is perhaps easier to envisage and define. It consists of breaking down a service or product into its constituent parts. These can then be produced independently, perhaps gaining from the low-cost attributes of mass manufacture. They are then assembled, including or omitting parts to the wishes of the customer to individualize the delivered service or product. This is often termed the 'MacDonaldization' of the process (Ritzer, 2000), involving modularization of the component parts of the service, allowing customer flexibility in the composition of what is delivered. It can be used to support lean production, and even in the service sector we expect the same or better quality of service at lower prices. Even holiday charter flights now allow customers to opt in or out of an in-flight meal, at extra cost. The concept has also been applied to the delivery of university degree programmes (Southern and Huczynski, 2003). The case of the choice of in-flight meal is a simple example of this, but even here the role of technology is obvious in automatically ordering the correct number and type of meals – there is always a vegetarian option – and in identifying the passengers they are to be handed to.

Summary

- The organization of production of goods and services has undergone a series of fundamental changes since the days of artisans making products for specific customers, with the manufacturing sector usually leading the way.

- Earliest changes were generally related to lowering price and controlling supply, as in the case of automated mass production and vertical integration exemplified by Ford. This relied on the technology of automation.

- In the second half of the 20th century, changes were related to offering perceived customer choice by modularization of parts or elements of service, as exemplified by all car manufacturers between 1950 and 1990. These changes relied on early computers and materials requirement planning to manage materials more effectively and efficiently.

- More recent changes use Internet technology to offer both customer choice and fast delivery, as exemplified by the BMW Mini (see Chapter 10).

- The changes were accompanied, or perhaps driven, by a series of management toolsets: work study (from Ford up to the 1960s), TQM (1980s), business process re-engineering (1990s) and a balanced scorecard approach to performance management (late 1990s).

- In all cases, a degree of evangelical conversion has occurred, sometimes resulting in over-expectation and ultimate disappointment and even disillusionment.

- No new toolset has replaced a previous one. Rather, it has consumed all previous toolsets while concentrating on a different aspect of management.

- Perhaps underlying all of the toolsets is the concept of a value-adding supply chain and the importance of managing it well. More recent developments have increasingly emphasized the importance of customer-centred thinking throughout the supply chain.

- There have always been difficulties in implementing any new management toolset, leading managers to recognize the fundamental importance of systems thinking and organizational development. This importance is demonstrated by developments in 'knowledge-based management', the 'learning organization' and change management theory in general.

- More recent terminology such as 'lean manufacture' and 'world-class' reflect the degree of evangelism still existing among gurus who label companies as such, and among companies who label themselves as such, although this may have more to do with reputation management (Chapter 13) and brand management (Chapter 18).

- Whatever the case, it does illustrate a continuing search for the secret of success in value chain management, leading to business success in general.

Chapter questions

1. Are improvements in the external value chain more associated with improving effectiveness, and those in the internal value chain more associated with improving efficiency? Justify your answer by reference to the contents of this chapter, or any other extended reading.

2. What are the basic generic differences between Hammer's (or our) processes, and Porter's activities in the process chain? How is this related to management culture of the time?

3. Has the development of IT been a driving force or just an enabling force in the move from activity-based systems to process-based systems? Justify your answer by reference to the contents of this chapter, or any other extended reading.

4. 'People can either make or break changes made in attempts to improve the value chain.' What evidence is there in this chapter to prove or disprove this statement?

References

Advanced Decorative Systems group (2006) [Online] http://www.advanceddecorative.com. Last accessed July 2006.

BBC (1994) White Heat, TV programme. (Off-air, 1994).

Benitez, T. (2003, January) 'Working class', *Incentive*, 177(1):31.

BMW (2006) [Online]. http://www.mini.co.uk/UK/index.htm. Last accessed June 2006.

Cortada, J. (1993) *Before the Computer: IBM, NCR, Burroughs, and Remington Rand and the Industry They Created, 1865–1956*, Princeton, NJ, USA: Princeton University Press.

Gittell, J. H. (2003) *The Southwest Airways Way: Using the Power of Relationships to Achieve High Performance*, New York: McGraw Hill.

Hill, T. (1985) *Manufacturing Strategy: The Strategic Management of the Manufacturing Function*, Basingstoke: Macmillan.

Huczynski, A., and Buchanan, D. (2001) *Organizational Behaviour: An Introductory Text*, 4th edn., Edinburgh: Pearson Education.

Kaplan, R. S., and Norton, P. P. (1996) *The Balanced Scorecard: Translating Strategy into Action*, Boston: HBR Press.

Krajewski, L. J., Ritzman, P., and Malhotra, M. K. (2007) *Operations Management: Processes and Value Chains*, 8th edn., New Jersey: Pearson Prentice Hall.

Macbeth, D. K., and Fergusson, N. (1994) *Partnership Sourcing: An Integrated Supply Chain Approach*, London: Longman.

Porter, M. E. (1980) *Competitive Strategy: Techniques for Analysing Industries and Competition*, London: Free Press.

Ritzer, G. (2000) *The McDonaldization of Society*, London: Pine Forge.

Southern, G., and Huczynski, A. (2003) 'Applying the Balanced Scorecard to Computer Aided Learning'. Proceedings of the BEST Annual Conference, Kendal, April 2003.

Walters, D. (1999) 'Marketing and operations management: An integrated approach to new ways of delivering value', *Management Decision*, 37(3):248–258.

Wild, R. (1980) *Essentials of Production and Operations Management*, London: Holt, Rinehart & Winston.

Zeithaml, V. A., Parasuraman, A., and Berry, L. L. (1990) *Delivering Service Quality: Balancing Customer Perceptions and Expectations*, New York: Free Press.

9

Customer relationship management and marketing insights

Len Tiu Wright and Merlin Stone

Introduction

This chapter begins with an explanation of customer relationship management (CRM) and looks at its network of relationships, in particular its close relationship with marketing. Relationship marketing's contribution to CRM development is examined. We look at how CRM helps business organizations focus their attention on interactions and key tasks in their relationships with customers, building the customer experience and long-term customer value. Case note examples are introduced. Throughout, insights are given about CRM's breadth of scope, its dependence on the use of managerial and marketing expertise, data and information technology, and business networks and processes to deal with customer service, care and feedback. Problems in CRM are identified and the QCi customer management model explained. The chapter ends with a summary of key inputs for successful CRM within business re-engineering for the future.

Learning objectives

- To introduce CRM and its network of relationships.

- To explain relationship marketing's contribution to CRM development.

- To examine interactions, building the customer experience and long-term customer value.

- To examine outsourcing and CRM problems that could affect customers' profitability.

- To show how the QCi model can be used to identify where a company stands relative to best practice in CRM.

- To consider a future view of CRM's contribution to management.

Customer relationship management and its network of relationships

Building new customer relationships and managing existing ones effectively are crucial roles for management. Businesses depend on their customers for cash flow and longer-term financial security. Irrespective of size (from sole proprietorships and partnerships to large companies), organizations now have at their disposal much more information about customers and their contacts with them than in the past, thanks to the use of call centres, direct mail and newer media such as the Internet, which has generated a proliferation of websites, company intranets, e-mails, bulletin boards, etc.

The importance of customer information that is current and usable should never be underestimated. Marketers understand this – hence the time, money and effort expended on profiling customer lifestyles and measuring customer purchases. Data captured on computerized databases, such as customers' personal preferences and products bought, their personal details and where they live (geo-demographic data), are providing genuine data. However, this must be turned into useful information if organizations are to succeed in their markets. Usage of data varies dramatically between different business enterprises no matter the size of their organizations. Poor data management, and weak processes governing its use, can lead to legal and regulatory problems, as evidenced by the constant poor publicity experienced by financial services companies in relation to their supposed marketing focus on initiatives and products which fail to meet consumer needs.

CRM emerged as a viable way of dealing with business-to-business and business-to-consumer relationships in the 1980s. It fits easily with business networks that make use of:

- Modern customer contact centres.
- Information technologies (IT) that centre on the Internet and integration with new forms of wireless applications.
- E-commerce that adds channels of communications to traditional ones via the Internet and the WorldWideWeb.
- Data warehousing to integrate operational and stored customer data for quick access and leverage of all data when and where needed.
- Data mining (extracting actionable information from large repositories of data) to gather and analyze information speedily.
- Marketing intelligence and information systems to handle such analyses and relationships within data to target customers across the world and cut lead times in responding to customer needs.
- Total quality management (TQM) to set targets and formally measure quality standards so that quality goods can be produced as economically as possible, by continuous improvement of processes and motivation of staff at every level of an organization and in its supply chain via devolved responsibility and decision making, so that goods and services are made available to the right customers, at the right time, as part of value for money propositions.
- Process management that forces the integrations of traditional functions within departments from enterprise resource planning and production to sales and personnel functions so that the technological capabilities and capacities of an organization meet with its strategic and operational objectives.

Our definition of *CRM* is as follows:

An all-embracing term to define the ethos of and networks used by companies to manage their customer relationships by harnessing the mix of information and communication technologies, e-commerce, data warehousing and data mining, marketing, TQM and business process management to achieve their strategic goals with customers.

We see the importance of networks within the CRM context as:

A complex set of interacting and interdependent arrangements for the management and exchange of information for a business purpose.

CRM's popularity rose in the 1990s as the ethos of being more customer oriented, a central plank of marketing theory, caught on with business organizations. It became a new fashion in management with growth in the number of organizations purchasing CRM systems followed by an increase in the volume of articles written about it in the academic and commercial literature (e.g., Winer, 2001; Plakoyiannaki and Tsokas, 2002; *DM Business,* 2004). The annual expenditure on CRM projects in software costs has been put at over US$3.5 billion and total systems costs (including implementation) to be worth around US$20 to $34 billion (Foss and Stone, 2001; Corner and Hinton, 2002). Investing in CRM systems also provides an image of corporate sophistication in a company's approach to its markets (Wright *et al.*, 2002).

Foss and Stone (2001) identified two main drivers of the growth of CRM:

- Customer acquisition and retention as top management priorities.
- E-business strategy involving the use of the Internet as a customer care and sales channel.

The first is fuelled by the realization of senior managers that, as a dimension of business strategy, good management of customer acquisition and retention would lead to increased profits. If handled badly, it could lead to the loss of the best customers and high acquisition costs for new ones.

Retaining customers through better care and efficient service builds customer satisfaction and, ultimately, customer loyalty. The cost of retaining customers is conservatively estimated at one-fifth of the cost of acquiring a new customer. Existing customers generate bigger margins and profits (per customer) than new ones. A customer retention level of 94 per cent yields profitability of just 50 per cent of what it would be at 98 per cent retention level (American Management Center, Europe, quoted by Smith and Taylor, 2004). So customer satisfaction makes the difference between short-term success and long-term growth and prosperity. Higher customer retention generates higher returns on investment.

The second driver, e-business strategy, has added a steep learning curve as business organizations have rushed to integrate old and new ways of managing customers. Adding the Internet as a new channel has created problems for traditional channels – personal selling, distribution and retailing. The urgent need to have an integrated view of the customer using e-channels has often led to the adoption of short-term tactical rather than long-term integrated IT solutions.

Relationship marketing's contribution to customer relationship management development

CRM has been, and still is, often identified by how the fruits of a long-term relationship with customers, built on trust and commitment, could create competitive advantage. However, one should be careful in interpreting the word 'relationship'. There are many approaches to managing customers. Just providing the right product at the right time and price is the classic marketing approach, and its track record is excellent. So, CRM is just one approach. There might be less confusion in the academic literature if the term 'customer management' (CM) was used instead of 'CRM'!

The interpretations of relationship marketing have supported the importance of building long-term contractual relationships. We define relationship marketing as:

> The sum of marketing efforts by a manufacturer, producer or supplier aimed at the establishment, development or maintenance of successful exchanges with a customer over time.

Relationship marketing focuses on establishing and maintaining good buyer–seller relationships. Organizations seek to move their interaction with customers along a 'marketing strategy continuum'. So the aim is to deliver goods and services, not through a series of discrete and casual transactions, but instead through continuous delivery within the context of an ongoing relationship (Grönroos, 1996). However, widening the interpretation of relationship marketing would lead to the inclusion of a broad range of activities which, when implemented, could mean quite different things to different organizations. There is a broad view of relationship marketing based on mutual exchanges and fulfilment of promises through co-operative and collaborative efforts of value to all in longer-term relationships (Parvatiyar and Sheth, 2000). Good relationships with suppliers are important for customers when purchases involve high levels of perceived risk and service benefits.

As organizations have grown, relationship building based on personal contact has become harder. Many organizations face increasing competition. Good products and services are no longer enough for competitive advantage. Powerful user-friendly databases and improved telecommunications allow large organizations to know more about their customers and competitors, but maintaining effective contact with their customers, which is at the heart of relationship marketing, can be hard when competitors can enter from any market or country, and when customers have more choices.

The notion of 'total relationship marketing' came about when researchers started to take an interest in relationships in internal marketing between managers and employees, i.e., the relationships existing or created internally between the people who worked for their organizations. For example, Ballantyne (2000) gave a case study example of the relationship development process in internal marketing activities. Gummesson (1999) had internal marketing as one of his 30 relationships. The implications are that internal marketing results from relationships that are created between management and employees and between those in different functional areas.

Relationship marketing activities with both external and internal orientation are easily incorporated into the ideas of CRM. This is partly because of relationship marketing's origins as a business-to-business concept (account management), developed because companies in a value chain needed to work together to improve quality. Business-to-consumer markets adopted the concept rapidly when the focus of competitive differentiation shifted from emphasizing the brand to that of giving more value to individual customers through products and services. It became linked with evolving ideas on improving customer loyalty and retention and heralded a change in business focus from customer acquisition to customer development, retention and loyalty.

A company could describe customer relationship marketing to its customers as:

> How we find you, get to know you, keep in touch with you, ensure that you get what you want from us in every aspect of our dealings with you, check that you are getting what we promised you, subject to it being worthwhile to us as well.

A prime aim of CRM can be said to be that of locking in high-value customers through identifying customers, serving their needs sensibly, using customer information tactically and overcoming customer dissatisfaction. In CRM, managing customer expectations and their experience of dealing with a company focuses as much on the emotional experience as on rational customer satisfaction and encourages feedback of information. The sharing of knowledge with customers and greater transparency, such as allowing customers to form their own communities and interact with each other, can provide the means for more word-of-mouth communications. Customer collaboration means major changes to the business model. Technology becomes a major enabler; anthropology and psychology provide analysis and policy perspectives.

CRM has much to offer when handled wisely, through effective management and adaptation of a broad range of network activities, communications and customer care approaches, and other organizational processes to the customer experience. However, poor CRM implementation harms customer relations. When the technology fails to deliver promised results or when an organization has not adapted its human resources and skills to meet customer expectations, CRM can become synonymous with technology and failure.

The five main reasons why CRM initiatives have generally failed to deliver on their promises are:

- A lack of senior executive ownership and leadership.
- A lack of building a CRM organizational culture.
- A lack of training about how CRM can deliver value.
- Poor implementation of CRM systems.
- Too much focus on technology, too little on understanding customers and what they want.

CRM is a common sense activity, with origins in straightforward ideas of direct marketing, sales management, customer service and quality. Treated as a management idea, developing slowly and applied consistently over many years, it usually brings good results. If it is done as a short-term fad, it usually fails.

Interactions, building the customer experience and long-term customer value

Interactions

To instil the disciplines of CRM, organizations need to change old attitudes, systems and procedures so that interactions at all levels bring in good results. Interactions and integration between different departments are crucial to effective CRM performance.

Building the customer experience and long-term customer value

CM has become a strong business focus. Information and communications technology allows organizations to do much more in terms of managing individual customers. Consumerism has put the spotlight on failures of organizations to use these new capabilities to satisfy customers. Consultants and researchers have focused on what is happening here, why and what problems companies are having. Suppliers of systems and software designed to help companies manage their customers have created a tidal wave of interest and aspiration, especially in CRM. As this wave has retreated, businesses are asking what value they are getting from their CRM systems.

There are difficulties in assessing value. Marketing and CM are challenged to prove their value. Worry about the 'value' of one or another business discipline is far from new. Debate about the value of IT, for instance, has been in the management press repeatedly, though many views expressed owe more to fashion than analysis. The value of any activity is hard to assess, because:

- Each activity has many stakeholders – internal customers, suppliers or resource providers – each with particular ideas about value. Actions that add value for some may cut value for others.

- Each activity is closely interlocked with others – so it is hard to identify the value that each adds.

- Business disciplines, such as process management and CM, have been hijacked by software suppliers so that the terms now seem to mean the software and not the management discipline that the software supports.

The main way to build customer value through relationships is to identify and acquire potentially valuable customers and then invest effectively to develop that potential through managing the customer experience. This is a combination of product, service and the 'feel-good factor' generated by a range of stimuli (e.g., visual, tone of voice, smell, atmosphere, care and attention to detail) at customer touchpoints (e.g., salespeople, call centre agents, advertising, events, debt collectors, receptions, product brochures and websites). It is based on customers' expectations, determined by:

- Brand promotion
- Word-of-mouth communication and reputation
- Previous experience of the company
- Previous experience of other companies and not necessarily of the competitors.

The customer experience is a step beyond customized service in the 'progression of economic value' and, like the product and the service, it requires design and management. The buying of art for reception and staff areas, the staging of themes at exhibitions, the attention to the details of navigation on a website, a supportive attitude in response to complaints and ensuring easy visitor car parking are all part of the same phenomenon, creates a positive customer experience around the value proposition.

In designing and managing the customer experience, one should aim to exceed expectations in the areas that really matter to a customer and just meet expectations for the rest. Relationship management research techniques can establish: what parts of the customer value proposition and experience are key and critical; which points

Process in action Gartner's eight building blocks of customer relationship management

Gartner's building blocks model is a key to success in CM, as expressed in Figure 9.1 (Gartner, 2003). The vision (1) sets the agenda for strategy (2) and what the fundamentals of the valued customer experience (3) are based upon. Efficiencies in

Figure 9.1 Gartner building blocks model

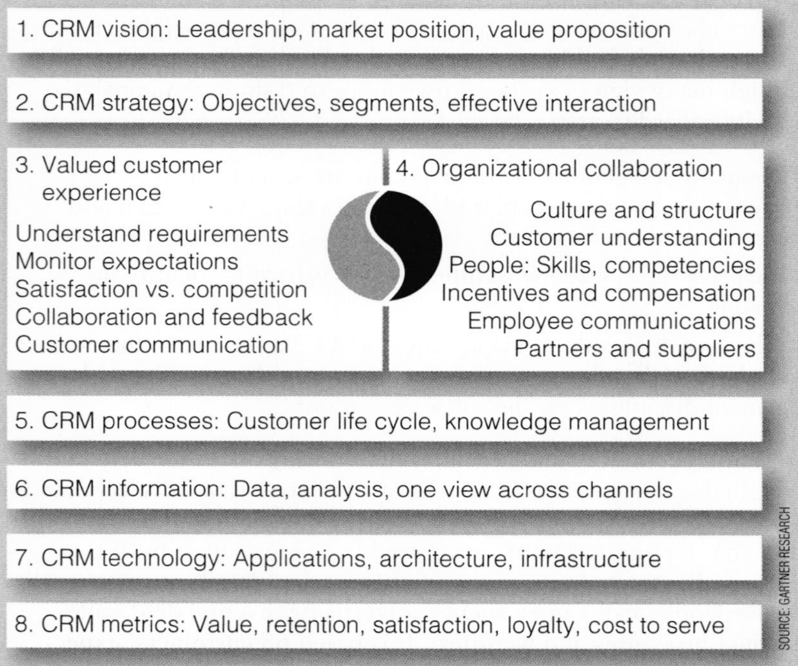

1. CRM vision: Leadership, market position, value proposition

2. CRM strategy: Objectives, segments, effective interaction

3. Valued customer experience

Understand requirements
Monitor expectations
Satisfaction vs. competition
Collaboration and feedback
Customer communication

4. Organizational collaboration

Culture and structure
Customer understanding
People: Skills, competencies
Incentives and compensation
Employee communications
Partners and suppliers

5. CRM processes: Customer life cycle, knowledge management

6. CRM information: Data, analysis, one view across channels

7. CRM technology: Applications, architecture, infrastructure

8. CRM metrics: Value, retention, satisfaction, loyalty, cost to serve

SOURCE: GARTNER RESEARCH

organizational collaboration (4) between departments are essential in defining and supporting the customer experience. Good CRM processes (5), information (6), technology (7) and metrics (8) support and enhance organizational performance to ultimately achieve the vision and strategy.

There are five requirements for success.

- **Set the strategic context** While it usually falls to the marketing function to make the case for CM to be part of strategy, a commitment to CM demands changes in product and customer service management departments and the bonus system.

- **Define customers and relationships** A CM initiative demands changes in many parts of the business. The first step is to identify and characterize customers – including types of customers you want but don't have. The analysis must include customer profitability as well as revenue. Many organizations find that 20 per cent of the customers generate 150 per cent of the profit. The next step is to decide what kind of relationship the business wants, from intimate through impersonal to anonymous to none.

- **Create the agenda for change** Customers or customer segments must appear in the structure and not just submerged within sales territories. Marketing, sales and service processes must be defined for each kind of relationship to be supported, from intense 'key account'–type relationships with very valuable customers, to near-automated processes for the large number of less valuable but still much-wanted customers. The choice of supporting software comes after that. There is a myth that CM IS software deployment is the main cause of dissatisfaction with CM. Software must be in the service of business objectives and never vice versa. A customer-focused enterprise also needs suitable metrics. The metrics – e.g., sales per customer, churn, customer profitability – may not be new. What is new is to report them by customer segment, and

individually for major customers, rather than by territory or product line. The rewards, usually bonuses, of the segment managers must depend on these metrics.

- **Change the organization** The change programme must be professionally managed and rolled out across the enterprise. A focus on relationships won't work. In fact, there won't be a focus on relationships unless people believe in it. So the programme must also explain the reasons for the changes and their detailed content.

Question

1. What are the business processes and organizational thinking specified by Gartner that will require changing for an organization to be successful in CRM?

of the life cycle, and via which channels, do customers value most; and which are merely necessities that all suppliers are expected to provide, being potential torch-points (as opposed to touchpoints). Exceeding expectations can be time-consuming and costly, so this must be done where it will have the most effect.

The major steps of designing the customer experience are:

- Confirm by research that the company's brand values and image are valued by customers and are seen as different from those of competitors.
- Carry out strategic relationship management research to establish relationship determinants, i.e., how customers currently feel about the experience, what they expect and value.
- Use a combination of touchpoint analysis, process-mapping of customer life cycle interactions and known relationship determinants, to map out the moments of truth in customer interactions (i.e., where the experience makes the most positive or negative impact on customers).
- Establish the gap between desired and actual customer experience at the moments of truth.
- Establish the employee experience at each moments of truth and compare to the customer experience.
- Design and pilot new customer and employee experiences.
- Recruit, train, coach and provide incentives to staff to support the customer experience.
- In the CRM strategy, build the required experience for each segment into the customer value proposition.

Outsourcing, customer relationship management problems and effects on customers' profitability

Customer insight

It is easy to assume that most companies – large or small – know and understand their customers. In fact, this is not correct. However, a new discipline of customer insight has arisen, merging market research and customer database analysis. Many large companies now have customer insight managers and teams, and these provide a vital building block for any CRM programme (Stone *et al.*, 2004).

Outsourcing

Outsourcing continues to be a growing part of new business as firms seek cost efficiencies by placing work with external partners that have suitable skill sets to service their brands. Manufacturers have for years sought to produce their products overseas where far lower labour costs, economies of scale in production and distribution and accessing global markets outweigh the advantage of manufacturing at home. The trend in outsourcing to call centres abroad is a relatively new phenomenon. The last decade has seen big companies such as BT following the outsourcing trend by transferring work to call centres in India where the presence of a large, trained, English-speaking and cheaper labour force combined with modern call centre facilities and international telecommunications networks to deliver quality in communications have been attractive incentives for the switch. Technology providers are broadening the abilities and reach of call centre operators. However, companies sometimes have to counter media publicity, some of it adverse, with tendencies to side with the domestic labour force (fears of loss of domestic jobs and incomes) and customers (fears about loss of quality and privacy). Good customer relations are very important to companies, and though

Process in action UIA

UIA Insurance is a mutual company with traditional roots in the trade union sector. Its business philosophy is anchored on socially responsible principles towards its members, customers, staff, partners and the community. UIA provides insurance to members of organizations in the not-for-profit sector and has maintained its in-house operations of its customer care centre. It also manages another trade union membership contact centre, UNISON Direct (*DM Business*, 2004).

The benefits of *not* outsourcing and handling the company's own call centre activities are cited as:

- Existing abilities in supporting implementation objectives across all business functions.

- Adequacy of its comprehensive staff-training programme.

- Facilitating speed and quality of communications and feedback between departments.

- Monitoring service quality such as enabling quick responses in resolving customer queries.

- Ensuring good customer care, thereby supporting the UIA brand.

- Facilitating efficiency and linkages in CRM processes.

Questions

1. What is the consistency of the customer experience in UIA that supports CRM processes?

2. What are the potential risks to the customer relationship and the integrity of the brand by outsourcing to a second or third party?

outsourcing can be tempting, companies should not risk embarking on this route and run the gauntlet of adverse publicity, unless the incentives are sufficient.

Problems that affect customers' profitability

CRM growth has not been without problems. Big investments in CRM systems require expertise and commitment in implementation efforts. These cannot be grown overnight. Figure 9.2 shows the typical configuration for CRM systems for a large financial services company. Day-to-day problems cause an acute shortage of relevant and different skills. Managers and their workers need to get systems to work efficiently and to know how to use such systems to manage customers properly.

Multi-channel strategies require different approaches, and switching investment from one channel can lead to the collapse of another. Customer privacy and security issues pose problems, and new regulations emerge almost every year as with new European directives to supersede national ones within the 25 member countries of the European Union.

There are also problems with customer acquisition and retention. With increased competition in satiated markets, discerning customers can find suppliers more willing to offer added value or better prices, thereby increasing customer choices. Despite CRM finding supporters amongst managers of marketing, service and information technology, and general managers, there has been little strong evidence that customers want to be 'managed' in a relationship and, indeed, in industrial markets, where many big buyers use their relationships with suppliers to extract maximum value while returning minimum value (Gartner, 2003). Customers can be fickle and switch from one company to another in looking for best value for their money.

CRM failures translate across with adverse effects on the businesses of customers. CRM investments are expensive, not just in money terms. Time spent is something

Figure 9.2
Systems requirements of customer relationship management

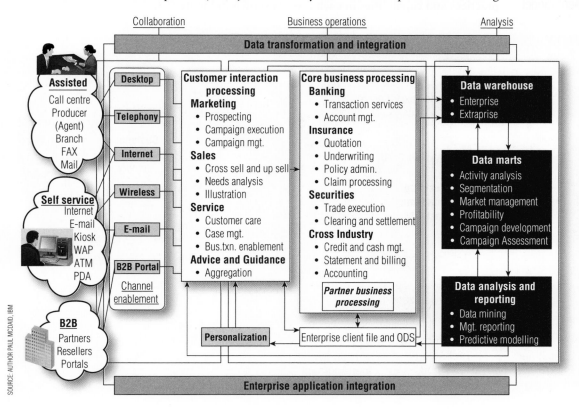

that cannot be recaptured. Loss of working capacity due to technological failures in CRM systems or poor management support from CRM providers have a knock-on effect on the profitability of customers.

Financial objectives are often set quarterly or at best annually. CRM approaches often take longer to pay back, unless activities are carefully planned. Managers are often in a role as a stepping-stone 'career development' move, and their performance is only judged over a short period. If managers do not see change through investment in CRM systems and in changing the behaviour and attitudes of employees, there is unlikely to be benefit for customers.

Some CRM suppliers might overcomplicate CRM; for instance, if a CRM programme design is removed from customer reality, customers will find it hard to use it to manage their processes.

Looking at the QCi model and what to consider in best-practice customer relationship management

QCi is a specialist CRM consulting company that has developed a way of showing what CRM entails. Rather than representing it as a high-level concept, QCi describes it as a list of management activities. It uses a CM assessment tool (CMAT) to seek 'hard evidence' for answers to 260 CRM best-practice questions that are known to be correlated to good business performance. Its results are supported by other studies (Stone *et al.*, 2002) that are concerned with effective CRM practices. Evidence is important because time and again there is a difference between what top management honestly believe happens within their organizations and the reality of what actually takes place. There is a gap between belief and reality. A CMAT assessment looks at practices and capabilities in each box, as shown in Figure 9.3.

Figure 9.3
The QCi customer management model

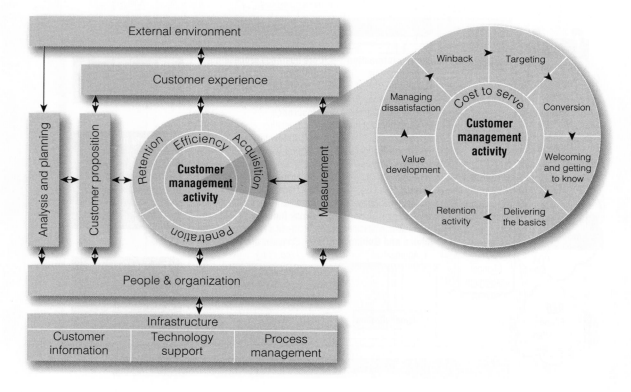

Despite all the problems and disappointments of sloppy CRM, there are many examples of very effective practices in companies and, after all, if it was easy, it would not give competitive differentiation benefits. Analysis of CMAT scores shows the characteristics and activities most closely associated with high (top quartile) scores, and thence overall business performance, as follows: analysis and planning, proposition development, CM, people organization, measurement, customer experience, information and technology, and process. Each of these are elaborated in Table 9.1.

Table 9.1

Characteristics most closely associated with high customer management assessment tool scores

Analysis and planning

- Determine your competitive arena and the competitive challenge facing your company.

- Determine which companies are trying to win your best present and future customers or increase their share of business from these customers.

- Ensure that the company's strategic objectives are communicated through the organization in a way that links them to the retention, efficiency, acquisition, penetration in CRM (we refer to these as the 'REAP measures').

- Be clear about profit and where it comes from, in particular, from which customers.

- Determine how much you can afford to spend on acquisition, development and retention of different customer groups and align resources to value (and maybe needs) segments.

- Be greedy for knowledge from customers, staff and partners.

Proposition development

- Develop clear and differentiated propositions aimed at those customers you want to manage.

- Determine how you can build loyalty amongst key value groups.

- Cascade the proposition from high-level brand values to influence the organization's behaviours.

- Communicate your customer propositions well to employees, partners and customers and measure the resulting behaviour and attitude change.

Customer management

Overall	▪ Develop practical and efficient acquisition, development, retention and efficiency plans.
Acquisition ▪ Targeting ▪ Enquiry management ▪ Winback	▪ Develop and measure effective enquiry management processes that identify future customers and business that will be good for your company (convertible, profitable, retainable, etc.). ▪ Develop winback programmes for selected former customers.

(Continues)

Table 9.1
(Continued)

Customer management	
Early retention ■ Welcoming ■ Getting to know	■ Provide thanks – as a courtesy and reinforcement of purchasing decision. ■ Ensure early relationship service-management works. ■ Monitor early transactions for indications of usage, higher future potential or risk of early attrition. ■ Build an understanding of customers – how they want to be managed and what their potential may be.
Repeat purchase ■ Ongoing management ■ Managing dissatisfaction	■ Let customers service (manage) themselves and their data. ■ Try to predict defections through customer feedback and contact analysis. ■ Proactively contact high-value groups regularly. ■ Manage key accounts in ways that are mutually beneficial. ■ Identify dissatisfaction and manage it timely and well. ■ Encourage a no-blame and learning culture in the whole organization. ■ Don't underestimate the value of good customer service. In these days of choice and when customers have the confidence to change, their service experience is key.

People organization

■ Provide CM leadership with cross-functional/departmental authority.

■ Ensure the organization is flexible enough to support customer-oriented decision-making.

■ Align objectives throughout the organization to focus on profitable CM.

■ Recruit and develop people with the right skills and orientation.

■ Ensure that incentives and rewards encourage desired CRM behaviours.

■ Understand employee satisfaction and commitment and its relationship with CM.

■ Actively manage those partnerships and alliances that affect your customers.

Measurement

■ Measure customer behaviours, attitudes and activities and their impact on return on investment (ROI).

■ Measure how different media (touchpoints and types) affect CRM results.

■ Measure and learn from campaigns.

■ Measure the effectiveness and efficiency of individuals.

Table 9.1
(Continued)

Customer experience
■ Understand how customer commitment (buying, responding) and customer satisfaction are related.
■ Understand performance in individual and combined (relationship) moments of truth at all customer contact points, absolutely and relative to competition.
■ Benchmark against others, in the company's competitive arena and outside it.

Information and technology
■ Understand priorities and dependencies that support ROI from CM.
■ Understand customer data application, acquisition and maintenance.
■ Increase visibility of appropriate customer data (to employees and partners).
■ Increase visibility of customer data (to customers).
■ Understand and implement support for the business integration requirements driven by CM.

Process
■ Define and integrate processes based around the proposition.
■ Replicate or grow successful processes for improved ROI.

The average overall CMAT score shown by the results of research with companies using the QCi model is 33 per cent – which means 'some commitment, some progress'. In most cases, this means that progress is patchy, uncertain and unconvincing, and therefore unlikely to have a solid and permanent effect on business performance. Companies appear to be experiencing real problems in implementing CRM. Expenditure on CRM trebled between 1999 and 2002, but the overall level of CRM competence appears to be falling as time goes on (Woodcock *et al.*, 2003). Much has been added to our understanding of good customer care and CRM through the use of QCi's CMAT.

What are the reasons behind poor scores? Many organizations realize that their future survival lies in their customers' current levels of satisfaction. New customers can be won, but at a much higher cost (five times) than that of retaining old ones. The everlasting customer can come back again and again if satisfied. Quality programmes and customer-care programmes require resources, including the '3 Ms' (men, money and minutes). Some argue that certain markets, depending on the stage in their life cycle, require less service than others. Managers constantly ask: How expensive are the trappings of service? What is the cost? Which service elements are more important to customers today? Is this different from last year? Does it have a direct effect on ROI? Can it be sustained? Does it retain customers and attract new ones? There is a correlation between customer satisfaction scores and the organization's stock market performance. Top companies are among the top scorers in customer satisfaction. Even the good management practice of measuring customer satisfaction has a correlation with successful commercial performance.

Companies have to understand that improving customer care may incur immediate or short-term costs, while some of the financial benefits will only emerge in the medium to long term. Quantified objectives can be set that can translate directly into turnover or bottom-line profits. Managers are constantly facing the question, 'Can costs be significantly cut by reducing the trappings of extra service?' This, of course, can affect the rest of the marketing mix, as reduced cost can allow prices to be cut or the savings enjoyed, to be spent on extra promotion or extra product improvements or kept in reserve for short-term profits. On the other hand, would a lack of service create a competitive disadvantage? Or perhaps there is a segment of customers who don't want the frills but would welcome a more cost-effective basic product or service, such as those who fly with the low-cost airlines such as Ryanair and easyJet. Can extra service create a competitive advantage, and for how long?

After the initial enthusiasm dies down, the real management task begins – sustaining and even improving the levels of customer care, satisfaction and retention. Competitive advantage may erode as other companies develop their own CRM systems. In the long term, customer service is not just about customer care or product quality. It is about serving customers and leveraging distinctive company capabilities to sustain a competitive edge. In a sense, this also requires clear communications with customers so that they are fully aware, at all times, of just how good the company is, how much it tries and succeeds and how much it cares.

While at Harvard Business School, Professors John Kotter and James Heskett ran an 11-year study to examine the effects of prioritizing three stakeholders: customers, employees and stockholders. Their 1992 study discovered that highly profitable companies serve the interests of all three stakeholders, while less profitable companies only satisfy one or two of these stakeholders (e.g., scored well on customer care but low on employee satisfaction). Over 200 major US companies were extensively surveyed. Those that successfully satisfied the three stakeholders increased sales (over the 11-year period) by an average of 682 per cent, compared with 166 per cent for those companies that satisfied only one or two of these stakeholders. Differences in stock performance were even more extreme: up 901 per cent and 74 per cent, respectively.

Another study (IBM, 2004) demonstrated that successful CRM implementation requires taking certain approach steps, which are all broadly related to good governance and management. Without them, CRM is unlikely to succeed (see Figure 9.4).

Today's companies need to address all three audiences and remember Peter Marriott's formula: happy employees = happy customers = happy stockholders.

Customer relationship management's contribution to management

As a management concept, CRM is important because acquiring customers is usually much more expensive than keeping them. To put this into perspective, on average it costs five times more to recruit a new customer than it does to keep an existing one. In direct marketing, this can actually be quantified, and in other marketing environments, estimates show the same.

The benefits of CRM can be shown through accounting techniques that reveal the:

- Costs of acquiring customers.
- Changes in the number of customers.
- Changes in what each customer is buying.

The benefits of CRM are usually in one or more of these areas:

- Improving customer retention and loyalty – customers stay longer, buy more and more often, increasing the *long-term value.*
- Raising customer profitability, not just because each customer buys more, but because of lowering costs of recruiting customers; there is no need to recruit so many customers to maintain a steady volume of business.
- Reducing cost of sales, as existing customers are usually more responsive.

However, acquiring the wrong customers and keeping them is often very damaging. Focusing on customer retention as a top business priority can be very damaging if most customers are not profitable. In many industries, such as banking, general insurance and utilities and also in many business-to-business situations, a high proportion of customers are unprofitable: The cost to serve them is much higher than the value derived from them. In such situations, CM techniques can be used to reduce costs to serve and possibly even to get rid of unprofitable customers. For future profitability, it is necessary to concentrate on customers who bring in higher revenue streams.

CRM is concerned with managing the customer experience. Companies need to understand their marketing and ask customers, for each experience they have with the companies, what the important considerations are for them. Asking questions about how well a company is doing for them, what it can improve on and what competitors can do better are all steps in the right direction. Getting the answers is a beginning to putting the CRM system in order. Customer satisfaction scores in 2003 compared to 1998 have fallen significantly (Smith and Taylor, 2004). Many experts believe CRM has delivered neither the promised ROI nor more satisfied customers. Although this is beyond the immediate realm of many marketing communications managers, they need to understand and influence CRM systems. They also need to be aware that many companies are going backwards rather than forwards in improving levels of customer satisfaction.

Figure 9.4
Drivers of customer relationship management success

Per cent of CRM initiative success predicted by performing the key CRM approach steps

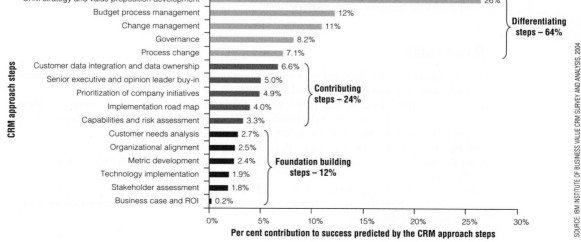

SOURCE: IBM INSTITUTE OF BUSINESS VALUE CRM SURVEY AND ANALYSIS, 2004

Summary

- The greatest business success will be achieved and sustained if the organization works towards an alignment of its culture, structure, goals, strategies, policies, processes and customer proposition with what its stakeholders, business partners and suppliers want.

- Customer experiences of product/service quality and customer service have a bigger impact on individual customers than any other communications tool. Outsourcing some functions to external partners may be suitable for some companies, but not others.

- Good strategic design is important and should be monitored with continuous improvement.

- Marketing activities, customer orientation, building customer value, care and feedback, are of prime considerations in building successful CRM.

- Customer acquisition is an expensive process, while customer retention boosts sales, profits and ROI. There is, therefore, an opportunity to carve out a competitive advantage through CRM programmes if they are carefully planned and executed.

- CRM is necessary as a way of managing the interactions between different functions, building customer value and integrating technology and communications for modern businesses.

Chapter questions

1. Why is CRM attractive to managers both as a management concept and as a tool to implement business processes?

2. What are the problem areas for CRM? Critically defend CRM as a viable method despite the problems.

3. Why is there a close relationship between marketing and CRM? What is involved in building the customer experience?

References

Ballantyne, D. (2000) 'Internal relationship marketing: A strategy for knowledge renewal', *International Journal of Bank Marketing*, 18(6):274–286.

Corner, I., and Hinton, M. (2002) 'Customer relationship management systems: Implementation risks and relationship dynamics', *Qualitative Market Research – An International Journal*, MCB University Press, 5(4):239–251.

DM Business (2004, Spring) 'Contact Relations', 6(1):50–52.

Foss, B., and Stone, M. (2001) *Successful Customer Relationship Marketing*, London: Kogan Page, pp. 3–5.

Gartner (2003) 'Strategy in the real world'. http://www.gartner.com.

Grönroos, C. (1996) 'Relationship marketing: Strategic and tactical implications', *Management Decision*, 34(3):5–14.

Gummesson, E. (1999) *Total Relationship Marketing*, Oxford: Butterworth Heinemann.

IBM (2004) *Global CRM study*.

Parvatiyar, A., and Sheth, J. (2000) 'The domain and conceptual foundations of relationship marketing', in Sheth, N., and Parvatiyar, A. (eds.), *Handbook of Relationship Marketing*, Sage, pp. 3–38.

Plakoyiannaki, E., and Tsokas, N. (2002) 'Customer relationship management: A capabilities portfolio perspective', *Journal of Database Marketing*, 9(3):228–237.

Smith, P. R., and Taylor, J. (2004) *Marketing Communications*, London: Kogan Page.

Stone, M., Woodcock, N., and Bryan, F. (2002) *The Customer Management Scorecard*, London: Kogan Page.

Stone, M., Foss, B., and Bond, B. (2004) *Consumer Insight*, London: Kogan Page.

Winer, R. S. (2001) 'A framework for customer relationship management', *California Management Review*, 43(4):89–106.

Woodcock, N., Stone, M., and Foss, B. (2003) *The Customer Management Scorecard: Managing CRM for Profit*, London: Kogan Page.

Wright, L. T., Stone, M., and Abbott, J. (2002) 'The CRM imperative – practice vs theory in the telecommunications industry', *Journal of Database Marketing*, 9(4):339–349.

10

Operations and marketing programming

Luiz Moutinho and Geoff Southern

Introduction

The traditional approach to the development of new products consisted of five distinct phases, with a handover associated between each phase.

- First, an idea was generated, either by an external need or desire, usually recognized by the marketing function, or by the internal expertise of a new technological development.

- Second, the idea was converted into a functional specification indicating what the product must do and how well it will do it. This stage was again directed by the marketing function.

- Third, the idea was converted into a detailed specification of the new product by the engineering design or research and development (R&D) function. In this phase, prototypes were developed and tested, and detailed design specifications created.

- Fourth, a product delivery system was designed and built, usually by a different team of technologists (production engineers).

- In the last phase, the production system was handed over to line managers who would be responsible for running it.

Learning objectives

- To consider differences in culture and opinion between engineers/ operations technologists and marketers by an overview of research on the subject.

- To consider how these differences can damage the performance of an organization.

- To outline concepts and techniques which are designed to reduce the barriers to integration between the two functions, and hence to improve organizational performance.

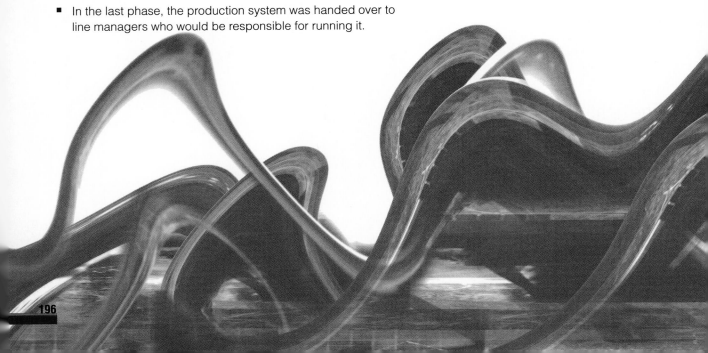

This arrangement of functional silos resulted in inefficiencies and friction between the parties involved: marketers, design engineers and production engineers.

It is now widely agreed that effective integration of marketing, product engineering and manufacturing is vital for the successful development and commercial development of new products. Anecdotal and empirical evidence also suggests that there is still much conflict between marketing, design and development and manufacturing personnel. Until now, much of this research has been concentrated in the USA and has tended to focus on the relationship between R&D/engineering and marketing personnel at a senior level.

This chapter will consider this conflict and how it has been reduced and can possibly be reduced further. It will first consider research on the way in which cultural differences are inhibiting a smooth product development process and then describe concepts and techniques which can alleviate the problem.

Research on barriers to integration

Given the importance of the R&D and marketing interface, Gupta *et al.* (1985, 1986) have studied the barriers to integration between personnel from the two functions. They identified five main barriers:

- Poor communications.
- Insensitivity towards each other.
- Lack of senior management support for an integrative approach to new product development.
- Differences in personality and culture between engineers and marketers.
- A lack of market knowledge on the part of the R&D personnel.

(The last point indicates that the researchers might have come from a marketing background, so perhaps we should add a sixth barrier: a lack of design and manufacturing knowledge on the part of marketing personnel.)

More recent studies, such as those of Griffin and Hauser (1992, 1996), also found that the common barriers between the two functions are primarily related to differences in personality, culture and language between the two functions, and by differences in organizational responsibilities and physical distances between them created by organizations. In their earlier work, Griffin and Hauser (1992) identified what they described as the different 'thoughtworlds' of the two functions as being a major barrier to effective co-operation. Differences in backgrounds have led to engineers having a greater product focus, whilst marketers were found to be more customer focused.

The conflict between engineering and marketing

Many researchers have found that a lack of integration between engineering and marketing leads to conflict (cf. Crittenden *et al.*, 1993; Souder, 1981; Weinrauch and Anderson, 1982). Weinrauch and Anderson (1982) give the following reasons for the existence of conflict:

- Differences in the tasks, goals and objectives of the two functions.
- Polarization of behaviour, with marketing wanting customized products and engineering wanting to manufacture standardized products.

- Stereotyping of personality traits.
- Overestimating the competitions and changes in the business environment.
- Ignoring difference in the power and organization of the two functions.

Improved communications between engineers and marketers, together with more networking, are their key recommendations for more effective integration.

Can engineers and marketers learn from each other?

The engineering viewpoint

In more recent international comparative work, Shaw *et al.* (2004) found that disagreement exists. For example, statements from their research, report that engineering and marketing are two separate functions, that a lack of understanding exists between the two, that engineering should come second to marketing, that engineers are more important to a firm, that marketing should be subservient to engineering and that there is a lack of trust between the two functions. Of course, all these statements should really be considered in the context of individual firms. In a bespoke or job-shop engineering firm, engineering and marketing will be forced to work more closely together than in a manufacturing mass production company. This is because the design of the product is part of what the firm offers, and engineers must become marketers to help gain the trust of customers.

Shaw *et al.* (2004) found that British engineers think they can learn a lot about customers. For example, several thought that they could learn about 'putting the customer at the focus of the firm's activities' and also 'finding out about customer needs and expectations'. They also thought that they could learn more about the business environment, typified by the comment 'we can learn about the marketplace, how it is changing and the need to be flexible'. Some admitted that 'technical superiority is not always the most profitable way forward'.

German engineers also took the view that they could learn more about customers and the business environment from their marketing colleagues. Many said that they needed to learn 'to put the customer first and discover their needs'. Many felt that they needed 'to listen to the customer more' and that marketing could also help them to learn more about 'legislation' and 'the different business environment in which they operate'.

These findings show that engineers in both countries recognize the important role that marketers play as an interface between an organization and its customers and the broader business environment. There is also a willingness on the part of the majority of engineers in this study to learn more about marketing activities and skills.

British engineers were particularly concerned that marketers needed to learn more about 'the constraints resulting from a lack of resources, competitive needs and technological difficulties and complexities' and 'the practical difficulties associated with engineering new products'. (The difference in attitude may be influenced by the relative reverence given to engineers in the UK and Germany, with German engineers having the greater esteem in their own country.)

The marketing viewpoint

In the work of Shaw *et al.* (2004), less attention was given to the marketing viewpoint, but marketers were also asked if they could learn anything from engineers. A significant number of them thought that marketers should learn more about 'the specific performance of products' as well as 'technical feasibility of the latest technical developments'. There was general agreement that marketers lacked 'specialist knowledge' and 'technical know-how' and that engineers could help their colleagues acquire this. In addition, marketers needed to gain a 'more realistic perspective of the company's product capabilities'.

The introduction of new technology, and the resulting change in the nature of the supply chain, gives marketers the opportunity to understand and participate in increasing efficiency. Marketers must learn how the procurement function explicitly works in their markets, particularly as purchasing-driven market hubs overhaul routine buying processes and put all levels of a supply chain in touch with each other. New technology requires marketers – the people at the 'sharp' end when matching company capabilities with customer needs – to approach their work from a perspective quite different from the traditional marketing model. Markets for manufacturers are diversifying, with small company start-ups and corporate mega-mergers making obsolete the concept of the 'average customer', that guides most marketing plans. Redesigning business marketing as a supply chain management function is one of the key new millennium recommendations.

Operationally, marketers must improve their ability to work within their industry supply chain by working closely with their own company's purchasing department so the firm can manage up and down the supply chain. In response, purchasers must recognize that good relationships can lead to long-term reliability and cost savings, albeit with a smaller supplier base. To keep such customers, suppliers must be prepared to work closely with buyers and look for system solutions. The buyer increasingly wants a relationship that delivers better performance through continuous improvement, innovation and cost reductions over time. In the long run, as prices and margins inevitably fall, demand capital, or reputation – akin to brand strength – is created. This becomes essential for business marketers.

It is standard practice in most organizations for manufacturing to control procurement. But in an age where building relationships is essential, marketing's goal becomes winning commitments from customers. To do so, marketers must play a strong part in controlling their own firm's sources of supply. They must help to manage up the value chain in order to ensure that both appropriate quality and timing levels are maintained in order to fulfil commitments to customers downstream. The McGavigan case, and their relationship with both their customers and their paint suppliers, is a good example of this (see Chapter 8).

Learning from each other

In the research by Shaw *et al.* (2004), the level of contact between engineers and their marketing colleagues was found to be relatively low. There was broad agreement on the need 'to define common goals based on customer needs'. Many engineers, however, were of the view that, whilst they as individuals could work towards an improved relationship, management also had a role to play by 'encouraging teamwork through offering appropriate incentives' and that 'management should measure engineering and sales/marketing people by long-term objectives and successful project realization rather than just successful sales'.

Researchers have suggested ways of improving the relationship, including working on communications, teamwork and training. However, techniques exist to channel efforts in promoting integration.

Techniques to promote integration

Quality function deployment

Quality function deployment (QFD) is a systematic technique, or framework, which enables the users to investigate relationships between the customer view, competitors' actions and the voice of the internal engineer or technologist. Originally devised by Bridgestone Tyre and Mitsubishi Heavy Industries in the 1960s, it gained popularity and its name from researchers at Tamagawa University in Japan in the late 1970s. Krajewski *et al.* (2006) say that the QFD approach seeks answers to six questions:

- **Voice of the customer:** What do our customers need and want?
- **Competitor analysis:** In terms of our customers, how well are we doing relative to our competitors?
- **Voice of the engineer:** What technical measures relate to our customers' needs?
- **Correlations:** Obviously there should be agreement between the voices of the customer and the engineer if we want our product or service to be commercially successful.
- **Technical comparison:** How does our product performance compare to that of our competition?
- **Trade-offs:** What are the potential technical trade-offs?

If we take the simple hamburger to illustrate these steps:

- **Voice of the customer:** The customer wants optimum size, good taste and healthy content, the last requirement being the most recent.
- **Competitor analysis:** Market research can help here.
- **Voice of the engineer:** For the technologist, size is easy to specify and control, but perceived taste relies mainly on fat and salt, both of which are unhealthy even at 'normally' acceptable content.
- **Correlations:** What are the relationships between the voice of the customer and the voice of the engineer?
- **Technical comparison:** This will measure the weight, fat and salt content and perhaps other content, of our own and our competitors' hamburgers.
- **Trade-offs:** This will be between unhealthy but tasty ingredients and the healthiness of the meal, and perhaps also between cost and size.

The QFD framework offers a prescriptive approach to addressing the six questions and a standardized mechanism to consider trade-offs and correlations. It is applied using a set of standardized presentation charts, the appearance of which has led to it being called 'the house of quality'. Perhaps its greatest advantage is that, when employing it, marketing and technical functions must communicate and collaborate with each other when concentrating on the same focal point.

Value engineering/analysis

According to Terry Hill (2005), the concepts of value analysis and value engineering were developed by Lawrence Mills in 1961. At that time, Mills said: 'On average, one-quarter of manufacturing cost is unnecessary. The extra cost continues because of patterns and habits of thought, because of personal limitations, because of difficulties in promptly disseminating ideas and because today's thinking is based on yesterday's knowledge.' While we may think we have improved in the past 40 or so years, we should still be on our guard against such waste. In short, we must make sure that we do not 'over-engineer' products.

Generally speaking, both value analysis and value engineering accomplish the same outcome, reducing the cost of a product by analyzing its design, although value analysis is undertaken for products already in production and value engineering is undertaken before production commences and is really part of the design process. The more current phraseology of 'continuous improvement' tends to concentrate on the processes of production, although this may necessitate changes in the design to allow process changes to be implemented.

There are many definitions of value. In accounting systems, we use the labels *book value* (what the item is worth having been depreciated since new) and *resale value* (the price it would achieve in the open market), although if our depreciation system is good, these will be the same. These are particularly important when considering the capital inventory of a firm, but we should also consider *use value*, or the properties and qualities that accomplish the function of a product. If we consider consumer goods, use value is important, although we must also introduce another component of value of equal importance: *esteem value*, or the properties, features or attractiveness that cause people to desire a product.

In both value analysis and value engineering, the product design is analyzed at a micro level in an attempt to reduce cost by:

- Eliminating or combining component parts.
- Reducing unnecessary accuracy in specification of dimensions or features.
- Increasing standardization of component parts across a range of products, thus achieving economies of scale.

The need for marketing and engineers to work together on such exercises is obvious.

One famous, now historical, example of value analysis was that of the woodworking single-blade plane by Stanley. In a value analysis exercise, and having identified that the two main use values of the tool were to remove wood and to achieve a smooth surface, a value analysis team consisting of engineers and marketers considered other methods of achieving the outcomes. One mechanism was the cheese grater, and it was observed that, while the resulting surface might not be as smooth, it required less skill to use and still fulfilled the objective of removing wood. In fact, it was capable of removing many other harder materials. The outcome was the development of the Stanley Surform, a hand-held 'grater' similar in shape to the woodworker's plane, but requiring less skill to use. This became popular with general handymen and do-it-yourself home improvers. (Skilled carpenters stayed with the woodworking plane, and its esteem value.)

Simultaneous or concurrent engineering

Simultaneous engineering (Hill, 2005) not only encourages integration of the engineering and marketing functions, but also reduces new product lead times and enables products to be put into production more quickly. It asks personnel to contribute at all stages of the new product supply chain, consisting of the stages of product concept, functional specification, product specification, product delivery system specification and finally production. Design, marketing, information technology (IT), production and even potential suppliers are required to work more in parallel, eliminating to some extent the traditional sequential approach described earlier (refer to the McGavigan case in Chapter 8). Early transfer of knowledge along the supply chain enables functional stages to begin work earlier on their aspects of development and, in addition, highlights decisions made at previous stages which may lead to problems needing rework.

The rationale behind simultaneous engineering is as follows:

- By identifying opportunities to overlap the traditional stages of product development, product concept, functional specification, product specification, product delivery system specification and production, the concept is brought to fruition quicker. It also forces the 'owners' of each stage to consult with each other sooner and problem-solve as the problems arise rather than after a handover.

- Overlapping may be achieved by greater use of standard parts and use of modular designs. Thus, elements of value engineering are instituted into the design process.

- Acceleration of the design process may also be achieved by contracting out activities and by working more closely with existing or potential suppliers. Macbeth and Fergusson (1994) describe how Toyota, rather than making a whole car seat (manufacturing the tubular frame, attaching springs and covering), subcontracted the whole design and production process to a single supplier after the functional specification stage. (This concept is also central to supply chain management; see the McGavigan case in Chapter 8.)

- These concepts and techniques not only need support from good teamworking, but also promote its development. They thus stimulate a virtuous cycle of improvement in communication and collaborative culture.

Not only do these initiatives within a simultaneous engineering framework result in incremental improvement, they can also lead to breakthrough innovations resulting from closer collaboration between specialists.

Hill's holistic approach

Terry Hill (2005) recommends that a firm should first define the order-winning criteria of a target market and then use these to help set manufacturing performance goals. In his framework for reflecting operations strategy issues in corporate decisions, he suggests that most firms follow a set sequence:

- They first set corporate objectives based on the *corporate strategy*, mainly in simple financial terms, although environmental targets may also be set.

- Then they develop a *marketing strategy* defining markets and segments to be targeted, the range, mix and volumes of products, policy on standardization (versus customization) and target level of innovation.

- They then consider how products qualify for and win orders in the marketplace: factors such as low price, conformance to specification, design leadership, brand name, delivery speed and reliability and the ability to meet demand increases.

Process in action ICI low-cost ammonia plant

Introduction

In the 1980s, ICI embarked on a programme to update their facilities for producing liquid ammonia, an important feeder component of their fertilizer products. There had been a series of major technological changes in ammonia production in the 1960s and 1970s, mainly concerned with changes in feedstock, from coke/coal to oil to natural gas. Liquid ammonia requires a great deal of energy to produce. Immediately prior to 1970, 'big was beautiful', and the economies of scale, particularly in energy efficiency gains emanating from a large plant, were sought. However, ICI had encountered problems in bringing large plants on stream. First they could not get the new 'single-stream' ammonia plants to work, and then they could not get them to work to the predicted level of efficiency. The time was near to replace two of the least energy-efficient plants in Europe, located near Bristol, which had been built in the early 1960s. But markets and environmental conditions had changed since the original plant had been commissioned. Reduction in growth rate in demand for fixed nitrogen, part of the ammonia production process, coupled with monetary constraints and a need to match the infrastructure of the Bristol region, had led to a new interest in smaller plants. Public opinion was also increasingly turning against large plants that issued noxious effluents. Finally, the world market in fertilizers was changing with markets arising in developing countries, and smaller plants would offer an opportunity to place plants nearer these markets, saving transport costs.

The target was clear – to develop a small plant technology that could:

- Maintain the energy efficiency of the best large-capacity plants and minimize waste during start-ups and upsets.
- Achieve high reliability by minimizing process steps.
- Maintain best-practice cost performance on a small plant by using a standard design and construction approach.

- Minimize inventories of hazardous materials and noxious elements from the process.

Development policies were specified to reflect these targets.

The development process

ICI did not wish to repeat previous mistakes. As the technical manager of the time recalled:

> We didn't think there were better ways of making fertilizers and gases, we slept for 5 to 6 years then woke up, almost too late and produced the famous steam reforming process that saved our necks. The engineering hadn't kept up with us and the ammonia plant we had built. We had a hell of a lot of trouble with materials and construction equipment.

In addition, strategic reforms undertaken by the chairman of ICI, Sir John Harvey Jones, transformed ICI to:

- Shift from its traditional production-driven to a market-driven approach.
- Move away from its policy of expanding by vertical integration.
- Force decision-making down to those nearer the markets by slashing middle management and move towards an organic form to meet the changing environment.
- Use task forces and committees to achieve momentum, allowing flexibility, creativity and opportunity to pursue desired goals.

In this new culture, a small multifunctional team – marketers, chemists, engineers, designers, process managers, procurement managers, etc. – gathered for two weeks in a 'remote' hotel to brainstorm the idea. What happened can be divided into three phases: before week two, during week two and after week two. These are described below.

Phase 1: Commercial considerations (before week two)

- Market orientation – consideration of the need for a small-scale ammonia plant with reduced capital cost.
- Relevance to the organization objectives – a major element of survival of ammonia plant.

Phase 2: Definition of draft functional specification (during week two)

- Brainstorming of creative ideas.
- Creating an organization receptive to innovation–culture of technological leadership.
- Gaining commitment of a few individuals and creation of a multifunctional team.

Phase 3: Detail design, supported by environment and market analysis (after week two)

- Development of an effective project selection and evaluation system involving a high degree of co-operation, mutual involvement and co-operation within project sub-teams.
- Effective project management and control – cost-control and milestone – based planning.
- Appointment of empowered and committed project manager, identified during the previous two weeks.

Two types of technique were available to create solutions to ICI's problem:

- Analytical – applying logical thought process within formal structuring of information.
- Non-analytical – stimulating imaginative thinking along unorthodox paths, deliberately aiming to free the mind from the constraints of analytical thought processes.

In the case of ICI, the problem was clear: how to develop a low-cost ammonia plant. In seeking a possible solution, ICI involved a group of experienced scientists, engineers and market analysts and brainstormed. After two weeks of brainstorming, cross-fertilization of ideas and probably much soul-searching, the group arrived at a consensus of what the aims of the full project should be and how they should be achieved. A flow chart plan was drawn up showing overall project timescales as accepted by the team.

Throughout the project, a simultaneous engineering approach was adopted. After the second week, many of the brainstorming participants returned to ICI headquarters and were appointed to a small multifunctional team to work to the remit of the study group and to complete the project. They were given the boardroom to continue their work until their own offices became available. The core team changed little throughout the project, but they were empowered to pull in experts from any field and from any part of the organization when required. Many members of the group were motivated by being members of the group, and although the project was kept as secret as possible, it became prestigious for other employees to receive 'the call'. Practical difficulties of group working, particularly when members come from different backgrounds and cultures, were overcome by creating a democratic group.

The team drew up a design during 1984 as a basis of evaluation which demonstrated that the project objectives could be met. There followed a period of testing and examination of problems in the laboratory, in the design office and with vendors and fabricators. An enormous quantity of information was reviewed by the team in a session in 1985, and a plan was selected which would be used as the basis for a design. Shortly afterwards, the reformer pilot unit came on line and demonstrated not only the viability of the process, but also the ability of the team to design and erect novel equipment and commission it over a short period.

The outcome

In describing a management training game used in the big organization of ICI, Sir John Harvey Jones said that:

> [I]t contained in it practically all the lessons that one needed about team work, involvement, mutuality of respect, the ability to recognise contributions no matter where they come from, the importance of multiple skills and the need to stay together and produce a solution which was good enough.

The ICI leading concept ammonia (LCA) process came to fruition in May and October 1988 with the opening of two ammonia plants of 450 MTD capacity. These replaced the existing large plant but had all the efficiencies of a single-stream facility at a considerably lower capital cost, incorporating advanced methods of heat, effluent and hazard waste management, and on a plot of land half the size of a typical large ammonia plant.

Question

1. Identify aspects of value engineering and simultaneous engineering which were applied in the ICI LCA project.

SOURCE: CASE BASED ON MBA DISSERTATION, SURESH MEDA, UNIVERSITY OF GLASGOW, 1992

- Generic choices are then made on the design of the delivery system to supply the product – choices such as whether a job-shop, batch or mass delivery system is appropriate; which type of flow system and material management approach is appropriate (associated with the previous choice); whether to make or buy some parts of products; and what size of facility is needed and where it is needed.

- Perhaps in tandem with the last stage, choices are made about the operations infrastructure – choices about operations planning and control systems, quality assurance systems, work structuring and organizational structure. These choices, together with the previous set, constitute the organization's *operations strategy*.

Hill argues that the pivotal view of the marketing function in understanding strategy development in an organization leads to the adoption of a marketing view which may be biased. He argues that, as a result, general words or phrases are used which can cause confusion – phrases such as 'customer service', which if not qualified in measurable terms can lead to a lack of clarity. Consideration of how a company qualifies and wins orders in the marketplace, the third traditional step, is central to success. Furthermore, the concept of order qualifying and order winning criteria must be considered. Qualifying criteria are those on which we must reach a threshold level of performance to get us onto a customer's short-list, and an order winning criteria is one that wins orders in proportion to our performance upon it. Finally, we must consider the relative importance of these criteria and assess them to improve clarity and understanding of our markets accordingly.

Hill comes from a background of researching and teaching in operations management, so he may be said to be adopting the operations viewpoint rather than the marketing or the integration viewpoint. However, he was in the vanguard of a school arguing that the operations function should have a greater say in deciding corporate strategy and that competitive priorities, the factors that qualify and win orders in the marketplace, are the link pin between marketing and operations. Hence, they should be considered by the marketing and operations functions equally in search of corporate strategy and mutually supporting marketing and operations strategy.

Value strategy approach

Walters (1999) suggests adopting a value strategy as a way to integrate marketing and operations and thus gain a competitive advantage. Calling upon definitions of value from both Porter and Kottler, he defines a value driver, in the context of products, as 'an attribute considered by a purchaser as a primary reason for selecting that product which in turn will either enhance the purchaser's lifestyle, in the case of consumer goods, or increase the value of the purchaser's output, in the case of industrial products'. In an earlier discussion, we suggested that this was a mix of use value and esteem value. Walters invokes Porter's concept of a 'productivity frontier' representing 'state of best practice', echoing the discussion of Porter's value chain and the two extreme strategies of price leadership and differentiation in Chapter 8. Walters quotes Porter's definition of the productivity frontier:

> [T]he maximum value that a company delivering a particular product can create at a given cost, using the best available technologies, skills, management techniques and purchased

input. . . . The productivity frontier is constantly shifting outwards as new techniques and management approaches are developed and as new inputs become available.

Walters develops Porter's ideas to define four categories of differentiation strategy:

- Customized value strategies
- Differentiated value strategies
- Stuck in the middle
- Commodity value strategies.

(The first two of these are non-price/value-led differentiation strategies, and the last two are price-led differentiation strategies.)

Following consideration of the relationship between marketing and operations strategy, Walters offers a framework for positioning the marketing/operations management dialogue, identifies four roles and indicates organizational features associated with these roles. This is summarized in Figure 10.1.

Business process re-engineering and performance management systems

More recent developments in business process re-engineering (BPR) in the mid-1990s and in performance management, noticeably the wide acceptance of the balanced scorecard approach, have been discussed in depth in other chapters. BPR was introduced in Chapter 1, and performance management, concentrating on the balanced scorecard, is covered in Chapter 16. Both schools of management thinking also feature strongly in Chapter 8. There is therefore little need to describe them further and in detail here.

However, it should be noted that in both BPR and balanced scorecard, there is an underlying principle to break down functional silo mentality and to get different management functions to work together on improvement initiative and problem-solving exercises. Specifically:

- The two underlying principles of BPR are: first, to concentrate on processes and to change the organizational mindset from specialist (knowledge-based) silos to cross-functional completion; and second, to focus on customers throughout the organization's supply chain. In BPR, product development is defined by the state change 'concept to prototype'. We suggested changing this process to 'product/ service development', and furthermore, that it could also be incorporated into the order acquisition process (Chapter 1). Hence we advocate the process incorporate input from marketers, design engineers and production (or system design) engineers, as many 're-engineered' companies do.

- In the balanced scorecard approach, managers should consider the links *between* scorecards. For example, an improvement in *learning and growth* may lead to reduced process times in *internal business processes,* which, in turn, leads to on-time delivery to *customers* and better productivity in *finance.* The improvement in *learning and growth* will also lead to improvements in product or service product quality for *customers*, resulting in customer loyalty, and will thus have a positive effect upon *finance.* In essence, these links represent causal relationships, a virtuous cycle and the value chain of the business (Chapter 16). These relationships cannot be considered without excellent communication and collaboration between marketers, design engineers and production engineers, hence application of the technique enhances the value of these virtues in an organization.

Hence both techniques require, and advocate, cross-functional working for success.

Customized value	**Marketer**	**Innovator**
	Organization:	*Organization:*
	Classic general job shop	Dedicated customer job shop
	Organizational aspirations:	*Organizational aspirations:*
	Expansive product range and features	Customized products and customer support
	Applied R&D	Dedicated R&D
	Extensive customer technical liaison	Customer partnerships in product/process development
	Strategy:	*Strategy:*
	'[F]requently used by organizations experiencing increased competition and their need is to enhance and extend standards of customer service they offer' (Sweeney, 1991)	'[A]ggressive, and the objective is to outperform the competition in terms of product performance ... is first to ensure that the firm's total management team maintains a customer focus in order to ensure the identification of any opportunities for improved competitiveness' (Sweeney, 1991)

Value-based strategy options

Stuck in the middle

Selective exclusivity	**Caretaker**	**Reorganizer**
	Organization:	*Organization:*
	Mass production	Similar to caretaker organization
	Organizational aspirations:	*Organizational aspirations:*
	Maintain cost-efficient operations to keep price/cost profile	Improve cost-efficient operations to improve price/cost profile
	Standard products	
	Standardized modules/ components	
	Process R&D	
	Market research activity	
	Strategy:	*Strategy:*
	'[T]o produce efficiently and to provide a reliable delivery service to customers' (Sweeney, 1991) Employed where differentiation offers little competitive advantage, i.e., cost leadership organizations (cash cow mentality)	'[A]dopted by manufacturing businesses to enhance the quality and the performance of their products and to change their manufacturing operations to reduce customer delivery lead-time.... Place greater emphasis on developing new production processes for new products and an efficient manufacture' (Sweeney, 1991)

Low relative cost value

Reactive ←———— Operations strategy ————→ Proactive

Process in action the BMW Mini

This case is complex in its conception and delivery. It demonstrates how close linkages between marketing in terms of the customer interface and operational engineering systems can work together to offer and deliver wider customer choice at reasonable cost. It shows how technology has been used by BMW to offer mass customization, i.e., a perception of wide customer choice, by combining a relatively small number of assembly modules. Of particular interest is the use of technology to manage these differences and to ensure that the manufacturing process is lean.

The customer view – customization and choice
'One in a million? Almost . . .'

'It's not only the Mini as a car that's unique – the chances are that the Mini you'll actually own is a one-off as well.'

'"Built to customer order" rather than "Built-to-stock" is the policy at Mini manufacturing.'

'Due to the varying standard specifications for different countries and the luxurious range of optional equipment available, calculations show that, out of every 1 000 000 Minis made, only 10 would be absolutely identical.'

The actual choice – Mini optional extras
Roof graphics – ten choices: union flag, silver union flag, Welsh flag, chequered flag (two alternatives), spider's web, Scottish flag, target, viper stripes, zebra print

Mobile communications – four extras: CD changer, hands-free phone kit, rear video screen, mobile navigation system

Internal accessories – four extras: additional instruments, automatic climate control, city floor mats, entrance

Safety – 19 extras: anti-theft alarm, baby seat, fog lights, heated windscreen washer set, junior seat (three alternatives), etc.

Transportation – 13 extras: anti-slip mats, roof base support system, bicycle lift, cool bag, tow bar, etc.

Total number of combinations $= (10 \times 2)^{40}$
$= 1.1081\mathrm{E}13$

The manufacturing view, or problem and technological solution
In view of the complexity and the sheer numbers involved – 2 415 different parts are involved in final assembly, plus 350 in the bodywork alone – it's not difficult to imagine what sort of mathematical wizardry is necessary at Oxford. Only a system which is working perfectly can ensure that each customer gets exactly the Mini they've requested.

One crucial factor for a successful logistics process is the so-called 'KISS system', a special IT development which ensures a full automated production process and electronic documentation for each vehicle: every Mini has a barcode and is scanned during all manufacturing steps, thus ensuring compliance with individual vehicle specifications as well as the top quality standards expected of a BMW Group product.'

But in case the customer is confused – a limited choice of preferences?
BMW offer six popular (or 'standard') variations of the Mini: Groover, Hipster, Business, Adventurer, Mover and Timeless.

Questions
1. What benefits does the consumer get from the BMW Mini purchasing system?
2. What benefits does the company get from the BMW Mini purchasing system?
3. What infrastructure is needed to support it?

SOURCE: EXTRACTED FROM BMW MINI WEB PAGES, 2006

Summary

- Research has demonstrated that there has been a lack of collaboration between marketers and engineers, and that as a result the product development process has suffered.

- However, marketers and engineers agree that they can learn from each other and that better communication and collaboration will enable them to do this.

- Several techniques already exist to aid this process. They include, in chronological order of development:

  - QFD

  - Value analysis and value engineering

  - Simultaneous (or concurrent) engineering

  - An holistic approach centred around competitive priorities (after Hill)

  - A value strategy approach (after Walters)

  - BPR

  - The balanced scorecard (and other performance management systems).

- The cultural differences between marketers and engineers are diminishing, but vigilance is still needed to reduce them further.

Chapter questions

1. What are the cultural differences between marketers and engineers and what are the reasons for that?

2. What do marketers and engineers think they can learn from each other?

3. If marketers and engineers agree that they can learn from each other, and that better communication and collaboration will enable them to do this, how do the following techniques (listed in chronological order) support this notion?

   - QFD
   - Value analysis and value engineering
   - Simultaneous (or concurrent) engineering
   - An holistic approach centred around competitive priorities (after Hill)
   - A value strategy approach (after Walton)
   - BPR
   - The balanced scorecard (and other performance management systems).

References

BMW Mini Web Page. http://www.mini.co.uk/UK/index.htm.

Crittenden, V. L., Gardiner, L. R., and Stam, A. (1993) 'Reducing conflict between marketing and manufacturing', *Industrial Marketing Management*, 22:299–309.

Griffin, A., and Hauser, J. R. (1992) 'Patterns of communicating among marketing, engineering, and manufacturing – a comparison between two new product development teams', *Management Science*, 38(3):360–373.

Griffin, A., and Hauser, J. R. (1996) 'Integrating R&D and marketing: A review and analysis of the literature', *Journal of Production Innovation Management*, 13:191–215.

Gupta, A. K., Raj, S. P., and Wilemon, D. L. (1985) 'The R&D-marketing interface in high-technology firms', *Journal of Production Innovation Management*, 2:12–24.

Gupta, A. K., Raj, S. P., and Wilemon, D. L. (1986) 'A model for studying R&D – marketing interface in the product innovation interface', *Journal of Marketing*, 50:7–17.

Hill, T. (2005) *Operations Management*, (2nd edn.), Basingstoke, UK: Palgrave McMillan.

Krajewski, L., Ritzman, L., and Malhotra, M. (2006) *Operations Management: Processes and Value Chains*, (8th edn.), New Jersey: Pearson.

Macbeth, D., and Fergusson, N. (1994) *Partnership Sourcing: An Integrated Supply Chain Management Approach*, London: Financial Times/Pitman.

Meda, S. (1998) 'Technological Development at ICI (C&P): The Hard and Soft Issues', MBA dissertation, University of Glasgow.

Shaw, C. T., Shaw, V., and Enke, M. (2004) 'Relationships between engineers and marketers within new product development – an Anglo-German comparison', *European Journal of Marketing*, 38(5/6):694–719.

Souder, W. E. (1981) 'Disharmony between R&D and marketing', *Industrial Marketing Management*, 10(1):67–73.

Sweeney, M. T. (1991) 'Towards a unified theory of strategic manufacturing management', *International Journal of Operations and Production Management*, 11(8).

Walters, D. (1999) 'Marketing and operations: An integrated approach to new ways of delivering value', *Management Decision*, 37(3):248–258.

Weinrauch, J. D., and Anderson, R. (1982) 'Conflicts between engineering and marketing units', *Industrial Marketing Management*, 11:291–301.

11

Distribution product category management and new delivery channels

Andrew J. Newman and Tony Conway

Introduction

Avital element in any marketing strategy is ensuring that goods and services reach the end-user at the right time and place as effectively and efficiently as possible. This 'order fulfilment' process involves distribution issues such as logistics management, channel decisions, channel management and retailing. Indeed, this aspect of marketing would seem to fit the business processing concept more easily perhaps than other marketing aspects, as it deals with decisions that critically and intimately affect all other marketing and strategic decisions.

Distribution is clearly at the heart of the marketing of many service industries (particularly retailing), but if the business processing approach is used, it is also relevant in all industries. Many aspects – from data processing through inventory management to deciding on whether to make or buy – need to be considered, and retailing is likely to be the ultimate link in many distribution channels.

Learning objectives

This chapter aims to provide understanding of the key processes and the changing nature of:

- Logistics management.

- Channel decisions and channel management.

The effectiveness and efficiency of such changes rely heavily on the development and maintenance of long-term relationships between the relevant parties concerned. This chapter, therefore, concludes with a deeper consideration of these relationships.

Logistics management

Logistics management is the term used for the management of the whole process which takes physical materials through the various production stages and through the distribution to the end-user. Its aim, therefore, is to ensure that goods and services are available for the customer to purchase.

In terms of physical goods, logistics management can be divided into:

- **Materials management,** which controls the movement through the production processes.
- **Physical distribution management,** which delivers the goods to the consumer.

Physical distribution tends to be closely linked to data processing and information systems. Two important aspects of this are:

- **Order processing,** which deals with the agreement made by the customer to buy.
- **Inventory control,** which is aimed at ensuring that inventory is available when a customer wants it but at the same time ensuring that there are no high costs involved in the storage of unwanted stock.

In terms of services, delivery may be rather different, but it is of equal importance and, indeed, the channel can actually be the service itself (e.g., retailing).

Channels

Channels decisions

There are many products and services where the sale is made through intermediaries who can spread their costs across a range of products or services from different producers. Although the retailer is the most obvious, other types of intermediaries can be found in a wide variety of situations. The relationships between intermediaries and the producers can be quite complex and can involve a wide range of organization types. It is important to remember that distribution channels generally involve relatively long-term commitments (Pitt *et al.*, 1999).

In the past, there has often been a chain of such intermediaries, through which goods or services are transferred from the original producer to the final consumer. This is known as the *distribution chain* or the *channel*. Members within the chain had their own needs that had to be taken into consideration. Indeed, each could be considered a customer of another.

Distribution channels can therefore have a number of stages or 'levels'. Doyle (1994) suggests three generic channel options:

- Direct marketing
- Via a sales force
- Via intermediaries.

Similarly, the simplest level can be considered to be the 'zero-level' where no intermediaries are involved (Kotler, 1991). The 'one-level' channel has one intermediary. A retailer would be of this type in consumer goods and a distributor would be of this type in industrial goods. A two-level channel involves an additional level, such as the wholesaler.

The term 'channel length' is sometimes used to denote these various levels of distribution. These days, however, a manufacturer has the opportunity to use a mixture of wholesalers, retailers, chains, buying groups and captive outlets. According to Stern and El-Ansary (1988), a distribution channel involves 'sets of independent organizations involved in the process of making a product or service available for use or consumption' and have three essential purposes:

- **Reassortment/sorting** (this includes sorting, sorting out, accumulation, allocation, assorting).
- **Routinizing transactions** to minimize costs of distribution.
- **Facilitating the searching process** for both producers and customers by structuring essential information.

If an organization can undertake distribution better than intermediaries at an equivalent or a lower cost, then direct distribution should be considered.

The aim of any marketing decision relating to distribution channels is to ensure that the relevant customers are reached in the most appropriate way, and the choice of channel to use is a major strategic decision. Consideration needs to be given to economic criteria such as pattern and level of costs, sales revenue and profit (if there is a direct link to the end-user, high costs can be incurred), control criteria (if there are a number of intermediaries, control over the relationship with the end-user can be reduced) and criteria relating to flexibility. In addition, Cravens (1991) identifies end-user considerations, product characteristics and manufacturer's capability and resources.

There are a number of distribution strategies:

- **Intensive distribution** involves maximizing the number of outlets where a product is available. This wide exposure means more opportunities to buy and this is typified by fast-moving consumer goods.
- **Selective distribution** is used where the choice of outlet or service offered is specifically relevant to the buying situation (e.g., electrical or photographic specialists).
- **Exclusive distribution** is a situation where there is only one exclusive company in any one geographical area.

In reality, the characteristics of the channel must be consistent with the organization's marketing strategy, and the choice of an efficient distribution channel relies on the needs and wants of customers. A customer's decision is likely to be based on issues such as cost, convenience and availability. Although there is a tendency on the part of intermediaries to emphasize the next customer rather than the end consumer (Svensson, 2001), this emphasis is shifting, particularly in the area of category management (CM).

Channel management

Channel management involves analyzing, planning, organizing and controlling an organization's channel of distribution, and an effective channel strategy can be a means of gaining differential advantage. Rosenbloom (1994) notes that this depends on:

- The degree to which customers demand a strong emphasis on distribution.
- The degree of competitive parity (the greater the parity, the more likely that channel strategy could make a difference).

- The level of vulnerability caused by distribution neglect.
- The degree to which there are opportunities for synergy within the channel.

There are three main channel-wide strategies: flow separation, flow postponement and flow acceleration (Bowersox and Morash, 1989).

- **Flow separation** requires different channel participants or intermediaries specializing in performing particular flow activities in an effort to increase channel efficiency and effectiveness.
- **Flow postponement** means that activities can be delayed to the latest reasonable point in time to minimize inventory risk arising from marketing uncertainties, information delays, etc.
- **Flow acceleration** requires the speedy processing of customer orders and payments to reduce uncertainty for the channel and to help in the planning of supply, production, labour, distribution and asset requirements.

Bowersox and Morash (1989) see a role for the co-ordination of these strategies to allow a firm to be more flexible in meeting competitive challenges. Whilst separation may have specialization benefits, it may also facilitate the efficient application of strategies to postpone or accelerate the commitment of specific order attributes to particular market segments or customers.

An organization can gain a degree of channel power when it develops or acquires products that can be marketed through its own existing channels. Firms are also exploring new relationships and alliances with customers, suppliers and intermediaries.

For Anderson *et al.* (1997), three forces are now changing the customary rules of channel management:

- Proliferation of customers' needs
- Shifts in the balance of power
- Changing strategic priorities.

In particular, there is now an emphasis on understanding and responding to customers' real requirements in order to deliver superior value and a willingness to cross artificial boundaries within the organization and challenge how all activities and processes that comprise value-added processes are linked. There is also an effort to perform activities only where they are the most effective, the assumption being that any activity that is not pivotal to the strategy can be performed better by another organization.

For Anderson *et al.* (1997), incremental change is not an option. There needs to be clear strategic decisions made where the requirement is to enhance effective delivery of the customer value proposition. In support of this, the channel must meet the requirements of effectiveness, coverage, cost-efficiency and long-run adaptability. Many suppliers seem to assume that once their product has been sold into the channel, their job is finished. However, if market orientation existed, the supplier should also be involved in the managing of all the processes in the chain until the product or service arrives at the end-user. This, therefore, involves decisions about channel membership, motivating owners and employees of organizations in the chain, and monitoring and managing the channels themselves.

Channel conflict

Conflict can arise in a channel where channel members have their own specific objectives, which may not complement those of other channel members. For Magrath and Hardy (1987), manufacturers can create channel conflict in designing and operating their distribution channels. A common action is the bypassing of usual channels to sell direct. This can only be made to work if the distribution channels understand the basis and rationale for such activity and accept the explanation, such as only dealing directly with some types of accounts. Sometimes, a manufacturer appoints too many resellers, reducing resellers' profits, or has too many links in the chain (e.g., requiring small dealers to buy from other master distributors). Conflict can also occur as a result of the opening of new untraditional channels that would seem to provide almost identical support. Sometimes, manufacturers can enfranchise resellers that are known as 'discount houses' or 'price cutters', which can be perceived by others in the channel as tarnishing the image of the product line. A major cause of conflict, however, is behaving arbitrarily with resellers, which can only be resolved when manufacturers establish ground rules and enforce their application with integrity.

According to Bucklin (1973), co-ordination left to market forces alone often results in less-than-optimal decision patterns for both members of the channel and the consumers it serves. Control problems occur because efforts by one firm in the system to influence the others have a differential impact upon the values of system members. Channel leaders also tend to emerge in distributive channels when the channel environment is threatening (Etgar, 1977).

Mutual dependency can be more important than control (El-Ansary and Robicheaux, 1974). Manufacturers need to recognize the impact of different channel strategies on the willingness of their resellers to be collaborative rather than combative. Indirect costs are associated with the use of power. The degree of conflict that the use of power may produce could disrupt channel performance. Firms, therefore, need to search for the least conflict-charged methods of using their power. Indeed, the firm's use of power is likely to affect its future power position through the feedback it produces (Wilkinson, 1996).

A way forward to overcome channel conflict has been the application of vertical marketing systems. Vertical marketing integrates the channel with the original supplier where producers, wholesalers and retailers work in one unified system. It may occur because one member of the chain owns the other elements, such as when a supplier owns its own retail outlets (vertical integration) or a retailer owns its own suppliers (backward integration). The integration can also be by a franchise or through co-operation. Vertical marketing aims to give all those involved control over the distribution chain. Co-ordination of the channel is supposed to eliminate conflict between individual members. The major advantage of this is the development of long-term relationships between the various parties.

An alternative approach aimed at gaining advantages for channel members is horizontal marketing. This is where two or more non-competing organizations agree on a joint venture.

A number of trends have impacted channel management:

- Electronic channels and virtual distribution.
- A new system of wholesaling.
- The focus on product CM.

Electronic channels and virtual distribution

Improvements in technology have enhanced the efficiency of distribution and influenced the development of database marketing and new retailing concepts. Through the use of new technology and better information, intermediaries can bring increasing sophistication to the buying process, resulting in more buying power being concentrated in fewer hands (Bower and Garda, 1985). Indeed, Pitt *et al.* (1999) contend that the Internet will change distribution dramatically. It could even obliterate channels themselves. Many intermediaries could die out while new channels may emerge. However, so far, few companies are managing to take full advantage of these new channels as channel opportunities are difficult to identify and channel decisions may tend to be governed by emotion rather than reason (Bucklin *et al.*, 1996).

E-procurement: from functions to processes

In this section, we consider the use of the Internet and electronic channels and the ways in which these are employed as trading conduits. First, however, two main issues must be considered that have bearing on the forthcoming discussion. It is important to remind readers that supply chain management (SCM) has an expansive role and seeks to integrate disparate functions across the entire supply chain, in particular, the various function-oriented relationships between suppliers and retailers (Graham and Hardaker, 2000). Figure 11.1 illustrates these.

Distribution is a major function, and one that impacts greatly on the efficiency and therefore profitability of both retailers and suppliers. The Internet as a medium transcends functionally based thinking and moves the business enterprise into a boundary-free environment. The speed and ease with which information can travel, and the 'real-time' advantages this creates, has had the effect of reshaping traditional methods of working.

Love and Tellefsen (2000) remind us that virtual networks have the most to offer if processes are repetitive and very explicit. Usually, these are areas where retailers tend to be organized around permanent, expertise-focused functional teams. It is perhaps in such functions and the processes that surround them that the most benefits in terms of cross-competitor collaboration can be achieved.

The importance that retailers place on the Internet as a means to reach additional customers may be conceptualized as transactional and/or informational tools used to reach new market segments (Reynold, 1997). However, the future holds much

Figure 11.1

Facilities, functions and activities for producing and delivering product or service from supplier to end consumer

Supply chain partners	Specific functions	Shared functions
Manufacturers	Planning	Forecasting demand
Warehouses	Warehousing	Selecting suppliers Ordering materials
Distribution centres	Distribution	Inventory control Scheduling production
Service centres	Delivery	Shipping and delivery Information management
Retailers	Procurement	Quality management Customer service

more for those organizations that realize the potential of an environment where information flows are limitless. It is the strategic use of informational tools to reshape the supply chain processes that are creating the major points of difference. With no boundaries and the traditional barriers that surround functions removed, the processes that relate to suppliers, distributors and customers are inevitably reduced (Christopher, 1998). This can reduce transactions for e-procurement by up to 70 per cent, and purchase order processing cycles by as much as 80 per cent.

In effect, this type of supply chain model requires a fundamental shift in thinking. Far from being bound to the physical movement of products and associated functions, in this complex, information-laden environment, the term *distribution* can have far-reaching consequences. It can, e.g., be used to describe the movement of data as well as the movement of product within the chain.

So what does the high-speed transfer of information, and the unrestricted flow of that information, mean for British and international retailers and suppliers? In essence, it makes selling higher volumes of goods and services across a world market unrestricted by the traditional geographical and political boundaries possible. Moreover, this can be achieved without a sales or purchasing team, or substantial input other than that required by the web-based communication processes (e.g., terminal operators). These advances in the manner in which goods are bought, sold and distributed have the potential to multiply the size of the potential market for products and services by several orders of magnitude. Inevitably, retailers and suppliers can reduce cost, make more money and add significant new dimensions that add value for customers.

Retail distribution models that utilize e-based informational tools are likely to incorporate sharing with several parties in the supply chain, thus enabling a high degree of cross-fertilization. This can result in 'adding value' to existing services in ways that evoke loyalty and induce customers to switch from competitors' offerings; such behaviours may arise in business-to-business or business-to-end consumer situations. In both cases, this fluidity and information sharing may be highly valued.

Traditional ways of adding value

The idea of adding value by undertaking various additional activities to existing processes is not unusual and has been widely adopted as part of the value chain management process. It presumes that delivering value to the consumer necessitates incorporating a range of value activities and processes at each stage in the purchasing and supplies functions. These may be divided into physically and technically focused ranges of activities, depending on the nature of the business (van Weele, 2002). Such activities typically commence with the manufacturer, and through suppliers filter down to the retailer and end consumer.

Based on Porter (1985), the value chain describes activities (ways in which the product is enhanced) and margins (levels of profit added that outweigh the cost of adding them) that result from these activities. The following are some of the activities that typically add value in the chain:

- **Logistical operations** – the order processing, handling, warehousing, storing and scheduling of products to the store or distribution centre (DC).
- **Marketing and sales** – the promotional activities such as advertising, merchandising displays and pricing, and the management of these activities through the channel may also include the task of organizing and sustaining relationships with channel members and the development of trust.

- **Support services** – a range of activities that include: warranty, repairs, returns, parts supply, installation and training; it also covers other elements of customer care such as advisory hot lines and quick response teams during peaks in the business cycle.

We can see how these value-added components fit into the supply chain process conceptually using Porter's (1985) model, which is illustrated in Figure 11.2.

As the model is oriented towards the manufacturers' and suppliers' processes, it fails to take into account less direct means of adding value. For retailers selling goods and services to the end consumer, the situation is somewhat more oriented towards perceptual processes and marketing concepts. This is because the retailer's primary goal is to serve the needs of the end consumer. The object is, where possible, to obtain and sustain customer franchise. For retailers, the concept of adding value is thus allied to loyalty, or the retailer's ability to convince customers that shopping in their stores offers significant advantages over the competition.

A value-added strategy for success

The term *value added* has been used to describe new methods of creating a point of differentiation between a company and its key competitors. In the case of proactive retailers, this objective not only satisfies goals that seek to engender customer loyalty, but also makes possible new levels of sophistication through the refinement of business processes. This may be achieved through consistency, competitiveness, etc.

For example, in the case of Internet shopping, a key reason why consumers are reluctant to buy over the web is that initial services offered little in the way of added benefits over conventional shopping (Anckar *et al.*, 2002). Moreover, deep-rooted shopping patterns and preferences for brick-and-mortar store visits undermined retail marketers' attempts to lure consumers into transactional websites. Hence, the

Figure 11.2
Value chain management Porter (1985) model

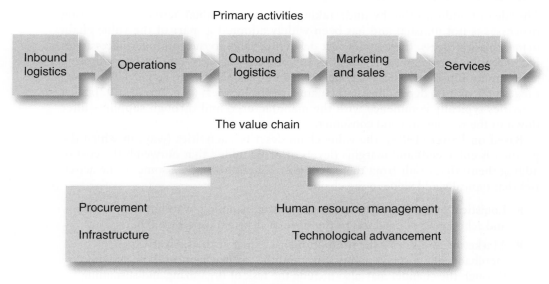

Primary activities

The value chain

Support activities

inherent need is to add benefits or value (perceived or tangible) in order to increase take-up and, where possible, switch behaviour. If a typical supermarket transactional website is considered, customer value can be created in a number of ways. For example (adapted from Anckar *et al.*, 2002):

- The retailer offers a competitive range of prices or discounts that only apply when purchased through the web shop.
- The retailer offers a much wider and more competitive assortment of products, some of which may be specialized.
- The retailer's website is a more convenient shopping medium for time-poor customers, with round-the-clock store access and variable delivery direct to the customer's home.
- The retailer prides itself on the superior customer service offered when compared with brick-and-mortar retail outlets and other competing supermarkets.

The difference between electronic channels and conventional methods of distribution is the unique manner in which the e-commerce exchange facilitates the integration (assuming access and interchange is granted) of numerous sources of data. Direct contact with numerous sources of information relevant to the customer permits not only the creation of bespoke order fulfilment, but also the additional added value creation (Bowersox and Daugherty, 1995).

Possibly the most important feature of electronic channel distribution has been the development of a total SCM perspective. This translates into collaborative working practices where numerous companies work together to create a degree of connectivity that transcends organizational boundaries. Hence, retailers can work together with wholesalers, suppliers, manufacturers and other trading partners; some of these may be competitors, as this practice will emerge with increased levels of trust.

A new system of wholesaling

In this section, we will consider the logistics functions and the specialist information technology (IT) that retailers and wholesalers have employed strategically to address changing commercial imperatives. The individual way in which new processes have evolved for the retailer and wholesaler means that we are obliged to place each fresh development within the context of the defining situations. We also examine the trading partners' individual and collective roles as the shifts in thinking take place. As in other sections, we make the assumption that the catalyst is consumers' expectations and the application of the marketing concept. However, it is worth noting that retailers in particular have not displayed consistency when it comes to quality marketing orientation (Newman and Patel, 2004). This is because most retailers, whatever the sector, tend to place merchandise rather than the consumer at the centre of attention.

Over recent years, the grocery and fresh food segment of the retail market has evolved with greater emphasis placed on vertically aligning sources of supply. These networks used by the major supermarket chains have, in effect, replaced the horizontal layers of growers, agents and retailers, and traditional methods of making purchases on the open market. The major catalyst for this change is the increasing pressure placed on food giants from competitors, and consumers demanding low-cost, high-quality merchandise. Indeed, for many consumers, fresh food became a destination category that tempted shoppers to switch stores (O'Keeffe and Fearne, 2002). Hence, the strategy has been to reduce costs through the reduction of suppliers and the consistency of that supply. This switch towards price differentiation and consumer awareness has brought the major supermarket chains increasing prosperity throughout the 1990s and into the 2000s.

Most multiple wholesalers face a dilemma that stems from the need to carry the items of stock necessary to satisfy their consumers' needs whilst attempting to lower the costs of carrying such stock. These stock holding costs relate to the usage of space, in both the front and the back of the store, and the significant investment in inventory. In the case of the latter, and with respect to food retailers, the cost of wastage due to fluctuations in demand can be considerable. Pressure is thus placed on sources of supply to meet tight delivery schedules and just-in-time (JIT) delivery methods, thereby reducing costs (Olorunniwo and Wood, 1998). In this rapidly moving, customer-focused climate, retailers require distributors and wholesalers to make smaller and more frequent store deliveries.

For major retailers, the precise physical distribution of merchandise became, and still is, the strategic goal, as it is no longer an option to offer in-store selections of merchandise. Sources of supply, and in particular the logistics function, are part of a complex long-term relationship with customers (Fuller *et al.*, 1993). As might be expected, this transformation in operational requirements places even greater pressure on sources of supply to improve the transportation costs and logistics data on which the schedules are based. For the traditional wholesaler and supplier, this has meant taking a new approach to the co-ordination and flow of materials (bulk items of merchandize) along the chain. Improved IT systems have been developed to optimize these processes (e.g., the movement of types, sizes and colours of fashion items) in modern supply chains (Das and Tyagi, 1994). This is illustrated in Figure 11.3.

Towards the end of the 1990s, wholesalers and suppliers turned increasingly towards warehouse management systems (WMS) and resource planning software

Figure 11.3
The traditional retailer-supplier order/shipping process

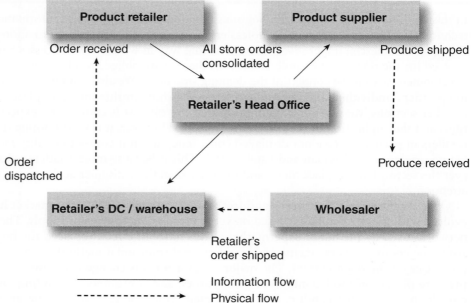

SOURCE: WALLER (2003).

(enterprise resource planning) to closely match inventory requirements (what stock is required) with actual customer demands (what the retailer wants). These systems track the shipping of products from a centralized warehouse, with multiple shipments to minimize costs, and the consolidation of deliveries. WMS are capable of comprehensive workload planning and task assignment functions that refine system management. Planners can define and modify the rules for allocating work tasks and equipment to the user-defined zones. Inventory management is a fundamental part of the system with rules-based processing for the maximization of storage, inventory, replenishment or order picking.

In the background, logistical information systems constantly monitor and update inventory status in real time and activate replenishment JIT. Inventory management systems update orders automatically or when processed via call centre systems. Figure 11.4 illustrates the various processes in a typical WMS.

A key factor influencing the progression of these systems has been software compatibility between parties in the chain. Manufacturers have the benefit of larger profit margins and thus the means to develop their own systems when compared with the narrow margins enjoyed by wholesalers and retailers. In addition, the JIT nature of payments has created a deterrent in some markets where retailers have not been prepared to pay suppliers using instant electronic transfers (Olorunniwo and Wood, 1998). However, retailers in the UK food, clothing and other sectors have a history of close collaboration with distributors to improve performance. The following illustrates some of the practices in existence:

- **Crossdocking** – Merchandise is transferred from the supplier's vehicle through the DC and directly onto a store-bound vehicle, with no stops in the picking area. This practice requires significantly greater co-operation and levels of communication between parties. In some sectors, such as fashion clothing, merchandise may be hung and store-ready.

Figure 11.4
Warehouse management systems

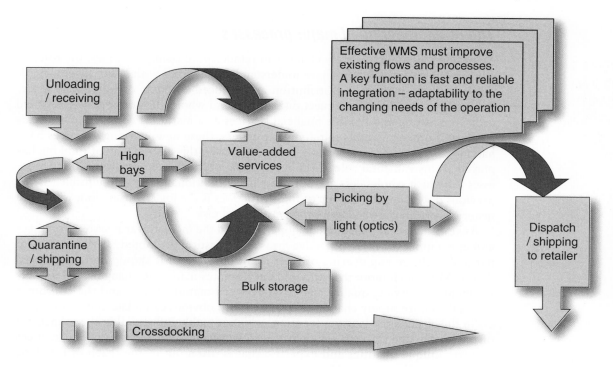

- **Store-ready dispatch** – Merchandise may be dispatched from the manufacturer or supplier, store-ready with, e.g., price tickets attached and bar coded, ready for sale. Garments, e.g., may be dispatched on hangers and rails for ease of movement from the DC to the vehicle. In the food sector, floor-ready pallets make for quick replenishment and stock holding solutions.

- **Electronic data interchange (EDI)** – This is a relatively well-established and embedded concept. Most major retailers now share stock holding and turnover data with suppliers to ensure smooth running and maximize control of the supply chain processes.

- **Efficient consumer response (ECR)** – These are computerized systems that scan stock keeping unit (SKU) data at electronic point of sale (EPOS) and then pass on this POS information to suppliers via the EDI networks. The main aim of ECR is to provide efficient replenishments by reducing ordering cycles and stock holding. This creates greater efficiencies within categories (ranges) by controlling the depth and breadth of goods for space allocation. For retailers wishing to implement ECR systems, the emphasis is thus placed on reducing the need for carrying stock and the minimal use of inventory.

In highly competitive sectors such as grocery and clothing, the implementation of pull systems that trigger stock orders based on actual sales is critical. Part of this process involves the rationalization of suppliers and maximized sharing of sensitive sales and SKU data to build long-term relationships with suppliers. The reality for many retailers is that traditional methods and deeply embedded ideals regarding the privileged nature of POS data, negate the potential advantages of fully implementing ECR. Hence, the principle of ECR, which hinges on the end-to-end paradigm, is still some distance to market.

The re-engineering of major processes

Alongside these revolutionary changes in retailer purchasing processes, the roles of wholesalers and distributors have understandably evolved with lower inventory requirements, economies in distribution and reduced amounts of warehouse space. For instance, retailers now expect distributors and wholesalers to provide electronic order processing and flexible financial services as a matter of course. However, as a result of other measures initiated by retailers, these new working practices have had far-reaching effects for wholesalers. Moreover, this altered way of thinking has played an instrumental role in the redesigning or, in some cases, removal of processes for which wholesalers and suppliers have traditionally been responsible. As the previous discussion shows, one of these processes is the logistics function, which has historically been classified as a supplier-oriented task.

As key retailers implemented major changes in the move towards systems redesign and integration, the more proactive firms enthusiastically adopted SCM practices, in particular, the re-engineering of their retail operations. It should be remembered that SCM is much more than this and encapsulates managing change to achieve refinements in service, quality and costs between manufacturers and the consumer across the entire supply chain (Waller, 2003). An obvious candidate and major process in the chain is the logistics function, which is highly influential in the refinement of the supply line through JIT delivery. However, introducing these new practices requires unique qualities and expertise that is often out of the reach of retailers, wholesalers and suppliers. More often than not, the capital investment in technology alone excludes most retailers and wholesalers anxious to focus on core IT systems for the management of stock replenishment and inventory. Specialists in physical distribution thus entered a relationship that had historically been reserved for retailer – wholesaler – supplier partners.

Strategic realignments in the sector as a whole compelled retailers to contract out the logistics function and obtain the wider range of services offered by logistics suppliers. Indeed, logistics research has identified that higher service quality is one of the key motives for outsourcing (LaLonde and Maltz, 1992). However, outsourcing logistics also gives retailers access to specialist expertise in firms whose core skill is logistics management, and more recently, the impact on the business processes of cost savings and service levels (e.g., ECR) has become major factors. This will of course vary according to the nature of the retailer and sector in which it operates.

In many ways, service, quality and reliability are interlaced and form part of the service offering. What may be considered to be high-quality service is determined by the nature and context of the service. For example, the third-party company must offer a responsive and friendly service that is mindful of the retailer's specific markets/customers. If the retailer's sales staff are obliged to say no to a loyal consumer, more than just the sale is lost. The image and reputation of the retailer can hinge on a slick order processing system and efficient call centre staff with high-quality communication skills and knowledge of individual customers (business-to-business).

Cost savings are varied, from overcoming internal labour problems and potential system failure to capital investment savings due to the reduced need for investment in new technology. Outsourcing the logistics function not only reduces the need for new investment in logistical facilities, but also releases capital already committed in warehousing and vehicle fleets for more productive use elsewhere in the business.

Several factors have forced suppliers to make greater use of shared-user services provided by outside contractors. These include demand for on-time performance, willingness to customize service and order cycle time and ECR pressures in the retailing supply chain which emphasizes increased frequency of delivery and reduced order size.

Dependence on technology

The evolution of the retailer – wholesaler business processes cannot be fully understood without consideration of the emerging technologies that have made this change possible. For example, the US retailer Wal-Mart has for some years operated a satellite system that transmits daily POS data to suppliers and distributors (Stalk *et al.*, 1992). Hence, a spectrum of critical supply chain technology has emerged that enables greater integration of flows and maintains on-time deliveries at minimal costs. Systems of this type include connectivity tools to ensure compatibility between users, and collaboration technology, which leads to the development of efficient collaborative trading networks.

The desire to make changes to business processes was not, however, confined to the retailer. On the supply side, a universal move towards 'lean' practices has also revolutionized this part of the industry, with dramatic effects. Successful distributors and wholesalers have responded to this general paradigm shift in chain activities by evolving with the help of WMS and other sophisticated technology. Clearly, this altered state of thinking owes its origins to the dramatic change in retailer requirements, such as ECR and short delivery times, and the wholesalers' need to drive out cost.

For wholesalers and suppliers, technology solutions hold other advantages, such as collaboration technology, which leads to development of efficient collaborative trading networks. The critical supply chain technology that enables the integration of flows includes:

- WMS (see Figure 11.4) that control the movement and volume of stock throughput.
- Order management systems for the placing, tracking and control of orders.
- Transportation management to meet ECR timelines and the maximization of load factors.
- Advanced planning and scheduling systems that better align supply with demand and optimize shipping solutions.
- Customer relationship management (Lancaster and Lassingham, 1988) applications that enable suppliers to anticipate customer (retailer) demand before an order is placed.

A fully integrated system of supply

A major feature of the proliferation of technology in the 2000s is that emphasis is placed on sophisticated decision tools to help companies automate their supply chains and achieve integration. This means that wholesalers and suppliers must be able to activate a comprehensive solution that fully integrates front-end order processing with back-end execution and, ultimately, the fulfilment of orders. The latter is ideally driven by customer requirements through the refinement of CM processes.

In a fully integrated system, products are shipped from a centralized warehouse, with multiple shipments to retailers consolidated into one co-ordinated delivery. Logistics information systems constantly monitor and update inventory status, triggering replenishment as required. Order and inventory management systems are fully integrated, and call centre systems are updated with order information. The more advanced systems offer retailers (the customers) access to accurate information via the call centre and online. A key goal, therefore, of so-called *re-engineered systems* is to remove the impact of sequential decision-making, which is reactive rather than proactive and is referred to as monotonic demand planning. What this means is that data is passed from stage-to-stage (e.g., store demand to DC) in a sequential fashion that precludes the essential component of new information (Sherman, 1998).

To fully accept the impact this has on the warehousing function, necessitates reflecting on our earlier comments on the importance of relationships in the supply chain. Trust is at the cornerstone of such relationships (Anderson and Narus, 1990), and partners must view themselves as trading partners with common goals. Replenishment planning needs to begin with customer purchases rather than store requirements based on capacity, historic patterns or order placements.

The new face of retailing: focus on product category management

The transformation in retail provision

Towards the late 1990s and on into the 2000s, the UK retail sector experienced a significant transformation in consumer shopping patterns and retailer trading styles. Particularly in the food sector, the demands of consumers and competitive actions necessitated a much more responsive and customer-focused approach to both in-store and so-called *back-end* activities. The latter have oftentimes been segregated from the retail change debate but account for a substantial resurgence in retailer operations. The precise catalyst for change is hard to determine but alterations in legislation, retail policy and planning restrictions impacted the level of retail provision and the structure of that provision. For example, the introduction of Sunday trading and 24 hours opening have fundamentally altered the way consumers shop. Measures by government at national, regional and local levels have curtailed the development of retail sites, with planning restrictions and unfair competition clauses. Several trends in shopping behaviour have emerged as a result of these and other transformations in the retail sector, some related to social and cultural practices. The following represent some of the key social drivers of change that have impacted retail operations across the entire sector:

- Increased pressure from employers has had the effect of extending the working week and thus reducing the time available to families to undertake the weekly shop.

- Time-poor consumers, rather than dispersing their visits across the week, have capitalized on new opportunities to vary the timetabling of shopping visits.

- Consumers' expectations of the level, nature, manner and standard of grocery and non-food provision have altered significantly. Retailers have responded with greater flexibility in terms of store access, product ranges, the diversity of services and involvement with community and social responsibility issues.

- More female professionals released from the role of homemaker require flexible shopping hours and products that free up time for other activities. Demands on the non-food, and in particular fashion, retailers are illustrated by yearly fluctuations in retail park and mall patronage footfall.

From the retailers' perspective, the sector became concentrated and less differentiated. Most food multiples faced a shrinking marketplace and rising levels of competition throughout the 1990s. Market saturation accounts for one of several factors that induce retailers to improve the retail offering and create a more compelling point of differentiation. For retailers, the great challenge in the evolution of retail provision was to avoid the tactic of 'trying out' merchandise on all groups of their customers and to develop clear-cut and distinctive strategies for specific groups of consumers (Dhar *et al.*, 2001).

It is therefore difficult to assign a definitive set of factors that should be classed as key drivers of retail change. We believe it is more relevant to consider in some depth the responses that retailers have made to these changes, as this is in alignment with the rationale of this chapter. Moreover, the techniques adopted by retailers have become 'cutting-edge' issues for retail businesses and aligned with current thinking.

A business process response to consumer change

There are a number of classic business process responses to the change that has taken place in the retail sector. The first of these is CM, which relies heavily on the restructuring of the traditional horizontal supply chains and the creation of significantly altered management thinking within retail organizations. The earlier development and refinement of the CM concept in the USA provided an off-the-shelf solution for UK retailers, particularly in the food sector. A significant factor in the emergence of CM stems from the continually expanding range of products offered, particularly by supermarket chains. The explosion of variety within product categories led to uncertainty for consumers due to the 'confusing' or even 'daunting' store fixtures (Anonymous, 1997a). On the supply side, continual invention of variety to leverage higher proportions of sales and profits is high risk, as around 80 per cent of new product launches fail within two years (McGrath, 1997).

At store level, the introduction of EPOS technology in supermarket checkouts and subsequent launch of customer loyalty cards has meant that retailers have had the technology to construct and analyze vast databases to improve the efficiency of their processes of replenishment and customer buying patterns (Newman, 2004). There is also evidence to suggest that the development of retailers' own-label products pioneered a new type of relationship between retailers and manufacturers. Such relationships are central to CM (Anonymous, 1997b).

At this point, it is useful for us to contemplate how CM differs from the traditional way of running a retail business, as there are some fundamental differences. The CM concept, e.g., treats each major product area as a strategic business unit i.e., a business in itself. However, unlike traditional approaches to managing product categories, where certain product groups may carry others, CM employs a range of computerized performance tools that objectively inform SKU decisions. These tools are then used to build performance analysis models to ensure that rational fact-based decisions are made about sourcing product ranges, merchandising and promotional events within categories. We can see the various stages of this process in Figure 11.5.

Category managers are thus obliged to judge products and categories in terms of performance against retail space, in-store fixtures, staff wages and net costs. CM typically uses quadrant analysis to identify relative performance across a number of performance dimensions such as margins and sales. Figure 11.6 illustrates how quadrant analysis is performed.

The allocation of retail space for merchandise is thus decided upon. More important, these issues are all related directly to the development of customer franchise. Hence, from a management perspective, the CM approach requires a critical adjustment in thinking from the more functional arrangements encountered in most retail businesses to a more vertical business structure. Thus, a portfolio or cluster of categories are developed and managed in an integrated fashion with individually targeted promotional programmes aimed at improving the performance of specific categories. In effect, this brings the business closer to customer needs and moves closer to achieving high-quality marketing orientation (Liu and Davies, 1996).

Supplier relationships make for contented customers

An overarching feature of CM is its long-term customer-focused strategy that engenders relationships across the entire chain from supplier to end consumer. This is a distinct departure from the 'deal-by-deal' approach that retailers have gravitated towards in the rush for market share. Hence, CM shifts the measurement process (e.g., quality, desirability) from the DC and quality control testing to the territory of the consumer, at store level (O'Keeffe and Fearne, 2002). Running the business is thus a function of reaching *both* backwards into the supply chain and forwards to ascertain customer needs and preferences. This maximizes both market and customer expectations. It also addresses three major issues in any business: the reduction of costs, the development of closer relationships with suppliers and the formulation of future plans. CM helps the retailer to foster closer relationships with suppliers, align activities with the needs of customers and assist in the minimization of costs within the chain. But this depiction remains supply driven. The aim is to put value in, and not just pull costs out. This is the essence of category leadership, where the greatest challenges and future gains will come from creating value in the retail store – and not from reducing supply chain costs alone.

It is important to emphasize that, as in the US models for CM, there is a need to demonstrate real financial investments and commitments in front- as well as back-end

Figure 11.5
Stages of category management

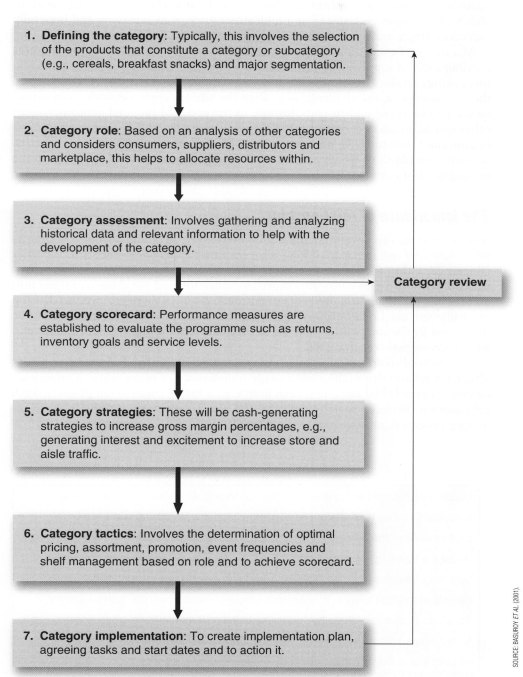

1. **Defining the category**: Typically, this involves the selection of the products that constitute a category or subcategory (e.g., cereals, breakfast snacks) and major segmentation.

2. **Category role**: Based on an analysis of other categories and considers consumers, suppliers, distributors and marketplace, this helps to allocate resources within.

3. **Category assessment**: Involves gathering and analyzing historical data and relevant information to help with the development of the category.

Category review

4. **Category scorecard**: Performance measures are established to evaluate the programme such as returns, inventory goals and service levels.

5. **Category strategies**: These will be cash-generating strategies to increase gross margin percentages, e.g., generating interest and excitement to increase store and aisle traffic.

6. **Category tactics**: Involves the determination of optimal pricing, assortment, promotion, event frequencies and shelf management based on role and to achieve scorecard.

7. **Category implementation**: To create implementation plan, agreeing tasks and start dates and to action it.

SOURCE: BASU ROY *ET AL* (2001).

activities, by retailers and suppliers (Dhar *et al.*, 2001). We can see how this may work in the fashion sector, e.g., where a quick response strategy adopted by many retailers is a prerequisite to survival. In the world of fashion, there is a fixed calendar of activities that surrounds exhibitions, fashion shows and fairs, and a retailer's selection process for specific ranges and styles. The critical buying cycles and lead times operate one year in advance of the new season and orders are placed about 6 months in advance of launch (Birtwistle *et al.*, 2003). For the valued fashion consumer, this converts to short catwalk to shop-floor lead times, ensuring the availability of cutting-edge fashions at a high street price, thus satisfying and hopefully exceeding target market expectations whilst maintaining a competitive edge.

Meeting and exceeding consumer needs and expectations, therefore, requires maximization of supply chain effectiveness with joint (supplier – retailer) planning, forecasting, product developments and CM (Giunipero *et al.*, 2001). Drawing on the US experience, the challenge is to align the whole supply network from manufacturer to store, or end-to-end, through to the needs of the final consumer, or in other words, to create a responsive system that could be quickly shaped to changes in consumer demands. At store level, the CM process involves a number of critical steps, the object of which is to create a strategic and controlled approach to the management of customer needs.

The importance of relationships

As can be seen, the developments highlighted above rely a great deal on the development and maintenance of long-term relationships between the various parties concerned within the chain. The issues of channel power and the resultant channel conflict need to give way to a more customer-focused perspective, taking into account the needs and requirements of partners. As such, there is a need to develop mutually beneficial relationships. Enduring relationships with customers cannot be duplicated by the competition and, therefore, such relationships provide unique and sustained competitive advantage.

Channels of distribution usually involve the development and maintenance of long-term relationships (although a single transaction can occur where a temporary channel is established for one transaction, e.g., a major engineering project). Such relationships between members need to be considered in this strategic decision-making process (Lancaster and Lassingham, 1988).

Figure 11.6
Quadrant analysis techniques for category management

Divide a whiteboard or flip chart into four quadrants and analyze the particular grouping (e.g., cereals, beauty care) in ways that are directly relevant to the performance of the category. For example, managers may wish to analyze categories under the headings of: 'the current situation', 'the way we want it to be', 'ways of obtaining these results', 'possible hindrances and/or threats'. Alternatively, using various evaluation criteria, a more appropriate approach may be: 'achievements', 'failures', 'problems', 'changes', or, using slightly different criteria, 'resources', 'skills', 'impediments' and 'needs'. Clearly, there are numerous ways of analyzing situations and management would determine the most appropriate.

Dwyer *et al.* (1987) distinguish between *discrete transactions* and *relational exchanges*, which differ on a number of dimensions. They believe that relational exchange can contribute to product differentiation and create barriers to switching. As a result, it can provide a competitive advantage. Co-operation leads to more satisfying supplier – dealer relationships, while conflict reduces satisfaction (Skinner *et al.*, 1992).

This approach sees a shift towards a value creation orientation based on incremental improvement and ongoing processes rather than one-time events (McKenna, 1991). This new marketing requires a company to master a high degree of knowledge of the technology in which it competes, its competition, its customers and its own organization. This leads to the development of an infrastructure for suppliers, vendors, partners and users whose relationships help sustain and support the company's reputation and technology. It also requires an emphasis on interactivity and creativity that ensures greater customer involvement with the company, creating and sustaining a relationship. Today, increasing technological knowledge is producing a need for skilled lateral relationships and modern channel relationships involve the use of integrated information systems. The desire to introduce relationship-marketing principles into buyer – seller relationships interacts with technology strategies in that a successful RM approach should mitigate the dangers of using buyer power to insist on supplier actions (Wilson and Vlosky, 1998). In a proactive approach to building relationships, buyers and sellers work together in joint problem-solving to ease the pressures on the buyer. However, there is the danger that firms are still too willing to use power regardless of the effect it may have on long-term relationships with suppliers.

Some have argued that this approach itself means that there is a need to look at the organization from a process management perspective rather than the functionalist view (Grönroos, 1996). He believes that those companies that want to adopt this approach should recognize that a significant change in business philosophy is required. Similarly, Boedeker (1997) sees relationship marketing as centring on developing a continuous relationship between buyers and sellers. These are usually long-term (Copulsky and Wolf, 1990) and dynamic. Marketing through relationships, as compared to transactional marketing, means that interactions between the parties concerned are connected to both previous and future interactions and that counterparts may become interdependent over time as they continue to interact (Holmund and Tornroos, 1997).

Boedeker (1997) believes that relationship marketing can be put to use on various levels, depending on the type and number of bonds used by the company to increase customer loyalty. The higher the level, the higher the potential payoff. At the lowest level, price incentives are used to increase the value of the customer experience, but this seldom offers long-term competitive advantage, as price is the most easily imitated tool. At the second level, besides price, social bonds are sought by establishing services beyond the ordinary. This is based on learning about clients' wants and needs, customizing the service and the relationships and continually reselling the benefits of the relationship. This develops to a third level, where structural bonds are created by providing clients with value adding systems which are not possible for the clients to build or use solely by themselves and are not available from other sources.

Christopher *et al.* (2002) note that there is recognition that quality customer service and marketing activities need to be brought together. This perspective is concerned with improving service quality through the integration of quality, customer service and marketing. All these together should lead to improved customer retention, and the stress on loyalty, customer retention and long-term relationships is a key to profitability (Gummesson, 1999). However, the relationship must be win-win if it is to be long-term and constructive, and the initiative must come from all parties to produce equal and respectful interactions. Relationships increase security, which aids the marketing effort and makes outcomes more predictable. Other key benefits include long-term service customers becoming better co-producers. This helps production and delivery and thus improves quality. This also means that service providers can gradually build up knowledge about their customers. In addition, customers tend to become less price-sensitive as the relationship becomes more important to them than price alone.

Components of successful relationships

A good deal has been written on the components of successful relationships, and although many factors have been identified in the literature as being of particular importance in the development of relationships, five seem to be the most commonly noted (Conway and Swift, 2000): (1) commitment, (2) trust, (3) customer orientation/empathy, (4) experience/satisfaction and (5) communication.

Commitment

Of central importance in developing relationships is the level of commitment a partner feels towards that relationship. Commitment is an intention to continue a course of action or activity (Hocutt, 1998). Indeed, Wilson (1995) identifies commitment as the most common dependent variable used in buyer – seller relationship studies. Morgan and Hunt (1994) see relationship commitment as a key characteristic associated with a successful marketing relationship as do Berry and Parasuraman (1991).

Commitment summarizes prior experiences of dependence and directs reactions to new situations and is a long-term concept (Rusbult and Buunk, 1993). Commitment can also be viewed as the desire to maintain a relationship (Hocutt, 1998) and this is often indicated by an ongoing 'investment' into activities, which are expected to maintain the relationship (Blois, 1998). Anderson and Weitz (1989) found evidence to suggest that the greater the level of investment made by a manufacturer in a relationship, the greater the increase in that manufacturer's commitment to its relationship with its distributor.

Trust

Trust is the precondition for increased commitment (Mietilla and Möller, 1990) and is a fundamental relationship model building block included in most relationship models (Wilson, 1995). Indeed, trust is often stated as a vital factor in successful relationships. Ford (1984, p. 18) sees trust as an important consideration, as '. . . many aspects of relations between customers and suppliers cannot be formalized or based on legal criteria. Instead relationships have to be based on mutual trust'.

Promises must be kept in order to maintain relationships, with mutual trust being a main factor in long-term relationships (Takala and Uusitalo, 1996). The challenge is to demonstrate commitment to a relationship and to inculcate trust in the partner.

A number of authors link trust to commitment. Morgan and Hunt (1994), e.g., argue that both trust and commitment are 'key' elements in a relationship as they encourage work at preserving relationship investments by co-operating with exchange partners. Trust and commitment also aid in resisting attractive short-term alternatives in favour of the expected long-term benefits of staying with existing partners. An environment of relationship commitment and trust produces a desire to provide excellent service. Trust and, most importantly, commitment are key components of value creation. For example, the committed customer is likely to trust the supplier. The likely outcome of this is a reinforcement of the relationship between the two partners. Managing this relationship will involve fine-tuning processes such as regulating the exchange of correct and timely information and the co-ordination of activities (Walter and Ritter, 2003). The closer the two partners merge in their relationship, the greater the chance of creating higher levels of value, expressed in terms of service quality, cost savings, and quick response and differential advantage.

Customer orientation/empathy

The word *empathy* really refers to an understanding of, or the ability to see a situation from, someone else's point of view. The greater the degree of empathy between the parties concerned, the fewer the barriers to relationship development. Empathy is a major influence in establishing relationships and, indeed, even where service delivery has failed, the ability to empathize with the customer can help build a relationship. Customer orientation encourages trust and increases the chance of developing a long-term relationship. Customer orientation requires the whole firm to satisfy customer needs more successfully than the competition.

Experience/satisfaction

Experience is another factor in successful relationships. The decision to continue in a relationship can be seen as dependent on the level of congruity between relationship expectations and performance so far (Levitt, 1981; Jackson, 1985). The more satisfied the customer, the more durable the relationship (Buchanan and Gillies, 1990). Relationship satisfaction is a multidimensional construct, which has been conceptualized as a prerequisite for relationship quality.

Hocutt (1998) links satisfaction with commitment and trust. Although trust directly influences commitment, the relationship between trust and commitment is mediated by both satisfaction with the service provider and relative dependence. Satisfaction, then, is an important component of relationships, both in its own right and in the way it can influence other components.

Communication

Communication is a vital component in the establishment of business relationships, as *all* other components are experienced through the medium of communication. Effective collaboration and co-ordination depend on effective communication, and communication becomes even more important when one is trying to establish business relationships. Seines (1998) agrees, hypothesizing that not only is communication an important element in its own right, but it has the propensity to influence levels of trust between buyer and seller. Similarly, Takala and Uusitalo (1996) see communication as being essential in relationships implying dependence and commitment.

Relationships for all?

Successful relationship development would seem to require a supportive culture. Organizational structures and rewards schemes geared to an understanding of customer expectations using a sophisticated customer database are also likely to be required.

However, recent research suggests that certain variables may make a relationship strategy less attractive (Sharland, 1997). These include the costs incurred in the development and implementation of a relationship marketing strategy (Nevin, 1995) and the extent to which the relationship enhances competitive advantage (Day, 1995).

It is important to note that costs are incurred when building and maintaining relationships (Johanson and Mattsson, 1985; Blois, 1998). Relationships are a 'market investment' or an asset and have positive and negative aspects, their value being determined by the relative importance of each. From the point of view of a specific customer, the balance between the positive and the negative may vary between suppliers for a variety of reasons.

Blois (1996) suggests that the participant's view of the desirability of entering into a relationship will be affected by perceptions of the likely size of the transaction costs involved. Similarly, Håkansson and Snehota (1995) note five negative factors or disadvantages which result from being in a relationship: (1) loss of control, (2) indeterminedness (i.e., difficult to predict), (3) resource demanding, (4) preclusion from other opportunities and (5) unexpected demands. The degree to which each is a disadvantage will vary with each relationship.

Process in action Tesco, a plethora of products and distribution channels

Tesco is one of the world's leading international retailers. Since the company first used the trading name of 'Tesco' in the mid-1920s, the group has expanded into different formats, different markets and different sectors. The principal activity of the group is food retailing, with over 2500 stores worldwide. Tesco employs over 380 000 people in its businesses around the world and aims to deliver a consistently strong customer offer on every visit and every transaction by focusing on the group's core purpose: to create value for customers to earn their lifetime loyalty. This core purpose is delivered through the Tesco values: 'no one tries harder for customers' and 'treat people how we like to be treated'. Tesco has a long-term strategy for growth, based on four key parts: to grow in the core UK business, to expand by growing internationally, to be as strong in non-food as in food and to follow customers into new retailing services.

Core UK
- Market leader
- Multi-format

- Competitive market
- Clubcard.

International
- Twelve markets
- Market leader in five countries
- Multi-format
- Local offer.

Non-food
- Fifty per cent of new space in UK
- Like-for-like sales growing twice as quickly as food
- Extending range.

Retailing services
- Tesco.com
- Tesco personal finance
- Tesco telecoms.

Tesco has four different store formats, each tailored to customers' needs:

Express (up to 3000 sq. ft.)
Express stores offer customers great value, quality and fresh food close to where they live and work. We opened our first Express store in 1994 and now we have over 650 stores selling a range of up to 7000 lines, including fresh produce, wines and spirits, and in-store bakery.

Metro (approx. 7000–15000 sq. ft.)

We opened our first Metro in 1992, bringing the convenience of Tesco to town and city centre locations. Metros cater for thousands of busy customers each week and offer a tailored range of food lines, including ready-meals and sandwiches.

Superstore (approx. 20000–50000 sq. ft.)

Tesco began opening superstores in the 1970s and, during the 1980s and 1990s, built a national network to which we are adding every year. We have an ongoing programme of extending and refreshing our superstores to improve the overall experience for customers. In recent years, we have introduced a number of new non-food ranges into superstores such as DVDs and books.

Extra (approx. 60000 sq. ft. and larger)

Since opening our first Extra in 1997, the one-stop destination store has proved extremely popular. Extra stores offer the widest range of food and non-food lines, ranging from electrical equipment to homewares, clothing, health and beauty, and seasonal items such as garden furniture. We have opened 18 new Extras in 2005, mostly through extensions to existing stores.

Broad appeal

In addition to a variety of formats, Tesco ensures it has broad appeal by continually innovating and investing in new lines to increase choice for our customers. From Value to Finest and lifestyle ranges such as Organic, Free From and Healthy Living, our various own brands enable customers to buy products to complement their lifestyle. We have recently introduced new nutritional 'signpost labelling' which aims to provide customers with the key information they need to help them choose a balanced diet; 2500 packs are already on the shelf and we plan to complete the range by the end of the year.

Distribution systems

Tesco uses a very technologically sophisticated distribution system. On 27 August 2002, it announced that it had rolled out a third-party (Paragon) system for efficient daily planning. Thus, an additional 15 Paragon systems were added to provide complete control of its vehicle routing and scheduling needs, increasing the total number of systems to 26. At that time, these systems were used for the daily planning of 4000 drops made by 1400 vehicles to over 700 stores throughout the UK and Ireland. Tesco's decision to implement the software across its entire food distribution operation reflected satisfaction with previous implementations, including its high-profile and highly successful Internet-based home shopping service.

Interfaced with Tesco's order processing system, Paragon helped Tesco meet its tight store replenishment timescales by completing the routing and scheduling process in several waves throughout the afternoon and evening. Unable to wait for a full day of orders to be received, Paragon got ahead with the scheduling task by processing its first set of orders at around 3 PM each day. Priority loads could then be 'frozen' and released to the pickers and loaders to ensure that despatch deadlines were met. Other loads were carried forward and merged with subsequent order downloads received. This enabled orders from different waves to be amalgamated into the overall distribution plan to maintain efficiency, whilst priority store deliveries were routed, picked and despatched even before the final orders for the day had been received.

In addition to calculating vehicle loads and maintaining an even distribution workload throughout the day, the Paragon system also took constraints associated with different product ranges into consideration. Some chilled produce, e.g., had to arrive at specific times, typically the beginning of the day – something that Paragon was able to build into the overall transport plan. Once scheduled, details of the routes, including planned store arrival times, were passed to an in-cab fleet management system for real-time monitoring.

In 2002, Tesco Distribution was also using Paragon to create scheduling 'routines', a series of best-practice guidelines already embedded into the everyday life of each depot. Not only did the guidelines encourage the same high-quality operational service across the whole of Tesco's business, they also promoted the development of common skills at all sites.

Overall, Tesco Distribution's choice of Paragon for all its temperature-controlled and ambient DCs in the UK and Ireland reflected satisfaction with existing systems. It also indicated a determination to ensure consistency throughout the network

(CASE CONTRIBUTED BY GEOFF SOUTHERN.)

covering 1,400 vehicles delivering to Tesco's 700-plus stores.

'The quality and reliability of the Paragon system made it the obvious choice for Tesco Distribution,' says Ken Davis, Transport Development Manager. 'This combined with the ease of implementation and the high level of support made available, has enabled us to install Paragon systems effectively within all of our 26 distribution centres. This ensures that we maintain a high standard of service throughout the operation. Paragon is a key operational system which we rely on every day.'

Tesco buying policy

Tesco is also re-engineering their supply system in a time of increasing customer concern about the ecological cost of moving food long distances. On 15 September 2006, they announced that they were opening six new devolved buying offices. These were regional buying offices aimed at increasing local sourcing and making it easier for small producers to sell goods through the UK's leading supermarket. The announcement marked the first time that any UK supermarket had opened nationwide regional buying offices and would result in hundreds of new local lines being stocked. The move, which was seen as a huge boost for small suppliers across the UK, was announced by Richard Brasher, the Commercial Director for Tesco, at Tesco's first regional roadshow. He addressed an audience of around 100 local Cornish producers gathered in Padstow to show off their wares to Tesco's senior buying teams with the hope of getting their regional lines stocked. He said:

> We know our customers want to be able to buy more regional products. We also know that smaller suppliers have sometimes found it hard to approach the supermarkets in the past. We want to solve both these issues.
>
> By opening regional buying offices with dedicated teams on the ground, we will achieve this and stock more local lines for our customers.
>
> We will also do more to promote them to customers including regional counters, improved promotional material in stores and a website that will allow them to recommend their favourite regional products to us.

The retailer thus began the process of recruiting regional food experts from across England and Wales. The regional teams were established with buying and marketing managers, as well as technical and merchandising support, and were based within the region they look after.

Question

Which elements of theory from this chapter do you think have informed the developments at Tesco?

Summary

The chapter has covered:

- Logistics management and channel decisions.
- Channel management and channel conflict.
- Value-added strategy and the re-engineering of major processes.

Chapter questions

1. Comment on key functions and processes associated with e-procurement.

2. Critically analyze the rationale behind new systems of wholesaling.

3. Is the focus on product CM going to prevail in future? Why?

References

Anckar, B., Walden, P., and Jelassi, T. (2002) 'Creating customer value in online grocery shopping', *International Journal of Retail & Distribution Management*, 30(4):211–220.

Anderson, E., Day, G., and Rangan, V. K. (1997) 'Strategic perspectives on channel decisions', *Sloane Management Review*, 3(4):59–69.

Anderson, J. C., and Narus, J. A. (1990, January) 'A model of distributor firm and manufacturer firm working partnerships', *Journal of Marketing*, 54:42–58.

Anderson, J. C., and Weitz, B. A. (1989) 'Determinants of continuity in conventional industrial channel dyads', *Marketing Science*, 8(4):310–323.

Anonymous (1997a, February) 'Regions to be cheerful', *Checkout*, pp. 35–40.

Anonymous (1997b, April) 'Retail marketing: Category management – key issue update', *ECR-NAMNEWS*, pp. 10–11.

Basuroy, S., Mantrala, M. K., and Walters, R. G. (2001) 'The impact of category management on retailer prices and performance: Theory and evidence', *Journal of Marketing*, 65:16–22.

Berry, L. C., and Parasuraman, A. (1991) *Marketing Services: Competing through Quality*, New York: Free Press.

Birtwistle, G., Siddiqui, N., and Fiorito, S. S. (2003) 'Quick response: Perceptions of UK fashion retailers', *International Journal of Retail and Distribution Management*, 31(2):118–128.

Blois, K. J. (1996) 'Relationship marketing in organisational markets: Assessing its costs and benefits', *Journal of Strategic Marketing*, 4(3):181–191.

Blois, K. (1998) 'Don't all firms have relationships?', *Journal of Business and Industrial Marketing*, 13(3):256–270.

Boedeker, M. (1997) 'Relationship marketing', *Journal of Marketing relationship and Planning*, 15(6):249–257.

Bower, M., and Garda, R. (1985) 'The role of marketing in management'. in Buell (ed.), *Handbook of Modern Marketing*, New York: McGraw-Hill.

Bowersox, D. J., and Calantone, R. J. (1998) 'Executive insights: Global logistics', *Journal of International Marketing*, 6(4):83–93.

Bowersox, D. J., and Daugherty, P. J. (1995) 'Logistics paradigms: The impact of information technology', *Journal of Business Logistics*, 16(1):65–80.

Bowersox, D. J., and Morash, E. A. (1989) 'The integration of marketing flows in channels of distribution', *European Journal of Marketing*, 23(2):58–67.

Buchanan, R. W. T., and Gillies, C. S. (1990) 'Value managed relationships: The key to customer retention and profitability', *European Management Journal*, 8(4):523–526.

Bucklin, L. P. (1973, January) 'A theory of channel control', *Journal of Marketing*, 37:39–47.

Bucklin, C. B., DeFalco, S. P., DeVincentis, J. R., and Levis, J. P. (1996) 'Are you tough enough to manage your channels?', *The McKinsey Quarterly*, 1:104–114.

Christopher, M. (1998) *Logistics and Supply Chain Management*, Pearson Education Limited, p. 265.

Christopher, M., Ballantyne, D., and Payne, A. (2002) *Relationship Marketing: Creating Shareholder Value*, Oxford: Butterworth-Heinemann.

Conway, T., and Swift, J. S. (2000) 'International relationship marketing: The importance of psychic distance', *European Journal of Marketing*, 34(11/12):1391–1414.

Copulsky, J. R., and Wolf, M. J. (1990) 'Relationship marketing: Positioning for the future', *Journal of Business Srtategy*, 11(10):16–20.

Cravens, D. W. (1991) *Strategic Marketing*, Homewood, Illniois: Imperial.

Dhar, S. K., Hoch, S. J., and Kumar, N. (2001) 'Effective category management depends on the role of the category', *Journal of Retailing*, 77:165–184.

Das, C., and Tyagi, R. (1994) 'Wholesaler: A decision support system for wholesale procurement and distribution', *International Journal of Physical Distribution and Logistics Management*, 24(10):4–12.

Day, G. (1995) 'Advantageous alliances', *Journal of the Academy of Marketing Science*, 23:297–300.

Doyle, P. (1994) *Marketing Management and Strategy*, London: Prentice Hall.

Dwyer, F. R., Schurr, P. H., and Oh, S. (1987, April) 'Developing buyer-seller relationships', *Journal of Marketing*, 11–27.

El-Ansary, A. I., and Robicheaux, R. A. (1974, January) 'A theory of channel control: Revisited', *Journal of Marketing*, 38:2–7.

Etgar, M. (1977, February) 'Channel environment and channel leadership', *Journal of Marketing Research*, xiv, pp. 69–76.

Ford, D. (1984) 'Buyer/seller relationships in international industrial markets', *Industrial Marketing Management*, 13(2):101–113.

Fuller, J. B., O'Conor, J., and Rawlinson, R. (1993, May–June) 'Tailored logistics: The next advantage', *Harvard Business Review*, pp. 87–98.

Giunipero, L. C., Fiorito, S. S., Pearcy, D. H., and Dandeo, L. (2001) 'The impact of vendor incentives on quick response', *International Review of Retail, Distribution and Consumer Research*, 11(4):359–376.

Graham, G., and Hardaker, G. (2000) 'Supply-chain management across the Internet', *International Journal of Physical Distribution & Logistics Management*, 30(3/4):286–295.

Grönroos, C. (1996) 'Relationship marketing: Strategic and tactical implications', *Management Decision*, 34(3):5–15.

Gummesson, E. (1999) *Total Relationship Marketing*, Chartered Institute of Marketing Professional Development, London.

Håkansson, H., and Snehota, I. (1995) 'The burden of relationship or who's next', *Proceedings of the IMP 11th International Conference*, pp. 522–536.

Hocutt, M. A. (1998) 'Relationship dissolution model: Antecedents of relationship commitment and the likelihood of dissolving a relationship', *International Journal of Service Industry Management*, 9(2):189–200.

Holmund, M., and Tornroos, J. K. (1997) 'What are relationships in business networks?', *Management Decision*, 35(4):304–309.

Jackson, B. B. (1985) *Winning and Keeping International Customers*, Lexington, MA: Lexington Books.

Johanson, J., and Mattsson, L. G. (1985) 'Marketing investments and market investments in industrial networks', *International Journal of Research in Marketing*, 2(2):185–195.

Kotler, P. (1991) *Marketing Management*, London: Prentice Hall.

LaLonde, B., and Maltz, A. B. (1992) 'Some propositions about outsourcing the logistics function', *International Journal of Logistics Management*, 3(1):1–11.

Lancaster, G. A., and Lassingham, L. (1988) *Essentials of Marketing, Text and Cases*, London: McGraw-Hill.

Levitt, T. (1981) 'Marketing intangible products and product intangibles', *Harvard Business Review*, 61(5):94–102.

Liu, H., and Davies, G. (1996) 'Marketing orientation in UK multiple retail companies: Nature and pattern', *International Journal of Service Industry Management*, 8(2):170–187.

Love, T., and Tellefsen, B. (2000) 'Constituent market orientation and ownership of virtual marketplaces', *Logistics Information Management*, 16(1):8–17.

Magrath, A. J., and Hardy, K. G. (1987, September/October) 'Avoiding the pitfalls in managing distribution channels', *Business Horizons*, pp. 29–33.

McGrath, M. (1997) *A Guide to Category Management*, Institute for Grocery Distribution, Watford, UK, p. 9.

McKenna, S. (1991) *The Complete Guide to Marketing*, New York: McGraw Hill.

Mietilla, A., and Möller, K. (1990) 'Interaction perspective into professional business services: A conceptual analysis', in Fiocca, A., and Snehota, I. (eds.), *Research Developments in International Industrial Marketing and Purchasing*, Proceedings of the 6th IMP Conference, Univesity of Bocconi, Milan, Italy.

Morgan, R. M., and Hunt, S. B. (1994) 'The commitment-trust theory of relationship marketing', *Journal of Marketing*, 58(July):20–38.

Nevin, J. (1995) 'Relationship marketing and distribution channels: Exploring fundamental issues', *Journal of the Academy of Marketing Science*, 29(4):327–334.

Newman, A. (2004) 'Retailing definitions', in Date Littler (ed.), *Blackwell's Encyclopedia of Marketing* (in press).

Newman, A. J., and Patel, D. (2004) 'Store image attributes: The marketing directions of two UK fashion retailers', *European Journal of Marketing* (special issue: Fashion Retailing, in press).

O'Keeffe, M., and Fearne, A. (2002) 'From commodity marketing to category management: Insights from the Waitrose category leadership program in fresh produce', *Supply Chain Management: An International Journal*, 7(5):296–301.

Olorunniwo, F., and Wood, D. (1998, May/June) 'Reengineering in the wholesale and retail industries', *Industrial Management*, pp. 8–11.

Pitt, L., Berthon, P., and Berthon, J. P. (1999, March/April) 'Changing channels: The impact of the internet on distribution strategy', *Business Horizons*, pp. 19–28.

Porter, M. E. (1985) *Competitive Advantage*, New York: The Free Press, pp. 11–15.

Reynold, J. (1997) 'Retailing in computer mediated environments: Electronic commerce across Europe', *International Journal of Retail & Distribution Management*, 25(1):29–37.

Rosenbloom, B. (1994) *Marketing Channels: A Management View*, London: Dryden Press.

Rusbult, C. E., and Buunk, B. P. (1993) 'Commitment processes in close relationships: An interdependence analysis', *Journal of Social and Personal Relationships*, 10(2):175–204.

Seines, F. (1998) 'Antecedents and consequences of trust and satisfaction in buyer/seller relationships', *European Journal of Marketing*, 32(3/4):305–322.

Sharland, A. (1997) 'Sourcing strategy: The impact of costs on relationship outcomes', *International Journal of Physical Distribution and Logistics Management*, 27(7):395–409.

Sherman, R. J. (1998) 'Supply chain management for the millennium', *Warehousing and Education Research Council*, pp. 1–16.

Skinner, S. J., Gassenheimer, J. B., and Kelley, S. W. (1992) 'Cooperation in supplier dealer relations', *Journal of Retailing*, 68(2):174–193.

Stalk, G., Evans, P., and Shulman, L. (1992) 'Competing on capability: The new rules of corporate strategy', *Harvard Business Review*, 70(2):57–69.

Stern, L. W., and El-Ansary, A. I. (1988) *Marketing Channels* (3rd edn.), Englewood Cliffs, NJ: Prentice Hall.

Svensson, G. (2001) 'Re-evaluating the marketing concept', *European Business Review*, 13(2):95–100.

Takala, T., and Uusitalo, O. (1996) 'An alternative view of relationship marketing: A framework for ethical analysis', *European Journal of Marketing*, 30(2):45–60.

Vaile, R. S., Grether, E. T., and Cox, R. (1952) *Marketing in the American Economy*, New York: The Ronald Press Co.

van Weele, A. J. (2002) *Purchasing and Supply Chain Management*, Thomson Learning.

Waller, D. L. (2003) *Operations Management – A Supply Chain Approach*, (2nd edn.)Thomson Learning.

Walter, A., and Ritter, T. (2003) 'The influence of adaptations, trust, and commitment on value-creating functions of customer relationships', *Journal of Business and Industrial Marketing*, 18(4/5):353–365.

Wilkinson, I. F. (1996) 'Distribution channel management: Power considerations', *International Journal of Physical Distribution and Logistics Management*, 26(5):31–41.

Wilson, D. T. (1995) 'An integrated model of buyer-seller relationships', *Journal of the Academy of Marketing Science*, 23(4):334–345.

Wilson, D. T., and Vlosky, R. P. (1998) 'Interorganizational information system technology and buyer-seller relationships', *Journal of Business and Industrial Marketing*, 13(3):215–234.

Part five

Getting new customer processes (order acquisition)

While good order fulfilment keeps existing customers, new ones must be attracted if a business is to grow. Hence, order acquisition is equally as important as order fulfilment for most organizations.

Chapter 12 explores marketing and resource allocation in financial management. It deals with issues such as allocation of resources, economic appraisal of capital projects and associated investment decisions, long-term capital budgeting, financial control systems, the mix of investments, operational budgeting, managing resources, cash flow and liquidity. 'Process in action' notes in this chapter consist of illustrations of comparisons of alternative methods of project appraisal and illustrations of budgeting techniques. In addition, illustrations of budgeting techniques cover the sales budget and the production budget.

Chapter 13 introduces reputation management, corporate image and communication. Reputation management is of immense importance to organizations and must be done well to achieve approval by stakeholders. Topics covered here include ethical environments, leadership, innovation, quality and relationships with stakeholders. It also discusses the boundaries between branding, image and reputation, as well as the transnational nature of reputation. A 'process in action' note illustrates how the reputation of Coca-Cola, accumulated over a century, was severely damaged by a delay in responding to a technical problem affecting product quality and how financial results were affected.

Chapter 14 tackles innovation management, marketing timing and solutions planning. It covers topics such as constant renewal, research data, technological innovations, novel solutions, short-lived new concepts, success factors, continuous innovation, competitiveness, risks, financial and intellectual resources, time management, market changes, market saturation, development costs and innovation strategies. The 'process in action' note returns to Tesco (previously used in Chapter 11), but now concentrates on their continuing innovation of service delivery modes.

12

Marketing and resource allocation in financial management

James Wilson and Luiz Moutinho

Introduction

This chapter deals with issues involving the allocation of resources to the various activities in which an organization engages. Marketing is one of those activities, supported by the other functional areas of the organization. Rather than seeing these as competing for resources, these should be considered complementary and mutually interdependent.

We will begin with a review of the economic appraisal of capital projects and associated investment decisions. In addition to these long-term investment allocation decisions – often called *capital budgeting* – there are also short-term issues that will be considered in the allocation of resources to operational concerns.

Case notes in this chapter will consist of illustrations of the various budgeting techniques described and comparisons of alternative methods of project appraisal.

Learning objectives

On reading this chapter, students should have knowledge of:
Long-term investments:

- Whether to invest in a single project.

- The choice of one project from a set of investment opportunities.

- The mix of investments when there are constraints on the total capital.

Short-term resource allocation and financial control systems:

- The use of operating budgets to allocate and manage resources.

- The impact of operations on the cash flow and liquidity of the organization.

The role of budgets in resource allocation

Organizations develop business strategies to recognize overall, long-term goals and to identify approaches suitable for attaining those objectives. Achieving these strategic objectives will require the organization to acquire what might be described as 'infrastructure' – the buildings, equipment, staff, products, intellectual capital, brands and distribution networks necessary to support their operations. These resources and organizational capabilities, and their development, typically require investment. Staff development requires recruitment and training; new products may require research and development; market development may require cultivation through marketing and advertising; growth may require new distribution and production facilities; and production systems may require investment in new equipment, processes and facilities.

These longer-term developments compete for an organization's capital, and it may be allocated between them through what is generally known as a 'capital budget'. Organizations may set aside a fixed amount for these developments, or they may take a more flexible approach, but regardless of the approach taken, these needs have to be prioritized and the capital allocated between them. These choices should reflect strategic and economic objectives. The underlying theory of capital budgeting is highly developed and its basics will be explored later in this chapter. The actual practice of capital budgeting may not be as sophisticated in its application, and examples of these approaches will also be explored.

It isn't only in the long term that an organization develops plans to co-ordinate the diverse activities of its various functions and units. These plans reflect the organization's goals and its efforts towards achieving them. Where these efforts involve different people, equipment and facilities, their shorter-term operations also need to be co-ordinated and directed. This co-ordination may be critical to succeeding in achieving the desired strategic goals. Unless there is effective co-ordination and control of the organization's activities, it may find that the resources it deploys are not acting in concert, and their individual efforts do not yield the desired results and may even be counterproductive. One major tool for co-ordination and control is an operating budget that allocates finance towards providing the physical resources required for fulfilling the organization's plans. The sales an organization makes require production, either during the period in which the sales arise or earlier, and that production will require staff, materials, equipment and inventory. The linking of sales with production activities and the demand derived from that for employment, training, working capital, etc., may be most effectively communicated by providing finance for them, and an operating budget is the chief mechanism for that. Budgets, then, represent a considered decision providing resources throughout the organization consistent with the requirements placed on each by the organization as a whole. In the short term, these are operating budgets that link current activities and those in the immediate future to current and short-term plans and goals.

A budget is a business plan defined in monetary terms that describes the resources to be acquired and used within an organization during a specified period. It facilitates planning. It provides accurate and clear communication to each part of the organization and co-ordinates their individual activities, and it provides control measures for assessing performance.

Budgets allocate resources

Finance can be considered a universal resource, as it facilitates the acquisition and use of all the other resources required and used by organizations. Every business plan or strategy may be reduced to a set of financial considerations and requirements. In the short term, an organization's plans for production, distribution, inventories, purchases, sales and employment require working capital. Each of these requires financial support, and that support must be explicitly allocated before the operational requirements for these resources and their use in the organization's activities arises. From a marketing perspective, the demand for sales dictates specific supporting activities in production and distribution with consequent impacts on raw materials, work-in-process, finished goods and distribution inventories. Sales are often facilitated by an organization's credit policies, and these too impose financial demands on an organization; the management of the short-term financial demands requires a clear plan for the organization's working capital. One key component of an organization's working capital is the cash it has available. A cash budget is often prepared to show projections of a company's cash flows so that it may carefully consider the monies it receives and has available in comparison to the varied demands for payment or the use of cash that it will face.

Unless an organization links its budget development to its strategic plans, it has little assurance that its resources will support those plans. Finance supports marketing, operations and staffing – everything that the organization does or uses in pursuing its objectives and purposes. No manager can effectively develop or implement a strategy unless they understand well how the resources can be provided and employed to support it.

Types of budgets: capital, operating and cash

It is useful to distinguish between the differing levels at which organizations use resources. In discriminating between resource use, the time frame in which demands for finance arise can be a very effective discriminating factor. In this we can discern financing requirements that arise in day-to-day activities, those that arise in the short or intermediate term, and longer-term needs for financial support. An organization must have a cash budget to provide cash and liquidity for meeting the demands it faces for payments, just as most people find it necessary to have some amount of cash available to enable them to make the economic transactions involved in their everyday lives. A company that cannot pay its bills or meet its obligations may be forced into bankruptcy. Organizations must balance their books and ensure that they have the necessary funds available when and where they're required. Failing to do so may have repercussions beyond simple finance: suppliers may refuse delivery unless orders are prepaid, vendors may charge higher prices or impose penalties for late payment and the unhappiness of unpaid staff may create significant management problems. The availability of cash balances and the effective short-term use of credit are critical for the smooth operation and financial credibility of an organization. A company's operations may then be judged in terms of their effects on a company's cash flows and the resources used or available.

The operating budget may be envisaged as representing the resource impact of the organization's short- and intermediate-term activities, covering as much as a year's efforts. These link to a business plan, which typically uses a 1-year planning horizon, subdivided into monthly (or, less commonly, quarterly) periods. The operating budget is a prime tool, whereby the organization's expected sales may be linked to the demands these sales place on current production and past inventories, on the production activities' demands for staffing and materials and on the demands for purchased components derived from those production activities (see Figure 12.1).

The key to understanding an operating budget is its focus on the operational activities necessary to support an organization's objectives as codified in its annual plan – a statement identifying what the company's sales objectives are and what inventories and production are needed to support them – and all the other activities needed in the short term for their satisfaction. The outputs produced by an organization generate income. This income may be reflected in the receipts of cash or customer debt. These cash inflows cannot arise without associated outflows – cash payments or promises to the company's suppliers and staff. An individual might have a personal budget that reflects anticipated income and various expenditures, and balances or attempts to match them over the planning/budgeting period. These short- and intermediate-term resource uses and their financial consequences are the focus of an organization's operating budget.

But not all of the resources used by an organization are completely used or created within its annual operations. These longer-term resources and changes in them reflect an organization's longer-term strategic plans and those resources required for making them possible. In the longer term, organizations use productive resources like equipment, buildings and intellectual property. These investments require financial support beyond the immediate or short term. Strategic policies require financial support in the longer term, and this requires a planned approach that accumulates finance over several years or that considers using long-term debt or finance and paying that off from the future operations it enables. In the context of personal finance, an individual might choose to save for a major purchase such as an automobile or an annual holiday or may commit to major borrowings such as a mortgage for a house or other long-lived asset that may be enjoyed for many years.

Budgets may then be seen as useful tools that assist organizations in implementing their plans, with capital budgets reflecting the longer-term interests of the organization in acquiring and paying for major capital assets, with operating budgets used to implement annual business plans and reflecting the costs associated and the revenues generated by those plans, and with cash budgets reflecting the short-term impacts of those activities on the liquidity of the company.

Budgets, motivation and co-ordination

Budgets provide more than simple financial information; they also serve to highlight those activities and involvements that an organization considers important. In both strategy and operations, money speaks louder than words when indicating what management really considers important and worthy of support.

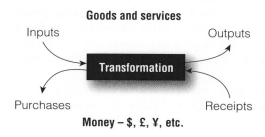

Figure 12.1

Financial flows match physical activities

Capital budgets and investment planning

Organizations raise capital and allocate (i.e., invest) it to the various activities needed. Thus, funds may be raised through the sale of shares or through borrowing from investors or financial institutions. These funds may then be used to invest in the capital resources used by the organization: its buildings, plant and equipment; patents and other intellectual rights and products the organization will exploit; and market development. Organizations make investments to support their strategies and long-term plans not just when they start up, but at numerous other times when new opportunities or threats emerge or resources become available. Capital budgeting may be identified by its concern with the organization's long-term investment decisions that necessarily involve the commitment of finance over a period of several years. These investments usually involve very large expenditures. Some capital assets may be bought and paid for quite quickly – buildings, land, equipment, product rights, etc. – while others may require expenditure over a number of years before the asset may be used, such as new product development, construction of a building, process improvement and building brand recognition. Capital budgeting allows managers to effectively consider the competing demands for investment and to direct finance to those developments that are most attractive or rewarding.

Financial analysis provides a critical tool that allows managers to compare investment alternatives across a variety of areas which may all present sound reasons for their support. These comparisons are a critical focus for financial analysts and for operational managers seeking support for developments in their areas.

Assessing individual projects

In capital budgeting, the first step is to assess the impact of the individual alternatives available. These may be very different, ranging from marketing initiatives such as new product or market development, advertising or other promotional campaigns to operational concerns such as investing in new facilities, equipment or production processes, staff issues involving training or longer-term staff development.

Regardless of the functional area, each alternative needs a clear definition of its costs and benefits, and when they occur. This is often described as 'cost – benefit' analysis, and it seeks to determine as fully and accurately as possible the net economic benefit associated with the proposed investments. This analysis can be very difficult in some cases. Most often, investments involve spending money today to obtain capabilities that can only be exploited in later years, making the problem one of comparing a known current cost to future forecast (and hence uncertain) benefits. This may be further compounded by the nature of the benefits contemplated. Many projects may yield financial benefits through increased sales or reduced costs. On the other hand, others may provide benefits that do not have an immediate or obvious financial reward. For example, a company may improve its products and processes to achieve a higher-quality product. This may attract customers or provide some competitive advantage, but the links may be very uncertain and difficult or impossible to measure. Nevertheless, organizations should assess both tangible and intangible costs and benefits for their projects. (See Table 12.1 for examples.)

It is useful to distinguish between a project's fixed costs, such as those incurred in developing and starting it up, and those that arise later during its operation. For example, new product development may involve initial research which would then lead to more product-specific applied development. Before production can start, there would be additional investment required in facilities or processes, tooling and staff training; the actual launch of the product may also entail a variety of costs. These may all be incurred before a single unit is either produced or sold. Costs like these may be identified as project initiation or start-up costs and may be of particular interest since they effectively are the first set of costs that a project imposes. The implementation phase, during which the product is produced and sold, may involve a number of operating costs: the costs of making and distributing the product, such as wages, materials, power, heating, storage, transport, sales commissions and taxes. All these may be described as 'ongoing costs', and they will generally vary with the scale of the activities and occur at the specific times when those activities occur. These running or operating costs are significant, but they will often be offset by revenues or income they generate, usually from the sales of the products and services provided. Once the project has ended, there may be costs (or revenues) associated with its closing: There may be disposal costs or salvage values for old equipment, or a new product development may finish with costs for patenting the product or revenues from its successful sale. Thus, a project may generate shutdown costs or revenues.

Any assessment of a project must consider all the associated costs and revenues – start up, operating and shutdown – in order to give a comprehensive and realistic understanding of its costs and benefits to the organization. In passing, it should be noted that there are distinct points where managers make decisions about projects – the initial investment decision is most commonly the major focus of interest in assessing projects and whether they should be supported with capital investment, but other points are appropriate for reassessing such investments. Most frequently, these arise at the point where the initial development work has been completed and organizations must then make a further commitment to production or operating, usually incurring major costs to do so. A reassessment of the likely benefits and costs of continuing is generally undertaken, looking *only* at the costs and benefits from that time forward. The initial costs may then be disregarded as having already been spent, and only the marginal or opportunity costs that remain should influence the decision. For example, an organization may find that its development costs have grossly exceeded what it had anticipated. But that fact shouldn't prejudice the assessment of the costs and benefits of going forward with the project, for

	Tangible	**Intangible**
Costs	Purchase price Installation costs Training costs Financing costs	Disruption to current activity Loss of staff morale/motivation Risk of failure
Benefits	Increased revenues Reduced operating costs Faster service – higher throughput	Improved product recognition Better customer relations Improved staff morale/motivation Reduced breakdowns

Table 12.1
Tangible and intangible costs and benefits – examples

it may be as profitable as previously forecast and attractive. Even if the excessive development costs are so great that they make the overall project run at a loss, that loss would be less than that incurred by simply killing the project after development. The benefits from its operations would reduce the loss, even if they cannot eliminate it entirely.

Simple methods for assessing projects

In industry, many firms use very simplistic methods for investment appraisal. Where capital has a cost, and this is usually the case, these basic methods are not recommended. However, because of their widespread use, they are described briefly here. They may be suitable for relatively small and short-term projects for which the more sophisticated methods might be considered too complex and analytical 'overkill'.

Process in action illustration of payback period and accounting rate of return

Table 12.2 indicates some of the difficulties with the payback method. Project A is preferred to B and C because it has the shortest payback period. Projects B and C are equally ranked, although Project C has a higher return over the whole of its life – the payback method ignores cash flows beyond the payback period.

A further problem may arise because the payback method simply looks at the time needed to recover the costs. This ignores the relative profitability of the projects; another simple alternative may choose to focus on profitability rather than simple cost as a means of trying to make better decisions in assessing projects.

The method used is the 'accounting rate of return' (ARR) that looks at the project's average accounting profit per unit of investment. It takes account of returns over the whole of the project's life. The lifetime income of each project is compared to its costs to yield a lifetime profit; this is then spread over the life to find a rough estimate of the average annual profit in terms of a percentage of the initial costs involved. The ARR is:

ARR = (Average annual profit / Investment) × 100%

Table 12.2
The payback method

	Project A	Project B	Project C
Investment	−£1,000	−£1,000	−£1,000
Return: Year 1	£740	£500	£500
Year 2	£500	£750	£750
Year 3	—	—	£50
Payback	Year 1:740	Year 1:500	Year 1:500
	Year 2:	Year 2:	Year 2:
	(1000 − 740)/500	(1000 − 500)/750	(1000 − 500)/750
	= 260/500	= 500/750	= 500/750
	0.52	0.67	0.67
	Shortest		

The 'payback method' is the simplest non-discounting approach. The payback period is the time a project must run for its cash flows to repay the initial investment. Projects with shorter payback periods are preferred, and the decision rule is to accept those projects with payback periods less than some target period. The method favours short-term returns, and cash inflows beyond the payback period are ignored. This may lead to worthwhile projects being rejected, particularly those with longer-term rewards. However, the method is very simple, and it does provide a means of allowing for risk by requiring 'risky' projects to be paid back earlier than others.

Time preference and discounting

Capital investment in a project involves making a payment now in the hope of generating a larger return in the future. To make rational investment choices, the decision-maker must be able to value and compare cash outflows and inflows which occur at different times and to value present and future consumption opportunities.

The projects shown in Table 12.2 are replicated and shown again in Table 12.3. Project B is now preferred to A and C on the basis of ARR. Although Project C provides the same returns as B in years 1 and 2, plus an additional return in year 3, the additional year's revenue works against it by yielding a lower-than-average return in that last year.

The ARR is a useful and easily understood technique, and it assesses projects in terms of their profitability and return on investment so that these may more easily be compared to the organization's financial objectives. It is a generally accepted method that provides consistent measures, and the ARR is a better performance index than the payback period, which excludes some returns. It is not without problems; the definition of the profits and investment may lack consensus, and while it is very useful where the annual profits are stable, it can introduce distortions in using an average for those cases where the profits differ significantly over the life of the project.

Both the payback period and the ARR provide useful and simple methods for comparing short-term, small projects, but they are inadequate for larger projects or for those having durations of several years or longer. The simplicity of these methods cannot cope well with the complexities of the cash flows and the need to consider the timings of those cash flows more fully. In these cases, more sophisticated methods are used based on the effects that time has on project valuation.

Question
Project A has the shortest payback period but Project B has the highest ARR. If you could only choose one, which would it be and why?

	Project A	Project B	Project C
Investment	−£1,000	−£1,000	−£1,000
Return: Year 1	£740	£500	£500
Year 2	£500	£750	£750
Year 3	—	—	£50
Profit	£240	£250	£300
Profit per year	£120	£125	£100
ARR	12%	12.5%	10%

Table 12.3
The accounting rate of return

In this section, a simple model is developed to illustrate the reasons why discount rates are positive and the economic rationale for borrowing. Consider a simple two-period model where an economic agent can consume a portion of their wealth in period 1 and invest the remainder in order to produce goods and consumption and reinvestment in period 2. Figure 12.2 illustrates the options open to the agent. They can choose to consume most of their stock in period 1 and be short in period 1, or they can invest heavily in period 1 in order to enjoy the fruits of that investment.

Figure 12.3 shows how the agent's preferences for goods in periods 1 and 2 can be represented by 'indifference curves'. Points A and B represent different consumption and investment patterns which the agent values equally. Indifference values are lines of equally desirable opportunities; they are analogous to isobars in weather charts or contours on a map. Point C represents an opportunity more desirable than either A or B; it is on a higher-level indifference curve. Figure 12.4 combines the previous two figures to show how, in the model, the economic agent will make this choice. They must choose

Figure 12.2

Time preference for money

Time preference for money; x-axis, quantity consumed in period 1; y-axis, quantity available to consumption and investment in period 2.

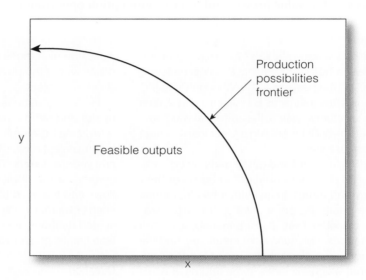

Figure 12.3

Indifference curves

Showing trade-offs between future and current consumptions preferences.

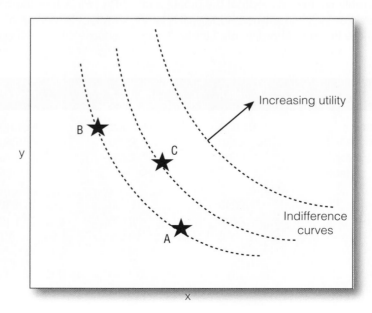

some mixture of consumption and investment within the range of feasible outputs. Any point along, e.g., EF indifference curve (1) would be equally desirable. However, more desirable alternatives exist, as there are feasible outputs on higher-level indifference curves. The optimum schedule, from the agent's point of view, is point D, where an indifference curve is tangential to the production possibility frontier.

Figure 12.5 introduces borrowing and lending into the model. If it is possible to borrow or lend at an interest rate of r, then consumption can be shifted between periods along a borrowing/lending line such as HI with slope $-(1 + r)$.

In this case, the agent borrows in order to produce at point D′ while adopting the consumption pattern of point G – the point where indifference curve (3) is tangential to the borrowing/lending line HI. HI is itself tangential to the production possibility frontier at D′.

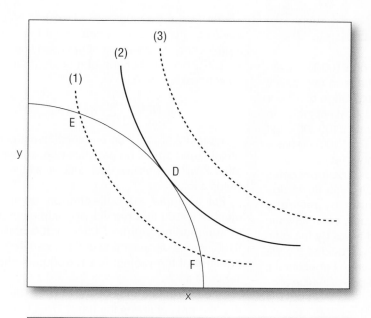

Figure 12.4
Consumption and investment

Borrowing and saving is used to shift consumption between periods.

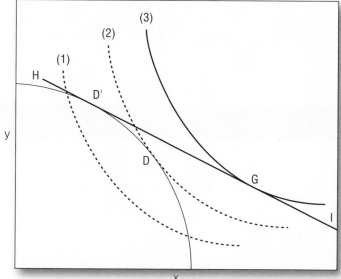

Figure 12.5
Consumption, investment and borrowing

It is the ability of borrowing, even at a cost, to uplift the consumption possibilities of producers to higher-level indifference curves, which causes a demand for borrowed funds and a market price for them in the form of a rate of interest.

Net present value

The relative values placed on capital held at different times can be represented by a set of exchange rates. This is illustrated in the following case note.

Process in action illustration of the concept of net present value and use in comparison of projects

If a firm places the same value on £100 000 available now as on £110 000 available in one year's time, it has an implied rate of exchange of 10 per cent. This is the firm's 'marginal investment rate': to obtain £110 000 in one year's time, £100 000 must be invested now at 10 per cent. The £100 000 has a discounted value now (a 'present value').

Hence all cash flows at 10 per cent becomes £110 000 in one year's time, all cash flows due in one year can be discounted by the ratio 100 000/110 000 or 1/1.1. Similarly, cash flows in two years' time are discounted twice by the ratio 1/1.1 to get their present values, provided the implicit interest rate remains the same. For example, £121 000 due in two years has a present value of:

$$£121 000 \times (1/1.1) \times (1/1.1) = £100 000$$

It would be necessary to invest £100 000 now at 10 per cent to obtain £121 000 in two years' time.

In general, the present value of a cash flow X, due in t years' time is:

$$X_t/(1+r)^t$$

where r is the discount rate expressed as a decimal (e.g., 10 per cent is equivalent to $r = 0.1$). If a project has a sequence of net cash flows X_0, X_1, X_2, … X_n over its horizon of n years, then its 'net present value' (NPV) is

$$NPV = \sum_{t=0}^{n} X_t/(1+r)^t$$

Typically, X_0 may be an initial investment in a project, and so will be negative (a cost), while the other X will be positive cash inflows as the project yields a return.

For example, suppose that an initial investment of £1000 in a project will yield cash returns in succeeding years of £500, £300, £400 and £100. With a discount rate of 5 per cent ($r = 0.05$), the NPV of the project is £176 000, as shown in Table 12.4.

The NPV of the project is £176.11. This means that the project saves the firm £176.11 compared with what it would have to invest at its marginal rate to achieve the same cash flow. Table 12.5 shows that an initial investment of £1176.11 at

Table 12.4
Net present value of a project

X_t				Present value (discounted at 5%)
Investment	X_0	−£1000	—	£1 000.00
Return=Year 1	X_1	£500	500/1.05 =	£ 476.19
Year 2	X_2	£300	300/(1.05)² =	£ 272.11
Year 3	X_3	£400	400/(1.05)³ =	£ 345.54
Year 4	X_4	£100	100(1.05)⁴ =	£ 82.27
Net present value				£ 176.11

➜

5 per cent is needed to give cash returns of £500, £300, £400 and £100 in successive years. The advantage of the project is that it gives the same cash flows for only £1000. The NPV is the present value of the surplus which the firm makes over and above what it could make by investing at its marginal rate.

In the example above, the cash flows in each year were all different. If the cash flows are constant for each time period, so that $X_1 = X_2 = \cdots = X_n = X$, the series of cash flows is called an 'annuity'. The present value of an annuity of n years' duration is:

$$NPV = (X/r)(1-(1/(1+r)^n))$$

The NPV of a project's future cash flows proves an immediate criterion for deciding whether to accept or reject the project. If the NPV is positive, investing in the project gives returns which are greater than the firm could get by investing the same amount at the firm's marginal investment rate; hence the project is worthwhile and should be accepted.

If the NPV is negative, the firm can get a better return by investing elsewhere at its marginal rate, and the project should be rejected.

Question
What is the advantage of the NPV project evaluation technique over the simple payback and ARR techniques discussed earlier?

Initial investment	1176.11
Interest at 5%	59.81
Balance at end of year 1	1234.92
Payment to shareholders X_1	500.00
Balance at start of year 2	734.92
Interest at 5%	36.74
Balance at end of year 2	711.66
Payment to shareholders X_2	300.00
Balance at start of year 3	471.66
Interest at 5%	23.58
Balance at end of year 3	495.24
Payment to shareholders X_3	400.00
Balance at start of year 4	95.24
Interest at 5%	4.76
Balance at end of year 4	100.00
Payment to shareholders X_4	100.00
Balance at start of year	nil

Table 12.5
An equivalent investment

Internal rate of return

An alternative to the positive NPV criterion for project appraisal is a requirement that the internal rate of return (IRR) of the project's cash flows exceeds the firm's marginal cost of capital. The IRR is the rate of discounting which equates the present value of the project's cash inflows with the present value of the investment. The IRR is the discount rate for which the project's NPV is zero. It is calculated by solving for r in the equation

$$\sum_{t=0}^{n} X_t/(1 + r)^t = 0$$

Solving this equation to determine the IRR generally requires an iterative trial-and-error approach, easily programmed if standard commercial software for doing so is not available.

The IRR may be interpreted as the maximum rate of interest that the firm should pay if the project is to be financed entirely by borrowing, and the project's cash flows are to be used to repay the initial loan and its interest charges. If the IRR exceeds the cost of borrowing, then the project should be accepted. Alternatively, if the firm is providing its own finance, the project should be accepted provided the IRR exceeds the return the firm could get by investing elsewhere at its marginal rate.

There are a number of problems associated with the IRR. The basis of these problems is that an IRR has a mathematical meaning as a root of an equation whatever its value, but an economic meaning only in relation to sensitivity analysis with respect to an appropriate marginal cost of capital. This is illustrated by the possibility of multiple IRR values. The equation must be solved to determine the IRR is a polynomial of degree n, so it has n – 1 roots. The number of real roots is equal to the number of sign changes. There may be several discount rates for which the NPV is zero, and there are no generally accepted criteria for deciding which is 'correct'. If a project requires an initial investment and thereafter returns positive net cash flows, there will be only one positive value of r. However, multiple rates may arise in projects that require frequent plant refurbishment or a cash outlay at abandonment. For example, a nuclear reactor must be demolished or made safe at the end of its useful life. There are methods of extending the IRR approach to avoid the problems of multiple solutions, but they are beyond the scope of this chapter.

The need to concentrate on an economically viable value is also illustrated by an assumption implicit in its use: The IRR method assumes that any borrowing or lending (e.g., the investment of cash surpluses generated by the project) takes place at the IRR. This assumption may be unrealistic if the inherent profitability of the project is considerably different from the firm's cost of capital.

Comparing net present value and internal rate of return

The NPV and extended IRR methods can be compared in the context of the main kinds of investment decisions that must be made. Acceptance and rejection occur when a firm is prepared to invest in all projects that are profitable given the firm's cost of capital. A project will be accepted if it has a positive NPV when its cash flows are discounted at the firm's cost of capital or if its IRR exceeds the cost of capital. Both NPV and IRR lead to the same accept/reject decisions for all projects, subject to dealing with any multiple roots in IRR, and the methods are equivalent in this case.

For consistency between the NPV and IRR criteria, the IRR decision rule must be modified so that the larger of the two projects is chosen provided the incremental IRR exceeds the firm's marginal investment rate. This selects the same set of projects as the NPV criterion. The incremental IRR has the advantage that the amount by which it exceeds the marginal rate indicates the 'risk' associated with the additional investment in the larger project.

Both NPV and IRR criteria require adjustment if they are to be used for ranking projects where there is a constraint or limit on some resource input. Problems of this nature will be discussed below under 'capital rationing'.

In many ways, the NPV and the modified IRR criteria are equivalent in that they lead to the same decisions. In practice, though, IRR may be preferred. Rates of return are more easily understood by business decision-makers and may be preferred to NPVs. They also allow the decision-maker to assess the 'riskiness' of a project, in a form of 'discounting for risk', although it will be seen later that there are more suitable ways of dealing with risk.

Process in action illustration of choosing between mutually exclusive projects using internal rate of return

When a firm must choose between mutually exclusive investments (either Project A or Project B, but not both), NPV and IRR may lead to different conclusions. For example, suppose Project A requires an initial investment of £2000 and yields £700 for each of the next four years, while Project B costs £500 and returns £200 in each of the next four years. Cash flows, NPV at the rate of 10 per cent, and the IRR for each project are shown in Table 12.6. Project A has the higher NPV, while Project B has the higher IRR.

The difficulty with the IRR criterion in this case is that it indicates a preference for a higher rate of return on a *smaller* investment; in other words, the projects are not strictly comparable. It is more appropriate to compare Project A's investment of £2000 at 15 per cent with Project B's investment of £500 at 21.8 per cent *plus* an investment.

The surplus £1500 is at the marginal market rate of 10 per cent. This can be done by examining the differential cash flows (the return from A less the return from B in each period) and determining the rate of return being made on the surplus invested in Project A. In this example, the IRR of the surplus is 12.6 per cent, which is greater than the firm's marginal rate, so Project A is preferred to Project B. Project A offers everything that Project B offers, plus a 12.6 per cent rate of return on the incremental capital investment of £1500 in Project A.

Questions

1. Which of the two projects would you prefer to invest in and why?

2. How would consideration of inherent risk affect your opinion?

	Project A	Project B	Differential A–B
Investment	−£2000	−£500	−£1500
Return: Year 1	£700	£200	£500
Year 2	£700	£200	£500
Year 3	£700	£200	£500
Year 4	£700	£200	£500
NPV at 10%	£219	£134	£85
IRR	15%	21.8%	21.6%

Table 12.6
Mutually exclusive projects

The IRR method does not require a value for the firm's cost of capital, at least when it is calculated initially for decision-making. Some cutoff rate is needed for project acceptance, but this can be a matter of management judgement in the light of the inherent riskiness of the project (noted above) and uncertainty about future market rates of return. Other forms of risk analysis may be appropriate at this stage, but they are beyond the scope of this chapter. A measure of the firm's costs of capital may be necessary with the IRR criterion, but it is used in a different way and at a different state in the decision process.

Choice of the discount rate

The NPV approach requires the decision-maker to have some set discount rate for use in the calculations of present values, and the IRR approach requires a discount rate that serves as the minimum acceptable rate of return. This discount rate is referred to variously as the 'marginal investment rate' or the 'cost of capital'; in the context of internal rates of return, it is also the 'hurdle rate' or the 'cutoff rate'.

In general, the cost of capital increases as the amount of borrowing increases. If projects are ranked in order of decreasing internal rates of return, the firm should continue to borrow until the marginal cost of additional funds is exactly offset by the marginal rate of return at which they can be invested (point A in Figure 12.6). The relevant discount rate for the firm is the marginal rate where the lines intersect at A in Figure 12.6.

The cost of capital includes the indirect costs of using a particular form of financing plus the undirected costs of using this form of financing on all other sources of funds. Hence, the total cost of capital will depend on its source and on the capital structure of the firm. The major sources of funds are debt, equity and retained earnings.

Fixed-interest stock includes debentures and preference stock as well as fixed-interest short- and long-term loans. The cost of this form of financing is the interest rate payable less any allowance for taxation.

Funding a project by means of an equity stock issue to existing shareholders should only occur if the return on the project is at least as good as the shareholders could get

Figure 12.6

Discount rates and the cost of capital

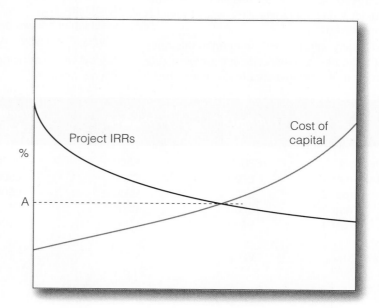

by investing elsewhere. The project's marginal rate of return must be at least as great as the shareholders' opportunity rate of return for marginal investments, i.e., the best return the shareholders could get by investing the same amount somewhere else.

The issuing of equity stock to new shareholders should leave the existing shareholders no worse off. For this to occur, the marginal project rate of return must equal the firm's current yield: If the marginal project rate is greater, then existing shareholders would be better off if they had the opportunity to buy additional equity themselves; if the rate is less, then existing shareholders are worse off because all the equity is devalued. (The restrictions here indicate why most equity capital is raised from existing shareholders by, e.g., rights issue.)

Projects can be financed from retained earnings. In the absence of tax, investments financed from this source cost the same as equity capital, since both represent cash flows that shareholders could otherwise invest at their own marginal rate. However, dividends may be taxed more highly than retained earnings. Calculation of the appropriate cost of capital in this case depends on the tax rates on earnings and capital gains.

Other discounting methods

There are several other discounting methods that can be used to value a project. The 'net terminal value' of a project values its cash flows in terms of what they will be worth at the end of the project life, analogous to the NPV at the beginning of the project. The calculation method is similar to that for NPV:

$$NPV = \sum_{t=0}^{n} X_t (1 + r)^{n-t}$$

Capital budgeting and discounting

Once a project has been assessed, it may then compete for limited capital against other projects. This competition may be considered in three broad analytic frameworks: one in which the organization has a fixed amount of capital to invest, a second in which the organization can obtain a flexible amount of capital at a fixed cost (rate) and a third in which the organization has available varying amounts of capital from different sources at differing costs. All these may be encountered in practice. The first occurs with organizations that have a fixed capital budget – many public bodies are in this situation, as are companies that have earnings to reinvest. The second case may arise when an organization has arranged a flexible line of credit and may call on that to fund its projects; this is usually bound by certain minimum and maximum amounts, but it allows for a degree of flexibility within those limits. The last case more nearly reflects the operation of capital markets, in which acquiring increasing amounts of capital will entail increasing costs – thus an organization may use its retained earnings as a relatively cheap source of investment funds. Selling treasury stock may also be inexpensive, authorizing and selling new shares more costly, and so on with secured and unsecured borrowings.

Capital budgeting with fixed capital

Organizations with a fixed amount to invest in projects may do so most effectively by ranking them in order of their IRR, showing those with the highest returns as worthy of funding before those with lower returns. The main difficulty with this approach to investing in projects follows from the likelihood that the capital available will not necessarily be enough to fund the most attractive of the projects available.

After investing in the most attractive projects, the organization may find it has used most of the capital available and that the next most attractive project requires more funds than are available; it may then have to forego that investment in favour of a less rewarding project with a smaller requirement for capital. An example of this case is shown in the following case note (Table 12.7).

This approach is unlikely to be entirely satisfactory – as noted, it is possible to pass over 'better' projects because they require too much investment. A more flexible approach that better attempts to match resources available to the potential investments is then desirable.

Capital budgeting with fixed rates

As noted in the previous section, providing a fixed amount of capital may not be the most effective approach in allocating resources between competing demands. An alternative is to provide a flexible amount of funding, with the sum actually used rationed to those projects that are best able to reward the organization and repay the costs of their investment. Once again, as for the previous method, the projects are to be ranked by their IRRs, with those projects yielding the highest returns deemed most worthy of support. In this case, the projects are now assessed relative to a required, or **threshold**, rate of return. This may be dictated by a number of concerns. At the

---

Process in action illustration of a fixed capital budget between projects

In the example shown, the £500 000 is invested first in Projects A and B, which are the most attractive; Project C is the next most profitable, but the funds left (500 − 150 − 250 = 100) are insufficient, so it would be passed over, and the funds invested in Project D will use the funds available and no more.

Overall return for the fixed capital approach:

$$\text{Returns/Investment} = (150 \times 0.25 + 250 \times 0.2 + 100 \times 0.1)/(150 + 250 + 100)$$
$$= 97.5/500$$
$$= 19.5\%$$

Questions

1. Is simple consideration of capital availability sufficient to make this decision?
2. Should the external cost of capital be considered?

Table 12.7
Distributing a fixed capital budget between projects

Project	Cost	Return	Balance to invest
Available capital of £500 000 to invest			
A	150	0.25	350
B	250	0.2	100
C	125	0.15	???
D	100	0.1	100
E	50	0.05	

very least, the threshold may represent the organization's cost of capital – how much the money invested 'costs'. No organization will want to make an investment that fails to cover the capital costs involved – that would create immediate losses. Typically, these threshold rates then represent rates of return that the organization expects on its projects – an opportunity cost. Organizations will not wish to invest in projects that are relatively less rewarding than the others that are available. At one level, the organization may look outside itself and see what returns it may obtain in investing in similar, external operations or projects to provide a benchmark against which its internal projects may be judged. Thus, an organization may find that it may borrow capital at an average cost of 8 per cent, but see that projects similar to those in which it might invest are yielding returns of 15 per cent elsewhere. In this case, it may wish to obtain similar returns from its own activities and set the threshold to reflect those aspirations. An example of this is shown in the following case note (Table 12.8).

Process in action illustration of distribution of capital between projects using a threshold internal rate of return

In this example, the 12 per cent capital cost is then taken as the threshold – no project will be accepted unless it repays those costs. The IRRs for Projects A, B and C are sufficiently high to do so and are accepted. The returns to Projects D and E are too low and they are rejected.

Overall return for the fixed rate approach:

$$\text{Returns/Investment} = (150 \times 0.25 + 250 \times 0.2 + 125 \times 0.15) / (150 + 250 + 125)$$

$$= 106.25 / 525$$
$$= 20.2\%$$

A simple comparison of the two approaches will show the second to be more effective in matching the capital used to the opportunities available.

Questions
1. What factors will influence the specification of the threshold IRR, 12 per cent in this case?
2. What are the skills and knowledge needed to make this decision?

Project	Cost	Return	Invest
Capital costs 12% to borrow – project must exceed or equal that to be acceptable.			
A	150	0.25	Yes
B	250	0.2	Yes
C	125	0.15	Yes
D	100	0.1	No
E	50	0.05	No

Table 12.8
Distributing capital between projects using a threshold internal rate of return

Although this approach is superior to the first, it may still suffer from limitations on the capital available; there is no guarantee that the funding provided will match that required by the investment opportunities available. The fixed capital approach left the organization choosing less profitable projects with lower capital needs over more profitable but more demanding projects. While the flexible approach may allow a better match between resources available and those used, there is still latitude for improvement. As noted, the funds available may still be limited; thus, attractive projects that yield more than the threshold rate may find insufficient funds to support them at the prevailing rate. The possibility that they could be funded using more costly sources of capital could offer potentially greater returns.

Capital budgeting

In capital budgeting, a balance is sought between the sources and costs of the capital employed and the uses to which it is put and their rewards. A highly profitable project may justify the use of very expensive capital; an unrewarding project may barely recover its operating costs and be a very unattractive proposition, unable to justify even modest financing costs. Capital budgeting relies on the economic theory of supply and demand: The organization's projects represent a demand for capital, while the capital resources available to the organization from various sources represent a supply of capital. Just as every project may be assessed and its worthiness as judged by its IRR assessed, so too may every source of capital be assessed and the funds available from that source identified along with an associated cost for using them. Thus, a firm might use its retained earnings and regard them as a relatively cheap, though limited source of capital; it might then rely upon secured borrowing as a somewhat more expensive source, up to a limit. If yet more capital is desired, the organization may then seek to borrow without security, with additional costs that may increase as the volume of borrowings increases.

The thinking underlying capital budgeting is that the organization will do best by using its cheapest capital first to fund its most profitable projects first. Once the cheaper capital (or most rewarding project) is fully used up, the next source (or use) is considered and funded so long as the returns exceed the costs. This is illustrated in the following case note (Table 12.9) and shown graphically in Figure 12.7. At the margin, i.e., for the last project funded and the last capital raised, the benefits must exceed the costs. For the next project and source, the organization should find that the costs then exceed the rewards and that investment would be unprofitable.

Process in action illustration of capital budgeting – a supply and demand approach

In the graph, the project shown at the 'equilibrium' point where the 'demand' and 'supply' lines cross may be problematic – its IRR is higher than the cost of capital initially available, but that is insufficient to fully fund the project, and capital that costs more than the project's return will be required. In this case, the average cost is compared to the project's return; if the return exceeds its cost, the project should be done. If the costs exceed the return, the organization would be better off not using the capital to fund it.

Question
1. What new factors does this technique bring to the capital budgeting decision?

Source of capital	Amount	Rate
Retained earnings	100	0.03
Unissued shares	100	0.6
Bank loan	200	0.12
New shares	150	0.15
Other loan	100	0.25
Louie the loan shark	250	0.4

Project	Amount	IRR (%)
A	100	50
B	50	40
C	200	25
D	75	17
E	125	10
F	150	8
G	50	1

Table 12.9
Capital budgeting –
a supply and
demand approach

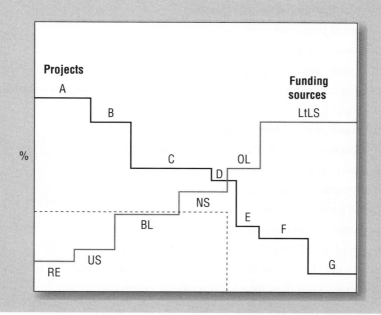

Figure 12.7
Capital budgeting

The budgetary process

Approaches to budgeting

A budget is a detailed plan outlining an organization's activities as defined in financial terms. It is a means of developing and communicating information about what the organization intends to do over a period of time. It identifies goals and assigns responsibilities and provides resources for achieving them. Budgets play a significant role in the decision-making, planning and control processes. A typical framework describing the development of a budget may be seen in Figure 12.7. This shows a top-down approach in which the organization's longer-term objectives serve to identify long-term plans from which shorter-term plans are derived and then used with cost and activity information to develop budgets. More generally, a 'management by objectives' approach may be used, in which interactions between the levels are recognized and explicitly incorporated within the planning process. This is desirable to involve a broader perspective in the planning process and to obtain more realistic plans based on the contributions of those involved with their short-term implementation. Effective planning (and budgets) depends on both leadership in identifying strategic issues and goals, and lower-level management most knowledgeable about the operational and practical issues, opportunities and constraints in their areas.

The budget is simply an expenditure plan based on some projected set of events. While the organization's strategy is ultimately responsible for driving operations as shown in Figure 12.7, the strategy does not itself define a useful plan at the operational level. It sets the long-term, major goal – but determining what to do in the short term, or day by day, involves a more detailed and clear set of goals and actions that must be planned as well. The links to the longer-term plan need to be explicit so that current activities support the organization's objectives. In the short term, the budget is a powerful financial and business planning tool.

It dictates:

- production of some **planned quantity of output**
- using **planned quantities of resources**
- available **at projected costs** to
- yield **some volume of forecast sales**
- sold at **some expected price** to
- provide a contribution to defraying **expected fixed costs and overheads**
- and planned **depreciation expense** to yield
- a **projected profit** before **interest and taxes**
- less **expected financing** costs of interest to yield an
- **expected profit**
- less **anticipated taxes** to give a
- **planned profit after tax**
- plus **planned depreciation**
- less any **planned variations in inventory**
- plus any **net changes in the credit taken or given** to yield
- an **expected cash flow** into (or out of) the company.

These provide an operational plan for the organization that reflect the links between the organization's marketing and sales activities, the production and distribution efforts needed to support them, the staffing required and use made of them and the finance needed to fund it all.

Historical budgeting with adjustments

The historical approach is one of the most widely used methods for developing a budget (see Figure 12.8). The basic idea is that the near future and the organization's activities in it are unlikely to change much from its current situation, and those changes that

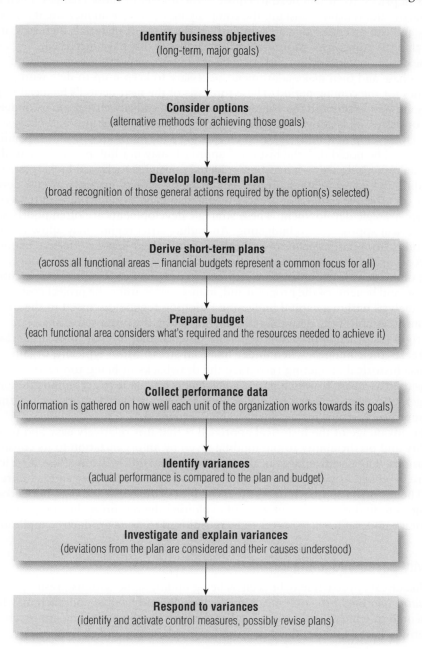

Figure 12.8
The budgetary process

Identify business objectives
(long-term, major goals)

Consider options
(alternative methods for achieving those goals)

Develop long-term plan
(broad recognition of those general actions required by the option(s) selected)

Derive short-term plans
(across all functional areas – financial budgets represent a common focus for all)

Prepare budget
(each functional area considers what's required and the resources needed to achieve it)

Collect performance data
(information is gathered on how well each unit of the organization works towards its goals)

Identify variances
(actual performance is compared to the plan and budget)

Investigate and explain variances
(deviations from the plan are considered and their causes understood)

Respond to variances
(identify and activate control measures, possibly revise plans)

are anticipated may be incorporated into the organization's plans and budgeted for. For example, a business may be experiencing a period of growth with sales increasing by 5 per cent annually. The company may then incorporate this information in its planning by estimating that next year's activities will need to increase by 5 per cent in order to cope with the expected increase in sales – thus, they may employ more staff or have current staff work longer hours, buy more materials and use more equipment or the equipment they already have more intensively and so on. Some of these increases may be very easily accommodated, while others may be more difficult and necessitate investing in new facilities or hiring additional staff. The company may also look at trends in prices, for it will need to consider the impact of those changes. Even if the volume of sales remains constant, the company may perceive an increase if it raises its prices and the revenues increase; similarly, if the price of materials increases, it may seem that the company is more wasteful since those costs have increased.

The common approach to historical budgeting is to use the previous period's budget as a base and then make adjustments necessary to keep it up-to-date with planned activities for the coming period. These forecasts of the next period's financial requirements must consider both the volume of the activity and any changes in its underlying costs or prices. This allows managers to review current operations and plans so that they may develop new budgets based on existing patterns of activity and expenditure.

It should be noted that the historical approach may not link particularly well with an organization's strategy – it may be considered somewhat backward-looking and static. In addition to adjustments that represent changing activity intensity or cost developments, an effective budgeting process would also need to reflect new initiatives that support strategic development. These strategic developments are often poorly served by historical approaches to budgeting. An unduly strict regime may allow few or no deviations from past expenditure patterns, a policy that may be effective in controlling costs in the short term but one that would stifle progress over the longer term. More often, new developments are required to present a case for support, identifying the costs and benefits of the proposal and, in most cases, using the project cost – benefit NPV analysis within a capital budgeting rationing regime discussed in the previous sections to establish the desirability of implementing the proposed change.

A rigid historical approach is generally unworkable, though some organizations do 'freeze' their budgets when under financial stress. More typically, organizations that use historical budgeting recognize the drawbacks of being too restrictive. The past is used as a base to which minor adjustments are made to accommodate forecast changes, and where major new developments are anticipated, more formal analysis and approval at senior management levels is provided.

The advantage of the historical approach is that it is relatively easy and provides stability and predictability to the funding given by an organization to its constituent operations. The disadvantages of this approach may follow from a 'use it or lose it' culture in which unspent portions of a budget are lost or not renewed for future periods. The historical approach treats the *status quo* as the norm and does not encourage managers to find more efficient ways of exploiting the resources they use, nor does it encourage underutilized resources to be redeployed to more productive applications.

Activity-based budgeting

The historical approach may be seen as being unduly static with its presumption that the *status quo* ought to continue. A more dynamic and flexible approach may be implemented in which activities are used as the base for the budgeting approach. With an activity-based budget, the past is no longer the base, and the organization goes beyond that to consider the intensity of the activities undertaken at different periods. The budget is then based on the costs of the various activities that would be undertaken. This approach would be most suitable when an organization finds that there will be periods of greater or lesser intensity in its work or output. The basic idea is that the actual activities incur costs and generate revenues, and those should be the basis for planning rather than an arbitrary period in which costs and revenues arise.

The key point is an understanding of the organization's variable and fixed costs. The fixed costs do not change with the intensity or volume of activity, while the variable costs do change. An activity-based budget would then provide resources using the projected fixed costs as a base, to which would be added additional resources as required by the levels of activity forecast. This would then reflect an expenditure plan based on anticipated activities. This flexibility may be valuable in allowing managers to direct resources more easily to those areas and periods where the activity is greatest.

An activity-based approach offers organizations a number of advantages: The flexibility allows for better allocation of resources, and it allows a more effective comparison of actual expenditure against plan with due consideration for actual and planned levels of activity. The approach allows for better cost control and management of variances. Performance assessments may then more accurately reflect the manager's control of the activities as well as the expenditures. The activity-based approach does, however, have some disadvantages. It requires a more sophisticated knowledge of an organization's costs and their interaction with activity levels. More data collection and analysis is required for the approach to be implemented and operate successfully.

Zero-based budgeting

The zero-based approach to budgeting was developed to help eliminate unnecessary expenditure that the historic approach would tend to keep renewing. The activity-based approach too will assume that operations should continue, though it is more flexible in handling resource allocation to them. The idea underlying zero-based budgeting is that all activities need to justify their continuation in order to receive funding. The budget process starts with a review of all activities and a judgement on their appropriateness for continuation. Effectively, every operation is cut back to nothing and all expenditure then has to be assessed and justified. This questions the costs and benefits of every activity and operational unit within an organization. Such a drastic approach has been found to be unduly disruptive, and even destructive, because managers become intensely concerned with the budgetary process and often neglect their operational duties. Staff morale too can suffer from the uncertainty introduced by such planning policies. Consequently, zero-based budgeting is rarely used for annual budget preparation. Nevertheless, the fundamental questioning and potential for rationalizing an organization's operations that zero-based budgeting offers can be attractive, and some organizations will undertake such reviews periodically (perhaps every 5 or 10 years) as part of a strategic review.

Operating budgets

The operating budget links costs incurred by the organization to the operations in which it engages. Sales revenues are generated by the provision of goods and services, and those in turn impose costs on the organization. In most instances, organizations produce operating budgets covering monthly periods – many of their operating costs arise and are paid on such a cycle, and it is the most commonly found planning period for the financial considerations associated with operations. This provides a short-term planning period for allocating and controlling resources.

The operating budget usually consists of an overall master budget that broadly reflects the layout and presentation of an organization's financial statements: a profit and loss 'budget' showing the financial impact of the organization's operations, a pro forma balance sheet showing the effect of operations on the assets and liabilities of the organization, and a cash budget to show the effects of the operations on the organization's liquidity.

The master budget can be seen as co-ordinating all the organization's activities. As such, it may be broken down into subsidiary budgets associated with particular areas of activity. For example, it is common to derive a sales budget from a master budget to identify sales targets, price and revenue expectations, promotional and advertising expenditures and the like. These activities and their associated costs would be the responsibility of the marketing and sales managers, and a focused budget specifically concerned with their activities may be made more detailed and sophisticated than necessary to the general managers concerned, more with overall performance and the organization as a whole. An example of part of a sales budget is shown in the following case note (Table 12.10).

Cash budgets and operations

The cash budget describes the impact of some period's activities on the organization's liquid resources. The cash flow generated by operations is of particular interest to organizations as it affects their ability to operate on a day-to-day basis. Their *working* capital can be severely affected by various demands placed on the organization.

Process in action illustration of sales budget

This case shows the planned sales for the first 6 months broken down by product. This information is useful for sales managers in showing what targets they may have. Such a budget might also have been broken down by sales region or even individual customers or salespeople. The key is to provide those managers concerned with the marketing and sales operations with the information needed from the overall plan as defined in the master budget. The sales managers can consider their sales targets and also look to the contribution margins to help provide incentives for reaching them and directing efforts where it will be most beneficial.

The master budget may also be used for deriving a production budget – there are obvious links between the sales an organization makes and its need to produce the items sold. This will also reflect the organization's production strategy, whether it chooses to hold little inventory and meet the bulk of sales from current production or whether it chooses instead to maintain a more stable use of its staff and facilities by using inventory stocks as a buffer, allowing inventories to build up during periods of lower sales and reducing them when sales are higher. Note that these are *planned* changes. The organization plans for these differences between its sales and production and moderates them through inventory buffer stocks. This policy then has implications for the organization's working capital budget – the funds provided to support operations.

Questions
1. How do you relate these four issues in terms of management decision-making level of production, achieved sales, profitability and long-term growth?

2. What is the role of the mean absolute percentage error in the estimation of accuracy between different sales forecasting methods?

Table 12.10
Sales budget
example

	January	February	March	April	May	June
Sales						
Product A	500	500	600	600	800	1000
Product B	600	700	600	700	600	700
Product C	400	300	300	300	200	100
Total	1500	1500	1500	1600	1600	1800
COGS						
Product A	300	300	360	360	480	600
Product B	360	420	360	420	360	420
Product C	200	150	150	150	100	50
Total	960	960	960	960	960	960
Contribution						
Product A	200	200	240	240	320	400
Product B	240	280	240	280	240	280
Product C	200	150	150	150	100	50
Total	960	960	960	960	960	960

A critical concept is the recognition that an organization's profits are not cash. A profitable company may have cash, but this is not necessarily so, because any company may do all sorts of things that affect how much money it has (or doesn't have) in the bank that are utterly unrelated to its profitability or even to its operations! For example:

- A company may sell an **asset** (even at a loss!) and thus have cash available.
- A company may borrow money and incur **liabilities** and thus have cash available.
- A company may buy **assets** and thus have less (or no) cash available.
- A company may repay borrowings and reduce its **liabilities** and thus have less cash available.

But more problematically, a company's operations may absorb (or free) cash in ways that are entirely unrelated to the profits or losses it generates. The profits created through an organization's operations are simply one factor in determining the cash flow generated by its operations. In order to determine the impact of operations on cash flow, it will be necessary to recognize how a company's operations and policies use its financial resources and require cash as a consequence.

Cash flow analysis

An organization's operations should generate a profit. How, then, does a business determine what cash it should have, if profit alone is not a sufficient guide?

The starting point will be the profits (or losses) that have been made. Profits should add to the cash available to the organization, while losses would be expected to reduce it. To the profit (or loss) would be added any non-cash expenses recognized as costs in the analysis of profitability. The prime example of this would be depreciation: an expense incurred in an earlier period that is carried into later periods and applied to the production activities it supports in those periods. Accountants use depreciation as a means of matching the costs of capital assets (such as buildings and equipment) to the revenues they help generate. Depreciation improves an organization's cash position. As shown in Table 12.11, inventories can require money. When inventories increase, they absorb money; when inventories decrease, their sales 'frees' money that was previously tied up in them. It is possible for an organization to sell off inventories for less than their production cost and thus incur a loss and find its cash flow improve due to the monies received for them. An organization's cash flow then needs to reflect changes in the inventories it holds: an increase in inventory reduces the cash available; a reduction in inventory would increase cash. An organization should also appreciate the effect that its operating policies may have on its cash flows; in particular, its use of credit as a substitute for cash can have important effects.

Many organizations use credit extensively. It may help in making sales, and many companies see credit as an essential marketing tool. If a high proportion of sales are made on credit, this may have the effect of rendering the profits all but invisible in cash terms. For example, if *all* of a company's sales are on credit, it might still determine that it has made a profit, but it cannot actually enjoy those profits or use them for other purposes until the customers eventually pay for the goods. Where a

Process in action illustration of production budget

An example of a production budget is shown in Table 12.11, one linked to the sales budget from Table 12.10. The organization has a policy dictating stable production output to allow a steady pattern of

Table 12.11 Production budget example

	January	February	March	April	May	June
Product A						
Sales	500	500	600	600	800	1000
Production	667	667	666	667	667	666
Inventory	167	334	400	467	334	0
Product B						
Sales	600	700	600	700	600	700
Production	650	650	650	650	650	650
Inventory	50	0	50	0	50	0
Product C						
Sales	400	400	300	300	200	100
Production	267	267	267	267	267	267
Inventory	200	150	150	150	100	50
	−133	−166	−200	−233	−166	0
Total investment in inventories	84	167	250	234	217	0

company sells a large proportion of its sales on credit, these may involve revenues significantly greater than their profit margins. Careful consideration of credit policies with monitoring and control mechanisms are critical in such businesses. Not just the loss of revenues due to bad debts can cause difficulty, the extended use of credit by customers can absorb monies the organization would prefer to use in other ways more effectively. Increases in the sales credit may result from large volumes being sold on credit or by customers taking longer in paying. These both can represent a reduction in the cash available to the organization. If credit sales can be reduced or customers encouraged to pay more quickly, the amount of credit provided may be reduced, with beneficial impact on the organization's cash flow.

A final factor would be the organization's own use of credit in buying from its suppliers. Just as the revenues identified could exist only as credit notations rather than cash payments, so too might some of the costs involved in making the sales be entirely nominal rather than actual. For example, a company might buy goods on credit and then sell them for cash. It would show a profit on the transactions, but the cash it holds would be much greater. At some subsequent point, the company would have to pay its suppliers. Then it would find that the cash held would equal the profits previously recognized.

work for its staff and regular purchases of materials. In this plan, the company will produce enough to satisfy its sales requirements over the 6 months, and no more or less. With Product A, which has increasing sales during the planning period, the organization produces more in the early months, and then stores it until the later months' sales use it. For Product C, which faces declining sales during the period, the organization would wish to produce less in the earlier months than are required for meeting sales. Unless there are inventories from an earlier time, it cannot meet the sales projections, and if there are existing inventories that could be so exploited, the production plans might then be reduced to reflect the availability of those stocks. The organization's desire to maintain a perfectly stable rate of production may not be feasible or practical. This projection would also highlight areas where production might not be able to cope with the sales volumes so that remedial action may be taken before sales are lost and customers disappointed.

The ideal is to effectively co-ordinate the activities across the organization and to allow any problems to be recognized early and their effects countered or minimized. It should also be noted that these production activities have an effect on the working capital used by the organization. In January, the increase in inventories will require an additional £84 000, and this will increase to a maximum of £250 000 in March. No organization can ignore these funding requirements without creating potentially significant problems with the people and other companies with whom it does business. Staff expecting to be paid will not be satisfied if the finance needed for their pay checks has inadvertently been diverted to inventories stored in the warehouses and can only be recovered once those are sold.

The production budget will have ramifications for other areas of the organization, such as staff schedules and wage bills, storage and delivery systems, materials purchases and working capital or cash. While all these areas might also have subsidiary budgets developed that look more closely at plans for those resources and their cost implications, most organizations feel the need for a cash budget. The cash budget reflects the effects of an organization's operations on its liquidity.

Questions
1. Could an economic order quantity model be applicable in this case?
2. What improvements could be through automated warehouses?
3. What is the role of a safety stock?

These adjustments should reveal how much cash is on hand. Mathematically:

Profits

+ depreciation

− the change in inventories

− the change in debtors

+ the change in creditors

= cash flow

Over the long term, the organization's profits should equal its cash, as the effects of credit given and credit taken work through the system, as inventories vary and eventually are all consumed and as the costs of capital equipment are paid and recovered.

The cash budget considers the organization's cash flow and the varied factors that affect it. It too is a critical management tool for managing an organization's short-term operations; it complements the operating budget by focusing clearly on a narrow area of concern.

Summary

- Marketing requires financial resources just as does every other activity in which organizations engage.

- New products, markets and other initiatives require investment. These may be considered alongside competing demands from other business functions.

- Marketing managers need to be familiar with the use of project assessment methods such as cost – benefit analysis and techniques such as NPV and IRR for making comparisons of costs and benefits when they are spread over time and between projects of varying risk.

- The use of these resources in operations will depend on budgets that make them available, so an understanding of the budgeting process and the various methods that may be used in formulating budgets such as the historical or activity-based approaches are necessary, too.

- The impact of business operations on the organization's cash flow may then be estimated and monitored.

This has been achieved through the chapter's discussions of:

- Investment analysis for single projects.

- Approaches to capital budgeting and the allocation of limited finance to projects.

- The development and application of operating budgets for short- and intermediate-term activities.

- Analyzing the impact of operations on the cash flow and liquidity of the organization.

Chapter questions

1. Discuss the role of budgeting within a resource allocation strategy. Further analyze the inner workings of different types of budgets: capital, operating and cash.

2. Critically comment on the following techniques for investment appraisal: the payback method and ARR.

3. Depict and dissect the overall framework related to the budgeting process and comment on its different stages.

References

Chapman, C. B., Cooper, D. F., and Page, M. J. (1987) *Management for Engineers*, Chichester, UK: John Wiley and Sons.

Dayananda, D. (2002) *Capital Budgeting: Financial Appraisal of Investment Projects*, Cambridge, UK: Cambridge University Press.

Hope, J., and Fraser, R. (2003) *Beyond Budgeting*, Cambridge, MA: Harvard Business School Press.

Peterson, P., and Fabozzi, F. J. (2002) *Capital Budgeting: Theory and Practice*, Chichester, UK: John Wiley & Sons.

Shim, J. K. (2005) *Budgeting Basics and Beyond*, Chichester, UK: John Wiley & Sons.

Srinivasan, S. (1999) *Cash and Working Capital Management*, London: Sangam Books.

Sweeny, A. (2003) *Handbook of Budgeting*, Chichester, UK: John Wiley & Sons.

13

Reputation management: corporate image and communication

Tom Watson and Philip J. Kitchen

Introduction

> Never do anything you wouldn't want to be caught dead doing. – Actor John Carradine advising his actor son, David

Reputation was, is and always will be of immense importance to organizations, whether commercial, governmental or not-for-profit. To reach their goals, stay competitive and prosper, good reputation paves the organizational path to acceptance and approval by stakeholders. Even organizations operating in difficult ethical environments – perhaps self-created – need to sustain a positive reputation where possible.

Argenti and Druckenmiller argue that 'organizations increasingly recognize the importance of corporate reputation to achieve business goals and stay competitive' (2004, p. 368). While there are many recent examples of organizations whose leadership and business practice behaviours have destroyed their reputations, such as Enron, Arthur Andersen, Tyco and WorldCom, the positive case for reputation is that it has fostered

Learning objectives

At the end of this chapter, the reader should be able to:

- Prepare their own working definition of reputation management.

- Identify best practices in reputation management.

- Understand the transnational nature of reputation and its management.

- Prepare strategies to plan, research and evaluate reputation in a corporate entity.

continued expansion of old stagers such as Johnson & Johnson and Philips, and innovators such as Cisco Systems, who top recent rankings of the most respected organizations in the USA and Europe.

What is evident is that reputation *does not occur by chance*. It relates to leadership, management and organizational operations; the quality of products and services; and – crucially – relationships with stakeholders. It is also connected to communication activities and feedback mechanisms.

This chapter will consider the definitions and nature of reputation and its management, best practice and evaluation. It will also discuss the boundaries between branding, image and reputation.

What is reputation?

Dictionary definitions of *reputation*, while normally focused on individuals, give strong indications of the elements that are relevant to organizations. Examples include:

1. The beliefs or opinions that are generally held about someone or something.
2. A widespread belief that someone or something has a particular characteristic.

(Oxford Compact English Dictionary, 2009)

Overall quality or character as seen or judged by people in general . . . a place in public esteem or regard : good name. *(Merriam-Webster)*

In the corporate world, reputation is seen as a major element of an organization's provenance alongside and included in financial performance and innovation. The academic-practitioner team of Paul Argenti and Bob Druckenmiller suggest that it is a 'collective representation of multiple constituencies' images of a company built up over time' (2004, p. 369). It is also linked to the organization's identity, performance and the way others respond to its behaviour.

The elements to note are that the reputation is a 'collective representation' of images and perceptions, not a 'self-promoted message'. It involves relationships with all stakeholders ('constituencies') and it is gained, maintained and enhanced or detracted from over time.

Murray and White's research amongst UK chief executive officers (CEOs) has found similar characteristics:

It's the role of public relations to make sure that the organization is getting credit for the good it does. Great reputations are built on doing this consistently over a period of time in which a track record of delivering on promises and engendering trust is evident to everyone. All members of an organization have a contribution to make to building and sustaining reputation. *(2004, p. 10)*

The elements of promoted yet sustainable image and performance are again identified, but an holistic factor – 'all members of an organization' – is added. Later in this chapter, the role of CEOs in defining and driving reputation is discussed. However, it is broadly accepted that good reputation is unsustainable without internal organizational support. Neglect of reputation by means of apathy, indifference or ineffective communication is leaving a key communication to the vagaries of other market forces.

Murray and White also point to relationship management as being 'at the heart of creating, enhancing and retaining a good reputation' (2004, p. 10). They see strong communication performance by organizational leaders and effective feedback mechanisms from stakeholders as essential for articulating relevant messages and making better-informed decisions that retain the support of stakeholders.

Developing a good corporate reputation

UK public relations industry leader Adrian Wheeler, taking cognisance of market research, that found 28 per cent of people do trust business leaders to tell the truth (meaning 72 per cent do not), has proposed six components of good corporate reputation. He also comments that 'corporate reputation is a slow-build proposition' (Wheeler, 2001, p. 8).

Wheeler's (2001, pp. 9–10) six reputation components are:

- **Be obsessed with your product or service:** Nothing comes close to superior product quality in influencing the way people feel about your organization.
- **Deserve confidence:** Lead from the front and engender trust from employees and customers.
- **Be available:** Don't hide behind a wall of middle managers and advisers. Build relationships with customers, employees and suppliers.
- **Admit mistakes:** If mistakes are made, admit them and respond rapidly.
- **Engage people's interest:** For CEOs and companies, taking up a public cause separates you or your company from the rest. Get all staff involved.
- **Have something to say:** Most people think business is boring, so make it interesting and human. CEOs can use their own and the business's personality to communicate with impact and colour.

Brand, identity and reputation

These three terms are sometimes used interchangeably – brand and image; image and reputation. Van Riel and Berens say, 'corporate identity can be defined as a company's *self-presentation*, that is, the managed cues or signals that an organization offers about itself to stakeholders' (2001, p. 45). It is also defined by Argenti and Druckenmiller as consisting of 'a company's defining attributes, such as its people, products, and services' (2004, p. 369). Van Riel and Berens also point to the corporate symbolism as part of the identity, which includes logos, house style and staff uniforms (2001, p. 45). The transmitted corporate identity is received by stakeholders as image, 'a reflection of the organization's identity and its corporate brand' (Argenti and Druckenmiller, 2004, p. 45). This image or set of images thus contributes to the reputation of the organization.

The corporate brand is also an expression of the organization's presentation to others. Argenti and Druckenmiller define it as: 'a brand that spans an entire company (which can have disparate underlying product brands); and . . . conveys expectations of what the company will deliver in terms of products, services, and customer experience' (2004, p. 369).

Argenti and Druckenmiller (2004, p. 369) proposed a taxonomy of questions which simplifies the differences between these terms.

Term	Question
Identity	Who are you?
Corporate brand	Who do you say you are and want to be?
Image	What do stakeholders think of who you are and who you tell them you are?
Reputation	What do all the stakeholders think of who you tell them you are and what have you done?

As can be seen, the primary (and important) difference between image and reputation is that reputation is a two-way relationship with stakeholders and thus open to managerial intervention.

Can reputation be managed?

The question of the validity of the term *reputation management* is also at the core of this chapter. In the new field of reputations management, there is academic research and a body of knowledge; a specialist academic journal, *Corporate Reputation Review*; as well as, many public relations consultancies are rebranding as 'reputation managers' (Hutton *et al.*, 2001, pp. 247–248). There is also an assumption that all organizations have a reputation, be it good, neutral or bad. But, how well can this be managed, controlled or directed? Hutton *et al.* (2001, p. 249) describe the dilemma succinctly:

(US public relations academics) David Finn, Doug Newsom and others have pointed out that concepts such as 'reputation' and 'image' are not generally something that can be managed directly, but are omnipresent and the global result of a firm's or individual's behaviour. Attempting to manage one's reputation might be likened to trying to manage one's own popularity (a rather awkward, superficial and potentially self-defeating endeavour).

On the other hand, some advocates see reputation management as a new guiding force or paradigm for the entire field, in keeping with Warren Buffet's admonition that losing reputation is a far greater sin for an organization than losing money.

So we see questions about the validity of reputation management balanced against the reality of the importance of reputation for businesses.

Charles Fombrun (1996) argues a different case: that reputation is built in a planned manner by organizations taking necessary notice of the environment in which they operate.

Better regarded companies build their reputations by developing practices which integrate social and economic considerations into their competitive strategies. They not only do things right – they do the right things. In doing so, they act like good citizens. They initiate policies that reflect their core values; that consider the joint welfare of investors, customers and employees; that invoke concern for the development of local communities; and that ensure the quality and environmental soundness of their technologies, products and services. *(Fombrun, 1996, p. 8)*

This paradigm of reputation management is that the organization's reputation is dependent on its behaviour as a corporate citizen, part of the societies in which it operates and not above or apart from these. Reputational considerations are embedded in policy and actions, not just bolted on when convenient. Hutton *et al.* (2001) and Fombrun (1996) are approaching reputational management from different perspectives – communications management versus organizational policy. This is a theme that is also part of the continuing debate of the nature of reputation management.

Good and bad reputation

The definitions of *reputation* tend to favour the positive, with emphasis placed on 'being well thought of', 'in public esteem' and 'delivering on promises'. But, as all readers know, reputation has two sides. In early 2000, Gardberg and Fombrun investigated the reputation of companies at both ends of the reputational spectrum. They sought the views of a sample of Americans and Europeans in 11 countries on companies with the best and worst corporate reputations (Gardberg and Fombrun 2002, p. 385) (see Tables 13.1–13.4). Using a combination of telephone and online polling, they garnered over 10 000 nominations.

On the positive side, Cisco Systems was one of the strong performers in the information technology (IT) business, while Johnson & Johnson had 'made' its reputation nearly 20 years earlier with its prompt and ethical response to the Tylenol extortion situation. Home Depot was more warmly regarded than Wal-Mart, which dominates

Table 13.1
Top five 'best overall reputation' in the USA (summarized by authors)

Rank	Company
1	Cisco Systems
2	Johnson & Johnson
3	Home Depot
4	Ben & Jerry's
5	Hewlett-Packard (HP)

Table 13.2
Worst-reputation nominees in the USA

Rank	Company
1	Firestone
2	ExxonMobil
3	Phillip Morris (now Altria)
4	Nike
5	K-Mart

US retailing. Ben & Jerry's, a niche ice cream brand owned by Unilever, had captured an immense place in the hearts of corporate America because it wasn't positioned as big and successful but quirky and human. Hewlett-Packard (HP), which was later racked by criticism for its takeover of Compaq, was then seen as part of the engine room of the US IT sector that was soon to be hit by the early-decade 'techwreck'.

On the negative side, Firestone was suffering (as was Ford) from catastrophic tyre failures on the Explorer SUV. ExxonMobil had become a long-term target for environmental groups after the Exxon Valdez pollution disaster in Alaska, while Philip Morris was constantly in the spotlight for its production and marketing of cigarettes, which also affected the reputation of non-tobacco brands and subsidiaries. Nike, once the darling of sports marketing, was under attack from public interest groups for sourcing productions from low-cost economies with abysmal labour practices, while K-Mart was suffering from poor financial performance and being seen as an also-ran compared with Wal-Mart and Home Depot.

In Europe, three motor vehicle makers were ranked in the top five in a list headed by a discount retailer, equivalent to Wal-Mart, and a long-established electrical and electronics manufacturer. Ironically, while Ford was being hammered in the USA for the failings of its Explorer SUV, it was simultaneously being lauded in Europe. Since 2000, Daimler Chrysler's star has been falling as the transatlantic motor manufacturing merger has failed to deliver value.

The negative picture contains two US-owned corporations, McDonald's and Microsoft, and two European oil groups (TotalFinaElf and Shell), along with Deutsche Bank. Yet all continue to be successful despite this negative reputation.

Rank	Company
1	Carrefour
2	Philips
3	Daimler Chrysler
4	Ford
5	Volkswagen

Table 13.3
Top five 'best corporate reputation' in Europe (summarized by authors)

Rank	Company
1	McDonald's
2	TotalFinaElf
3	Shell
4	Deutsche Bank
5	Microsoft

Table 13.4
Worst-reputation nominees in Europe

SOURCE: TABLES ADAPTED FROM GARDBERG AND FOMBRUN, 2002, pp. 387–390.

The conclusions drawn by Gardberg and Fombrun (2002, p. 391) were:

- Positive nominations are given to companies with strong corporate brands that have identifiable subsidiary brands often of the same name. The gaining of favourable 'top-of-mind' visibility speaks to the historical associations created in the minds of the public through strategic communications.
- Negative associations with some equally strong mega-brands whose names have become synonymous with crisis speak to the inability these companies have in adjusting public perception.

Links to relationship management

A recurrent theme in public relations and corporate communications theory is whether the paradigm should be changed from message delivery–type process activities to management of relationships. There have been parallel tracks of development that emphasize the use of negotiation techniques, the embedding of corporate social

---

Process in action Coca-Cola – reputation damaged by delay

In 1999, around 200 people in Belgium and France complained of illness after drinking Coca-Cola products. Soon after, it was claimed that this had had two causes – defective carbon dioxide in a Belgian bottle plant and cans tainted by a fungicide at a French unit. As a result of these allegations, governments of seven northern and western European countries issued bans or partial bans on Coca-Cola products.

Coca-Cola responded at local, national and European levels with response teams to counter allegations and restore customer and staff confidence. Its chief executive, Douglas Ivester, came from the USA to meet Belgian government officials and to express apologies. Other actions were put in place with company-wide communications to staff and by corporate advertisements in key European markets.

Although Coca-Cola was not slow to attend the situation and – unlike Perrier when faced with claims of benzine taint in its bottled waters – did not mount a long period of denial, it was criticized. Sales suffered with a drop of 6 per cent in Europe and there was a stock price fall of 28 per cent.

As one newspaper in Coca-Cola's hometown, Atlanta, commented, 'As the hours fly by, the precious Coca-Cola brand is threatened, with one country and then another registering levels of concern about the beverages.' (Roughton and Unger, 1999)*

Wakefield asks, 'What went wrong with Coke?' (2000, p. 61). Essentially, 'its efforts were too late and insufficient'. The CEO's first comment came four days after the first allegations were made, and he did not travel to Europe until a week after the crisis started. As PR commentator Paul Holmes noted at the time, 'waiting several days to issue a response from corporate headquarters . . . raised serious questions about the company's sensitivity to customer safety concerns'.

Wakefield also comments that Coca-Cola failed to anticipate the issues and show significant understanding of the European public health environment in which public concerns over food safety had been heightened by dioxin scares, the BSE scandal and other agricultural threats. 'Aside from ignoring the immediate context, Coca-Cola also failed to properly gauge some long-term issues related to differences between conducting business globally versus the US domestic market,' he concludes (2000, p. 62).

The accumulated reputation of more than a century stood for little because Coca-Cola did not recognize the gravity of the issue as it broke and then tried to manage it from thousands of miles away. The cost was very high, both financially and in lost trust with customers and staff.

SOURCE: CASE STUDY BASED ON WAKEFIELD, I. (2000)

responsibility in corporate policies and symmetrical (equal two-way) communications. These have been brought together by Ledingham (2003), who has proposed relationship management as the core of a general theory of public relations. This moves theory and practice away from message creation and dissemination to a problem-solving management function. It fits into a framework of mutual understanding and can be closely associated with negotiation techniques where the outcome sought is mutual gain. Relationship management fits closely with community relations, corporate social responsibility and consultative processes used in corporate issues management.

As noted earlier, the development and maintenance of reputation is based on numerous relationships with internal and external stakeholders, so relationship management as a new paradigm of public relations can be aligned with reputation management. Bruning and Ledingham's (2000, p. 169) argument is based on very similar grounds to those expressed for best practice in reputation management:

> Organizations that develop a relationship management programme that focuses on mutual benefit will maximize the influence that relationships can have on consumers while concurrently acting as a good citizen because the organization will be engaging in activities, actions and communications that are in the best interests of both the consumer and the organization.

Although some public relations academics, notably Hutton *et al.* (2001), strongly question reputation management as a separate discipline, there appear to be strong enough operational and applied theoretical links between reputation management and relationship management to indicate the need for closer dialogue.

Costs of crises

The financial and reputational cost of catastrophe can be extremely high and may not be fully apparent for months and years after the event, according to examples given by Regester (2001, p. 93):

Exxon (Valdez spill)	$13 bn
PanAm (Lockerbie crash)	$652 m
P&O Ferries (Zeebrugge sinking)	$70 m
Union Carbide (Bhopal)	$527 m
Perrier (benzene accident)	$263 m
Occidental Oil (Piper Alpha explosion)	$1.4 m
Barings Bank (collapse)	$900 m

Best practice in reputation management

In a recent eight-country study, Kitchen and Laurence (2003) explored corporate reputation management practice, with an emphasis on the role of the CEO and the management of reputation across cultures and national borders. Table 13.5 shows that corporate reputation is of the greatest importance in achieving corporate objectives, with the highest ranking in the Anglophone (the USA, Canada and the UK) world.

As for measurement of this 'very important' element, Kitchen and Laurence comment that 'despite the apparent importance devoted to corporate reputation, sustained increase in systematized formal measurement procedure was not in marked evidence in the countries concerned' (2003, p. 108) (see Tables 13.5 and 13.6). More than half the respondents in The Netherlands and Canada undertook formal measurement, but there was little or no progress in other countries. It should be noted that this situation of low investment measurement is similar for measurement of public relations and corporate communications programmes in general.

Table 13.5
The importance of company reputation in achieving corporate objectives (summarized in percentage ranking)

Country	Very important	Somewhat important
USA	94	6
Canada	90	8
UK	89	10
Belgium	86	14
France	86	14
Italy	83	17
The Netherlands	76	24
Germany	71	29

Table 13.6
Formal systems to measure a company's reputation (summarized in percentage ranking)

Country	Yes	No
The Netherlands	62	36
Canada	52	48
USA	42	57
France	50	56
Belgium	37	63
UK	37	63
Germany	33	67
Italy	29	71

NOTE: 'NOT SURE' DATA OMITTED

Corporate reputation measurement

Where evaluation took place, the majority of companies in the eight countries nominated 'custom research' as both their main method of monitoring and measuring reputation and the one metric that is 'most meaningful'. Kitchen and Laurence (2003, p. 110) comment that 'custom research' is a category that covers a wide range of quantitative and qualitative research techniques that can be undertaken by in-house facilities and external suppliers. However, the very interesting factor identified is that 'media coverage' is much less important than 'custom research' and 'informal feedback' in most countries and was lowly ranked as a 'most meaningful' metric in only three out of eight countries (The Netherlands 7 per cent, USA and UK 5 per cent each). As media relations is the main activity in most corporate communications programmes, it is revealing that it appears to have so little importance in the measurement of (and thus contribution to) corporate reputation. Perhaps this information can potentially preface a fundamental change in corporate communications activity to more effective activities.

Kitchen and Laurence (2003, p. 113) (see Table 13.7) comment that, apart from the third-ranked role of CEO reputation, it is notable that print media has a higher ranking (3.24) than broadcast media (2.29). The Internet (2.90) also ranks higher than broadcast media, despite its often unmediated and unchecked content. Another observation is 'the very low ranking awarded to labour union leaders', which may indicate that the power and importance of unions is well on the wane, a trend very noticeable throughout Europe.

Rank/influence	Mean
Customers	4.58
Employees	3.92
CEO reputation	3.70
Print media	3.24
Shareholders	3.05
The Internet	2.90
Industry analysts	2.87
Financial analysts	2.78
Regulators/government	2.64
Broadcast media	2.29
Labour union leaders	2.29
Plaintiff's lawyers	2.03

5 = extremely influential; 1 = does not influence at all

Table 13.7
Corporate reputation influencers (summarized in mean rank order)

A theme of this study is the weight given to the CEO's reputation in determining corporate reputation. Citing van Riel (1999) that there is a close inter-relationship between corporate reputation and the reputation of the CEO, Kitchen and Laurence found that it is 'most important in Italy, closely followed by Canada, then the USA'. On the reverse, it is' . . . least likely to impact on corporate reputation in Belgium, the UK and France' (2003, p. 113) (see Table 13.8).

'The CEO's reputation becomes more important when choosing a successor to move the company on to new and better heights,' with the USA (64 per cent), Germany (55 per cent) and Italy (52 per cent) placing greatest weight, and Canada (38 per cent) and France (34 per cent) placing least emphasis on this factor (Kitchen and Laurence, 2003, pp. 113–114).

Summarizing the eight-country study, Kitchen and Laurence (2003, pp. 115–116) offer six conclusions:

- Corporate reputation has increased and is increasing in importance.
- The need to systematize measurement is growing in importance.
- The key influencers on reputation are – despite some caveats – customers, employees and then the CEO.
- A good corporate reputation precedes and helps business grow internationally and in preparing the ground in new markets among key constituencies.
- CEO reputation and corporate reputation are increasingly intertwined. The CEO is inevitably cast in the role of chief communicator.
- The responsibility for managing reputation is a key management responsibility and – led by the CEO – it must be managed in an integrated manner.

It is clear that if the organization or its CEO cannot communicate its mission, brands or values, some other organization, stakeholder or irate public with communication capabilities can or will . . . corporate communication must be mastered by the corporation and those duly appointed to speak on its behalf; or it will master the corporation. *(Kitchen and Laurence, 2003, p. 116)*

Table 13.8
What percentage of your company's corporate reputation is based on the CEO's reputation? (summarized in percentage ranking)

Country	50–100
Italy	83
Canada	66
USA	54
The Netherlands	44
Germany	42
France	36
UK	33
Belgium	26

Multinational reputation management

As the case study on Coca-Cola demonstrated, transnational enterprises (TNEs) have to defend their reputations with speed and understanding of local situations if they are to retain their high standing. Kitchen and Laurence (2003, p. 116) reinforce the point that the corporate reputations of TNEs are open to scrutiny around the clock:

> Corporations in the global economy need to exercise social responsibility and exercise due accountability for their actions and if not at their peril. And all forms of communication offer global potentiality. As the multiple medias undergo further development, so the imperative will be to monitor what is communicated, how it is communicated, through which media and with what potential outcomes. That means measuring outcomes by all media contacts including the WorldWideWeb.

This argument brings reputation management back to corporate communication structures that operate 24/7 and which have a direct line of responsibility to the highest levels of management or preferably are managed by those at board level.

Lancaster says that because of global communication, the 'old rules . . . have to be re-written. Thus, committee-written responses to news inquiries have to be replaced with scenario planning' (2001, pp. 37–38). He says that early-warning systems are needed, along with role-playing of situations and preparation of responses for unlikely situations. 'Instantaneous media demands instantaneous responses.' (Lancaster, 2001, p. 38) So corporate communication in TNEs has to be organized to handle these demands.

Measuring reputation

Although Kitchen and Laurence's eight-country study found that the majority of organizations do not measure reputation well, there is a wide range of literature that propose reputational measurement. Two are identified in this section: Fombrun's taxonomy from which he developed the proprietary 'reputation quotient' (RD) offered by public relations group Weber Shandwick, and the qualitative approach developed by Grunig and Hon.

From a study of data collected by Harris Interactive and analysis of focus groups, Fombrun (2000) has proposed an index to summarize people's perceptions of companies. Based on respondent's comments on companies they liked and disliked, he has nominated six categories of factors:

Emotional appeal	How much the company is liked, admired and respected
Products and services	Perceptions of the quality, innovation, value and reliability of the company's products and services
Financial performance	Perceptions of the company's profitability, prospects and risk
Vision and leadership	How much the company demonstrates a clear vision and strong leadership
Workplace environment	Perceptions of how well the company is managed, how good it is to work for and the quality of its employees
Social responsibility	Perceptions of the company as a good citizen in its dealings with communities, employees and the environment

From these factors, he has developed a RQ to 'benchmark the reputations of companies as seen by different stakeholder segments' (Fombrun, 2000). This, he claims, is a valid instrument for measuring corporate reputations.

Fombrun argues that corporate reputation has economic value, but 'unfortunately, efforts to document this value have run up against the fact that a company's reputation is only one of many intangibles to which investors ascribe value' (2000). He says that three factors – crisis effects, supportive behaviours and financial analyses – confirm 'reputations have bottom-line financial value' (Fombrun, 2000).

For *crisis effects*, he points to the recovery that corporations such as Johnson & Johnson (Tylenol), ExxonMobil (Exxon Valdez) and Motorola (brain tumours and mobile phones) have had after crises. This has varied in financial and reputational terms, with research by Gardberg and Fombrun (2002) identifying Johnson & Johnson as one of the most respected companies and ExxonMobil as one of the least respected companies in other research published in 2002.

Supportive behaviour is evidenced by the attitude of resource holders (banks, suppliers, regulators and staff). Most companies are not in a crisis state and thus their reputation remains stable if not improving. That, says Fombrun (1996), creates a value cycle when perceptions and performance '[demonstrate] approval of the company's strategic initiatives and [are] made possible by more attractive financial valuations'.

Financial analyses can also support the value of corporate reputation with measurement of intangible assets such as patents and goodwill (reputational capital). Other technical devices, such as notional licensing of a corporate name, can demonstrate value. Fombrun points to research by Srivastava *et al.* (1997), who compared companies with similar risk and return but different average reputation scores in 1990. This study found that a 60 per cent difference in reputation score was associated with a 7 per cent difference in market value. Since this average capitalization was $3 bn, 'a point difference in reputation score from 6 to 7 on a 10-point scale would be worth an additional $52m in market value' (Srivastava *et al.*, 1997, p. 67). Later studies of Fortune 500 corporations between 1983 and 1997 indicated that one point difference on the scale was worth $500 m in market value (Black *et al.*, 2000).

A challenge to Fombrun's analysis and methodology has been mounted from public relations academics. Hutton *et al.* (2001, p. 258) argue that there is a confusion between correlation and causality: '. . . reputation researchers have claimed significant correlations between reputation and financial performance; unfortunately such studies are largely meaningless and circular in their logic, given that *Fortune* and other reputation measures they are studying are largely *defined* by financial performance.'

The relationship between reputation and spending on corporate communication activities has been studied by Hutton *et al.* (2001). They did not find a smooth, consistent relationship between corporate communication spending and reputation, with the overall correlation being just 0.24. They also found that the correlation between company size and reputation was 0.23. 'In other words, there was a modest correlation between reputation and spending on communication activities, but most of that was accounted for by the fact that larger companies – which presumably benefit from greater visibility – tend to have better reputations.' (Hutton *et al.*, 2001, p. 249) The significant correlation between corporate activity and reputation was 'foundation funding' (charitable donations), which was 0.69. High levels of expenditure for investor relations, executive outreach and media relations were other activities that correlated highly with positive reputation. Acidly, they noted that social responsibility, corporate advertising and industry relations have negative correlations (Hutton *et al.*, 2001, pp. 252–253).

Thus, there is a mixed picture in the academic debate over corporate reputation. Simple verities that good behaviour and practice equals good reputation are challenged by the correlation between sheer size of a company and its expenditure in some areas of communication.

Assessing relationships between organizations and publics

Public relations evaluation commentator Walter Lindenmann has identified 'measuring the success or failure of long-term relationships' as an important element in the measurement of public relations and corporate communications activity.

> As important as it can be for an organization to measure PR outputs and outcomes, it is even more important for an organization to measure relationships. This is because for most organizations, measuring outputs and outcomes can only give information about the effectiveness of a particular or specific PR programme or event that has been undertaken. *(Lindenmann in Hon and Grunig, 1999, p. 2)*

Hon and Grunig (1999) reviewed research that shows value is contributed to an organization when its communications programmes lead to quality long-term relationships with strategic publics (stakeholders). They identified two types of relationships, with four characteristics. The relationships are:

- **Exchange**, where one party gives benefit to the other only because the other has provided benefits in the past or is expected to do so in the future. A party that receives benefit incurs an obligation or debt to return the favour. Exchange is the essence of marketing relationships between organizations and customers. But, Hon and Grunig argue, it's not enough for a public, which expects organizations to do things for the community, without expecting immediate benefit.

- **Communal**, where parties are willing to provide benefits to the other because they are concerned for the welfare of the other – even when they believe they might not get anything in return. 'The role of public relations is to convince management that it also needs communal relationships with publics such as employees, the community, government, media and stockholders – as well as exchange relationships with customers.' (Hon and Grunig, 1999, p. 24) Communal relationships are important if organizations are to be socially responsible and to add value to society as well as client organizations.

The quality of relationships

Hon and Grunig (1999) also nominate four outcomes that are indicators of successful interpersonal relationships but can be applied with equal success to relationships between organizations and their publics. Importance declines down the list:

- **Control mutuality:** The degree to which the parties in a relationship are satisfied with the amount of control they have over a relationship. Some degree of power imbalance is natural, but the most stable, positive relationships exist where the parties have some degree of control. It doesn't have to be exactly 50:50. The ceding of some control is based on trust.

- **Trust:** The level of confidence that both parties have in each other and their willingness to open themselves to the other party. Three factors are important:
  - **Integrity:** An organization is seen as just and fair.
  - **Dependability:** It will do what it says it will do.
  - **Competence:** It has the ability to do what it says it will do.
- **Commitment:** The extent to which both parties believe and feel the relationship is worth spending energy to maintain and promote.
- **Satisfaction:** The extent to which both parties feel favourably about each other because positive expectations about the relationship are reinforced. Each party believes the other is engaged in positive steps to maintain the relationship.

The suggestion is that relationships are evaluated through a questionnaire that asks a series of agree/disagree statements (using a 1 to 9 scale). Table 13.9 gives Walter Lindenmann's shortened list of statements used to measure relationships outcomes.

These questions can be used in two ways. A questionnaire can be administered with a 1 to 9 scale to indicate agreement or disagreement with the statements. The data from all participants can be collated and an overall mean deduced. Alternatively, the questions can be used as a basis for focus groups, discussion to probe the attitudes of participants.

The results from either (or both) methodologies can assist the organization to develop strategies that address identified strengths and weaknesses. The qualitative route will give more information on attitudes which can assist the development of behavioural objectives. That then feeds back into the development and maintenance of reputation in the organization.

Table 13.9
Measuring
relationship
outcomes

Control mutuality

1. This organization and people like me are attentive to what each other says.
2. This organization believes the opinions of people like me are legitimate.
3. In dealing with people like me, this organization has a tendency to throw its weight around. (Reversed)
4. This organization really listens to what people like me have to say.
5. The management of this organization gives people like me enough say in the decision-making process.

Trust

1. This organization treats people like me fairly and justly.
2. Whenever this organization makes an important decision, I know it will be concerned about people like me.

Table 13.9
(Continued)

3. This organization can be relied on to keep its promises.
4. I believe that this organization takes the opinions of people like me into account when making decisions.
5. I feel very confident about this organization's skills.
6. This organization has the ability to accomplish what it says it will do.

Commitment

1. I feel that this organization is trying to maintain a long-term commitment to people like me.
2. I can see that this organization wants to maintain a relationship with people like me.
3. There is a long-lasting bond between this organization and people like me.
4. Compared to other organizations, I value my relationship with this organization more.
5. I would rather work together with this organization than not.

Satisfaction

1. I am happy with this organization.
2. Both the organization and people like me benefit from the relationship.
3. Most people like me are happy in their interactions with this organization.
4. Generally speaking, I am pleased with the relationship this organization has established with people like me.
5. Most people enjoy dealing with this organization.

Exchange relationships

1. Whenever this organization gives or offers something to people like me, it generally expects something in return.
2. Even though people like me have had a relationship with this organization for a long time, it still expects something in return whenever it offers us a favour.
3. This organization will compromise with people like me when it knows that it will gain something.
4. This organization takes care of people who are likely to reward the organization.

Communal relationships

1. This organization does not especially enjoy giving others aid. (Reversed)
2. This organization is very concerned about the welfare of people like me.
3. I feel that this organization takes advantage of people who are vulnerable. (Reversed)
4. I think that this organization succeeds by stepping on other people. (Reversed)
5. This organization helps people like me without expecting anything in return.

Summary

This chapter demonstrates that reputation is at the heart of all organizations, irrespective of stakeholders' perspectives as to whether these organizations are good or bad.

- Reputation is organic and thus ever-changing, which means that it must be monitored, understood and nurtured.

- The companies with the best reputations are those who have close and interactive relationships with their stakeholders. They also have policies and practices that offer continuing, ongoing and mutual benefit to these stakeholders, who include employees, customers, shareholders, regulators and suppliers.

- Companies with good reputations have strong communication cultures, both internally and externally.

- They are prepared to listen and be flexible in their operations.

- Their CEOs are the lead communicators and their communication staff are involved in high-level decision-making.

- These companies understand that their reputation has great value, not just in leveraging financial performance; they take a 'long view' in the decision-making.

- Managing reputation is an integral part of the organization's operations and not confined to a special group.

- Poor reputations are a necessary consequence to organizations which are poorly led with low levels of engagement with stakeholders and weak ethical performance.

- In the short term, many of these companies may still enjoy good financial performance, but the cost of their operations will become greater if they ignore reputational issues.

- Continued poor communication may mask managerial inefficiency for a while, but market performance will undoubtedly unmask pretensions in this area.

- Measurement of reputation is still in its infancy in some countries and, while there is debate over methodology, the chapter indicates two routes that can be taken and recommends their adoption.

Chapter questions

1. Discuss the differences between image and reputation.

2. Draft your own definition of *reputation management*.

3. Track media coverage of a major organization in print, broadcast and on the Web for a month. Identify the reputational issues that impact upon it.

4. Use the data from the tracking study undertaken to draft a corporate communications advice to the organization's CEO.

5. If you are working in a classroom or online situation, poll fellow students for their list of organizations with positive and negative reputation and prepare a report on the outcomes.

6. Identify major organizations, research them and apply Fombrun's taxonomy of six factors to them.

7. Discuss the reality that some firms – even with poor or negative reputation – may still have good sales and profit. Does that mean that reputation can be treated with disdain? (Justify your response with examples.)

Further reading

Argenti, P., and J. Forman (2002). *The Power of Corporate Communications: Crafting the Voice and Image of Your Business*, McGraw-Hill, New York.

Handy, C. (1995). *The Empty Raincoat*, Arrow Books, London.

Kitchen, P. J., and D. E. Schultz (Eds) (2001). *Raising the Corporate Umbrella: Corporate Communications in the 21st Century*, Palgrave, Basingstoke.

Ledingham, J. A., and S. D. Bruning (2000). 'Background and current trends in the study of relationship management,' in Ledingham, J. A., and Bruning, S. D. (Eds), *Public Relations as Relationship Management: A Relational Approach to Public Relations*, Lawrence Erlbaum Associates, Mahwah, NJ.

Schultz, D. E., and P. J. Kitchen (2000). *Global Communications: An Integrated Marketing Approach*, NTC Business Books, Chicago and Macmillan London.

Watson, T., and P. Noble (2007). *Evaluating Public Relations* (2nd ed.), Kogan Page, London.

References

Argenti, P. A., and Druckenmiller, B. (2004) 'Reputation and the corporate brand', *Corporate Reputation Review*, 6(4):368–374.

Black, E., Carnes, T., and Richardson, V. (2000) 'The market value of corporate reputation', *Corporate Reputation Review*, 3(1):31–42.

Bruning, S. D., and Ledingham, J. A. (2000) 'Organization and key relationships: Testing the influence of the relationship dimensions in a business to business context', in Bruning, S. D., and Ledingham, J. A. (eds.), *Public Relations as Relationship Management*, Mahwah, NJ: Lawrence Erlbaum Associates.

Fombrun, C. J. (1996) *Reputation: Realizing Value from Corporate Image*, Cambridge, MA: Harvard Business School.

Fombrun, C. J. (2000, December 4) 'The value to be found in corporate reputation', *London Financial Times*, p. 2.

Gardberg, N. A., and Fombrun, C. J. (2002) 'For better or worse – the most visible American corporate reputations', *Corporate Reputation Review*, 4(4):385–391.

Hon, L. C., and Grunig, J. E. (1999) 'Guidelines for measuring relationships in public relations', The Institute for Public Relations, Gainesville. [Online]. http://www.instituteforpr.com. Last accessed 21 April 2009.

Hutton, J. G., Goodman, M. B., Alexander, J. B., and Genest, C. M. (2001) 'Reputation management: The new face of corporate public relations', *Public Relations Review*, 27:249.

Kitchen, P. J., and Laurence, A. (2003) 'Corporate reputation: An eight-country analysis', *Corporate Reputation Review*, 6(2):103–117.

Lancaster, G. (2001) 'Global campaigns and communications', in Jolly, A. (ed.), *Managing Corporate Reputations*, London: Kogan Page.

Ledingham, J. A. (2003) 'Explicating relationship management as a general theory of public relations', *Journal of Public Relations Research*, 15:181–198.

Merriam-Webster. [Online]. http://www.m-w.com. Last accessed 21 April 2009.

Murray, K., and White, J. (2004) *CEO Views on Reputation Management*, London: Chimes Communications.

Oxford Compact English Dictionary (2009) [Online]. http://www.askoxford.com/results/?view=dev_dict&field-12668446=reputation&branch=13842570&textsearchtype=exact&sortorder=score%2Cname. Last accessed 21 April 2009.

Regester, M. (2001) 'Managing corporate reputation through crisis', in Jolly, A. (ed.), *Managing Corporate Reputations*, London: Kogan Page.

Roughton, B., and Unger, H. (1999, June 22) 'Multifront effort seeks to restore confidence', *The Atlanta Journal-Constitution.* [Online]. http://www.ajc.com.

Srivastava, R. K., McInish, T. H., Woods, R. A., and Capraro, A. J. (1997) 'The value of corporate reputation: Evidence from equity markets', *Corporate Reputation Review*, 1(1):61–68.

van Riel, C. B. M. (1999) *Corporate Communications*, New Jersey: Prentice Hall.

van Riel, C. B. M., and Berens, G. (2001) 'Balancing corporate branding policies in multi-business companies', in Kitchen, P. J., and Schultz, D. E. (eds.), *Raising the Corporate Umbrella: Corporate Communications in the 21st Century*, Basingstoke: Palgrave.

Wakefield, R. I. (2000) 'World class public relations: A model for effective public relations in the multinational', *Journal of Communication Management*, 5(1):59–71.

Wheeler, A. (2001) 'What makes a good corporate reputation?', in Jolly, A. (ed.), *Managing Corporate Reputations*, London: Kogan Page.

14

Innovation management: market timing and solution planning

László Józsa and Judit Pakai

Introduction

The world of business is driven and dominated by the compulsion to constantly renew and innovate. Substantial research information and data prove that a significant part of the profits made by successful companies results from the launch of new products into the market. The main tendency is to apply technological innovations on an ever-broader scale, and companies create newer and newer product concepts. Successful new product concepts and novel solutions are then quickly copied/taken up by the competitors. Therefore, the central question in specialist literature on innovation is the analysis of the will to innovate as well as the determination of and research into the success factors of new products, product development strategies and product development processes. Innovation, management, marketing and company success are closely related concepts and phenomena. Porter (1980) claims that it is highly likely that continuous innovation results

Learning objectives

- To understand the concept and forms of innovation.

- To be able to analyze the characteristics of innovation strategies.

- To be able to summarize the theories on the process of the development of new products.

- To understand the role of time in market appearance.

- To know the strategic issues of market testing and expansive market launch.

- To be able to identify the most common forms of innovation in company structure.

in a company's ability to maintain its successful operation and that companies innovate in order to adapt to the changing circumstances. Drucker (1985) points out that the competitiveness of companies is determined by two main factors: continuous innovation and marketing.

Innovation, however, is not only a necessity but also a risk. It is necessary because it is the condition for companies to survive and maintain their competitiveness and it is risky because it necessitates substantial financial and intellectual resources as well as time while market success itself is not ensured.

The urge to innovate demands that companies continuously develop new products and manage the related risks no matter whether innovation is a result of technological development or the change in market needs. Companies also need to face the fact that, in most industrial sectors, saturated markets and a wide choice of products make it increasingly difficult to explore new consumer needs and identify new niches in the market. They also generate higher product development costs and slow down the acceptance of new products.

Concept and forms of innovation

Innovation means a new idea or a renewal. The concept is associated with a positive meaning: the assumption of progress and development. There are several ways to create novelties; therefore, the concept and types of innovation can be defined in various ways. According to the first approach, innovation means new knowledge, ideas, methods, procedures, products and services. Its two main forms are product innovation and process innovation, which may come about in any sphere of life, within the framework of arts and sciences, technology, economy or social institutions.

Drucker's (1985) definition reflects the management approach to company activities in claiming that innovation is organized, planned and purpose-oriented work during which companies strive to create some new value and satisfy new needs or to reorganize existing resources so that they generate more profit. The definition highlighting a company approach is also customer centred. According to this latter definition, innovation is a new way of satisfying consumer needs at a higher level of quality.

Innovation according to Schumpeter

According to economists, the most widely quoted definition is Schumpeter's (1930). According to Schumpeter, there are five basic forms of innovation:

- **Product innovation**, i.e., the production of new goods or goods with a new quality yet unknown to consumers.
- **Process innovation**, i.e., the application of new manufacturing or commercial procedure related to a product.
- **Market innovation**, i.e., the opening of a new market related to a sales task.
- **Purchase innovation**, i.e., the exploration and acquisition of new purchase sources of raw materials and semi-manufactured products.
- **Organizational innovation**, i.e., the creation of a new type of organization.

The definition accepted by the OECD (1993) is also widely applied: Innovation is the transformation of an idea into a new or updated product launched onto the market or into a new or further developed procedure used in industry and commerce, or it is a new approach to some social service.

Absolute and relative innovations

Innovation does not only relate to inventions and discoveries, i.e., radically new products or methods, but also relates to the improvement and perfection of previously manufactured products, applied technologies or ways of production organization and management. Modified products and procedures are relative innovations. In the case of radical innovations, it is quite frequent that product and process innovation are closely related to each other, unlike in the case of innovations which are merely product improvement and repositionings.

The technological approach to innovation

The technological approach often limits the concept of innovation to research and development (R&D) activities. The 'engineering design' approach represents a broader approach than new product developments and uses the 'engineering design' concept so that it can be seen as a modern interpretation of product and new product development. Engineering design is the transformation of an idea or a market need into detailed information on the basis of which a new product or technical system can be developed (Hales, 1993).

The concept of 'technomanagement' relates to technical innovation from the outset, and it perceives innovation as an activity present in innovation management approaches on both company and national economic levels. Inzelt (1998) defines technomanagement as: 'Technomanagement is an economic activity which concentrates on the management of technology innovation, realization and dispersal through company and governmental organizations.' Technology management implemented in the commercial context connects the natural sciences, technical engineering sciences and management sciences in order to plan, develop and introduce new technological opportunities as well as the strategy to carry them out.

From a technical viewpoint, we can talk of those innovations making a major change to technology (major innovations) and those with smaller technological significance (minor innovations) (Altshuller, 1984). The category of major innovation accounts for only a small percentage of all innovation. Based on the analysis of 400 000 patents, an American study, concentrating on the significance of technical development, identified five categories of innovation:

- Innovations related to discoveries, e.g., penicillin or the transistor, amounted to 0.3 per cent of the patents.
- Innovations which represent a new product or system concept, e.g., the development of personal computers, amounted to 4 per cent.
- Innovations representing a radical modification of an already existing product or system, e.g., the ballpoint pen (biro) or the Ford Model T, amounted to 19 per cent of the patents.
- Innovations representing a non-essential, but qualitative modification of an already existing product or system, such as the addition of a new luxury

function, e.g., the automatic electric car window, amounted to 45 per cent of the patents.

- Innovations representing the improvement of the functions of a product or system amounted to 32 per cent of the patents.

Models of the innovation process

The modelling of the innovation process centres on two core questions. The first: What is to be considered the starting point of the innovation? And the second: Do we see the individual phases of the process as phases representing activities separate from one another and occurring in a strictly defined time sequence?

As far as the first basic question is concerned, there are two opposing standpoints associated with the research of Schumpeter (1930) and Schmookler (1996). One emphasizes the effect of technological development and new scientific achievements (technology push), while the other gives a central role to market needs (demand pull). The development of science, especially with the development of radical innovation, is a prerequisite for progress. Relative innovation representing modifications, however, can come about without it on the basis of the identification of market needs and possibilities.

The traditional interpretation of views emphasizing the primacy of scientific-technological development sees innovation as a passive adaptation process resulting from technology push and claims that the individual phases of the process represent separate activities. The traditional approach is based on a linear and hierarchical model of innovation (see Figure 14.1). According to this view, innovation is realized through the following phases: invention, first application and spreading. The model presupposes a strictly set time sequence of the activities involved in the innovation process, starting from basic research and ending in the market launch of the innovative product.

Figure 14.1
The linear model of innovation

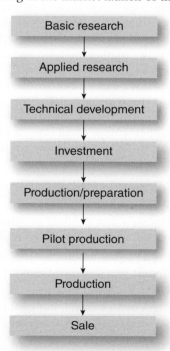

The interactive model of innovation (the chain-linked model, Kline and Rosenberg, 1986)

According to modern research, the innovation process is not made up of linear and hierarchical activities, nor does it begin with research and end with some scientific result. Rather, the main characteristic of the process is the continuous and interactive relationship between the activities. The innovation process consists of links embodying different activities, and it starts with the companies recognizing a market or business opportunity on the basis of research or other effects and changes. They then devise a product idea and concept through iteration, test it, manufacture the new product and launch it onto the market.

The starting point of the model is in line with the results of some research on technical patents, namely that the basis of an innovation decision for companies on the industrial market is the prospective profit which can be made on the potential markets of new investment goods.

The model of the national innovation system

In some countries, the development of innovations is supported by an institutional network on the national economic level (Inzelt, 1998). The purpose of a national innovation system is to facilitate the realization of scientific-technical development in economic processes. In a narrower sense, it includes organizations and institutions that are supported by the national government and that create knowledge and participate in research, as well as the spread and exploitation of new scientific results. Its main constituents are:

- The educational system
- The research system
- The innovation legal system of the economy
- The system of financing the innovations.

In a broader sense, it also includes all the organizations and mechanisms including the business sphere that contribute to the creation and spreading of knowledge and the creation and utilization of innovation.

Product innovation strategies

We can distinguish between two types of product-innovation strategies depending on whether the company reacts to changes (reactive strategy) or initiates changes in the market (proactive strategy). Both have a number of variations.

The essence of *reactive strategies* is adaptation or reaction to market needs and challenges. The bulk (90 per cent) of new product categories appearing on the market are the result of a reactive strategy. It has four main variations:

- **Defensive strategy,** which aims to defend the existing goods of a company against the growth in market share of the competition's product. Its main means are through product modification, the broadening of the product family, the launch of new brands and repositioning. Product modification may mean new product variations of better quality or lower production costs.

- Copying strategy, where the launch of the company's own brand results from the copying (with some minor modifications) of a successful new product of a competitor.
- Second but better strategy, where, in comparison with the new product of a competitor, a more developed and better brand is launched onto the market.
- Responsive strategy, where the company develops a new product on the basis of well-identifiable consumer needs.

The choice of the reactive strategy is the most expedient in the following cases (Urban and Hauser, 1993):

- If the market of the existing products of the company is still expandable.
- If the potential market of a new product is not big enough for development costs to be recovered.
- If the company cannot defend its new products against being copied.
- If companies to copy new products seriously threaten the success of the new product.
- If it is difficult to find suitable suppliers for the production of the new product.
- If marketing other companies' control channels.

Proactive strategies

The proactive strategy is adopted by those companies that take initiatives in the market. It is the marketing, collection of orders, strategic alliance and innovative enterprise that makes the proactive strategy and the launch of new products possible.

Research and development

Companies usually make applied research into the direction of the application of new scientific and technical results. In these cases, product innovation shows up primarily in the field of technical development. In the course of technical innovation, a specific new product will be created.

Marketing: identification of market demands

Research into market demands and consumer needs requires the activity of marketing. Manufacturers of consumer goods and service providers follow the strategy outlined above. The majority of new products are therefore created on the basis of marketing initiative.

Acquisition

The acquisition of the right to use patents, licences and company properties provides a good opportunity to acquire and launch brand-new products.

Strategic alliances

Temporary alliances are often entered into between competitors in order to develop certain new products under joint ventures. This process contributes much to the launch of a new product of competitive advantage by the combination of resources and abilities.

Innovative enterprise

The expression above refers to an organization within the company that carries out product development in the form of entrepreneurial activity. This organization provides the basic foundations for commercial success.

The choice of the proactive strategy is the most expedient in the following cases (Urban and Hauser, 1993):

- If the company can acquire a quick and significant rise in the amount of sales, it can enter new markets – consequently, the new product can offer significant profit.
- If the company is able to protect its new product from imitators with the help of either patents or any other orders.
- If the company is able to protect its market from the imitators that are superior to the original product.
- If the suppliers necessary for the creation of the new products are available.
- If the company is able to control marketing channels to a desired extent.

Timing of market entry

A successful product launch or market entry depends also on good timing and takes the characteristics of the target groups into account. In the case of timing as a strategic dimension, three basic possibilities can be differentiated:

- Be the first to launch as a 'first mover'
- Launch in parallel
- Launch with delay.

We often come across the view that it is worthwhile to be the first on the market because there is then a great chance for an enterprise to gain the highest profit. Even though this phenomena is true from many points of view, still, the reality is more complex. There are enterprises that have been defending their business positions from the very beginning, but others also have very much to expect even if they enter the same field of business at a later point in time. We can regard an early access to be the best opportunity to obtain abundant competence and better market conformity. Not only do cost efficiency and low prices emerge here, but in the case of a registered patent, the market entry of a new competitor can also be prevented. Consequently, a monopoly position will be secured in an artificial way. There is a great risk in this, however. If by any chance the technology is not perfect, the product cannot be perfect either, so competitors might leave the first mover behind.

It is not easy to create new consumer demands, especially in the field of marketing communication. In the case of subsequent enterprises, there is no need to create the primary demand because it already exists. Therefore – with a view to ultimate success – it is essential that the first mover leverages its powers, possibilities and the strengths of the enterprise as well. A well-planned and well-accomplished primary entry can result in high market share and accelerate the pace of growth as well as good profit potentials.

A great number of ventures have been striving to come onto the market simultaneously with competitors. Gillette, IBC, Coca-Cola and Pepsi Cola, for instance, always launch an innovation on the market once competitors do so. A parallel entry is usually considered significant on those markets where a strong venture with great expectations can be found beside the leading enterprise. Sometimes a considerable degree of challenges are achieved through a certain number of subsequent ventures. This is the case, for instance, in the case of the market of TV channels.

A severe competition in the case of parallel entries can be explained by the fact that both enterprises aim to launch something new and also want to come on market first. This usually arouses the curiosity of the competitor's venture. If they succeed in finding their own niche in the market, others might also get the chance to make their dreams come true. It is difficult to challenge TV channels as BBC or NTV; however, the specialized Discovery (science), MTV (music) and others can still enter and develop, and do not fail. There is a strong need for resources in the case of a parallel entry in particular, but it can also imply an intense pace of growth and reasonable profit and might also contribute much to a dynamic rise in market share.

We can talk about delayed entry if it happens either at a late phase of the intensive advance (in the period of turbulent competition) or in the phase of the maturity of the product according to its life cycle. These types of entries can be realized in the following forms:

- As imitators
- As innovators
- As a combination of the two forms above.

In the case of imitators, the 'new' product launched is one and the same as the competitor's product. We often encounter imitators in the fields of banking and fast-food services. In the case of innovators, for instance, it is the e-banking system that has been transformed into a solution that all the market players are using.

The innovator enters the market in order to come through on a revolutionary programme, which differs radically from its predecessors. Accordingly, this helps various consumers switch over to another product. The launch of 1800 MHz mobile phones in Hungary has had similar results. By these means, Vodafone – a new market participant – has already tried out the market.

It is simply not fair to copy another's achievement. It is more acceptable to come up with a little modification. For example, in the insurance market, both Allianz and Union say that 'Our life insurance is at least as nice as the one of ING, but you can get much farther with it.'

Simple consecutive enterprises can expect merely a short career, but as new opportunities are found they can also improve their original product and supersede the lingering competitor. For an innovative entrant, however, who is creative at the same time, success is still attainable. The nature of economy constantly provides opportunity for successful introduction of new ideas and for career making. Lagging entrants cannot normally expect a reasonable market share.

The process of product and service innovation

There are two main approaches to the description of innovation process:

- Technical planning and development of new products – engineering design (Hales, 1993).
- Marketing conception of a product – innovation and innovation management. Technical development and technical innovation in general do not belong to this category. It rather refers to the requirements of communication and co-operation.

We can differentiate three basic model types that can depict product innovation:

- Conceptual models that refer to the process as a whole (Crawford, 1994; Urban and Hauser, 1993).
- Models for managers, which are parts of the models above. Their task is basically to assure managers that a sub-field or sub-activity conforms to the conceptual model and with the direction and supervision of the process itself.
- Specific sub-models that refer to certain sub-activities, models and decisions such as demand forecast, pricing and calculating of advertising costs.

On the level of conceptual models, product innovation can be modelled in many ways. The main types (Hart and Baker, 1994) are as follows:

- **The model of batch production according to functions** refers to a conventional approach. The development of a new product is organized such that the responsibility for the particular sub-tasks of development should be given to various departments within the company. The R&D department is responsible for the idea, the department of technical innovation is responsible for the designs of the product, the production department is responsible for the organization of the manufacturing process and the marketing department is responsible for the plans of market entry. The main problem concerning this model is co-ordination, controlling and the time factor.
- **The model of batch production according to activities** depicts the process of product development according to the tasks to be carried out. This model is rather similar to the one mentioned previously, but it does not put the emphasis on the function itself but rather on the activity.
- **The model of batch production according to decisions** puts the emphasis on the stages of decision-making. *Decisions* refers to the lay-off or restart of a particular project. Planning can be continued only if the project meets the fixed requirements. It is important to draft this criteria well in advance. Decisions can be as follows: the project can be continued, stopped or resumed with certain modifications.
- **The transformation model** focuses on the so-called *black box theory*. Accordingly, functions, tasks and information are simultaneously taken into account and represented as inputs in the course of the process of development. This model is holistic and information is regarded as the key question.
- **The model of parallel development** considers product innovation so that certain functions cannot be carried out in succession but parallel with one

another. This model presupposes certain integrated organizations that are able to co-operate even with outside partners. The model described above complies with the following requirements:

- The technical know-how of various fields of interest should be easily put into practice in the course of the development process.
- The necessary information should be made available for every single function that is in connection with all other business activities and market feedback.
- The loss of time should be eliminated in the development process.

Testing of new products

The main task of testing in this case is to reduce risks in the process of product innovation. We can highlight three different spheres of testing as follows:

- Product testing
- Testing of the sub-sections of the marketing mix
- Testing of the entire marketing programme.

Product tests, on the one hand, aim at controlling the operation and applicability of the product; on the other hand, they check whether the products meet the expectations of the consumer. We can differentiate three types: **alpha**, **beta** and **gamma** tests.

The *alpha test* refers to an in-company quality test. It is possible to check the way in which the colour, size and weight of the product can affect the potential consumer.

In the *beta test* (product use test), the examination concentrates mainly on the way products operate or how they are employed and utilized under current usage. In this method, it is the potential consumer who puts an experimental product to use; consequently, their opinion is of great value as far as further developments are concerned. Beta testing is particularly preferred in computer and car production.

Gamma tests are set up to examine the appropriateness of the product in the market, and basically analyze the conformity of the product to customer needs in terms of both utility and value. This method not only can depict the main characteristics of the product but also contains valuable references concerning the price and further features of the product. This method is often used in the pharmaceutical industry.

The type of method applied for product testing depends on the basic aim of the experiment. The following questions should be considered:

- Does the product meet the original requirements of the project?
- Where can the product be improved?
- Is price reduction possible?
- Where and how is the new product used?
- Is it worth proceeding with product innovation?

Consumers' perceptions and evaluation also play a crucial role in the testing phase. These aspects are the following:

- The physical appearance (size, form, colour), style and flavour of the product.
- The operation of the product: how the product accomplishes the expected functions.
- Whether the product works as expected, e.g., whether a detergent is really able to remove an iron stain.
- Product image – is it a type of product or brand that people buy because of its public image?

The type of testing carried out with the help of consumer reports is usually put into practice according to four main methods:

- Blind test
- Evaluation of alternative product types
- Individual product evaluation
- Comparison of different brands.

In the *blind test,* consumers evaluate similar products without being aware of their brand names. In this case, test designers aim to conduct selling-point analysis. This method is fairly well known in the food industry and household-chemical engineering.

Alternative product types (Urban and Hauser, 1993) are experimental products that differ from each other in certain significant aspects. People participating in the survey test the variations and give their opinions concerning the characteristic features of the product. On the basis of this method, we can define the best product type. This experiment proves to be most successful in the case of products that people prefer to buy most often. This method is generally applied to the market of industrial products and durable goods.

In individual product evaluation, a test scale of five to seven stages is normally applied. The consumers report their opinion about the particular product without references. They do not compare the product with a preconceived mental schema. It is therefore very important to use the methods of *brand comparison.*

A survey on all the elements of the marketing programme is a crucial part of new-product testing. This method basically covers the field of survey that examines packaging, brand name and advertising. When a new product enters the market, it is crucial to discover the role that the price can have in the sales appeal. It is important to define how many consumers are willing to test the product at the pilot study stage at a certain price. The most regular methods of price testing are: price-simulation, conjoint analysis and store panels (Holbert and Speece, 1993). Simulation is suitable for measuring the flexibility of the price. The conjoint analysis technique which involves various combinations of product characters are associated with different price levels. Furthermore, the survey can also reveal the type of product that consumers normally prefer to buy, but we also have to take the indicated price into account. In the case of the store panel method, a price-acceptance survey is also usually carried out in order to reveal the volume of products being sold at a particular price level.

Testing of packaging

When planning packaging, specialists have already examined the different functions of packaging. During testing, they examine if packaging is really suitable for these functions. According to Holbert and Speece (1993), functional testing of packaging can be done by examining the protection of the product.

Examining the protection of the product is done by laboratory and consumer testing. In the latter case, the consumers express their opinions about the practicability of the packaging. Their classification is usually stricter and more critical than the examination carried out in one's own laboratory.

The aim of testing the product is to determine if packaging enhances the use of the product. This function mainly asks about the shape, size and colour of the packaging.

It also matters, e.g., how much space a tube of toothpaste takes up on a shelf and how easily its contents can be removed. The third test aims at the control of the aesthetic-communication function. It can be tested with scale methods if the packaging suits the potential customers from an aesthetic point of view and to what extent it is attractive and informative. During aesthetic testing, consumers express how much they like the product, but with a focus group interview, it also can be asked why they like or don't like it.

By observation we can determine how the packaging attracts attention. We can observe, e.g., the eye movement of customers in front of the shelf. If we want to know if the packaging indicates the quality of the product, we can analyze it by test sale, during which a product is offered for test sale in different kinds of packaging and, after using it, customers are asked about the product. Customers usually report that a product is of good quality if its packaging is attractive.

A specific requirement of packaging is to help shopkeepers with handling, transporting and storing the product. It is in the manufacturers' own interest to respect the shopkeepers' attitude; that's why they ask shopkeepers as well about the packaging of new products. Shopkeepers give information not only about their own expectations but also about their customers' wishes and problems.

Brand name testing

The brand name has an influence on the image of the product and, through this, on its demand. A good brand name is:

- Distinctive
- Short
- Memorable
- Convincing
- Specific.

The brand name is usually tested together with the packaging. In a test, the brand name must be exposed to consumers to trigger perceptions. First the test name is tried out on the inner circle of the company, and then it goes to a consumer panel. During testing, several brand names are shown and consumers are asked what a particular brand name reminds them of and what associations it evokes in them. The brand provides product advantages and communicates to consumers. At the same time, it is used to express the image of the company. When naming a new product, the following things should be considered.

- The branding policy of the company (special brand name, brand families, company name and their combinations).
- The hallmark policy of the company.
- General requirements in relation to the trade name.
- Graphic and aesthetic viewpoints having a connection with the brand identification.
- The image policy of the whole company.
- Special points of view connected with the new product.

The decision about brand name is in close connection with quality, positioning, packaging and advertising.

Advertising test

During testing of the advertisement, the main aim is to find out how potential customers react and if the advertisement will be effective. By testing, you can measure:

- Access to consumers through the selected media.
- Attracting the attention of the public.
- Understanding the message of the advertisement.
- The credibility of the message.
- The convincing power of the message.
- Arousing of purchasing willingness.

The two methods of testing are the home and the laboratory test. In the case of the home test, the examination is carried out in real circumstances. For example, for a newspaper advertisement, it is measured if the public remembers and understands it, if they can identify it and what they think about it. The laboratory test simulates the real circumstances. In such a case, the reactions of the invited public can be observed more closely and exactly during the presentation of the advertisement and after it.

Market testing

Prior to a wide-ranging introduction of a new product into the market, it is practical to examine the designed product within narrow market conditions. The examination focuses on trial and repurchase of the product. Its aim is to explore:

- How big the expected interest is?
- How big the expected sale is?
- How efficient the planned marketing programme will be?

During the simulated market test, the methods of sales testing and market testing are available, which have different examination cycles, expenses and time demands.

For testing, it is advisable to use the services of professional market research companies (see Figure 14.2).

Simulated market test

Here, customers are invited to constructed shopping environments through advertising or personal recruitment.

The customers try the purchase at home and then give their opinions in person or by telephone. The key of the examination is to put the customer in a shopping situation and record their opinion and repurchasing intention immediately. The testing can be performed by sending off free samples where the customer can order the product after trying it. It can be successful, especially in the case of consumer goods. Compared with other methods, it is cheaper, it takes less time, and the interest and reaction of the competitors can be better assessed. If this testing is successful, there is no reason to choose more expensive methods. By means of simulated market testing, the market share attained by a new brand can be estimated as follows:

$$MS = W \times R \times SR$$

where MS indicates the market share, W is willingness to try, R is repurchasing rate and SR is shopping rate.

If, e.g., the ratio of people trying is 20 per cent, repurchasers spend 10 per cent of their expenses on the new brand and they buy by 30 per cent more, the index of market share is as follows:

$$PR = 0.2 \times 0.1 \times 1.3 = 2.6\%.$$

The trying willingness is estimated by observation or questioning, and the repurchase willingness is estimated by questioning.

Test sale

The test sale happens in real shopping circumstances. The new product is put on the shelves of selected existing specialists shops in the market. Usually, different marketing mix strategies and solutions can be tried in each shop.

Figure 14.2
Market test methods
for various contexts

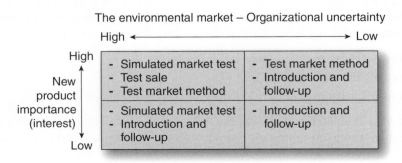

Test market method

The method of test markets is also called a marketing test. The whole marketing programme is tested. The method is expensive and takes a long time. The number of shops involved in sale is high. Accordingly, it is used before the introduction of new products when the risk is high and product manufacture requires significant investment. The results are used to make an ideal marketing programme in order to make maximum profits. Two to three towns and one or two geographical regions are chosen for testing, which represent anticipated typical demographic conditions from the point of view of replicating the consumer decision-making process. Advertising media must be selected and the intensity of advertising must be set so as to fit the target goal in terms of potential customers. As test marketing demands a lot of company resources, before its application it must be considered if the examination doesn't place the company in a disadvantaged position with regard to its competitors. In the electronic version of the test market method (the behaviour-scan model), shopping and advertisement influence can be measured at the same time. In a selected area in the selected shops, the new product is put into circulation and, by means of the optical reading device used at the cash register, sales can be measured.

Testing of production equipment

The testing of production equipment usually takes place first in-house, as the number of potential customers is low. The examinations carried out by the manufacturer during alpha testing are related to the qualities of the product.

The beta tests are carried out at the users in real circumstances of application by the technicians of the manufacturing company. Product use and safety conditions are observed. During the gamma test, information is collected about the extent to which the product meets potential users' demands and what they think about it. On the basis of the results of the testing carried out with the users, it is possible to change certain attributes of the product, but the information can also be utilized during the final design of the awareness building process and service architecture.

The representatives of the manufacturing company can observe what value the user attaches to their product. This information can be important during the calculation of the price.

In order to test and attract attention, product demonstrations are common at trade fairs and in exhibition rooms where a great number of experts are present. Interest can be gauged as well as the reaction of customers to individual technical attributes of the new product. As competitors can easily get information in this way, it is advisable to hold the demonstration when everything is ready for introduction.

Product launch and follow-up

If the market testing is successful, the final plan must be prepared to introduce the new product onto the market, which consists of strategic and tactical decisions. The strategic decision points are as follows:

- Timing of market entry (mentioned earlier)
- The scale of launching the product

- The intensity of market entry
- Determining the target group
- Product positioning
- The evaluation of the product advantage
- The choice of the brand name (mentioned earlier).

The tactical decisions are about the product range, the marketing communication, the price and the distribution.

The scale of market entry

Market entry can be realized on a narrower or wider scale. You can enter the market by occupying one segment, some segments or completely (in all segments of the potential market). Of course, it can also happen that with the combination of the two a gradual market entry is realized, so that after being successful in a segment or in some segments, the business moves towards the whole market. When starting a gradual entry, we usually meet two main target groups: innovative consumers or customers of a geographical area. If the introduction happens in a narrower circle in the beginning, the processes can be followed and controlled more easily and it's easier to intervene if necessary.

The intensity of launching a product

The intensity of launching includes how the new product is announced on the market; it also includes the effect that the announcement elicits. The announcement is a part of the communicational tasks. Its aim is to create an atmosphere in which the market is full of expectations and to help ensure the favourable reception of the product. Usually, intensive marketing communicational means are used. The effect depends on the efficiency of the means and the attractiveness of the product.

The target market

In the phase of introduction, we can apply mass, differentiated or concentrated marketing. In mass marketing, the market is considered homogeneous and we aim at the average consumer. We offer the same programme to every potential customer, i.e., the same product at the same price on the same channel with the same communication. In differentiated and concentrated marketing, we don't consider the market homogeneous: We get to know the main customer groups by means of market segmentation and, accordingly, form the marketing programme considering their demands.

Selling point/product advantage

The basic selling point has been determined in the planning phase of the product. When a product is designed, this advantage should be enforced through technological development. In addition, some other characteristics should be developed that represent added value. Added value is mainly found in marketing, such as packaging, guarantee, services connected to the product, terms of payment and delivery, brand development and product availability. Essential points to consider are:

- The customers' demands and expectations
- The customers' reactions at product testing

- Costs that might arise from better quality
- Findings from comparing with competitors.

Added value is differentiated according to the target groups' demands, which affects the company's competitive position and competitive advantage.

Positioning

Positioning gives the answer to the following question: Why will the potential customers of the target market buy that product? It's difficult to choose if there are more options. In such cases, the following should be focused (Lendrevie and Lindon, 1990):

- The largest target market
- The most competitive advantages
- The most credible advantages.

Good positioning can be achieved if:

- The product has real advantages
- The advantages have been tested through the development procedure
- The selling point matches the customers' demands
- The planners are familiar with competitive products
- The selling point conforms to the corporate image.

Positioning aims at having very consistent marketing elements.

Product range is the first element of market introduction. The question is, whether in the introductory stage – i.e., one year after the appearance of the product – what sort of product range should be offered around the new product, should we offer a wide range of it. Product varieties can differ from one another in the number of services, their quality, format, size and price. Several aspects must be considered. If the product is brand new, the customers might be confused if we offer too many new models. In other cases, the company can increase its potential market and can expand its scale of competitive advantages.

The decision is affected by (Hultink and Hart, 1996):

- The degree of novelty
- The strategic aspects of product development
- Whether it is a new product or product line or expands the current product line
- The number of customers in the target market.

Those companies that are among the first to introduce the new product have greater advantage and offer wider product range. However, those who enter the market later decide on fewer ranges.

Price

In the introductory phase, we can decide which pricing to use: penetration or skimming prices. Penetration pricing promises the biggest market share. It is advantageous if (Kotler, 1994, pp. 304–306):

- The market pricing sensitivity is high
- The high turnover balances the low price
- The low prices discourage both current and potential competitors.

Skimming pricing means high prices in the introductory stage. It is reasonable to apply if:

- The number of customers is large and there is a large demand
- The high price does not attract more competitors
- The high price shows high quality
- The selling point is big.

Marketing communication

Marketing communication strategy is very important when introducing a new product. Companies spend a great deal of money in this field. It includes advertising, retailers' motivation and the improvement of sales staff's motivation and customer awareness. It belongs to the promotional decisions whether the focus is on push (focus on trade) or pull (focus on end consumers) strategy. The push strategy targets the intermediary and the pull strategy targets the end consumer.

Tracking the product on the market

Tracking the product is important both in the introductory stage and during its life cycle. It should ensure its successfulness and, if needed, it should apply amendments in the introductory stage. Basic tasks in this phase include:

- The analysis of product acceptability
- Tracing competitors' reactions
- Taking necessary measures in order to achieve goals.

Life cycle management serves the achievement of long-term objectives adapting these to the specific stages of the life cycle.

Product innovation in organizations

Companies operate in different organizations; therefore, there are several types of functional solutions. Each company is looking for the best and most efficient organizational structure. There are several approaches to product innovation based on:

- Corporate level
- The level of concrete development projects
- The level of network
- Informal structures.

In a traditional functional organization, the development of a new product can take place in several organizational structures: the R&D departments, marketing departments, product managers and new product departments. In the traditional organization, some functions are co-ordinated with one another. The task of product innovation is done by functional sectors. This is only effective if risk is low: it only focuses on the alteration of the product. It is essential that the work of departments is co-ordinated by the board of directors. The product management organization in the frame of functional organization represents an individual stage. Product innovation is one of its tasks. The product management system is mainly used by those corporations that have several product lines or products and very high turnover. Procter & Gamble first applied it in 1931. Today, it is widespread. Advantages include: The product manager is able to create a cost-effective marketing mix; they can react to the problems of the market; and they can keep an eye on less important brands. Disadvantages include the setback role of the co-ordination activities and the conflicts that emerge, and that the product managers often change their positions (they remain in this position for only a short time; therefore, it is hard to maintain continuity, and long-term planning is out of the question). In order to solve this problem, production teams were set up (Kotler, 1994) and the category management system was introduced, in which they focus on the product categories.

There are three characteristic types of production teams:

- **The vertical production team,** led by the line manager, who is responsible for co-ordinating the other managers; a deputy line manager and an assistant helps their work.
- **The triangle production team,** consisting of a line manager and two assistants.
- **The horizontal production team,** consisting of a line manager and other experts such as a marketing manager.

The category management system is mainly applied by those companies that have several competitive products, have the same position and compete with each other. Several category managers are led by a brand manager, who is in charge of positioning, distributing the budget and developing new brands in the given category. Divisional organizations are suitable for those transnational organizations that have a lot of products and markets. They set up autonomous organizational units or divisions for big production lines or market groups. This means some kind of decentralization.

Concerning innovation, there can be four solutions:

- Each division sets up their autonomous innovation.
- Co-operative and divisional product development.
- The co-operative and divisional sector has the leading role in developing new products.
- The divisions are responsible only for some simple development tasks.

In matrix-type organizations, the innovation is realized according to the above-mentioned aspects.

In an enterprise, the product development organizational units can have several solutions. However, without the company's support, none ensures the success of the new product.

The main forms of corporate subsidies are:

- Determination of a clear innovation policy (objectives, resources).
- Creation of product innovation projects.
- Creation of a suitable co-ordination and supervision organization.
- A suitable corporate culture.

Process in action new service products at Tesco

(This case expands on the Tesco case from Chapter 11 and considers it from an innovation viewpoint. Innovation in this chapter concentrates on the development of new products, but the same theory can also be applied to new services or new service delivery modes.)

Tesco has four different store formats, each tailored to customers' needs. They started with a superstore 'product':

Superstore (approx. 20000–50000 sq. ft.)

Tesco began opening superstores in the 1970s and, during the 1980s and 1990s, built a national network, to which we are adding every year. We have an ongoing programme of extending and refreshing our superstores to improve the overall experience for customers. In recent years, we have introduced a number of new non-food ranges into superstores such as DVDs and books.

They then introduced a bigger store 'product' . . .

Extra (approx. 60000 sq. ft. and larger)

Since opening our first Extra in 1997, the one-stop destination store has proved extremely popular. Extra stores offer the widest range of food and non-food lines, ranging from electrical equipment to homewares, clothing, health and beauty and seasonal items such as garden furniture. We have opened 18 new Extras in 2005, mostly through extensions to existing stores.

. . . and then a convenience store 'product' . . .

Express (up to 3000 sq. ft.)

Express stores offer customers great value, quality and fresh food close to where they live and work. We opened our first Express store in 1994 and now we have over 650 stores selling a range of up to 7000 lines, including fresh produce, wines and spirits and an in-store bakery.

. . . and finally a town and city centre 'product'.

Metro (approx. 7000–15000 sq. ft.)

We opened our first Metro in 1992, bringing the convenience of Tesco to town and city centre locations. Metros cater for thousands of busy customers each week and offer a tailored range of food lines, including ready-meals and sandwiches.

Questions

1. Do you consider that Tesco are innovators in their business?

2. If so, what models and frameworks of innovation could they have adopted from this chapter to ensure success in their innovation ventures?

(Case note contributed by Geoff Southern. Please see Chapter 11 for more background information on Tesco and sources of quotations.)

Summary

- This chapter deals with the concept of innovation and its main types.

- We have analyzed the process of product development and introduced the most widespread models.

- Besides the innovation strategies, we have looked at the role of time in relation to the new product's success and showed the basic testing methods of new products.

- We have highlighted the problems of market introduction strategies.

- Finally, we have introduced those organizational solutions that are most frequently used in innovations.

Chapter questions

1. Introduce and compare the models suitable to describe innovation.

2. Give examples to illustrate time as the strategic element in the success of a new product.

3. Analyze the new product testing methods and compare their deployment.

4. What are the strategic problems of introducing a new product in the market?

5. What sort of organizational solutions would you recommend to those involved in innovation at a national or transnational company? Support your idea.

References

Altshuller, G. (1984) *Creativity as an Exact Science*, New York: Gordon and Breavh Science.

Crawford, C. M. (1994) *New Products Management*, (4th edn.), Irwin Inc.

Drucker, P. F. (1985) *Innovation and Entrepreneurship, Practice and Principles*, London: William Heinemann Ltd, p. xv.

Hales, C. (1993) *Managing Engineering Design*, London: Longman, p. xv.

Hart, S., and Baker, M. J. (1994) 'The multiple convergent model of new product development', *International Marketing Review*, 11(1):77–92.

Holbert, N. B., and Speece, M. W. (1993) *Practical Marketing Research: An Integrated Global Perspective*, Prentice Hall, pp. 206–209.

Hultink, E., and Hart, S. (1996) 'The World Path to a Better Mousetrap: Myth or Reality?', Paper for ESOMAR CONFERENCE, Budapest.

Inzelt, A. (ed.) (1998) *Bevezetés az innovációmenedzsmentbe (Introduction to Management of Innovation)*, Müszaki, Budapest.

Józsa, L. (2003) *Marketing Strategy*, KJK- Kerszöv, Budapest.

Kline, S., and Rosenberg, N. (1986) 'An overview of innovation', in Landau, R., and Rosenberg, N. (eds.), *The Positive Sum*, Washington: National Academy Press.

Kotler, P. (1994) *Marketing Management: Analysis, Planning, Implementation, Control* (8th edn.), Prentice Hall International Editions.

Lendrevie, J., and Lindon, D. (1990) *Mercator: Theorie et Pratique du Marketing*, Dalloz, Paris.

OECD. (1993) *Frascati Manual.*, (5th edn.), Annex 2, Para 29, p. 116.

Porter, M. E. (1980) *Competitive Strategy: Techniques for Analyzing Industries and Competitors*, New York: The Free Press.

Schmookler, J. (1996) *Invention and Economic Growth*, Harvard University Press.

Schumpeter, J. A. (1930) *Business Cycles*, New York: McGraw Hill.

Urban, G. L., and Hauser, J. R. (1993) *Design and Marketing of New Products* (2nd edn.), Prentice Hall Inc.

Part six
Organizational development and co-ordination (infrastructure processes)

Every organization needs an infrastructure – processes of organizational development, evaluation, and co-ordination – to support the order fulfilment and order acquisition processes.

Chapter 15 presents the concept of solutions design. It highlights the process of seeking and evaluating solutions to problems. The nature of problems ranges from strategic to operational (tactical). Valuable methodologies and supporting techniques are introduced. One 'process in action' note consists of a marketing investigation on trends and strategy in the cigarette industry, which students are asked to undertake with the support of notes by the authors. Another describes a problem-solving technique employed at John McGavigan (see also in Chapter 8).

Chapter 16 explores the effectiveness of strategic planning and performance measurement. It discusses issues such as flexibility, quick management reaction, recent developments in management theory, interfaces between strategy and performance management, operational measures, integrated management, strategy formulation process, marketing performance and strategic integration. The first 'process in action' note considers the (strategic) mission statements of two organizations, Merck (a US pharmaceutical company), and Wal-Mart (a major US/international retailer). A second returns to Oticon (see Chapter 5), to discuss operational implications of the strategic change from a task-based organization to a project-oriented one. The final note simulates the development of a balanced scorecard performance management system derived from the corporate mission and objectives of the British Broadcasting Corporation (BBC).

Chapter 17 introduces marketing implications for financial management. It calls for a good understanding of accounting principles and stresses the fact that accounting information is central to planning, measuring and controlling many marketing activities. Its content revolves around the discussion of financial accounting related to marketing effectiveness, budgeting techniques, project appraisal, accounting systems and balance sheets. 'Process in action' notes in this chapter consist of illustrations of the various budgeting techniques described, and comparisons of alternative methods of project appraisal. They are concerned with activities in a provisions company (Smith's Grocers), investment in a new product and the benefit of advertising in accounting terms.

Chapter 18 focuses on strategic brand management. Its content covers issues such as innovation, time management, market centricity, customer-facing business processes, customer value viewed within the organization, brand strategy and value gaps. The 'process in action' notes illustrate this changing relationship and positioning frameworks in First Direct Bank, and in McDonald's.

Chapter 19 addresses the issue of managing the marketing and e-business interface. The Internet could be considered as the largest market of all. The chapter delves into e-business and e-commerce models linked with business plans and strategies, web-design criteria and Internet-marketing strategies. It also discusses the concepts of viral marketing, relationship marketing and contextual marketing. The 'process in action' note considers a Taiwan bookseller, the Caves Book Company, and its transition from a traditional (B2C) (brick-and-mortar) bookshop to an electronic retail seller (still B2C), to an electronic wholesaler business-to-business-to-customer (B2B2C) and, to a virtual 'book club', delivering literature-associated services and exploiting individual customer data to build relationships.

Finally, Chapter 20 takes a look at developments in international and global management from the marketing perspective. The content covers issues such as the divergence and convergence paradigm, the impetus for internationalization, global marketing opportunities, entry strategies, global competition and strategy, the future of global marketing, cross-functional processes, global sourcing, international fluxes, trade barriers and theoretical frameworks. The 'process in action' notes use international business events as illustrations addressing the convergence and divergence paradigm of international business, and in particular the global marketing environment. Various companies operating in different parts of the world are considered. A comparison of the behaviour of several companies in international markets is also made.

15

Solutions design

Geoff Southern and Luiz Moutinho

Introduction

This chapter looks at the process of seeking and evaluating solutions to problems in business and management. These problems may be on a scale from strategic (whether there should be fundamental changes in what the business does) to tactical (whether a company should enter a new market or develop a new product) to operational (what kind of marketing programme to use). The chapter will attempt to describe techniques and methods used to solve problems. It will make reference to other parts of this book where appropriate to avoid repetition of methodology of analysis and evaluation, but will also introduce other techniques. It will end with a specific marketing problem which students are asked to solve, with the support of notes from the authors.

Learning objectives

- To become acquainted with problem-solving methodologies and supporting techniques.

- To become skilful in the choice of techniques and in the application of some of them.

The general problem-solving process

The problem-solving process is a combination of scientific method and artistic creativity. It is scientific in that it requires a logical approach to the analysis of current situations and simulation of future scenarios (with and without change). However, creativity is needed because solutions are seldom obvious; otherwise, they would not be problems, and the generation of solutions needs what de Bono called 'lateral thinking' (de Bono, 1995). The process calls upon:

- Experience of what has happened in the past.
- Experience in the process of problem-solving.
- Ability to work with others in idea generation.
- Ability to seek out data to define problem, scope and scale.
- Ability to model scenarios and communicate those models to others.

This chapter will follow the natural sequence of problem solving, which consists of the following stages:

- Situation analysis/prediction
- Resource/competence analysis
- Solution formulation
- Synthesis
- Evaluation.

At each stage we will identify and briefly describe appropriate supporting techniques.

Situation analysis/prediction

This stage begins with environmental scanning and also forms the first step of strategic planning. The most frequently prescribed method of environmental scanning is the PESTEL analysis framework (political, economic, social, technological, environmental and legal). This is fully explained in Chapter 16. However, it is opportune here to look at environmental scanning from a marketing problem-solving viewpoint rather than as a strategy-supporting technique, if the two can be separated.

Environmental scanning procedure: a problem-solving approach

There is no way to introduce a foolproof environmental scanning system into a corporation from the beginning. Like any other new programme, it evolves over time. Of course, if conditions are favourable – for instance, if there is an established system of strategic planning in place and the chief executive officer is interested in a structured effort at scanning – the evolutionary period shortens, but the current internal state of the art may not permit the introduction of a fully developed system at the outset. Besides, behavioural and organizational constraints require that things be done over a period of time. The level and type of scanning activity that a corporation undertakes should be custom designed – and a customized system takes time to emerge into a viable system. Figure 15.1 shows the process by which environmental scanning is linked to marketing strategy.

Practical advice

However, any approach to environmental scanning can never be completely prescriptive, and at each step practical advice is needed to support the relationship between environmental scanning and marketing strategy. This is as follows:

1. **Keep a tab on broad trends appearing in the environment.** Once the scope of environmental scanning is determined, broad trends in the chosen areas may be reviewed from time to time. For example, in the area of technology, trends in mastery of energy, material science, transportation capability, mechanization and automation, communications and information processing, and control over natural life may be studied.

2. **Determine the relevance of an environmental trend.** Not everything happening in the environment may be relevant for a company. Therefore, attempts must be made to select those trends in the environment which have significance for the company. There cannot be any hard-and-fast rules for making a distinction between relevant and irrelevant. For instance, one of the major threats to

Figure 15.1
Systematic approach to environmental scanning

1. Pick up events in different environments (via literature search).

2. Delineate events of interest to the SBU in one or more of the following areas: production, labour, markets (household, business, government, foreign), finance, research and development. This could be achieved via trend-impact analysis of the events.

3. Undertake cross-impact analysis of the events of interest.

4. Relate the trends of the noted events to current SBU strategies in different areas.

5. Select the trends which appear either to provide new opportunities or to pose threats.

6. Undertake trend forecasts
   a. Wild card prediction
   b. Most probable occurrence
   c. Conservative estimate

7. Develop three scenarios for each trend based on three types of forecasts.

8. Pass on the information to strategists.

9. Strategists may repeat steps 4 to 7 and develop more specific scenarios vis-à-vis different products/markets. These scenarios will then be incorporated in SBU strategy.

10. Require that all ad claims be substantiated.

11. Publish corporate actions that endanger workers or the environment.

the future growth of commercial airlines may originate not from other transportation companies but from communication firms, and in particular from the development of the 'television phone' and web-based conferencing. As this technology is perfected and as the costs of using it are lowered, it may eliminate completely the need for many business flights, with consequent substantial impact upon the future growth of airlines.

3. **Identify relevant trends in the environment.** Here, creativity and farsightedness can play an important role in a company's ability to pinpoint the relevant areas of concern for a large corporation. General tips are:

   - Place a senior person in charge of scanning.
   - Identify a core list of about 100 relevant publications worldwide.
   - Assign these publications to volunteers within the company, one per person. (Selected publications considered extremely important should be scanned by the scanning manager.)
   - Review (each scanner) stories, articles, news items, books, and conference proceedings in the assigned publication that meet predetermined criteria, based on the company's aims.
   - In a few lines, prepare an abstract on the item, giving it a predetermined code. For example, a worldwide consumer goods company can use the following codes: subject (e.g., politics); geography (e.g., Middle East); function (e.g., marketing); application (e.g., promotion, distribution).
   - Submit the abstract, along with the code, to a scanning committee consisting of several managers. They determine the relevance in terms of effect on corporate/strategic business unit/product-market strategy. An additional relevance code is added at this time.
   - Computerize the codes and the abstract.
   - Prepare a newsletter to disseminate the information company wide. Managers whose areas are directly affected by the information are encouraged to contact the scanning department for further analysis.

4. **Study the impact of an environmental trend on a product/market.** An environmental trend can pose either a threat or an opportunity for a company's product/market; which one it will turn out to be must be studied. The task of determining the impact of a change is the responsibility of the strategic business unit manager. Alternatively, it may be assigned to another executive who is familiar with the product/market. If the whole subject appears controversial, it may be safer to have an ad hoc committee look into it, or consultants, either internal or external, may be approached. There is a good chance that a manager who has been involved with a product or service for a good many years would look at any change as a threat. He or she may, therefore, avoid the issue by declaring the impact to be irrelevant at the outset. If such sabotage is feared, perhaps it would be better to rely on the committee or a consultant.

5. **Forecast the direction of an environmental trend into the future.** If an environmental trend does appear to have significance for a product/market, it is desirable to determine the course that the trend is likely to adopt in the future. In other words, attempts must be made at environmental forecasting.

6. **Analyze the momentum of the product/market business in the face of the environmental trend.** Assuming the company takes no action, what will be the shape of the product/market performance in the midst of the environmental trend and its direction into the future? The impact of an environmental trend is usually gradual. While it is helpful to be 'first' to recognize freedom of action, a serious effort would have to be undertaken to 'open up' line managers to new ideas and to encourage innovation in their plans.

Scanning techniques

In the past, environmental scanning has been implemented mainly by using conventional methodologies such as marketing research, economic indicators, demand forecasting and industry studies. But the use of such conventional techniques for environmental scanning has not been without pitfalls, for two major reasons. First, these techniques have failed to provide reliable insights into the future. Even the most careful and sophisticated market demand forecasts have been useless, and no technical improvements are on the horizon to change matters.

Second, these techniques provide a narrow view of the environment in any event. Direct competition is only one of the basic dimensions of the company's total strategic environment. A competitive audit must be augmented by assessment of the broader governmental, social, economic, ideological and other forces which all influence the company's character, purpose and strategies over the longer term.

Table 15.1 tabulates a variety of techniques that have been adapted for use in environmental scanning.

Table 15.1 Techniques which have been adapted for use in environmental scanning

Technique	Description/comment
Extrapolation procedures	These procedures require the use of information from the past to explore the future. Obviously, their use assumes that the future is some function of the past. There are a variety of extrapolation procedures which range from a simple estimate of the future (based on past information) to regression analysis.
Historical analogy	Where past data cannot be used to scan an environmental phenomenon, the phenomenon may be studied by establishing historical parallels with other phenomena. Assumed here is the availability of sufficient information on the other phenomena. The turning points in the progression of these phenomena become the guideposts for predicting the behaviour of the phenomenon under study.
Missing-link approach	The missing-link approach combines morphological analysis and the network method. Many developments and innovations that appear promising and marketable may be held back because something is missing. Under such circumstances, this technique may be used to scan new trends to see if they provide answers to the missing links.

(Continues)

Table 15.1
(Continued)

Model building	This technique emphasizes construction of models following deductive or inductive procedures. Two types of models may be constructed: phenomenological models and analytic models. Phenomenological models identify trends as a basis for prediction but make no attempt to explain the underlying causes. Analytic models seek to identify the underlying causes of change so that future developments may be forecast on the basis of a knowledge of their causes.
Delphi technique	The Delphi technique is the systematic solicitation of expert opinion. Based on reiteration and feedback, this technique gathers opinions of a panel of experts on happenings in the environment.
Intuitive reasoning	This technique bases the future on the 'rational feel' of the scanner. Intuitive reasoning requires free thinking unconstrained by past experience and personal biases. This technique, therefore, may provide better results when used by freelance think tanks than when used by managers on the job.
Scenario building	This technique calls for developing a time-ordered sequence of events bearing a logical cause-effect relationship to one another. The ultimate forecast is based on multiple contingencies each with its respective probability of occurrence.
Cross-impact matrices	When two different trends in the environment point toward conflicting futures, this technique may be used to study these trends simultaneously for their effect. As the name implies, this technique uses a two-dimensional matrix, arraying one trend along the rows and the other along the columns. Some of the features of cross-impact analyses that make them attractive for strategic planning are: (1) they can accommodate all types of eventualities (social or technological, quantitative or qualitative, and binary events or continuous functions); (2) they rapidly discriminate important from unimportant sequences of developments; and (3) the underlying rationale is fully retraceable from the analysis.
Morphological analysis	This technique requires identification of all possible ways to achieve an objective. For example, the technique can be employed to anticipate innovations and to develop the optimum configurations for a particular mission or task.
Network methods	There are two types of network methods: contingency trees and relevance trees. A contingency tree is simply a graphical display of logical relationships among environmental trends that focuses on branch-points where several alternative outcomes are possible. A relevance tree is a logical network similar to a contingency tree, but drawn in a way that assigns degrees of importance to various environmental trends with reference to an outcome.

Process in action trends and strategy in the cigarette industry

The marketing strategist of a consumer goods company may want to determine if market trends have any relevance for the company. To do so the marketing strategist will undertake *trend-impact analysis* (Exhibit 1). This will require the formation of a Delphi panel to determine the desirability (0-1), technical feasibility (0-1), probability of occurrence (0-1) and probable time of occurrence of each event listed above. The panel may also be asked to suggest the area(s) which may be affected by each event, e.g., production, labour, markets (household, business, government, foreign), finance or research and development.

The above information about an event may be studied by managers in areas that, according to the Delphi panel, are likely to be affected by the event. If their consensus is that the event is indeed important, the scanning may continue.

Next, *cross-impact analysis* may be undertaken. This type of analysis is planned to study the impact of an event on other events. Where events are mutually exclusive, such an analysis may not be necessary. But where an event seems to reinforce or inhibit other events, the cross-impact analysis is highly desirable for uncovering the true strength of an event.

The cross-impact analysis amounts to studying the impact of an event (given its probability of occurrence) upon other events. The impact may be delineated either in qualitative terms, such as critical, major, significant, slight, or none, or in quantitative terms, in the form of probabilities.

Exhibit 2 shows how cross-impact analysis may be undertaken. The cross-impact ratings or probabilities can best be determined with the help of another Delphi panel. To further sharpen the analysis, it may also be determined whether the impact of an event on other events will be felt immediately or after a certain number of years.

The cross-impact analysis provides the 'time' probability of occurrence of an event and indicates

other key events which may be monitored to keep track of the first event. Cross-impact analysis is more useful for project-level scanning than for general scanning.

To relate the environmental trends to strategy, consider the following assumed environmental trends and strategies of a cigarette manufacturer:

Trends

T1: Requiring that all ad claims be substantiated

T2: Publishing corporate actions that endanger workers or the environment

T3: Disclosing lobbying efforts in detail

T4: Reducing a company's right to fire workers at will

T5: Eliminating inside directors

Strategies

S1: Heavy emphasis on advertising, using emotional appeals

S2: Seasonal adjustments in labour force for agricultural operations of the company

S3: Regular lobbying effort against further legislation imposing restrictions on the cigarette industry

S4: Minimum number of outside directors on the board

The analysis in Exhibit 3 shows that strategy S1, heavy emphasis on advertising, is most susceptible and requires immediate management action. Among the trends, trend T5, eliminating inside directors, will have the most positive overall impact. Trends T1 and T2, requiring that all ad claims be substantiated and publishing corporate actions that endanger workers or the environment, will have a devastating impact. This type of analysis, shown on the following page, indicates where management concern and action should be directed.

Event	Requiring that all ad claims be substantiated	Reducing a company's right to fire workers at will
Desirability	0.8	0.5
Feasibility	0.6	0.3
Probability of occurrence	0.5	0.1
Probable time of occurrence	2003	2010
Area(s) impacted	Household markets Business markets Government markets Finance R&D Production	Labour Finance
Decision	Carry on scanning	Drop from further consideration

Exhibit 1
Trend-impact analysis: an example

Event	Probability of occurrence	Impact								
		a	b	c	d	e	f	g	h	i
a. Eliminating inside directors	0.6		0.3*							
b. Requiring companies to meet the cost of "unfriendly" proxy contests	0.3									
c. Barring nominee ownership of stock	0.5									
d. Reducing a company's right to fire workers at will	0.1									
e. Guarding worker privacy	0.4									

Exhibit 1
(Continued)

Event	Probability of occurrence	Impact								
		a	b	c	d	e	f	g	h	i
f. Mandating due-process procedures for grievances	0.3									
g. Disclosing lobbying efforts in detail	0.4									
h. Requiring that all ad claims be substantiated	0.5									
i. Publishing corporate actions that endanger workers or the environment	0.4								0.7**	

Note: Two to three rounds of Delphi would be needed to arrive at the above probabilities
*This means that elimination of inside directors has no effect on the probability of event b.
**This means that if publishing corporate actions that endanger workers or the environment occurs (probability 0.4), the probability of requiring that all ad claims be substantiated increases from 0.5 to 0.7.

Exhibit 2
Cross-impact analysis: an example

Trends	Strategies				Impact (I1)	
	S1	S2	S3	S4	+	−
T1	−8	0	+2	−2		8
T2	−4	−2	−6	0		12
T3	0	+4	−4	+2	2	
T4	0	−4	0	+6	2	
T5	−2	+6	+4	+2	10	
Impact (I2) +	+	−	4	−	8	
Impact (I2) −	14	−	4	−		

Exhibit 3
Use of matrix
to determine
the impact of
selected trends on
different corporate
strategies

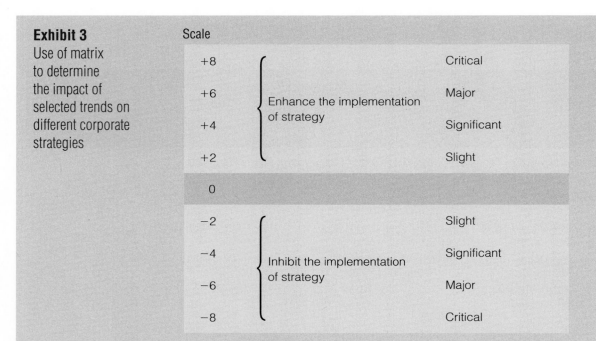

Scale

+8		Critical
+6	Enhance the implementation of strategy	Major
+4		Significant
+2		Slight
0		
−2		Slight
−4	Inhibit the implementation of strategy	Significant
−6		Major
−8		Critical

Thus, it will be desirable to undertake forecasts of trends T1 and T2. The forecasts may predict when the legislation will be passed, what will be the major provisions of the legislation, etc. Three different forecasts may be obtained:

1. Extremely unfavourable legislation
2. Most probable legislation
3. Most favourable legislation

Three different scenarios (using three types of forecasts) may be developed indicating the impact of each trend. This information may then be passed on to product/market managers for action. Product/market managers may repeat steps 4 to 7 (see Figure 15.1) to study the selected trend(s) in depth.

Questions

1. Define both areas and discuss the link between the concepts of environmental scanning and strategic planning.

2. Give and explain some examples of classic market opportunity analyses which have recognized key environmental trends.

3. What are the organizational behaviour implications pertaining to the area of environmental scanning, especially when dealing with (1) responsibility; (2) key tasks to be implemented and (3) staff training and motivation?

4. Describe and comment on the trend impact analysis approach as well as on the Delphi technique.

Resource analysis

There is a wide variety of general terminology to describe this stage of the problem-solving process. For example for *resource* read *skills, competence, capability* or *capacity* and for *analysis* read *audit*. However, within all of these terms and combinations of terms there is an attempt to define product and service flexibility in a combination of three ways:

- **Product and service design flexibility.** What we can do?

  (What we are capable of doing, related to scope, variation of skill sets in our labour force and variety and flexibility of plant and equipment.)

- **Product and service volume flexibility.** How much we can do?

  (What volume variation we can cope with, related to number of workers in each skill set, and numbers of plant and equipment by type.)

- **Geographical flexibility.** Where we are capable of doing it?

Resource analysis is superficially covered in the first two stages of the classic SWOT (strengths, weaknesses, opportunities, threats), and in greater depth in consideration of supply and value chains in Chapter 16. However, the concept of customer (and quality) chains is also important here. This is an important underlying principle of total quality management.

Total quality management (TQM) is a philosophy underpinned and supported by a number of techniques. It stresses three principles:

- Customer satisfaction
- Employee involvement
- Continuous improvements in quality.

This has implications for the need for standards of performance. For customer satisfaction, we must have product or service quality standards related to their expectations. For continuous improvement, we must have standards to demonstrate improvement. The value of performance measurement, discussed in detail in Chapter 16, is therefore self-evident.

For successful continuous improvement of quality (termed *Kaizen* – from Japanese), employee involvement is vital. Coupled with this, and perhaps resulting from it, is a fundamental change in the role of managers from controllers (of people) to trainers, developers and team builders. At an organizational level, a customer-oriented culture must be developed where everyone has either external customers, who buy the product or service, or internal customers who rely on the output of other employees. Hence, there is a chain of customers leading to the external customer.

At the level of the individual, workers must learn more generic skills so they are more flexible; they must also learn skills of problem solving and team working. Managers must learn to develop and train their subordinates, and to lead rather than direct them.

Teams are important, and members must have a common commitment and purpose and 'share' leadership. People are judged collectively as well as individually. Successful teams have meaningful objectives with well-defined performance measures, and are committed to them. They work in a positive environment and foster accomplishment, are constructively confrontational and seek outside advice when necessary. Perhaps most important, they have management support. All of these attributes involve some level of employee empowerment, moving both authority and responsibility down the organization.

Quality circles is a technique developed in Japan under the umbrella of TQM. It involves small groups of people drawn from different skill bases and different departments looking at individual quality problems. It is effective because it reduces compartmentation, chooses the right problems to look at, increases job enrichment and involves the natural affinity of most people for group working. It assumes that Douglas McGregor's theory Y – that most people have an affinity to work and enjoy improving how they do it – is correct. However, there is also a need for management to support groups, and to train members in use of the tools of quality analysis and improvement: simple tools such as flowcharts, check-sheets, histograms and, pareto (ABC) analysis and cause-effect diagrams. It also helps, particularly in mass production systems, if members understand the underlying principles and techniques of statistical quality control.

Thus the concept of a chain (or network) of customers and continuous improvement, and the importance of performance standards, are underpinning factors in resource analysis.

Solution formulation

As previously indicated, the problem-solving process is a combination of scientific method and artistic creativity, and it is at this stage where creativity is most needed. While de Bono maintains that creativity can be taught to – or at least developed in – people, others say it is inherent. Research on teams indicates that the creative productivity of management teams is greater than that of the composite individuals. Such teams, however, need tools and techniques of group working and problem solving to facilitate the process. Three such interrelated techniques will be briefly described here: brainstorming, Ishekawa diagrams and the talking wall technique.

Brainstorming

The objective of brainstorming is to generate quickly as many ideas as possible. The quality of ideas is not analyzed: this will be done later 'off-line'. Here it is the quantity and variety that count, and a principle of deferred judgement is applied. The value of brainstorming in the work of teams such as quality circles is self-evident, but there are pitfalls such as the possibility of 'groupthink' (where everyone follows the same thought path and ideas generated become narrow in scope), and deferment to 'senior' opinion when all members should be equal. To reduce the likelihood of these pitfalls there are several tips concerned with the brainstorming process:

- If the team is new, make sure there is a warming-up period. The cycle of forming, storming, norming and performing should be considered, and ice-breaker exercises are useful here.

- The physical arrangement is important. Have a focal point; whiteboards are useful here, but flip-charts are possibly even more useful as they ensure that all ideas are recorded and not erased.

- Record all ideas. Simple lists are useful here, and development of diagramming skills, mind maps, systems maps, influence diagrams and Ishekawa (or 'fishbone'; see next) diagrams is to be encouraged. (For more details consult Giles and Hedge (1998).)

- All ideas should be recorded at the focal point, and it is advisable not to allow members to make individual notes; these are distracting and possibly divisive. There is also a danger that the person recording the ideas builds up an undue influence, so rotate the task amongst members of the team, and perhaps limit what the recorder can say. The seating arrangement should be informal; a semicircle is ideal.

- Generate only one idea at a time, but move on quickly. There should be little evaluation. Hijacking the ideas of others to improve them or to develop associated alternatives is to be encouraged; that is the whole point of the process.
- Finally, on the personal-behaviour front, give praise for good ideas but don't patronize, and if criticizing ensure that the criticism is constructive.

Ishekawa diagrams

Ishekawa – or, as they are colloquially termed, fishbone – diagrams were first used in the field of quality management and popularized in the west in a book by Taguchi *et al.* (1989). However, the technique can be adopted to help solve any problem. A problem is presented as shown in Figure 15.2, using low productivity as an example.

Ishekawa diagrams form an ideal focal point for brainstorming problems, and enable a problem to be cascaded down through various levels of causes. For example, the 'aging equipment' reason above could be caused by a poor depreciation/replacement policy, or by technological obsolescence. The diagram would be used to identify possible causes for the problem very quickly, and the outcome causes would then be independently analyzed to assess their contribution to the final problem, perhaps using pareto analysis.

Talking wall technique

The talking wall technique is similar in nature to the Ishekawa technique. The version described here is very useful as a mechanism for including more people in the analysis procedure, hence increasing the potential for consensus and ownership on any outcomes, and thus improving the likelihood of success of any ideas for improvement which may be generated. An example of its use in developing a strategy for small UK companies entering EU markets was described by Paton *et al.* (1989).

In essence, the process is as follows:

- The problem is discussed by the whole (large) group and aspects of it are identified and agreed upon.

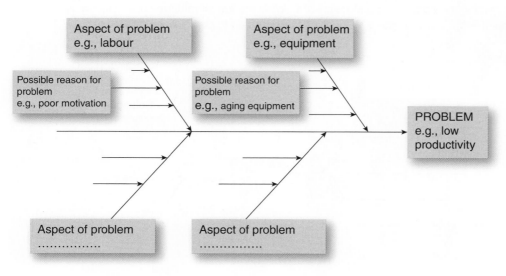

Figure 15.2
Ishekawa
presentation

- One flip-chart sheet is prepared for each identified aspect and placed on walls, spaced around the room.
- All participants are given sticky notes and asked to write questions or statements related to aspects, and stick them to the relevant flip-chart sheet.
- The group is divided into smaller teams, one for each aspect, and each team analyzes the questions and statements produced for its aspect and develops proposed actions. This entails grouping the sticky notes and then making a statement in the form 'the organization should . . .'. (At this point, teams inevitably suggest that some of their sticky notes should be on another team's sheet, and a good response is simply to duplicate the sticky note.)
- The statements generated are then checked to eradicate duplication, and an agreed, limited number are taken to the next stage.
- The whole group are then asked, as individuals, to rate in some way the importance of allocating limited resources, i.e., funds, to each proposed action. (Give each participant, say, ten points to divide among the statements.)
- The actions are then listed in rank order for group discussion, and taken forward for deeper consideration.

Process in action brainstorming at John McGavigan

In another example, as part of a John McGavigan TQM programme, the Ishekawa technique (Figure 15.3) was combined with brainstorming using the talking wall technique to enable a continuing dialogue to take place within the company workforce. (See Chapter 8 for the McGavigan case study.)

On a company notice board an Ishekawa chart was left for employees to stick sticky notes to.

Employees used colour-coded sticky notes to contribute suggestions to both sides of the chart, and a large number of valuable suggestions resulted.

Question
1. What are the advantages of this technique when compared to conventional brainstorming?

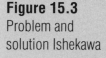

Figure 15.3
Problem and
solution Ishekawa

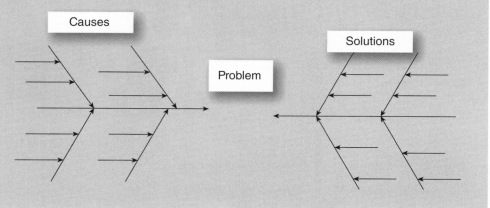

Synthesis

Synthesis methods include:

- Systems maps
- Flow diagrams
- IDEF diagrams
- Queuing
- Discrete event simulation
- Value trees
- Financial simulation (BE analysis).

These are covered elsewhere in the text.

Evaluation

Evaluation of different solutions to problems, or any change proposals, is made difficult in many situations by the intangible nature of both the objectives and the factors or attributes which influence the outcomes. Almost always, the decision-maker has to compare the value of different types of income to a change situation to the requirement to satisfy different outcome requirements. For example, in the seemingly simple location of a shop, incomes include not only costs (tangible and measured in simple financial terms), floor space, frontage and distance to parking (all seemingly tangible but using differing metrics) but also appearance and esteem of location (which are intangible and subjective).

The primary outcome is profit, but the company will also want to ensure that the new shop adds to the public perception of the company. So we have a problem with several solutions, different locations and with multiple objectives and multiple attributes, both a mixture of tangibles and intangibles. A mechanism is needed to help the decision-maker. Goodwin and Wright (2006) proposed a technique they call SMART (simple multiple attribute rating technique), developed by Edwards (1991), to help address such problems. In fact, the technique is generalized, and about the same time had been advocated by Wild (2002) to solve operational problems such as factory location. Here we will concentrate on the generic version, SMART, considering the principles rather than demonstrating the detailed calculations.

Simple multiple attribute rating technique

SMART is a method of arriving at a numerical score for each course of action where there is more than one objective to be met in making a decision.

We first need to establish terminology:

- An **objective** is an indication of preferred movement (e.g., minimize costs, maximize market share).
- An **attribute** is used to measure performance in relation to an objective (e.g., costs, market share – predicted?).
- If the decision involves no element of risk and uncertainty, we will refer to the score as the **value** of this course of action.

- If the decision involves risk and uncertainty we will refer to the score as the **utility** of this course of action.

Now we can describe the stages of the generic process:

1. Identify the decision-maker(s).

2. Identify the alternative courses of action.

3. Identify the attributes that are relevant to the problem.

4. *For each attribute*, assign values to measure the performance of the alternatives *on that attribute*.

5. Determine a weight *for each attribute*.

6. *For each alternative*, take a weighted average of the values assigned to that alternative.

7. Make a provisional decision.

8. Perform sensitivity analysis.

Stage 1 is self-explanatory.

Stage 2 may require the application of the techniques described earlier for solution formulation, or at least some kind of brainstorming exercise.

In Stage 3 construction of a value tree is a useful way of identifying both major objectives, and the attributes that, if properly addressed, can lead to achieving those objectives. A value tree, in most situations, takes the form of a generic cost/benefit analysis framework within which different solutions can be compared. An example value tree for the relocation of a business school is shown in Figure 15.4.

The value tree itself needs to be evaluated before continuing, and five criteria are suggested: completeness, operationality (or ease of understanding and use), decomposability, absence of redundancy and optimum size.

In Stage 4 we measure how options perform on each attribute. As previously indicated, measures are tangible (e.g., costs) or intangible (e.g., appearance), and for both we want to convert the measure (or opinion) to a 'dimensionless' and comparable function. This is achieved by the use of scaling mechanisms to compare each solution against the others for each attribute.

For intangibles (e.g., appearance) this can be done by asking the decision-maker(s) to rate the alternatives on a scale of, say, 1 to 100. This is called **direct rating.**

For example, if we are rating attractiveness of premises, say a shop, and there are five possible locations A, B, C, D and E, we ask stakeholders (i.e., managers and staff):

Which is the most attractive ...... A ..... allocate score of 100

Which is the least attractive ......C..... allocate score of 0

We now ask stakeholders to rate the others on a scale of 0 to 100: B = 30, D = 70, E = 50.

Then the score of A = 100 / (100 + 0 + 30 + 70 + 50) = 100 / 250 = 0.4

B = 30 / 250 = 0.12

C = 0 / 250 = 0

$$D = 70 / 250 = 0.28$$

$$E = 50 / 250 = 0.2$$

(Note that the sum of these is 1.)

For tangibles we can construct a curve with the attribute value as the X axis, and the 'dimensionless' function as the Y axis. The optimum attribute value will register as 100 on the Y axis (the maximum). Such curves are shown in Figure 15.5.

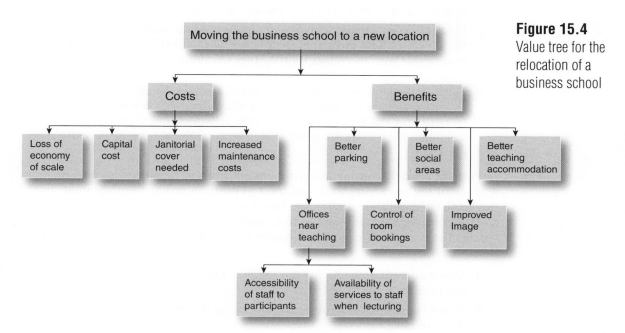

Figure 15.4
Value tree for the relocation of a business school

Figure 15.5
Examples of curves for rating tangible attributes

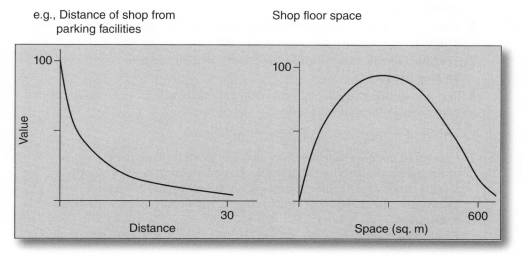

In Stage 5 we determine a *weight* for each attribute. This is a measure of the perceived importance of the attribute to the decision-makers(s). Again, we ask the decision-maker(s) to rate the importance of the attributes on a scale of 1 to 100, and then normalize by totalling the weights and dividing each original weight by the total. (The total of the normalized weights should equal 100.)

In Stage 6 we determine the weighted values. For each alternative, multiply the value of each attribute by the weight of each attribute, and add the results to give our measure of the performance of the alternative.

In Stage 7 for each alternative solution, we total the weighted values of all the attributes. This gives us a single value for each attribute which is directly comparable with the values for the other solutions.

Finally in Stage 8, we conduct a sensitivity analysis. This is necessary when two attributes are not independent, or when the decision-maker may be worried how much the value of an attribute will change with a change in weighting factor. (We are really testing how flat the bottom of an optimization curve is.)

Product replacement is the most common form of new product introduction. A study of the marketing strategies used to position product replacements in the marketplace found eight approaches based upon a combination of product change, and other marketing modifications (e.g., marketing mix and target market changes). Companies use one of eight replacement strategies, or a combination of some of them.

1. Minor alteration, modifying the product appearance, but not the marketing.
2. Minor technological substitution, modifying the product appearance, but not the marketing.
3. Re-formulation of marketing approach, but keeping the same products.
4. Modifying product appearance and re-launching with a new marketing programme.
5. Modifying product technology and re-launching with a new marketing programme.
6. Perceptual repositioning, approaching a new market segment with the same product.
7. Tangible repositioning, approaching a new market segment with a new-looking product.
8. Technologically tangible repositioning, approaching a new market segment with a newer technology product.

Examples of the application of these are as follows:

1. Cars often undergo facelifts midway through their lifecycle by undergoing minor styling alterations. Japanese companies constantly facelift current electronic products, such as video recorders and camcorders, by changing product features, a process known as **product churning.**

2. Here the technological change is not brought to the consumer's attention. For example brand loyalty to instant mashed potatoes was retained through major technological processes and product changes (powder to granules to flakes) with little attempt to highlight these changes through advertising.

3. Here a modification of name, promotion, price, packaging and/or distribution occurs, while maintaining the basic product. For example, an unsuccessful men's deodorant was successfully re-merchandized by repackaging, heavier advertising, a higher price and new brand name: Brut.

4. Here both the product and other marketing mix elements are changed. Re-launches are common in the car industry when every four to five years a model is replaced with an upgraded version. The replacement of the Ford Sierra with the Mondeo is an example.

5. Here a major technological change is accompanied by heavy promotionals (and other mix changes) to stimulate awareness and trial. The replacement of the IBM PC by the IBM PS/2 is an example.

6. Here the basic product is retained but other mix elements and target customers change. Lucozade is an example of a product which kept its original formulation but was targeted at different customer segments over time.

7. Here both the product and target market change. In the UK, Kendalls – a down-market women's accessories chain – was repositioned as Next, a more up-market women's clothing store.

8. Here a fundamental technology change is accompanied by target market and mix changes. For example, Compaq became a market leader in computers for a time by replacing its down-market inexpensive IBM PC-compatible machines with up-market premium-priced computers based on the 286 chip.

Companies, therefore, face an array of replacement options with varying degrees of risk.

Process in action product replacement strategies at Volvo

The Volvo View
Volvo is a global name that is successful in its chosen markets. Volvo pays much more than lip service to the idea of change. Although Volvo is exceptionally well-established in its market, it recognizes that they will stay at the top only by embracing constant change.

Volvo sees marketing as more than a technical function confined to a specialist department. In Volvo Care UK, marketing pervades the whole company. Managers at all levels are involved and recognize that they have a role to play in the company's success.

Volvo has set itself the ambition of becoming the 'most desired and successful speciality car brand and the most customer-focused organization in the world, achieving exemplary standards and support which will match or exceed customer expectations'. But when it speaks of being customer focused, who, exactly, is the customer?

At one level, it is the dealer network. At another, it is Volvo's corporate customers. Regardless of how a car is purchased, the customers who matter most are those at the end of the chain – the people who drive the cars. Ultimately, it is they who decide whether Volvo achieves its objectives. Clearly, there would be no point in Volvo developing successful business-to-business relationships if the employees of corporate customers did not want to choose Volvos as their company car.

To tackle this issue, Volvo has two programmes. The first is Corporate Account Relationship Experience (Care). This is a corporate account programme aimed both internally and at selected dealers. It has 'the specific purpose of ensuring that everyone involved with our corporate customers delivers a level of service and professionalism consistent with our global ambitions'.

The second is One Customer One Relationship (Oncore). This is a dealer programme designed to satisfy the end customer. Volvo describes it as 'the creation of a differentiated customer experience, an experience that will match the new products and services that Volvo will launch over the coming years'.

These two programmes work together to satisfy both the business needs of the corporate customer and the human needs of the driver. They reflect the fact that looking after corporate customers is a shared responsibility for Volvo and its dealers, the common factors being drivers, their spouses and families. Both programmes concentrate on developing the skills of all those people who touch the customer, whether they are employed by Volvo or a dealer. The two programmes dovetail together. Care is a business-to-business management process. When a car is delivered or a driver calls in at a dealership, Oncore takes over.

Volvo deals directly with its largest customers. Dealers are involved pre- and/or post-sales with all organizations that have company Volvos. The larger dealers have a business centre with a business sales manager, trained in all aspects of fleet customer requirements.

This manager's main role is to develop business-to-business relationships not handled directly by Volvo. Dealer business centres are typically in main towns and cities. They are responsible for most of Volvo's sales. But the company has wide geographic representation and service cover.

One of the interesting features of the way Volvo develops customer relationships is how it uses multiple relationships. For example, a person who drives a company Volvo is involved in as many as six relationships. Significantly, Volvo has a direct impact on every one of these relationships.

- Volvo and its corporate customers

  Relationships between Volvo and its corporate customers govern Volvo's inclusion in entitlement lists.

- Corporate customers and their employees

  The agreements reached affect which models are available to employees.

- Corporate customers and Volvo dealers

  The local dealer usually delivers and then services the cars, however they are acquired.

- Volvo and Volvo drivers

  Volvo maintains a direct marketing relationship with all drivers of its cars.

- Volvo and its dealers (some of which it owns)

  Volvo works hard with its dealer network to maintain and improve its standards.

- Volvo dealers and Volvo drivers

  Volvo dealers are the front line of meeting the drivers' expectations.

The Oncore and Care programmes are designed to ensure systematic approaches and consistent treatment across all these relationships. Volvo is seeing the benefits of its programmes. Its combined direct and dealer focus, coupled with its deliberate, near dramatic, image shift over recent years has lifted UK business purchases to 70 per cent of sales – behind competitors such as BMW and Mercedes, but still growing.

Of course, all high-engineering products are different and so are their markets and potential customers. But both British Aerospace and Volvo demonstrate that a willingness to change and develop multi-layered relationships with customers are key ingredients of success.

Questions

1. Out of eight product replacement strategies discussed; which do you feel applies more directly to the Volvo example?

2. What is the thinking behind the 'facelift' and 're-launch' product replacement strategies?

Summary

- The generic problem-solving process consists of five stages: situation analysis, resource analysis, solution formulation, solution synthesis and solution evaluation.

- The problem solver(s), or decision-maker(s), need to combine logical analytical thinking with creativity.

- There are many systematic techniques available to help the decision-maker in both analyzing current situations and predicting future scenarios (see Table 15.1).

- The resource analysis phase is closely related to the study of supply and value chains.

- The solution formulation stage requires the most creative thinking. This is best done in groups, and there are various techniques which support this creativity and record the outcomes. These include brainstorming, Ishekawa diagrams, and talking wall.

- There are also techniques to synthesize solutions and changes.

- Evaluation is made difficult because of the intangible nature of many contributing factors and outcomes. In addition, even tangible factors and tangibles are measured in different currencies, so comparison is impossible. Consequently, a rating and weighting approach is needed so that attributes can be measured on a non-dimensional scale for comparison. The SMART process is such a technique.

- While such techniques cannot usually be applied prescriptively, they are a good foundation for undertaking and marketing a business or management problem.

Chapter questions

1. Situation analysis

Year	Visitors	Year	Visitors
1995	76,890	1990	54,890
1994	73,500	1989	52,765
1993	67,500	1988	46,750
1992	66,780	1987	42,125
1991	56,000	1986	34,400

Swing-Rite is one of the leading producers of hinges for garage doors. The product is comparable to any on the market but if it is not available contractors will switch to one of three other brands. It is your responsibility to set production levels based on sales forecasts. A multiple-regression model was used to estimate sales. The estimate for 1997 is 14,000,000 units with a standard error of 1,560,000 units. What do you recommend?

2. Marketing Investment Decision

With limited funds, Volvo (see Process in action) must decide whether to invest in selling through dealers to the public, dealing directly with the public using Internet selling or selling directly to corporate account customers (fleet owners, company cars and rentals). By referring to the Volvo case study, construct an objectives/value tree which can be used to analyze the three alternatives, identify attributes which will affect the decision and then consider how these will be processed in the SMART technique to help make the decision.

References

de Bono, E. (1995) *Parallel Thinking: From Socratic Thinking to de Bono Thinking,* London: Penguin.

Edwards, W. (1991) 'Social Utilities', *Engineering Economist,* Summer Symposium Series No 6.

Giles, K., and Hedge, N. (1998) *The Manager's Good Study Guide,* Milton Keynes, UK: Milton Keynes.

Goodwin, P., and Wright, G. (2006) *Decision Analysis for Management Judgement,* 3rd edn., Chichester, UK: John Wiley.

Paton, R. A., Southern, G., and Houghton, M. (1989) 'European strategy formulation: The small company European analysis technique', *European Management Journal,* 7(3): 305–309.

Saunders, J., and Jobber, D. (1994) 'Strategies for product launch and deletion', in Saunders, J. (ed.), *The Marketing Initiative,* Hemel Hempstead: Prentice Hall, p. 227.

Taguchi, G., Elsayed, E. A., and Hsiang, T. C. (1989) *Quality Engineering in Production Systems,* London, UK: McGraw Hill.

Wild, R. (2002) *Operations Management,* 6th edn., London: Continuum.

16

Strategic planning effectiveness: performance measurement

Geoff Southern and Luiz Moutinho

Introduction

Strategic planning is now recognized as being more than 'high-level planning'. It has progressed from simply making plans for, say, 1- and 5-year periods, given an understanding of the current business situation and forecasts of changes in the operating environment of an organization, to encompass the idea of developing an organization which is flexible and can react to opportunities which have not been forecast. Recent developments in management theory, and in management practice, have emphasized the importance of relating strategy to performance management, and in particular the importance of making sure that the implementation of a strategy is cascaded through operational measures to all levels of an organization. Operational measures must reflect and drive the implementation of an organization's strategy; otherwise, results expected from that strategy will not be forthcoming.

Learning objectives

- To provide an overview of the traditional strategy formulation process, models, tools and strategic performance (financial) measures.

- To consider performance management in an historical context.

- To provide an overview of current concepts of relating strategic objectives to performance management: strategic integration.

- To consider performance management in marketing.

- To consider if concentration on performance management is a fashionable panacea, or if it had always been there and is here to stay.

In this chapter, we will consider how the planning, and more particularly the implementation, of strategy is measured and managed. The chapter aims to briefly describe historical developments in theory of business strategy as a foundation to enable the reader to study more recent developments in depth, and to evaluate these developments and their value to practicing managers today.

Strategy: an academic history

> Strategy making is considered the high point of management activity. But bombarded by fads and fixes, most managers have been groping blindly to get their arms around the proverbial elements. (Mintzberg *et al.*, 1998)

In the flysheet of the textbook from which this quotation is taken, the authors list and describe, in chapter order, 10 schools of strategy formulation.

So strategy is not easy and strategic theory is not fixed. The number of schools identified by Mintzberg *et al.* bear witness to that, and even since the publication of the text in 1998, more recent publications have stressed that the difficulty in strategy is not in its formulation but in its implementation. It is now inextricably linked to performance measurement, and current thinking is that the performance management systems of an organization must not only be compatible with the formulated strategy but should be capable of driving its delivery.

Mintzberg *et al.* break their 10 schools of strategy formulation into three that are prescriptive, i.e., concerned with *how strategy should be formulated*, and seven that are descriptive and study *how strategy is formulated* in practice. They are as follows.

Prescriptive schools:

- **Design school.** A process of conception, informal in nature.
- **Planning school.** A formal process, detached and systematic.
- **Positioning school.** An analytical process, more concerned with the content of strategies and their position in the marketplace.

Descriptive schools:

- **Entrepreneurial.** A visionary process of a 'great leader'.
- **Cognitive.** A mental process.
- **Learning.** An emergent process.
- **Power.** A process of negotiation.
- **Cultural.** A collective process.
- **Environmental.** A reactive process.
- **Configuration.** A process of transformation.

In a footnote in this text, Mintzberg *et al.* point out that others map the schools into fewer divisions, and that the last seven of their own schools really consider specific aspects of the process of strategy formulation.

We would further argue that strategy formulation comes from a set of viewpoints:

- **The marketing manager's view.** Opportunities in the environment (stable or constantly changing).
- **The operations manager's view.** The company resources or capabilities of the organization in terms of output, and in particular their degree of embeddedness and ease of copying.

- **The human resource manager's view.** The capabilities of the workforce to do what they do at the moment, and their capability to be inventive and change to do something different.

In our overview of strategic planning effectiveness and performance measurement, we will first consider prescriptive schools of theory and their process of strategy formulation. We will then consider descriptive schools, classifying these in terms of their focus on competences, and labelling them as such. Finally, we will discuss the latest views in terms of the flexibility of the organization to react to external change, concentrating on effectiveness, and performance management within it, concentrating on efficiency. Throughout the discussion, we will indicate various conceptual models and factors for consideration where we think they best fit, although all will have value throughout.

The prescriptive school: strategy formulation process

Strategy formulation follows the path of any decision to be made: diagnosis, design formulation, action and measurement. Throughout the formulation process, features from all three prescriptive schools can be drawn upon: informal conception from the design school, more systematic analysis of an organization's relative position from the positioning school to look at the 'big picture', and systematic formality from the planning school to devise an appropriate plan and control system.

Diagnosis: first, analyze the present situation

Factors for consideration here are key issues related to the business environment and the strategic capability of an organization that are most likely to impact on strategic development. There are several well-established prescriptive analysis frameworks from the positional school of strategy that can help: PESTEL, Porter's 5 forces and SWOT.

The PESTEL framework is useful for scanning and analyzing the holistic external environment and changes in it. Table 16.1 identifies the aspects considered and factors for exploration.

Porter's 5 forces framework (Porter, 1985) focuses on the more immediate operating environment of an organization from a competition viewpoint. Concentrating on the intensity of rivalry in an organization's market, it suggests looking at the relative bargaining power of buyers, the relative bargaining power of suppliers, the ease and threat of new competitors and the threat of substitutes to the products or services of the organization.

The classical SWOT analysis fulfils a similar purpose in what might be considered to be a more pragmatic way, considering the strengths and weaknesses of the organization related to competitors, opportunities in the marketplace and threats to the current customer base of the organization.

Design formulation: then, formulate a desired outcome situation

This usually begins by specifying a corporate mission, or reappraising an existing one.

Underlying strategy theory, especially its design aspects, is an irrefutable business performance principle: Strategic business units (SBUs) with a clear sense of purpose outperform those that do not have a clearly defined vision, mission and strategic intent. The concepts of vision and mission are thus central to strategy, and indeed central to more recent work on performance management where it drives associated systems. (See reference to balanced scorecard later in this chapter). It is therefore worth pausing here to consider the role and value of corporate mission statements. According to one firm of consultants (Business Resource Software, 2006):

> The mission statement should be a clear and succinct representation of the enterprise's purpose for existence. It should incorporate socially meaningful and measurable criteria addressing concepts such as the moral/ethical position of the enterprise, public image, the target market, products/services, the geographic domain and expectations of growth and profitability.
>
> The intent of the mission statement should be the first consideration for any employee who is evaluating a strategic decision. The statement can range from a very simple to a very complex set of ideas.

Business Resource Software (BRS) says that a corporate mission should define some or all of the following features of the organization:

- The moral/ethical position of the enterprise
- The desired public image
- The key strategic influence for the business
- A description of the target market
- A description of the products/services
- The geographic domain
- Expectations of growth and profitability.

Table 16.1
PESTEL analysis
framework

Aspect for consideration	Factors for exploration
Political	Stability, taxation, trade regulations, social welfare
Economic	Business cycles, GNP trends, interest rates, money supply, inflation, unemployment, disposable income
Socio-cultural	Demographics, income distribution, social mobility, lifestyles, attitudes, education
Technological	Government spending on research, focus on technological effort, new technologies, speed of transfer, rates of obsolescence
Environmental	Protection laws, waste disposal, energy consumption
Legal	Monopolies legislation, employment policy, health and safety, product liability

Mission statements are usually simple, and the content is indisputable. They often consist of a bold statement of intent with no indication of how that intent is to be realized, but they are usually supported by a set of organizational values. See the following case study for examples.

The Merck mission statement seems to address most of the criteria of the BRS list. Merck is a mature organization that adopts a highly moral stance in its corporate mission, as do most mature organizations. The chronological development of the Wal-Mart mission statement implies that companies move from a financial emphasis to a more moral stance. Perhaps this reflects a change within the company to greater stability and an increased feeling of financial security, or perhaps it just reflects an increased need over recent years for companies to be morally acceptable to society in general. This general trend may be explained by a framework which considers the relationship between the position of drivers of strategy and the ethical stance taken by the organization (see Table 16.2).

In the case of Wal-Mart, the growth, from a central-US company to a US-wide company and, then to a worldwide operator, is certainly reflected by changes to the mission statement.

Process in action examples of mission statements

Example 1: Merck, a US pharmaceutical company, state their mission as:

The mission of Merck is to provide society with superior products and services by developing innovations and solutions that improve the quality of life and satisfy customer needs, and to provide employees with meaningful work and advanced opportunities, and investors with a superior rate of return.

They then support it with the following set of (summarized) value statements:

Our business is preserving and improving human life.

We are committed to the highest standards of ethics and integrity.

We are dedicated to the highest level of scientific excellence and commit our research to improving human and animal health and the quality of life.

We expect profits, but only from work that satisfies customer needs and benefits humanity.

We recognize that the ability to excel – to most competitively meet society's and customers' needs – depends on the integrity, knowledge, imagination, skill, diversity and teamwork of our employees, and we value these qualities most highly.

Example 2: Wal-Mart, a US/international retailer, demonstrating that the mission is dynamic:

In 1990, the Wal-Mart mission statement was *'To be a $125 billion company by the year 2000.'* (Business Resource Software, 2006)

In 2000, it was 'To give ordinary people the chance to buy the same things as rich people.' (Business Resource Software, 2006)

In 2006, it was 'In everything we do we're driven by a common corporate mission – to improve the quality of life for everyday people round the world.' (Wal-Mart, 2006)

Questions
1. Is there a fundamental difference between the two companies in terms of competitive priorities – the factors on which companies compete?
2. How has the Wal-Mart mission statement changed between 1990 and 2006?

But deciding on a mission is only the beginning. A clear statement of strategy involves the formulation of desired outcome situations and at least an indication of tactics for getting there. Traditionally, this is where functional management plays a part and where an overall business plan is first formulated. The overall business plan is then employed to formulate a finance plan, a marketing plan, an operations plan and an HR plan, as described in Figure 16.1.

This is very much a market-driven approach to strategy formulation, and many researchers argue that in some companies, especially companies with a large investment in specialized resources, a resource-driven approach is more appropriate. Terry Hill (2005) argues that it is essential to reflect operational strategy decisions in corporate decisions, and that the question 'How do you qualify and win orders in the marketplace?' is pivotal in the strategy formulation process, linking the marketing strategy to choices made in designing the delivery system and supporting infrastructure systems. Krajewski *et al.* (2007) have consistently identified seven 'competitive priorities' in several editions of their well-established operations management text,

Table 16.2
Ethical strategy framework

		Ethical stance	
Drivers of strategy		Legal minimum	Ideological
	Internal managers	Culture and strategy are secretive in nature.	Culture and strategy are evangelical.
	External stakeholders	Strategy and culture are set and controlled by regulations and procedures.	Strategy and culture are political.

Figure 16.1
Traditional strategy formulation model

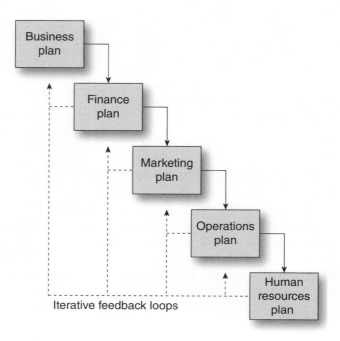

Iterative feedback loops

which represent generic answers to Hill's question. These are listed in Table 16.3, and the value of each to the customer is assessed.

In various editions of their text, Krajewski and Ritzman have added other competitive priorities reflecting the previous argument that strategy is dynamic and should reflect changes in the environment. For example, in the late 1990s, they added a factor reflecting the need for organizations to be seen as environmentally friendly, but in the last two editions (6th and 7th) they have added 'development speed', i.e., how quickly an organization can get a new service or product to the customer. These chronological changes also relate to the previous discussion on corporate missions.

An organization is most likely to benchmark itself against its competitors on each of these competitive priorities. It is also likely to consider customer expectations on each of them, e.g., if there is a threshold level which must be met before customers will even consider dealing with us (indicating a market-qualifying attribute), or if we get a bigger market share the better we perform (an order-winning attribute).

The desired outcome from the formulation stage is presented in a format which corresponds to Figure 16.1, i.e., as interrelated business, finance, marketing, operations and human resource plans. The questions that must be answered in each of these is as follows.

Business plan:

- What new services or produces are we going to introduce to our portfolio?
- What current services or produces are we going to eliminate?
- What new markets are we going to enter?

Table 16.3 Competitive priorities

Competitive priority (Krajewski and Ritzman)	Advantage to customer
Low-cost operations	The customer pays a low price.
Top quality	Prestige: Specification of service or product includes latest technology or fashion.
Consistent quality	Peace of mind that the specification is always met.
Delivery speed	The customer gets the service or product without waiting long.
On-time delivery	The customer knows that delivery will relate to their own plans.
Customization	A service or product will be changed to meet the customer's specific needs.
Variety	The customer is offered a wide variety of 'standard' services or products, even before customization.
Volume flexibility	The customer will never have to wait long for a service or product because the delivery rate can be increased quickly. (Alternatively, the price will remain the same if demand drops.)

- What existing markets are we going to withdraw from?
- What are the timescales for all of these?

Choices concerned with expansion into new products and markets are represented in Table 16.4, but relinquishment of non-profitable products or markets is not considered. In the BSG Boston Matrix (Stern and Stalk, 1998), dividing products into question marks, stars, cash cows and dogs is a further useful analysis framework for making decisions.

The plans for the functional areas will set targets in numbers and/or income for each of the changes identified in the business plan, usually in the form of budgets:

The finance plan (overall budget) will define spend and income plans for each product or service in each market. This will be an aggregation of the marketing and operations plan factors.

The marketing plan (marketing budget) will define planned spend to promote each product or service in each market, and will estimate sales increases, all in fulfilment of the finance (and hence business) plan.

The operations plan (operations budget) will define spend on new facilities and cost of closing old facilities, and changes in costs of logistics supply network to support operating volumes defined by the marketing plan.

The human resource plan (HR budget) will define spend on payroll – labour skills and volumes to support operating volumes from operating plan, all in fulfilment of the operations and marketing plans.

Action: implementing the plan

The grounds for action are laid when preparing the above budgets. Staff within the functional areas of the organization will have already been thinking of the actions needed to deliver them. They will have been using aggregated work standards of some kind, often based on historical performance measures, and forecasting techniques (see Chapter 4), to simulate the outcomes of various alternative actions. Now they will develop more detailed implementation plans describing ways of getting to the desired outcomes, having modelled and evaluated the options (see scenario building, Chapter 3). Eventually, financial budgets will be converted to detailed plans of resources to be deployed, although these will already have been considered in defining the financial budgets; such is the iterative nature of the strategic planning process.

Table 16.4
Choices concerned with expansion into new products and markets

	Existing markets	New markets
Existing products	Increasing market share – market penetration Low risk and return	Increasing market size for existing products – market enlargement Medium risk and return
New products	Product diversification – exploiting 'brand' image and market knowledge Medium risk and return	New products in new markets High risk, unknown return

Measurement: check whether the plan is being adhered to

In the above process, budgets are 'cascaded' from organization level to business unit level to departmental and functional level. Of fundamental importance here is the unit cost of a service or product, or the cost per unit of a service or process. These alternatives are termed *product-based costing* and *process-based costing*, respectively, and each lower-level budget will define the volume or value of business unit or departmental output expected, and the cost of delivering it. Costs are a product of volume of resource to be deployed and cost per unit volume. Thus, departmental and business unit budgets are used to monitor adherence to plan, and when aggregated will determine whether the business plan is being met. Measures of performance (to budget) in the business plan are almost always financial in outcomes; in other words, they are not known until the planning period is finished. Examples are profitability and liquidity values, rates of return, return on capital, economic value added, cash flow and payback periods. However, these are 'driven' by measures embedded in departmental budgets, measures such as output volume per unit of resource employed, but unless these are monitored continuously, there is a danger of warning signals appearing too late. So a business unit budget will be divided into, say, monthly time periods, and a departmental budget may even be presented on a weekly basis.

When it occurs, deviation from budget, or the plan, can be for two generic reasons:

- More or less resource is being used than was expected; this can be termed *volume variance*.
- The unit cost of resources is more or less than was expected; this can be termed *cost variance*.

When resources are shared between business units, departments or even products or services, it is not easy to apportion volume or cost variances. Examples of such resources are the salaries of strategic or senior financial managers, and management accounting techniques are employed to allocate them to services or products. Traditional costing systems date from the 1900s and rely on arbitrary cost allocations. In a more recent innovation from the 1980s, activity-based costing, cause-and-effect relationships are considered and used to allocate costs.

When deviation from budget does occur, either the plan was not a good one or the implementation has been poor. In either case, detailed analysis and feedback will lead to the development of better planning skills and to better planning within a 'learning organization'.

Descriptive schools: coping with change

The prescriptive approach described so far is best suited to times of stability, with slow changes in the social, political and economic environment, and in technology. However, such stability no longer exists, so while the prescriptive approach still has value (any plan is better than no plan at all), newer developments in the descriptive strategy schools advocate that the ability of an organization to grasp emerging opportunities moves a company in the direction of its corporate mission. In this view, strategy becomes a compromise between a fixed plan and ability to change.

Descriptive schools, therefore, are more concerned with creating enterprises that are conducive to, and embrace, change. Indeed, they are contemporary with developments in change management, and in particular the organizational development school within it. Here the concepts of 'learning organization' (Senge, 1992), organizational culture (Hofstede, 1991) and knowledge-based organization (Harrison and Kessel, 2004) are central in the aim of creating a team of people who constitute the key resource to corporate success. These concepts are also reflected in many of the descriptive school names: entrepreneurial, cognitive, learning, cultural, environmental and configuration (transformation).

In order to create an enterprise that embraces change, we need to consider several aspects of the enterprise:

a. **The structure of the organization**, and the power relationships within it, must be conducive to change.

b. **The culture of the organization**, and the styles of management associated with it, must be conducive to change.

c. **The competencies and skill of the organization**, the teams within it and individuals within those teams must be conducive to change.

d. It is necessary to develop **an organization that intuitively improves**, i.e., a 'learning organization'.

Structure and power

Classic pyramid organizations, with vertical lines of communication, place barriers to change. Chains of communication are long, and departments tend to become insular under heads whose power comes primarily from their position in the organization, which is referred to in the literature as *legal* or *legitimate* power (Handy, 1999). Such structures also indicate that the organization is systematically controlled, which again tends to inhibit creativity and change. Hence change is imposed from above, rather than organically introduced from below.

While it may be argued that an organization needs a pyramid structure to assert control, and that lack of such a structure might lead to a high degree of anarchy and excess waste, it can also be argued that individuals and teams need freedom to experiment in order to improve. A compromise between these two extremes may be facilitated by improvements in communication and information systems that reduce the need for a limited span of control for an individual manager, enabling them to multitask better and to keep track of a greater number of activities and what a greater number of people are doing.

Culture and management style

The culture of an organization and the style of management prevalent within it are closely related. Early writings by Handy (1976) classified culture into four categories:

- **Power culture.** Where control is centralized and exerted through a few individuals; small entrepreneurial organizations provide most examples here.

- **Role culture.** Typified by the classical formal organization with strong functional or specialist areas (finance, marketing, personnel).

- **Task culture.** Job or project oriented; organizations exhibiting this culture are flexible and adaptable, but do need managers who can multitask.

- **Person culture.** Not found in many organizations; people can obtain power by having specialized skills or knowledge, or can even influence people charismatically; sometimes, such 'stars' form co-operative arrangements within an organization where their skills complement each other (in other words, they network).

Different types of managers, classified by the management style they adopt, will prefer to work in organizations with specific cultures. Even as early as 1938, Kurt Lewin identified three management styles: autocratic, democratic and laissez-faire (Lewin, 1964). Likert (1961) identified four categories of leadership: exploitive-authoritative, benevolent-authoritative, consultative and a style where decisions were jointly made by managers and workers. He called these Systems 1 to 4, respectively. Tannenbaum and Schmidt (1958) presented a fuller picture, when they described managerial style as a continuum from boss-centred autocratic (the author's phrase), with extensive managerial authority, to subordinate-centred democratic, with freedom for subordinates. Pugh (1983) added markers along the continuum indicating typical managerial actions, from *telling* at the autocratic end to *delegating* at the democratic end: tells (orders), sells (decisions), tests (ideas), suggests (ideas), consults (on problems), joins (workers in decision-making) and delegates (decisions). However, at the democratic end of the continuum, the manager will still always set limits within which subordinates can, or are empowered, to act (Open University, 1994).

Competencies for strategic performance and change

The strategic performance of an organization depends on the competencies it has to deliver. Competencies may be based on technical expertise in product (or service) design and delivery, on expert knowledge in terms of data sources and systems to turn them to competitive advantage, or on management skills to plan and control or adapt to a changing environment quickly.

Considering the managerial competencies, two early pioneers addressed the question 'what do managers do?' In 1916, Fayol and Taylor came up with a set of activities reflecting the influence of the school of scientific management at the time. They were:

- **Forecasting.** Looking ahead.
- **Planning.** Deciding what to do.
- **Organizing.** Constructing relationships and structures, i.e., systems.
- **Commanding.** Inspiring and enthusing (perhaps we would now call this 'leading'?).
- **Co-ordinating.** Checking consistency of actions in the organization within the overall plan.
- **Controlling.** Checking that the plan is being implemented.

Sixty years later, Mintzberg (1973) concentrated on the roles of managers that emphasized the art (or craft) of management. He identified three role categories:

- **The interpersonal role.** Dealing with people.
- **The informational role.** Dealing with information.
- **The decisional role.** Making decisions.

Both scientific and artistic elements of management were combined in the early 1990s by the management charter initiative (MCI) into a competency framework. This consisted of two sections: the first concerned with the functional aspects of management (operations, finance, people and information) and the second concerned with more behaviourally-based personal skills, such as leadership and decision-making. In fact, lower-level skills were combined into 'competence clusters', needed for managers to practice higher-level outcome skills. For example, to practice leadership, an individual might need the lower-level skills of listening, presenting, negotiating and persuading, to name but a few. [See also work by Boyatzis (1982) on personal competencies.]

The MCI framework was embedded into the UK National Vocational Qualification (NVQ) system for training and assessing managers, administered by the Chartered Management Institute (Management Charter Initiative, n.d.).

The learning organization

In the late 1980s and 1990s, attention moved to consideration of how to manage change in organizations, as indicated by a plethora of books (cf. Mayon-White, 1986, a collection of 'themed' prepublished academic papers to support a UK Open University postgraduate course, and Burns, 1992; Carnall, 1995; McCalman and Paton, 1992).

There are two schools of managing change: the systems intervention (SI) school, which tends to consider organizations as hard bureaucratic or technical systems, and the organizational development (OD) school, which thinks of them as softer socio-political and economic systems (McCalman and Paton, 1992). Change in the SI school is analyzed and planned at higher management levels, and implementation is supported by communication and persuasion. Change in the OD school is driven from the bottom and requires a culture which looks for improvement, and by individuals who are empowered to seek it. Referring to the previous discussion, one can relate the SI approach to 'power and role'-type organizations, and to the 'telling, selling' end of the managerial style spectrum, while OD can be related to 'task and person'-type organizations and to the 'suggesting, consulting' end of the managerial style spectrum. In terms of schools of strategic thinking, the prescriptive and descriptive categories, the SI school is aligned to the first and the OD school to the second.

The influence of the SI school of change can be easily recognized in business process re-engineering, a strategic level change model where change is initiated at the top and driven down by telling and selling. This reached its zenith in terms of popularity in the mid-1990s, shortly after the publication of the seminal text by Hammer and Champy (1993). However, at the end of the 1990s, both academics and practicing managers were questioning the value of the approach, as it was rarely delivering the expected improvements (Moorag et al., 1999). Lack of good measurement and monitoring systems, and lack of employee support, were thought to be primary reasons for this failure.

The OD school encourages the study of the culture of an organization as part of the change process, attempting to identify where an organization wants to be in terms of culture, where it is now, and how to manage the transition. This process is embodied in a classic framework for analysis, Pugh's OD matrix (Pugh, 1983). This considers current states of behaviour, structure and context at individual, group, inter-group and organizational levels, looking for improvements and suggesting mechanisms to effect them. Out of the OD approach to managing change has evolved the concept of the 'learning organization'. Senge (1992) has defined the learning organization as a place 'where people continually expand their capacity to achieve the results they truly deserve, where new and expansive patterns of thinking are nurtured, where collective aspiration is set free and where people are continually learning how to learn together'. The value of this approach to internal OD in organizations, where learning itself is the key product delivered to customers, is obvious but can be overlooked.

It is now recognized that learning and growth are central to the improvement and continuing success of an organization, and as such they are a foundation stone for more recently developed performance management systems, such as the balanced scorecard (Kaplan and Norton, 1992, 1996) and its derivatives. These are being increasingly employed in business to underpin improvements in financial outcomes.

Closing the loop: the importance of performance management

The importance of measuring performance has always been recognized, but it has not often been practiced holistically across all levels of the organization. At the macro-organizational level outcomes, i.e., those associated with financial performance of the organization, have always been measured. At the micro-organizational level, operational performance has been measured by the scientific management process of work study, or more specifically work measurement, since Taylor (and Fordism) in the early 20th century. Although efforts have been made to introduce intermediate performance measures, e.g., in the definition of key performance indicators (KPIs) and the related practice of management by objectives (MBO), a systematic model attempting to relate strategy implementation and operational performance measures was not available. The balanced scorecard represents an attempt to fill this gap by combining the SI and OD schools of managing change.

The balanced scorecard (Kaplan and Norton)

Following studies at the Harvard Business School, Kaplan and Norton launched a technique known as the 'balanced scorecard' (BS) (Kaplan and Norton, 1992). Their original concepts were later expanded into a more prescriptive process

Process in action Oticon

(Please refer to the Oticon case in Chapter 5 on page 94)

Question

1. Where would you place Lars Kolind in the context of schools of strategic management thinking? [In 2006, Oticon was still thriving and featured on a 'Business Excellence of the Danish Exporters' web page (Danish Exporters, 2006).]

SOURCE: OFF-AIR BBC, CRAZY WAYS FOR CRAZY DAYS (TOM PETERS), 1992 (SEE ALSO BODDY, 2002).]

(Kaplan and Norton, 1996). Kaplan and Norton promote the use of the BS to link business strategy to operational performance (Figure 16.2) by defining measures of performance. They make the link in two complementary ways:

- By developing measures which support the strategy of the organization.
- By using performance, as indicated by the measures, to influence 'emergent' strategy.

The BS approach is a prescriptive approach that has been widely adopted in industry and commerce by management consultants. The framework presented by Kaplan and Norton encompasses all aspects of business and management, including:

- Operational measures of performance, financial, production and customer satisfaction.
- Development of the organization (learning and growth).
- Alignment of operational performance measures, and hence operating system design, with strategic management targets.

The BS approach also owes much to earlier, fashionable prescriptive approaches such as activity-based costing, total quality management, managing change and business process re-engineering. However, outcomes of these earlier approaches appear

Figure 16.2
Balanced scorecard: translating strategy into operational items (based on Kaplan and Norton, 1996)

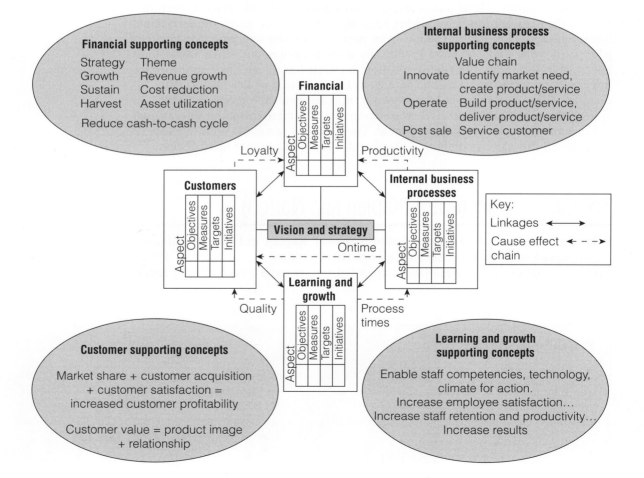

to be of less practical value to operational managers and to controllers of the business than those offered by the BS approach. The core of the BS approach is the development and specification of operational measures of performance under the headings of finance, customers, internal business processes, and learning and growth – all in support of the vision and strategy of the business unit (see Table 16.2). Under each of these headings, managers identify aspects which affect performance. For each aspect, they then identify objectives, measures and targets. Finally, they identify initiatives to create improvements.

When developing a scorecard for each of the four headings, managers are expected to draw on existing concepts and techniques. For example, the concept of the value chain is pertinent when considering internal business processes. Some of these supporting concepts and theories are indicated in Table 16.2. Managers should also consider the links *between* scorecards, such as the generic ones that are shown in Table 16.2. Here, an improvement in *learning and growth* may lead to reduced process times in *internal business processes,* which, in turn, leads to on time delivery to *customers* and better productivity in *finance*. The improvement in *learning and growth* will also lead to improvements in product or service quality for *customers*, resulting in customer loyalty, and will thus have a positive effect upon *finance*. In essence, these links represent causal relationships, a virtuous cycle and the value chain of the business. The final stage of the BS process is to re-evaluate the scorecards and their value in the context of evolving strategy.

Recent developments in the field of performance management

Since the publication of the paper describing the BS in the *Harvard Business Review*, and particularly since the publication of Kaplan and Norton's first text on the technique, many academics and practitioners have analyzed the value of it. For example, Otley (1999) compared the BS with the budget system in his work using a five-issue analysis framework. His findings are summarized in Table 16.5.

It is not surprising that the budgetary control system is relatively strong on control aspects, while the BS is stronger on planning. However, it is surprising that Otley finds that targets are not considered in the scorecard, as they are included within each of the four scorecards which are central to the framework: financial, customer, internal business processes, and learning and growth (see Table 16.4). However, he does highlight potential weaknesses of the BS.

Kennerley and Neely (2002) seem to agree with the structure of the BS. Based on their research, they conclude that:

- A performance measurement framework should provide a balanced picture of the business.
- It should provide a short but important overview of the organization's performance.
- It should be multi-dimensional.
- It should provide comprehensiveness.
- It should be integrated across the organization.
- It should identify how outcomes are driven by performance drivers.

They then propose an alternative framework called 'the performance prism', which includes the following five perspectives.

Perspective	Question
Stakeholder satisfaction	Who are our key stakeholders and what do they want and need?
Strategies	What strategies do we have to put in place to satisfy the wants and needs of these key stakeholders?
Processes	What critical processes do we need to operate and enhance these processes?
Capabilities	What capabilities do we need to operate and enhance these processes?
Stakeholder contribution	What contributions do we require from our stakeholders if we are to maintain and develop these capabilities?

Table 16.5
Comparison of budgetary control system and the balanced scorecard Five Perspectives of the Performance Prism

Kennerley and Neely (2002) claim that this alternative framework addresses the shortcomings in existing performance measurement frameworks and provides an integrated framework to view organization performance. It certainly links strategies, capabilities and processes of the business through consideration of the interests of its

Issue	Budgetary control	Balanced scorecard
Objectives	Financial objectives: profit, cash flow, and return on capital employed	Multiple objectives based on strategy
Strategies and plans	Means/end relationships not formally considered, although budget is based on a plan of action	Implicit in selecting some performance measures; no formal procedures suggested
Targets	Best estimates for financial planning; literature on target-setting gives some guideline for control	Not considered despite being central to 'balanced'
Rewards	Not addressed, despite many rewards now being made contingent upon budget achievement	Not addressed
Feedback	Short-term feedback of budget variances; Incremental budgeting from year to year	Reporting of performance assumed, but no explicit guidance given

SOURCE: OTLEY (1999)

stakeholders. However, stakeholders usually consist of financial shareholders, customers and employees, and it can be argued that their interests are considered in, respectively, the financial scorecard, the customer scorecard and the learning and growth scorecard of the full BS. As processes and capabilities are considered in the internal business process scorecard, it can be argued that Kaplan and Norton's and Kennerley and Neely's frameworks fulfil very similar objectives, and map against each other very closely.

More recently, when assessing the potential ignorance within current financial accounting practice, Lev (2001) questions the lack of consideration of the value of intangible assets. He argues for the importance of this. While economic performance based on the traditional production function is sustained by a company's physical, financial and intangible assets, future earnings and growth potentials could be enhanced by intangible performance as reflected in company valuation (Lev, 2001). Increasingly, researchers are concerned about the presence of knowledge-based assets (KBA) and their impact on financial performance, and it can be further argued that this is a shortcoming of both the BS and the performance prism performance management frameworks, particularly in service organizations, and is a good area for future research.

Process in action building a balanced scorecard for a public broadcasting organization (simulation only)

This case study consists of the outcomes of a simulation exercise undertaken with an MBA class to demonstrate and test the process of developing a balanced scorecard for a public broadcasting organization. The British Broadcasting Company (BBC) was chosen to test the procedure.

The BBC: mission, purposes and limitations

The BBC is the national public broadcasting organization of the UK. It operates under a Royal Charter of 1926 and under a constitution, both of which are now under review (in July 2006).

The motto of the BBC is 'Nation shall speak peace unto nation'.

The mission of the BBC is embedded in the latest revised draft royal charter (July 2006), which describes the BBC's public nature and its objects as:

1. The BBC exists to serve the public interest.

2. The BBC's main object is the promotion of its public purposes, which are:

a. Sustaining citizenship and civil society

b. Promoting education and learning

c. Stimulating creativity and cultural excellence

d. Representing the UK, its nations, regions and communities

e. In promoting its other purposes, helping to deliver to the public the benefit of emerging communications technologies and services and, in addition taking a leading role in the switchover to digital television

3. In addition, the BBC may maintain, establish or acquire subsidiaries through which commercial activities may be undertaken to any extent permitted by a framework agreement. (The BBC's general powers enable it to maintain, establish or acquire subsidiaries for purposes sufficiently connected with its public purposes.)

The BBC promotes its public purposes by means of its mission, **to inform, educate and entertain, through the provision of output which consists of information, education and entertainment.** This is supplied by means of (a) television, radio and online services, (b) similar or related services which make output generally available and which may be in forms or by means of technologies which either have not previously been used by the BBC or which have yet to be developed. The BBC is also allowed to carry out other activities which directly or indirectly promote the public purposes, but such activities should be peripheral, subordinate or ancillary to its main activities (i.e., must be in proportion to them).

Finally, the BBC is independent in all matters concerning the content of its output, the times and manner in which it is supplied and the management of its affairs.

(The reader should consider this information in the context of theory on corporate missions described earlier.)

Sources: http://en.wikipedia.org/wiki/BBC. Last accessed June 2006. http://www.bbc.co.uk. Last accessed June 2006.

Setting system boundaries

Although the BBC transmits both radio and television programmes, the biggest part of the broadcasting business, in terms of both consumers (listeners and viewers) is in television. This part of the business is expected to expand in the future with the development of satellite and digital broadcasting systems. It was therefore decided to concentrate on television for this exercise, although developing a balanced scorecard for radio would be a very similar process.

The process of developing a balanced scorecard is indicated here by the diagrams that were developed. However, in a real situation, underpinning these diagrams would be group strategy meetings with both internal and external stakeholders to try to gain the consensus necessary for successful implementation.

The systems map

In developing a balanced scorecard for the BBC, a systems map was first drawn to present an holistic view of the organization, the subsystems within it and the lines of influence connecting them. The systems-mapping technique is primarily a tool from the systems intervention school of change management.

The objectives tree

The objectives tree, very similar to a value tree used in systematic decision-making (Goodwin and Wright, 1991), is also a tool which is frequently used in both the SI and OD schools of change management. It cascades the corporate mission down to operational objectives. In its development, the quality and financial aspirations of the business are developed within the political and legal constraints imposed upon it. It is obvious that cause-effect relationships which should be embedded in a balanced scorecard are beginning to be identified.

The strategy map

Strategy maps were introduced by Hamel and Prahalad in the *Harvard Business Review* in the early 1990s, and expanded upon in a subsequent strategy text (Hamel and Prahalad, 1994). The strategy map here is presented in levels reflecting the balanced scorecard framework, in effect by rearranging the objectives tree. The causal relationships are more obvious here, and strategic outcomes at each level are linked to the factors that drive them. 'Outcome' boxes are labelled for reference.

The balanced scorecard

The strategy map, with the objectives tree before it, enables us to identify attributes to be measured, and the causal relationships between them. The balanced scorecard now allows us to develop ideas for detailed measures on these attributes. The attributes have been listed in the balanced scorecard framework, with a reference for each one linking it to the strategy map. These references are then used within the scorecards to indicate the causal linkages already identified in the strategy map (the 'driving' formulas). Finally a bundle of measures for each attribute are identified as potential performance measures, and either one can be selected or some kind of weighing formula can be applied to calculate a composite value.

Question

1. Evaluate the use of the balanced scorecard exercise used in the BBC here, and the value of the diagrams produced in that exercise.

Practice in action diagram: BBC systems map

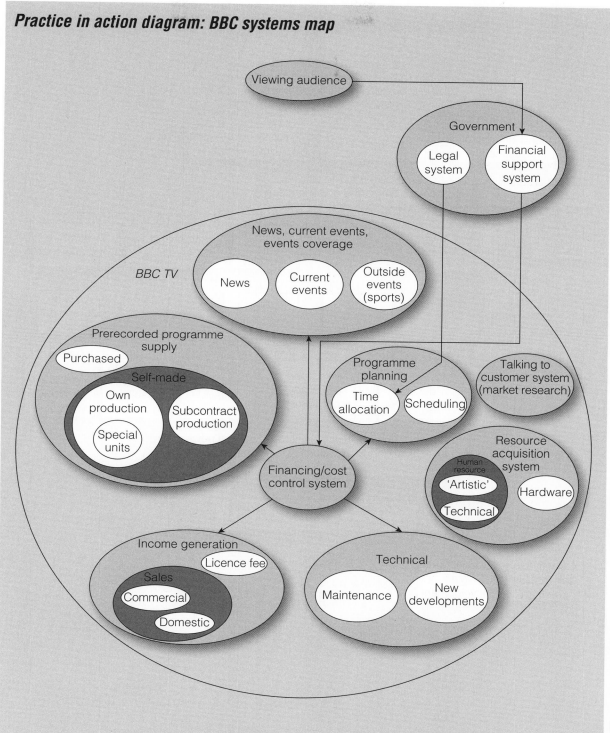

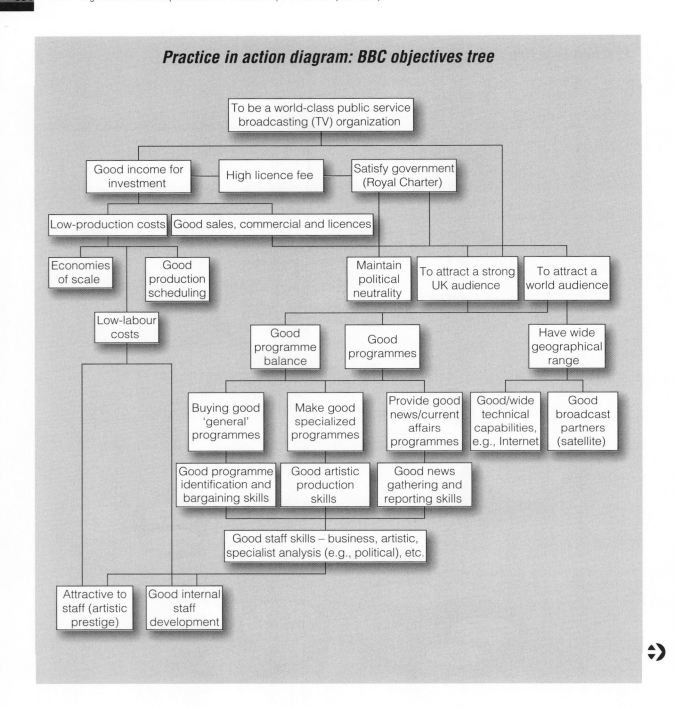

Practice in action diagram: BBC objectives tree

Practice in action diagram: BBC strategy map

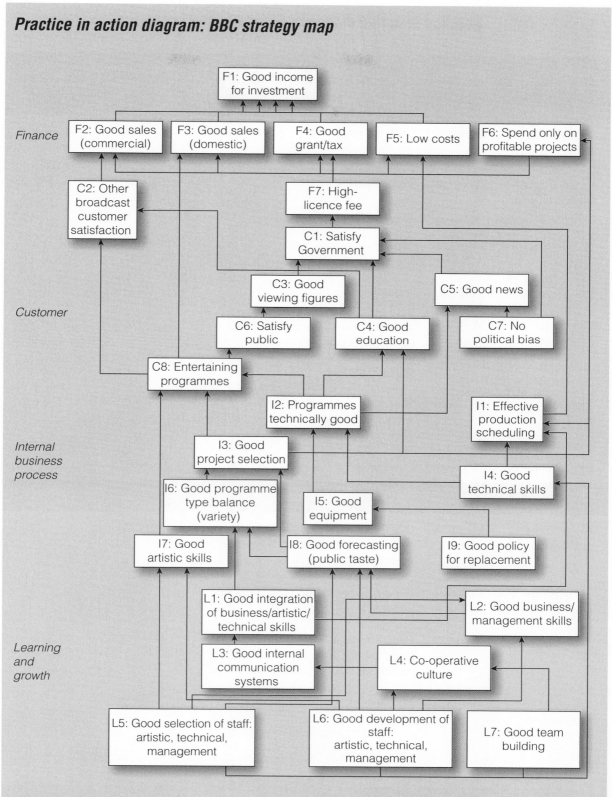

Practice in action diagram: BBC balanced scorecard

Attribute	Objective	(Output) measures	(Driving) Formula	Ref
Finance scorecard				
Total income	Maximize	Direct measure	$= F2 + F3 + F4 - F5$	F1
Commercial broadcast sales income	Maximize	Direct measure	(Function of) f(C2, F6)	F2
Domestic sales income	Maximize	Direct measure	f(C8, F6)	F3
Licence income	Maximize	Direct measure	f(F7, F6)	F4
Low costs	Minimize	Actual measure = labour + consumable materials + equipment (hire and depreciation) + overheads . . . i.e., from budgets	f(F6, I1)	F5
Profitable projects	Maximize	Statistical analysis of projects on time and within budget, based on records for each project	f(I3)	F6
High-licence fee	Maximize	Direct value	f(C1)	F7
Customer scorecard				
Government satisfaction	Maximize	Qualitative opinion of ministers. Number of complaints (and balance between all political parties). *As C7*	f(C3, C4, C5, C7)	C1
Commercial satisfaction	Maximize	Repeat purchases and preproduction orders	f(C8, C4)	C2
Viewing figures	Maximize	Direct measure. Statistical sampling, electronically collected from TVs monitoring of scientific sample	f(C6)	C3
Educational programme value	Maximize	Survey of teachers and subject specialists? Focus groups (statistically designed?) Questionnaire surveys. (Viewing figures?)	f(I2, I3)	C4

Attribute	Objective	(Output) measures	(Driving) Formula	Ref
Customer scorecard (continued)				
News programme value	Maximize	Viewing figures (quantitative) and survey (qualitative). Awards received? Speed of reporting, accuracy of reporting (number and magnitude of errors reported). Percentage of moving pictures and interviews/talking heads	f(I2, C7)	C5
Public satisfaction	Maximize	Qualitative surveys, focus groups	f(C8)	C6
Political bias	Minimize	Qualitative opinion of ministers. Number of complaints (and balance between all political parties)	None	C7
Entertainment programme value	Maximize	Viewing figures (quantitative), and surveys/focus groups (qualitative)	f(I7, I3, I2)	C8
Internal business process				
Production scheduling	Optimize	Percentage of labour/equipment hours inactive	f(I3, I4, L1)	I1
Technicality of programmes	Optimize	Prizes won for technical aspects, critical reviews	f(I5, I4)	I2
Quality of project selection	Maximize	Viewing figures, profit profile (outcomes)	f(I6, I8)	I3
Technical skills	Maximize	Qualifications of staff. Experience	f(L5, L6)	I4
Quality of equipment	Maximize	Age. Technical specification	f(I9)	I5
Programme balance (variety)	Optimize	Percentage by category. Critical and public view (survey, focus groups)	f(L1)	I6
Artistic skills	Maximize	Staff training (drama schools etc.), previous work and achievements	f(L5, L6)	I7
Forecasting accuracy (public taste)	Maximize	Forecast error tracking signals	f(L5, L6, L2)	I8
Equipment replacement policy	Optimize	Life cycle, replacement policy	None	I9

(Continues)

Attribute	Objective	(Output) measures	(Driving) Formula	Ref
Learning and growth				
Integration of business, artistic, and technical skills	Optimize	Number of inter-departmental meetings, average percentage time spent attending	f(L3)	L1
Business/ management skills	Maximize	Qualifications and experience of staff	f(L5, L6)	L2
Effectiveness of internal communications	Maximize	Staff opinion, surveys	f(L4)	L3
Internal co-operation	Maximize	Staff opinion, surveys	f(L6)	L4
Quality of staff selection	Maximize	Selection process and criteria set for selection	None	L5
Quality of staff development	Maximize	Average staff time, selection of staff for training, advancement of staff after training (an outcome)	None	L6
Quality of team building	Maximize	Number of team meetings. Time spent in team meetings (both to be optimized)	None	L7

Summary

- This chapter has presented a chronological view of the development of strategic thinking, up to the current time when strategy is closely interrelated with theory on performance management and measurement.

- This theory brings together classical planning and motivational theories, combining them with concepts of how to best plan and manage change situations.

Chapter questions

1. Analyze where the following theory is applied in the BBC balanced scorecard exercise, and evaluate its value in leading to a successful implementation.

2. It has been suggested that in a service organization, particularly in a public service organization such as the BBC, that the customer scorecard should be

at the top and the finance scorecard should be at the bottom. What are the arguments for and against this proposal, and how would the decision be related to the organization's strategic mission?

3. The BS developed for the BBC has 31 attributes to be considered, and many of these attributes have 'bundles' of several suggested measures. In addition, some suggested measures apply to more than one attribute. How easy would the BS be to use? How would you simplify it for easier use?

References

Boddy, D. (2002) *Management: An Introduction,* 3rd edn., Harlow: Pearson Education.

Boyatzis, R. E. (1982) *The Competent Manager: A Model for Effective Performance*, Chichester: John Wiley.

Burns, B. (1992) *Managing Change*, 4th edn., Harlow: Pearson Education.

Business Resource Software (2006) [Online]. http://www.brs-inc.com/advice-mission.asp. Last accessed June 2006.

Carnall, C. (1995) *Managing Change in Organisations*, Hemel Hempstead: Prentice Hall.

Danish Exporters (2006) [Online]. http://www.danishexporters.dk/scripts/danishexporters.

Goodwin, G., and Wright, P. (1991) *Decision Analysis for Management Judgement*, Chichester: John Wiley.

Hamel, G., and Prahalad, C. K. (1994) *Competing for the Future*, Boston, MA: HBS.

Hammer, M. and Champy, J. (1993) *Re-engineering the Corporation: A Manifesto for Business Revolution*. London: Nicholas Brearley.

Hammer, M., and Champy, J. (2001) *Re-engineering the Corporation: A Manifesto for Business Revolution*, London: Nicholas Brearly.

Handy, C. B. (1976) *Understanding Organizations*, Harmondswort, UK: Penguin Books.

Handy, C. B. (1999) *Understanding Organisations*, 4th edn., London: Penguin Books.

Harrison, R., and Kessel, S. J. (2004) *Human Resource Development in a Knowledge Economy: An Organizational View*, Basingstoke: Palgrave Macmillan.

Hill, T. (2005) *Operations Management,* 2nd edn., Basingstoke: Palgrave Macmillan.

Hofstede, G. (1991) *Cultures and Organisations: Software of the Mind*, London: McGraw Hill.

Kaplan, R. S., and Norton, P. P. (1992, Jan–Feb) 'The balanced scorecard: Measures that drive performance', *Harvard Business Review*, pp. 71–81.

Kaplan, R. S., and Norton, P. P. (1996) *The Balanced Scorecard: Translating Strategy into Action,* Boston: HBR.

Kennerley, M., Neely, A. (2002) 'Performance management frameworks: A review', in Neely, A. (ed.), *Business Performance Measurement: Theory and Practice*, Cambridge: Cambridge University Press, pp. 144–145.

Krajewski, L. J., Ritzman, P., and Malhotra, M. K. (2007) *Operations Management,* 8th edn., New Jersey: Pearson Prentice Hall.

Lev, B. (2001) *Intangibles: Management, Measurement, and Reporting*, Washington: Washington Brookes Institution Press.

Lewin, K. (1964) *Field Theory in Social Science: Selected Theoretical Papers*, New York: Harper Torchbooks.

Likert, R. (1961) *New Patterns of Management*, London: McGraw Hill.

Management Charter Initiative (n.d.) Introduction to the Management Standards. Implementation Pack. [Online]. http://www.managers.org.uk.

Mayon-White, B. (ed.) (1986) *Planning and Managing Change*, Milton Keynes: Open University.

McCalman, J., and Paton, R. A. (1992) *Change Management: A Guide to Effective Implementation*, London: Paul Chapman.

Mintzberg, H. (1973) *The Nature of Managerial Work*, London: Harper Row.

Mintzberg, H., Ahlstrad, B., and Lampel, J. (1998) *Strategy Safari*, Hemel Hempstead: Prentice Hall.

Moorag, S., Oyon, D., and Hostettler, D. (1999) 'The balanced scorecard: A necessary good or an unnecessary evil?', *European Management Journal*, 17(5):481.

Open University (1994) *Managing Development and Change*. Course B751 Course Material, Milton Keynes: Open University.

Otley, D. (1999) 'Performance management: A framework for management control systems', *Management Accounting Research*, 10(4):363–382.

Porter, M. J. (1985) *Competitive Advantage, Creating and Sustaining Superior Performance*, New York: Free Press.

Pugh, D. (1983) *People in Organisations*, London: Penguin.

Senge, P. M. (1992) *The Fifth Discipline: The Art and Practice of the Learning Organisation*, London: Century Press.

Stern, C. W., and Stalk, G. (eds.) (1998) *Perspectives on Strategy from the Boston Consulting Group*, Chichester: John Wiley.

Tannenbaum, R., and Schmidt, W. (1958, March–April) 'How to choose a leadership pattern', *Harvard Business Review*, pp. 95–101.

Wal-Mart (2006) [Online]. http://www.Wal-Martfacts.com. Last accessed June 2006.

17

Marketing and its implications for financial management

Luiz Moutinho and James Wilson

Introduction

A basic understanding of accounting principles and practices is essential for marketing managers. Accounting information is central to planning, measuring and controlling many marketing activities, and managers who understand and can use this information effectively can act on it more effectively than those who do not. The learning objectives then focus on those dimensions of financial accounting most relevant to a marketing manager's effectiveness.

Case notes in this chapter will consist of illustrations of the various budgeting techniques described, and comparisons of alternative methods of project appraisal.

Learning objectives

- To understand that accounting systems and reports may be adapted to marketing needs.

- To develop a comprehension of the profit and loss statement and the effects of marketing on it.

- To appreciate the differences between profit and cash flow and the effects of marketing on cash flows.

- To present a perspective on the balance sheet that reveals its relevance for marketing managers.

- To show how marketing interacts with accounting measures and the impact different elements have on an organization's finances.

Accounting implications of marketing

Many of the systems used by financial accountants are also useful for marketing purposes. The prime orientation of financial accounting systems focuses on acquiring the financial information necessary for keeping accounts – tracking sales, cash, stocks, etc. – in an organization's day-to-day operations. But just as an accountant is interested in knowing exactly how much was sold and the incoming revenues in order to prepare the financial statement reporting on the organization's assets and liabilities, and its profits and losses, so too will marketing and sales managers have their own interests in knowing what products are selling, where those sales are occurring, who is buying the products, what prices are being paid, whether a recent promotion is having an effect and a myriad of other sales-related aspects. Financial data may be mined extensively for useful marketing information if the appropriate information systems are in place. Even relatively small organizations will generate thousands of sales and financial transactions in a day. In the past, the effort required to separate, extract, categorize and then analyze that information for marketing has been too onerous to consider. The legally mandated financial controls and reports produced by accounting systems may, through design and implementation efforts that consider the organization's needs, be more broadly augmented by further controls and reports that provide information beneficial for marketing. Accounting information may now be used as never before to help with an organization's understanding of its marketing and sales efforts and their impact.

The fundamental unit of financial activity is a **transaction**: the exchange of money for goods or services. Financial accounting monitors these transactions and records their effect. When something is purchased, the customer surrenders either cash or a promise to pay in exchange for goods or a service, or for the organization's promise to provide it in the future. No single transaction generally has much significance but, when all are taken together and their collective effect is gauged, the organization may then understand how well it is doing, or how poorly. With thousands of transactions occurring, the volume of data can be enormous and its analysis and presentation very difficult. Accounting information systems have been developed to handle these demands and to provide summarized reports and controls required to effectively manage the finances. These systems have also been exploited by non-financial managers; both operations and marketing managers share an interest in knowing what stocks remain after sales have occurred, and understanding what is selling provides insight into what needs to be produced and how it might best be distributed. Finance, marketing and operations all interact, and the information vital to one is often just as important within the other functions.

A brief consideration of the main financial statements will illustrate the interests that marketing managers will have in the financial information acquired and used by accountants. One key issue and potential problem is that such accounting information only describes what has *already* happened, and while this may be useful for short-term responses in the immediate and near future, its value for longer-term decisions and marketing developments is more limited. Nevertheless, a sound understanding of the past is usually necessary for a well-founded extrapolation or consideration of how future developments might unfold.

Financial statement analysis from a marketing perspective

The two main financial statements developed by accountants are the profit and loss statement and the balance sheet. These are required by law for all corporations for their annual reports and they are also useful to managers in providing an overview of an organization's operations. From a manager's perspective, these are particularly useful when produced more frequently or in greater focus and detail to allow specific marketing (or other) questions to be investigated. For example, a profit and loss statement for a particular product or sales region might help in analyzing the latter's economic benefit. The balance sheet is rather less useful, but some real benefit may be obtained through an analysis of the assets and liabilities that are affected by marketing initiatives and policies.

The chief difficulty with most treatments of financial statement analysis is their focus – a consideration of the information from an accountant's point of view rather than that of a functional manager. However, managers with interests in operations, personnel and marketing could find much value in this data if only it were refined in ways to maximize its usefulness in those areas. So long as the preparation of these statements is dominated by purely financial and regulatory requirements, organizations will find they are not extracting the maximum benefits from the data collected. A proactive approach may help design systems that produce information more useful than that seen in the usual sets of accounts produced.

One point to recognize with financial statement analysis is that the information is all historical – it shows the effects of past policies and decisions. In their most commonly seen format, analyses can reveal what happened over the past year (or quarter, if public accounts are produced that frequently). Yet managers will require information more frequently – generally monthly, and perhaps even weekly or daily. But even the most current accounting reports will always describe events that have already occurred. This information can be very valuable, but it does not necessarily allow marketing efforts to be managed as they are happening.

The profit and loss statement and how marketing managers can use it

The profit and loss statement is perhaps the most useful of the accounting reports commonly used. It summarizes the organization's income from sales, the costs incurred in generating those sales and the overhead expenditures necessary to support the sales activity. This information is presented in a coherent format that allows the different pieces of information to be considered individually and in relation to other relevant issues. Marketing managers may easily see what the sales revenues for the period have been. Going beyond that simple information, they may then look at related information: how much the costs of making those sales were, or how the current period's sales changed from the previous periods, or even how the current period's sales compare with the same period in a previous year, if that is more relevant. The profit and loss statement can be constructed to provide a more precise

Table 17.1
Profit and loss
statement and
implications for
marketing

focus if necessary – it may be broken down to focus on specific products or regions (and their costs), or any other aggregation that the manager may have a specific interest in assessing. The information can be acquired and a close working relationship with an organization's accountants can help design systems that allow this information to be easily and effectively collected and reported from the mass of accounting information handled.

Table 17.1 illustrates a commonly seen format for a profit and loss statement. This also provides a line-by-line synopsis of the value of each entry for marketing and sales management. Besides the raw figures from the profit and loss statement

Profit and loss statement	This year (£)	Last year (£)	Implications for marketing
Sales revenue	1500	1250	The level of sales in monetary terms. Are sales reaching desired levels? Is there a minimum level of sales necessary? Are sales increasing, decreasing or stable? Related: Are revenues per unit sold stable, increasing or decreasing? Is the item's price 'right'? Is it being discounted? Are competitor's products affecting sales – and if so, is it volume or price most affected? Not only are changes in value considered but also proportionate changes. A £1 million increase in sales might be great for a small company but not so impressive for a much larger one. Comparative changes are important too, for a company may find that its results should not be considered in isolation but in reference to its nearest competitors and the industry or economy more widely. Thus a set of 'good' results may lose some of their shine if others are doing even better; or gain more if those competitors are doing more poorly.
Cost of goods sold	750	650	This reflects the unit costs of the items sold. These may include purchase or production costs not usually a marketing concern, but also distribution costs and direct sales commissions that are. Are these increasing or decreasing proportionately with sales? These can be a measure of efficiency in production, or a measure of how effectively suppliers are controlled. Also note that accounting policies on inventory valuation may have an effect – policies that increase the COGS reduce profits (and the tax on them).
Gross profit	750	600	Also called a contribution margin. This is a broad measure of the profitability of the goods and services sold. Its interest to marketing is that it is a better guide for sales incentives than simple price or volume. Increasing the sales of the most profitable items is one financially oriented objective that marketing managers may be given.
Selling and administrative	500	400	General administrative costs would not necessarily be a concern for marketing, but selling overhead costs certainly would be closely considered. These would include such issues as advertising and other promotional costs.

Table 17.1
(Continued)

Profit and loss statement	This year (£)	Last year (£)	Implications for marketing
Other fixed costs	100	100	Outside the day-to-day control of managers, though these may be varied over the longer term by investment or disinvestment, or changes to the assets base of the organization. Examples of such costs could be items such as depreciation of assets, insurance, rent and utility costs. One point to recognize is that investment in new product development may be classified as an overhead in this category.
Profit	150	100	How much money is being made from the organization's operations before interest and tax. This is an important number, for it represents a measure of the organization's performance independent of the manner in which it has financed itself. Thus, two companies might be equally successful in their marketing and production activities but find that the choices made in financing their operations create cost differentials. This value is thus more suitable for comparisons between periods or companies that finance themselves differently.
Interest charges	50	50	The costs of money borrowed to sustain operations. This too may not generally be a concern for marketing managers *but* if extensive credit is offered to customers to promote sales these costs may then become very relevant.
Taxes	50	25	Again, not usually a concern for marketing.
Net profit	50	25	How much money is being made.

there are a number of relationships that may also be used to explore the organization's performance. Some of the commonly used ones follow from the accounting statements directly. These interesting relationships are most often identified through financial ratio analysis, an important tool used by accountants in generally assessing organizational performance. Some of these ratios reflect an organization's competitive and marketing performance and so have a specific relevance to marketing managers.

A frequently used measure of marketing performance is the gross profit margin: gross profit divided by sales revenue. Effectively, this is the difference between an item's selling price and its direct costs. The key point to recognize is that this should be considered as showing 'symptoms' of a problem and is not itself the problem. For example, a company's gross profit margin may fall from one year to the next. This may cause concern, but without further investigation the correct response cannot be identified from that simple measure. The margin may have fallen because prices have 'softened'. That could be due to competitor pressure: price-cutting by existing competition, improved competing products, new entrants into the market, etc. Or it could also be due to customer behaviour – tastes may change, incomes may not rise as expected – or to even more general macro-economic factors such as interest rate changes, inflation or exchange rate variations. The ratio provides an insight into performance, but does not explain why that varies. Explanation requires a closer review of revenues, prices, volume sold, unit costs, etc. – the whole range of factors that affect gross profit.

While selling and administrative expenses are generally presented as an aggregate, an analysis that breaks these down so that the selling costs may be considered on their own is most useful for marketing managers. In this, the ratio of selling overheads to sales revenue would be a critical interest. Advertising and other promotions often require expenditure prior to the realization of sales – these fixed costs then need to be recovered by the sales they help generate. If the level of sales is greater than expected, a lower cost/revenue ratio may be seen; if sales are not stimulated as much as desired, a lower ratio may be observed. The 'target', or desired ratio, may be set arbitrarily or taken from past experience. Differences from the target or from experience in past years may again be explained by other factors: Advertising costs may be increasing faster than sales revenue, yielding a higher cost/revenue ratio, or a promotion may be more successful in stimulating sales revenues than expected, yielding a lower cost/sales ratio. A disaggregated set of revenues and costs would then attempt to link specific overhead expenditures for a given product's or service's selling, advertising, promotion and development costs to the revenues it yields. This information may then be compared with the marketing plans previously developed and performance against the plan assessed. Questions may then be posed: Was the plan successfully implemented? If not, what problems were there? Higher than expected production or distribution costs? Delays in promoting the product? Delays in delivery? Problems in distribution? In essence, the effectiveness of the plan and its implementation may be assessed. A proper 'audit' of the marketing may then indicate successes to be emulated or failures to be avoided in future plans and activities.

Other ratios of specific interest to marketing that may be derived from accounting data are such parameters as gross profit per product. This may be used to help identify sales commissions to stimulate sales of those items that are most profitable. Similarly, the company might focus on regions or countries and assess its marketing efforts within those more effectively than looking at the whole; some products may vary in popularity and profitability between regions. This may be due to price differentials, but there may well be cost variations in serving different areas.

Profit and loss information is just one tool accountants use to manage an organization's operations. It is usually supplemented by a cash flow analysis. Managers recognize that profits are only part of the story in running their organizations. No organization can survive long if it doesn't earn profits, but it also needs to generate sufficient cash flow to meet its obligations. Profit alone does not necessarily permit that. Profits can be used for numerous purposes, and these uses may sometimes be greater than are the profits! For example, a marketing manager may argue that using a greater number of outlets could increase sales. The implications of this policy may not be immediately obvious: There may be higher operating costs if additional transportation costs are incurred. Going beyond that, it may almost certainly increase inventories of stock held in a larger number of outlets and increase the inventories in transit. The sales revenue generated might increase, only to be reduced by higher transportation costs (higher cost of goods sold (COGS), so the gross profit may not increase proportionately with sales. The profits generated may then be seen as eaten up by the greater level of inventories needed in the greater number of outlets and in transit to them. So while profits might increase from this initiative, it may demand additional investment in stocks that use up some of or even more than the profit generated. The profits then turn out to exist entirely as 'paper profits' without more cash in the bank.

Adjustments to 'profit': cash flow and its impact on marketing

Following consideration of profit and loss, we analyze cash flow. In cash flow analysis, a number of 'adjustments' must be made in order to fully understand the impact of operations over a period on the organization's cash position.

Profit is the starting point. But some of the fixed costs deducted generally are depreciation – simply an allocation of past investment in productive assets to the current and future periods with the purpose of more accurately reflecting the true costs of doing business over the life of an asset, rather than forcing all of its costs onto the period when it was acquired. Thus, depreciation is a non-cash expense for an organization, one that it has to recognize to properly assess its profitability, but not one that currently costs it any money. Depreciation is effectively money spent in the past that is treated as a current cost, so the true cash position for an organization would look to its profits and add back to them the depreciation previously paid. This generally improves the situation (more cash available for paying debts and other uses), but against that there may be a number of deductions.

First, there are inventories to consider. An increase in inventories will require money. These inventories are not shown on the profit and loss statement but will be shown later on the balance sheet. A decrease in inventories has an effect like depreciation: Stock created and paid for in the past is currently being sold. Those earlier costs are now shown on the profit and loss as a cost, but they were paid in the past. So current sales of inventories previously created brings in more cash through recovering those earlier costs. In effect, the profits from past sales have been stored in inventories until those stocks have been sold off and converted into cash. Marketing managers should consider inventories as working capital just as accountants do, and ask whether those stocks are being deployed most effectively.

Second, there are organizational credit policies to consider. Many organizations will operate using inventories bought on credit from their suppliers. This may be an effective means for raising working capital, but it may be expensive in terms of the cost of the goods, sold. Supplies acquired on credit might be priced higher than they would be otherwise. Does the organization pay a premium for the easy credit it enjoys? While not directly a marketing concern, it is an issue of some interest, for it will reduce gross profit. Similarly, an organization may offer credit terms to its own customers as a means for stimulating sales. The benefits of increased sales revenues will be reduced somewhat by higher costs for bad debts and the costs of providing credit as well as the cost of the capital used. Marketing managers should also consider whether the profits generated by these additional customers attracted by credit are sufficient to meet the additional costs of providing it.

The working capital employed in an organization's operations will be greatly affected by its marketing policies, and it is useful for marketing managers to understand those effects.

A summary of adjustments:

CASH = Profit

+ Depreciation

− Change in Inventory

− Change in Creditors

+ Change in Debtors

The profit and loss statement shows the effect of operations over a period on an organization. The cash flow analysis shows the effect of those operations on the organization's working capital – the monies it relies on in its day-to-day activities. But organizations also use resources such as buildings, equipment, patents and brands, and capital borrowed or invested for long term. These are not working capital but are still necessary for the organization to operate. The profit and loss statement simply describes an organization's activity within a specific period, but its existed before that, and will generally continue afterwards. The organization started the period with various assets and liabilities – these are described by the balance sheet. The balance sheet will be changed by the activities described in the profit and loss statement. Sales (and production) will possibly alter the organization's inventories. If sales are made on credit, that will affect the monies owed to the organization. These interactions between the profit and loss statement and the balance sheet are also interesting for marketing management.

Balance sheets and current assets used in marketing

In broad terms, the balance sheet describes the resources available to the organization and their sources. Marketing activities will not generally be too concerned with where their organization obtains financing – it would not matter much whether the capital was all contributed by investors or borrowed. But marketing can be affected by organizational policies on how resources are used, and marketing strategy should work to ensure that its needs are properly resourced and financed. Long-term assets most generally relate to resources used in the production processes: physical plant and equipment, for example, though product patents and rights may also be included. Long-term assets of a specific marketing character may focus on product rights and brands. But more often, the marketing resource requirements might be most readily seen as they relate to short-term operational needs: the current assets as shown on a balance sheet. In this the two main foci are inventories and debtors.

Inventories are goods held for later sale. This is usually set by policy, either proactively by marketing in identifying stock levels necessary to support projected sales requirements, or reactively by finance in limited stock levels to minimize demands on the organization's working capital. Ideally, a marketing plan will forecast demand and then ensure that the organization has either the productive capacity to meet needs as they occur, or the ability to build up inventories beforehand so that demands may be met as they occur by using these too. These anticipation inventories help balance productive capacity with sales that may vary significantly.

A further use of inventories may be to buffer production from sales fluctuations – even when demand is stable, it may vary more than desired for productive efficiency. Thus, inventories may be used to decouple and stabilize production. Inventories in the form of 'safety stocks' may also provide for minor, unanticipated fluctuations in demand. These operational concerns with buffer and safety stocks may be quantitatively assessed, and there are numerous operational research models available for that. These can be used to establish safety stocks so that the risks or costs of running out of inventory are reduced to an acceptable level.

A more problematical issue arises with assessing the appropriate level of inventory to carry in order to support sales. In this, the difference in perspectives between financial managers and marketing and operations managers is notable. Providing inventories for any purpose places a demand on financial resources. A financial manager may then wish to restrict such working capital investment to a fixed level as a *total* commitment. However, marketing (and operations) managers are concerned with *specific* uses of inventories to support sales, distribution and production activities. Their focus is on specific items rather than on the whole, and it may be very difficult to ascertain the aggregate impact of numerous product-specific obligations. It is thus highly possible, for example, that marketing policies on credit sales or dictating inventory levels as a fixed proportion of expected sales may in aggregate demand more working capital than would be made available. This highlights the need for marketing plans to be consistent with overall business plans to ensure that the needs of marketing are well co-ordinated with financial and operational planning.

In using balance sheet information about the working capital assets employed in supporting sales, marketing managers may assess this aspect of performance through inventory turnover – how long it takes to sell inventories. This is usually expressed as a ratio:

$$\frac{\text{Cost of Goods Sold}}{\text{Inventory}}$$

(yielding an estimate of the number of times inventory is sold out during a period), or

$$\frac{\text{Inventory}}{\text{Cost of Goods Sold}} \times 365 \text{ days}$$

(yielding an estimate of the number of days' stock held). Both ratios are commonly seen. The balance sheet records inventories at their cost to the organization. Turnover is then calculated using the COGS rather than revenue. The revenue value includes a mark-up to provide profit and cover fixed costs, while the COGS is the value consistent with the inventory valuation on the balance sheet.

The COGS divided by inventory gives a number crudely interpreted as how often the stockroom may be emptied during the period. This is crude because there will be variations in how quickly different items held in inventory sell – the most popular items may turn over much more quickly than the unpopular items. It is entirely possible for this ratio to mask a very wide range of variation – some items may sell out almost immediately, while others may linger for several years on the shelf. In fact, inventories should be closely analyzed, for there may be substantial obsolete or unsaleable stock hidden in that value. These stocks then reduce overall performance, but recognizing that they cannot be sold will involve writing them off or selling them as salvage – reducing profits by accepting that these have been a loss. It should also be noted that too high a ratio may hide other problems from not having sufficient stock – lost sales are nowhere recorded in financial statements. Reducing the number and variety of items held in inventory is beneficial, but at some point such financially motivated reductions may create greater losses in current and future sales than they are worth. Inventory may thus have a value rather greater than its cost might indicate.

The alternative inventory turnover ratio (Inventory / Cost of Goods Sold × 365 days) provides the same information, although expressed differently. Some managers find it more tangible to speak of days' stocks, though the import of the ratio is unaffected by its expression. An organization that reduces its inventories from 30 days' stock to 20 days' worth may be more readily perceived to have improved than one that has improved its turnover from 1/12 to 1/18, yet the two are the same. The use of 'days' as a measure is particularly useful for accounting managers, for they can combine that with the average time debtors take to pay to understand the demands these uses place on working capital. To illustrate: If items are in inventory an average of 30 days before being sold, and if the buyers then take an average of 60 days to pay for what they've bought, the combination of the two means that working capital is tied up for 90 days – the total time needed before the monies invested in the inventories are recovered from payments by customers. The implications for marketing are quite clear: Increasing the volume and variety of inventories and easing credit policies to stimulate sales has an immediate impact on the need for working capital.

Financial managers often regard inventory as underused capital – money idly sitting in warehouses or on shelves. The role inventory plays in supporting sales and facilitating operations needs to be clearly understood and presented. And underused inventory must be recognized for the drain it is on organizational resources – particularly when it might be better invested in more productive marketing activities.

Marketing often uses credit policy as a promotional tool – with 'loose' credit seen as a method for stimulating sales. The financial effects can be seen in the profit and loss statement through increased sales revenues. The net effect is to increase the gross profits, but against that gain there are costs. With credit sales it is inevitable that some proportion will be bad debt losses. Other costs reflect the capital devoted to supporting credit sales. This capital could otherwise be earning interest if banked, or it might be generating profit if invested. If the organization has to borrow money itself to provide credit, the costs can be yet greater. Credit policy may be dictated by competitive pressures, so simple financial analysis may not be decisive. It can, however, give an estimate of the real costs of meeting these competitive pressures, and indicate pricing policies that might help recover these costs.

One point from this analysis is the observation that the attractiveness of credit sales is affected far more by the incidence of bad debt losses than by the underlying costs of the money so invested. If careful credit policy and debtor management can reduce these losses, such a policy may become more attractive, though those restrictions may mean less increase in sales growth. It also, e.g., allows Smith's Grocers to appreciate the potential demands the policy has on their cash flow and financing needs (see the following Process in action). Such a financial analysis allows such policy to be considered and implemented in a more profitable and effective manner than might otherwise be the case.

Process in action Smith's Grocers

Smith's Grocers has recently increased their store's internal capacity and sales potential by 20 per cent.

This involves little additional investment, so depreciation of their building and shop fittings will be modest.

They anticipate no significant increase in other overhead costs – some additional utility costs for heating, refrigeration, lighting and overheads such as cleaning and property tax.

They anticipate that this will increase their sales by 30 per cent and intend to use the additional space for those items in the greatest demand and for other, higher-mark-up stock. In the past, the COGS averaged 90 per cent of sales revenues. The expansion will be used to provide goods and services that are more profitable than their current product lines, and the COGS is estimated to fall to 80 per cent.

In addition, the company is considering the re-introduction of credit sales. It provided such a facility several years ago, but stopped because it found the effort too great and the rewards inadequate. If reintroduced, its past experience leads Smith's to expect an increase in their sales by a further 20 per cent. Furthermore, they also expect roughly 50 per cent of total sales to be on credit, and to see roughly 5 per cent of credit sales become bad debt losses. Smith's own cost of capital is 9 per cent per annum, or roughly 0.75 per cent for a month's lending. Smith's expects its credit customers to take an average of one month to pay their accounts. Although the company did lose some unknown volume of sales when it stopped credit sales previously, its estimate of the sales increase is the maximum likely, and the effect could well be less.

Profit and loss (typical month)	Current (£)	After expansion (£)	After expansion and credit extension (£)	Remarks
Revenues	100 000	130 000	156 000	Proportionate increases (+30%, and then +20% 'on top' of that increase)
COGS	90 000	104 000	124 800	COGS was 90%, with expansion and higher mark-ups expected to fall to 80%
Cost of credit			3900	Expected credit sales: 50% of (£)156 000 = (£)78 000
			585	Expected bad debt losses: 5% of (£)78 000 = (£)3900 Expected cost: 75% of (£)58 000 = (£)585
Gross profit	10 000	26 000	26 715	
Fixed costs	5000	6000	6000	A crude estimate, fixed costs are unlikely to rise proportionately – utility and other fixed costs (such as property tax) may increase some, but this is likely to be an overestimate.
Profit	5000	20 000	20 715	
Tax	2500	10 000	10 358	Rate = 50%
Net profit	2500	10 000	10 357	

The impact on Smith's cash flow may be assessed:

	Current (£)	After expansion (£)	After expansion and credit extension (£)	Remarks
Annual profit	30 000	120 000	124 290	Monthly profit × 12
+ Depreciation		6000	6000	£500 for 12 months, change from past – these reflect the depreciation charges for the investment in the expansion for the building alterations and new shop fittings.
Inventories				Smith's generally turns its stock over 4 times a month. It has on hand one quarter of monthly COGS invested in its inventories.
Starting	22 500	22 500	22 500	
Ending	22 500	26 000	31 200	The starting inventory is without the expansion; the others then reflect the anticipated increases in sales and stocks needed to support them.
− Change:	0	3500	8700	
Credit sales				With no credit sales, Smith's doesn't need to 'invest' any of its working capital in this area. With credit sales, it is effectively lending half of its annual profits to its customers!
Starting	0	0	0	
Ending	0	0	78 000	
− Change:	0	0	78 000	
Credit purchases	135 000	135 000	135 000	Smith's, like many businesses, uses supplier credit a great deal, typically owing 150% of its monthly COGS. The company policy intends to minimize its own need for its own working capital.
Starting	135 000	156 000	187 000	
Ending	0	21 000	52 000	
+ Change:				
Cash	30 000	143 500	95 790	Profit + Depreciation − Δ Inventory − Δ Credit sales + Δ Credit purchases
Net impact	No change	+113 500 Increase	−47 710 Decrease	

An assessment shows that the expansion of Smith's Grocers is beneficial, with after-tax profits increasing substantially from £30 000 to £120 000. The 30 per cent increase in sales volume has yielded a 400 per cent increase, quadrupling profits. The cash position of Smith's is improved too. With the expansion, Smith's will need to hold greater inventories, and while this might seem to absorb working capital, the fact that Smith's buys on credit expecting to sell stocks within a week and then itself takes an average of six weeks to pay for them means that the company actually benefits and has more working capital rather than less from its inventory and payment policies. So Smith's sees its cash position benefit slightly from depreciating the expanded facilities *and* from having more of its supplier's cash. Thus, the expansion is well-justified on financial grounds as well as marketing ones – increased sales volume and revenue as well as other considerations such as improved facilities, larger and more varied products and services.

The proposed extension of credit offers a more mixed promise. It does act to increase sales, but the relatively low gross profit shows that the expected losses from bad debts and costs for the capital tied up make the policy virtually unprofitable. With expansion, monthly profits increase to £10 000 and the looser credit policy will only improve on that by £350 despite an apparently attractive large monthly sales increase of £26 000. With the proposed extension of credit to its customers, the cash situation will worsen considerably. In this case, substantial monies (£78 000) are now being lent out rather than kept, and losses (£3900 monthly) due to bad debts are incurred. Again, the low gross profit works against credit sales, for the margins offer relatively

little profit to pay for such losses. Even with a 20 per cent gross profit margin, Smith's then has to sell £5 of goods to recover £1 of bad debt. So the small margin on the £26 000 increase in sales has to then compensate for the losses on the larger £78 000 increase in credit used. And there are the costs (nearly £600 monthly) of that lending. Thus, there is a modest increase in profit of roughly 3.5 per cent (£10 357 vs. £10 000) to be made from credit sales. Given the effort and risks involved in setting up and running such a scheme, it is unlikely that these would be sufficient to make credit sales attractive, unless there are other pressures – for example, such policies may be common and competitive pressure may force Smith's to do so, despite the lack of financial appeal.

Questions

1. How much would you trust the numbers used in this analysis?

2. How would you evaluate and perhaps specify the risk that some of them are wrong? (Consider each business initiative separately.)

Balance sheets and fixed assets used in marketing

The distinction between fixed and current assets reflects the need to distinguish between the working capital used within the day-to-day operations and marketing efforts of an organization and those assets used to support those operations and marketing efforts in the longer term. For example, it is necessary to have both materials and manufacturing equipment to use on those materials – but the materials are inventory that is regularly bought and sold, while the equipment remains in the organization's possession. In marketing, a similar situation arises: It may be necessary to promote the product in numerous ways – advertising, discount coupons, trade expositions, etc. – in the day-to-day activities of the organization, but products also need to be developed. Marketing management focuses on the strategic development of 31 product portfolios, product lines, product variants, brands and customer relationships. Without these developments of what may be considered marketing assets, short-term marketing and sales operations will be handicapped. These longer-term developments may well have a presence seen in financial accounts: on the balance sheet. The key issue is whether these have a measurable, marketable value. For example, an organization may purchase a franchise and have the rights to use a brand and product in its operations. These represent an asset. Similarly, new product development can involve expenditure over several years to yield an asset that may then be exploited. This expenditure will often be treated as an expense in the period in which it's made – there are significant tax benefits in doing so, as it effectively shields current profits from taxation. These expenditures may yield a product capable of generating later profit streams, so they are in actuality investments.

Similarly, many marketing efforts create brand identities through effort and expenditure over periods of time. These may also be considered to represent an 'asset' in providing an economically exploitable identity. But valuing such expenditure as an investment is difficult: How can a distinction be made between advertising that promotes current sales and its lingering effect in helping future sales? How can such costs be allocated? The implication is that some of these costs should really be spread over the whole time horizon for which they help sales. If so, these residual effects need some consideration as an asset just as any other that depreciates over time.

Balance sheets are excellent at representing things on the basis of their cost. They are much less effective at presenting things in terms of their value. An example used earlier for current assets should be recalled: Inventory may be carried on the balance sheet on the basis of what it cost to produce or purchase, but it may be obsolete and have no monetary value. While the accounting principle of valuing assets at the lower limit of cost or market value should provide some protection against such cases, it only does so if inventory valuation is comprehensively and critically applied on a regular basis. This may be particularly true for the fixed assets of an organization: They are shown on the books at cost, yet the company keeps them because it believes they can all be exploited to yield greater income now and through their life than if sold off.

The intangible dimensions of marketing – building brand identity, customer relationships, etc. – are almost impossible to effectively value in the first instance, and prove even more difficult to convert into a marketable form; how can a customer relationship be 'sold' to another party to realize its value? Should the organization go into liquidation? Thus, many of the financial interests involved in marketing create intangibles difficult in the first instance to quantify a value for, and impossible to render into a marketable form even if values may be determined.

It might be useful nevertheless to think of a 'marketing' balance sheet in which such intangibles have a presence. This cannot replace the true financial balance sheet but ought to serve a parallel purpose – to formally and honestly assess the long-term marketing 'investments' that may be considered assets for any organization. Some suggestions along these lines are proposed in the following discussion.

While a brand may not show up on a financial balance sheet, it may show up on one used for marketing, but this forces a number of difficult and potentially unwelcome questions to be confronted: Is this to be valued at cost, or should its exploitable market value be used? Most would argue that some idea of the present value of future benefits should be used – but these may not be readily expressed monetarily.

Other marketing assets, such as customer relationship development, may be similarly assessed in terms of their future exploitable value. There may, however, be objections to so doing, for such an attitude reduces everything to issues of pounds and pence. But such is the nature of a balance sheet – and numerous other intangible assets of organizations (staff skill and loyalty, for example) are similarly disregarded or treated in a mercenary way.

Indeed, there is much confusion about the concept of value as distinct from cost. A customer may be asked the 'value' of what they have purchased (or, more to the point, a marketing manager may be asked the value of a customer). In almost every case, the customer will respond by saying that the value of an item was the price they actually paid for it. Yet a moment's reflection would show the fallacy of that perspective. The customer chose to exchange money equal to the item's price in order to obtain it, presumably because they valued it more than the money, or the other things they could have bought with it. This perspective is clear from the basic idea of a demand curve in economics: When prices are high, the quantity demanded is low, but as prices fall and the quantity demanded increases, those first customers remain and enjoy a 'consumer surplus'. They're able to obtain the product which they valued so greatly, and for which they were willing to pay a high price, for the lower price needed to attract customers not so eager to buy the item. Similarly for producers, the most efficient may be able to produce very cheaply, but if prices rise they will then enjoy extra profit on those efficiently produced units.

Developing customer relationships can be a costly exercise, involving time, effort and even the investment in physical facilities to support the relationship and its servicing. The value in terms of current and future sales and profits should exceed current and future costs, else there is little economic justification for it.

Customer relationships and their financial impact

Customer relationships are one of the key assets of a business. Each relationship is unique; its value may vary over time in ways that are hard to predict, and customer relationships are not saleable and can be hard to transfer. Valuing a relationship involves collecting data about customer behaviour and having the financial tools to analyze that data.

Interest in the concept of customer profitability is very strong, with 92 per cent of respondents to a study by the Economist Intelligence Unit with Anderson Consulting across North America, Europe and Asia indicating that they thought customer profitability would be a critically important customer-related performance measure by 2002. The same study found that most companies tracking customer profitability were doing so in a simplistic way, with a focus on the size of transactions, the level of purchases and changes in order volume. Indirect costs were then allocated in proportion to total sales volume to each customer. This reflects the differing perspectives of accountants and marketing managers. For accounting purposes, the *internal* focus is readily understandable: The products have been produced using existing equipment and current staff, and consequently 'absorb' their costs as the relevant overheads. For marketing, an *external* focus is more appropriate: The concern is with sales and the customers making purchases, and the objective is often to extract the maximum benefit from those exchanges over the long term – past, present and future. Under that perspective, the recovery of current overhead costs may be a peripheral consideration. The internal focus of accounting staff on recovering overheads can conflict with the external focus of marketing staff on maximizing sales and profits.

Arriving at an accurate picture of customer profitability is problematic, particularly where direct product costs are a relatively low proportion of total costs. In other words, the higher the proportion of indirect costs (sales expenses, administration and service costs), the more misleading a simple proportional allocation of such costs can be. Different customers use company resources very differently; e.g., inventory holding and delivery requirements, payment terms, order entry and customer and sales support may all vary considerably from customer to customer. Allocating such costs proportionate to volume, as is often done, may well fail to reflect the true pattern of the customer's usage of the company's resources. The allocation of sales and general administration costs is a particular concern, as this item has grown significantly, now representing 20 to 40 per cent of the total costs in some *Fortune* 500 companies and continuing to grow much more rapidly than product costs (in one case, growing almost four times as quickly as manufacturing costs between 1985 and 1989).

Accurately assessing customer profitability may be problematic, particularly where product costs are a relatively low proportion of the overall costs of serving any given customer. All sales involve a mix of both goods and services, and the costs of *both* must be accurately assessed and allocated between the organization's customers. So long as customers use the organization's services proportionately to the volume of goods they purchase, traditional cost allocation methods used by accountants will render fairly accurate allocations of the service overhead costs between customers. This is considering each product not as a single entity but instead as a 'bundle' of identifiable goods and support services. Bundling in marketing usually considers the combination of two products that may have a natural affinity for the consumer – strawberries and cream, for instance. But virtually all products carry an invisible bundle of supporting services that may constitute some of the cost of producing, selling and delivering the product. A difficulty arises, however, when customers vary significantly in the services they require in support of the goods bought. In these cases, the traditional cost allocation approaches, which treat service support as a general overhead to be distributed evenly across all goods produced, fails to reflect the uneven distribution of service demands that actually arise. In these cases, those customers who place fewer demands on support service effectively pay more for their goods, implicitly subsidizing those customers with heavy demands whose product price fails to fully reflect that dimension of the service costs. To some extent, the variability in service demand may reflect product variability: quality variations, warrantee requirements and the like. These may quite properly be averaged out between customers as a form of 'insurance' in which these expected, but randomly occurring, costs are spread across all customers. But difficulties arise when the variations in the service demands arise not from the product sold or its performance but variations in customer behaviour.

For example, some products have a small element of service associated with them. Commodities such as a loaf of bread, bottle of milk or packet of writing paper would be typical examples. For these, there is little service involved: The commodity itself offers little variability and both buyer and seller hold well-understood expectations of the product. The service component may exist in ancillary aspects of the product mix – the packaging or delivery of the goods, for example – but the products themselves offer little scope for contention between buyers and sellers. Other products consist almost entirely of services, with little goods involved in their production or consumption. A service such as hairdressing would be a typical example. For this, there is little physical product involved: The service itself involves the application of the employee's time and skill, but little physical product. In hairdressing, there may be small and inexpensive amounts of shampoo, hair gels and mousses, colouring, etc., but the bulk of the effort and cost arise from the staff time used. To the extent that prices may be varied to reflect the effort involved, these relatively fixed labour costs can be effectively allocated between customers – thus, a customer who requires twice the labour time of another may be charged proportionately more. But if such pricing differentials are not possible, these more labour-intensive services will consume more resource than paid for. The pricing of products that involve a more balanced mix of physical goods and intangible services may be very problematic, for the price may be based entirely on the product involved and the service dimension given little consideration. A personal computer may fall into this category. An experienced and knowledgeable user may buy one and need virtually no support in installing or operating it, thus putting no load on the product service facilities. On the other hand, an inexperienced and inept user may pay the same price as the experienced one and place far heavier demands on the service facilities provided. In this example, products are sold in a highly competitive and very price-conscious market to consumers who differ very widely in their understanding of the product and the service support they consequently require. In other markets, customer behaviour may vary significantly, with aggressive customers demanding more extensive support *and* lower prices than more passive customers. These aggressive customers may demand special packaging, delivery and service, as well as being tough negotiators on price. The balance of power between customer and supplier is likely to affect the profitability of their relationships; the stronger the customer, the more concessions they can wring from their suppliers and the less profitable that relationship may be.

This goes beyond the aforementioned desire to break down profit and loss statement entries for overheads into more precise categories for assessing product profitability – at the extreme it goes to the question of the profitability of each product for any given customer.

An incorrect allocation of indirect costs can lead to a misleading picture of customer profitability.

New IT tools and analysis techniques can help companies better understand the profitability of their customers. Customer data can now be collected in data warehouses, and new financial tools, particularly activity-based costing (ABC), are helping companies understand customer profitability. Where general corporate overheads are substantial and customers are very different in their purchasing behaviour (particularly where the demands that customers make are not proportional to the quantities they buy), ABC is appropriate. ABC examines the actual time and costs spent on sales and support activities associated with specific customers, and enables organizations to apportion more accurately the real costs of serving individual customers. This gives a better basis for managerial action by enabling managers to focus their attention and energy on improving activities that will have the biggest impact on the bottom line.

Product costing needs to expand beyond the traditional perspective in which the direct costs were only those of the physical goods produced to include an element of service costing too. This is essential (and actually done) in service organizations and is also becoming important in those industries where the mix of goods and services sold increasingly demands more service in the balance. The role of marketing in this is self-evident, for the price setting in such circumstances may need to shift from the easily implemented and usually noncontroversial 'one price for all customers' to the more difficult pricing based on discriminating between high- and low-service-demand customers. The acquisition of goods may bring little or no appreciation of the associated services or their costs, and great customer resistance to any pricing scheme that specifically charges for these. In the computer example mentioned above, vendors may circumvent this through the use of telephone support services that charge customers for the time used. Thus, customers who need little support pay little or nothing for these services, while the more demanding ones do contribute to the cost of the services they require. In effect, an 'unbundling' of product and support services has been achieved, and the acquisition of the product no longer brings with it an unlimited right to the formerly bundled service. Aggressive customers may be particularly resistant to paying the higher prices needed to defray the additional costs their service demands impose. Marketing managers need to assess customer demands for *both* the goods and services used, and identify mechanisms for pricing that more fully reflect the true total costs of serving each customer. Where there are significant differentials, mechanisms for unbundling those dimensions susceptible to varying demands may be financially beneficial in generating revenues from those with heavy demands and in attracting cost-conscious customers unwilling to subsidize the more intensive service users.

Profit or value?

However, customer profit – whether in a single period or over a relationship life-time – might not be the best foundation on which to base decisions about customer strategies. As a measure, profit is subject to distortions. Accountants and financial consultants are now arguing that it is value, not profits, that companies should be measuring. It has been clear for some time that it is possible to perform very well on conventional accounting measures but destroy value. Accounting measures of profit can be misleading, showing apparent growth whilst providing minimal or negative returns to shareholders. Customer value analysis serves as a valuable adjunct to traditional accounting measures of profitability.

Accounting measures of profit deduct financing costs, and accountants regularly differentiate between organizations that fund themselves through equity and those that rely on debt with interest payments reflecting a cost of capital i.e., EBIT. This isn't the full story, for even equity has a cost, but in a totally debt-financed organization it seems that the cost of capital would be fully incorporated within a profit calculation, while for other firms there would be a clear understanding that even a totally equity-financed firm would have expectations of risk-adjusted returns. Traditional profit measures do not necessarily reflect value creation. It is only if the return on capital exceeds its cost of capital that an investment creates value. The critical difference between measuring performance using accounting profit that reflects *average returns* and measuring using value is that the latter does take into account the *specific, marginal* costs of serving a customer when calculating returns on the organization's 'investment' in the customer relationship. Value is only created when marginal returns exceed the marginal costs, a more demanding requirement than that of making an accounting profit – something that may occur even if marginal costs exceed marginal revenues because of earlier, even greater profits.

The economic value of a customer

Applying this concept of value creation to customers enables companies to think about the economic value, rather than the profitability, of their customers. This is particularly important where a company has to make a significant investment in order to serve a customer or group of customers. In order to determine the economic value of a customer, the cost of capital associated with the customer has to be established. This is a function of the amount of capital invested in serving that customer and the cost of capital. This might include investment in bespoke products and consequently stock, custom paperwork or software, or even the cost of time. Customers who require significant individual investment have a higher cost of capital than customers who do not. Using accounting profit rather than a value measure in such cases will tend to overstate the amount of shareholder value the company is creating by doing business with high-investment customers. In this case, direct costs of serving a particularly demanding customer are not properly allocated. That is to say, the COGS fails to include significant elements of the direct services and support required. In a bespoke product, the example is a customized one used for no other customers – clearly, those customization costs should be a *direct* cost and are not by any consideration a general overhead. If a customer requires investment to support their requirements, this too should be considered a cost that can be specifically allocated.

When companies apply this thinking to their customer portfolio, it is likely that they will find a dispersion of customer economic value. It may be that some customers will be yielding more than the company's weighted average cost of capital (WACC), and some will be yielding less. While it might be thought that so long as the return on the total customer portfolio is higher than the company's WACC, the company is creating value for its shareholders, this thinking is erroneous, for it implies that the company may be using more costly finance to serve less rewarding customers. An economic analysis would suggest that the average returns vs. average costs would still be positive for a while *after* the marginal costs exceed the marginal returns and would thus lower the average return. This is a more stringent perspective than the focus on averages. But the company can increase the returns to its shareholders by attracting and retaining more value-creating customers, and also by improving the performance of its existing customers, in particular those customers who yield less than they cost to serve. Figure 17.1 illustrates the principle of shareholder value creation. The higher the risk associated with a customer, the higher the return required by the company to create value for its shareholders. Customers in the area below the line may appear to be profitable, but are destroying value. Only customers above the line create value. As Figure 17.1 indicates, there are many routes to value creation. Nevertheless, there will be times when highly risky customers may fill a role in a well-considered customer 'portfolio', just as highly risky investments may also be included in an investor's financial portfolio.

The cost of capital can be reduced either by reducing the *amount* of capital used in the customer relationship or by reducing the *cost* of that capital. Here, the notion of customer relationships becomes important. It may not always be possible to reduce the amount of capital needed to look after a customer, although sometimes customers will agree to bear certain capital costs such as equipment or software, which is used only for a customer's own, bespoke products. However, it may be

Figure 17.1

The customer portfolio and value creation

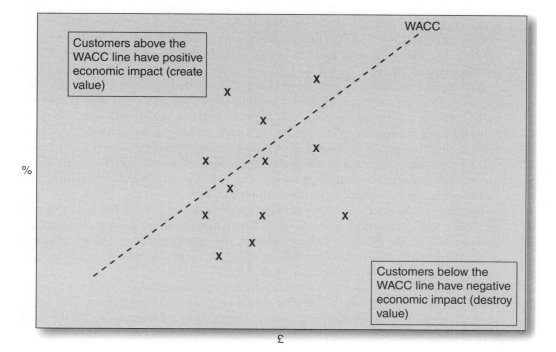

possible to reduce the cost of capital. The amount that a company has to pay for its equity or debt is a reflection of the amount of risk that investors perceive they are taking on by lending to that company. If the risk is reduced, the cost of borrowing is reduced.

It is important not to confuse the cost of capital *used* with the returns on the *use* of that capital. In finance, it is common to raise funds for investment in risky projects, and the perceived riskiness of an organization will be affected by the *average* riskiness of the projects in which those funds are invested. If I borrow money at 5 per cent, that is my cost of capital regardless of whether I then invest it in blue-chip shares or the South Sea Bubble, but if the balance of the investment portfolio includes few blue-chip shares and many speculative investments, that risk will be recognized by investors. Companies in highly volatile markets are naturally riskier than those in stable markets – with corresponding differences in their costs of capital – and returns to equity investors are generally lower for companies in stable markets and higher for those subject to greater fluctuations. While true for markets, this perspective is more difficult when applied to customers.

In the context of a customer relationship, risk is about the *volatility* of the returns from that customer. The more volatile the returns, the riskier the customer. Sudden variability in buying patterns cause difficulties for the retailer, and unexpected up-swings can be just as difficult to deal with as unexpected downturns. This is just as, or even more, true for manufacturers whose equipment may be tied up with other customers' work and who may have difficulty with their own suppliers in getting sufficient materials in a timely fashion. A customer who buys regularly is more valuable than one who buys the same amount but whose buying pattern is unpredictable. If the variability in demand can be made predictable or controllable, much of the risk due to the randomness of its occurrence may be managed out of the system. A proactive approach that tries to ascertain customer intentions beforehand may be one approach to coping with the natural fluctuations in demand, not by trying to forecast them but instead by trying to obtain early warnings of those variations that create risk.

Implementing relationship management entails certain changes in the way in which companies view their customers and manage their contact with them. These are summarized below.

A customer relationship perspective will shift towards customer value analysis and away from product profitability or single-period customer profitability analysis. Value analysis is forward-looking, unlike profit analysis, which relies on historical data. Existing management accounting systems may have to be adjusted to accommodate this change. To analyze the economic value of their customers, companies will need to make forward projections of income, costs and risk. This will entail investment in data warehouses to collect and manage customer information, and customer-facing technology to facilitate communication.

Positive management of customer relationships as an asset of the business will mean developing customer strategies over the lifetime of the customer relationship. In order to manage all aspects of the value of the customer, these strategies should deal with maximizing returns, minimizing risks and obtaining benefits from the customer relationship (Christopher and Ryals, 1999).

Customer relationships do involve significant cultivation and represent a real investment of marketing effort, one that would be worthy of recognition – for there are real, tangible costs to building these intangible but economically valuable and exploitable assets.

Table 17.2
Balance sheet and implications for marketing

Balance sheet	This year (£)	Last year (£)	Implications for marketing
Fixed assets (at cost minus accumulated depreciation)	110000	120000	Fixed assets are the long-term capital used by the organization, in the form generally of physical facilities – buildings, machinery, equipment, shop fittings, etc. Intellectual property such as patents is included, as are such things as acquired 'rights' to manufacture products or use a franchise. Whether a 'brand' constitutes a fixed asset is somewhat controversial. And the suggestion that customer relationships too are assets is one totally alien to accounting, though any marketing manager would regard these as critical.
Current assets			The basic criterion is whether the asset will last longer than one year, or be fully used up or sold in less time.
Inventories	25000	20000	Inventories are goods produced and held for later sale. They may be created on purpose to decouple sales activities and production processes, or to provide an immediately available supply to support sales. There are two dimensions of particular interest for marketing – the volume and variety of stock available. The balance sheet simply shows the total value – a disaggregated view may be more useful. One useful relationship is inventory turnover – how quickly these stocks could be sold.
Creditors (minus bad debt allowance)	15000	10000	Creditors are customers who have bought on credit and this reflects the monies owed to the organization. Credit policies may be a critical issue in supporting sales – with 'loose' credit stimulating sales. Such policies have associated cost – first is the opportunity cost of the monies lent: they could be deposited in a bank and earning interest. A second cost is the possibility of non-payment – bad debt.
Cash and securities	2000	2000	These funds are almost immediately available to settle the organization's own debts and liabilities.
Total assets	152000	150000	
Liabilities			Current liabilities are those that will demand payment within one year – long-term liabilities are those that do not have to be paid that quickly.

(Continues)

Table 17.2
(Continued)

Balance sheet	This year (£)	Last year (£)	Implications for marketing
Current portion of long-term debt	6000	6000	While the bulk of long-term liabilities do not require payment in the current year, there is usually some obligation to service the debt by making periodic payments on the debt. This figure represents the amounts due in the current period.
Debtors	12000	10000	The organization may have bought on credit itself. This represents the amounts owed. This may be of some interest to marketing if the credit taken on purchases is reflected in higher purchase costs that will be reflected in higher COGS in the profit and loss, and lower profits.
Long-term debt	20000	22000	The outstanding balance of the long-term debt excluding the portion currently payable. The long-term debt represents borrowings and reflects the organization's financial strategy – whether to use debt or equity in funding its operations. Debt incurs fixed payments, while equity does not.
Share capital	100000	100000	Organizations typically incorporate and have shareholders who have invested. The share capital describes the sums of money so invested.
Retained earnings	14000	12000	Retained earnings are profits earned in previous periods that have been kept by the organization for its own investments and to support its future activities. Such profits could have been paid to the shareholders as dividends, but most organizations find that keeping these for reinvestment is more effective than having to raise new equity funding or borrowing.
Total liabilities and equity	152000	150000	

Marketing decisions and their financial effects

The marketing mix may be used as a framework to describe the financial ramifications of common marketing decisions. This provides a comprehensive overview of both operational and strategic issues. One perspective may be seen in Figure 17.2 [taken from Wilson (1999) and revised slightly] that shows contrasting orientations taken by marketing-dominated and finance-dominated companies. It illustrates the intersection of concerns between marketing and financial managers, with finance tending to emphasize the issues on the right side [return on investment (ROI) and those factors that affect it] and marketing the ones on the left side (market penetration and related factors). A more balanced view would be more beneficial for the organization as a whole – where one dominates, the other may not be given due consideration.

The objective in taking a balanced perspective is to ensure that the relative concerns of both financial and marketing managers are mutually understood, and that the effects of decisions in each area for the other may be more fully appreciated within the decision-making process. To assist in this, a commonly used framework within marketing employs the 'four Ps': *product, price, promotion* and *place*. These foci describe the major decisions confronting marketing managers and will thus provide a context for the application of the tools financial analysts may apply.

Product

A key decision in marketing is the identification and development of products for markets. Marketing research and product development are essential elements in the marketing mix and may represent a significant demand for finance. Some examples of the activities subsumed in this aspect of the marketing mix are those concerned with identifying what products to produce and sell:

a. New products to be introduced, or old ones to be withdrawn or improved.

b. Product ranges, lines and portfolios.

c. Product positioning vis-à-vis competitors, direct competition or differentiation.

d. Branding.

e. Product design/performance characteristics.

Figure 17.2
Marketing vs. financial orientations (taken from Wilson, 1999)

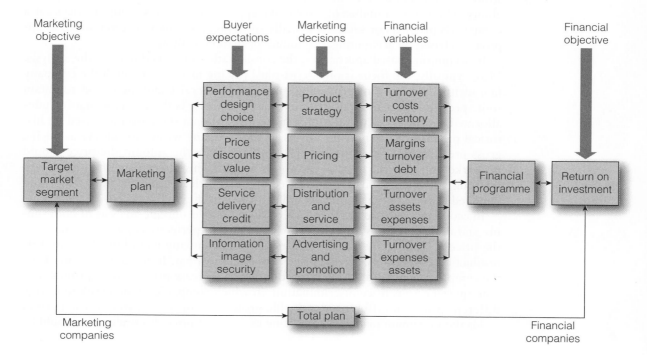

This investment in marketing is made with a view to potential returns from the successful exploitation of the products later. Similarly, marketing research that helps understand markets and their needs is also clearly a form of investment, though quantifying the economic returns to such studies may be virtually impossible. Marketing information does have value, but this is derived from its subsequent use. Product development may then act on this information and yield a new (or updated) product with better potential for being profitable than if no such study were undertaken.

The issue is one of balancing the costs of market research and product development against the potential economic benefits. In this there may be a number of analytical tools useful to assist in managing the risks involved in market analysis and for assessing the attractiveness of alternative product investments.

Make-or-buy decisions

Many businesses are now considering 'outsourcing' – the use of external suppliers to provide goods or services that could be, or have been, provided within the organization. While there are numerous issues involved in the decision – capacity loading, staff attitudes and morale, and control over the outsourced goods and services – it very often hinges on an assessment of the costs and returns to in-house or outsourced provision.

New product introduction

Businesses also need to consider the implications of new product intervention by modelling them.

Price

The price of a product is one of the most important decisions made. There will be strategic implications, but the usual effects relate to short-term volume and profitability. There are a number of alternative approaches to the setting of prices for a company's products or services. Broadly speaking, these may be categorized as approaches based on accounting, economics or market analysis.

In accounting-based approaches, the consideration of costs dominate the analysis. Most typically, the focus is on a 'cost-plus' pricing method in which the company first identifies the cost of producing some good or service and then seeks to obtain some premium over that cost. In most cases, the base is the full cost that includes allocated overheads. The additional mark-up is often a standard one based on historical practice or on industry norms. If the company wishes to achieve a specific gross profit margin, that too may be used to dictate the amount the price should be marked-up over the costs of the goods bought. This policy may often be seen in retailing, in which goods are purchased and then priced using a standard mark-up intended to recover the overheads and provide a profit.

In economic approaches, there is a reliance on an economic analysis of both supply and demand curves as seen by the company. In perfectly competitive markets, the price is dictated by market factors, and the company would produce until its production costs rise above the price consumers will pay. In monopolistic markets, the company would effectively restrict output to increase prices and its profitability. One special case is price discrimination, in which companies would seek to charge different prices to different identifiable groups of consumers so that each group yields the maximum profit possible. One example of price discrimination would be

Process in action Smith's Grocers (cont.) – outsourcing

Make or buy, part 1

Smith's Grocers is considering outsourcing its cleaning services. At present, the company employs its own team of cleaners. During the day, shelf-stackers are regularly used to deal with any minor cleaning demands (breakages, spills, etc.) in addition to their regular duties, but once the store closes the shelves are restocked and the store prepared for the next day's business. In the morning, before a day's trading, a team of cleaners then undertakes the major cleaning – sweeping, mopping and polishing so that the store is clean and presentable.

At present, Smith's employs 5 people for 3 hours per day, 6 days per week at a cost of £5 per hour. These staff are entitled to employee benefits such as 2 weeks paid holiday per year, pension contributions, sick-leave entitlements and discounts on purchases. The company's accountants estimate that these add another 40 per cent to the wage costs. The company has approached a cleaning contractor and been given estimates of monthly costs for cleaning. Should it choose to employ these contractors, it would have to transfer the cleaners to other duties or dismiss them. If cleaning staff are suitable for other work there are likely to be little or no costs in redeploying them; the retraining involved would have to be done for any new employee taking such a position. If no other work is available, the costs per employee dismissed would be of the order of £500 each for their accrued unpaid holiday and sick leave and statutory redundancy payments. The company estimates that other work can be found for three of the five but not the remaining two.

Financial assessment:

Current monthly cleaning costs:

$$5 \text{ people} \times 3 \text{ hours} \times 6 \text{ days} \times 4.3 \text{ weeks/month} \times £5 \text{ hour} \times 1.4 \text{ overhead rate} = £2709$$

Contractor proposal: Redi-Kleen will provide a cleaning team (size unspecified) to provide cleaning to the required specifications, finishing before store opening but requiring free access at any earlier time. They require a 1-year contract, with 3 months' notification if it is not to be renewed, and will charge Smith's £2 500 per month.

This offers Smith's an opportunity to save some £200 a month on its cleaning costs or £2400 per year. Against that saving, Smith's would have to set the change over costs that are expected to be £1 000 for the two employees it does not think will take other jobs within the company. The net benefit for the first year's operation would be £1 400.

Make or buy, part 2

After the first year's operations, which have proven broadly satisfactory, Redi-Kleen have approached Smith's with their contract for the second year. Smith's are now surprised to see the monthly fee increased by 15 per cent to £2 875 per month.

The savings they'd initially gained from the outsourcing now appear to be threatened with ensuing higher costs than if they had continued with their own in-house cleaning.

Smith's managers reconsider the situation. They could restart their own cleaning services. Wage costs will have risen by 5 per cent, so the monthly costs of running their own services would now be £2844, offering a potential benefit. Against that should be set the costs of advertising, interviewing and training five new employees – costs estimated at roughly £150 each, or a total of £750.

The restarting of the cleaning service would then offer the company some modest savings of roughly £350 per year, but the start-up cost of £750 means that Smith's would take more than 2 years before recouping those costs.

Questions

1. What are the practical dangers of subcontracting in a situation such as this?

2. Should financial return be the only consideration?

Process in action new product introduction

A new product has been developed and is proposed for introduction. The question of its potential profitability and economic attractiveness has been raised. The product will cost £250 000 to introduce, inclusive of all necessary equipment, staff training, vendor support, introductory promotions and initial advertising. The product has a 5-year life expectancy and during that time is expected to yield sales revenues of £300 000 in the first year increasing by £100 000 annually until they end in the fifth year, with direct costs of 70 per cent of revenues and allocatable overheads (advertising, warranty support, management, etc.) of £75 000 per annum. The new equipment will be depreciated by £20 000 per annum and have no salvage value at the end of the period. The company pays 40 per cent tax on its profits. Similar projects in the past have been evaluated using a 15 per cent discount rate.

The table provides a time-phased analysis of the impact of introducing the new product. It shows the sales revenues in each year based on the starting volume and projected growth, the associated

New product assessment		Year			
	1	2	3	4	5
Sales revenues (£)	300	400	500	600	700
Direct costs (£)	180	240	300	360	420
Gross profit (£)	120	160	200	240	280
Selling and administrative (£)	75	75	75	75	75
Depreciation (£)	20	20	20	20	20
Profit loss (£)	25	65	105	145	185
Tax (£)	10	26	42	58	74
Profit (loss) after tax (£)	15	39	63	87	111
Cash (£)	35	59	83	107	131

direct production, distribution and selling costs, and the gross profit. The fixed costs for the selling and administrative overheads and depreciation are deducted to yield the profits, from which taxes are deducted to yield the after-tax profits. The cash flow due to the new product is then determined by adding the depreciation to the after-tax profits.

The cash flow generated by the product can then be compared to the costs of undertaking the project.

➔

A simple comparison might just total the cash flow from the project and compare the total income to the start-up costs: Total income is £415 000, while the start-up costs are £250 000 yielding an apparent net gain of £165 000.

But the difficulty in this simplistic approach is its failure to appreciate that the benefits are spread over a period of 5 years' time, while the start-up costs are paid beforehand and could have been earning interest instead. What is necessary is to look at the future cash flows and ask what would be their equivalent value at the time the product was introduced. This value will be lower due to the time value of money. Applying the discounting rate of 15 per cent, the implication is that cash received in 1 year's time would be worth less than its full value. If the organization invested £100 and earned 15 per cent interest on it, in 1 year's time it would have £115; in 2 years, £132; in 3 years, £152, etc. Conversely, if the company were offered £100 in a year's time, that money would be worth only £87 today, for the company might invest that £87 and the interest earned over the year would bring it up to £100. Thus, the 'discount factor' of 0.87 would describe the present value of a cash inflow in 1 year's time for a discount rate of 15 per cent. For this product, the projected discounted cash flows (in £) are:

Discount factor (0.15)		$1/(1.15)$	$1/(1.15)^2$	$1/(1.15)^3$	$1/(1.15)^4$	$1/(1.15)^5$
		0.870	0.756	0.658	0.572	0.497
Cash × Discount factor = Discounted income		$35 \times 0.87 =$ 30	45	55	61	65
Total discounted income	256					
Cost	250					
Net benefit	6					

The comparison is now much closer – the undiscounted cash flows seemed to be very much greater than the product introduction costs. But this consideration of the impact of time and alternative investments that might be made significantly reduces the economic attractiveness of this proposal. The total discounted income is now reduced to only £256 000 compared to the costs of £250 000, leaving a discounted benefit – the net present value (or NPV) – of only £6000. So long as the NPV is positive, the proposal is considered viable, but there may well be other proposals with higher NPVs competing for limited investment capital.

Questions

1. Would you invest in this new product?

2. What other information would you like to have to help you decide?

'peak' vs. 'off-peak' pricing – this may have the objective of maximizing profits as well as attempting to shift demand from peak periods to off-peak periods.

With market analysis, the company will generally know its own costs but go beyond those to consider its customers and competitors in determining pricing policy. This may result in a variety of alternative pricing strategies. In practice, companies may use 'reference' pricing, based on the prices charged by their competitors, and set their price relative to the competitor's given issues such as perceived quality, availability, etc. Other approaches include a 'skimming' policy, in which a product is introduced at a relatively high price, which is then reduced once those people willing to pay the high price have been satisfied. A similar policy is 'penetration' pricing, in which a relatively low price is charged to achieve a higher sales volume and market share than might otherwise be the case, or to attempt to break up existing buying patterns. Such a policy should be considered very carefully since it may induce competitors to reduce their price to retain market share. The consequence of such a response is that neither company may earn the profits it might normally expect.

One interesting development is the idea of target pricing, and target costing based on that information. Here, a new product is assessed against consumer expectations, and priced to fall into the range of prices acceptable to consumers. With target costing, this analysis is carried one step (or several) back into the organization. If the consumers are only willing to pay a relatively low price for the product or service, its producers might then ask how the costs may be reduced to allow that demand to be met profitably. This may revolutionize product design, with greater interest in cost as a critical design dimension along with product performance, quality and other traditional engineering concerns. In the traditional approach, it is usually assumed that the product is defined first and then a price determined for it from consumer behaviour – a more integrated approach sees product design and pricing as interrelated.

All pricing policies have financial implications. Some plainly look at maximizing sales volumes or sales revenues, and these might be considered as possibly suboptimal since they consider only one aspect of the overall impact. Besides these measures of sales, a well-founded decision should also consider the costs associated with generating sales and the potential profitability.

Breakeven analysis

One of the most basic analyses of pricing is a breakeven analysis. In this approach, an organization simply needs to identify the fixed costs associated with developing and producing a product, its direct production and distribution costs and the proposed price for which it would sell. The product 'breaks even' when the sales volume yields total revenues that exceed the total costs.

Promotion

Promotion involves a wide range of competitive activities used to increase sales and to attract and hold customers. Promotional activities include advertising, public relations and customer-oriented sales promotions. Promotional activities may be directed at customers or at the distribution channel with the intent of increasing demand or improving product availability. Some promotional activities may involve discounts that affect the revenues from sales, but most are more appropriately considered product-related overheads. The introduction of a new product will typically be accompanied by a number of promotional activities – advertising directed at the product's end-buyers, point-of-sale materials for retailers, training programmes and

Process in action new product introduction (cont.)

Consider the earlier example. The product had start-up costs of £250 000 and allocated overheads of £375 000 (£75 000 for 5 years) for a total fixed cost of £625 000. The product's direct costs were described as being 60 per cent of revenues, but a more effective approach would consider the actual purchase or production costs instead. These have been estimated as £100 per unit. The price initially considered is £165 (providing a mark-up roughly equal to a 60 per cent COGS-to-price ratio).

How many units would need to be sold in order for the organization to break even on this product?

The breakeven point would look at the contribution (price-direct costs per unit) each unit sold makes towards recouping the start-up and overhead costs. Each unit sold thus yields £65 contribution to repaying the £625 000 'invested'. At that rate,

the company would need to sell some 9616 units to break even.

Breakeven point:
625 000 / (165 − 100) = 9616

If the actual sales are greater than 9616, the product will yield a profit; if the actual sales are less than that, a loss will result. This breakeven point provides a threshold against which forecast sales can be assessed. In most instances, the introduction will depend on exceeding the breakeven point by a healthy margin.

Looking back at the projected sales revenues of £300 000 in the first year, rising by £100 000 annually, we can estimate the first year's sales volume to be roughly 1800, with annual increases of approximately 600 units for a total sales volume over the 5 years of about 15 100 units, well above the breakeven point. This analysis is illustrated below.

With the identified relationships, the breakeven point is exceeded by roughly 5500 units, yielding a contribution of £65 per unit that becomes profit once the overheads have been fully recovered. The total profit then is £357 500.

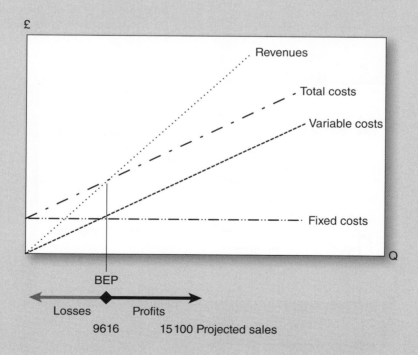

Issues

This may be used to judge the financial impact of differing prices on the breakeven point – higher prices mean that fewer units need be sold in order to recover the investment. Lower prices would dictate that it would take a longer period. But the process ignores the time needed to generate sales. This is significant for two reasons: future returns should be discounted particularly if several years' revenues are needed to reach the breakeven point; and the time may exceed either the productive life of the facilities used or the product's life cycle.

Caveats

The breakeven model is very simple and straightforward in application, but its results need to be carefully considered. Is the volume of sales required to break even feasible? In the example, the product life was sufficiently long to allow these costs to be recovered, but if its life were much shorter, the sales volume would then be inadequate. If the price were much lower, the volume of sales needed to break even might exceed the life of the product substantially.

A further difficulty arises from the use of fixed prices and unit costs. Basic economic theory suggests that prices need to fall in order to induce customers to buy more. The implications are that the total revenue doesn't simply keep increasing at a constant rate, and that the effect of reducing prices to stimulate further sales would cause total revenues to 'flatten' and fall. Similarly, direct costs might be subject to variations – perhaps exhibiting 'learning curve' effects in which the unit costs decrease as experience is gained and allow for more efficient production – and the fixed costs may prove to be quasi-fixed and exhibit a step-like behaviour with fixed increments of capital required to accommodate capacity increases. This more complex analysis is illustrated below.

In this more complex environment, the breakeven analysis may still be used, recognizing the effects of the non-linear relationships – the flat fixed costs have been replaced by a set of fixed costs that increase in steps as increases in the sales volume make additional capital investment necessary. The variable cost is no longer a simple line as would be the case for a constant production cost, but now curves and becomes 'flatter' as the learning effects reduce unit costs. The total cost is now a stepped curved line, against which the total revenues are plotted as they increase and then decrease to reflect the impact that lower prices and increasing volumes sold have on total

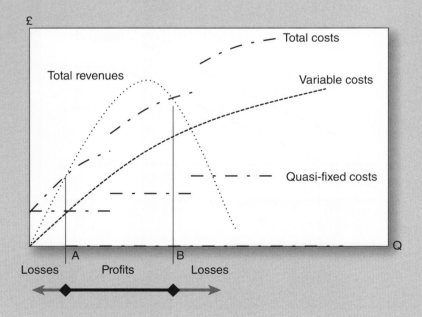

revenues. The result is a range of output which allows the organization to break even; below point 'A' costs exceed revenues, as they do above point 'B', but for the points between 'A' and 'B', the total revenues exceed costs and the organization breaks even. The profit-maximizing point may be identified where the difference between total revenues and costs is greatest.

Questions

1. Can we expect yearly income from a new product to be linear?

2. What historical data can we use to predict non-linearity?

3. How can we predict what is called the 'product life cycle' to use in this technique?

Process in action advertising

One controversy arises over the benefit of advertising: Do organizations really benefit from this expenditure? This issue may be addressed in accounting terms. The analysis proceeds by investigating the impact advertising has on increasing

revenues relative to the costs involved in both the advertising and in supporting those sales.

In this example, advertising does increase sales substantially, by 20 per cent, a gain of £20 000 in revenues compared to the advertising costs of only £5000. This apparent gain is not actually realized because it ignores the costs of providing the product – the relevant increase is not from revenues but instead the gross profits. Advertising has increased these by £2000, which is less than the

Profit and loss (typical month)	Without advertising (£)	With advertising (£)	
Revenues	100 000	120 000	Advertising increases sales by £20 000
COGS	90 000	108 000	COGS increases proportionately. Note: Some promotional activities may involve disproportionate changes – discounting or higher sales commissions, for example.
Gross profit	10 000	12 000	
Fixed costs, general overheads	5000	5000	The general overheads will not be affected by increased advertising.
Advertising	0	5000	Cost of advertising.
Profit	5000	2000	
Tax	2500	1000	Rate = 50%
Net profit	2500	1000	

costs of advertising of £5000, so the organization is then worse off despite the increased sales volume and revenues.

Question

1. Once again, how can we determine the relationship between advertising spend and sales?

dealer incentives for wholesalers or intermediaries, etc. These consequently may be considered overheads that can be allocated to that product specifically, though no individual customer or sale can be identified with those costs. If more products are introduced, the organization will have more of these promotional activities to perform and pay for. Some promotional activities may not be associated with specific products – such things as public relations that have the intent of promoting the organization as a whole rather than any specific product. In those cases, the promotional activities would constitute part of the general marketing overheads.

Sales incentives case

Sales commissions are frequently used to help motivate salespeople in their work. These may be considered a direct cost because these commissions are directly linked to the sales volumes achieved – if they increase, so too do the costs of selling the goods. In many cases, sales incentives operate on a sliding scale (see table below); for example, a salesman may be paid a base salary plus an incentive of 5 per cent for all sales over £10000 per month, 10 per cent for sales over £15000 and 20 per cent on sales greater than £20000 monthly. So long as the gross profit margin is greater than 20 per cent, the organization will benefit from these incentives.

Profit and loss	Salesperson basic salary (£)	Salesperson 5 per cent commission (£)	Salesperson 10 per cent commission (£)	Salesperson 20 per cent commission (£)
Revenues	5000	12500	17500	22500
COGS (70% of revenues)	3500	8750	12250	15750
Sales commissions		125	500	1250
Gross profit	1500	3625	4750	5500
Fixed costs	500	500	500	500
Profit	1000	3125	4250	5000
Tax	500	1562.5	2125	2500
Net profit	500	1562.5	2125	2500

The increasing sales commission percentages are intended to motivate salespeople; by looking at the midpoint of each sales range, it can be seen that the sales commissions increase substantially. The profits also increase, but not so much as the salespeople's commissions.

The key is to recognize that the costs of promotion are paid not from the increase in total revenues but from the increase in gross profits. This is true both for fixed, general promotional costs involved in advertising, public relations, etc. and for variable, sale-specific promotional costs such as price discounts and sales commissions.

Place

Place is the 'P' in the mix that reflects the distribution aspects of marketing: how the product gets to the customer (what kind of channel to use, how many outlets or channels should be used and where and when should the product be available).

The consolidation of inventories and the reductions in risks due to individual operations carries significant financial attractions. Against those may be set the increased possibility of store-level stock outs and a heightened need for point-of-sale IT systems that can closely monitor stock levels and automatically generate replenishment orders, dynamically considering demand patterns.

Process in action Smith's Wholesalers distribution

Smith's Wholesalers is considering changing its distribution network through increasing the number of outlets from six to nine. At present, Smith's uses two warehouse facilities that receive incoming goods from manufacturers, hold them in storage and then ship daily replenishment stocks to their retailers as required by sales. The increase in the number of outlets will increase a number of costs to the company: the number of staff will increase by 50 per cent, the shop rental costs will also increase by 50 per cent, etc. Against those increases there are a number of other fixed costs that will remain unchanged – the general administrative costs will not be affected, nor will Smith's advertising or marketing that exist independent of store operations (e.g., introductory offers to attract people to the newly opened stores would be attributable promotional costs for each store, while Smith's advertisements in the national press would not be). Distribution costs, however, are not so clear. They will increase, as more goods will be handled, but the increase will be less than 50 per cent because there will possibly be economies of scale and lower costs from consolidating risks.

Consider one of Smith's warehouses. At present it serves three of the six stores. Each store averages sales of £1.5 million annually, with a standard deviation of £0.25 million. In aggregate, these demands on each warehouse are for an average of £4.5 million with a standard deviation of £0.43 million. The demand on the warehouse from the three stores is thus relatively lower than the demands seen by the individual stores. The underlying explanation is that fluctuations in the demand experienced by a particular store may be offset by variations in other stores, and the larger the number of stores, the more stable the pattern of demand for the central service supporting them.

If Smith's added a fourth store (also with annual average sales of £1.5 million having a standard deviation of £0.25 million) to the warehouse's operations, the variability of the demand on the warehouse would increase too, but only from £0.43 to £0.5 million.

This allows Smith's to make significant savings on its inventory stocks. If each store was required to hold sufficient inventory to provide protection against selling out for 90 per cent of its products, they each would then have to hold £1.82 million ($1.5 + 0.25 \times 1.28$) in stock through the year, or a total of £5.46 million for the three combined. For the warehouse inventories, the equivalent protection would be provided by £5.06 million in stock, a savings of £0.4 million in capital with further savings in interest expenses (or revenues if those could be invested and earn interest).

Questions

1. Present this information as a cost/benefit analysis to help the manager decide.

2. Are there any intangible costs or benefits which might negate the theoretical cost saving?

3. How would these be assessed? (See Chapter 15 for ideas.)

Conclusions

This chapter has presented a perspective on accounting that reveals the financial consequences of common marketing decisions and policies. Marketing managers cannot ignore the economic effects of their decisions and actions, and a better understanding of those should improve both decision-making and performance. The chief focus is usually on the profit and loss statement because it reflects sales activities directly, and marketing strategy and planning more generally. Simple but important developments such as sales revenues and costs can be measured and potential problems recognized. Financial analysis will not provide a solution, but it is a vital tool in identifying symptoms of problems and suggesting avenues for investigation. Relationships, too, can be recognized – trends in sales or the impact of credit policies on sales. The underlying need to justify marketing decisions and actions in terms of profitability or cost-effectiveness makes a grasp of these relationships most useful.

Summary

The importance of financial considerations in marketing decisions has been demonstrated through this chapter's discussions:

- The accounting systems reports and their relevance to specific marketing needs.

- Analysis of the profit and loss statement and the effects of marketing.

- Analysis of the balance sheet and its relevance for marketing managers.

- Analysis of the differences between profit and cash flow and the effects of marketing on cash flows.

- A review of how the marketing mix of price, product, place and promotion can impact on accounting measures and the organization's finances.

Chapter questions

1. Critically comment on the use of balance sheets and current assets in marketing.

2. Discuss the limitations associated with the use of breakeven analysis.

3. Comment on the undervalued assets that may be found in a company's customer portfolio.

References

Christopher, M., and Ryals, L. (1999) *International Journal of Logistics Management*, 10(1):1–10.
Haigh, D. (1994) *Strategic Control of Marketing Finance*, London: FT Prentice Hall.
See, Ed. (2006) 'Bridging the finance-marketing divide', *Financial Executive*.
Walters, D., and Halliday, M. (1998) *Marketing & Finance: Working the Interface*, London: Allen & Unwin.
Ward, K. (2003) *Marketing Finance: Turning Marketing Strategies into Shareholder Value*, London: Butterworth-Heinemann.
Wilson, R. M. S. (1999) *Accounting for Marketing*, London: Thomson Learning.

18

Strategic brand management

Simon Knox and Stan Maklan

Introduction

As customers become ever more demanding in a business environment where competition is fiercer (Day, 1999) and innovation faster (Datar *et al.*, 1997), the key challenge facing business leaders today is how to further increase the value of the products and services they sell. The more enlightened ones know that they will not be able to achieve this through the traditional product-led approach to brand management; customers expect products to work reliably and what creates value for them today is the ability of an organization to respond to their individual needs over an extended time frame. Consequently, strategic brand management now needs to focus on the organization's brand and its customer-facing business processes that create and deliver customer value consistently and in a timely fashion (Knox and Maklan, 1998a).

This chapter explores the changing relationship between customer value and how it has been traditionally interpreted *within* the organization. It also provides a practical framework which enables senior management to develop and market the customer-value proposition at a broader level *across* the organization. The role of the business leader in leading this transformation is discussed and the efficacy of the traditional brand strategy to respond is brought into question.

Learning objectives

After studying this chapter, students should be able to:

- Understand the relationship between the value of brands and perceived customer value.

- Comprehend the meaning of 'value gaps'.

- Understand the meaning of strategic brand management and organizational core processes.

The value of brands

Oscar Wilde wrote that a cynic is someone who knows the price of everything but the value of nothing. He may well have been talking about the attitude many business leaders have towards their brands and, indeed, the ways in which the organization itself is managed as a brand. It is only relatively recently that senior managers have started talking about brands as assets and brand equity as a major component of their organization's marketplace value (Davidson, 1998; Ward and Perrier, 1998). If anyone is in any doubt about the value of brands, they need do only two things: look at what companies are prepared to pay for top brands and observe the extent to which the market capitalization of brand-led organizations exceeds the value of their tangible assets.

During the past decade, there has been a spate of acquisitions by European consumer goods companies to increase their product portfolio and accelerate their geographic expansions. In many instances, large premiums were paid for the companies they acquired. For instance, Nestlé paid £2.6 billion for Rowntree, though the latter's balance sheet value was only £0.4 billion. While this premium reflects the potential value of Rowntree's distribution, customer relationships and branding know-how, without doubt the largest share of the premium was for its confectionery brands, which the company's management had carefully nurtured for decades: Kit-Kat, After Eight and Polo mints. Each of these brands now carries the Nestlé brand name, and their distribution in Europe has increased dramatically, as one would expect from this powerful multinational (Kotler *et al.*, 1996; Shamoon, 1999).

Coca-Cola calculates that only about 4 per cent of their value can be attributed to their plants and machinery. The real value of the soft drinks giant lies in their intangible assets, and first amongst these is their brand. Likewise, the microprocessor company Intel, which makes more profit than the world's 10 biggest PC makers combined, believes that 85 per cent of their worth lies in their brand equity and intellectual capital: their brand name, patents, know-how, people and processes (Hope and Hope, 1997).

During the late 1980s and early 1990s, brand management practices spread to services and business-to-business organizations. In some business-to-business markets, brand preferences can be quite marked. Dell Computer Corporation and Accenture are both very good examples. In 1998, worldwide sales of Dell's PCs overtook IBM's and Dell's PCs became the number-two brand. Dell is now the market leader on a global basis with over 13 per cent market share (Abrahams, 2001); Michael Dell started the corporation in the back of his garage as an 18-year-old entrepreneur in 1983. Accenture, formerly Andersen Consulting, had increased its turnover from $800 million to $2.5 billion within 5 years of repositioning itself in the IT-led change management marketplace. The firm ran the largest-ever business services advertising campaign on TV, a first for a management consultancy selling multi-million-dollar services.

In simple terms, a brand is an entity which offers customers (and other relevant parties) added value based on factors over and above its functional performance. These added values, or brand values, differentiate the offer and provide the basis for customer preference and loyalty. Traditionally, marketers use the marketing mix – the 'four Ps' of product, price, place and promotion – to position the brand and to create brand values around a coherent set of policies for each of these Ps (Jain, 1993; Kotler, 1997; Lancaster and Reynolds, 1995). Over time, the marketing community's knowledge of the effect of these various stimuli on customer perceptions increased and brand managers became brand engineers, manipulating well-tried stimuli to achieve predictable levels of customer value and generate superior profits.

Brand and customer value

The key issue facing business these days is how to build more value into the products and services they sell in the face of product commoditization, faster innovation, global competition and more demanding customers (Court *et al.*, 1999).

At the heart of the matter are fundamental shifts in what customers perceive as value, and this is challenging the traditional role of brand management. Customers traditionally rely upon brands as the antidote to the perceived risk of the product or service failing to provide its promised functional benefits (de Chernatony and McDonald, 1998). And, at a psychological level, a trusted brand minimizes the risk that the image created for customers using the product or service falls short of that desired. Therefore, brands create customer value by managing the customer's performance risk through a promise of sameness and predictability (Keller, 2003) and psychological risk through the image and social acceptability it confers. These value-creating roles are being challenged by customers who are developing more sophisticated strategies for managing risk. Business buyers are now much more inclined to develop partnerships with suppliers, involving closer relationships characterized by more openness and risk sharing. Continuous improvements in consumer product performance, reliability and choice are generating more confident, less risk-adverse customers (Knox *et al.*, 2000). The promise of sameness and predictability is no longer a compelling-enough customer proposition.

In the search for superior customer value, managers are realizing that their organization has to touch customers in a myriad of ways that go far beyond marketing communications about individual products and services (Mitchell, 1999). Customer value today involves creating more comprehensive solutions for customer problems that cannot be solved through one-off transactions; customers want a stream of value over time. This is true for consumer, business and service marketing. For example, consumers don't just buy a car, they expect that a new car will provide them trouble-free mobility for a number of years; the manufacturers' brands must credibly convey the reliability of design, technology and production. Moreover, car warranties are comprehensive, and dealers remove the onus of servicing problems from the customer to the manufacturer. Similar examples can be found in IT business services, where IBM's renaissance and retention of its status as the world's leading IT firm were generated more from developing comprehensive, long-term customer service (outsourcing) solutions than from new computer introductions. High availability of computing and information generates more customer value than do the computers themselves. This transition from product brand value to company brand value is equally reflected in the rapidly growing markets for customer services. Banks, for example, need to manage individual customers through all the points of customer contact regardless of the product or service that the customer needs on any one occasion. This customer management must be integrated across branches, call centres and a company's website. Each experience provides a context for customers to evaluate and test the organization's image and reputation, and its ability to deliver against expectations. To develop an integrated approach to these endeavours, the context of the brand has to change to embrace culture, know-how and organizational systems and processes – as well as products – if senior management is to use these assets and capabilities effectively

(Doyle, 1998). Without such a transformation in strategic brand thinking, traditional brand-building activities are unlikely to create value.

The value gap

In the 1990s, it became evident to a number of commentators that there was a growing gap between brand and customer value, with the latter stemming increasingly from processes outside the remit of marketing, such as supply chain leadership and customer relationship management (Christopher, 1996). Many iconic consumer brands, even though they were well managed and well funded, could no longer automatically command price premiums in the face of credible lower-priced alternatives. Perhaps the most famous example of this occurred on Friday, 2 April 1993, when the Philip Morris Company announced very large price reductions on its flagship Marlboro cigarette brand which suffered loss of share value. In what became known as 'Black Friday' amongst marketers, $20 billion was wiped off the value of Philip Morris that day (Knox and Maklan, 1998b). Similar pressure on premium pricing strategies was experienced by a large number of other leading brands, including Coca-Cola and McDonald's (Knox and Maklan, 1998b). Owners of these brands looked hard at the gap between customer and brand value, and, amongst other measures, re-engineered their core business processes to close that gap. Where the costs of creating brand value failed to generate commensurate customer value, they had to be scrutinized very carefully. Mercedes-Benz in the USA provides a very clear example of such re-engineering. The car marque had long been one of the world's most powerful brands in terms of engineering quality, luxury and exclusivity. But by the early 1990s, the range no longer met customers' perceptions of good value and they were not willing to pay Mercedes-Benz prices. Mercedes was losing its following in the USA to Toyota's Lexus, a competitor whose corporate brand initially appeared to lack credibility in the relevant market segment. But Lexus was quickly recognized as offering better perceived value against the costs of ownership. This superior value was primarily a result of Toyota's breakthrough developments in its manufacturing processes and resultant cost management capabilities, in conjunction with excellent design and customer care. When brand value is not commensurate with customer value, a company faces a stark choice: change or fail. In a frank interview, the then-CEO of Mercedes-Benz acknowledged that his cars were overengineered, and he began to address the problem (Lorenz, 1993). His stated intent was to change the company from being a producer of only luxury cars to an exclusive, full-line manufacturer offering high-quality vehicles in all segments. Mercedes was forced to look beyond the traditional four Ps of brand management as its definition of 'premium' positioning was no longer working.

Customer value and the organization

Today's customers are highly sophisticated and confident in their own ability to decide between products and suppliers' offers (Mitchell *et al.*, 2003); these days, they need much less brand reassurance to validate their choices. In most markets, the customer can choose between a large number of high-quality products made by renowned companies. In the modern economy, value is no longer exclusively created by marketers branding what their organization wishes to produce.

From the customer's point of view, value is created when the benefits (*perceived quality*) they receive exceed the costs of owning it (*perceived sacrifice*). These components of customer value can be disaggregated further into the benefits derived from the core product and customized service against the purchase price and the consumer's transaction costs.

In many consumer goods markets, brands can no longer command premium prices or even shelf space by virtue of advertising-generated awareness and affinity, because the price of a brand is no longer what customers pay for it. The real price includes everything the customer has to do to realize its value: time and money spent searching for the right product and sales outlet, travel and purchasing costs, consumption and disposal costs (Mitchell, 1998).

Taking this broader view of value – and customizing it – is transforming the marketing agenda. This is how the former chief executive of First Direct transformed the perceptions of customer value in the banking world.

Process in action customer value at First Direct

Kevin Newman, the former CEO of the world's first telephone bank, had a very clear vision of how customer value could be constructed in his bank:

> I believe that in going forward [at First Direct], three things need to be developed. We have to be utterly low cost. We must be able to individualize the manufacturing process and recognize that all our customers are individuals. Thirdly, we must build a strong brand as people need to identify with institutions they can trust.[1]

Since opening for business in October 1989, First Direct representatives have signed up over 850 000 customers for their telephone-banking services. Without a branch network to support, First Direct's staff costs are about half those of a typical retail bank and an efficient information system has been instrumental in keeping these costs down.

Information technology is critical for accessing the bank's online customer database, the hub of its operations. Using an automatic call distribution system, customers' calls are routed to unoccupied operators across its four call centres. Each banking representative has instant access to each customer's accounts and business history. Day-to-day transactions, such as balance enquiries, electronic payment of bills or a transfer of funds between accounts, can all be completed by the same representative without having to transfer the customer. For more specialized information, such as loans and mortgages, customers are transferred to trained advisors. In most instances, the full range of traditional banking services is offered in a friendly and efficient manner – 24 hours a day, 365 days a year – for the price of a local telephone call.

These components of customer value delivered by First Direct's banking representatives can be summarized in the customer value monitor (Figure 18.1) and shows the bank's commitment to *increasing* service and product benefits through customization of its CRM software, and *decreasing* transaction costs through quick, efficient responses and 24/7 access.

Overall, the customer value monitor depicts First Direct's customer-driven focus (current position -------) based on relationship marketing, customer retention and lifetime value, rather than the traditional banking approach of selling products and servicing customers on a transaction basis.

What sets First Direct apart from high-street banks are the perceptions its customers have of a convenient, well-informed service which provides access to a broad range of financial, travel and information products in a speedy and efficient fashion.

Because the bank is able to provide superior customer value, it enjoys a level of customer retention and loyalty that is second to none. Ninety-seven per cent of First Direct customers remain with the bank year on year, and about one-third of its new customers are referred by existing loyal customers.

Question

1. How do you think your own bank compares to First

2. Direct in terms of 'customer value'?

[1] From the case study on First Direct: Branchless Banking, Parmenter, D., J. C. Larréché, and C. Lovelock (1997). Insead Case No. 597-028-1.

Figure 18.1
First Direct customer value monitor

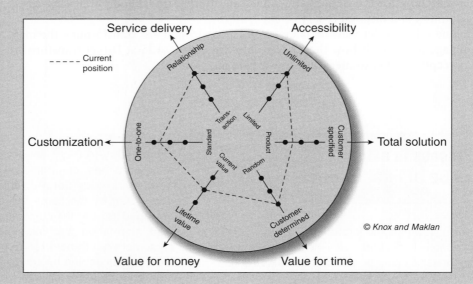

Reintegrating customer and brand value: the challenge for strategic brand management

As products become more sophisticated and customer demands for service and performance grow, few companies, if any, find they can offer a total solution to what customers require. The traditional brand marketing response to these demands is to add levels of service to augment the product offer. But this tends to create complexity and cost rather than value (George *et al.*, 1994). Referring again to IBM and its renaissance in recent years, the company was the leading exponent of 'solution selling' during the 1960s and 1970s, and its methods were widely copied by companies such as Xerox. It created a company brand based on its product line, augmented with layers of added value services and systems support. The positioning of the IBM brand was about being the IT manager's supporter, and the selling proposition was about certainty and predictability. But the infrastructure needed to deliver that promise proved unequal to the challenge of client server architecture: Leaner competitors, such as Novell, and new demand-chain models such as Dell's, unbundled IBM's offer through new business processes and alliances that delivered combinations of more powerful solutions, lower prices and better service. No amount of traditional product-focused brand strategy was able to address these issues. IBM has successfully responded by redefining its brand and the customer problem it seeks to address. However, to do so required IBM to create business processes and an organizational structure commensurate with its new brand promise. These examples illustrate that strategic brand management creates customer value by integrating the company's suppliers and business processes to create value-adding business systems rather than the more limited product solutions of traditional brand management. The structure of alliances and processes needed within the supply chain to create the total customer experience is beyond the scope of traditional product management (Prahalad and Ranaswamy, 2000).

The realities of brand strategy today

Business leaders increasingly acknowledge that competition is based on entire value or supply chains rather than the efforts of their individual organizations, its product portfolios battling head-to-head with those of adversaries (Christopher, 1998). This understanding has profound implications for how the company is organized to create and deliver customer value. At the heart of this transformation is the strategic requirement to shift marketing from a narrow departmental approach, positioning and selling product lines, to a broader activity that includes positioning and branding the organization in the supply chain (Knox and Maklan, 1998a). Business leaders must accept the need for new business models and brands built upon those models both to create customer value in the first place and then to differentiate their organization's offer, or they will find themselves increasingly irrelevant both to their customers and business partners.

Marketing the organization

Marketing the organization or a strategic business unit requires a very different approach from the conventions of four-Ps product marketing (de Chernatony, 1999) that are associated with traditional brand strategy. There are a number of very good reasons for this. First, the organization's good name and reputation is at stake rather than the name associated with a product or service in a particular market (London, 2003). As the portfolio increases or the company diversifies into different market segments, the risk of a service or product failing becomes magnified with increasing scale and operational complexity (Doyle, 1989). Second, the reputation of the organization or business unit is much more challenging to manage than that of a single product, since the former is constructed by customers from multiple reference points which extend well beyond the products and their projected images (Keller and Aaker, 1998). The key elements of a company's reputation derive from its commitments, values, policies and risk management techniques (Maitland, 2003). Although the risk associated with developing this broader approach to marketing is greater than traditional product marketing, the rewards can be dramatic. Neither individual marketing managers nor the product portfolios they manage have the necessary scope or authority to commit the entire organization in these areas or to manage the full range of stakeholder relationships necessary to create reputation.

In marketing an organization, business leaders need to consider four components to develop its brand positioning in the supply chain: its overall reputation, product/service performance, product and customer portfolio, and networks (Knox and Maklan, 1998b). Again, the First Direct brand can be used to illustrate how to interpret customer value across the entire organization.

Process in action (cont.)
positioning the First Direct brand

The First Direct brand tries to communicate and deliver a no-frills, hassle-free approach to banking, more in tune with customers' lifestyles than the traditional high-street bank. Customer feedback through surveys suggests that First Direct is achieving these brand objectives: customer satisfaction levels are running at 90 per cent[2], compared to less than 60 per cent in a typical retail bank. Commercially, the telephone bank is very successful, enjoying a return on equity of over 25 per cent and an equally attractive return on investment.

How has First Direct managed to create these brand values and position itself as the bank of choice in the minds of its customers? By analysis of the four components of the First Direct brand (Figure 18.2), the organization's value proposition becomes clear. In contrast to product branding based on the four Ps, product positioning and market share metrics, the First Direct Brand is positioned (current position ---------) as an organization that has a select customer base, strong customer relationships and a growing network of value-adding partners.

Reputation
The First Direct brand is not seen as depending on any one product; its reputation is built upon the compete portfolio of the company's activities and values. It engenders trust and commitment by being

Figure 18.2
The First Direct brand monitor

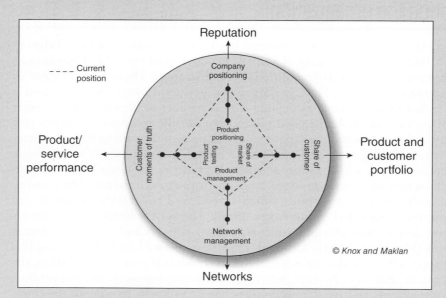

© Knox and Maklan

flexible, responsive and accessible, as well as highly competitive. All aspects of the company's operations contribute to this positioning; it is not a by-product of the marketing efforts behind individual brands.

Product/service performance

This component has to do with the way customers perceive the bank's products and service delivery. It is about the 'moments of truth' customers experience in their day-to-day dealings with the bank and its representatives. The relationship customers have is with the bank rather than individual representatives, but the representatives' thorough training and knowledge of the customers' usual needs, which is instantly accessible through information technology, mean that the company culture is very customer oriented and keen to serve. The relationship is based upon 'listening and serving' rather than 'selling financial services'.

Product and customer portfolio

In building up its customer portfolio, the new-customer team rejects about 50 per cent of applicants. The profile of its existing customer base is the young professional working in a metropolitan area who tends to make extensive use of the bank's product portfolio. The bank's strategic focus is to balance the share of spend targets, aimed at encouraging existing customers to spend more across the bank's product portfolio by cross-selling and up-selling, with growth in market share from new customers generated by referrals.

As a result of matching customer and product portfolios, the bank generates superior profits. A *New York Times* journalist has estimated the average balance of a First Direct customer to be 10 times higher than that of a typical high-street bank, while the overall transaction costs are 60 per cent less. The bank makes money on 60 per cent of its customers compared to 40 per cent at the average British bank.

Networks

To help deliver its service, the bank uses a number of IT providers for transaction clearing, card service processing and credit scoring. Likewise, the management team has developed its product portfolio through establishing networks both within the HSBC group, which owns it, and among external insurance and assurance companies. But these networks of relationships are not overtly branded. Over time, the network could become part of the company brand proposition; when you 'buy' First Direct, you get access to a large number of value-adding partners.

Overall, the First Direct brand is positioned to offer outstanding customer service by skilfully managing each customer's moments of truth with an individualistic style that is both respectful and open. Thus, the strength of the brand lies in its customer relationship management capabilities and the service values the senior management team has inspired its staff to support and believe in.

> We like to think that we are not really in banking but distribution. We just happen to supply financial products. . .[3]

Question

1. How much do you agree with the last statement and whether First Direct can justify making it?

---

[2]First Direct won the Management Today/Unisys service excellence award (Financial Services) in 1998, and this figure is taken from an interview with Guy Davis, First Direct's Customer Director, *Management Today*, October, p. 90.
[3]From the case study on First Direct: Branchless Banking, Parmenter, D., J. C. Larréché, and C. Lovelock (1997). Insead Case No.597-028-1.

Positioning and branding the organization

The First Direct 'process in action' example suggests that the marketing mix and the positioning of the organization brand can be determined by reputation, the performance of its products and services, its product and customer portfolios and the network of relationships which management has developed in the supply chain. Clearly, it is possible to place a different emphasis on each of these components according to how you wish to position your offer and the nature of market competition. The UK airline industry in the 1990s provides an example of companies whose brands were competitively positioned at the corporate level (Table 18.1).

British Airways (BA) aimed to be the choice of the highly profitable long-distance business traveller. It was determined to keep its hold on the business's most profitable customers and create the world benchmark for reliable global travel. It delivered an effective and predictable service to time-obsessed business travellers, provided a comfortable and convenient business-class service and had a network of relationships integrated into the brand proposition to meet customers' global needs.

However, these global ambitions have been frustrated as new competitors operating with much lower cost structures called into question how much of a premium BA could charge to fund the customer experience it delivered. The increased competition, coupled with the impact of 9/11, coincided with BA reporting its worst results since privatization 15 years ago and the loss of some 7000 jobs. The company is now restructuring its short haul network to fight competition from low-cost carriers (Done, 2002a).

Virgin, referred to by some marketers as the 'challenger brand', wisely avoided trying to become a 'mini-BA', a strategy that was unsuccessfully attempted by Mercury when it was the challenger brand to British Telecom. Virgin's appeal was more emotional than BA's, and its service performance reflected this: massages, free ice creams, baseball caps on flights and so on. It appealed to those disposed towards the Virgin brand and all that it stood for. This concept will be much harder to extend to business partners, and one wonders about its ability to compete for business travellers should the industry consolidate into a number of global players.

The 'no-frills' proposition is not new in the airline industry and many early successes have closed down – none with more publicity than Laker. Nonetheless, easyJet entered the market in 1995 with a highly credible brand positioning: limited European destinations but effective and low-cost. With the takeover of Go – formed by a management buyout from British Airways in 2001 – easyJet became a significant low-cost airline last year (Done, 2002b).

Table 18.1

The positioning of airline brands in the UK

	BA	*Virgin*	*easyJet*
Reputation	Reliable, predictable	Challenging, exciting, unconventional	Cheap
Product and service performance	Extensive routes, range of service, excellent recovery from problems	Limited routes, innovative services	Fit for purpose, few routes
Product and customer portfolio	Strong business class sub-brand, focus on long-distance business traveller	Trade on corporate name mostly, target 'Virgin' likers	Corporate brand focused on budget traveller paying for own trips
Networks	Emerging global alliances deliver worldwide capability, Air miles scheme a major part of loyalty strategy	Focused on Virgin to appeal to Virgin-likers	Not as part of the brand

SOURCE: KNOX ET AL. (2000), IN *THE EXPRESSIVE ORGANISATION*, p. 223.

While four-Ps marketing remains central to product and sales strategies, the organization's marketing mix is more appropriate in an environment where customer value is created through the activities of the entire company. But these credentials – or what the organization is known for by customers – are sustainable only if the core processes that run end-to-end through the company are suitably aligned. Thus it is the positioning of the organization brand in conjunction with its core processes that creates and delivers customer value through the organization.

The organization marketing mix described here provides the framework for senior management to align processes. Once the processes are aligned, the proposition moves deep into the organization, because process leaders and their teams understand the priorities that determine customer value among their important customer segments. The core processes which deliver value to customers will vary by industry and by company within industry. If one considers the organization as an input–output system, then there are broadly five generic processes: customer development,

Process in action (cont.) the First Direct brand and core processes

The brand values of First Direct are delivered through very effective customer development and asset management processes (Figure 18.3). Both processes support a positioning based upon product/service performance (customers' moments of truth) and a company-wide reputation (culture,

identity and image development), as we have already identified in Figure 18.2. Arguably, these processes represent the investment priorities for the CEO, and it is critical that he ensures that these processes are aligned. Resource transformation and supply partnership are less well developed within the bank.

As market understanding grows within the bank, and the management teams develop their resource transformation process to meet a wider set of their customers' needs (innovation in both financial and non-financial areas), stronger alliances, new modes

Figure 18.3
The First Direct process monitor

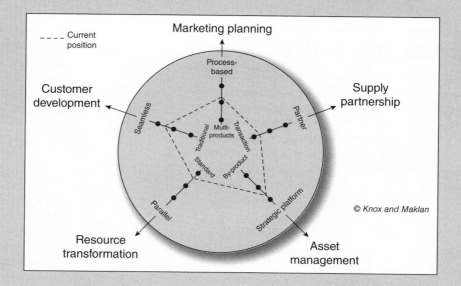

of distribution and networks will be needed within the bank's supply chain.

The challenge facing the bank's new CEO will be to develop the supply partnership process to enable effective management of these more complex relationships with supplier networks.

The mode of distribution is changing – at the moment we definitely see it as person-to-person over the telephone. Do we believe that people will bank electronically over the next 10 years? We are not fussed about how quickly or by which means our customers choose to access all or part of their banking electronically. The elements for us are: when they do so, what is

the role of our bank and how do we deliver a competitive advantage in this environment? We must always remember that our moments of truth are the telephone contacts with banking representatives. Creating value in an electronic world will be a key issue in the future of First Direct.[4]

Question
1. Do you agree that the First Direct initiatives will help them grow the business? How would you justify your opinion?

[4]From the case study on First Direct: Branchless Banking, Parmenter, D., J. C. Larréché, and C. Lovelock (1997). Insead Case No.597-028-1.

resource transformation, asset management, supply partnership and marketing planning (Knox *et al.*, 1999). However, the framework discussed in this chapter works across most process designs.

Two examples are used to illustrate this close alignment between the positioning of the organization brand and its core processes.

Retail franchises and brand development

Retail franchise brands in fast food, printing and car repair businesses are built upon effective supply chains and supply partnership. McDonald's provides an excellent example of supply partnership.

Process in action McDonald's

For McDonald's, branding and service delivery, supported by first-class supply partnerships (from buns and burgers to new store design and build), deliver the majority of its customer value (Macrae, 1991). Marketing at McDonald's is as much about supporting training and company brand developments as it is about the four Ps of its product portfolio.

The McDonald's brand positioning consists of:

Reputation	family fun, value for money, hygiene
Performance	consistency in taste of food, speed of service, cleanliness of restaurants
Portfolio	clear product portfolio strategy based upon burgers, fries and soft drinks and a customer portfolio of families with young children
Networks (Co-branded)	Disney for joint promotion
	Cadbury's flake in its ice cream desserts (UK)
	Coca-Cola has been introduced through branded founts and paper cups

Much has been written about the McDonald's service model and its business process design (cf. Treacy and Wiersema, 1995; Keen, 1997). While not minimizing the importance of all of its business processes, it does not have close customer relationships, nor is the company's food preparation process particularly unique. However, people management and extensive training across the whole organization is regarded as essential to sustaining brand values and business growth. In the USA, McDonald's Hamburger University is the centre of management and operative training across the franchises. To support training in the workplace, senior management everywhere in the world has a special affiliation with one or more restaurants in order to share their experiences and knowledge with retail management and operatives. In fact, some members of senior management go back into the regions for extended periods to operate a franchise, or a group of McDonald's-owned restaurants, to ensure that best practices in product and service performance are continuously improved through their leadership.[5]

Question

1. How has McDonald's created and enhanced its brand by networking and by developing its people?

---

[5]Personal interview with McDonald's CEO (UK), Feb. 2001, East Finchley, London.

Summary

- Business leaders must continuously view brand investment in light of the need to close the gap between customer and brand value. Strategic brand management today is not just about advertising messages and image.

- As marketers find it increasingly difficult to achieve breakthroughs in customer value, business leaders should be reviewing not only how judiciously marketing budgets are spent but also how effectively the company is creating a differentiated set of business processes that creates real customer value.

- It may be that the traditional approach to product brand marketing and the functional structures usually associated with this are no longer appropriate and are destroying rather than creating value.

- A sequential approach to processing customer feedback through marketing and sales departments may be costing the business dear in terms of time to market, customer satisfaction performance and missed opportunities (Hammer and Champy, 1993; Boehm and Phipps, 1996).

- In today's flat-structured organization, end-to-end process management encourages the involvement of customers at one end and suppliers at the other (Hammer and Stanton, 1999).

- Neither the marketing department nor sales should act as the final arbiter of customer needs or market developments.

- Similarly, supply partners must have access to all parts of the organization; purchasing should not impose itself between supplier and company.

- The traditional marketing department, perversely, can act as a barrier to strategic brand marketing if it does not support process management in this broader approach to delivering customer value.

- If the framework suggested here is used, it should become clear just how pervasively the marketing principles are used in appraising customer value and the lead which the marketing department provides.

- It should also reveal how closely the organization's positioning and delivery of brand value are aligned to the value expectations of key customer segments.

- Although many of the value-adding processes in an organization fall outside the remit of the marketing department, the effects of marketing should be present in them.

- In a process-based organization, the degree to which the marketing department has adapted to the new challenges should be apparent throughout the company.

- If it is not, then the company may wish to restructure marketing and sales to strike a better balance between their functional tasks and cross-functional process involvement.

Chapter questions

1. Comment on the growing gap between brand and customer value.

2. Critically discuss how to reintegrate customer and brand values as a major challenge for strategic brand management.

3. Discuss the interrelationship between brand value and the core processes of an organization.

References

Abrahams, P. (2001, June 26) 'Compaq goes into training for its next big fight', *The Times*, p. 23.

Boehm, R., and Phipps, C. (1996) 'Flatness forays', *The McKinsey Quarterly*, 3:129–143.

Christopher, M. (1996) 'From brand values to customer value', *Journal of Marketing Practice, Applied Marketing Science*, 2(1):55–66.

Christopher, M. (1998) *Logistics and Supply Chain Management*, 2nd edn., London: Financial Times Pitman.

de Chernatony, L. (1999) 'Brand management through narrowing the gap between brand identity and brand reputation', *Journal of Marketing Management*, 15:157–179.

de Chernatony, L., and McDonald, M. H. B. (1998) *Creating Powerful Brands*, 2nd edn., Oxford: Butterworth-Heinemann, p. 42.

Court, D., French, T. D., McGuire, T. I., and Partington, M. (1999) 'Marketing in 3-D', *The McKinsey Quarterly*, 4:6–17.

Datar, S., Jordan, C. C., Kekre, S., Rajiv, S., and Srinivasan, K. (1997, February) 'Advantages of time-based new product development in a fast-cycle industry', *Journal of Marketing Research*, 34(1):36–49.

Davidson, H. (1998) 'The next generation of brand measurement', *Journal of Brand Management*, 5(6):430–439.

Day, G. S. (1999) *The Market Driven Organisation*, New York: The Free Press, p. 22.

Done, K. (2002a, May 21) 'BA report worst results since privatisation', *Financial Times*, p. 23.

Done, K. (2002b, May 17) 'Go executives to gain from easyJet takeover', *Financial Times*, p. 23.

Doyle, P. (1989) 'Building strategic brands: The strategic options', *Journal of Marketing Management*, 5(1):77–95.

Doyle, P. (1998, Spring) 'Brand equity and the marketing professional', *Market Leader*, 1:38–42.

Economist (1996, October 5) 'Selling PCs like bananas'.

George, M., Freeling, A., and Court, D. (1994) 'Reinventing the marketing organization', *The McKinsey Quarterly*, 4:43–62.

Hammer, M., and Champy, J. (1993) *Re-engineering the Corporation*, London: Nicholas Brealey.

Hammer, M., and Stanton, S. (1999, Nov–Dec) 'How process enterprises really work', *Harvard Business Review*, pp. 108–118.

Hope, J., and Hope, T. (1997) *Competing in the Third Wave*, Boston, MA: Harvard Business School Press.

Jain, S. C. (1993) *Marketing Planning and Strategy*, 4th edn., Cincinnati, OH: South-Western.

Keen, P. G. W. (1997) *The Process Edge*, Boston, MA: Harvard Business School Press.

Keller, K. L. (2003) *Strategic Brand Management*, 2nd edn., Englewood Cliffs, NJ: Prentice Hall, p. 9.

Keller, K. L., and Aaker, D. A. (1998) 'The impact of corporate marketing on a company's brand extensions', *Corporate Reputation Review*, 1(4):356–378.

King, S. (1991) 'Brand building in the 1990s', *Journal of Marketing Management*, 7:3–13.

Knox, S. D., and Maklan, S. (1998a) 'Brand marketing in transition', *The Journal of Brand Management*, 6(1):50–56.

Knox, S. D., and Maklan, S. (1998b) *Competing on Value*, London: FT Pitman.

Knox, S. D., Maklan, S., and Thompson, K. E. (1999) 'Pan-company marketing and process management', *Irish Marketing Review*, 12(1):36–45.

Knox, S. D., Maklan, S., and Thompson, K. E. (2000) 'Building the unique organisation value proposition', in Schultz, M., Hatch, M. J., and Larsen, M. H. (eds.), *The Expressive Organisation*, Oxford: Oxford University Press, p. 216.

Kotler, P. (1997) *Marketing Management: Analysis, Planning, Implementation and Control, International Edition*, Englewood Cliffs, NJ: Prentice Hall.

Kotler, P., Armstrong, G., Sanders, J., and Wong, V. (1996) *Principles of Marketing: The European Edition*, Hemel Hempstead, UK: Prentice-Hall, pp. 120–126.

Lancaster, G., and Reynolds, P. (1995) *Marketing*, Oxford: Butterworth-Heinemann.

London, S. (2003, April 4) 'All new HP... with added Shrek', *The Times*.

Lorenz, A. (1993, April 11) 'Mercedes slump forces overhaul at German giant', *The Times*.

Macrae, C. (1991) *World-Class Brands*, Wokingham, UK: Addison-Wesley, pp. 22–27.

Maitland, A. (2003, March 31) 'Reputation: You only know its worth when it lies in tatters', *The Times*, p. 14.

Mitchell, A. (1998, October) 'New directions', *Marketing Business*, pp. 12–15.

Mitchell, A. (1999) 'Out of the shadows', *Journal of Marketing Management*, 15:25–42.

Mitchell, A., Bauer, A. and Hausruckinger, G. (2003) *The New Bottom Line: Bridging the Value Gaps that Are Undermining Your Business,* London: Capstone Wiley.

Prahalad, C. K., and Ranaswamy, V. (2000, Jan–Feb) 'Co-opting customer competence', *Harvard Business Review*, pp. 79–87.

Shamoon, S. (1999, January 16) 'Shares in Nestlé will build up bottom line', *The Times*, p. 51.

Treacy, M., and Wiersema, F. (1995) *The Discipline of Market Leaders*, London: HarperCollins.

Ward, R., and Perrier, R. (1998) 'Brand valuation: The times are a-changing', *Journal of Brand Management*, 4(5):283–289.

19

Managing the marketing and e-business interface

Kunhuang Huarng and Charles S. Chien

Introduction

Customers all over the world have become connected to the Internet, and far greater numbers of customers are expected to become connected in the future. If the size of the population can be referred to as the size of a market, the Internet should become the largest market of all. Hence, e-business and e-commerce models are increasingly gaining the attention of businesses and academia as they are used to develop business plans and to realize these plans through websites, to implement all kinds of marketing strategies, to ensure a flow of incoming revenues and to increase profits through the use of the Internet. This chapter introduces these e-business models, e-business plans, web-design criteria and Internet-marketing strategies.

Learning objectives

- To introduce e-business models and e-business plans.

- To describe web-design criteria that are directly relevant to marketing.

- To map these web-design criteria into marketing strategies.

- To cover some popular Internet-marketing strategies, such as viral marketing, relationship marketing and contextual marketing.

- To discuss some novel analytical methodologies for marketing research.

Business models

In this era of the Internet, business models are considered critical to the success of e-business or e-commerce. These business models can help companies create entry barriers so that other companies experience difficulty entering the market. The innovative companies can easily dominate the market, thus making it difficult for the other companies to follow. There are various ways in which these business models may be specified. In this chapter, we adopt an intuitive approach to categorize business models in terms of their transaction flows on the Internet: from the consumer/business to the consumer/business. Hence, based on the different combinations of the consumer and business, there are four basic business models:

- business to business (B2B)
- business to consumer (B2C)
- consumer to consumer (C2C)
- consumer to business (C2B)

Afuah and Tucci (2001) have summarized a taxonomy of business models. In B2B models, a group of companies (including buyers, sellers and intermediaries) conduct business transactions among each other via the Internet (Greenstein and Feinman, 2000; Schneider, 2003). Users of B2B models include Internet access providers (Eisenmann, 2002), application service providers (Eisenmann, 2002), distributors (Afuah and Tucci, 2001; Morgan Stanley Dean Witter, 2000) and market makers (Afuah and Tucci, 2001; Morgan Stanley Dean Witter, 2000).

Users of B2C models, simply put, allow consumers to shop directly on the Internet (Schneider, 2003), and include e-shops (Rappa, 2000), content providers (Eisenmann, 2002; Hoque, 2000; Laudon and Laudon, 1999), retailers (Eisenmann, 2002; Hoque, 2000), registration models (Rappa, 2000), brokers (Eisenmann, 2002), generalized portals (Eisenmann, 2002; Rappa, 2000) and service providers (Afuah and Tucci, 2001; Hoque, 2000; Laudon and Laudon, 1999; Lumpkin and Dess, 2004).

In C2B models, consumers determine their prices and the companies decide whether to accept the prices (Afuah and Tucci, 2001). Some examples include reverse auctions (Rappa, 2000) and buyer-oriented aggregators (Rayport and Jaworski, 2001). In C2C models, transactions take place among consumers (Afuah and Tucci, 2001). One example is online auctions. The transaction flows for these models are depicted in Figure 19.1. From that figure, we can easily see that other models can be derived, in addition to the above basic models. For example, a B2B2C model represents transactions from one company to another company and then to consumers. As a result, complex business models can be derived.

E-Business plans

Business plans are used to implement business models. Most business plans cover similar subjects, such as missions, objectives, competitive strategies, marketing, financial analysis and so on. e-Business plans, however, should place more emphasis on marketing, especially Internet marketing. The reasoning behind this is simple. INSEAD *et al.* (1999) predicted the marketing trend for the year 2005 by listing 11 hot items. Almost half of these items are Internet relevant, and are concerned with the removal of intermediaries, B2B, customer database analysis, virtual companies, interaction with customers via computer screens and e-learning. Indeed, the Internet makes many marketing strategies possible, such as viral marketing, relationship marketing, contextual marketing, and facilitates the implementation of these marketing strategies, such as market segmentation. Furthermore, existing mobile technologies empower the so-called mobile commerce. Hence, the Internet has become ubiquitous, and ubiquitous marketing is made possible. However, before discussing how to realize these Internet-marketing strategies, we will first review some web-design criteria and then discuss how Internet marketing can be implemented via these criteria.

Web design

It is paradoxical that the design of a website should be simple and straightforward. Even worse, many people are used to relating HTML programming to web design. In fact, there are systematic guidelines for web design, which may not be as straightforward as many people think. Rayport and Jaworski (2001) have proposed seven criteria for web design, namely, context, content, community, communication, customization, connection and commerce. The top five criteria are relevant to Internet marketing and are elaborated as follows. **Context** is concerned with the design of a website being more functional or aesthetic, or a combination of both. Functional style focuses on, e.g., how to lay out information in an organized way, and to speed up the exchange of information. Many portals are considered to be typical functional ones, with well-known examples including Yahoo and eBay. On the other hand, many artwork-oriented websites are regarded as being more aesthetic, such as those of film makers and animation firms. Nevertheless, one recent trend has been to integrate both styles to locate information efficiently as well as to impress customers with sophisticated designs.

Content was once considered to be the king of e-commerce (Angehrn, 1997; Huizingh, 2000; McCarthy, 1995). Only proper content can attract customers to

Figure 19.1
Internet business models

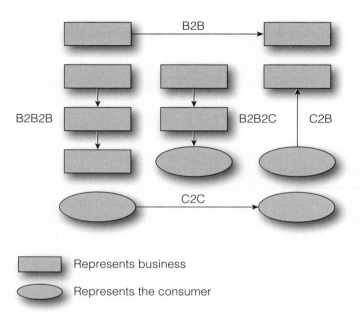

visit and revisit (Huarng, 2003). In Rayport and Jaworski (2001), two types of content were introduced: the offering mix and the appeal mix. The offering mix provides products, services or information. In other words, the offering mix focuses on what is being sold. On the contrary, the appeal mix focuses on promotion.

Community relates to the sharing of ideas, thoughts or feelings among customers without interference from the operators of the websites. Community customers usually attract other customers to join, and they share similar interests (such as sports and movies), concerns (such as politics and education), experiences (such as unemployment and sickness), etc.

On the contrary, **communication** represents means by which the websites convey their messages to their customers. The websites use all kinds of marketing strategies to send accurate and appropriate messages to their customers via this communication tool.

Customization provides custom-made surfing environments created either by the websites or by the customers themselves. Customized environments can assist in attracting customers. To that end, the websites need to analyze their customers' data so that the firms can understand their purchasing preferences and behaviour. For example, Amazon provides customers with lists of the most recently published books, the most popular books, etc., based on the customers' previous purchasing histories. It is assumed that the customers are still interested in similar topics during their subsequent visits to Amazon. The customers certainly like this type of custom-made service. Websites can also analyze customers' preferences based on the types of environments that are formed by the customers themselves. Similar results from such analyses can be obtained.

From web design to Internet marketing

These five web-design criteria are related to Internet-marketing strategies. A community on the Internet comprises customers who share certain similar characteristics, which can be referred to as market segmentation. Communication, community and content provide the means by which the websites can communicate valuable information with their proper segments, which can facilitate viral marketing. Customization and context provide custom-made environments to realize one-to-one marketing or relationship marketing. Content, communication and community are concerned with how the websites can be properly promoted via proper channels to proper segments, which can implement contextual marketing. The mapping from web design to Internet marketing is summarized in Table 19.1.

Web-design criteria	Internet-marketing strategies
Community	Market segmentation
Communication, community and content	Viral marketing
Customization and context	Relationship marketing
Content, communication and community	Contextual marketing

Table 19.1
Mapping from web design to marketing

Market segmentation

A community on the Internet comprises customers who share certain similar characteristics (demographics, psychographics, etc.). The customers may be of similar age; e.g., a community of video-game enthusiasts may essentially consist of teenagers. The customers may be interested in particular events, such as sports, and in issues, such as political issues and educational topics. Understanding the special interests and even purchasing behaviours of the community members is critical for serving these community members.

The effects of analyzing the communities are very similar to those in relation to market segmentation in conventional marketing studies. Usually the demographic data regarding the customers are worth analyzing, such as ages, jobs, genders. Furthermore, more advanced information concerning the customers in the community is even more valuable, such as acquisition and retention expenses and rates (Thomas *et al.*, 2004). Hereafter, proper marketing strategies can be applied.

As the Internet becomes increasingly popular, the amount of customer data increases drastically. Meanwhile, computing power has also increased tremendously, which facilitates the complicated computations of these data. Thanks to this, data-mining methodologies have been developed and have become very popular. Therefore, we can apply data-mining methodologies to customer data in order to arrive at very meaningful results. The topic of data mining is discussed in the next section.

Viral marketing

Communication provides the means for websites to communicate with their customers. Reminders, routine notices and news of promotions can be sent to customers. Content can be referred to as valuable information or promotions and community as the proper segments. Communicating valuable information to these proper segments activates viral marketing. First, valuable information is delivered to customers. These customers will widely broadcast these messages within their social networks, as the information is considered valuable. As a result, this strategy will encourage the customers to pass on marketing messages to others (who are segmented by the customers), ultimately creating a potentially exponential influence (Brewer, 2001; Wilson, 2000). This effect is very similar to that of a computer virus that automatically reproduces itself on other computers.

e-Magazines and e-newspapers routinely apply the viral marketing strategy. *USA Today*, for example, allows readers to print their favourite articles as well as to e-mail them to others. Allowing readers to share what they think is valuable with those they think will be interested is an example of viral marketing. In this case, those who receive the interesting articles may further distribute the articles to others who may be interested in them. As a result, the readership of such articles may grow exponentially.

Relationship marketing (one-to-one marketing)

Relationship marketing (or one-to-one marketing) lays a fundamental basis for competition in the marketplace by focusing on customers rather than products (Peppers and Rogers, 1993). Market research suggests that many customers are willing to establish a relationship with suppliers (Chablo, 2001). Hence, after identifying profitable segments, tailored marketing messages should be delivered. This form of marketing is referred to as one-to-one marketing (Teklitz and McCarthy, 2001). Customization and context provide tailoring and personalization to facilitate one-to-one marketing.

Website management can tailor the user interface for the customers, just as Amazon tailors sales messages for its customers when they log on to Amazon. Meanwhile, some websites also allow customers to personalize their user interfaces, such as the personalized headlines, images and layouts at http://mylook.com. In addition, websites can provide personalized content according to the customer's needs.

Meanwhile, in e-commerce, aliases allow customers to use different names for convenience and to maintain confidentiality (Web Associates, 2001). e-Commerce also allows different levels of interaction. Customers can even choose when and how they would like to receive and reply to a communication (Web Associates, 2001).

Contextual marketing

Bringing customers to websites may not be enough in this highly competitive business. How to bring the right messages to the right customers at the right moments when they are in the right environments has become a critical issue, and for this the term *contextual marketing* has been coined (Kenny and Marshall, 2000). Content, communication and community can facilitate contextual marketing. For example, a company that sells headache relief tablets will display its web banners only when the stock index drops drastically, and restaurant ads will only be shown around meal times.

On the other hand, recent developments in mobile techniques (or mobile commerce) can also enhance contextual marketing. In driving a car on a motorway, for instance, the driver may need various kinds of information at different times. For example, during meal times, they may need information on restaurants near their current location. When about to run out of gas, a driver will need information regarding the surrounding gas stations. Hence, to win over drivers on the highways, the necessary information should be delivered to drivers at the right time.

A case study (Kenny and Marshall, 2000) mentioned that a car-manufacturing company could collect information regarding their cars. Gas stations are very interested in knowing how much gas is left in the cars around the stations. Proper information, such as maps and promotional materials, could be sent to drivers when they are running out of gas. Other stores, such as retailers, restaurants and auto-repair shops, would also be interested in information relevant to them. Hence mobile commerce enables contextual marketing to take place.

Data mining

As computing technologies have progressed, many analytical methodologies have been proposed. Data-mining methodologies are just one type. Data-mining methodologies can be classified as supervised or unsupervised (Roiger and Geatz, 2002). Supervised learning involves the application of induction-based supervision; in short, it builds models by using inputs to predict outputs. A popular application of supervised learning is classification. On the contrary, unsupervised learning builds models from data without predefined patterns. In other words, only inputs are used for building the models. One popular application is clustering.

Some of the currently popular techniques regarding data-mining methodologies are introduced below, and include market-basket analysis, neural networks, clustering and decision trees.

Market basket analysis

The purpose of market-basket analysis is to find possibly useful relationships among events or products. The results of the analysis may help in the design of promotions and the development of cross-marketing strategies (Roiger and Geatz, 2002). The relationships are usually represented in the form of an IF-THEN rule. For example:

IF {bread} THEN {milk}

There are two indicators used to show the degree of matches. In the above example, *confidence* is the number of customers who buy both bread and milk divided by the number of customers who buy bread. *Support* is the number of customers who buy bread divided by the total number of customers. In other words, the probability that a customer will buy bread (i.e., that the antecedent is true) is referred to as the support for the rule. The conditional probability that a customer will purchase milk given that bread is purchased is referred to as the confidence. Hence, market-basket analysis can be used to analyze customers' purchasing patterns between one product and others. This feature can facilitate cross-marketing.

Decision trees

Decision trees aim to induce decision procedures with discriminative bias for the classification of other samples (Janikow, 1998). ID3 and CART are the two most important discriminative learning algorithms that work by recursive partitioning. C4.5 (Quinlan, 1993) is an improved version of ID3. CART is different from C4.5 in that CART always performs binary splits on the data and uses test data to help prune and generalize a created binary tree (Roiger and Geatz, 2002). Decision trees can be used to classify customers according to their demographics, psychographics or other important variables. Hence decision trees can facilitate market segmentation.

Neural networks

Neural networks are mathematical models that attempt to mimic the operations of human brains. There are three types of layers: input, hidden and output layers (von Altrock, 2001). The input layer contains nodes, with one for each input variable. The output layer contains one or more nodes, also with one for each output variable. There may be one or more hidden layers. Each hidden layer contains several nodes. The input and output layers are connected by the hidden layer(s). Neural network learning is accomplished by modifying the weights on the connection by repeatedly passing the values of the input variables through the network. Once the learning is completed, a new set of inputs (out of sample) will create new output(s) (forecasts) at the output layer when the inputs pass through the network.

Neural networks can be used to classify customers if certain purchasing patterns are known. They can be used for complicated analyses such as analyses of retention and loyalty. Neural networks can also be applied to cluster customers when specific purchasing patterns are unknown.

Clustering

Clustering is a process of grouping objects that are similar in that they share certain characteristics. A cluster is therefore a collection of objects that are 'similar' to each other, and are 'dissimilar' in that they are different from the objects belonging to other clusters. Various algorithms have been proposed. K-means (MacQueen, 1967) is one of the simplest unsupervised learning algorithms for clustering. The main idea is to define k centroids, with one for each cluster, and to then regard the objects that are located close to the centroids as a cluster. A self-organization map (SOM) is an unsupervised neural network model devised by Kohonen (1982). The SOM consists of two layers of nodes: an input layer and an output layer. The neurons in the output layer are arranged in a grid and are influenced by their neighbours within this grid. The goal is to automatically cluster the inputs in such a way that similar ones are represented by the same output neuron (Kim and Han, 2001; Mangiameli *et al.*, 1996).

A two-step cluster is a two-step clustering method. The first step involves making a single pass through the data, during which the raw inputs are compressed into a manageable set of subclusters. The second step involves using a hierarchical clustering method to progressively merge the subclusters into larger clusters. Clustering is good for clustering customers into groups when specific purchasing patterns are unknown.

Applications

Data-mining methodologies have been applied to various problems related to marketing. In one study (Kim *et al.*, 2001) data-mining methodologies were suggested for personalized recommendation. It has also been shown that market-basket analysis can be useful for personalized recommendation (Lee, 2000). Shin and Sohn (2004) used K-means, SOM and fuzzy K-means (a fuzzy version of K-means) to segment stock-trading customers into normal, best and VIP categories for two different modes: a representative-assisted and an online trading system. According to the segmentation, different brokerage commission rates were suggested. Decision trees were applied to improve the website's retention (Pabarskaite, 2003). Furthermore, neural networks were applied to learn customers' repeat purchase patterns in direct marketing (Baesens *et al.*, 2002).

Process in action Caves Book Company, Taiwan

Caves has been a brick-and-mortar book company in Taiwan since 1952. Its recent strategy has been to increase its market share by opening branches. The 23rd branch has newly opened. Caves mainly sells language books and sells directly to its end consumers. Hence, its business model belongs to the B2C category. It plans to establish its own publication line to expand its business model in the near future. Until then, the published books will be sold to other retailers and then to the end consumers. In other words, the business model will be expanded to B2B2C.

Caves started its website (http://www.cavesbooks.com.tw) in 2001. The virtual bookstore basically sells the same content as in the traditional outlet. The virtual store was not intended to replace the brick-and-mortar counterpart. Instead, it was intended to work as a complement. As a result, brick-and-mortar and virtual bookstores can serve consumers who can and cannot reach the physical stores.

The website provides online catalogues, promotion, chat rooms, etc. The online catalogues belong to the offering mix in the content. The promotion belongs to the appeal mix in the content. The chat room belongs to the community. With regards to the context criterion, the website (as in Figure 19.2) is full of colourful design; hence it is more aesthetic than functional.

Comparatively, it is easier to collect the transaction data from the web, which facilitates the analysis of consumer behaviours. In addition, the web design is used to reinforce its marketing strategies. It sends customized e-news to its members according to members' education levels, favourite collections, purchase histories, etc. It also provides different discounts and credits for various classes of members. These members may share the valuable information with potential consumers. From the transaction database, market segmentation is clearly defined by using data-mining technologies. Hence market strategies can be implemented accordingly and efficiently.

Questions

1. What is the business model of Caves?
2. How does Caves perceive its brick-and-mortar and virtual stores?
3. What is the web design of Caves' website?
4. How can the Caves website implement viral marketing?

Figure 19.2
The website for the Caves Book Company

SOURCE: K.-H. HUARNG, 2006. COURTESY OF CAVES BOOK COMPANY.

Summary

- As the Internet has become increasingly ubiquitous, new marketing strategies have emerged and marketing has consequently become popular.

- e-Business models and e-business plans provide clear e-marketing strategies to win more customers on the Internet.

- To this end, web-design criteria can be applied to implement these e-marketing strategies.

- Meanwhile, thanks to the Internet, an increasing amount of customer data is becoming available and being collected.

- Methods are needed to analyze and use these data to understand customers' needs, and then to provide relevant services.

- Data-mining methodologies constitute one of the tools used to delve into such an abundance of data.

- Hence, Internet marketing can rely on the analyses obtained from these data-mining methodologies and apply the web-design criteria to win customers and continuously make profits.

- This chapter has provided some insights into applying data-mining methodologies to facilitate customer data analysis.

- In addition, it has also described the methodology of implementing e-marketing strategies.

Chapter questions

1. What are the four basic business models? What can be derived from these basic models?

2. Why should e-business plans place more emphasis on marketing?

3. What are the seven web-design criteria proposed by Rayport and Jaworski? Which ones are relevant to Internet marketing?

4. What are viral marketing, one-to-one marketing or relationship marketing, and contextual marketing? How can they be implemented by web-design criteria?

5. What are data-mining methodologies? What are their major applications to marketing?

References

Afuah, A., and Tucci, C. (2001) *Internet Business Models and Strategies: Text and Cases*, Maidenhead, UK: McGraw Hill.

Angehrn, A. (1997) 'Designing mature internet business strategies: The ICDT model', *European Management Journal*, 15(4):361–369.

Baesens, B., Viaene, S., den Poel, D. V., Vanthienen, J., and Dedene, G. (2002) 'Bayesian neural network learning for repeat purchase modelling in direct marketing', *European Journal of Operational Research*, 138:191–211.

Brewer, B. (2001, February 22) 'Tips for optimizing viral marketing campaigns', [Online] http://www.clikz.com/837511. Last accessed 13 May 2009.

Chablo, E. (2001) 'The importance of marketing data intelligence in delivering successful CRM', *Customer Relationship Management*, pp. 57–70.

Eisenmann, T. M. (2002) *Internet Business Models: Text and Cases*, Maidenhead, UK: McGraw Hill.

Greenstein, M., and Feinman, T. M. (2000) *Electronic Commerce: Security, Risk Management, and Control*, Maidenhead, UK: McGraw-Hill.

Hoque, F. (2000) *e-Enterprise: Business Models, Architecture, and Components*, Cambridge, UK: Cambridge University Press.

Huarng, K. (2003, April) 'A framework for official web site design', *Journal of Management and Systems*, 10(2):10–21.

Huizingh, E. K. R. E. (2000, April 1) 'The content and design of web sites: An empirical study', *Information & Management*, 37(3):123–134.

INSEAD, J. L. Kellogg Graduate School of Management, London Business School, and Wharton School of the University of Pennsylvania (1999) *'Financial Times' Mastering Marketing: Your Single Source Guide to Becoming a Master of Marketing*, Financial Times/ Prentice Hall.

Janikow, C. Z. (1998) 'Fuzzy decision trees – Issues and methods', *IEEE Transactions on Systems, Man, and Cybernetics*, 28(1):1–14.

Kenny, D., and Marshall, J. F. (2000, Nov–Dec) 'Contextual marketing – The real business of the internet', *Harvard Business Review*, pp. 119–125.

Kim, J. W., Lee, B. H., Shaw, M. J., Chang, H.-L., and Nelson, M. (2001, Spring) 'Application of decision-tree induction techniques to personalized advertisements on internet storefronts', *International Journal of Electronic Commerce*, 5(3):45–62.

Kim, K. S., and Han, I. (2001) 'The cluster-indexing method for case-based reasoning using self-organizing maps and learning vector quantization for bond rating cases', *Expert Systems with Applications*, 21(3):147–156.

Kohonen, T. (1982) 'Self-organized formation of topologically correct, feature maps', *Biological Cybernetics*, 43(1):59–69.

Laudon, K. C., and Laudon, J. P. (1999) *Management Information Systems*, 8th edn., Upper Saddle River, NJ: Prentice Hall.

Lee, K. (2000) 'Personalized Advertisement Techniques for One-to-One Marketing on internet Stores', Masters thesis, Chungnam National University.

Lumpkin, G. T., and Dess, G. G. (2004) 'e-Business strategies and Internet business models: How the Internet adds value', *Organizational Dynamics*, 33(2):161.

MacQueen, J. B. (1967) 'Some methods for classification and analysis of multivariate observations', *Proceedings of Fifth Berkeley Symposium on Mathematical Statistics and Probability*, Vol. 1, Berkeley: University of California Press, pp. 281–297.

Mangiameli, P., Chen, S. K., and West, D. A. (1996) 'Comparison of SOM neural network and hierarchical clustering methods', *European Journal of Operational Research*, 93(2):402–417.

McCarthy, V. (1995) 'The web: Open for business', *Datamation*, 1:30–36.

Morgan Stanley Dean Witter (2000) The B2B internet report – Collaborative commerce. [Online]. http://www.morganstanley.com/institutional/techresearch/pdfs/b2bp1a.pdf. Last accessed 7 May 2009.

Pabarskaite, Z. (2003) 'Decision trees for web log mining', *Intelligent Data Analysis*, 7:141–154.

Peppers, D., and Rogers, M. (1993) *The One-to-One Future: Building Relationships One Customer at a Time*, New York: Currency and Doubleday.

Quinlan, J. R. (1993) *Programs for Machine Learning*, San Francisco: Morgan Kaufman.

Rappa, M. (2000) 'Business models on the Web'. [Online]. http://ecommerce.ncsu.edu/ business_models.html#anchor1516683. Last accessed 9 May 2009.

Rayport, J. F., and Jaworski, B. J. (2001) *e-Commerce*, Irwin, Boston: McGraw-Hill.

Roiger, R. J., and Geatz, M. W. (2002) *Data Mining: A Tutorial-Based Primer*, New Jersey: Pearson Prentice Hall.

Schneider, G. P. (2003) *Electronic Commerce*, 4th edn., Boston, MA: Thomson Learning.

Shin, H. W., and Sohn, S. Y. (2004) 'Segmentation of stock trading customers according to potential value', *Expert Systems with Applications*, 27:27–33.

Teklitz, F., and McCarthy, R. L. (2001) 'Analytical customer relationship management', *Customer Relationship Management*, pp. 277–300.

Thomas, J. S., Reinartz, W., and Kumar, V. (2004, July–August) 'Getting the most out of all your customers', *Harvard Business Review*, pp. 76–85.

von Altrock, C. (2001) *Fuzzy Logic & Neurofuzzy Applications in Business & Finance*, Upper Saddle River, NJ: Prentice Hall.

Web Associates (2001) 'e-Everything: Technology-enabled customer relationship management', *Customer Relationship Management*, pp. 45–56.

Wilson, R. F. (2000, February 1) 'The six simple principles of viral marketing', *Web Marketing Today*, 70:1–3.

20

Cross-boundary and global (international) management: some considerations on recent events

Carlos Lucas de Freitas

Introduction

In this chapter we will take a look at developments in international and global management, starting from the marketing perspective. Using very recent and current international business events as guides, and without any pretence of being too systematic or exhaustive, we will address the convergence and divergence paradigm of international business, and in particular the global marketing environment. Then we will discuss the impetus for internationalization, and the assessment of global marketing opportunities. This leads to new market and/or production site selection abroad – to be discussed with other entry strategies (which may be oriented towards sales in that market and/or to production for other markets). Finally, we will briefly discuss global competition and strategy and the future of global marketing.

We will attempt to bring into play the 'process-based view of marketing management', which implies a consideration of a cross-functional perspective directed at the various process(es) involved in what is really cross-boundary and global

Learning objectives

To enable the reader to discuss some recent events in international marketing with respect to:

- International marketing theoretical frameworks.

- Current environmental conditions and trends.

- Future directions of international marketing.

(international) management. Global marketing, like global sourcing, involves the efficient use of worldwide human material and capital resources, via a co-ordination of such flows powered by the much easier informational and logistical fluxes.

What makes international marketing worthy of specific treatment? Most of the specificity of international marketing can be summed up by the word 'distance' (more encompassing than 'difference'). Too narrow and old-fashioned, you might say, but this encapsulates both *geographical* distance and *psychic* distance.

In the middle there are the 'barriers', such as trade barriers – political, fiscal, etc. – so one might say global management is about overcoming *distance* and *hurdles*.

On marketing definitions

The working definition proposed by Bradley (2005) is relatively complete, and includes the need to sense/research:

> International marketing means identifying needs and wants of customers in different markets and cultures, providing products, services, technologies and ideas to give the firm a competitive marketing advantage, communicating information about these products and services and distributing and exchanging them internationally through one or a combination of foreign market entry modes.

We would add the provision of *empathy* as an increasingly important complement to research in the definition. Empathy, a requirement in marketing, may be more difficult to achieve but is very important in the international arena and the future of marketing within it. It is important for both the market-sensing and relationship-building activities at the market levels (B2C and B2B) and at the network-building level. An ethnocentric attitude is no way to an ethically sustainable business future.

Another attribute which needs to be increasingly considered is *politics*, mainly at the macro-level but with some impact at the micro-level. This is often reflected in the country-of-origin effect (with a strong supra-country regional effect in Europe). But political skills are also very important for the relationship-creation and maintenance (never-ending) processes which have been highlighted in the most recent American Marketing Association definition of 'marketing' (American Marketing Association, 2009). Implicit in that definition is the importance of technology, in value creation, value communication and the potential to power up and manage the relationships with customers and other stakeholders.

This general definition naturally extends to international marketing. Marketing is an organizational function and *a set of processes* for:

- Creating, communicating and delivering *value* to customers.
- Managing transnational relationships with customers and other partners, in ways that benefit the organization and its stakeholders.

The international arena: marketing vs. other functions

Marketing is not just a functional area concentrated in one or a few departments. It is also a set of processes that cross between departments, converging on the fulfilment of the objectives listed above. These processes are also naturally cross-border for internationalized firms. They go beyond *organizational integrated* (or *integral*) marketing into what might be labelled 'diffused marketing', with its principles being widely accepted.

Diffusion is good for the organization, but it can be contentious for marketing as a discipline. The situation is analogous to when a product brand name becomes so widely known that it becomes a pseudonym for the product category, perhaps losing brand strength. This current ubiquity of the marketing concept indicates a need for marketers to redefine their positions in the business place, or risk being replaced by professionals from other areas (in particular, operations management and quality), which have already assimilated the marketing philosophy and attitude.

Marketing is thus rapidly becoming a core operating philosophy of organizations. Drucker (1954) asserted that there were only two basic 'functions' in a business enterprise: marketing and innovation. If this is the case, how can marketing really assert itself as a managerial function?

Marketing, business policy and strategy courses have a great deal of synergy. It follows that synergy occurs between international/global marketing and international/global business educational courses. The difference lies in a greater consideration of economic, financial and operations aspects in the latter courses (which are naturally more encompassing in terms of disciplines), and more detail in terms of marketing tools in the former courses. However some critical issues are the same, e.g., international market entry, market selection and the process of internationalization.

Whatever the arguments, an 'I was here first' response from the marketing function is no longer acceptable. It is not in the interest of business to constrain marketing to a functional area. In fact, it is important to have that mindset spread all over the organization. So will marketers and marketing become diluted within the organization, part of the scenery, just when marketing is so relevant? Marketers should get involved in co-ordinating activities in cross-functional marketing processes, emphasizing integration and co-ordinating the activities across departments towards the achievement of marketing goals. This requires competence to gauge the marketplace impact of the various functional units.

The customer then becomes the real driver of the business – a principle also adopted by business process re-engineering in the operations view. As Drucker rightly observed, customers increasingly play a critical role in defining value. It is up to the marketer to identify and monetize that added value – always a challenging task, but particularly so in an international environment.

Supply chain design, redefinition and management

As firms disperse across borders [from the classical multinational to the more 'modern' global meta-national, ironically designated 'mini-national' by Czinkota *et al.* (2004)], understanding the consumer becomes imperative. It is driven by growing simultaneous demands from customers and consumers for lower costs and increased innovation, speed and flexibility (or the overall value offer). There is an increasing need to focus on the inner processes of the supply chain and on the outer processes of the demand chain. Both can and do span across not one but several borders, in series and in parallel.

Supply chain management (SCM) refers to the co-ordination of flows (e.g., material, information and finance) along the value chain from manufacturer to end-user. Building on IBM Research to build and operate an open and adaptive framework (IBM, 1999), An and Fromm (2005) advocate the use of *business process integration and management*

(BPIM) technologies (see Table 20.1). The end objective is a supply chain solution with agility, responsiveness, resiliency and dynamism. BPIM technologies focus on the structure and behaviour of business systems, of which marketing, operations and logistics are critical functions at the domestic – but to an *n*th degree at international – levels.

Lee (2004) recommends that supply chains (see Figure 20.1) should not only be fast and cost effective but agile, adaptable and aligned (the 'three As'). Some diversity/'adaptation' can be provided through processes focused on servicing demand (demand chain management, i.e., pull oriented).

Farrel (2004) (see Table 20.2) sees offshoring as an intrinsic component within a five-stage model of global restructuring, evolving from a less global to a more global position. (The model is not necessarily sequential.)

International (regional and country) borders will criss-cross this chain at different and various points.

Table 20.1
The supply chain reference (SCOR) process model

SOURCE: ADAPTED FROM AN AND FROMM, 2005.

Deliver	Source	Make	Deliver	Source	Make	Deliver	Source	Make	Deliver	Source
& return	& return		& return	& return		& return	& return		& return	& return
Supplier's supplier	Supplier (internal or external)			Company			Customer (internal or external)			Customer's customer

Table 20.2
Supply chain – five-stage model

SOURCE: MODIFIED FROM FARRELL, 2004.

New market entry	Production delocalization (displacement) abroad	Disaggregation of the value chain	Re-engineering of the value chain	New market creation
Value derives from basic improvements to business practices			Value originates from process innovation and market expansion	
Less global — — — — — — — — — — —			More global	

Figure 20.1
Supply chain

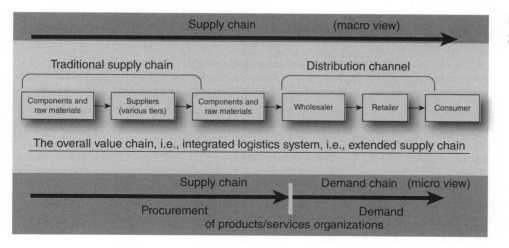

Convergence and divergence paradigm, and politics in the global marketing environment

The term *cross-boundary* is quite generic and comprehensively qualifies the phenomena usually associated with international marketing. It involves not just crossing country frontiers, but also regional differences both at the supra-national [e.g., European Union (EU)] and intra-national (e.g., Flemish and Walloon regions in Belgium) levels.

When dealing with large yet not widely explored markets such as China or Russia, these particular differences must be taken into account. Foreign company officials in China who believe it is enough to deal with national politicians may be shocked when they find that regional and local officials have the power to obstruct or smoothen business processes. Moreover, there are structural differences between regions in terms even of law, not to mention the personal rivalries (which may or not be connected) between the governors of each province. China also has important spoken language differences, with Cantonese being spoken (and deeply rooted) in the economically very important southeast, while the central government is sponsoring a move towards the generalized use of Putonghua (modern Chinese).

This 'divergence' perspective is much more general than one might assume. Past 'convergence' ideas stemmed from a dominant Western, mainly Anglo-Saxon, point of view, where the rule of law was considered the norm, or desired, or inevitable. Rule of law would supersede the inter- and intra-country differences – a guiding belief of the EU. Differences are nevertheless now gaining recognition by talk about the 'Europe of Regions', increasing with the growth in the number of eastern European country members.

After a period of 'bipolar' convergence (with the nuclei then being the USA and the USSR), which continued even after the creation of the 'non-aligned' movement by a group of nations voicing their independence from both blocks, the collapse of the USSR led to a feeling that a one-system world was a possibility, given the existence of a single hegemonic superpower. Nowadays, China is positioning itself as a counterbalance to US hegemony. Recent US foreign policy coupled with Chinese pragmatism (and strong market attractiveness) has created a surge of sympathy towards this option, to the point of ignoring unaddressed issues that may or not be naturally corrected with China's economic evolution. Russia also benefits from some good grace for similar reasons, coupled also with its status as an oil and gas supplier, and a feeling that there is less internal chaos (something established businesses abhor).

The EU 'superpower' has the disadvantage of poor demographic evolution, and furthermore has been 'successfully' conditioned and contained by the USA-UK tandem into its current position of both producer and large market in terms of current purchase power. It is difficult to predict the future of the EU both politically and as an 'economic powerhouse' as the current production advantages have been eroding for some time and will continue to be so at the intellectual capital level. This is because the current leadership position reflects what might be considered a declining level of entrepreneurship, creativity and innovation. In the authors' opinion, the UK is a case apart. It is formally inside but attitudinally outside the EU. It is strategic ally of the USA and shares with it a desire for a weak-willed and low-initiative EU, basically reduced to the 'large-market' dependent status. However, this is an untenable situation in the long term because it will simply lead to a decline in purchase power, and faster replacement by Far Eastern markets.

In the past, the bipolar convergence (around USA and USSR, plus a 'third way' of the non-aligned countries) has kept some stability within economic blocks, and has increased the importance of micro (i.e., firm-level) actions. However, current shifting situations indicate a need to bolster the macro (country-level and international) forces, and a need to advance under their protection away from markets where the macro movements will draw 'fire' based on negative company country of origin perceptions.

Economic diplomacy, often strong-armed, has long been a fact of life, but its importance has been played down officially in a politically correct narrative. Recent events are ripping apart some carefully constructed tales. For example, one can say that the World Trade Organization (WTO) has been expanded to include China and Vietnam, and in the future will include Russia, but it took the barbaric 9/11 events to shift the US perception of China from its main potential foe to a close ally. This ideological pendulum is likely to swing back again in the not too distant future, and WTO membership will not prevent the execution of policies that will condition companies' activities. Just consider the 30 per cent tariff imposed on steel imports by President Bush in March 2002 and the subsequent retaliatory reactions by other countries, not ending with the March 2003 WTO ruling that the steel tariffs were illegal under world trade law, nor with the December 2003 lifting of those US tariffs.

> Nations have no principles, only interests (*attributed to Henry Kissinger*).

One may argue that all this is just background, one more external 'environmental' force that needs to be considered (scanned) when preparing, say, a marketing plan. But would that be too simplistic a perspective? Wars have been waged for economic reasons, but recently ethical standards and moral high ground seem to many of us to be the desirable and inevitable way to the future, along with a common trade framework.

The two new 'heavyweights'

Two new heavyweights have recently exploded into international business: the so-called Chinese 'dragon' and the Indian 'tiger'. China in particular is a significant factor in the development of the rules (and praxis) of international trade, but India is close behind. They are good students, but on their own terms.

> China is modernizing, not Westernizing. The country's goal is to modernize but retain the Chinese 'essence', which it is still struggling to define. (*McGregor, 2005*)

There is plenty of anecdotal evidence that major international players force the rules to their advantage:

- The USA has been on a drive towards extending the application of some of its laws extra-territorially, to companies from other countries.
- China considers ethnic Chinese to be subject to their own laws without regard for the nationality of the said citizen. This will inevitably create some conditioning on ethnic Chinese born in other countries when dealing with and in China, since they benefit from little outside protection.

Process in action Pepsi in India

Companies must choose whether to standardize (centralize) or adapt (localize). In India, PepsiCo, perhaps falsely, signalled their intent to 'adapt' to India 'centrally' – all the way to corporate headquarters in the USA.

> Ms. Nooyi joined the $33 billion global convenient foods and beverages company in 1994 and has served as President and Chief Financial Officer since 2001, when she was also named to PepsiCo's board of directors. As the fifth CEO in PepsiCo's 41-year history, she brings vast and unique skills to the job. She has directed the company's global strategy for over a decade and was the primary architect of PepsiCo's restructuring . . . [*excerpts from PepsiCo news release, August 14, 2006* (PepsiCo, 2006)]

Even if the new CEO choice seemed natural, the timing was simply too convenient to be a simple coincidence, a sign of the importance of a market like India for a global company like PepsiCo. Indra Nooyi (originally from India, and a graduate of Yale School of Management) had been appointed (chronologically after this controversy) as President and CEO of PepsiCo from October 2006 (at the same time that the retirement of the current chairman was announced for May 2007). Nooyi had already been mentioned as a key player in the company's strategic planning.

In December 2006, the *London Times* reported that Muhtar Kent, originally from Turkey and a senior executive at Coca-Cola's North Asia and Middle East division, had been promoted to the reintroduced position of global chief operating officer. It also mentioned the possibility that he might soon have the top job at Coke.

Relationships and public relations in particular are very visible in this case. Is it all relationship 'mending' – macro-marketing or micro-politics?

In December 2006, Indra Nooyi was reported as saying that PepsiCo's products in India were totally safe, and that PepsiCo would abide by any (Indian) government standards. Perhaps this was aimed at Coke's previous problems?

The Indian 'revolt' also illustrates two other points:

1. Importance of other actors besides competitors and politicians: the Centre for Science and Environment (CSE), a New Delhi-based NGO, had been at the centre of this controversy, with its third damaging report against Coke and PepsiCo on the subject since 1993. There was, in effect, a fight over public opinion, and it seems PepsiCo had decided it is simply too large to be in the hands of PR, but rather should be addressed at the new CEO level.

2. *Intracountry* political differences have led to different actions in various states.

Contemporary sources

TIME Asia magazine (August 14, 2006): 'India's Storm in a Cola Cup: Reports of Pesticides in Soft Drinks Prompt a Nationalist Backlash against Coke and Pepsi' reported by Aryn Baker.

BusinessWeek Asia (August 10, 2006): 'India: Pesticide Claims Shake Up of Coke and Pepsi' reported by Brian Bremner and Nandini Lakshman.

International Herald Tribune (August 7, 2006): 'India Widens Ban on Coke and Pepsi' reported by Amellia Gentleman.

http://www.pepsico.com

http://www.businessweek.com/globalbiz/content/aug2006/gb20060810_826414.htm?chan=top+news_top+news

http://www.cseindia.org (Centre for Science and Environment (CSE), New Delhi, India)

http://www.reuters.com

Reuters India, New Delhi (August 12, 2006 7:40 AM IST): Interview – 'McDonald's India Sees Sales, Profits Surging', conducted by Shailendra Bhatnagar.

Reuters, Monday, August 14, 2006 3:47 PM: 'Nooyi Expected to Ease into Pepsi's Top Job', reported by Martinne Geller.

Associated Press, August 14, 2006 03:47 PM:
'PepsiCo Names Its First Female CEO', reported
by Vinnee Tong.

http://www.businessweek.com/globalbiz/
content/aug2006/gb20060810_826414.
htm?chan=top+news_top+news

Questions

1. How do you think the appointment of the new CEO will alleviate the problems of PepsiCo in India?

2. What theory do you think explains the appointment? (You may wish to read further before answering this question.)

- In India, there is ongoing litigation against US flag carrier Coca-Cola. Even as early as 1977, Coke chose to leave India after the government insisted that it reveal the formula. Coca-Cola returned to India in 1993, but with Pepsi now dominating the soft-drinks market (80 per cent). In a different initiative, the state of Kerala (approximately 30 million inhabitants) banned the Indian subsidiaries of both companies from making or selling their beverages, and several other regions instituted partial bans on the sale of Coke and Pepsi (e.g., schools and government offices). In fact, six state governments had stopped the sale of carbonated beverages made by Coca-Cola and PepsiCo at or near state-run schools, colleges and hospitals. They are now once again the target of Indian justice after analyses have shown high levels of pesticides in the soft drinks – apparently from the local water used for the bottling process. There is now a campaign accusing Coca-Cola of depleting the ground water. In August 2006, the Supreme Court of India ordered Coca-Cola and PepsiCo to provide information on the chemical composition and ingredients of their products or face a ban in India. Is this a pollution issue, or one of breaking up the market dominance? Sales have dropped by over 30 per cent. The USA is warning of possible investment fallout. Some businesspeople argue that it is a matter of local politics that needs to be perceived in the Indian context.

These events indicate that relationship marketing, as compared to single-dimensional, or one-transaction merit-based marketing decisions, is considered increasingly important. However, the world is going through a period of upheaval and instability which may require very careful monitoring of political relationships, as they can seriously impede relationship-marketing efforts.

Intracountry political differences are also an issue in China, where some perceive fierce interregional strife, and could become an important issue for international marketing in several other countries. This is a strong argument for localization and adaptation options.

After a period of much touted homogenization, where the underlying assumption was of an ever-increasing client and consumer commonality allowing for the use of standardized strategies (e.g., product, price, communication and distribution for marketing), at least in propensity, we seem to be at a point of paradigm shift or, less dramatically, one more turn in a cycle of history. Rigby and Vishwanath (2006) report the ending of standardization due to increased diversity (in ethnicity, values, lifestyle and wealth) of consumer communities. This is also true in the international arena, with increasing affirmations of ethnicity, values and lifestyle.

Recent trends in international environment: convergence or divergence?

It seems that we are witnessing a surge of divergence with several hot-points. Furthermore, these divergences are occurring often in regions within countries, which advocate a focus that is finer than just country-based. Naturally, marketing is about segmentation (including geographical segmentation) but this requires extra attention at the supra-segment regional level. Examples include:

- Flemish-speaking Belgium, where questions in French are listened to and politely replied to in English.
- Québec in Canada, where there has been an anti-English movement and affirmation of French cultural values.
- Catalonia, where Catalan was officially recognized as a nationality in the Catalan Statute of Autonomy enacted in 1979. In June 2006, Catalonia voted to adopt a new Statute of Autonomy, including a provision defining Catalonia as a nation.
- Scotland, where a semi-autonomous parliament was installed in the 1990s, and law, education and health-care systems are separate from the rest of the UK.

Maybe these European examples can be seen as understandable in the context of the EU as 'a Europe of regions', and while worrisome in terms of peace and harmony, they still represent a drive further away from standardization.

In Eastern Europe, there are two examples, one solved peacefully, and the other still in development after a dramatic conflict: Czechoslovakia, which split peacefully into the Czech Republic and Slovakia in January 1993, and Yugoslavia, which contentiously broke up into Bosnia, Herzegovina, Croatia, Montenegro, Republic of Macedonia, Serbia and Slovenia – some of which still harbour strong inner tensions.

Indonesia, the country with the largest Islamic population, is currently trying to implement Sharia (Islamic law) in the troubled province of Aceh, where the indigenous people have been fighting for independence for more than 30 years. Apparently, other Indonesian provinces are waiting to see whether they should follow this example. It remains to be seen whether this constitutes intracountry divergence or a future convergence towards another paradigm: Indonesia.

Process in action wrong country of origin – Arla Foods

In May 2001, the Danish-Swedish dairy giant Arla Foods (the world's second-largest dairy producer) announced the creation of a new subsidiary in the Middle East (Arla National Food Products LLC, in the United Arab Emirates (UAE), its second-most important market in the region after Saudi Arabia) in a joint venture with one of its long-time local business partners, with the stated objective of obtaining full control of the distribution of their products and taking charge of the company's future development in the UAE. In August 2005, it revealed plans to move a production plant to Saudi Arabia as part of a strategy to develop its market position in that country (doubling sales by 2010) and the Middle East. This meant an increase in commitment to that market (both country and region – the Middle East is Arla's largest market outside the EU). Arla Foods had experienced few problems in 40 years of building up its business in the Middle East.

Then, at the turn of 2005–2006, a few newspaper cartoons were published, physically depicting Mohammed, an illegal act in Muslim law. Arla found themselves with a 'wrong' country of origin label in the Muslim world, and facing a boycott of Danish goods called by Muslim leaders. A news item dated 30 January 2006 indicated that, by then, the boycott of Danish products in the Middle East was almost total.

(Notice that Arla's long-established subsidiary in Saudi Arabia is designated 'Danya Foods' – which gives some clue to the country of origin – understandably, as Denmark adds value to dairy products. On the other hand, the LEGO group, a privately held Danish toy-maker group, doesn't market its toys as being Danish, considering LEGO to be perceived as an international brand. Because of this and because the Middle East is a small market for LEGO, the boycott was considered by that group to have little consequence – despite the fact that it was put in several boycott lists.)

Interestingly, these events can be construed as an example of globalization: Paul Reynolds wrote on the BBC News website (Wednesday, 22 February 2006, 15:06 GMT) that 'the spread of protests against the cartoons of Muhammed is another manifestation of globalization' – and so is the spread of Islamic terrorism. These are extremely powerful 'environmental' factors that must be factored in business decisions, both by themselves and considering other parties' possible reactions to these trends.

At about the same time that Arla was experiencing 'Danish problems' in the Muslim world, it was stepping up its involvement in the Chinese market. In the spring of 2002, Arla Foods Ingredients had established a 'first base' in China, consisting of a sales office in Beijing. Its purpose was to assess the potential of the growing dairy market to determine the best direction for its own expansion in China. Following 2 years of exploratory activities, Arla made its first appearance at the Food Ingredients China trade fair in Guangzhou in 2003. The sales office was also the base from which Chinese Lillie Li Ekhard, a qualified medical doctor with a background in the Chinese industry, scouted out possible local partners for Arla, from which resulted a joint venture with the China Mengniu

Dairy Company in October 2005. Ownership of the venture consists of 49 per cent equity owned by Arla and 51 per cent by Mengniu. The joint venture, called the Inner Mongolia Arla Mengniu Dairy Company, is located in Hohhot in Inner Mongolia, a semi-autonomous region in Northern China. (This region has a population which is already used to drinking milk, though the Chinese government is actively building that consumption all over China. Production started with milk powder; China is the world's largest market for milk powder).

Lillie Li Ekhard is currently responsible for Mengniu Arla's marketing operations. She was born and bred in Shanghai and lived in Denmark for several years with her Danish husband. She considers this mixed cultural background to have been extremely important in her work. This case is thus an example of cultural-bridging competencies, which can be critical to foreign operations, and where attention to local details – such as the choice of a joint venture with a resourceful local partner – is imperative. (In this case, the local partner owned production capabilities, and had market knowledge and networking competencies.)

Contemporary sources

ChinaNews (2005, December). 'Arla in Milk Powder Joint Venture in China', unattributed.

Newsweek International (2006, August 21–28). 'Iranians Rename Danish Pastries', unattributed.

http://www.arla.com

http://www.arlafoods.com

http://www.arlaingredients.com

http://www.arlafoodsingredients.com

http://www.chinadairy.net/english/List.Asp?ListID=176

http://www.giract.com/food_industry_news/

Questions

1. Could Arla have predicted the problems that arose between Denmark and the Muslim world?

2. What could they have done to prevent the problem before it happened?

3. Is there any theory or advice they could have consulted to help them?

In summary, rather than moving towards homogeneity, recent years have witnessed prolific affirmations of linguistic, cultural, racial and religious differences. Alternatively, one may argue that some of these 'schisms' are naturally part of a *transnational* movement – including the Kosovo and Tchetchen separatist movements with an affirmation of Islamic identity.

Theory of new market selection and market entry strategies

There are several 'step models' purporting to explain the internationalization process. The best known pertains to the Nordic or Uppsala School theory of Johanson and Vahlne (1990), which is a process theory of internationalization (PTI).

This model must be seen in the light of the conditions at the time of its conception in 1973, and contrasted with the conditions prevalent in most countries nowadays, as well as the interim periods. It can be called the 'gradualist' or 'incrementalist' approach, and is concerned with the state and change aspects of internationalization. The state aspects include market knowledge and current market commitments, while the change aspects comprise both commitment decisions and current activities.

There is an implicit assumption of learning from experience, with competence development – this may lower the risk perceptions (internal barriers in the mind of managers), enabling the consideration of more 'distant' markets.

In parallel to this external pathway to internationalization, there are internal organizational changes which the literature sees occurring, as portrayed by Luostarinen (1994) (see Figure 20.2).

Figure 20.2
The stages of internationalization and the structural evolution of international operations

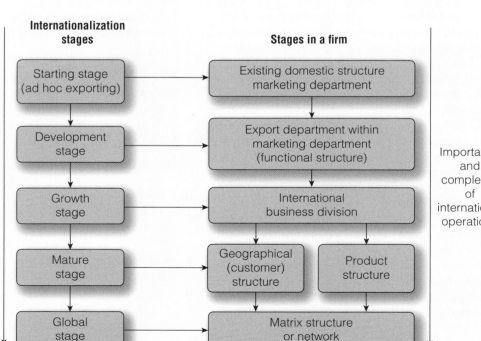

SOURCE: ADAPTED FROM LUOSTARINEN (1994, 2006).

Structural evolution of international operations

According to the PTI, internationalization proceeds incrementally and sequentially as the company acquires more *experiential knowledge* and *foreign organizing knowledge* (see Figure 20.3).

A firm gains experiential knowledge from its current business activities, and PTI sees market commitment decisions depending greatly on that experience. When experiential knowledge increases, the company is more prone to a decision to commit more resources to specific foreign operations. As gaining experiential knowledge about foreign markets takes time, the additional market commitment will be made in small, incremental steps.

The PTI sees the internationalization processes as causal cycles, where the firm's current activities (i.e., the change aspects) affect market knowledge and market commitment (designated the state aspects) which in turn affect the change aspects.

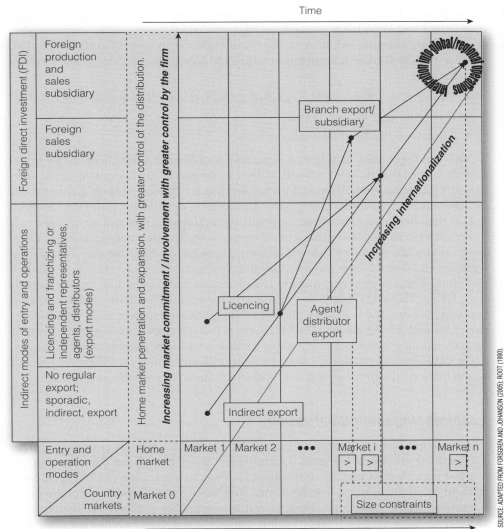

Figure 20.3
Increasing geographic market diversification: incremental (stepwise) model of internationalization

SOURCE: ADAPTED FROM FORSGREN AND JOHANSON (2005); ROOT (1990).

However, even then, some firms do not follow that pure stepwise approach. Some 'disobedience' to this almost normative theory would also be a good way to differentiate from competitors. Furthermore, some rationales might not be easily perceived from superficial observation – e.g., the internationalization of a medium-sized company to a geographically and psychically distant country because the owner's wife hailed from there, as in the Arla case. In fact, Arla is almost a textbook example for the PTI model of internationalization, starting with domestic development and exports to neighbouring countries (Arla's largest regional market is the EU, where it is the largest dairy producer). These initial steps would then be followed by an increase of commitment to those markets up to the installation of subsidiaries for marketing and production. Concurrently, there would be a movement towards more distant markets. In recent incarnations of this theory, it has been generalized by going beyond geographical distance to psychic distance. For example, New Zealand and the UK are very distant in geographical measurements but very close psychically.

The causal cycle theory attempts to explain both the increasing level of involvement with a foreign market, and the expansion activities to more 'distant' foreign markets (considering psychic distance). The model depicts an increasing commitment of the firm to international markets with time. There is an underlying dimension of learning and knowledge acquisition, through which firms get the competencies which enable them to risk developing those higher involvement (and investment) modes. Typical for the incremental change models is that the enterprises are assumed to:

- Evolve from a low to a high level of activity, resources or commitment.
- Evolve in small or large steps.
- All steps assumed to be unidirectional.

The 'unidirectional' assumption is notably problematic since there are plenty of market entries that do not end well, with total or partial abandonment of the market, in some cases going from full ownership to partial ownership or complete sale of that venture. Sometimes this is part of a move by the firm to consolidate its position in the international markets, rationalizing its global or regional operations.

Lasserre (1996) suggests generic *entry modes* from two subsequent phases of operational modes: *development* and *consolidation*. Lasserre espouses the use of greater integration and control entry modes when going from *platform* markets (e.g., Singapore and Hong Kong) to *emerging* markets (e.g., Vietnam and Cambodia), *growth* markets (e.g., China, Thailand, Indonesia, Malaysia, India and the Philippines), *maturing* markets (e.g., Taiwan and Korea) and finally to the *established* market (e.g., Japan). Concurrently, and synchronized with PTI, there is in each market an evolution towards operational modes representing greater commitment (with possibly some dispersion in the development phase), followed by a rationalization and consolidation towards an integration into global or regional operations (even for the emerging markets).

Leapfrogging into globalization

The staged models presented in Figure 20.4 have become less prevalent due to a growth of vicarious learning. Learning by experience is an extremely effective method, though not the most efficient. Vicarious learning can be much more efficient – and universities, in general, and business schools, in particular, have propagated important knowledge. Thus, an increasing number of relatively small but relevant companies have been leapfrogging multiple stages of the traditional process of 'gradual internationalization'. Many have indeed been created with the sole intent to 'export', i.e., to be international in one form or another, from inception.

Many of these firms behave in ways that contradict the PTI theories, and have been given titles that represent 'immediate' internationalization. Such titles include *INVs* (international new ventures) (McDougall *et al.*, 1994), *born globals* (Knight and Cavusgil, 1996; Madsen and Servais, 1997), *global startups* (Oviatt and McDougall 1994), *instant internationals* (Preece *et al.*, 1999), and *metanationals* (Doz *et al.*, 2001). They are often small, agile firms who chase customers. They then work in close association with the customer, even becoming imbricated within its value chain and production process, eventually living in close symbiosis with the 'host' partner. Sometimes, significant company personnel work for periods within the client's facilities at an international, regional or even global level.

Born globals tend to get a high degree of international involvement soon after creation, sharing with older global firms similar characteristics of international orientation, export strategy, competitive advantage and market situation (Moen and Servais, 2002). The firms start up with high-involvement exporting, i.e., without gradual build-up (by comparison, ordinary firms who start with low involvement usually remain with low involvement). This is in clear contradiction to the PTI models. In such companies, the attitude of the decision-maker in terms of global orientation, as well as the prevailing market conditions, seemed to be of paramount importance. Furthermore, decisions made around the time of the creation of the company seem to be critical to the surge of this type of company, exhibiting rapid and high-involvement internationalization.

> We define an international new venture [INV] as a business organization that, from inception, seeks to derive significant competitive advantage from the use of resources and the sale of outputs in multiple countries. The distinguishing feature of these startups is that their origins are international, as demonstrated by observable and significant commitments of resources (e.g., material, people, financing, time) in more than one nation.
> *(Oviatt and McDougall, 1994)*

Figure 20.4
Global marketing evolution: some international forms of organization

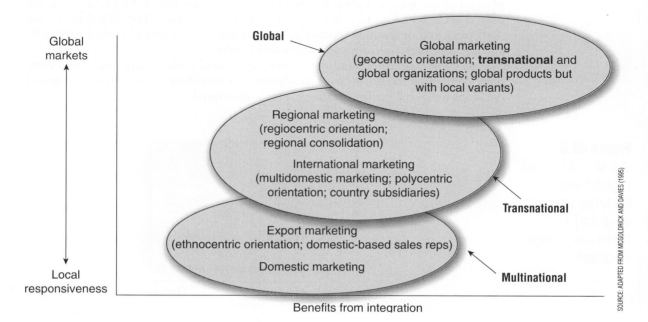

SOURCE: ADAPTED FROM MCGOLDRICK AND DAVIES (1995)

One can argue that the existence of such shortcuts result from vicarious learning from other companies (made easy by the natural creation of clusters that in turn reflect the phenomena), and from increasing exposure to vicarious learning through education media such as universities. But one should not neglect the opening up of communications such as television and, more recently, the Internet, making the world seem a much smaller and less scary place. At present, business education is more widespread and communications are easily, widely and cheaply available. Thus, it is possible for young upstart companies to have multiple worldwide contacts, and to keep them going on acceptable budgets.

Other theories of internationalization include:

- Comparative advantage theory
- Oligopolistic models of foreign direct investment
- Transaction cost theory
- Dunning's eclectic paradigm
- Nordic or Uppsala theory of internationalization
- Resource-based and knowledge-based theory

The application of the resource-based view of the firm (Barney, 1991; Conner, 1991; Peteraf, 1993; Wernerfelt, 1984, 1995) to international marketing (de Freitas, 2000; Zou and Cavusgil, 1996) has been fairly recent and, through the incorporation of the importance and intrinsic stickiness of resources, capabilities and skills, can be used to explain the PTI models. In fact, it goes further into the INVs and born global phenomena (Knight and Cavusgil, 1996; Oviatt and McDougall, 1994).

A search for markets and/or factors of production

However, the step models ignore the *duality* of domestic and global locations affecting marketing and production. The reduction in the cost of communications, both voice/data and physical, has made viable the location of production, and increasingly product or service conception and R&D, in distant countries with output often imported back 'home' or to other countries. As a consequence, bonding between the marketing and operations functions is increasing, with a mix of complementarity and overlap: they are truly and inextricably intertwined.

Canel and Das (2002) consider a four-stage global evolutionary model of a company, combining the functions of marketing and operations, in an attempt to model decisions on global facility locations. This is illustrated in Figure 20.5.

Figure 20.5
A 2.M × 2.O model of global evolution. Marketing (domestic vs. global) × Operations (domestic vs. global)

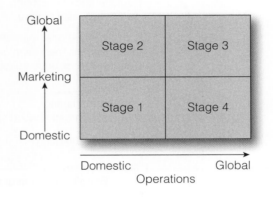

In the model, there is a suggestion of sequentiality, as represented by the stage numberings (and the 'stage' designation itself). Stages 1 and 2 represent an evolution towards international marketing, and Stages 3 and 4 a progression towards international sourcing and production. But does manufacturing abroad for international operations (Stage 3) appear first, or manufacturing abroad for home operations? Wal-Mart could be depicted as going from Stage 1 to Stage 4 and now to Stage 3 (through outsourcing). (See Wal-Mart case note later.)

> Global sourcing is 'the integration and co-ordination of procurement requirements across worldwide business units, looking at common items, processes, technologies and suppliers'. *(Moncza and Trent, 1991)*

Naturally, this simplified model does not fully depict the complexity of international expansion of manufacturing operations, with locations influenced by, for example, country, technological and product factors. It is not simply the duality of home vs. abroad but, in the latter case, the continuous dynamics of concentration vs. dispersion. It does relate to, but cannot fully and unequivocally identify with, and detail, the four stages of the development of global sourcing.

According to Monczka and Trent (1991), international procurement implementation follows four phases (reflecting also the acquisition of information and consolidation of knowledge about possible overseas suppliers):

Phase 1: Domestic purchasing only.

Phase 2: Foreign buying based on need, where companies use subsidiaries or other corporate units for international assistance and designate domestic buyers for international purchasing.

Phase 3: Foreign buying as part of procurement strategy, where companies start establishing international purchasing offices.

Phase 4: Integration of global procurement strategy, where firms integrate and co-ordinate worldwide sourcing strategy and assign design, build and sourcing to specific worldwide business units.

There is a mirror effect when we simultaneously consider the stage model of internationalization of marketing. In effect, sourcing is an activity immersed in marketing effects, including plenty of what can be called reverse marketing activities.

There is another dichotomy missing from these model depictions: business to customer (B2C) and original equipment manufacturers (OEM)/service suppliers vs. business to business (B2B) businesses. The 'markets' are different in each case. In B2C and OEM, the market is the final customer and consumer market, but in B2B it is business customers who are increasingly outsourcing a proportion of their value chain. Often, supplier firms will follow their customers in their internationalization efforts, and global firms are increasingly looking for global suppliers of goods, and increasingly for services such as consultancy and advertising agencies.

The right side of the model represents the intricacies of modern partner relationships along the supply chain. Even in a transnational one, where partners work side by side, outsiders often find difficulty 'drawing the line' between supplier and customer. Is it just an outside perception difficulty, or does boundary confusion also happen from within? In fact, both situations arise, and it is even more complex when country–region boundaries criss-cross the supply-manufacture-distribution value-chain. It is difficult to establish boundaries, particularly when low equity (less than 50 per cent) modes are used, since that does not necessarily represent the strength of the control over the venture.

Outsourcing involves some severe blurring or even dissolving of organizational boundaries. Its potential derives from its capability, capacity and distribution leveraging – without proportionately increasing its own costs on human resource, capital assets, logistical network, etc. However, as with any outsourcing, there are increased risks compared with their own operations. Organizations must not mistakenly opt for outsourcing to relax and yield responsibility – the need for responsibility remains, albeit of different nature, within the parent company.

Process in action approaches to internationalization – Logoplaste and COLEP CCL

Logoplaste presents itself as an outsourcing packaging company intimately integrated into the value chain of its clients (e.g., P&G, Reckitt-Benckiser and Danone). They often locate processes within the clients' premises or as close as possible. In this way, they have a presence in more than 30 plants in Europe, South America, Portugal (the 'home' or 'originating country'), Spain, Italy, UK and Brazil. Naturally, Logoplaste is always trying to increase what they offer to these clients, adding and extracting value from such close relationships, which require specific investments.

In a less 'dedicated' way, COLEP CCL defines itself as a pan-European supplier of packaging services, with six plants in Europe (Germany, Poland, Portugal, Spain and the UK). From these facilities, it has now started to offer contract manufacturing operations and specialty custom manufacturing, going up and down the clients' (e.g., Johnson Wax) value chains. Thus, its clients can rely increasingly on a full-service production package, almost limiting their own activities to R&D and marketing. Customers buy some products that are not just packaged, but completely manufactured and delivered by this company.

Both of these firms have based their internationalization strategy on long-term customer relationships, with close operational integration.

Questions
1. Place Logoplaste and COLEP CCL in the model in Figure 20.6.
2. Explain and discuss your placement.

Figure 20.6 Task complexity, co-ordination required and security of subcontracting alternative typologies

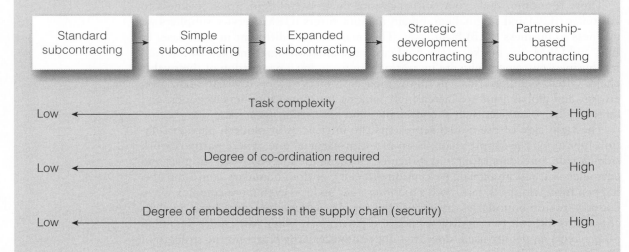

Global marketing comprises activities that precede, accompany and follow the production process (from core product conception, which may be more centralized, to product development and market communications and sales, which are more localized).

The increasing recourse to outsourcing, or offshoring, is also leading to the surge of network organizations (or 'virtual' organizations). (Some offshoring, when done to foreign subsidiaries, is not strictly outsourcing but can be considered to be the same in practical terms.) Though network or virtual organizations should not be confused with web-based organizations, they in fact do benefit from such an increasingly ubiquitous infrastructure. These networks appear as a more or less co-ordinated or loose set of organizations spread throughout the world and working together as if they were a single organization, whilst many are formally and *de facto* independent. Trust is a critical issue for these networks, and relationship creation and development – or business to business (B2B) relationship marketing activities – are fundamental.

As El Ansary (2006) points out, marketing strategy is one of the functional area strategies (including e.g., human resources, finance, operations and logistics) and furthermore, it is also conceived and implemented together with the other strategies of the firm. (These cross-function aspects are shown in Figure 20.7.) Similarly, an internationalization process is one expression of a more fundamental competitive strategy for the firm (e.g., growth, market development, diversification, etc.), and therefore it cannot be isolated from the overall strategy.

The conception and implementation of the marketing strategies will, of necessity, escape the control of formal marketing structures to some degree, especially for implementation. These tasks, one hopes, will be assigned to several processes running concurrently to create, communicate and deliver value to the customers, and always going to and fro across 'borders' of one kind or another.

Global marketing evolution: outsourcing and process-based marketing management

There is an ongoing move towards outsourcing as a way of reducing fixed costs and thus gaining flexibility to weather low periods in economic cycles, the vagaries of demand and generally maintaining competitiveness.

Plenty of this outsourcing is offshored. The help desks and call centres of both American and British companies that were displaced to India provide good anecdotal evidence to support this statement, though at the current low end of the scale in terms of skills and competencies required, and value-added capability. However, examples have also since occurred of consumer reaction to such moves, arising from issues of service quality such as poor language comprehension or a feeling of perceived strangeness and remoteness. Conversely, there is now a reaction in India, with many companies rejecting simple call-centre business, unless it is coupled within a wider service relationship. Many companies are now much 'pickier' and are stating interest in higher-value outsourcing, such as high-tech outsourcing activities with more value adding and learning potential for themselves. This is happening naturally, as the success of the software industry is providing higher salaries to many competent technical people who would otherwise be saying 'Good morning, you have called XYZ company, and my name is Singh [or a Western name for customer contact]. How may I help you?'

Some companies still resist offshoring, and the privately owned Zara is one such case, producing mainly in Europe and thus benefiting from a flexibility and speed that enables very quick introductions of new models/products into the market. Its closest competitor in Europe is H&M, which outsources and offshores in the Far East, apparently with some damaging impact on conception-to-market timescales. Of course, one may also argue that privately held Zara is taking a stance on being European and having strong ties to local producers and communities, but it has done well with its SCM policies.

Figure 20.7
Value-creating functions and cross-functional processes

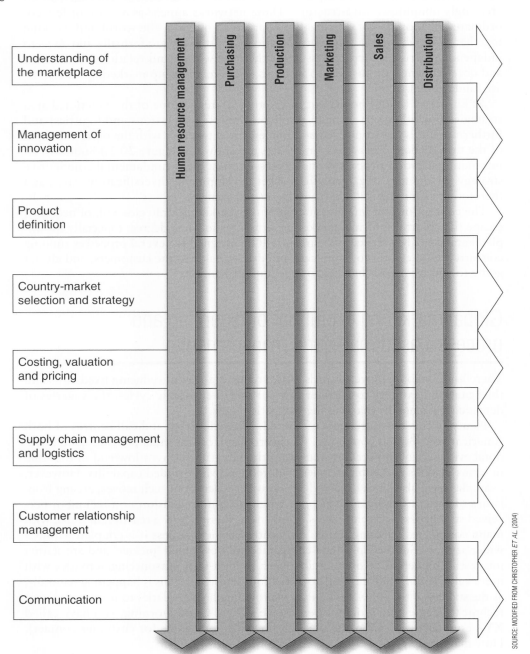

SOURCE: MODIFIED FROM CHRISTOPHER *ET AL.* (2004)

Silhouette (eyewear design and manufacture), on the other hand, goes even further and still manufactures spectacle frames in its home-based factory in Lienz, Austria – considering it the only way to control the process from start to finish. (This attitude can be said to reflect an almost compulsive need for control when dealing with top-end products.) There is a trade-off between incurring opportunity costs (of not outsourcing) and paying higher costs of control and co-ordination should you outsource. The latter may be very high if the manufacturer is extremely demanding in terms of quality control, but one should not reduce this to a pure financial equilibrium – intangibles such as manufacturing prestige, 'made in . . .', and the feeling of total control to offset eventual manufacturing mishaps cannot be completely explained from a financial point of view, but can make or break an image.

Returning to process-based management – and even process-based marketing management

Examples have often been given in the past portraying companies with wide supply networks, such as a car manufacturer with assembly plants in both the UK and Germany, being supplied from diverse countries. In fact, the car industry, with dual assembly and dispersed suppliers, is still hailed by some as a paradigm of modernity. However, more recently we have seen greater rationalization-by-concentration moves, as well as some attitudinal changes. These changes have been reflected in the literature (Ghemawat, 2003, 2005; Rugman, 2005). This work reflects both marketing and production/operations changes, such as:

a. A growing importance of localization and adaptation.

b. The need to have more concentrated and better-integrated networks, for greater rationality; costs matter and time matters when responding to final market demands.

In fact, there is an ongoing movement of concentration at all tiers – both at the business client levels and at the supplier levels. This trend is reflected in geographic rationalization, supplier concentration and concentration of the outsourced components into fuller assemblies.

Ghemawat (2005) reports on the superiority of a strong global-region-co-ordinated strategy to a pure worldwide strategy. This is in line with growing evidence of the importance of regions, and intraregional trade. Ghemawat's 'The Forgotten Strategy' (2003) focuses on the strategy of differences, and states that rather than simply having strategies focused on minimizing differences between countries, we should also be exploiting those differences for advantage. This also points to a proactive stance of exploring those differences rather than a defensive attitude, which might have occurred naturally when it was considered *de rigueur* that globalization as standardization should be the ultimate objective, with everything else as flaws to be glossed over.

After a period of denial, *globalization by standardization* (i.e., developing standard products and marketing mixes to be promoted worldwide), has evolved conceptually to *global localization* (i.e., adaptation of products and mixes). Needless to say, aspects of aggregation/concentration, adaptation and arbitraging need to be weighed and considered in the context of local circumstances. (Basically, standardizing when feasible, and adapting when necessary – according to the internal/external analysis and fit.) Consequently, there is a mix of standardization and customization to balance the needs of cost minimization with the maximization of customer satisfaction. In effect, this represents a return to the essence of marketing – segmentation with appropriate differentiation. In this situation, marketing activities and processes are in effect distributed between the central headquarters and the regional or local subsidiaries. So, marketing must consider the value chain and make choices according to the perceived customer requirements, situational conditions, internal resources, competencies and processes, and proceed to enable the delivery of the most adequate value offer to the customers.

Rigby and Vishwanath (2006) report results by Bain & Company, suggesting that the era of equating globalization with homogeneous products is at an end. They consider the keyword to be *localize*, both at the retail and consumption levels. These authors say that consumer product multinationals are already abandoning the 'myth' of global consumer segments. Nevertheless, they advise against a return to 'ultra-segmentation' tactics advocated in the 1990s – such an option would increase the operational complexity, causing a steep increase in costs vs. benefits. Though intellectually seductive, this could become an economic problem, given that the increase in operational complexity would create more costs than benefits. Internationally, as domestically, it is important to reach a balance between uniformity and diversity of product (and brand) offers. The dominance of the former can lead to market feelings of offer inadequacy and boredom, whereas the latter causes rising costs and loss of brand potential. This desired equilibrium at international level requires a 'central control with a local touch', i.e., supplying the diversity demanded by the market,

Process in action linguistic localization

- The Mitsubishi Pajero is known in Spain and Portugal as the Mitsubishi Montero. 'Pajero' is definitely not an acceptable word to use in either Spanish or Portuguese. For this reason, it is known as the 'Montero' in all Latin American countries also.

- The Toyota 'MR2' designation is not used in France, where this coupe is simply called 'MR'. This is due to the nasty homophonetic thought which comes to mind when pronouncing 'MR2' in French.

- Differences also occur between regions. For example, the VW Golf (in Europe and almost everywhere) has been called, intermittently, the VW Rabbit (in North America) for communication (imagery)

reasons. Similar reasons apply to the Honda Jazz (Europe and Asia) and Fit (Japan and North America).

- Besides the visible designations, there are naturally also other differences, e.g., in engine size, and sometimes in design. Notice the diversity, especially in size and power, between North American, European and Asian car models. Japanese automakers also have very specific models for the USA, as well as for East Asia, not easily saleable in other countries. (They are gaudier or trendier, depending on taste and culture.) Honda unveiled the 'Civic Concept' – a five-door hatchback design exclusively developed for the European market – at the Geneva Auto Salon. In the UK, General Motors is also aware that it cannot replace the Vauxhall brand with that of Opel, which is of German origin, due to country sensitivities. That problem, however, is not felt so strongly by BMW and Mercedes, partly because of the segments served and existing reputation.

whilst still actively seeking economies of scale, scope and experience. Once again: 'think globally; act locally'.

Rugman (2005) states that a global strategy of economic integration and standardization is only feasible for a few sectors, in particular consumer electronics. He advocates the use of regional strategies for other manufacturing sectors (including automobiles, chemicals and energy) and for all services sectors (particularly retail and banking).

This regionalization trend (or also past reality) has been picked up by Rugman (2005) and by Ghemawat (2003, 2005). Rugman asserts that multinationals tend to have most of their trade within regions. It also points to a localization (at least regionalization) of many processes.

Kotler and Kartajaya (2000) propose that companies consider the relationship connection between three factors (Figure 20.8).

Thus, the global company would remain mostly a myth, with the usual suspects such as Coca-Cola, and to a lesser degree McDonald's, as its idealized examples. We all know that McDonald's has adapted many of its elements worldwide – whilst retaining its core values.

This move towards a localized global company means a localization of many of the supply chain elements and even (related) of the internal value chain elements. Marketing activities, consumer related in all dimensions, but including consumer communications and market sensing (linked with product development), have a natural tendency to be adapted, despite all the moves towards gaining economies

---

Case notes: Moves to concentrated and better-integrated networks.

- Opel moved out of its assembly unit in Palmela (Portugal), displacing production to a factory in Spain (with higher labour costs, but closer suppliers).

- Autoeuropa, of the VW group (currently producing units under the brands VW and Seat), has decided to stay in Portugal, benefiting from a local group of suppliers closely integrated with its production process. In fact, some suppliers which in the past were located elsewhere within this (quite small) country have moved closer to the client's plant.

- Ford had already left this country (both from its former partnership with VW in Autoeuropa, and from its plant in Azambuja in 2000). The latter moved its production to the UK, seeking consolidation and thence higher overall efficiency.

These examples illustrate the fact that the higher costs of a supply chain for the auto industry, which

includes Portugal (the westernmost and southernmost European country), are no longer easily offset by lower wages, when the major markets are elsewhere.

Time matters; distance(s) matters; differences matter; energy matters. Transportation costs have been under pressure given the recent hikes in oil prices – and with its expected future trend given the increasing consumption from emerging economies (China in particular, which has been planning and executing well ahead its strategy of securing ample supplies worldwide). Costs of overseeing subcontractors may become too high in many cases when the product is going to be imported back to the 'home' country. However, expansion abroad may increase with the objective of establishing regional strategies elsewhere.

Question

1. In what ways have these companies thought globally and acted locally, or vice versa?

of scale and centralizing, e.g., ad film production. In fact, what many companies are vying for is suppliers who follow them internationally (be it by organic growth or through acquisitions). This reflects the importance of the trust issue – and the associated costs of supervision, relationship building, etc. For example, GM, still the number one auto manufacturer, though reaping some global benefits from standardization, has European operations such as Opel and Vauxhall with strong European product development and market communication systems. GM does not seem to minimize the design preferences in the European market, as well as the PEST factors which lead to different car sizes and power purchase preferences between the USA and Europe.

As Ghemawat points out, the comparatively low price of petrol in the USA explains a lot. This may also have been a reason for Ford's problems with 'across the pond' standardization.

Globalization or localization – ongoing examples

In this section, we will ask the reader to consider how a single company, Wal-Mart, has set about becoming a global player, and how their actions can or cannot be explained by theory. It may be worth looking at the reference to the development of the Wal-Mart corporate mission over the last 15 years in the first case note in Chapter 16.

The teacher and the student: 'globalizing back'

Possibly the first noticeable backlash of the internationalization movement was the successful invasion of the USA by Japanese manufacturers of motorized vehicles (motorcycles, cars, boat engines and now even plane engines). It is a classic example of success, both in segmentation and overall competitive strategy, and is exemplary not only in its current dominance but also in the overall impact on the way their competitors do business. Toyota will soon become the largest automaker in the world. This was a case of the student 'bettering' the teacher – in fact leapfrogging by adopting total quality concepts from American intelligentsia well ahead of US manufacturers. Overall, these Japanese developments were strongly influenced by the powerful Ministry of International Trade and Industry and other governmental policies.

Figure 20.8
Globalization –
factors for
consideration

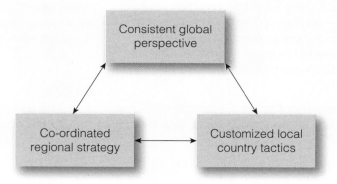

Process in action Wal-Mart

If Arla Foods seems to have adapted to local markets, Wal-Mart in Germany can provide a different example as an (initial) attempt at standardization.

On July 28, 2006, Spiegel Online headlined: 'Retail Giant Humbled: Wal-Mart Admits German Defeat.' There seems to be a broad consensus on the reasons behind this failure, foretold by, amongst others, Knorr and Arndt (2003). Common consensus says that Wal-Mart made three mistakes.

The first error seems to have been a bad market entry choice. Wal-Mart entered by acquisition. Nevertheless, this could be considered *a priori* a sensible choice of entry mode considering the maturity and strong competitiveness of the German market, as it could remove some of the existing competitors (which a *greenfield* or entry by *organic growth* would not do). However, the acquisition seemed to have been quite inadequate for Wal-Mart's purposes, with inadequate locations and disparate sizes, and they were not successful in expanding sufficiently in order to achieve benefits of scale. So it seems that rather than having made an incorrect *a priori* choice of entry mode, they erred in persisting with that choice when its implementation was not viable (at least in view of their efforts).

Other mistakes have been linked to the choice of applying a standardized strategy, applied successfully in the USA and the UK, in Germany. The strategy involves using a specific discount formula and business.

Thus, a second mistake seems to have been a grave underestimation of the competition. Germany is a paradigmatic example of a market where the discount format and chains are very strong (pioneer and leader ALDI foremost, but also Lidl, and others). Wal-Mart's purchasing power is quite strong worldwide in non-perishable goods (e.g., procuring from China), but many of the products from the grocery side of the business have to be sourced from nearer suppliers and, given their smallish size in Germany, they could not compete with the other main local chains. Furthermore, they gave up some of their distinctiveness arising from a broader range of products in order to try and control their losses,

rather than possibly attempting a different positioning strategy in Germany. In fact, the various 'restructuring' attempts went in several different directions over time (and gave rise to big price fluctuations), possibly contributing to a loss (or non-creation) of a clear identity in the market. Some of these changes involved a reduction of the broad scope of the products offered and, conversely (near the end), the addition of both trendy clothing and organic food with the objective of attracting higher-margin shoppers – seemingly incoherent moves.

Hubris and *arrogance* have been common words associated with Wal-Mart, and not only by historically persistent detractors. (They have been given as reasons for the exit from Germany at a loss of $1 billion.) Such assumptions are easily understood in light of the experience of Wal-Mart and its position in the distribution sector, a recognizable and recognized number-one spot. It can also be the downside of an uncheckered application of the RBV: overconfidence due to sheer volume of resources, skills and capabilities. It is not only resources like factories that are inherently risky (particularly when there are barriers to exit); the same can be said of knowledge – and Wal-Mart's experience is very much USA-centric.

However, Wal-Mart's German exit does not seem to reflect these problems. Rather, it highlights the failure of an intended process implementation and not a failure of process-based management.

This leads us to the third error. Wal-Mart was unable to replicate in Germany the success of its formula for selling discount goods, mainly due to the specifics of that market, competition-wise (as discussed) and customer-wise.

Wal-Mart in Germany had one head office and three distribution centres, a logistical infrastructure prepared for a large retail network. The failure resided, on one hand, downstream – with the diminutive growth of its retail chain of hypermarkets, which in turn caused an upstream inability to guarantee favourable procurement conditions for grocery items. This third mistake depicts a lack of market orientation – which may sound strange considering Wal-Mart's ethos and history. The mistake is linked to a misguided perception (or simply an assumption?) of strong customer homogenization across countries. Wrong assumption, as it turned out, even for two 'Western' countries, the USA and Germany,

➡

which have been in such close contact. American culture and products are well known and generally well accepted in Germany. Wal-Mart focused at first on the customer, with a wide range of products at discounted prices complemented with 'Wal-Mart' service. Okay? Apparently not so for the German customer and market. It was shown that 'the devil is in the details': too much standardization and not enough localization in that market entry process. It may not have been an obvious sign of marketing (orientation) myopia, but it is a sure case of what could be labelled 'marketing strabismus', or what we could call 'cross-eyed marketing'.

Germany is a discounter-dominated country market, and the German consumers, despite enjoying a healthy disposable income, could be regarded as the epitome of parsimony. Having learned by experience with competing discount networks to recognize value for money, informed German consumers are self-confident and have more autonomy from brands (products or retailers). For these reasons, Wal-Mart could not compete on price – maybe the dominant attribute of its overall offer in the USA – and was unable to offer a consistent and acceptable alternative value proposition, i.e., a different marketing strategy, with viable segmentation and positioning choices. However, other attributes of the offer were off, considering local preferences. The Wal-Mart spirit aggravated both local customers and employees – the smiling, the greeter, even the shopping 'packers' made customers uncomfortable (reading too much effusivity, even aggressiveness).

In many cases, customers were unable to decode that behaviour – or did so mistakenly, e.g., assuming flirting where there was only company-mandated smiling.

Wal-Mart, on the other hand, seems to be enjoying successful operations (both greenfield and through acquisition) in China, where it now has plans for the purchase of a Taiwanese-owned chain. It has also reached an agreement towards the formation of an equal-stakes partnership in India, with a local partner (due to restrictions still imposed by the Indian law). Perhaps it will be more successful there?

Contemporary sources

The New York Times, (2006, August 1). 'Wal-Mart's Overseas Push Can Be Lost in Translation', reported by L. Landler and M. Barbaro.

http://www.service.spiegel.de/cache/international/0,1518,429137,00.html

http://www.chinadaily.com.cn/world/2006-07/30/content_652859.htm

http://www.freerepublic.com/focus/f-news/1673629/posts

http://www.reason.com

Questions

1. What theory explains the failure of Wal-Mart in Germany?

2. What lessons should they take from this failure to have a better chance of success in China, Taiwan and India?

There is a Western tendency to dismiss governmental directives, with good reason in many cases. But that contempt may be a weakness when it comes to gauging the impact of the Asian economic tsunami being formed. Maybe this alert will prove to be unfounded due to the depth of demand rapidly being built in China with the stunning growth of its middle class, soaking up an increase in production that could otherwise prove to be a Noah-grade deluge directed to other markets. The Chinese government has been very directive, and the Chinese have been all too happy to follow – and lead – so much so that internal brakes had to be applied to ease the growth trend. (Europe should beware, lest another USA blocking move diverts it into their shores, even though at the time of writing Obama had replaced Bush and such moves seemed less likely.)

In any case, the Japanese auto-propelled invasion of the USA, now providing local jobs and adapted products, is a clear demonstration of the transferability of skills. We have other more recent examples of this phenomenon, many of which are in connection with outsourcing.

Process in action internationalization via the supply chain, from supplier to branded vendor

Acer and Asus are now well-known computer brands. Both are manufacturers from Taiwan. Acer is one of the top five branded computer vendors, and it has recently raised awareness and even launched a co-branded line of laptops with Ferrari to reposition its brand image upwards into the luxury segment. Asus has launched co-branded products with Lamborghini. Most consumers did not know of Asus a few years ago, but they have been around for a while – as business-to-business (B2B) supplier Asustek Computer Inc. They started supplying parts for computer OEM, and increasingly became suppliers of complete machines under other brands. The next logical step was to market under their own brand. (Acer did the same some years previously – in fact, Asus founders were formerly engineers with Acer, which shows a clear process of knowledge transfer.)

Asus is, with Samsung, one of the first manufacturers to have launched products with the specifications of what was formerly known as Microsoft's Origami project, also known as the UMPC (ultra-mobile personal computer). Given the increased interconnectedness of OEM and suppliers, reaching the phases of strategic development subcontracting and partnership-based subcontracting, with the corresponding 'diamond model' of interfacing, it is much easier for knowledge transfer to occur.

These and other companies started out as suppliers to branded vendors who outsourced an increasingly large proportion of their product, to the point of supplying its conception. Many decided to take the next step and reap the value benefits associated with the branded relationship with the customers. For those who outsource, it is a medium- to long-term 'flip side', which needs to be considered when pondering what to outsource and what to hold back (for a while, whilst developing the next idea) to keep some advantage.

HTC (High Tech Computers, also from Taiwan) has been a major manufacturer of advanced PDA phones, marketed under different brands. HTC supplied phones e.g., to i-mate, but also marketed it under its own Qtek brand, which had some prestige. Recently, it decided to concentrate its own branded sales under the HTC (corporate and product) brand. Following this change, i-mate decided to source from other vendors, rather than deal with such direct competition.

Contemporary sources
http://www.htc.com.tw
http://www.myqtek.com/europe/about.aspx
http://www.theunwired.net/?itemid=3099
http://www.acer.com

Questions
1. What lessons do these cases have for companies who offshore source or subcontract?
2. How could those companies have defended their core competencies?

Summary
- The concept of diffused marketing places the responsibility for marketing on all parts of an organization. This indicates that organizations are shifting from a specialist function focus to a process focus, if they haven't already done so.

- When internationalizing, there is a need to redefine the supply chains of an organization to create diffusion and to promote the 'three As': agility, adaptability and alignment.

- In all marketing, there is a need to understand the customer. When internationalizing, there is danger of stereotyping; so a company needs to understand each country, and the regional variations within each country.

- In internationalization, and globalization, there is a paradigm of optimizing convergence and divergence. Convergence assumes that a standard product or service fits all (globally). Divergence assumes that regional differences must be considered, and that products and services must be adapted appropriately.

- Convergence is easier for products than for services, but almost all companies now offer some element of service to the customer.

- The two new 'heavyweights' in the international marketplace, China and India, offer vast market opportunities, but entrants have sometimes forgotten the convergence/divergence paradigm.

- The process theory of internationalization (PTI) suggests that internationalization precedes incrementally and sequentially as the company acquires more experiential knowledge and foreign organizing knowledge. PTI sees the internationalization processes as causal cycles where market knowledge and market commitment are affected by the firm's current activities and commitment decisions, which in turn affect the change aspects.

- However, the advent of vicarious learning (from the increase in management education) and better communications (terrestrial and personal) has enabled some companies to leapfrog within the PTI process. As a result, some companies, mainly in the small-to-medium sector, were even launched as international organizations from the start.

- Work on process-based marketing (and management) has indicated a need to consider:
  - The growing importance of localization and adaptation.
  - The need to have more concentrated and better-integrated networks, for greater rationality; costs matter and time matters when responding to final market demands.

Chapter questions

1. Will a process-focused company find the process of internationalization easier than a traditional (management) function-focused company? Why or why not?

2. What are the modes of entry into different national or regional markets? What factors will affect the choice of mode for a company for a specific country or region?

3. The process theory of internationalization suggests that internationalization proceeds incrementally and sequentially, but some companies leapfrog it. How? What developments have allowed this to happen?

4. If a company decides to subcontract offshore for financial reasons there are dangers. What are they? How can they be reduced?

References

American Marketing Association (AMA) (2009) [Online]. http://www.marketingpower.com/_layouts/Dictionary.aspx?dLetter=M. Last accessed 10 May 2009.

An, C., and Fromm, H. (2005) Supply chain management on demand: Strategies, technologies, applications, in *Interdisciplinary Aspects of Information Systems*, Physica-Verlag HD, Heidelberg DE, pp. 147–153.

Barney, J. B. (1991) 'Firm resources and sustained competitive advantage', *Journal of Management*, 17:99–120.

Bradley, F. (2005) *International Marketing Strategy*, New York: FT Prentice Hall

Canel, C., and Das, S. R. (2002) 'Modeling global facility location decisions: Integrating marketing and manufacturing decisions', *Industrial Management & Data Systems*, 102(2):110–118.

Christopher, M., Payne, A., and Ballantyne, D. (2004) *Relationship Marketing: Creating Stakeholder Value*, Oxford, UK: Butterworth-Heinemann.

Conner, K. R. (1991) 'A historical comparison of the resource-based theory and five schools of thought within industrial organization economics: Do we have a new theory of the firm?', *Journal of Management*, 17(1):121–154.

Czinkota, M. R., Ronkainen, I. A., and Donath, B. (2004) *Mastering Global Markets: Strategies for Today's Trade Globalist*, Kentucky: Thomson/South-Western Independence.

de Freitas, C. L. (2000) 'International market entry choice: A resource-based perspective'. Proceedings of the European Marketing Academy Conference, EMAC, May 2000, Rotterdam, The Netherlands.

Doz, Y., Santos, J., and Williamson, P. (2001) *From Global to Metanational: How Companies Win in the Knowledge Economy*, Boston, MA: Harvard Business School Press.

Drucker, P. (1954) *The Practice of Management*, New York: Harper & Brothers.

El-Ansary, A. I. (2006) 'Marketing strategy: Taxonomy and frameworks', *European Business Review*, 18(4):226–293.

Farrell, D. (2006, June) 'Smarter offshoring', *Harvard Business Review*, 84:84–92.

Forsgren, M., and Johanson, J. (eds.) (2005) *Managing The Embedded Multinational: A Business Network View*, Cheltenham: Edward Elgar.

Ghemawat, P. (2003, November) 'The forgotten strategy', *Harvard Business Review*, pp. 76–84.

Ghemawat, P. (2005, December) 'Regional strategies for global leadership', *Harvard Business Review*, pp. 98–108.

Hollensen, S. (2004) *Global Marketing: A Decision-Oriented Approach*, 3rd edn., New York: FT Prentice-Hall.

IBM (1999) [Online]. https://www.research.ibm.com/journal/sj/441/kapoor.html. Last accessed 13 May 2009.

Johanson, J., and Vahlne, J.-E. (1990) 'The mechanism of internationalization', *International Marketing Review*, 7:11–24.

Knight, G. A., and Cavusgil, S. T. (1996) 'The born global firm: A challenge to traditional internationalization theory', in Cavusgil, S. T. (ed.), *Advances in International Marketing*, 8th edn., Greenwich, CT: JAI Press, pp. 11–26.

Knorr and Arndt (2003) [Online]. http://www.iwim.uni-bremen.de/publikationen/pdf/w024.pdf.

Kotler, P., and Kartajaya, H. (2000) *Repositioning Asia: From Bubble to Sustainable Economy*, Chichester. UK: John Wiley.

Lasserre, P. (1996) 'Regional headquarters: The spearhead for Asian Pacific markets', *Long Range Planning*, 29(1):30–37.

Lee, Hau L. (2004, October) 'The triple-a supply chain', *Harvard Business Review*, pp. 102–112.

Luostarinen, R. (1994) 'Internationalizing the Doctorate Education in Business'. Paper presented at the Roundtable on Internationalizing Doctoral Programmes in Business, 11–13 September 1994, Michigan State University, East Lansing, MI.

Madsen, T. K., and Servais, P. (1997) 'The internationalization of born globals: An evolutionary process?', *International Business Review*, 6(6):561–583.

McDougall, P., Shane, S. A., and Oviatt, B. M. (1994) 'Explaining the formation of international new ventures: The limits of theories from international business research', *Journal of Business Venturing*, 9(6):469–487.

McGoldrick, P. J., and Davies, G. (1995) *International Retailing: Trends and Strategies*, London: Pitman.

McGregor, J. (2005) *One Billion Customers: Lessons From the Front Lines of Doing Business in China*, New York: Free Press/Simon & Schuster.

Moen, Ø., and Servais P., (2002) 'Born global or gradual global? Examining the export behavior of small and medium-sized enterprises', *Journal of International Marketing*, 10(3):49–72.

Monczka, R. M., and Trent, R. J. (1991) 'Evolving sourcing strategies for the 1990s', *International Journal of Physical Distribution & Logistics Management*, 21(5):4–12.

Oviatt, B. M., and McDougall, P. P. (1994) 'Toward a theory of international new ventures', *Journal of International Business Studies*, 25(1):45–64.

PepsiCo news release. [Online]. http://www.pepsico.com/. Last accessed 14 August 2006.

Peteraf, M. A. (1993) 'The cornerstones of competitive advantage: A resource-based view', *Strategic Management Journal*, 14(3):179–191.

Preece, S. B., Miles, G., and Baetz, M. C. (1999) 'Explaining the international intensity and global diversity of early-stage technology-based firms', *Journal of Business Venturing*, 14(3):259–281.

Rigby, D., and Vishwanath, V. (2006, April) 'Localization: The revolution in consumer markets', *Harvard Business Review*, pp. 83–92.

Root, F. R. (1990) *International Trade and Investment*, South-West, Florence, KY.

Rugman, A. M. (2005) *The Regional Multinationals: MNEs and 'Global' Strategic Management*, Cambridge: Cambridge University Press.

Wernerfelt, B. (1984, April–June) 'A resource-based view of the firm', *Strategic Management Journal*, 5(2):171–180.

Wernerfelt, B. (1995, March) 'The resource-based view of the firm: Ten years after', *Strategic Management Journal*, 16(3):171–175.

Zou, S., and Cavusgil, S. T. (1996) 'Global strategy: A review and an integrated conceptual framework', *European Journal of Marketing*, 30(1):52–69.

Part seven

The future

21 Future trends in marketing

What does the future hold?

Part seven consists of a single chapter that asks readers to consider future trends in process-based marketing management under three topic headings: Consumer Behaviour, New Social Values and Paradigm Shifts; The New Consumer; and New Consumer Applications. This consideration is directed by the authors, and supported by links to appropriate reading and websites. The authors then summarize their own thoughts on future trends in marketing programming.

21

Future trends in marketing

Luiz Moutinho and Paulo Rita

Introduction

This chapter tries to forecast the future, and the effects of globalization, technological developments and other environmental changes. The implications for organizational system design, and particularly for marketing, will be discussed. As a result, there are no case notes; they have not happened yet, so their role is taken by 'Topics for consideration', and these topics form a basis for a discussion modelling the future.

We also need to change the language we use. New concepts will arise and they will need new names. We therefore begin by suggesting what some of this terminology will be, although most of the terms are already coming into use and are therefore used in this chapter.

The chapter ends with a more general discussion on future trends in marketing programming.

Learning objectives

- To highlight trends in globalization.

- To discuss the future role of technology.

- To analyze a myriad of future trends related to consumer behaviour, e.g., socioquake, downshifting, prosumption and zones of tolerance.

- To comment on new business ecosystems.

- To give an overview of key developments in the area of marketing programmes.

New terminology

Affluenza

A counter-trend based on social values that emphasize 'inner richness' as opposed to the maximization of personal economic goals viable in the 'trappings' and signs of an over-focused affluent society.

Consumer agency

A company works as a consumer agency when its marketing concept, philosophy and activities really start to be at the service of consumers, resulting in a whole new marketing paradigm.

Customer contempt

An increasing state of frustration felt by consumers triggered by companies who engage in marketing deception, shoddy practices, misleading messages, lack of value and fairness in exchanges, and patronizing and narcissistic behaviour.

Contingency mentality

Consumers today possess a multi-dimensionality of traits and personal facets that defy preconceived consumer behaviour frameworks. They purchase products/services depending on multiple occasion factors and modes of existing, which demonstrates the increasing non-linearity of human behaviour.

Customer bonding

To seek truly fair exchanges with consumers which would lead to their maximization of expectations and therefore the establishment of strong ties/relationships/associations between needs and brand values which will last in the long run.

Feminization of markets

The important role played by women in society – education, industry, government, science and other fields – in terms of performance, decision-making power, consumption and action leadership.

Hard-on-hard, soft-on-soft

Consumers are less willing to 'fall' for gimmicks and deception (soft pushes), and are looking for true product attributes of functionality, innovativeness and tangible product benefits. Overall, consumers prefer that companies pursue a policy of marketing transparency (hard features).

Neomarketing

A new marketing philosophy which encapsulates a clear customer centricity, integrated management and an information technology focus.

Neuromarketing

The utilization of imaging technology – MRI (magnetic resonance imaging) – to understand the workings of the brain and how consumers make decisions in the purchase of products and services.

Parity markets, parity products

In most industries, the markets are experiencing signs of stagnation and low growth rates, compounded by the consumers' perception of little differentiation between competing products and services.

Particle marketing

A concept borrowed from physics and derived from the use of personal technologies enabling organizations to customize micro-individual offerings to the market.

Prosumption and prosumers

Those consumers who will go a step further and be actively involved in the design, assembly/production, communication and distribution of products and services knowing that these want-satisfying outputs will be for them.

Smaller zones of tolerance

The difference between designed and adequate expectations experienced by consumers is being reduced all the time.

Time to market

This is a new intervention process that encompasses some of the traditional new product development activities but is supported by a multidisciplinary team of managers who work under new premises – concurrent development, non-sequential, faster and very short time frames for each developmental stage.

Voluntary simplicity/downshifting

A new social values movement which attempts to redress the work – private life balance, it focuses on a return to family and friendship as opposed to pursuing a career- and work-obsessed life pattern, and seeks an outwardly simpler life and an inwardly richer life.

The why generation

The new value system adopted by younger generations seeking world cultures, knowledge and travelling as an antecedent stage to a professional career.

Global trends

Economic 'globalization' is a historical process, the result of human innovation and technological progress. It refers to the increasing integration of economies around the world, particularly through trade and financial flows. The term sometimes also refers to the movement of people (labour) and knowledge (technology) across international borders. There are also broader cultural, political and environmental dimensions of globalization; hence, globalization is characterized by unrestricted flows of information, ideas, cultural values, capital, goods and services, and people, leading to a borderless, free-market, mono-cultural world. The last three decades have indeed evolved in that direction. But the road towards globalization is paved with many hurdles, and that is not the only likely scenario. In fact, several organizations have projected future scenarios, all coming up to three alternatives: a globalized world, a fragmented world and an intermediate world in which globalization is partly achieved.

Some experts (NIC, 2000) believe that the process of globalization is unstoppable and will be driven by political pressures for higher living standards, rising foreign trade and investment, an increasingly dynamic private sector and the diffusion of information technology. In particular, technologies such as the Internet create the basis for the development of global virtual marketplaces that make national borders irrelevant. The virtual corporation can be viewed as a collaborative network comprised of a focal business, its suppliers and customers whose activities are integrated and co-ordinated by the extensive use of information technology. As globalization has progressed, living conditions (particularly when measured by broader indicators of well-being) have improved significantly in virtually all countries. However, the strongest gains have been made by the advanced countries and only some of the developing countries.

But this evolution will come at a huge cost: a widening economic divide. That the income gap between high-income and low-income countries has grown wider is a matter for concern. And the number of the world's citizens in abject poverty is deeply disturbing. Those feeling left behind will face deepening political and religious extremism and will force the developed world to manage simultaneously new economy technologies and old economy challenges.

Others (Rodrick, 1997) argue that the social fabric in the developed world will be increasingly undermined by globalization because of the use of cheaper workers as substitutes, the difficulty for governments to provide social insurance, and more conflicts within and between nations over domestic norms. This may lead to regionalization as an alternative (Rugman, 2000). He projects that, instead of a free flow of goods, services, people and capital across the world, regional 'fortresses' may emerge as the dominant form of economic structure.

Yet others, namely militant groups, express a more negative view towards globalization and actually defend the contrary: deglobalization (Bello, 2000). It is argued that social and environmental issues should be driving the economy and not the other way around, as happens today. Actually, the environment will become a mainstream issue (water supply, global warming, deforestation), particularly in the developed world.

When one looks at the future, one has to identify the ideological, social, demographic, political and scientific developments that may affect the world's economies and businesses. Some of these are already visible today; some others are hidden or are present only in the form of 'weak signals'.

In demographic terms, the world population is expected to top 7.5 billion by 2015. The increase will come from the developing world, whereas industrialized nations will keep facing an ageing population. An asymmetric development between these two clusters of countries is a factor of instability that can generate conflict and even disrupt global trade. According to Huntington (1997), future conflicts will be rooted primarily in cultural differences due to increasing ethnic and cultural fragmentation, and will thus occur between different 'civilizations'.

Based on the assumption that globalization is progressing and that global firms are the main vectors of that progress, the future global corporation may take either an individualized corporation or a metanational approach. The individualized corporation model (Ghoshal and Bartlett, 1997) is described by a portfolio of three key processes – entrepreneurial, management and renewal – by which new management competencies and roles are defined. The metanational model (Doz *et al.*, 2002) considers a networked organization implying the co-ordinated combined effort of 'unbundled' business units, some internal (e.g., subsidiaries) and some external (e.g., partners, suppliers and distributors) to a corporation.

The future of technology

Now that the Internet is mainstream, information technology is a part of most business strategies and the economy is on an upturn, and we are again in a position to expect big changes in e-business. One reason is that the profitability of many Internet firms renewed confidence in e-business strategies after the dot.com bust. Another stimulus is the rapid adoption of broadband services, which allows for faster and more stable Internet connections. Interconnectivity will increase in both depth and reach. Fast Internet means that users can watch video, enjoy high-quality Internet telephony and move quickly from website to website, even when large graphics and photos are presented. Speech commands will replace typed commands and software will greatly reduce security concerns. Other important trends include the rise of customer power, the rise of trust, Internet strategy integration, refined metrics, wireless networking, media-usage fragmentation appliance convergence and the semantic web.

The rise of customer power

Customer power will increase as an increasing number of people use digital technology for more activities. When television, radio, print media, entertainment and shopping all converge seamlessly on a device of choice, consumers will truly have information and entertainment on demand. The ability of consumers to uncover the truth, share stories about products or search for alternative suppliers means that companies will need to improve quality and create win-win relationships with customers. Marketers will lose control over brand images due to the expansion of blogs, online bulletin boards and other forms of online communication, and must consistently underpromise and overdeliver or be found out under the bright lights of the globally networked community.

The rise of trust

The rise of customer power, with its increasing demand for information, and the reduction in the cost of maintaining relationships will lead more companies towards selected or fully trust-based marketing approaches, including new tools to customize products and services, and advisors to help customers make the right decisions.

Improved Internet strategy integration

In the future, organizations will increasingly integrate information technology as just one more tool to communicate with prospects, generate transactions and build customer relations. This integration is particularly evident in multichannel marketing – offering customers more than one way to buy something, such as a website, retail store and catalogue. Consumers will use multiple channels by entering an order over the Internet, choosing a pick-up time on the cell phone on the way to the mall, inspecting the goods and making impulse purchases in the store, and paying for the purchase with an online payment transfer to the retailer. Overall, the result will be much more intensive co-ordination among a growing number of channels, creating 'one face to the customer' regardless of how the customer chooses to interact with the company. The rise of digital technology will force marketers to create new depth to their content as customers are especially demanding of good content before, during and after the sale. This technology will also provide the tools to design, stimulate, test and implement the rollout of new innovations, accelerating new product development.

Refined metrics

In the future, some interesting but not-too-useful metrics such as 'site stickiness' (how long a user stays on a page) will yield to more direct measures that indicate corrective action, such as cost per acquired customer, cost per retained customer, customer lifetime value based on cost per retained customer and customer-level return on marketing investment. Firms will sort through the array of clickstream data to create metrics dashboards that display key metrics tied to goals or other success measures.

Wireless network increases

The rapid growth of wireless access points, when coupled with the huge numbers of cell phones, PDAs and notebook computers worldwide, indicate a continuing growth in wireless networking. As this trend plays out, customers will demand information, entertainment and communication whenever and however they desire, and in small file sizes for fast downloading. Thus, there will be a widespread adoption of wireless handheld and other non-computer Internet access devices. With increased digitization of content and the promise of widespread broadband delivery in the near future, the personal computer will not necessarily be the prime receiver of Internet content. Currently, other Internet receivers include digital telephones, handheld computers and video-game consoles. Indeed, many experts believe that either the interactive television set-top box or the video-game console will emerge as the preferred 'gateway entry' (over the personal computer) for accessing the web at home. Moreover, in-house wireless technology will allow greater widespread ubiquitous web access throughout the home without the need for a modem or other accessories.

Media-usage fragmentation

The continued proliferation of television channels and services as well as other media outlets will lead to a considerable increase in audience fragmentation. Consumers will be presented with a more diverse range of media choices powered by advances in wireless technology, digital compression, two-way networks, and digital and high-definition television.

Appliance convergence

Television programmes, radio shows, news, movies, books and photos are sent by their creators in electronic/digital form via satellite, telephone wires or cable, and then viewed by the audience on receiving appliances such as televisions, computers, radios, cell phones and PDAs. Thus, the receiving appliance is separate from the media vision programming. This idea of separating the medium from the appliance opens the door to new types of receiving appliances that are also 'smart' (e.g., Internet refrigerator), allowing for saving, editing and sending transmissions.

Semantic web

This is an extension of the current web in which information is given well-defined meaning. Whereas the current web carries text documents, photos, graphics, and audio and video files embedded in web pages that search engines struggle to catalogue for users to find, the semantic web will make it easier by providing a standard definition protocol so that users can easily find information based on its type, such as the next available appointment for a particular doctor (found by searching a doctor's database). The value of the semantic web is truly 'information on demand'. Consumers will define tasks for their personal digital agents, which will search for pieces of data and return them as movies to the television set, appointments to the PDA, contact information to the address book and so on. There will be multiple concurrent website access where sites will be held on the screen all at the same time to allow easier comparison shopping (multitasking). In addition, there will be visualization, virtual reality, even holographic images so customers can 'feel' products.

So, what will be the digital lifestyle of the future? Consumers will be able not only to access e-mail, chat with others, surf the web and watch their favourite shows, all on the same technological appliance, but they will also have access to a wider range of media services over the web, from downloading books to videoconferencing to exchanging video clips with family members.

Three topics for consideration

Instead of case notes, this chapter considers changes in marketing practice resulting from globalization and new technological development by discussing three topics.

- Topic 1 introduces a number of selected social values and paradigm shifts which provide critical understanding and background into *the new shaping and behaviour of consumers in the future.*
- Topic 2 deals specifically with a *myriad of examples that define the new consumer.* These topics range from downshifting and the why generation to affluenza and intelligent agents.
- Topic 3 focuses on *new consumer applications*, in particular in the areas of neuromarketing and particle marketing.

These topics will be introduced, discussed and summarized.

New social values, such as cocooning, voluntary simplicity, save our society, evolution, feminization of markets, deconsumption, mancipation and vigilante consumers, are determining a number of paradigm shifts in the area of consumer behaviour. Moreover, they are reversing the flow of marketing from company-to-customer into customer-to-company. This new paradigmatic view shows that consumers not only are more educated, discriminating and demanding, they also increasingly seek the value in my life goal. This phenomenon gives rise to a new consumer behaviour paradigm called 'consumer agency', which should alter the way organizations analyze markets, deliver want-satisfying outputs and communicate with sophisticated consumer audiences. The new consumer will move towards prosumption, seek new bonds with companies, be more aware of product and market parity, have smaller zones of tolerance, buy goods and services on the basis of a contingency mentality, know what lies behind the brand, be more savvy about the commercial realism and, above all, increasingly embrace a feeling of consciousness.

Topic 1 new social values and paradigm shifts

Topic objectives

After studying this topic, students should:

- Understand paradigm shifts such as reversing the flow of marketing (from supply chain to demand value chain), the move away from patronizing and business ecosystems.

- Be familiar with new social values such as cocooning, contingency mentality, icon toppling and deconsumption.

- Be able to explain the feminization of markets, consumer agency and the value in my life concept.

Topic discussion

Marketing evolution and revolution should be considered in the context of who is the new consumer, ranging from prosumption and downshifting to particle marketing and neuromarketing.

Companies are designed to deliver what we call 'value' from their own operations. The Profit Impact on Marketing Strategy is a database that was developed 34 years ago by a non-profit institute named Strategic Planning Institute in Massachusetts with 3800 strategic business units as its database. Member partners pay fees to receive data that are analyzed in multiple ways and using multiple variables. The impact of all these variables is measured on two dependent variables: cash flow and return on investment. In the last 2 years, they have been reporting that variables that contribute to what we call 'operational efficiency' only contribute around 15 per cent to cash flow or return on investment, whereas everything that contributes to environmental scanning, new ways to look at the market, consumer, competitors, etc., contributes around 65 per cent to fixed costs and profits.

The environment is changing. Technology is transforming what companies do, how they do it and how they communicate their product and service offerings. Distributors are becoming new 'virtual manufacturers'. These are distributors and retailers who, as a result of the shift in power from manufacturing to distribution, can dictate policies and indirectly 'produce' their own-label products. There are dramatic changes in consumers and media. We are rapidly becoming an information-intense society and entering the digital era and the realm of virtual marketspace. The world and the business environment can change more rapidly than most managers can make decisions. This requires the ability to operate with rapid decision cycles. Companies will become increasingly dependent upon the global market to achieve best-in-class services and minimize costs. The backlash against offshore outsourcing will increase as it becomes a political focus when the companies using poor-quality outsource firms get low scores for customer service and their business declines. Companies have spent the best part of the past decade re-engineering business processes, but they have ignored customer processes.

Paradigm shifts

Neomarketing

Information technology has driven employees to work within groups of integrated management. Neomarketing involves new business structures and a new marketing philosophy that encapsulates a clear customer centricity, integrated management and an information technology focus.

Time-based decision-making

One of the biggest challenges to management for the next 20 years will be to change rapidly enough to keep pace with changing consumer behaviour in the marketplace. The vertiginous speed with which markets, technologies and social values are changing makes it hard for managers to absorb information, make decisions and take actions in real-time.

Moving away from patronizing

Many companies have been treating consumers as if they are children. They claim to be market- and consumer-oriented, stating, for example, 'we understand the customer, we know what the customer wants and needs'. They do market research and segmentation, and so they think they know what consumers need. Thus, old-fashioned marketing people assume that they know everything. However, consumers nowadays are more educated, knowledgeable and demanding.

From supply chain to demand value chain

Firms are going to reverse the marketing flow from company-to-customer to customer-to-company. Nowadays, there are a number of examples, such as online or cyberspace, where it is the market that is going to the company. The demand value chain depicts the full range of activities that occur from the inception of demand backward through the steps necessary to fill the demand. Rather than focusing more on the physical flows (logistics) that relate to production, the demand value chain focuses more on the flow of delivered value. In many situations, companies do not understand the business they are in because they have not clearly considered the source of demand. Moreover, in the last 5 to 20 years, companies have opened multiple distribution channels beyond the traditional ones to help their customers to contact them directly. So, this reverse from supply chain to demand value chain and this paradigmatic change will be very important to the new market structure in the future. This new model of demand value chain should also be applied to non-profit and social or political marketing organizations.

Business ecosystems

This is a complex system of products or services that are connected to a chain of other values. For example, Campbell Soup now has an academy or clinic for health and has other services or products that complement or add value to or reinforce their core product; this is related to the complete vision of consumer behaviour.

> 'Business ecosystem' is a strategic planning concept originated by James F. Moore and widely adopted in the high-tech community, starting in the early 1990s. The basic definition comes from Moore's book, *The Death of Competition: Leadership and Strategy in the Age of Business Ecosystems* (HarperBusiness, 1996).

The business ecosystem concept was introduced by Moore in the *Harvard Business Review* in May/June of 1993, and won the McKinsey Award for article of the year. Moore (1993) wrote:

> An economic community supported by a foundation of interacting organizations and individuals – the organisms of the business world. This economic community produces goods and services of value to customers, who are themselves members of the ecosystem. The member organizations also include suppliers, lead producers, competitors and other stakeholders. Over time, they co-evolve their capabilities and roles, and tend to align themselves with the directions set by one or more central companies. Those companies holding leadership roles may change over time, but the function of ecosystem leader is valued by the community because it enables members to move towards shared visions to align their investments and to find mutually supportive roles.

The concept and associated methods became part of the standard practice of strategy making among companies, including Intel, Microsoft, Hewlett-Packard and SAP.

The concept has since been applied more broadly to a variety of problems in network-centric strategy making, including foreign policy and national and regional economic development.

Creating value in your business ecosystem

Wal-Mart's and Microsoft's dominance in modern business has been attributed to any number of factors, ranging from the vision and drive of their founders to the companies' aggressive competitive practices. But the performance of these two very different firms derives from something that is much larger than the companies themselves: the success of their respective business ecosystems. These loose networks – of suppliers, distributors, outsourcing firms, makers of related products or services, technology providers and a host of other organizations – affect, and are affected by, the creation and delivery of a company's own offerings.

Like an individual species in a biological ecosystem, each member of a business ecosystem ultimately shares the fate of the network as a whole, regardless of that member's apparent strength. From their earliest days, Wal-Mart and Microsoft – unlike companies that focus primarily on their internal capabilities – have realized this and pursued strategies that not only aggressively further their own interests but also promote their ecosystems' overall health.

The keystone advantage

Keystone organizations play a crucial role in business ecosystems. Fundamentally, they aim to improve the overall health of their ecosystems by providing a stable and predictable set of common assets – think of Wal-Mart's procurement system and Microsoft's Windows operating system and tools – that other organizations use to build their own offerings.

Keystones can increase ecosystem productivity by simplifying the complex task of connecting network participants to one another or making the creation of new products by third parties more efficient. They can enhance ecosystem robustness by consistently incorporating technological innovations and by providing a reliable point of reference that helps participants respond to new and uncertain conditions. And they can encourage ecosystem niche creation by offering innovative technologies

to a variety of third-party organizations. The keystone's importance to ecosystem health is surely that, in many cases, its removal will lead to the catastrophic collapse of the entire system. For example, WorldCom's failure had negative repercussions for the entire ecosystem of suppliers of telecommunications equipment. By continually trying to improve the ecosystem as a whole, keystones ensure their own survival and prosperity. They don't promote the health of others for altruistic reasons; they do it because it's a great strategy.

Keystones, in many ways, are in an advantageous position. As in biological ecosystems, keystones exercise a system-wide role despite being only a small part of their ecosystems' mass. Despite Microsoft's pervasive impact, for example, it remains only a small part of the computing ecosystem. Both its revenue and number of employees represent about 0.05 per cent of the total figures for the ecosystem. Its market capitalization represents a larger portion of the ecosystem – typical for a keystone because of its powerful position – but it has never been higher than 0.4 per cent. Even in the much smaller software ecosystem, in which the company plays an even more crucial role, Microsoft's market cap has typically ranged between 20 and 40 per cent of the combined market cap of software providers. This is considerably lower than the 80 per cent of total market capitalization of the much larger ecosystem of computer software, components, systems and services that IBM held during the 1960s.

Broadly speaking, an effective keystone strategy has two parts. The first is to create value within the ecosystem. Unless a keystone finds a way of doing this efficiently, it will fail to attract or retain members. The second part, as we have noted, is to share the value with other participants in the ecosystem. The keystone that fails to do this will find itself perhaps temporarily enriched but ultimately abandoned.

Keystones can create value for their ecosystems in numerous ways, but the first requirement usually involves the creation of a platform: an asset in the form of services, tools or technologies that offers solutions to others in the ecosystem. The platform can be a physical asset, like the efficient manufacturing capabilities that Taiwan Semiconductor Manufacturing offers to those computer-chip design companies that don't have their own silicon-wafer foundries, or an intellectual asset, like the Windows software platform. Keystones leave the vast majority of value creation to others in the ecosystem, but what they do create is crucial to the ecosystem's survival.

The second requirement for keystones' success is that they share throughout the ecosystem much of the value they have created, balancing their generosity with the need to keep some of that value for themselves. Achieving this balance may not be as easy as it seems. Keystone organizations must make sure that the value of their platforms, divided by the cost of creating, maintaining and sharing them, increases rapidly with the number of ecosystem members that use them. This allows keystone players to share the surplus with their communities. During the Internet boom, many businesses failed because, although the theoretical value of a keystone platform was increasing with the number of customers, the operating cost was rising as well. Many B2B marketplaces, for example, continued to show an increase in revenue despite decreasing and ultimately disappearing margins, which led to the collapse of their business models.

A good example of a keystone company that effectively creates and shares value with its ecosystem is eBay. It creates value in a number of ways. It has developed state-of-the-art tools that increase the productivity of network members and encourage potential members to join the ecosystem. These tools include eBay's Seller's Assistant, which helps new sellers prepare professional-looking online listings, and its Turbo Lister service, which tracks and manages thousands of bulk listings on home computers. The company has also established and maintained performance standards that enhance the stability of the system. Buyers and sellers rate one another, providing rankings that bolster users' confidence in the system. Sellers with consistently good evaluations attain PowerSeller status; those with bad evaluations are excluded from future transactions.

Additionally, eBay shares the value that it creates with members of its ecosystem. It charges users only a moderate fee to co-ordinate their trading activities. Incentives such as the PowerSeller label reinforce standards for sellers that benefit the entire ecosystem. These performance standards also delegate much of the control of the network to users,

diminishing the need for eBay to maintain expensive centralized monitoring and feedback systems. The company can charge commissions that are no higher than 7 per cent of a given transaction – well below the typical 30 to 70 per cent margins most retailers would charge. It is important to stress that eBay does this because it is good business. By sharing the value, it continues to expand its own healthy ecosystem – buyers and sellers now total more than 70 million – and thrive in a sustainable way.

Match your strategy to your environment

A company's choice of ecosystem strategy – keystone, physical dominator or niche – is governed primarily by the kind of company it is or aims to be. But the choice also can be affected by the business context in which it operates: the general level of turbulence and the complexity of its relationships with others in the ecosystem. If your business faces rapid and constant change and, by leveraging the assets of other firms, can focus on a narrowly and clearly defined business segment, a niche strategy may be most appropriate. You can develop your own specialized expertise, which will differentiate you from competitors and, because of its simple focus, foster the unique capabilities and expertise you need to weather the turbulence of your environment.

If your business is at the centre of a complex network of asset-sharing relationships and operates in a turbulent environment, a keystone strategy may be the most effective. By carefully managing the widely distributed assets on which your company relies – in part by sharing with your business partners the wealth generated by those assets – you can capitalize on the entire ecosystem's ability to generate, because of its diversity, innovative responses to disruptions in the environment.

If your business relies on a complex network of external assets but operates in a mature industry, you may choose a physical dominator strategy. Because the environment is relatively stable and the innovation that comes with diversity isn't a high priority, you can move to directly control the assets your company needs, by acquiring your partners or otherwise taking over their functions. A physical dominator ultimately becomes its own ecosystem, absorbing the complex network of interdependencies that existed between distinct organizations, and is able to extract maximum short-term value from the assets it controls. When it reaches this end point, an ecosystem strategy is no longer relevant.

If, however, your business chooses to extract maximum value from a network of assets that you don't control – the value dominator strategy – you may end up starving and ultimately destroying the ecosystem of which you are a part. This makes the approach a fundamentally flawed strategy.

This is a new paradigm whereby products are not 'sold to'; instead, they are 'bought from'. This is the best validation consumers can give a firm – empathy, transformation and passion. Currently, the emphasis is on the promotion, distribution and selling of manufacturer/distributor-led efforts, as opposed to having an exchange process being directed by expectations, elaboration of information, choice and effective post-purchase evaluation by increasingly more educated, discriminating and demanding consumers.

New social values and new socioquake

The time lag for diffusion of information for events or trends occurring in different locations is becoming shorter. For instance, there are social values spreading from North America to northern Europe and then to southern Europe. Faith Popcorn is one sociologist who has been studying the future of social values in the USA that may later be present in other countries.

Some of the trends discussed in this topic, as described by Popcorn (2002), include cocooning, small indulgence, egonomics, vigilante consumers, save our society, 99 lives, icon toppling, deconsumption, anchoring and clanning, all from Faith Popcorn, as well as the Golden Mafia and deconsumption.

Cocooning

Consumers are staying home longer, without as much contact with the outside world, and thus are more isolated. For example, home is used as an entertaining island with flat-panel screens for entertainment. Also, the elderly even have self-help kits to monitor their health.

Shular (2005) discusses new social trends in Canada. According to the author, the earlier trend of 'cocooning' is on its way out and social cocooning, or 'hiving', is in. Cocooning implies the desire to escape from the stresses and realities of life by retreating into the comfort of one's home. This was best represented by renting videos instead of going to the movies, or ordering takeout instead of dining at a restaurant. Hiving is about reaching out to others, not retreating. While cocooning was about disconnecting from the outside world, hiving is about connecting to others from within one's home. The home has essentially become the hub for a range of activities involving other consumers, most significantly entertaining and socializing.

Golden Mafia

Another social trend is the Golden Mafia, i.e., retired seniors over 65-years-old who have money and some social cultural background. They are mature, affluent and indulgent, and have longer life expectancies. They are using the money they saved throughout their lives to move into senior communities. One of the market segments exhibiting higher growth rates for motorcycles is the Golden Mafia as they travel in groups of four to six people together to different places.

Small indulgence and egonomics

There is a growing trend towards consumers emphasizing self-pleasure and small personal indulgences (to please myself), as well as looking for what is going to benefit them (what is going to benefit me?).

Vigilante consumer and save our society

Companies should behave correctly with consumers. Failing to may lead to brand boycotts. Indeed, there is an increasingly active voice against companies. Firms are being expected to act more like consumer agencies.

99 lives

Nowadays, there is too little time for consumers to assume many roles. However, in the future, there will be even more plurality of roles. In fact, our society is demanding from consumers a more polyvalent and flexible role-playing, in the family unit, with friends and at work.

Icon toppling

Many luxury market segments are directed to brand names that are growing, such as Burberry and Pierre Cardin. In the past, the influence of opinion leadership and reference groups in consumer decision-making was strong. However, there are examples of celebrities or stars who were paid over a million dollars to endorse a product that they actually do not like, thus affecting the credibility of those advertisements. Now, there is a clear trend from *trickle-down* theory to *trickle-across* theory, i.e., from stars to common people – online bulletin boards, Internet chat rooms, web communities or second-generation shopping agents. Mergers and acquisitions leading to fewer but larger companies are considered bad for consumers as the resulting firms tend to be more distant and less concerned with attending to particular customer needs, as they look for more global, standardized approaches to larger markets.

Deconsumption

During the economic recessions of the 1980s and early 1990s, consumers moved to buy cheaper products. However, in the last recession, consumers moved to buy less rather than more cheaply in order to keep the quality standards of the products they purchase. There are 28 000 items in an average 110-square-foot connect. In the European Union, there are 220 alternative products for hair care. Hence, there is a proliferation of products and brands that somehow tie up the consumer. Indeed, they may feel that most of the products are the same. For example, the basic ingredients in a personal grooming product are the same. However, the customer is faced with a huge number of options to choose from in terms of packaging, brands, etc.

Anchoring and clanning

Consumers tend to anchor social, moral and philosophical values related to family, friends, respect and tradition. The next step in the evolution of relationship marketing is the establishment of brand communities. In order to build up loyalty to a brand, a product has to have an active social life. A brand community is a specialized and bounded community based on a structured set of social relationships of admirers of a brand. The group is marked by a shared consciousness, rituals and traditions, and a sense of moral responsibility. Examples are groups and even tribes, such as the Harley-Davidson Hogs (Harley-Davidson owner group).

Feminization of markets

We are living in an era of 'eveolution' and 'mancipation'. Women are having an ever more important role as key decision-makers in a household (family and single-unit). Their education levels and their achievements have never been so high. These trends imply a clear feminization of markets. Women are moving targets, thus demanding from companies a continuous monitoring of their needs and wants, and there is also a role reversal (e.g., house-husband) taking place.

In her book on eveolution, Popcorn (2001) also states that there are essential truths that should be considered by a company: connecting female consumers to each other connects them to the firm's brand; products/services should be targeted to the different lives and roles of women; and companies should anticipate women's needs, secure women's loyalty, invest in a long-term relationship across different generations, have a co-parenting approach and not try to hide behind a logo, as for women, everything matters.

Today's women make 80 per cent of all purchasing decisions. A firm cannot succeed in business or successfully start one without understanding how to market to women. Hence the new trend of the feminization of markets.

Consumer agency

We are in a new period, maybe at the crossroads, where we hear a lot about brand building and customer relationship management/marketing. However, firms must go beyond all of this and move towards a new consumer agency role. This new type of comprehension of the consumer is much more directed. It is not so much to know *about* customers but more about knowing *with* them (understanding them). This is, once more, related to prosumption: to understand and collect live data, to do market research with the consumers, to communicate with them and to have the products designed with them. So this phenomenon of consumer agency is going to have huge repercussions in the marketing programmes of the future.

Nowadays, many contemporary consumer marketing actions do not take the consumer agency perspective into consideration and are not focused on the real needs of the customer. They are focused on the company's objectives and how to change consumer attitudes and behaviour to adjust them to the company's objectives.

In the larger markets, this understanding of the consumer is very important. But in fact, many times, this approach to consumer understanding, especially how we get there, and what for, is going to hide not a customer-centric but a seller-centric approach. This approach is dominated by company objectives and not by consumer objectives. So, it is an ideology of control from marketing. The successful companies of the future will break free from this seller-centric command ideology – 'we know and understand the market', or 'we know all about our consumers, our marketing department has eighteen people' – because this is not enough, as it is company dominated or seller-centric. What is really important is to be consumer-centric, whereby a company seeks to provide solutions to consumer needs via its products or services and only then to achieve its organizational goals.

In emerging markets, the main actors in the globalization process are widely considered to be governments and multinational corporations (MNCs). Eckhardt and Mahi (2004) examine the role of a key player who has largely been left out of the globalization debate: the consumer. Viewed through a lens of consumer agency, the authors outline important factors that influence whether new foreign goods that enter the marketplace are accepted, rejected or transformed by consumers. This is investigated in the context of the Indian marketplace, an emerging market that has only recently had access to foreign goods. The authors' analysis suggests that consumers are not merely pawns of MNCs or governments. The framework developed to understand the complexities of consumer agency in an emerging market provides the first such effort to guide future empirical consumer globalization research.

Value in my life

The notion of value – fairer market, value-based marketing and brands, value gaps – is of utmost importance. In saturated markets with huge competition, traditional companies are selling finance products. Firms approach consumers such as this way: 'Come to me and I will give you £35 in your account.' But this barely pays for one meal in the UK; hence, what is the real value provided by the company to its client? As another example, a credit card company might propose to you: 'Do you like animals? Would you like to protect a whale? If you buy this credit card at 18.9 per cent APR and spend £5000 a month, we will give £100 to charity.' Where is the equity and value in this offer to the consumer? Is this a notion of value?

Marketers who have a wider vision must try to collaborate more with the consumers to create a dialogue (a brain-to-brain model) whereby new processes will be created to develop value for the two sides of the equation, or we risk consumer contempt or even their immunization to the marketing process. Although hard-selling strategies are being used, they are not fair to consumers.

Most companies are designed to create value from their operations – they are not designed to deliver the consumer value in my life. Thus, where is the value? Where are the benefits for which consumers pay?

Nowadays, consumers buy more if they are treated well. Honesty, human transparency and care from the salesperson may help clinch the deal more than discounts. Since there is no perceived differentiation in the minds of consumers, the latter seek products and services that give them 'value in their lives', which is something that goes beyond the basic attributes of products and services. But what is this value in my life? *Value in my life* means to look for and find the best value, sourcing to genuine products that can be adjusted to the consumer request or personalized in terms of services, designed solutions to better serve the two building blocks: the personal productivity and the emotional authenticity. For example, if a consumer buys a printer, it would be really nice if, when they purchase a defective product from one shop, they may return and exchange it easily. Hence, companies should help individuals to manage some aspects of their lives in a more comfortable way, helping consumers reach personal goals and acting as partners. However, when marketing people get so involved with all the rules to follow (segmentation techniques etc.) they forget about the customer, and use the traditional marketing pressure, losing track of their main focus: satisfying the needs of their customers.

Topic summary

This topic looked at paradigm shifts, namely, neo-marketing, time-based decision-making, moving away from patronizing, moving from supply chain to demand value chain, and business ecosystems. New social values and the new socioquake were also outlined, such as cocooning, Golden Mafia, small indulgence and egonomics, vigilante consumers, save our society, 99 lives, icon toppling, deconsumption, and anchoring and clanning. Finally, the feminization of markets, consumer agency and value in my life were analyzed.

Suggested reading
Cocooning
http://en.wikipedia.org/wiki/Cocooning

Deconsumption
http://mathewgross.com/community/
aggregator/sources/6

http://deconsumption.typepad.com/

Anchoring
http://en.wikipedia.org/wiki/Anchoring

Commonsense marketing
http://www.commonsensemarketing.com/

Key terms
Consumer agency
Feminization of markets
Neomarketing
Time to market

Topic 2 the new consumer

Two trends are happening simultaneously: everything is becoming the same, and differences are becoming greater. Today, we increasingly think in terms of qualities rather than quantities. Consumers do not want more of the same, but different and better, from matter to mind. Indeed, products and services are increasingly being consumed by the mind as experiences as opposed to first perceiving the functionality of product or service attributes. This trend is linked with the fact that marketing actions should be geared towards having a full impact on the five human senses. The greatest challenge to management in the next decade will be to change rapidly enough to keep pace with new technology, new markets and new values. Either we take hold of the future or the future will take hold of us.

Topic objectives
After studying this topic, students should:

- Know new consumer trends, namely, the consciousness paradigm, prosumption and zones of tolerance.
- Be able to describe downshifting, voluntary simplicity and affluenza.

Topic discussion
Parity markets, parity products
The perceptual parity of the consumer in products and services is becoming higher due to their common features, such as in cars, hotels and computers. The differential advantage is becoming more illusory or virtual. It is more difficult to find true differentiation. With parity markets and smaller zones of tolerance, the consumer is more organized and more in control, is an intelligent agent and has more power.

Consciousness paradigm
Consumer contempt
Sometimes, marketing actions performed by companies are so bad that they stimulate consumer contempt towards products and brands, and may even lead to brand boycotts.

Exit and disconnected consumers
If products and services are not being delivered in the way clients and consumers are expecting, their tolerance zones become smaller, and every day we will have higher psychological deficits. In other words, customers will disconnect on exit companies and leave companies with them compounded by today's real-time, time-based paradigm (consumers strive for an immediacy effect and instant gratification). Consumers are time starved and effort starved.

Integrity
In B2B transactions, there are situations where a person who is selling a product works so much with the customer that they almost end up being a part of the decision-making unit of the customer. But in terms of ethics, if the seller knows that a new company with new technology, a new price and a new offer is in the market and has a better offer than theirs, the critical question is to learn which of the following options available to the marketer will

be selected: (1) the seller pursues a dual loyalty (whereby ethics and human integrity are paramount) and hence they stand by their loyalty to the decision-making unit of the customer, and even sells their competitor's products if they are better; or (2) the seller always tries to persuade the customer to buy their product, even if it is worse than competitors' offers.

Downshifting, voluntary simplicity, affluenza and the why generation

Consumers are downshifting and voluntarily simplifying their lives and consumption behaviours. Voluntary simplicity, a practice that is inextricably linked to consumer behaviour, means choosing to limit material consumption in order to free one's resources, primarily money and time, to seek satisfaction through non-material aspects of life.

Huneke (2005) identified a number of underlying dimensions of voluntary simplicity, namely, ecological and social responsibility, community and maintaining a spiritual life. Consumers of moderate income were found to be more likely to practice voluntary simplicity than was previously believed.

Consumers are rejecting the ideas of customer satisfaction, customer ecstasy and customer delight, as they want no fuss. For many companies, CRM is used only to benefit the company, for doing cross-selling and making cold calls.

There is a shift away from an obsessed career orientated and work path as a lifestyle into a way of having a life outwardly simpler and inwardly richer (an enriching lifestyle) (i.e., your money or your life). Dixon (2004) reports on two studies that are relevant to this discussion. In one study of 10 000 American, British and Japanese managers, the most important factor was the balance between their working and personal lives. In another study involving 1000 young managers, this work – life balance was the second most important concern. Consumers are keen in giving or trading off 15 to 20 per cent of their total fringe benefits and salary to achieve more flexibility (e.g., work 4 days a week and have more time to be with their family and friends).

There is also a movement towards affluenza (Hamilton and Deniss, 2006), i.e., a condition when consumers are disillusioned with affluence. These consumers want to have a simpler life but a more enriching and wealthier internal life. The affluenza virus is spread by marketing, which is, unremittingly, predicated on perpetuating and promoting the search for happiness. Happiness can only be found by inoculation with massive doses of choice. The symptoms of marketing and choice are the creation of desires and intensified feelings of deprivation and hastening obsolescence. Consumers suffering from affluenza do not know what they want, yet they want everything.

This is related to the why generation. Until recently, youth would finish their undergraduate academic degree and then start on a masters programme or a PhD degree, or go to the job market (careerism). Now, instead of starting up a new job or career as, for instance, assistant brand manager, they think they should first travel and know the world. They want to know more about new cultures and become culturally and humanly wealthier. Then, they come back and go to work. This is a truly talented generation that aims for immediate gratification and is eager to acculturate itself with new values and travel the world to discover new human perspectives.

Prosumption

The consumer is no longer just waiting for new products – mere consumption. They are having a more active behaviour in consumption. Indeed, the consumer is producing and giving ideas, and even co-creating new products. They are becoming more active in the conception, assembly and co-creation – and even in the production – of products and services.

There is a conscience paradigm. Consumers are looking for value and want to know what is behind a brand name. To reinforce the idea of prosumption, those consumers who buy can go a step forward and become prosumers, i.e., consumers who desire to take part in the design, shaping and even production of a product, knowing it is for them (co-creation). For example, http://www.customatix.com allows the client to design or co-create their own sneakers.

Contingency mentality

Traditional consumer life stages are fragmenting. Today, trends such as fractured career paths, redundancy and self-employment, rising divorce, and SSWD (single, separated, widows and divorcees) are disrupting the conventional patterns. They are changing the shape of the family life cycle, patterns of consumption, information gathering, intervention and decision-making processes, use of purchase, and post-purchase evaluation – in summary changing the overall patterns of consumer behaviour. These changes are fostering a 'contingency mentality'. This means that consumers are buying products according to their context and multi-dimensionality of consumption situations. Every day, we see more contingency marketing that is no longer straightforward.

Consumers today possess a multi-dimensionality of traits and personal facets that defy preconceived consumer behaviour frameworks. They purchase products/services depending on a multiplicity of occasion factors and modes of existing which demonstrate the increasing non-linearity of human behaviour.

Brain-to-brain model

The brain-to-brain model is a pattern of truthful and commonsense communication between human beings, in this case within the realm of economic transaction. Markets cannot be treated as pure demographics, geodemographics or psychographics in terms of segmentation bases and with simple labels. There are human beings involved, new consumers claiming to save our society and aiming for a work–life balance, so above all we need relations which are based on a brain-to-brain model. This is a big challenge for marketers – to understand consumers in a very complex environment – and we cannot think of consumers as behaving in one-, two- or three-dimensional models. Consumers use different devices (e.g., mental heuristics, shopping strategies, information gathering processes) in different ways to react to marketing, giving rise to more immunization (e.g., consumers are reacting to the 'bombardment' of 3000 stimuli a day using perceptual defences: blocking out junk mail and preventing cold calls by requiring privacy lines from telephone operators). Consumers participate in different transactions at different times of the day. Hence, there is multi-plurality and multi-dimensionality associated with consumer behaviour.

Any company may have a marketing department, but not every company has a marketing soul. In the consumer behaviour area, it is not enough to say that we know and understand the consumer; it is not enough to say that we have been in the market for a long time. Customer focus has become a cliché among marketing departments keen to have a competitive edge. But it deserves to be taken more seriously, as it disguises a paradigm shift from 'share of brand' to 'share of customer'. Firms should adopt an intelligent and integrated marketing and management approach. They must undertake an 'intelligent dialogue' with customers using a brain-to-brain model based on shared emotion. Many opportunities may be missed because old-fashioned marketers still assume they know everything there is to know about knowing their customers.

Zones of tolerance

Marketing is a service for the consumer. A service worth buying is rapidly becoming the new consumer's expectation. This value and expectancy are making the tolerance zones of the consumer shrink, i.e., they are becoming smaller because consumers are more demanding. Zone of tolerance is the difference between desired and adequate expectations.

The new consumer is becoming more 'hard on hard – soft on soft'. Consumers find differences between advertised promises and real services which make them unhappy. Moreover, consumers are more demanding of the real attributes of the products (hard) rather than relying on advertising glitz and packaging (soft). For example, consumers are giving more emphasis to the fundamental attributes of a shaver, such as smoothness, quality and price.

Companies in all industries face problems pertaining to the issue of retaining customers and securing satisfaction through service quality management. The repeat-purchasing behaviour at an individual level is affected by the level of a customer's 'zone of tolerance', a term not always fully understood. Gilbert and Gao (2005) examined the relationships that customer tolerance has with customer experience, brand trust and customer emotions for travel agency businesses. Customers who had had recent experience with travel agencies were sampled from two UK travel agencies situated in London and Guildford. One hundred and twenty customers were surveyed face-to-face through a questionnaire. The results, using Spearman-ranked order correlation, showed that there is a relationship between customer tolerance and customer experience. However, it was found there is no relationship between customer tolerance and customer emotion. In addition, the tests revealed that there is no relationship between customer tolerance and brand trust. The conclusion is that travel agencies are failing to keep in mind the importance of carefully handling customer tolerance and understanding the level of customer tolerance and its influence.

Sense and respond

A real-time organization must always be available to all customers. Time to market for products and services is becoming shorter, and company response to consumer queries and needs should be given on time. Hence, market research nowadays does have a much shorter life as values and motivations are changing with so much speed. Businesses need to operate within this model of 'sense and respond'. This sensing of the market will give the answers to what the market really needs in real-time. Indeed, in today's rapidly changing marketplace, a business cannot expect to thrive by just making products and selling them. For a company to succeed nowadays, it needs to know how to adapt to customers – even before they themselves know what they want. When unpredictability is given, the only strategy that makes sense is a strategy to become adaptive – to sense early and respond quickly to abrupt changes in individual consumer needs.

However, firms must have critical mass resource assets to answer the needs in those markets/segments. The best way to reach that objective is to have a real-time sense-and-respond model, which is going to be very important in the future.

The market-sensing capability acts as an antecedent to market orientation. Foley and Fahy (2004) propose that the market-sensing capability is comprised of four dimensions, which have specific resonance in market-sensing activities: organization systems, marketing information, organization communication and learning orientation. They emphasize a positive relationship between these dimensions and market orientation, and ultimately performance. For example, the greater the commitment to learning, the more developed the marketing information system, and the greater the degree to which organizational values and norms are customer oriented, the greater the market orientation. Moreover, learning orientation, marketing information and organizational communication are positively associated with the market-sensing capability.

The decisions consumers make and the desires they have are going to influence the outcome of our decisions in the company, but they should also direct and guide our decision-making. Nevertheless, this is not the case most of the time. For example, when it comes to budget allocation, firms use a cascade approach, i.e., they look at total market, market share, growth rate, aggregate competition, price for next year, contribution margin, fixed cost, advertising and promotion. In most companies, the leftover goes to marketing and marketing research. The new idea is completely different because, if one has a sense-and-respond model, it is possible that the numbers attached to the market size and its growth will be influenced by the firm's strategy.

The 'real-time' organization strives to be available to its customers 'all the time', and its marketers must expand their toolkit of sensors. This is not just abstract theory. Success is down to a new model: to operate on a sense-and-respond basis. One of the main sources of ideas for new products and services is sensing customers' needs in 'real-time'. Similarly, the whole idea of partnership sourcing or virtual integration is an application of the sense-and-respond model. The idea is that consumers' desires should not only influence our business decisions, they should direct our business operations.

Customer bonding

Keeping customers is more important than attracting new ones, but satisfying a customer is not good enough. Leading companies are moving from marketing to customers or customer segments to bonding with each customer. In a difficult business environment, enterprises that succeed in permanently bonding with their customers have an advantage.

Customer bonding is based on seeking truly fair exchanges with consumers that lead to their maximization of expectations and, therefore, the establishment of strong ties/relationships/associations between needs and brand values which will last in the long run.

Businesses are increasingly driven by consumer pressure. Consumers have never been totally powerless, but the balance of power is tilting in their favour and will continue to do so. Marketing lives and breathes two core functions: matching supply to demand, and connecting buyers and sellers as efficiently and effectively as possible. Both these functions are critically dependent on consumer understanding. The creation of the unique customer value proposition – customer bonding as the foundation of economic value creation – is paramount.

Customer loyalty develops from personal relationships and trust between the company and the customer, and deepens over time. This includes keeping customers involved throughout the product life cycle as well as developing products and/or services to meet changing customer needs and desires. This bond results from effective one-on-one communication, mutually beneficial interaction, the company's genuine interest and involvement in the customer's life and lifestyle, a combination of customer allegiance and company advocacy, and a shared sense of purpose.

Topic summary

This topic addressed the new consumer, including parity markets and products, and the consciousness paradigm (consumer contempt, exit and disconnected consumers, integrity). Downshifting, voluntary simplicity, affluenza and the why generation were described. Prosumption, contingency mentality, zones of tolerance, the sense-and-respond model and customer bonding were discussed.

Suggested reading

Huneke, Mary E. (2005). 'The face of the un-consumer: An empirical examination of the practice of voluntary simplicity in the United States', *Psychology & Marketing,* 22(7), 527–550.

The new consumer
http://www.newconsumer.org/

Consciousness paradigm
http://www.enformy.com/ionsnewparadigm.htm

Downshifting
http://www.abc.net.au/religion/stories/s1115995.htm, http://www.downshiftingdownunder.com.au/

Voluntary simplicity
http://www.simpleliving.net/

Affluenza
http://www.affluenza.com/

Why generation
http://en.wikipedia.org/wiki/Generation_Y

Sense and respond
http://senseandrespond.com/

Topic 3 new consumer applications

Topic objectives

After studying this topic, students should be able to:

- Discuss neuromarketing and its relationship with consumer behaviour
- Discuss particle marketing and micromarket segmentation

Topic discussion

The digital revolution of the marketplace allows much greater customization of products, services and promotional messages. This revolution has introduced several drastic changes into the business environment. Consumers have more power; they can use intelligent agents to locate the best prices for products and services, bid on various market offerings, buy directly from producers and shop for goods 24/7 and worldwide. Consumers have access to more information since they can easily find reviews from products, compare their features and subscribe to virtual communities.

Marketers can offer more customized services and products as well as promotional messages. Marketers can gather information about consumers more quickly and easily, analyzing increasingly complex data on consumers' buying patterns and personal characteristics. The exchange between marketers and customers is increasingly interactive and instantaneous as digital communication enables a two-way interactive exchange in which consumers can instantly react to the marketer's message. Thus, marketers are now able to build and maintain relationships with customers on a greater and more efficient scale.

An aid to the anytime/anywhere purchasing and consumption need is the mobile phone. Transactions made using mobile phones are marking a fundamental change in consumer behaviour dynamics. Consumers are using their mobile phones to purchase goods from vending machines, buy cinema and train tickets and shop on the Internet. Wireless Internet services can be made more personalized for customers than any other means of communication. As mobile phones are usually with customers, wireless network operators are now able to identify a user and send them personalized communications, and the operator is able to pinpoint the exact user location, hence presenting the user with an array of new applications.

Recent developments in technology are also offering new opportunities for the Internet customer in the area of telematics. For example, in the next few years, consumers can expect the car, the refrigerator and the television to be Internet-ready. The car may be able to keep track of the date when it is to be serviced next, the refrigerator may automatically order items that fall below a particular stock level and interactive TV may enable consumers to order products through the television. This concept of ubiquitous Internet may be also applied to any other place where the customer is physically present, such as parking garages and airport lounges.

Neuromarketing

Researchers are starting to look at what is going on inside the consumer's brain. Neuromarketing, through functional MRI, may be used to analyze memory and chunks of information to better understand the behaviour of consumers.

Wilkinson (2005) examines the significance of marketers and advertising agencies turning to neuroscience in a bid to better understand consumer reactions to brands, products and marketing messages. He found functional MRI useful in mapping the degree to which certain areas of the brain are activated when exposed to different stimuli, and investigated the utility of the technique to assess the merits of new product development and packaging design.

Particle marketing and micro-market segmentation

In the postinformation age, we often have an audience of one. Everything is made to order, and information is extremely personalized. Companies now have the ability to remember the tastes and preferences of individual customers. As a result, product marketing is being supplanted by relationship marketing. The ability to remember a customer from one event to the next is the primary requirement for sustaining an ongoing relationship, and is becoming the main reason why a customer will remain loyal to one product. In this context, the Internet comes to age, not as a new mass medium but rather as a totally new peer-to-peer medium. As a matter of fact, we are witnessing the necessity of focusing on the right content for the right audience.

Particle marketing is a concept borrowed from physics and derived from the use of personal technologies enabling organizations to customize micro-individual offerings to the market. In the last 15 years, there has been an advance in this concept. In fact, a huge change has been occurring, driven by vendors who are selling technologies such as customer relationship management (CRM). However, many companies do not know how to use it and what to do with it.

In particle marketing, via direct broadcasting systems, a company can communicate to consumers through split-screen television geodemographics, scanning and identifying the location of one's house, its price, one's vehicle registration, knowing that one has a new doctor, suggesting the best type of food for one's children and so on. These layers of information are a more revolutionary idea than database marketing. However, there are many ethical problems related to particle marketing, as firms would quickly find out everything about the consumer. The technology is here, but will consumers allow this intrusion in their homes, as if Big Brother is watching them all the time?

Ali and Rao (2000) proposed a neural network model (NNM) as a viable alternative for micro-market segmentation. Traditional market segmentation methods and their unsuitability for micro-market segmentation purposes are dealt with, as well as various business applications of neural network techniques, and managerial implications of NNM.

Topic summary
This topic focused on new consumer applications. Specifically, it considered neuromarketing, and examined both micro-market segmentation and particle marketing.

Suggested reading
Wilkinson, Amanda (2005) 'Neuromarketing: Brain scam or valuable tool?' *Marketing Week*, 28(5), 22–23.

Neuromarketing
http://en.wikipedia.org/wiki/Neuromarketing
http://www.wisegeek.com/what-is-neuromarketing.htm

Future trends in marketing programming

Many factors will impact on the way organizations conduct and apply their marketing controllable programmes. Here is a synthesis of some of the most important trends.

Trends in product policy, brands and new product developments

- The tremendous role of disruptive technologies.
- The importance of detailability due to competitive parity.
- Product, service and brand architectures.
- Speed, cost and quality not seen as trade-offs.
- Product and service sensitivity.
- High quality and non-conformity, as high quality is already the norm and just the 'start of the race'.
- Sales vs. sensitivity (economies of scope but also with market sensitivity).
- Vertical quality integration throughout the company.
- Brand information as a major product differential.
- Super brands, 'brand strength' and axing brands; the focus will be on concentrating on those brands that carry 'consumer franchise' in the long-term memory of the consumer.

The impact of new disruptive technologies has had a tremendous influence on how companies manage their product portfolios. Because of perceived parity by consumers, the importance of managing the detail (detailability) is crucial and paramount not only in the design of the product, service and brand architecture, but in any area of marketing. Increasingly, the product mix has to be seen as a complete architecture which includes the product itself and the amount of service that goes with it as well as the sustainability of the brand. Because of the requirement for more detail management, companies should have more product and service sensitivity. Sales volume and economies of scope should be equated with customer, market and product sensing and sensitivity. A truly felt and implemented policy of integrated quality is critical for the survival of the company. Brand information posture and trust are now major arenas to foster competitive differentiation. Companies are reducing their product mix in order to concentrate on super brands – the ones that carry positive associations in the neurons of consumers and can, therefore, develop true customer franchise.

We used to think of speed, quality and cost as trade-offs, but suddenly we noticed that if you do it right, all three can go together.

High quality is simply the entry price to start in the race. Look at this equation for quality:

$$CPQ = COC + CONC + CDA$$

where:

CPQ = cost of quality

COC = cost of conformity (with market standards)

CONC = cost of non-conformity

CDA = cost of sustainable differential advantage

The test of values lies in what and how companies sell.

Increasingly, the true cost of quality derives from these three elements. Most companies are only interested in conforming with the standards of the market (COC). Those that do not want to conform with competitor benchmarking (CONC) will appropriate more resources but will also have a higher return on their investment. The highest payoff is derived from a measured investment policy to improve overall quality and the search for true differentiation, which will then translate in the achievement of sustainable corporate results.

Value-based marketing

The value of brands no longer lies just in their ability to deliver superior margins, but in their ability to forge business relationships that deliver the assets and resources that make the difference between perishing and prospering. So, mind the (brand) gap!

'Branding the future' can be encapsulated by a vision which involves:

- The total brand experience.
- Value-led marketing, which will create stronger brand relationships.
- Brand spirit (cause-related marketing), brand storm (consumer power) and brand essence and vision.
- Brand equity is really what people carry around in their heads.
- Global co-branding is on the increase, as well as elastic brands (innovative point-on-purchase plus creative field marketing techniques).
- What about *no branding*?
- The corporate brand will be the main marketing mode of the future.

Companies need to address erroneous value gaps in the market. Value-led marketing will create stronger brand relationships based on the total brand experience by consumers. Cause-related marketing (brand spirit), the awareness of consumer power (brand storm) and brand vision are essential ingredients for the future. Although there are more elastic brands (triggered by innovative point-on-purchase and creative field marketing techniques), brand content is still the imperative element of a branding strategy.

Brand ubiquity

Brands have become omnipresent. They come in all the shapes and sizes, from *corporations* (Microsoft, Virgin, Starbucks) to *products* (Gillette Mach III, Mini, Mars) to *events* (Glastonbury, Super Bowl) to *locations* (New Zealand, the French Riviera) to *ingredients* (Lycra, Intel, Dolby) to *endorsers* (ISSO 9000, Woolmar) and even *individuals* (Madonna, David Beckham). Whilst they are essential guides through the cluttered multiple-choice world we live in, they are in danger of losing their edge. Backlash from books like Naomi Klein's anti-branding bible *No Logo* and brand evangelists like Michael Eisner, Chairman of Disney, who commented on branding as 'overused, sterile, and unimaginative', are also adding to the debate.

Brand management is interface management. The organization has to manage every link with its customers – through its departments of personnel, finance, operations, media relations, etc. – in order to explain its brand values. Responsibility for the brand moves beyond the marketing department.

The customer, not the brand manager, is the key specifier. A brand is not a product, but an invitation. Nowadays, marketers want to extend their contact with customers through time. The brand promise is about the quality of a relationship. The price of a product is not what customers pay for it. The price of a product includes everything the customer has to do to realize its value: time and money spent searching for the right product and sales outlet, travelling to the shop, paying, transporting, unpacking, preparing for use, disposing of it, etc. Taking a broader view of what constitutes value is transforming the marketing agenda. The brand is an experience, not a product. In a time-pressured world, customers want value for time as well as value for money. They either 'outsource' unsatisfying, time-consuming tasks or expect the time they spend to be as fulfilling as possible. Increasingly, the way to win a greater share of the purse is to win a greater share of customer time. Brands are spilling across corporate boundaries. The corporation is only a halfway house. Increasingly, brands represent not just the activities of one company but the combined activities of many companies.

Paradoxically, although brands will become more important, their influence over individuals may weaken. Ultimately, the most successful brands will be those that most effectively serve the customer. At present, a service ethos is widely promoted, but frequently it is 'skin deep'. The future is likely to bring more strenuous attempts to serve the customer in ways that invite them to take ownership of a brand (i.e., 1:1 MK).

Often, the most enthusiastic proponents of 'brand experience' are victims of marketing's most prevalent occupational hazard: rampant brand narcissism, where everything the marketer does is for the glory of their brand – not for the benefit of the consumer. Not for much longer. How a brand goes to market can either add extra value for its customers or snatch value from them. That is why competing along this dimension of 'go-to-market' value is heating up so quickly.

Sometimes it is better and more credible to be *brand-anonymous* than *brand-hyperventilated*. Brand makeover is not enough. The key is to explore the brand space between the company and the customer. The whole 'brand management thing' has moved on. A few years ago, people were running internal marketing programmes to script the whole thing, but recently, people have begun to understand that coaching people to recite brand values parrot-fashion is not the way forward. It is about much more fundamental things, such as: Do we understand how our customers need to be treated, what the nature of our business is and how we can translate the promises we make into *real products and services*? The staff have to be part of the *brand definition process* rather than the unwilling back-end of it.

Branding is not just about how companies present themselves to customers. Rather, brands are becoming a sort of supply or value chain 'superglue' – something that can forge better connections between each player in the supply chain, thereby unleashing bigger, better and more fruitful flows of economic energy between them. The content of branding will also change. Under the old paradigm, brands stood for quality, consistency, ubiquity and affordability. Under the new paradigm, brands will increasingly stand for *inconsistency* (i.e., customized offers), variable distribution and variable pricing. Branding will increasingly be about 'living the brand' – bringing the brand experience inside so that it becomes real to the employees who deliver the brand promise. Brand strategy needs a new perspective, where both the customer and employee experience are explicitly *linked*.

One of the most striking marketing dilemmas can be defined as follows:

> A brand is only successful if it has enough devoted followers who are happy to stand up 'and be counted'. The brand has to be kept relevant to the group against which it is targeted as they, and their needs, change over time.

Another important trend relates to tribal marketing. All great brands create tribes. For example, they have behind them a brand community (e.g., Nutella, Sara Lee, Gillette, Saks). One of the basic assumptions behind tribal brands is that companies needed a strategic transformation by acquiring a 'we believe in you' attitude, personal care, new technology, better data and no central 'control', and having brands with a 'human face'.

With consumers even more in the driving seat, the most successful brands will be those that abandon the traditional top-down approach – 'we market to you' – in favour of bottom-up strategies. There is also the *brands' role reversal*. Currently, and up to now, brands (and marketing) have been all about helping sellers to sell. Brands are the producer's agent. Many of tomorrow's megabrands will be the consumer's agent, and that changes everything. The days of mindless marketing are over; it is time to transform brands from trademarks into trust marks using trust-based marketing.

Some of the key trends in product policy and new product development will be in these areas: talking packages, chatty packages, self-destructing packages and shrinking packages, micro-marketing, and smart packaging. Furthermore, there will be dynamic messages based on remote telecommunications, technology-new metrics for brand valuation and brand equality, a high technological turnover rate in innovation as well as the impact of disruptive technologies, ranging from computerized plano-programming to virtual reality.

In terms of micro-marketing and smart packaging, it is expected that evolving technology will enable the planting of information specific to individual consumers in each pack via electronic home shopping. The smart packs will 'get the product to think'. It is realistic to expect packs whose graphics can be changed remotely by communication technologies, either on the shelf or at the point of sale. Dynamic messages within the graphics are another step. Consumers will be able to interrogate the brand directly – and the can of beans will be able to answer back. Companies must innovate if they are to survive in the new millennium. Producing good products will no longer be enough. They must be clever, original, well designed and creatively marketed. The problem is never how to get new innovative thoughts into your mind, but how to get old ones out. Every industry on the planet is being reinvented from the customer backwards. Companies need to bring as much innovation to the demand chain as they brought to the supply chain. Innovation management needs to be an ongoing competitive effort woven throughout the entire corporate value chain. All the technological knowledge we work with today will represent only

1 per cent of the knowledge that will be available in 2050. Virtual reality will be pervasive, enabling companies to provide lifelike illustrations of product models and permitting prospective customers an 'experience' of production machinery.

As late as World War II, it took 30 years to go from a theoretical idea to the release of competing products in an established market; in computing, it now takes 18 months or less. Some Japanese companies have squeezed the cycle even further. They aim for no more than 4 months from the start of R&D for one product through the introduction of the next product.

A message for phobic market-facing companies is: A company that is managing itself for operational excellence cannot create a market for a radical innovation. The skill sets, organizational structure, cost structure, goals and metrics are all different. The allocation or derivation of power is all different as well.

There is usually some corporate process by which a potentially great value-balanced innovation gets adulterated into something 'mundane'. In many companies, there are screening criteria which seem effectively to get rid of the more adventurous, breakthrough ideas – or to subject them through the Inno Funnel to 'death by a thousand cuts'.

People drive innovation – period: all other factors may merely 'influence' innovation

Examine the extent to which company leadership causes employees to use their brains at work. The brain controls creativity, innovation, productivity, motivation and commitment. A superior leadership strategy turns on brains to the maximum extent and thus greatly enhances innovation. Values are the centrepiece of this strategy because employees respect actions that reflect high standards of all good values, values such as fairness, compassion, honesty and trust. Otherwise, why not just 'leave your brain at the door'? Innovations get slowed down (or stopped) by different functions, consumers, R&D, marketing, supply chain, etc., all pursuing their own agendas, spelling disaster for innovation and a heavy brake on progress. Also, marketing research often gives negative feedback on innovations. Furthermore, consumers/customers generally see the world through rear-view mirrors when addressing the future.

Examining the trends in product policy, branding and new product development, some of the key underpinnings of these trends can also be highlighted. The new product development process is very short (4 months), more non-sequential and based on concurrent stages of development; innovation is a route to improving the perceived value of a brand. Virtual reality will have a role to play in the research and development processes. There will be faster access to knowledge and faster innovation; connect and develop (C&D) replaces R&D; there will be more shared innovation; and most 'real innovations' will come from small, fast, hungry companies with few corporate overheads to feed.

Companies need to balance scale vs. market sensitivity. Integrated marketing (integration, agility and flexibility) is needed as well as brand integrity. By addressing a corporate DMU rather than a customer, the brand can identify its target on the basis of a shared vision. In a major attitude shift, companies are sharing once-secret new ideas and outsourcing innovation.

There is also the rise of 'infomediaries' – third-party mediators who help companies fill 'structural' gaps in market understanding, such as poor access to competitors, customers or to their own customers who do not feel 'close' enough to a particular company to bother providing ideas.

The competitive advantage related to innovation and sustainable strategies derived from innovation (INNO) can be analyzed in Table 21.1.

The innovation station will be formed upon:

- A cluster of transparent free-thinkers.
- A culture of innovation.
- An 'out-of-the-box' remit.
- The use of technology creatively.
- A market-driven innovation methodology and tools.
- INNO networks to spin out innovations.
- Will be SYS^3 (a systematic systemic system).
- Will foster INNO(vation) KNOW(ledge) representing.
- A move from INNO confusion to representing an INNO fusion.
- Companies also need a strategy *canvas* (to integrate strategy).

Table 21.1
From the INNOVANTAGE (innovation advantage) grid to INNOSUSSTRAT (IS^2) (innovation sustainable strategy)

INNO criteria \ INNO type	Incremental	Continuous	Radical	Breakthrough	Distinctive	Sustainable
Strategic vision						
Want-satisfying outputs						
Knowledge 'reservoir'						
Human-factor-based processes						
Technology-based process						
Process-based management						
Implementation						

But the ultimate pure marketing approach sees innovation as:

Integrity

HoNesty

BalaNced Exchanges

VisiOn

Value and values

TrAnsparency

Trust brands

True consumer solutIons +

COmmon

SeNse

Technologies, human sensing, co-creation of value and marketing with meaning will drive innovation in the future.

Trends in pricing

Some of the key trends in this area can be encapsulated as follows:

- Transformation of cost structures.
- Downward price pressure and new lower price points because of the appearance of a new buyer psyche.
- Japanese companies such as Olympus and Komatsu developed target costing based on monetary perceived value attached to product/service attributes by consumers. These monetary benefit levels determine price points. This is called **target costing** (bundles of benefits and their perceived value).
- The battle for brand loyalty is heating up, but is this true brand loyalty?
- Rapidly advancing technology is continually transforming underlying cost structures and creating endemic pricing instability.
- Globalization, removal of trade and regulatory barriers mean more price pressures by opening new low-cost sources of supply and new competition. Therefore, there will definitely be new, lower price points.
- A new non-inflationary environment is transforming buyer psychology, making it much harder to make price rises stick.
- The markets will go beyond the era of everyday low pricing.
- There will be more one-to-one pricing; individualized pricing and customer-specific pricing will become more prevalent. Some companies (e.g., Dell Computers) are even 'sacking' individual customers because of profitability levels.

Also, looking at the cost behaviour, e.g., the ratio of fixed to variable costs, will also be an important trend. Just try to grasp the meaning of these scenarios.

Scenario 1 $\quad\quad\quad\quad\quad\quad\quad\quad$ $\downarrow$P VC(+), Vo$\uparrow$, TVC$\uparrow$, Po$\downarrow$

$$> GR$$

Scenario 2 $\quad\quad\quad\quad\quad\quad\quad\quad$ P$\downarrow$ FC(+), Vo$\uparrow$ UNC$\downarrow$ Po$\uparrow$

Scenario 3 $P\downarrow$ VC($-$), AC$\downarrow$, Vo$\uparrow$, Po$\uparrow$

$> P\downarrow$

Scenario 4 $P\downarrow$, Vo$\uparrow$ Only if VC$\downarrow$

Why ?

TVC$\uparrow$, Vo$\uparrow$, Po$\downarrow$

Scenario 5 $P\uparrow$, PE-1 Only if VC = Vo$\downarrow$

VC = $->$, P$\uparrow$, TVC$\downarrow$, Po$\uparrow$

Why ?

Vo$\downarrow$

where:
P = price   Po = profit   GR = growth in revenue
VC = variable costs   PE = price elasticity   AC = average costs
FC = fixed costs   UNC = unit variable cost   TVC = total variable costs
Vo = volume

Some of these scenarios can be interpreted as follows. Scenario 1 is telling us that if a company plans to decrease its price level, and it has a large proportion of variable costs, as it lowers its price, volume goes up, but its total variable costs will also go up. If this increase in TVC is greater than the growth in revenue generated by the lower price, then profitability will also decrease. In Scenario 2, the company has a large proportion of fixed costs, and as the volume goes up, the average unit cost is spread out over the volume and the profitability will go up. Scenario 3 is demonstrating that if the company has a somewhat lower proportion of variable costs, as the volume goes up, with the decreasing price, the average costs will also decrease. If these savings in the reduction of average costs is greater than the lowering of sales revenue due to the decreased price, then the profitability will increase. The warning in Scenario 4 is that you can lower the price and have a subsequent increase in sales volume, but only if you can lower your variable costs: with the increase in volume, your total variable costs will also go up and your profitability will decrease. Scenario 5 deals with a price increase and a unitary level of price elasticity. With the price increase, the volume will come down and, if the variable costs could be maintained, then the profitability will group. This is because with the price increase there will be less sales, and consequently a lowering of total variable costs.

Trends in advertising

Trends in advertising can be encapsulated by referring to these main areas: fragmentation of audiences, narrowcasting, multi-unit advertising, time-compressed TV commercials and grazing, digital compression technology, video on demand, advertising on demand, advertising diseffectiveness, place-based advertising, experience planning, participative advertising and consumer-generated advertising. Other trends in integrated marketing communications advertising, sales promotion and public relations include non-interrupted advertising, brand velocity, increased sales promotion spending, strategic role of PR, reputation management and CIC (corporate image and communication).

The way companies communicate with their markets will surely change. Due to the digital compression technology, there is more narrowcasting, fragmentation of audiences and media atomization. More companies will advertise several brands in the same advertising campaign. Commercials are being reduced to 8 seconds, although some companies, e.g., Hovis, are 'bucking' the trend with longer advertisements (more than 1 minute). Split-screen technology coupled with particle marketing are allowing individual advertising messages to be delivered, supported by direct satellite broadcasting systems. Well beyond the current and traditional 'monologue' approach, we will see more participative advertising and voluntary advertising: you request the campaigns, or parts of the advertising message, according to your needs. The current trend of advertising diseffectiveness is on the rise. There will be more concentration on captive audiences, and media planning will be increasingly replaced by experience planning (based on extracts of product/service experience by consumers) (e.g., Philips, Volkswagen and Adidas). Advertising messages will be increasingly generated by consumers. Do we really want more intrusive and non-interrupted advertising? Companies are also trying to have more continuity of market response in terms of the balancing of effects between advertising and sales promotion.

The commercial message

The nature of the message will change as we move from the mass to the multi-mediated world of interactive communication. The message will become multi-dimensional, with interactive advertising pods of product information that can be peeled like an onion and will move from an 'intrusive commercial' to an 'invited conversation'. The message will be less ephemeral and more embedded and will move from a 'glib' intangible style to a substantive, value-added tangible style.

Still other trends in advertising can be summarized as follows:

- More 1:1 media
- More Internet/CD-ROM
- More interactive advertising
- More voluntary/individualized advertising
- Advertising will have a new ecology through use of message-engineering technologies and new artificial intelligence methodologies, which will be applied in order to maximize consumer response and involvement with the message.

Therefore, the new ecology in advertising will be focused on cost per 'involved' viewer/reader, cost per earned attention, cost per touch, message maximization modelling, simulated advertising concept testing and test marketing by seeking to yield the maximal level of market response, as well as measuring competitive response (modelling technology), through knowledge-based systems, expert systems and artificial intelligence.

Trends in integrated marketing communication related to selling can be expressed as follows: value-balanced selling; sales automation tools, interactive systems and online transactions; partnership selling and non-manipulating techniques; time-based competitive selling, sales without selling (a philosophical stance whereby the sophistication, knowledge and a myriad of other developments on both sides of the exchange process – suppliers and consumers – will make the selling itself redundant, since both parties know exactly what the other one wants).

Selling – but not just selling, also marketing as a whole – needs to be more value balanced. Value should be provided with equity to both sides of the exchange process. Sales automation tools and interactive systems will be increasingly adopted by companies. By around 2013, 10 per cent of global sales will be based on online transactions. In B2B, partnering and partnership selling will be the norm, as well as the increasing use of non-manipulative techniques. Transparency, trust and an intelligent dialogue between sellers and buyers will be prevalent; it's about time!

Time-based management will have an impact on every facet of the business, including the selling function and sales management. Marketing without marketing (marketing as we know it) and selling without selling will be two strong philosophical stances to be pondered by business systems in the future.

Partnership selling

In the 21st century, non-manipulative selling techniques will be the key to survival, because increasingly sophisticated clients will not fall for gimmicks or deception. Salespeople must assume the role of lifelong learners. In the future, sales will become almost incidental – a natural outgrowth of a long-term relationship. In order to stay current with clients' long-range plans to which their input could be invaluable, 'relationship selling' is *de rigueur*. The challenge for an organization is to move to a situation where the customer starts buying from you rather than being sold to. New approaches to doing business are emerging, e.g. contract-plus-relationships – where both sides freely 'give' each other more than is, or can be, specified by a formal legal contract. This means *trust*-based marketing, and that is what organizations and markets need. CRM is based on simple, common-sense ideas. Making it happen, however, is difficult. Customers are not data; they are people. To manage a customer relationship, you need a single, rounded view of each customer. But that is still a dream for many companies with many separate legacy-product or division-based databases. Equally vital is a coherent, unified customer experience across all possible 'touchpoints' (call centre, website, billing, retail outlet and so on), but achieving such consistency remains a nightmare. There is some woolly thinking. Core CRM notions such as lifetime customer value seem clearer than they are. The best customers are those from whom the company learns from the most. The customer's contribution can go further. Partnership-sourcing programmes and open cost book policies recognize that the more suppliers that involve their customers in new product and service development, the better the outcome. The customer contributes 'consultancy' for free. Likewise, at the heart of most relationship marketing is the recognition not only that repeat business is valuable but that customers potentially could contribute much more in terms of information and insight.

Putting the C into CRM

Bad CRM practices over many years and in most industries turned CRM into 'customer rejection of management' and 'customer removal management'. With human beings becoming increasingly empowered by technological accessibility, traditional approaches of CRM are being redefined as CMR – customer-managed relationships. It is the customer who decides and manages whatever relationships they want to have with organizations.

Distribution trends

Some of the main distribution trends can be described as follows: category management will still prevail in the future; multi-dimensional competition will be a major feature (the appearance of many non-traditional competitors, of different sizes, locations and industry origin); scanning technology and the high-tech superstore; marketspaces; and Internet shopping as well as virtual shopping.

Category management will keep its crucial role as the interface between the product mix and strategic retailing decision-making processes. Multi-dimensional competitors, as well as non-traditional ones, will change the retailing landscape. The impact of scanning technology and other disruptive technologies (e.g., pathway technology) will redefine our store (high-tech) experience. We will see more of experimental store atmospheres, attentive environments, electronic kiosks, eye-tracking devices, etc. New marketspaces will emerge through the appearance of vertical search engines, visual search engines and the semantic web, as well as the increased use of virtual reality shopping.

Marketspaces are developing where the crucial issue is access to information. Distribution is now essentially an information system. New distribution strategies entail the development of new levels of partnership based on the mutual sharing of data. We already had 2 billion Internet uses by 2005. Global Internet retailing was worth $0.6 trillion in 2000 (Datamonitor, 2008). By 2013, it is predicted to account for 10 per cent of global retail and distribution expenditure. We are rapidly becoming an information-intense society and entering the digital era and realm of the virtual marketspace. Also, forget boundaries; online cohorts are the future (e.g., twinsumers, brand communities, brand boycotts, tribal brands, infomediaries, trusted sites, Internet-free zones and others).

Organizational, cultural, regional and national boundaries will disappear, replaced by *online cohorts*, attitudes and interests being the glue that binds people into future marketplaces. Online Oxygen is another massive trend: 780 000 000 consumers worldwide are beginning to see online access as an absolute necessity, and there are no signs that the pace of integrating online access into their daily life is slowing down.

Convergence matrix

Consumers do not fall neatly into two categories, although marketers assume they do: the old, traditional consumer for whom the Internet is an irrelevance, and the super-cool cyberconsumer who has not left their flat for months, ordering everything via the Web. The vast majority of people are in fact **hybrid consumers**, centaurs, who move easily between the online and off-line worlds.

We will also see more strategic paths being developed on the basis of a diagonal integration, which is driven by information technologies, and is a process by which companies move into new and different activities, with tremendous gains, synergies and scope economies derived from integration and mutual sharing of data. Companies that once had little in common, such as banks, supermarkets, travel companies and TV stations, are discussing new partnership structures that will give exclusive access to each others' customers. The new technologies will enable multiple channel marketing. And there is also the invasion of the infomediaries (e.g., virtual retailers), which will transform the way we purchase goods and services by, at the same time, minimizing our time and efforts. These trends will create a totally new marketsphere of electronic retailing (e-tailing), electronic distribution patterns and flows (d-tailing) and a continued trend towards downward price pressure because of the impact of the cyberspace (p-tailing). We will also witness a counter-trend towards brand ubiquity (called 'generica' in retailing, with most super-brands having a presence pretty much almost everywhere in the global market) by favouring local brands and retailers – locavores – who can really address and meet a growing trend towards satisfying local micro-belief systems of consumers (a trend towards market divergence). The blurring of retailing with entertainment will also be growing in importance – 'retailtainment' – as well as sensory and experiential shopping by going back to livening the five human senses in retail shopping.

Efficient consumer response (logistics)

The length of the supply chain is having to move faster all the time. Trans-shipment centres are replacing traditional warehouses. Stock is held for hours rather than weeks. JIT (or cynical 'just-too-late') is old hat. It is near-zero inventory now. Speed, response and integration are watchwords. It is the efficient transmission and management of information which can make or break a business.

In summary, and overall, there will be a new interactive mix based on superior market sensing, particle marketing and a neighbourhood and marketing persona orientation, based on the use of disruptive technologies and marketing with memory. We will see more cybersegmentation, (e.g., CLIP, a classification of Internet people), as well as smart packaging. The new marketing approaches will range from brand vision to living brands and from individualized pricing to media narrowcasting. There will be more advertising on demand, place-based advertising, participative advertising, ambient media and corporate concern about brand velocity. We will also see more sales automation tools and the philosophy of 'sales without selling' being implemented. Within the trends of marketing programming, we will have more diagonal integration, e-tailing, a counter-trend against ubiquity in retailing and retailtainment. Experimental marketing and experience will become more visible.

Since common sense is as rare as genius (Emerson, 1844.), making sense of marketing is imperative. Furthermore, we need common-sense marketing. Simplicity marketing. Marketing with meaning.

Summary

This chapter has been designed to highlight and analyze the following key topics:

- Trends in globalization.

- Future roles of technology and its impact.

- Future trends in consumer behaviour.

- The concept of business ecosystems.

- An overview of the many developments and future trends related to the controllable marketing programmes, ranging from innovation and pricing to integrated marketing communication and distribution.

Chapter questions

1. Critically comment on the phenomenon of 'deglobalization'.

2. Comment and bring your own critique of the new strategic planning concept called 'business ecosystems'.

3. Discuss the following related trends: downshifting, voluntary simplicity, 'affluenza' and the why generation.

References

Ali, J., and Rao, C. P. (2000) 'Neural networks model: A viable approach for micro market segmentation', *American Marketing Association Conference Proceedings*, 11:320–321.

Anonymous (2004, May 10) 'E-Biz strikes again!' *Business Week Online*. [Online]. http://www.businessweek.com.

Bello, W. (2000) [Online]. http://www.corpwatch.org. Last accessed 10 May 2009.

Berners-Lee, T., Hendler, J., and Lassila, O. (2001, May) 'The semantic web', *Scientific American*. [Online]. http://www.scientificamerican.com.

Datamonitor (2008) *Internet Access: Global Industry Wide*.

Dixon, P. (2004) *Futurewise: The Six Faces of Global Change*, 3rd edn., London: Profile Books.

Doz, Y., dos Santos, J., and Williamson, P. (2002) *From Global to Metanational: How Companies Win in the Knowledge Economy*, Boston, MA: Harvard Business School Press.

Eckhardt, G. M., and Mahi, H. (2004) 'The role of consumer agency in the globalization process in emerging markets', *Journal of Marcomarketing*, 24(2):136–146.

Foley, A., and Fahy, J. (2004, December) 'Towards a further understanding of the development of market orientation in the firm: A conceptual framework based on the market-sensing capability', *Journal of Strategic Marketing*, 12:219–230.

Gilbert, D. and Gao, Y. (2005) 'A failure of UK travel agencies to strengthen zones of tolerance', *Tourism and Hospitality Research*, 5(4):306–321.

Ghoshal, S., and Bartlett, C. (1997) *The Individualized Corporation: A Fundamental Approach to Management*, New York: HarperCollins.

Hamilton, C., and Deniss, R. (2006) *Affluenza: When Too Much Is Never Enough*, Sidney: Allen & Unwin.

Huneke, M. E. (2005) 'The face of the un-consumer: An empirical examination of the practice of voluntary simplicity in the United States', *Psychology & Marketing*, 22(7):527–550.

Huntington, S. (1997) *The Clash of Civilizations and the Remaking of the World Order,* London: Simon & Schuster.

Iansiti, M., and Levien, R. (2004, March) 'Strategy as ecology', *Harvard Business Review,* 82:68–78.

Moore, J. F. (1993) 'Predators and prey: A new ecology of competition', *Harvard Business Review,* 71(3):75–86.

NIC (2000) 'Global Trends 2015: A Dialogue about the Future with Non Government Experts', National Intelligence Council, United States.

Popcorn, F. (2001) *Eveolution: The Eight Truths of Marketing to Women,* New York: Hyperion.

Popcorn, F. (2002) *Dictionary of the Future.* New York: Hyperion.

Rodrick, D. (1997) 'Has Globalization Gone Too Far?', Institute for International Economics, Washington, D.C.

Rugman, A. (2000) *The End of Globalization: A New and Radical Analysis of Globalization and What it Means for Business,* London: Random House.

Shular, S. (2005) 'A new buzzword', *Marketing,* 110(25):20.

Wilkinson, A. (2005) 'Neuromarketing: Brain scam or valuable tool?', *Marketing Week,* 28(5):22–23.

http://www.publicinternetproject.org

http://www.trendwatching.com

Index